DATE DUE

APR 7 1993 MAR 1 7 1993			
MAR 1 7 1993			
GAYLORD			PRINTED IN U.S.A.

**Developmental Biology
of the Sea Urchin Embryo**

DEVELOPMENTAL BIOLOGY
OF THE SEA URCHIN EMBRYO

Giovanni Giudice

Istituto di Anatomia Comparata
Università di Palermo
Palermo, Italy

ACADEMIC PRESS   New York and London   1973
A Subsidiary of Harcourt Brace Jovanovich, Publishers

ACADEMIC PRESS, INC.
111 Fifth Avenue, New York, New York 10003

United Kingdom Edition published by
ACADEMIC PRESS, INC. (LONDON) LTD.
24/28 Oval Road, London NW1

LIBRARY OF CONGRESS CATALOG CARD NUMBER: 72-88335

PRINTED IN THE UNITED STATES OF AMERICA

Contents

Preface

Developmental biology owes a tremendous debt to sea urchins and amphibians. Indeed, since the very beginnings of experimental embryology, embryos of these animals have proved to be experimental jewels, and fundamental ideas of development have been derived to a large extent from the study of these organisms. In more recent times they have also proved to be extremely well suited for the analysis of developmental processes at the ultrastructural, biochemical, and molecular levels. The amount of data that have accumulated and continue to accrue is so great that it requires considerable and even painful effort to acquaint oneself with the present-day "state of the art." Hence it seemed appropriate for someone in the field to make an effort to correlate the available information in one source.

The aim of this work is to attempt to answer the following questions: What have we learned of development in general from the study of the sea urchin embryo? What advantages and limitations does the use of the sea urchin embryo present in the study of developmental problems?

In referring to experimental observations I have always quoted the original data, indicating when and in what way they were amended as a result of further experimentation. Indeed, it is a curious fact that quite often an interpretation suggested by the original author has eventually become the observation of another investigator. This may be very misleading to anyone who does not take the trouble to refer to the original source and, in fact, can cause considerable confusion in the literature.

I have tried to present the biochemical data in a manner that will be understandable to those not specialists in this discipline, always warning against the temptation of too simple an interpretation. Technical detail was included to aid in interpreting data correctly where necessary and to endow the work with some of the properties of a "technical handbook."

Although most of the recent works in which sea urchin embryos have been used deal with the molecular aspects of development, due emphasis has been given to the morphological, both structural and experimental, observations. Indeed, experimental embryology — the *Entwicklungsmechanik* — laid the foundation for the analysis of development and uncovered some of the key events governing embryonic development such as morphogenetic localization, cell lineage, regulation, and embryonic induction. In spite of much effort, interpreting these events at the biochemical and molecular level appears to be a rather remote goal; yet it should be borne in mind that these are key problems for the understanding of development.

As we say in Italian, "Non c'é rosa senza spine" (No rose without thorns), and that of the sea urchin is the lack of genetic information. The lack of genetic markers is indeed a very serious limitation for the analysis of development. Yet I am convinced that because of its many obvious advantages, the sea urchin egg will be the material of choice for the developmental biologist for many years to come.

To Professor A. Monroy I wish to express my gratitude for having introduced me to developmental biology and my appreciation for many years of pleasant cooperation. I sincerely thank Professors E. Anderson, J. Brachet, G. B. Metz, J. M. Mitchison, J. W. Michejda, and E. Scarano for critically reviewing individual chapters. I am also indebted to Miss D. Raccuglia, Mr. D. Cascino, Mrs. A. Cascino, and Drs. S. G. Sconzo, A. Pirrone, and G. Cognetti for their cooperation in preparing this book.

GIOVANNI GIUDICE

PART I

MORPHOGENESIS AND RELATED PROBLEMS

Introduction

The literature on sea urchin embryology has been accumulating throughout this century at an ever increasing rate.

The motivation of the biologists' interest in this animal has changed with time. And yet, this embryo has turned out to be as suitable for a molecular approach to the study of development as it must have appeared to the first students of experimental embryology. The very accumulation of data in such a field has rendered it ever more suitable for the study of new problems by reason of the considerable background of literature available.

The following are among the reasons that have stimulated work on sea urchin embryos:

(a) The availability of large amounts of these animals along the shores where two of the most outstanding laboratories of marine biology have been founded, the Stazione Zoologica of Naples and the Marine Biological Laboratory of Woods Hole, Massachusetts. Here the founders of classic embryology have devoted a great deal of time to the study of the embryos of two species, *Paracentrotus lividus* and *Arbacia punctulata*.

(b) The transparency of the eggs of many species, which allows a good *in vivo* microscopic observation of the morphology of development.

(c) The ease with which the eggs can be experimentally fertilized or parthenogenetically activated and the clarity of some phenomena related to fertilization, such as elevation of the fertilization membrane.

1

(d) The relative synchrony of development.

(e) The rapidity of development, which leads to the larval stage in about 2 days.

(f) The feasibility of experiments of transplantation during the early stages of development.

To these advantages can be added others that encourage the use of the sea urchin embryo for an approach to the problem of differentiation from a biochemical and molecular point of view. They are:

(a) The possibility of obtaining eggs easily in gram amounts. It must be remembered that since the egg is oligolecithal, at least 50% represents living cellular material rather than a storage of yolk as is the case for telolecithal eggs.

(b) The lack of egg envelopes resistant to homogenization or impermeable to metabolic precursors.

(c) The fact that, until the early pluteus stage, active cell multiplication is not accompanied by a net increase of mass. This allows study of the processes related to cell division and differentiation independent from growth.

Many additional advantages, as well as some disadvantages, will become apparent in the course of this monograph. Among the disadvantages, is that this animal is not especially suitable for genetic work, because of the difficulty of raising the larvae through metamorphosis under laboratory conditions and the long period (at least 6 months, according to Hinegardner, 1969) required by the metamorphosized larvae to reach sexual maturity.

Chapter 1

Experimental Embryology of the Sea Urchin

A. Some Technical Notes on Handling Sea Urchin Embryos for Embryological Studies

1. SPECIES USUALLY STUDIED

Several sea urchin species have been employed for the study of development. Most of them are listed in the extensive monograph by Harvey (1956a) and in the more recent book edited by Boolotian (1966). Table 1.1 gives pertinent information on the season when ripe eggs of the Echinoidea class can be obtained, the place where they can be easily found, and their size.

2. COLLECTING THE GAMETES

For most species of sea urchins it is impossible to distinguish between the two sexes from an external inspection of the intact animals. Swann (1954) has, however, reported that the male gonopores of *Echinus esculentus, Paracentrotus lividus,* and *Psammechinus microtuberculatus* are located at the apex of a small hemispherical papilla, while the female gonopores are lodged within an ovoidal escavation, as can be seen under a dissecting microscope.

In species such as *Paracentrotus lividus,* gametes can be usually collected by cutting open the animals, scooping out the gonads, and gently shaking them in seawater. Practically, only ripe eggs are released in such a way during the breeding season.

3

TABLE 1.1

GEOGRAPHICAL DISTRIBUTION, BREEDING SEASON, AND EGG SIZE OF SOME SEA URCHINS

Classification	Place	Season	Size (μ)
I. Order Centrochinoida			
Suborder Stirodonta			
Family Arbacidae			
Arbacia lixula	Mediterranean; Atlantic coast of North Africa; some of the Atlantic islands; Brazil	Entire year, except summer; at least in south Mediterranean	79
Arbacia punctulata	East coast of United States and part of Central America	Summer in the north; spring and and winter in the south (all year round in southern United States)	74–80
Suborder Camarodonta			
Family Echinidae			
Echinus esculentus	Baltic sea; North Sea and west coast of Europe	Spring and summer	150–180
Psammechinus miliaris	Norwegian, Baltic, and North Seas; northwest coast of Africa	Spring and summer	98–115
Psammechinus microtuberculatus	Mediterranean		
Lytechinus variegatus	Bermuda; West Indies; United States Gulf and east coast north to North Carolina	Winter	100–120
Lytechinus anamnesus	Southern California	Summer	111
Lytechinus pictus[a]	Southern California	Summer	111
Family Strongylocen-trotidae			
Paracentrotus lividus	Mediterranean; Atlantic islands; northwest African coast; Ireland and Scotland	Entire year, except summer, at least in Mediterranean	90–100
Sphaerechinus granularis	Mediterranean and West Atlantic	November through July	98
Strongylocentrotus dröbachiensis	Circumpolar seas in the Arctic and other north seas	Winter	136–160

TABLE 1.1 *(continued)*

Classification	Place	Season	Size (μ)
Strongylocentrotus franciscanus	Pacific coast of North America; Japan	Winter (in northern United States)	120
Strongylocentrotus purpuratus	Pacific coast of North America	November to March	80
Strongylocentrotus pulcherrimus	Japan; north coast of China	Jan.–March (Misaki) Feb.– May (Asamushi)	96
Pseudocentrotus depressus	Southern Japan	End of October to December	95
Heliocidaris crassispina	Southern Japan	June and July	96–100
Family Echinometridae			
Echinometra lucunter	East Florida; Central America; Mexico; West Africa	Summer	80–120
Echinometra mathaei	Indo-West Pacific; Red Sea; East coast of Africa; Australia, Japan, etc.	Winter (southern United States)	
II. Order Exocycloida Suborder Clypeastrina Family Clypeastridae			
Clypeaster subdepressus	Florida	April to October	150–170
Clypeaster japonicus, Döderlein	South Japan	End of June to end of July	108
Family Scutellidae (sand dollars)			
Echinarachnius parma	Coasts of North America; Japan (?)	Summer	145
Dendraster excentricus	Pacific coast of North America	Summer	114–120
Mellita quinquies- perforata (keyhole urchin)	Florida up to North Carolina	Summer	120
Suborder Spatangina (heart urchins) Family Spatangidae			
Echinocardium cordatum	Baltic Sea; North Sea; Mediterranean; Japan; Australia	Winter in Mediterranean	110–125
Briossips lyrifera	All Europe and South Africa		

[a] Probably the same species as *anamnesus*.

The eggs can now be separated from the emptied gonads and other impurities by filtering them through a few layers of gauze or a "plankton net."

Sperm can also be collected by removing the gonads, but should be left undiluted up to the moment they are used for fertilization.

In some species, spawning can be induced by injection of 0.5 M KCl into the body cavity through the peristomal membrane. A volume of 0.5 ml of such a solution is generally suitable for an average-sized *Arbacia*. With this genus, however, the release of a fertilization inhibitor from the epidermis or from the perivisceral fluid has been noted, and this needs to be carefully washed away from the eggs, which otherwise will prove unfertilizable. After the injection, the animals are held over a dish or beaker full of seawater, with their genital pores below the surface; the gametes will be exhaustively shed within a few minutes. It should be noted that spawning can also be induced by injecting seawater instead of KCl.

In some genera, such as *Arbacia,* a convenient method to induce shedding of a limited quantity of gametes is electric stimulation. An alternating current of about 10 V is passed by applying the electrodes on the shell; shedding usually stops as the current is shut off.

Both methods, particularly the latter, leave the animal viable after shedding.

Before fertilization it is advisable to wash the egg suspension twice by sedimentation or low-speed centrifugation, in order to remove impurities which might affect future development.

3. FERTILIZATION

Fertilization is easily obtained by mixing an egg suspension with a slight excess of sperm.

The relative proportions can be varied within a very large range (Branham, 1969). We have, however, found it convenient to use the following proportions: 3 drops of thick (dry) sperm suspension diluted with 20 ml of seawater and mixed with 250 ml of egg suspension at the concentration of 30,000 eggs per ml.

Higher sperm concentration may cause polyspermy.

The mixture should be left undisturbed for at least 2 minutes, i.e., the time required for the fertilization membrane to be elevated and hardened.

4. EMBRYO CULTURES

It is usually very easy to obtain a good development of sea urchin eggs under laboratory conditions up to the larval stage, provided the following rules are observed.

Remove the excess sperm from the fertilized eggs by washing them at least twice in sterile (Millipore-filtered) seawater. Washing can be performed either by letting the eggs sediment and removing the supernatant seawater by suction, or by centrifuging the eggs in a fixed angle rotor at about 2000 *g* for 1 minute. Excessive centrifugation may result in damage to the eggs; sensitivity to centrifugation varies to a certain extent in different species. Resuspend the embryos in sterile seawater, with the addition of 100 IU of penicillin, 50 μg of streptomycin, and 50 μg of 3-sulfonamidomethoxypyridazine per ml of seawater, and allow them to develop under gentle stirring.

Sterilization of seawater is not necessary, nor is the addition of antibiotics and sulfonamides. Their use, however, has become routine to avoid bacterial growth that may interfere with metabolic assays, especially when performed with radioisotopes. Bacterial growth is favored by the presence of excess sperm (see Chapter 10).

Stirring of the seawater is necessary to provide adequate oxygenation. This has been achieved by the use of rocking trays, by air bubbling, or by rotating propellers. The use of 4-pole propellers, rotating at 40 rpm, has been found to be the most convenient.

The standard concentration used in our laboratory is 5000 eggs/ml. Higher concentrations can be used; however, it has been observed that as the concentration increases the rate of development decreases.

Embryos can also be cultured without stirring; in this case they should be kept in a monolayer in shallow water to ensure proper oxygenation.

The pH of the seawater is of the greatest importance. For optimal development, it should be kept between 7.7 and 8.3. Buffering of the seawater with 0.01 *M* Tris at pH 8.0 is permissible.

The temperature of seawater has to be kept at optimum, which obviously varies for the different species, being close to the temperature of the local seawater during the breeding season. It is about 18°–20°C for the Mediterranean species *Paracentrotus lividus* and *Arbacia lixula*. Higher temperatures speed up development, but at the same time render it less synchronous and regular. Lower temperatures slow down development. Unfertilized eggs remain fertile for about 1 month when kept refrigerated in the presence of antibiotics and sulfonamides (Mertes and Berg, 1962). In our experience a great variability is observed in this respect in different egg batches. Hultin and Hagström (1954) have reported that *Psammechinus miliaris* eggs can be stored frozen for 2–15 hours and still remain fertilizable in a few instances. We have not been able to preserve frozen-stored *Paracentrotus lividus* eggs.

Sperm can be stored refrigerated for weeks, provided they are not diluted with seawater.

B. Morphogenesis of the Sea Urchin Embryos

A thorough description of the developmental stages of *Psammechinus miliaris,* with extensive comments on the morphogenetic movements, can be found in Gustafson and Wolpert (1967). The development of the *Arbacia* egg is thoroughly described by Harvey (1956a). The development of several species has been described in detail by Mortensen (1921). This author has also listed a useful summary from which earlier morphological work concerning development of all echinoderms can be traced. A list mostly derived from Mortensen (1921) and comprising some of the available information on the development of the most common sea urchin species, is reported below:

Arbacia lixula (L.) (syn. *Arbacia pustulosa* Gray; *Echinocidaris aequituberculata* Blv.): reared by W. Busch and A. Krohn, in 1853 and 1854, to first larval stage; the fully formed pelagic larva identified by Joh. Muller in 1853; reared through metamorphosis by Giesbrecht in 1909 (see von Ubisch, 1913a,b,c, 1927, 1932b, 1950).

Arbacia punctulata (Gray): reared to full larval shape by Fewkes, in 1880; through metamorphosis by Garman and Colton, in 1882 (see Fewkes, 1881; Garman and Colton, 1883; Harvey, 1956a).

Psammechinus miliaris (Mull.) (syn. *Echinus, Parechinus miliaris*): pelagic larva identified by Mortensen in 1898; reared to full larval shape and through metamorphosis by McBride in 1898 and 1903; and by Théel in 1892; by Shearer, De Morgan, and Fuchs in 1909 (see Mortensen, 1898, 1921; McBride, 1903, 1914a; Shearer *et al.,* 1913).

Psammechinus microtuberculatus (Blv.) (syn. *Echinus pulchellus* Ag.): reared to first larval stage by Joh. Muller in 1852; Selenka in 1879 (wrongly named *Echinus miliaris*); Seeliger in 1896; reared through metamorphosis by Giesbrecht in 1909 (see von Ubisch, 1913b).

Echinus esculentus (L.): reared to full larval shape and through metamorphosis by McBride in 1898 and 1903; Shearer, De Morgan, and Fuchs in 1913 (see McBride, 1903; Shearer *et al.,* 1913; Shearer and Lloyd, 1913).

Echinus acutus (Lamk.): reared to full larval shape and through metamorphosis by Shearer *et al.* in 1913 (see Shearer *et al.,* 1913).

Paracentrotus lividus (Lamk.) (syn. *Strongylocentrotus lividus*): reared to young larva by A. Derbés in 1847; Krohn in 1849; to initial metamorphosis by J. Müller in 1852 (for references and latest descriptions, see von Ubisch, 1913a,b,c, 1927, 1932b, 1950).

Strongylocentrotus drobachiensis (O. F. Mull.): young pluteus reared by A. Agassiz in 1864 (see Agassiz, 1867, with the caution that other pelagic larvae have been wrongly described as the later stages of this larva by the same author).

Strongylocentrotus franciscanus (Ag.): young larva reared by Loeb in 1909 and by Hagedorn in 1909 (see Hagedorn, 1909).

Strongylocentrotus purpuratus (Stimps.): young larva reared by Hagedorn (1909).

Lytechinus variegatus (Lamk.) (syn. *Toxopneustes variegatus*): reared to beginning metamorphosis by Tennent in 1910 (see Tennent, 1912a).

Sphaerechinus granularis (Lamk.) (syn. *Echinus brevispinosus* Risso): young larva reared by Krohn in 1853; fully formed, pelagic larva identified by J. Müller in 1855 (see Müller, 1846–1855; Müller *et al.,* 1971).

Echinarachinus parma (Lamk.): pelagic larva identified by A. Agassiz in 1864; reared through metamorphosis by Fewkes in 1886 (see Agassiz, 1867).

Echinocardium cordatum (Pennant): pelagic larva identified by Mortensen in 1898; reared through metamorphosis by McBride in 1914 (see Mortensen, 1898, 1921; McBride, 1914b).

Moira atropos (Lamk.): reared through metamorphosis by Grave in 1902, but with no description given of the larva; young larva reared by Tennent in 1910 (see Mortensen, 1921).

1. DESCRIPTION OF NORMAL DEVELOPMENT

Development of the Mediterranean *Paracentrotus (Strongylocentrotus) lividus* will now be described in greater detail, including some consideration on the mechanics of development fundamentally derived by the observations of Gustafson and co-workers on the *Psammechinus* larvae, which show very similar developmental patterns.

The unfertilized egg (Fig. 1.1b) is 90–100 μ in diameter, and is an orange-yellow color determined by the different proportion of carotenoid pigments in different animals, so that the eggs may appear at times more yellow or more red; usually the eggs become paler toward the end of the breeding season.

The unfertilized egg is surrounded by a jelly coat, which will be discussed later.

Selenka (1883) and Boveri (1901a,b) have described a reddish band owing to the concentration of pigment in the sub-equatorial region of the egg. This band has been extremely useful in recognizing the animal (upper) and the vegetal (lower) pole of the the unfertilized egg. It is, however, observed only in the eggs of a few animals, at least in animals from the south Mediterranean.

Upon fertilization (Fig. 1.1c), a "fertilization membrane" is lifted from the surface of the egg. Within about two minutes, the membrane becomes quite tough and contributes to the prevention of polyspermy.

Within about 60 minutes, the egg undergoes the first cleavage; the furrow is meridional, i.e. from the animal to the vegetal pole, thus giving rise to the two first blastomeres (Fig. 1.1d). A second furrow, also meridional but at a right angle to the first, divides the egg into four blastomeres (Fig. 1.1e). The third cleavage furrow is orthogonal to the former two and divides the egg into an animal (upper) quartet and a vegetal (lower) quartet. This 8-cell stage is reached about 3½ hours after fertilization (Fig. 1.1f). At the following cleavage, the animal and vegetal blastomeres are cut in a different way: in the animal half each blastomere is divided by a meridional furrow, while in the vegetal half cleavage occurs along a plane parallel to the equator, but very close to the vegetal pole. As a result, a 16-cell embryo arises which is made up of 8 mesomeres in the animal part, 4 subequatorial macromeres, and 4 micromeres at the vegetal pole (Fig. 1.1g). In the next division a transversal furrow divides the mesomeres into two rings of 8 cells each, while the macromeres and the micromeres divide meridionally. This is the 32-cell stage (Fig. 1.1h). The two rings of mesomeres have been designated (Hörstadius, 1931, 1935, 1939, 1949) as "an_1" and "an_2," moving from the animal pole. In the next stage of 64 cells, the macromeres also become divided by an equatorial furrow into two rings which have been called veg_1 and veg_2, respectively, moving from the equator toward the vegetal pole (Fig. 1.5).

Through further division, the egg reaches the morula stage (Fig. 1.1i); about 6 hours after fertilization, the blastomeres have become progressively smaller and have acquired the shape of epithelial cells, which surround the blastocoel in a single layer. The outer surface of the embryo appears regularly smooth. This is the early blastula stage (Fig. 1.1j and k). The formation of the blastocoel can be traced back to the 16-cell stage (Wolpert and Gustafson, 1961b). Several hypotheses have been proposed to interpret the formation of the blastocoelic cavity. K. Dan (1952, 1960) has suggested that the adherence of the cells to the hyaline layer surrounding the egg holds them away from the center of the embryo, which at the same time becomes filled with fluid by an osmotic mechanism. The observation that the volume of the blastocoel is reduced if the blastulae are immersed in seawater containing nondiffusible substances with high osmotic pressure supports this view. Monné and Härde (1950) too have proposed an osmotic mechanism. According to Wolpert and Gustafson (1961b), the attachment of the cells to the hyaline layer,

Fig. 1.1. The early development of the sea urchin *Paracentrotus lividus* ($\times$ 400). (a) fully grown oocyte (slightly flattened with the coverslip); (b) unfertilized egg (slightly flattened with the coverslip); (c) fertilized egg; (d) 2-cell stage; (e) 4-cell stage, seen from the animal pole; (f) 8-cell stage; (g) 16-cell stage (the micromeres are toward the bottom); (h) 32-cell stage; (i) morula; (j) early blastula (the external edge has not yet become uniformly smooth); (k) blastula; (l) hatching blastula (10 hours after fertilization).

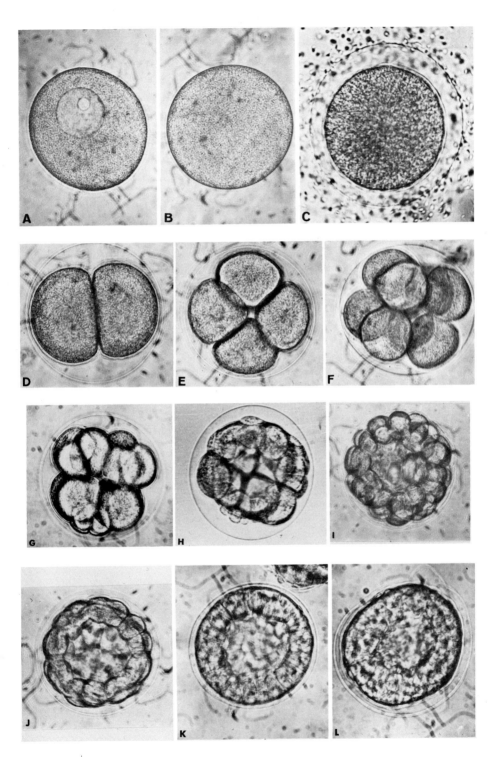

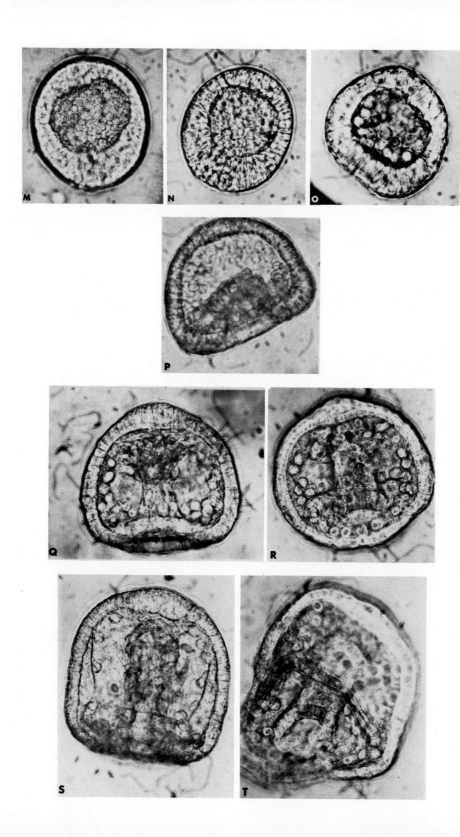

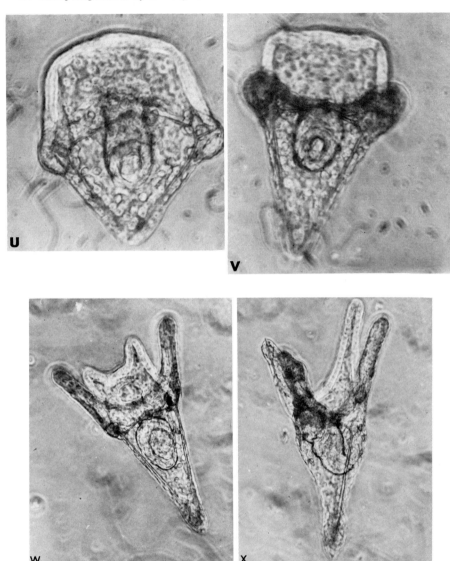

FIG. 1.1 (*continued*). (m) Swimming blastula; (n) early mesenchyme blastula; (o) late mesenchyme blastula; (p) early gastrula; (q) late gastrula; (r) early prism, viewed from the ventral and vegetal side; (s) prism viewed from the ventral side; (t) same as in (s), further rotated toward the vegetal side; (u) a developmental stage between the prism and the pluteus [same orientation as in (t)]; (v) pluteus [same orientation as in (t) and (u)]; (w) late pluteus (48 hours after fertilization) viewed from the vegetal side; (x) same as in (w), viewed from its right side. (Magnification of w, x: × 180.)

together with the radial pattern of cleavage and the change in cell shape, are enough to account for the blastocoel formation without resorting to an osmotic mechanism. The problem then arises on how the change in cell shape occurs. This change, which during cleavage goes from spherical to conical and then to cubical, is attributed to changes of the cell membrane tension tending to round up the cells, and of the intercellular adhesion tending to flatten them against each other. The radiality of cell division prevents the cells from piling up in several rows.

About 8 hours after fertilization, because of the formation of a motile cilium from each cell, ciliation occurs. The embryo now starts rotating within the membrane. Ten hours after fertilization, the fertilization membrane breaks up at one point (Fig. 1.1l) and the embryo hatches. This is the swimming blastula stage (Fig. 1.1m), an apical tuft of long, stiff cilia develops at the animal pole, while the vegetal pole begins to flatten, forming the so-called "vegetal plate," and the larva thus becomes more or less pear-shaped. At this time, a pulsatory activity of the cells at the vegetal pole can be observed by time-lapse cinematography (Gustafson and Kinnander, 1956a,b). According to Gustafson, this activity is due to the reduced adhesiveness of the cells to each other and to the hyaline layer; as a result, they become loose and move singly inside the blastocoelic cavity giving rise to the primary mesenchyme (Fig. 1.1n and o). It is of interest that the number of primary mesenchyme cells is species specific: 33 ± 4 cells in *Sphaerechinus* and 55 ± 4 cells in *Echinus,* according to Driesch (1898). As the primary mesenchyme cells are shifted inside the blastocoel, they initiate an active pseudopodial activity (Gustafson and Wolpert, 1961a). The pseudopodia are about $0.5\ \mu$ thick and up to $30–40\ \mu$ long; they can reach their full length in about 3 minutes. Time-lapse cinematography shows that the pseudopodia move very actively as if they were exploring the blastocoelic wall, to which they get attached. The displacement of the mesenchyme cells along the blastocoelic wall is caused by the attachment and retraction of the pseudopodia. The points of contact of the pseudopodia with the inner surface of the blastocoelic wall are continuously broken and renewed so that eventually the cells move toward the areas where adhesion of the pseudopodia is stronger. At the gastrula stage, the primary mesenchyme cells are grouped in a ring at the base of the intestinal invagination; two cellular rods rise from the ring, one on each side of the intestine, along the ventral side of the embryo, i.e., the one where the stomodaeum will differentiate. Meanwhile, the pseudopodia of primary mesenchyme cells fuse with each other, thus giving rise to a continuous cablelike structure within which the matrix of the skeleton is deposited (Chapter 11).

The process of gastrulation has been thoroughly investigated by Gustafson and collaborators (Gustafson and Kinnander, 1956a,b, 1960; Gustafson and Wolpert, 1961a,b, 1962, 1967; Gustafson, 1963; Kinnander and Gustafson, 1960; Wolpert and Gustafson, 1961b) by means of time-lapse cinematography. According to Gustafson, invagination of the primitive intestine, up to one third of its final length, is an autonomous process, i.e., it is the result of the continued pulsatory activity and of change of adhesiveness of the cells of the vegetal plate once migration of the primary mesenchyme cells is over (Fig. 1.1p). At this point, the cells at the tip of the archenteron start to bud off (this is the secondary mesenchyme) and, by means of pseudopodia, establish contact with the inner surface of the ectoderm at the animal pole. The shortening of these pseudopodia pulls the intestine toward the animal pole, i.e., brings about its further invagination (Fig. 1.1g). How invagination may be generated by a decrease in cell-to-cell adhesiveness, with no concomitant decrease of adhesion to the hyaline layer, and coupled with a pulsatory activity, is illustrated in Fig. 1.2. The fact that the forces involved in the first invagination of the primitive intestine are confined to the vegetal plate was first recognized by Moore and Burt (1939). These authors show that isolated vegetal plates can continue invagination. Moore (1941) has calculated that the force necessary to produce invagination is of the order of 10^{-2} erg. This calculation is based on experiments that take advantage of the fact that the blastocoel is easily accessible (through the intercellular spaces, according to Moore) to salts and water but not to organic molecules, as for example, sucrose. Gustafson and Wolpert (1963b), by measuring the elastic properties of the cell wall of blastula and gastrula, have calculated that the maximum force required for gastrulation to occur is about 0.1 dyne.

The role of pseudopodia in the second part of invagination of the primitive intestine has also been suggested by Dan and Okazaki (1956) and K. Dan (1960). Indirect evidence for this also derives from observations that the conditions that impair pseudopodial movement also adversely affect gastrulation. No pseudopodial activity has been observed in *Lytechinus* early gastrulae (Trinkhaus, 1965); this is the only observation questioning the role of pseudopodia in gastrulation.

While the intestine completes its invagination, the larva becomes flattened along its dorsoventral axis, and in a sagittal section it appears roughly triangular. Meanwhile, the skeleton appears; its development will be described later. The cells at the animal pole have thickened to form the so-called "animal plate." This is the prism stage (Fig. 1.1r–t). The next important morphological event is the constriction of the animal end of the intestine into a vesicle, which is the first rudiment of the coelom. At the same time, the ectodermal wall, at its ventral side close to the animal pole, forms a small invagination; its upper edge with its apical tuft forms the ciliated band; the invagination is the first rudiment of the stomatodaeum. Indeed, the tip of the intestine now bends toward it, apparently again through the action of the pseudopodia of the cells of the secondary

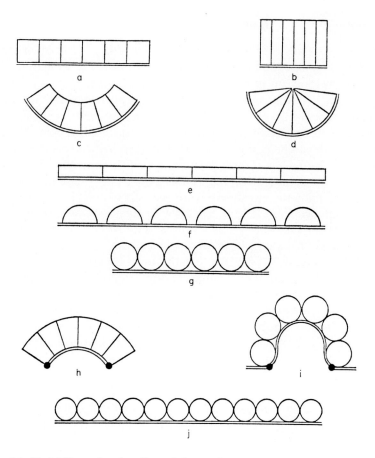

Fig. 1.2. Model illustrating the effect of changes in contact between cells, and between cells and a supporting membrane, on the form of a cell sheet. For convenience only six adjacent cells are considered. The cross-sectional area of the cells is fixed. (a) Moderate contact between the cells and between the cells and supporting membrane. (b) Increased contact between the cells and loss of contact with the supporting membrane; the cells become columnar. (c) Effect of increased contact between the cells if the cells do not alter their contact with the supporting membrane; the sheet becomes curved. (d) Effect of a further increase in contact between the cells, compared to that in (c), if the cells do not lose their contact with the supporting membrane; the sheet is maximally curved. (e) Effect of stretching the supporting membrane if the cells are able to increase their contact with it; the cells are flattened. (f) Effect of stretching the supporting membrane if the cells are able to increase their contact with the membrane, but not to the same extent as in (e), and lose contact with one another; the cells tend to round up owing to the tension in the membrane. (The free edges in the other figures are not drawn rounded since they are still in contact with other cells in the sheet.) (g) Effect of the cells in (a) rounding up; the sheet becomes longer. (h) Effect of the cells in (b) reducing their contact if the ends of the sheet are fixed; the sheet becomes curved. (i) Effect of rounding up of the cells in (b) if the ends of the sheet are fixed; the sheet curves maximally in a direction similar to (h). (j) Effect of doubling the number of cells in (g) by division; the sheet becomes longer. (From Gustafson and Wolpert, 1963b.)

mesenchyme and of the coelomic cells. The coelom is then pulled by its own pseudopodial activity into two small sacs at the right and left side of the intestine, which thus makes direct contact with the ectodermal wall (Fig. 1.3). At this time, two constrictions divide the intestine into three successive segments: the esophagus, followed by the stomach and the intestine.

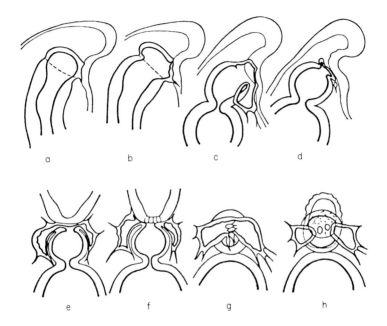

Fig. 1.3. Semischematic drawings from time-lapse films and fixed material showing various stages in the development of the coelom and the mouth. (a–d) Larvae in optical median section; (c) somewhat to the right of the median plane; (e–f) dorsoanimal view; (g–h) ventral view.

The pictures show the progressive constriction between the coelom region and the esophagus rudiment (a, b, and d); in later pictures the constriction between the esophagus and the stomach rudiment has also appeared. The unpaired coelom rudiment in (a) and (b) increased its contact with the oral ectoderm, which shows a progressive invagination associated with pulsatory activity at the inner border. The coelom is pulled out to the right and the left into two sacs by means of pseudopods (c); downward there is little coelom surface to pull out (see a, b, and d) and only a few cells are released in that direction. As a result of the bilateral extension of the sacs the median unpaired section connecting the sacs (the isthmus) becomes more and more reduced and is finally very small and slitlike (c, d, and e). The coelom sacs are extended laterally and downward and also more and more backward along the esophagus. As a result of this pull the anterior isthmus sheet finally ruptures (f and g) and the upper edge of the esophagus can make direct contact with the oral ectoderm and the two coelomic sacs make further contacts with the oral ectoderm (f). The pull also contributes to tease the ectodermal sheet until it ruptures (h). The oral invagination is indicated by dotted contours in (h). (From Gustafson and Wolpert, 1963a.)

According to Gustafson and Wolpert (1963a,b), it is the pseudopodial action of the coelomic cells that stretches the ectoderm sideways at the site of the stomatodaeum, thus contributing to its breakage, and allowing communication between the esophagus and the outside.

The coelomic cells with their pseudopodia then give rise to bundles of contractile cables along the major axis of the esophagus. It is through the contraction of these pseudopodia, according to Gustafson and Wolpert (1967), that the peristaltic movements of the esophagus are brought about. These consist of peristaltic waves that originate at the oral end and move backward thus forcing the water through the cardiac constriction into the stomach. When a high hydrostatic pressure has been built up in the stomach its pyloric constriction opens, letting the water pass into the proctodaeum.

By this time, the embryo has changed its shape into that of the mature larva, the pluteus. The skeleton, which at late gastrula stage appears as two triradiated spicules whose rays are at first randomly oriented (Wolpert and Gustafson, 1961a), has now elongated following the pattern laid down by the matrix (see Chapter 11).

Three pairs of rods grow along the plane of the vegetal pole in three different directions. The first pair represents the ventral rods (one per side), which grow toward each other; their tips eventually come in contact with each other on the ventral side of the anal opening (Fig. 1.1w–x). The second pair of rods elongates dorsally pushing the dorsal side to form an acute angle, at the apex of which the two rods will touch and stop growing. These are the so-called body rods. A third rod grows from each spicule toward the ventral side forming the anal rods, i.e., the skeleton of the anal arms. From the ventral rods, close to the point of confluence with the anal rods, another rod grows upward from each spicule; i.e., toward the animal pole. They soon bend ventrally thus forming the oral rods, i.e., the skeleton of the oral arms. In this way the mouth of the pluteus will eventually be framed by the oral arms at its animal side and by the anal arms at its vegetal side. The pluteus moves with its arms forward; the cilia derived from the ciliated band give rise to a stream that conveys the food to the mouth.

According to Gustafson and Wolpert (1961c), growth of the arms depends on the pushing action of the growing skeleton over the ectoderm. Since it is possible, however, to completely inhibit the formation of the skeleton with low doses of actinomycin, according to Peltz and Giudice (1967), and still obtain formation of the arm buds and of the apex, which, however, fail to grow to full length, it is more likely that the first formation of the bud is independent of the presence of the skeleton which only influences its further growth.

The morphology of the skeleton is one of the main features that differentiate the larvae of different sea urchin species; indeed, it has been used as a major marker for the recognition of maternal or paternal characters in hybrids (see Fig. 1.4).

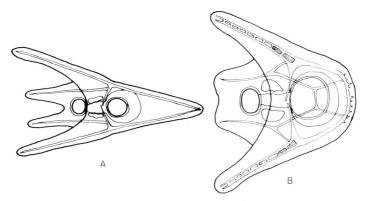

Fig. 1.4. Drawing of a pluteus of *Paracentrotus lividus* (A) and of *Sphaerechinus granularis* (B) showing the different morphologies of the skeleton.

While the skeleton elongates, bright red pigmented cells make their appearance; they are scattered throughout the larva but are preferentially grouped along the skeleton.

At the pluteus stage the left coelomic sac attaches to the dorsal ectoderm and eventually opens to the outside, thus forming the rudiment of the pore canal.

For a better understanding of the different phases of development the reader is referred to the diagram of Fig. 1.5.

Under standard laboratory conditions the plutei survive only for a few days. In order for them to metamorphose, food must be added to the sea water. This may consist of diatoms or other planktonic organisms. Harvey (1956a) reports that the diatom *Nitzschia closterium* (identified as *Phaeodactylum tricornatum* by Hendey, 1954) is a suitable nourishment. These diatoms can grow in pure culture in a sterile solution of 0.002% $Na_2HPO_4 \cdot 12H_2O$ and 0.01% KNO_3. A recent discussion on the food to be used in these cultures can be found in the work by Hinegardner (1969).

It is outside the scope of this book to give a description of the complex process of metamorphosis. For a general survey of sea urchin metamorphosis, the book by Hyman (1955), the article by Fell (1948), and the "Traité de Zoologie" of Grassé (1948), can be consulted. Metamorphosis of *Paracentrotus lividus* embryos has more recently been studied by Cziahk (1960, 1965a).

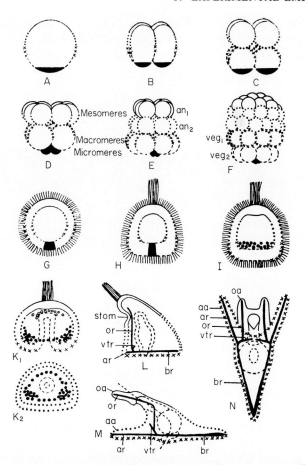

Fig. 1.5. Diagram of the normal development of *Paracentrotus lividus*. Indication of the layers: an_1, continuous lines; an_2, dotted; veg_1, crosses; veg_2, broken lines; micromeres, black. (A) Uncleaved egg; (B) 4-cell stage; (C) 8-cell stage; (D) 16-cell stage; (E) 32-cell stage; (F) 64-cell stage; (G) young blastula; (H) later blastula, with apical organ, before the formation of the primary mesenchyme; (I) blastula after the formation of the primary mesenchyme; (J) gastrula: secondary mesenchyme and the two triradiate spicules formed; (K) transverse optical section of the same gastrula; bilateral symmetry established; (L) so-called prism stage; stomodaeum invaginating; (M) pluteus larva from the left side: broken line indicates position of the egg axis; (N) pluteus from the anal side. Abbreviations: *aa*, anal arm; *ar*, anal rod; *br*, body rod; *oa*, oral arm; *or*, oral rod; *stom*, stomodaeum; *vtr*, ventral transverse rod. (From Hörstadius, 1939.)

Hinegardner (1969) has described the conditions for raising, through metamorphosis, eggs of *Arbacia punctulata, Lytechinus pictus, Lytechinus variegatus, Strongylocentrotus purpuratus,* and *Echinometra mathaei.* A brief morphological description is also reported and the interesting point is stressed that these larvae can reach sexual maturity in about 6 months, a period that is not much longer than the generation time of some other biological materials, like corn or mice, that are extensively used in genetic studies.

2. DETERMINATION OF THE POSITION OF THE EMBRYONIC AXES

A sea urchin larva offers two main axes: (a) a dorsoventral axis, the ventral side of the larva being the one where the stomatodaeum opens, and the dorsal side being the one where the body rods meet; (b) an animal–vegetal axis, which runs from the animal to the vegetal pole. A plane of bilateral symmetry through both axes cuts the embryo in two symmetrical halves, right and left (see Fig. 1.6).

The question has long been debated as to when during development these axes become fixed.

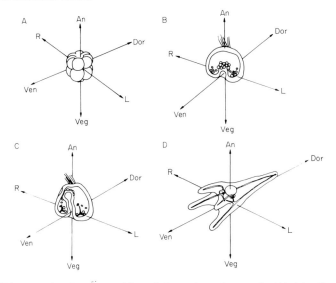

Fig. 1.6. Diagram showing the position of the embryonic axes in (A) 16-cell embryo; (B) an early gastrula; (C) an early prism; (D) a pluteus. Abbreviations: An, animal; Veg, vegetal; Ven, ventral; Dor, dorsal; R, right; L, left.

a. The Dorsoventral Axis

The most important recent reviews on the subject belong to Hörstadius, to whom we owe the major contributions to the solution of the problem (Hörstadius and Wolsky, 1936; Hörstadius, 1939, 1949, 1957).

It has been shown by Selenka (1883) and Boveri (1901a,b) that in *Paracentrotus* the first two cleavage furrows lie meridionally, i.e., along the animal–vegetal axis.

By means of vital staining it has been shown (Hörstadius, 1928) that the point of sperm entry bears no relation to the position of the first furrow.

Various ideas have been expressed as to the relationship between the two first meridional furrows and the plane of bilateral symmetry. According to Boveri (1901b, 1902, 1905, 1907), Garbowsky (1905), Herbst (1907), Jenkinson (1911), and Runnström (1914), the first furrow coinsides with this plane of symmetry. However, von Ubisch (1925a) and Hörstadius and Wolsky (1936) have shown by means of vital staining that in fact there is no relationship between the position of the first two furrows and the plane of bilateral symmetry. The position of the dorsoventral axis, and, therefore, of the plane of bilateral symmetry, does not seem to become fixed, at least irreversibly, in the early stages of development. Experiments in which the egg or the embryo are longitudinally cut have given the following results: If an unfertilized egg of *Paracentrotus* is cut longitudinally, using as a marker the pigment ring, and the two halves are fertilized, each half (one is haploid and the other diploid) develops into a more or less normal larva. Both exhibit various degrees of defects of ventral structures (Hörstadius and Wolksy, 1936). These results agree with the hypothesis (Lindahl, 1936) of a ventral center being present in the unfertilized egg, which, however, becomes gradually irreversibly fixed in the course of development.

Again, if the two first blastomeres are separated, each one may give rise to a normal pluteus, even if defects are often observed at the side originally facing the removed blastomere (Driesch, 1891, 1892, 1900, 1903). In this case, each blastomere shows a more or less pronounced tendency to form structures that are characteristic of the ventral side, possibly depending on the amount of ventral material it contains. In some instances it has been observed that the ventral side is formed on both blastomeres on the formerly outer side. This result would argue against the existence of any irreversibly fixed ventral side. It may at most be taken as indicating that the dorsoventral polarity has been reversed in the presumptive dorsal blastomere.

If the blastomeres are separated at the 4-cell stage, they usually develop as rather normal, dwarf plutei; the results, however, suggest that the early differentiation of those that happen not to contain the ventral side is delayed. Indeed, it should be recalled that in the pluteus the spicules and the stomatodaeum, which account for two thirds of the original egg material, differentiate at the ventral side (Fukushi, 1959).

That the dorsoventral axis is not irreversibly fixed at these early stages is best shown by the experiments of Hörstadius (1957) of exchange of meridional halves of 16-cell embryos. In 41 out of 43 cases a perfect pluteus is obtained. This suggests that the deficiencies observed in the isolated blastomeres may be owing to the quantitative reduction of the overall embryonic material more than to a prefixed position of the dorso-ventral axis (Fig. 1.7).

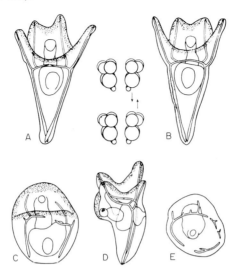

Fig. 1.7. Exchange of meridional halves between two eggs. (A and B) Pair of typical plutei; (C) pluteus with typical bilateral symmetry but without arms; (D) pluteus with two esophagi and a supernumerary ciliated band on part of the dorsal side; (E) irregular larva. (From S. Hörstadius, 1957, *J. Embryol. Exp. Morphol.* **5**, 60.)

That the determined condition of the ventral side is reinforced as cleavage proceeds is indicated by further experiments of Horstadius in which 32-cell embryos were longitudinally split, flattened, and combined (Fig. 1.8). All kinds of larvae were obtained, ranging from perfect gigantic plutei to larvae with two ventral sides. These results were interpreted by Hörstadius as suggesting that many sides of the egg are potentially able to become a ventral side; however, one dominating ventral center that represses all others must exist. This view is also supported by the fact that by constricting the eggs so as to drastically reduce the communication between the two parts, some embryos with two ventral sides are obtained.

Fig. 1.8. Fusion of two 32-cell stages to form a giant larva with unitary animal–vegetal axis. (A) The egg is placed on its animal pole and cut along a meridian from the vegetal to the animal pole (thick line); (B) the 32-cell stage flattened as one layer; (C) one flattened egg placed on top of another, as seen from their animals ends. (From S. Hörstadius, 1957, *J. Embryol. Exp. Morphol.* **5**, 60.)

In later stages, the ability to form a ventral side becomes progressively restricted. If an early gastrula is cut meridionally into two halves, ventral and dorsal, each one will give rise to exactly half a pluteus.

Hence, the beginning of gastrulation is the turning point for the dorso-ventral axis to become irreversibly fixed.

In early stages it is also experimentally possible to alter the orientation of the dorsoventral axis. Lindahl (1932a, 1936) achieved this result by sucking eggs into a pipette with an inner diameter smaller than that of the egg; the outer end of the stretched egg was then vitally stained and proved to be the ventral side. However, if the staining was too intense, the stained end became dorsal. Interpretation of these experiments is very difficult. Centrifuging the eggs before fertilization alters the plane of symmetry (Runnström, 1926; Lindahl, 1932b; Pease, 1939). It is also pertinent to recall that Mazia (1958a) has been able to obtain twin embryos of *Dendraster* by treating them with mercaptoethanol during metaphase of the first or second cleavage. This treatment is effective in breaking the contact between the first two or four blastomeres, which is followed by a rearrangement of the dorsoventral axis of the egg. Many other authors in the past have also been able to obtain twins from single sea urchin eggs through a variety of treatments (reviewed by Hörstadius, 1939).

What is the mechanism that brings about determination of the dorso-ventral axis? What are the conditions that determine appearance of the skeleton and formation of a stomatodaeum at one specific side of the embryo? Studies of time-lapse cinematography by Gustafson (see above) lead to the conclusion of a preferential adhesion of the pseudopodia of the cells at the tip of the archenteron with the ventral rather than with any other part of the ectoderm, thus providing one of the late steps through which the oral side is formed. What makes ectodermal cells more adhesive for mesenchymal pseudopodia is still a matter of conjecture. Gustafson and Sävhagen (1949) have found that treatment of the eggs with diluted detergents like dodecylsulfate abolishes the dorsoventral axis, and larvae with radial symmetry originate. At the dilution used, according to the authors, the most likely site of action of the detergent is on the cell surface, and, therefore, on adhesiveness.

Experiments aiming at inhibiting nucleic acid and protein synthesis throw little more light on the problem: Hörstadius and Gustafson (1954) have showed that a treatment of the embryos with 8-chloroxanthine and β-phenyllactic acid, which are supposed to inhibit RNA and protein synthesis, respectively, resulted in a marked inhibitory effect on the establishment of the bilateral symmetry. Similar results were obtained with 3-acetylpyridine (an analog of nicotinic acid). Although the effect on metabolism was not tested, the authors were inclined to believe that their results might be due "to the surface activity of the agents used rather than to their anti-metabolic properties in a restricted sense."

Other results point to a role of the synthesis of RNA in the establishment of an oral field, which is one of the late features of dorsoventral organization. Runnström (1966a) has observed that treatment with actinomycin concentrations, which do not affect the distribution of the primary mesenchyme cells (i.e., close to the ventral side), inhibits formation of the oral field. Markman (1966) has observed autoradiographically a higher incorporation of RNA precursors in the cells of the ventral side. However, experiments with inhibitors, even barring the possibility of side effects, are difficult to interpret. In the case of actinomycin, since its effect is on the RNA synthesis of the whole embryo, there is little hope of understanding at what level RNA synthesis plays a role, if any, in the establishment of the bilateral symmetry of the oral field. The experiments of Markman, on the other hand, are open to the more general question of the lack of information as to the permeability to radioactive precursors and the size of the internal precursor pool in the different territories of the embryo. Histochemical techniques (Czihak, 1961, 1962) have revealed an accumulation of cytochromoxidase in the ventral side of the embryo, as from the blastula stage. Taken together, these results suggest that, at least from the blastula stage, the oral field is characterized by a particularly active metabolism with respect to RNA synthesis and energy production.

Nothing more than a faint light in the darkness of the problem, yet the key to a complex phenomenon may lie in a very simple mechanism.

The key question is: What is the structural or molecular basis for a certain area of the egg to become the ventral and another the dorsal side? The centrifugation experiments suggest that whatever the factor may be that determines this localization, it seems to be bound to structures affected by centrifugation.

b. Animal–Vegetal Axis

A tremendous amount of data has accumulated on the establishment of this axis of the embryo. Among them, the ones obtained by operative methods have been reviewed by Hörstadius (1939).

The time at which this axis becomes fixed in the egg should be ascribed to some point before fertilization. While Driesch (1902) had reached the conclusion that all parts of the egg are totipotent, Hörstadius was able to show (1928) that, while vegetal halves are usually capable of giving rise to entire larvae, the isolated animal halves give rise only to animalized larvae, i.e., to larvae with a strongly unbalanced development, with excessive development of those structures deriving from the animal half of the egg. This latter conclusion agrees with the previous results of Zoja

(1895), Boveri (1901b, 1902), Terni (1914), von Ubisch (1925c, 1929, 1932a), and Plough (1929). This may seem in contradiction with the results of Harvey (1932, 1933a), who reported on the occasional development into normal dwarf plutei of nucleated halves of *Arbacia* eggs (obtained by splitting the eggs by means of centrifugation). According to Hörstadius (1939), however, the few nucleated halves that develop into plutei may have been those that, as a result of the random orientation of the eggs during centrifugation, happened to contain the vegetal side of the egg.

On the other hand, it seems definitively proved that the position of the animal–vegetal axis is already laid down in the ovary. Actually, it has been suggested that micromeres are formed at the site where the egg is attached to the ovarian wall during oogenesis. The animal pole is located at the opposite side where the polar bodies are extruded (Jenkinson, 1911; Lindahl, 1932a,b).

To what extent are the vegetal and animal potentialities fixed in the different parts of the egg? As already mentioned, the experiments of equatorial section of the unfertilized eggs argue in favor of an irreversible distribution of at least the animal potentialities before fertilization.

Let us discuss first the criteria on which to rely for the evaluation of the animal potentialities.

On the basis of the mapping of the presumptive areas, one criterion may be the ability to develop a ciliated epithelium. It is indeed from the animal half that two thirds of the ectoderm of the larva arises; it is from the animal pole of the egg that the apical tuft of the blastula will originate. Another criterion may be based on a negative condition, i.e., the inability of a territory to give rise to structures different from the ectoderm, i.e., mesenchyme, intestine, and skeleton. Knowledge of the structures to be considered as derivatives of the vegetal pole, and of the ones from the animal pole, come from the work of mapping of the presumptive territories on the egg (Fig. 1.5). Bearing these criteria in mind, it becomes apparent from the results of experiments of equatorial cutting of the embryos at various developmental stages (as indicated in Fig. 1.9) that the animal properties are irreversibly fixed in the egg before fertilization. Cutting an embryo before the early blastula stage results in the development of a hollow ectodermic sphere from the animal half; the animal potencies have now spread over the entire larva. After the blastula stage, a restriction of the animal potencies must take place; indeed, if animal halves are cut after that stage, blastulae with normal extension of the apical tuft that lack vegetal structures are obtained. A different interpretation of these results might be that a critical mass of embryonic material is needed for the vegetal structures to be formed. This is ruled out by the observation that meridional halves or isolated blastomeres after the first or second cleavage, and even isolated vegetal halves of eggs, may give rise to more or less normal embryos.

If the ability to form mesenchyme, intestine, and skeleton is taken as an expression of vegetal potencies, then it may be said that these are also irreversibly fixed in the unfertilized egg; indeed, these structures appear in embryos deriving from isolated vegetal halves of the egg. These latter are sometimes able to give rise to entire dwarf plutei, i.e., small larvae containing structures that would normally be formed from the animal pole. This shows that it is difficult to assess that in the vegetal half of the egg only vegetal properties are contained. Sometimes, however, the embryos

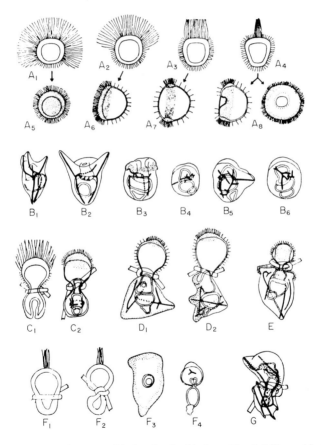

Fig. 1.9. (A_1–A_8) Development of isolated animal halves. (A_1–A_4) Young blastulae with more or less enlarged apical tuft; (A_5–A_8) fully differentiated halves. (B_1–B_6) Development of isolated vegetative halves. The animal and vegetative halves on the left represent equatorial eggs, those to the right, subequatorial halves. (C–E) Equatorial constriction in early cleavage stage. (F–G) The originally loose hair-loop has been more tightly constricted at the blastula stage. (From Hörstadius, 1935.)

obtained from vegetal halves do actually contain all of the vegetal structures and lack the animal ones, like stomatodaeum and ciliated band. For
a better understanding of such results, the diagram derived from Hörstadius (1935, 1938) and reported in Fig. 1.9 should be examined. One can
observe various degrees of animalization obtained by isolated animal
halves of eggs in the first two rods, and various degrees of vegetalization
obtained by isolated vegetal halves in the third row. Among the latter, we
observe larvae that range from a dwarf pluteus up to a vegetalized form,
with little skeleton and almost no ectodermal structures. This result
appears particularly puzzling, especially in view of the fact that the
animal halves always fail to differentiate vegetal structures. An explanation that the author proposes is based on the theory of the two gradients,
which will be discussed later.

Proceeding with development, we observe that the most vegetal part
of the early embryo, the micromeres, are endowed very precociously with
vegetal properties. This is clearly demonstrated by experiments of
implantation of micromeres, which causes the formation of a secondary
archenteron and of a supplementary skeleton at the site of implantation
(Fig. 1.10). A series of transplantation experiments have been performed, especially by Hörstadius, aimed at investigating the details of
distribution of the animal–vegetal potentialities along the animal–vegetal
axis of the egg and embryo. All of them seem to fit nicely in a general
scheme proposed by Runnström (1928a,b) of the existence of two gradients of animal and vegetal potentialities, with a maximum of intensity
at the respective poles and decreasing toward the opposite pole.

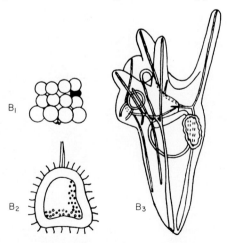

Fig. 1.10. Implantation of four micromeres between an_1 and an_2 of a 32-cell stage. (From
Hörstadius, 1935.)

By microsurgical experiments, Hörstadius has made an accurate quantitation of the distribution of these properties along the egg axis. Figure 1.11 demonstrates the effect of the implantation of different parts of a vegetal half on the developmental fate of an animal half. It appears that the animal properties of the animal half of the egg (which, if isolated, would develop into the usual hyperciliated blastula) are the more balanced the closer to the vegetal pole is the origin of the implanted blastomeres. On the other hand, a weakly vegetal fragment, while unable to balance the animal properties of a whole animal half, will succeed in balancing the animal properties of one third of the animal territory.

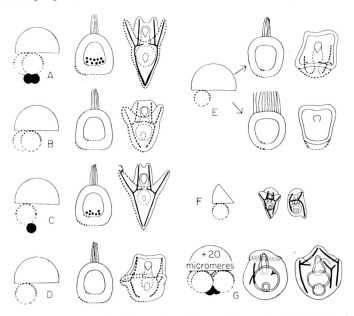

Fig. 1.11. Diagram of gradual diminution of vegetative material (A–E). Animal half, half circle; veg_1, crosses; veg_2, broken line; micromeres, black. (A) $8 + 2 + 2$; (B) $8 + 2 + 0$; (C) $8 + 1 + 1$; (D) $8 + 1 + 0$; (E) $8 + \frac{1}{2} + 0$; (F) if the animal material also is diminished, this small larva will differentiate more harmonically, as the animal and vegetative qualities are more typically balanced; (G) if a whole egg be filled with micromeres, it will differentiate like a vegetative half. (From Hörstadius, 1935.)

In Fig. 1.12, the effect of implanting micromeres on animal or vegetal fragments is quantitized. In agreement with the above, it is also shown that from vegetal fragments on which micromeres have been implanted, larvae arise which get more vegetalized the closer to the vegetal pole are the fragments that have received the micromeres. The results also depend on the number of micromeres implanted. In extreme cases, a larva is formed with a disproportionate development of intestine, i.e., an exogastrula; skeleton is not formed in these larvae, probably because of the lack of the guidance exerted by the ectoderm on the skeleton-forming cells. Ectoderm is indeed practically absent in these larvae.

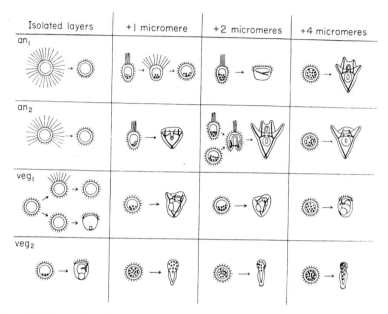

Fig. 1.12. Diagram of development of the layers an_1, an_2, veg_1, and veg_2 isolated (left column) and with 1, 2, and 4 implanted micromeres. (From Hörstadius, 1935.)

The above results have been questioned by von Ubisch (1936) on account of the poor reproducibility of some of them. Even if we do not feel qualified to definitively settle this question, we should like to stress here the tremendous amount of work performed by Hörstadius, which adequately appears to support the above conclusions.

The theory of the double gradient may explain the results of the experiments of Hörstadius, summarized in Fig. 1.9, where variable results were obtained with isolated developing animal or vegetal halves. The author reports that usually the best development, i.e., the one closest to normal, is yielded by those vegetal halves whose animal counterpart had shown the highest degree of animalization. In such cases, the line of equivalence of the two gradients should have been below the equator of the egg. After transection, the animal half had, therefore, contained no vegetal potentialities at all, or almost none, while the vegetal half still contained some of the animal potentialities that enabled it to give rise to a rather normal larva. The opposite result was obtained, according to this idea, when the line of equivalence was above the equator.

Several attempts have been made in an effort to answer the question as to the nature of these gradients. The earlier attempts were directed toward chemically affecting either one of them. Some of these attempts were successful and gave rise to tremendous enthusiasm; however, the number of chemicals effective in modifying such properties, i.e., orienting the egg toward an animal or vegetal development, has grown to an almost endless list. One is thus led to the conclusion that the egg is in a state of unstable equilibrium between its animal and vegetal potentialities. All the chemicals that are artificially introduced into the egg, by the very fact that they modify its metabolism, may have a 50% chance of shifting this delicate equilibrium in either direction. This does not necessarily imply that the chemical in question is actually involved in, or even mimics, the regulatory factors that underlie the animal or vegetal type of development. Because of the great instability of this equilibrium, it seems, therefore, unlikely that any clear answer can be found as to what controls or favors either type of development by the simple addition of chemicals to the developing system.

A list of the compounds that exert an animal or vegetal effect has been given by Lallier (1964a).

The first attempt of this kind goes back to Herbst (1892, 1893, 1896, 1901, 1904) with his study of the development of the sea urchin eggs in artificial seawater with the addition or the omission of various components. Among the various and interesting results, the one that concerns us in this chapter is the effect of the addition of lithium ions. This deserves a special mention because it represents the basis for the experiments that follow.

Treatment of the eggs for the 18 hours following fertilization with 0.066 M LiCl in seawater brings about a hyperdevelopment of the entomesodermic structures. This result is called vegetalization (Lindahl, 1933). Different degrees of vegetalization can be obtained under different conditions (Fig. 1.13). In the extreme case, one obtains an exogastrula, in which an excessive growth of the entoderm, combined with the extreme reduction of the ectoderm, prevents the former from invaginating. The result is a small ectodermal vesicle on top of a large entodermal sac,

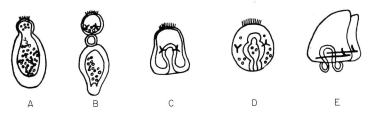

Fig. 1.13. Various degrees of vegetalization. (A) the highest; (E) the lowest. (From Lallier, 1966h.)

filled with mesodermal cells; pigment cells differentiate but no skeleton is formed. The vegetalizing effect of lithium ions is well illustrated by a parallel between figures of abnormal development obtained either by removal of the animal material or by treatment with lithium (Fig. 1.14). Indeed, animal halves of blastulae, if treated with lithium, may gastrulate (von Ubisch, 1925b,c). Moreover, Hörstadius (1936a) has shown that if an animal half is treated with lithium, the most vegetal part of it, when transplanted into another embryo, behaves as micromeres do, i.e., it is able to induce an animal half to develop into a normal pluteus. Finally, the work of Bäckström and Gustafson (1953) provides details on the sensitivity to lithium treatment at different developmental stages, and that of Runnström and Immers (1970, 1971) on one of the latest morphological descriptions of the lithium effect.

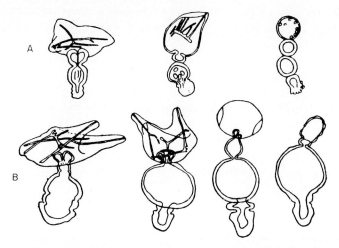

Fig. 1.14. Embryos of vegetal type (exogastrulae). (A) obtained by reducing the animal material; (B) by lithium ion treatment. (A: from Hörstadius, 1935; B: from Lindahl and Öhman, 1938.)

It was Herbst (1895) who found that a treatment with thiocyanate resulted in a developmental alteration which, in a way, can be considered as opposite to that of lithium, i.e., it caused an exaggerated development of the ectoderm with very little, if any, development of entoderm and mesenchyme. This effect is called animalization. Again, various degrees of animalization can be obtained under different conditions (Fig. 1.15), as discussed by Runnström (1928a). The strongest effect is obtained by a treatment of the unfertilized egg with 10–15 parts of isotonic thiocyanate solution in 90–85 parts of Ca^{2+}-free seawater, for 12–16 hours (Lindahl, 1936; Runnström, 1967b). Thiocyanate is able to counteract the effect of

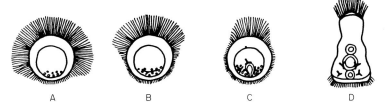

Fig. 1.15. Various degrees of animalization, from (A, the highest), to (C); (D) radialized larva. (From Lallier, 1966h.)

lithium when the two ions are administered to the eggs at the same time (Gustafson and Hörstadius, 1956).

Many other inorganic anions and cations exert an animalizing effect on the sea urchin embryo. A good correlation between the hydration radius of an ion and its morphogenetic properties has been known for a long time. If the ions are ordered according to Hofmeister's series, i.e., according to their valence, charge, and hydration, one finds that lithium and thiocyanate, which are the strongest vegetalizing and animalizing ions, respectively, are located at the opposite extreme ends; the former has a very high and the latter a very low hydration. The animalizing or vegetalizing properties of different ions vary according to their position in this classification (Tamini, 1943). For example, perchlorate, which is close to thiocyanate, exhibits animalizing effects (Lallier, 1957a). Among the heavy metals, zinc (Lallier, 1955, 1959) and cadmium act as strong animalizing agents. Also iodine, bromine and sulfate ions are animalizing ions (Lindahl, 1936). Changes too in the ionic balance of the seawater may result in animalization or vegetalization. For example, deprivation of sulfate ions leads to animalization (Herbst, 1897, 1904), whereas an increased concentration of potassium decreases the vegetalizing effect of lithium (Runnström, 1928b; Lallier, 1960a).

Organic components too may produce animalizing or vegetalizing effects. Among the organic anions some are able to induce animalization. They are usually polyanions and possess acidic functions such as the sulfonic or carboxylic groups. Examples are bile acids (Lallier, 1954), anionic detergents (Gustafson and Savhagen, 1949), some azo dyes such as Evans blue, sodium polyanethosulfonate and germanin. The three latter compounds are endowed with strong animalizing action (Lallier, 1957b,c; O'Melia, 1971). Among those dyes, the strongest animalizing effect is exhibited by the ones that have the highest affinity for proteins. Other dyes that show animalizing effect are uranin and Bengala Pink, which possess a carboxylic group (Lallier, 1957d, 1966b).

Animalizing effects may also be produced by organic cations of different composition such as polylysine, polyamines, and cobalt-containing molecules (Lallier, 1963a). Among the polyamines, the ones that have the highest molecular weight show the strongest effect. Glutamine has been reported to have an animalizing effect (Hörstadius and Strömberg, 1940), whereas little or no effect is obtained by treatments with some amino acids such as arginine, alanine, serine, glycine, and aspartic acid. Vegetalizing effect has been reported for treatments with valine, leucine, isoleucine, proline, oxyproline, methionine, glutamic acid, cysteine hydrochloride, lysine dihydrochloride, and tryptophan (Hörstadius, 1949). Gustafson and Hörstadius (1957) have reported a reproducible animalizing effect by L-glutamine and L-lysine. Vegetalizing effect for tyrosine and no effect for several other amino acids have been reported by Fudge 1959). That compounds normally contained in the egg may bring about development anomalies depends upon the high concentration at which they have been experimentally used. This also partly accounts for the differences among the data reported by different authors.

Treatment with trypsin causes animalization (Hörstadius, 1949, 1953, 1965; Runnström and Immers, 1966). Among the metabolic inhibitors, chloramphenicol and streptomycin, which inhibit protein synthesis and are known to cause misreading of the messenger RNA in bacteria, exhibit a vegetalizing power when used above certain concentrations (Lallier, 1962a,b,d, 1966g, 1968; Hörstadius, 1963).

Many more substances than those listed above have been tested for their morphogenetic effect on sea urchin embryos, but it would be too long to deal with all of them, especially if one considers that the mechanisms through which they act are not yet understood. Among the papers that have been left out of our brief discussion, the reader may, for the sake of completeness, consult Lallier (1960b, 1964b, 1965a–e, 1966a,c,d,e,f), Brice (1959), Gustafson and Hörstadius (1955), Immers (1965), Mizejewsky (1969), and Barber (1971).

Gustafson and Toneby (1970) have investigated the morphogenetic effect of 223 neuropharmacological agents and other agents known to interfere with the turnover of biogenic amines. The results point to the suggestion that many morphogenetic cell movements are initiated by serotonin and acetylcholine.

A fruitful discussion on the action mechanisms of these compounds should rest on knowledge on the nature of the animal and vegetal potentialities. Since this knowledge is far from adequate, it seems appropriate here to limit ourselves to summing up the known facts and then trying to establish, whenever possible, some correlation between some of them and the mechanism through which the above chemicals may have acted. First, the question may be asked as to whether those potentialities are bound to any specific structure of the cytoplasm of the egg and/or the embryo.

In this respect, the only visible territorial difference has been reported by Gustafson and Lenicque (1952), who have found an accumulation of mitochondria in the animal half of the mesenchyme blastula stage of *Psammechinus miliaris*. No such difference is observed in younger stages. Lenicque *et al.* (1953) too have reported that the implantation of micromeres into animal halves causes a decrease in the mitochondrial population density of the host halves. It should be mentioned, however, that the finding of a preferential accumulation of mitochondria in the animal territories of the embryos has been questioned by Shaver (1955, 1957), who used a different technique for counting mitochondria in *Lytechinus pictus* and *Strongylocentrotus purpuratus*. An electron microscopic study by Berg and collaborators (Berg *et al.*, 1962; Berg and Long, 1964) has also denied any differential distribution of mitochondria along the embryonic axis at any one of the developmental stages studied in *Lytechinus anamnesus, Strongylocentrotus purpuratus,* and *Dendraster excentricus*. These authors have found that after the blastula stage, mitochondria of the primary mesenchyme cells or of the endoderm cells appear larger than those of the cells belonging to the animal part of the embryo. No such differences are, however, found at the 16-cell stage. Nor has any differential distribution of mitochondria throughout the cytoplasm of the egg been observed at the electron microscope level by Pikò (personal communication).

It has been known that alteration in the distribution of the subcellular components of the egg by centrifugation does not alter the polarity of the egg (Runnström, 1926; Lindahl, 1932b; Pease, 1939). This, according to Motomura (1949), depends on the fact that at the used centrifugal forces the outer part of the cytoplasm, the so-called cortical cytoplasm, is not moved. The author reports (1948) that if a fertilized egg of *Strongylocentrotus pulcherrimus* or of *Temnopleurus hardwickii* is centrifuged at 40,000 *g* for 12 minutes, the subcellular components are stratified in several layers. Starting from the centripetal pole, they are (1) a centripetal oil drop; (2) a layer of cortical cytoplasm, recognizable in *Strongylocentrotus pulcherrimus* because of its yellow pigment; (3) a layer containing the nucleus; (4) layers containing granules of various type (presumably mitochondria and yolk and pigment). Under such conditions, i.e., under conditions where the cortical cytoplasm too has been moved, the egg axis is changed as well, and the vegetal pole will now be at the centripetal pole, where the cortical plasma has collected. On the other hand, there is evidence that the cortical plasma contains both animal and vegetal potentialities. This is suggested by experiments where part of the inner cytoplasm of the egg is sucked out with a micropipette without causing any alteration of the animal–vegetal axis (Hörstadius *et al.,* 1950). This rules out the hypothesis by Dalcq (1941) that the animal potentialities might be located in the cortex and the vegetal ones in the internal cytoplasm.

The experiments of egg constriction (Hörstadius, 1938) are also relevant to this question. If during early cleavage an egg is partially constricted at the equator by means of a hair loop and the constriction maintained thereafter, the upper half of the embryo will appear clearly aninalized, while the lower half will show some sign of vegetalization (Fig. 1.9). These experiments have been interpreted by Lindahl as meaning that the action of the vegetal principle is mediated by means of substances the diffusion of which has been partly impaired by the constriction.

However, experiments by Berg and Chang (1962), aimed at finding out if diffusible morphogenetic substances are produced by blastomeres isolated at the 16-cell stage, have given negative results. This result is not critical in view of the difficulties connected with the detection of factors present, most likely in very minute amounts and which may also be easily destroyed when forced to move into an outer medium. More recently Berg and Akin (1971) have reported that the blastocoelic fluid added to seawater inhibits gastrulation. It must be remembered, however, that the gastrulation process is sensitive to a variety of nonspecific inhibitors. Diffusion of substances has been advocated as a basis for the gradients (Crick, 1970). Indeed, a factor has been extracted from egg homogenates that, after elaborate purification, has exhibited animalizing activity (Hörstadius *et al.,* 1967); more recently, Josefsson and Hörstadius (1969) have isolated from eggs of *Paracentrotus lividus* several substances that exhibit animalizing or vegetalizing effect.

It should, however, be considered that since the egg is a labile system which can be easily animalized or vegetalized, the finding of substances with animalizing or vegetalizing activity, even if extracted from the egg itself, does not necessarily imply that these are the factors responsible for the balancing of the vegetal or animal tendencies — unless one could prove that these factors are actually localized in the animal and vegetal territory, respectively.

A key question is, of course: Do metabolic differences exist between the animal and vegetal part of the egg? A number of attempts have been made, however, without any conclusive result.

Cytochemical experiments (Child, 1936) have suggested the existence of a "reduction gradient" from the animal to the vegetal pole. Holter and Lindahl (1940) by means of the Cartesian diver, have not detected, however, any respiratory difference between isolated animal and vegetal halves. Nor can any significant correlation be found between inhibitors of the respiratory metabolism and deviation of morphogenesis toward the animal or vegetal differentiation.

More recently, the rate of oxygen consumption of animal and vegetal halves has been reinvestigated by De Vincentiis *et al.* (1966). Again no differences between the two halves have been found at a stage that corresponds to the time when the corresponding control embryos are mesenchyme blastulae. At earlier stages, on the other hand, the isolated vegetal halves show a somewhat higher rate of oxygen uptake than the corresponding animal halves. Treatment with 2,4-dinitrophenol at both stages causes a considerable increase of the rate of oxygen consumption only on the animal halves. The authors suggest that the latter might have a higher content of high energy compounds. Bäckström *et al.* (1960) have suggested that the pentose phosphate cycle is correlated with ecto-dermal differentiation and, conversely, the glycolytic pathway with the development of the intestine. The experimental support for this view is rather tenuous: it is based on the observation that during gastrulation there is a shift from the pentose phosphate pathway to glycolysis (see Chapter 8), and that this is more pronounced in animalized embryos. Moreover, the activity of glucose-6-phosphate dehydrogenase and 6-phosphogluconate dehydrogenase, which normally undergoes a sharp decrease during gastrulation, remains at a somewhat higher level in animalized embryos. Apart from the fact that the latter evidence is only indirect, it should be considered that differentiation is blocked as a whole during animalization, and hence other alterations might be responsible for the changes in the pattern of enzymatic activity.

The increasing attention that in recent years has been directed to the role of nucleic acid and protein synthesis on morphogenesis has prompted a number of investigations directed toward solving the riddle of the bio-chemical basis of animalization and vegetalization. Unfortunately, most of these attempts have been performed with unsatisfactory methods.

With respect to protein synthesis, Markman (1961a) has suggested that the rate of amino acid incorporation (judged by autoradiography), is the highest in the animal part of the early blastula stage, while the situation is reversed in the mesenchyme blastula and gastrula. These results, together with similar ones obtained by Immers (1959, 1961b), do not agree with the observations of Bosco and Monroy (1962), who found, also by autoradiography, that in the mesenchyme blastula amino acid incorporation proceeds at a higher rate in the animal than in the vegetal pole. Markman (1961c), on the other hand, has observed that isolated animal halves, at the time when the control embryos have reached various stages from cleavage to gastrula, show a higher rate of amino acid incorporation into proteins than the corresponding vegetal halves. This correlates with the finding that in the animal halves mitotic activity is greater.

If, however, the rate of amino acid incorporation is calculated as percent of uptake, then (at least in *Lytechinus anamnesus*) the rate of protein synthesis is found to be comparable in animal and vegetal halves (isolation at the 8-cell stage) (Berg, 1965).

This way of calculating the results seems to be the most correct one, since it takes into account changes in permeability (see Chapter 4).

The observation by Markman (1961b), and confirmed by Runnström *et al.* (1964), that the sum of the amino acids incorporated by isolated vegetal and animal halves exceeds the one incorporated by whole embryos (due to the increased rate of incorporation by the animal halves), can perhaps be explained as due to differences in the internal amino acid pool. The difference of incorporation in fact has not been observed when high concentrations of external radioactive amino acids were supplied, which minimize the effect of radioactivity dilution into the internal pool (Berg, 1968a).

Spiegel and Tyler (1966) have succeeded in isolating the micromeres of *Arbacia punctulata* in more substantial amounts than can be obtained by microsurgery. Their method involves dissociation of the blastomeres from 16-cell embryos by means of Ca^{2+}-free seawater, followed by their sedimentation through a sucrose layer in which micromeres sediment slower than the other blastomeres. The rate of amino acid incorporation into the isolated micromeres have proved to be the same as in the other blastomeres (results calculated per unit of volume). Hynes and Gross (1970) have reached the same conclusion in experiments where micromeres are labeled either before or after their removal from the entire embryo.

An interesting result has been obtained by Berg (1968b) who has shown that in Li-treated embryos the rate of protein synthesis fails to undergo the characteristic increase at the gastrula stage. This suggests that the increase is in fact correlated with the morphological event of gastrulation.

Attempts have also been made to correlate nucleic acid metabolism with the animal or vegetal determination (Markman, 1961c, 1963, 1967; Markman and Runnström, 1963; Lallier, 1962c, 1963b,c,d; Berg, 1968a). These investigations are all concerned either with variations in the rate of uptake of precursors into the total RNA fraction, under conditions that favor vegetal or animal development, or with the overall inhibition of RNA synthesis. Several considerations, however, can be made that bias the interpretation of the results. First is the frequent lack of knowledge in such factors as permeability, changes in the internal precursors pool, and exchange at the terminal pCpCpA sequence of transfer RNA (which, in the sea urchin embryos, is of major importance) as opposed to incorporation into newly synthesized RNA. Next, one may wonder how meaningful it is to try and get information on the overall RNA synthesis short of knowledge as to the different classes of RNA that are being synthesized at any given time. In other words, measures of the rate of synthesis of RNA have a meaning only when one has to deal with a homogeneous class of RNA. With the exception of ribosomal RNA, this has not yet been done in sea urchin embryos. Furthermore, it seems very unlikely that information on the overall rate of synthesis of proteins and RNA can ever provide the key to the problem of the role of these macromolecules in establishing of the animal and vegetal properties. RNA and protein synthesis results in the synthesis of hundreds or thousands of different molecules, with as many different functions. Hence, there seems to be no justification for the idea that a certain metabolic pattern, such as the one leading to animal or vegetal differentiation, should depend on an overall increase or decrease of the synthesis of so many different products.

It seems more reasonable to imagine that a slight difference in a few metabolic activities might bring about a different morphogenetic pattern.

We will not, therefore, go into details of these investigations, but will limit ourselves to mentioning the findings of Czihak and collaborators (Czihak, 1965b,c; Czihak *et al.,* 1967), who reported that the nuclei of the micromeres, as shown by autoradiography, at the 16- to 32-cell stage, are particularly active in the incorporation of uridine into RNA.

These findings have been partially confirmed by Hynes and Gross (1970) and by Spiegel and Rubinstein (1972). These latter authors, in fact, find a somewhat lower difference between the pattern of uridine incorporation in micromeres and in other blastomeres. These findings, together with the suggestion by Czihak and Hörstadius (1970) that the micromeres may exert their inductive effect through transfer of their RNA into the other blastomeres, will be discussed in greater detail in Chapter 10.

Experiments by Giudice and Hörstadius (1965) have shown that, during the period between fertilization and the 16-cell stage, no RNA synthesis is required for the animal and vegetal potentialities to be fixed in the embryo territories. This conclusion, which agrees with the animal–

vegetal axis being already fixed in the unfertilized egg, is based on the following experiment: Embryos were raised to the 16-cell stage in the presence of actinomycin at a concentration known to strongly inhibit RNA synthesis. The micromeres of such embryos, if implanted into animal halves from untreated embryos, have shown a normal inducing ability.

Recently, Markman and Runnström (1970) have found that the animalizing effect on vegetal halves of trypsin and of the animalizing factor described by Hörstadius *et al.* (1967) are to a certain extent counteracted by actinomycin. De Angelis and Runnström (1970) have also found that the effect of lithium on animal halves is counteracted by actinomycin D.

Lallier (1961) has reported that adenosine can counteract the vegetalizing effect of lithium. It is not known, however, through which mechanism adenosine brings about its effect.

Finally, Pirrone *et al.* (1970) have demonstrated that embryos treated with doses of LiCl which, while causing strong vegetalization, do not cause embryo degeneration, allow ribosomal RNA synthesis to proceed normally. On the other hand, a treatment with doses of $ZnSO_4$, which produce a high degree of animalization (again without embryo degeneration), very strongly inhibits ribosomal RNA synthesis (Fig. 1.16).

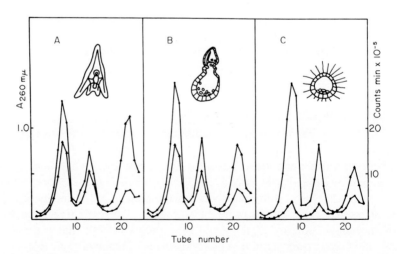

Fig. 1.16. Sucrose density gradient profiles of RNA extracted with cold phenol from embryos at 23 hours after fertilization, prelabeled with ^{32}P for the first 13 hours following fertilization under the following conditions: (A) in plain seawater; (B) in the presence of $4.6 \times 10^{-2}\ M$ LiCl; (C) in the presence of $10^{-3}\ M\ ZnSO_4$. The inserts show the morphology of the embryos at 36 hours after fertilization. ●——●, $A_{260\,m\mu}$; ▲——▲, counts/minute $\times 10^{-5}$. It should be noted that the specific activity of the α phosphate of the nucleotidic pool was the same in the three cases. (From Pirrone *et al.*, 1970.)

The search for differences in single enzymatic activities specifically linked to the animal or vegetal metabolism might be more rewarding. An investigation along these lines has been performed by Gustafson and Hasselberg (1951).

The assays were carried out on whole homogenates of different species. Their overall picture shows that those enzymes whose activity normally increases at the stage of mesenchyme blastula, like apyrase, cathepsin II, glutaminase, and succinodehydrogenase, undergo partial inhibition in Li^+-treated embryos. Other enzymatic activities, like adenosinedeaminase, pyrophosphatase, and hexametaphosphatase, whose activity remains constant throughout the embryonic development, do not undergo any change following LiCl treatment.

At present, it is impossible to decide whether it is because of the lack of these metabolic changes that gastrulation does not take place or whether, conversely, it is the lack of morphogenesis that prevents the metabolic changes. As the authors point out, the changes in enzymatic activities at mesenchyme blastula do correlate with the increase in mitochondrial population in the normal embryos, all of these enzymes being mitochondrial. No changes in the content of mitochondria take place in the LiCl-treated embryos.

The cholinesterase activity, absent in the unfertilized eggs, appears during development and, in *Paracentrotus,* undergoes a marked increase at the pluteus stage. This may be tentatively correlated with the appearance of the coordinate ciliary and intestinal movements of the larva. Once again this increase is reduced in the Li-treated embryos (Augustinsson and Gustafson, 1949).

In conclusion, attempts to correlate any one of the effects of chemical treatments with specific metabolic alterations that bring about animalization or vegetalization seem, to say the least, premature; essentially because we have no hint as to the possible biochemical basis of the two types of metabolism. Finally must be mentioned the attempts to correlate the results obtained by removal of sulfate ions from seawater, with a possible role of sulfates in the polysaccharides of cell surfaces. The original observations of Herbst (1897) and of Lindahl (1936, 1942), which showed an animalizing effect of sulfate deprivation on entire embryos, were followed by the experiments of Runnström et al. (1964) and by Immers and Runnström (1965), who found that the same treatment increases both the animalization of isolated animal halves and the vegetalization of vegetal halves. The hope, therefore, of finding a specific effect of sulfate seems to drop considerably. Experiments aiming at investigating the metabolism of the sulfate ions (Hörstadius et al., 1966) have failed to show any difference in the rate of sulfate uptake between whole embryos and animal or vegetal halves when the data are referred to equal volumes.

Our review of the problem concerning the mechanism of determination of the animal–vegetal axis has not presented any final solution. It has chiefly the value of listing the attempts so far made. Even if their results are not conclusive, however, these attempts represent a necessary step toward a solution that has to come from a molecular approach to the problem.

Chapter 2

Ultrastructure

The structure of the sea urchin egg has been studied by classic cytological methods as well as by electron microscopy. The egg contains the usual complement of organelles common to all animal cells. It also contains some peculiar structures that have been investigated by cytochemical methods as well as by electron microscopy.

The scheme of intracellular organization is preserved, with some modification, during embryonic development. Associated with the plasma membrane of the egg is the vitelline envelope, which undergoes dramatic changes after fertilization.

A. Oogenesis

It seems convenient to begin the description of the structure of the egg with oogenesis. This should give a better account of the significance of several structures characteristic of the mature egg.

A section of a sea urchin ovary shows several distinct layers. One of these represents the germinal epithelium, which contains two cell types: accessory cells and germ cells (Tennent *et al.,* 1931). The reciprocal proportion of these two kinds of cells undergoes seasonal variations, as has been thoroughly described by Dawydoff (1948), Holland and Giese (1965), Holland (1967), Pearse and Giese (1966), Fuji (1960), and Chatlynne (1969). The accessory cells are found in the spaces between the oocytes and, as a consequence, are found in greater number out of the breeding season, i.e., when the gonad does not contain growing oocytes but only oogonia as representatives of the germ cells. Conversely,

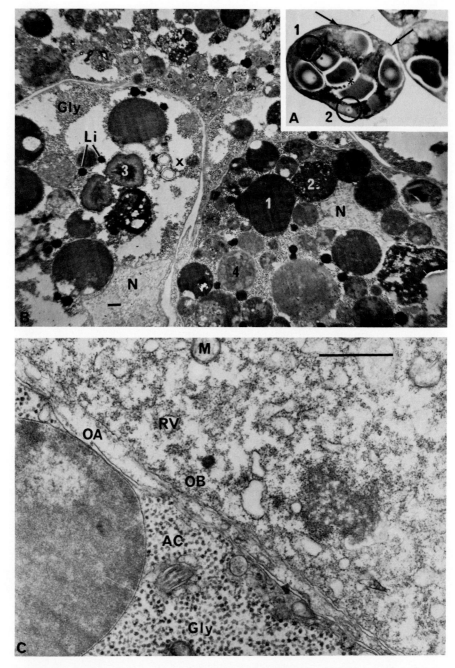

Fig. 2.1. *Lytechinus pictus*. (A) Cross section of ovary fixed in osmium tetroxide and embedded in Epon-812. Arrows indicate cells of germinal epithelium. Circle 1 surrounds a cluster of accessory cells; other accessory cells extend between oocytes at the asterisk.

an ovary filled with growing oocytes shows very few accessory cells. These latter contain four different kinds of yolk granules, according to the description of Verhey and Moyer (1967) (Fig. 2.1). They also contain lipid droplets and glycogen (Takashima and Takashima, 1965). They do not seem to contain mitochondria, at least the typical kind. The presence of reserve material, coupled with the finding that injection of radioactive amino acids into a female results in a heavy accumulation of isotope in the accessory cells (Monroy and Maggio, 1963; Immers, 1961b), suggests that these cells play a role in the synthesis of some storage material for oocytes (Tennent and Ito, 1941).

Takashima and Takashima (1966) have reported the presence of processes and pinosomes on the surface of young oocytes.

The germ cells have been described more recently by Millonig *et al.* (1968).

It is apparent that the investigations of these and other authors working on the morphology of oogenesis have focused mainly on the nucleoli and the formation of the cortical granules. The reason for this interest in nucleoli is that during oogenesis, synthesis of ribosomal RNA is very active, as described in oocytes of other species, while it ceases at the maturation of the oocyte (see Chapter 10).

The formation of the cortical granules is of especial interest because, as will be shown later, these structures are concerned with the physiology of fertilization.

According to Millonig, the female germ cells of the ovary of *Arbacia lixula* and *Paracentrotus lividus* frequently appear in the stage of secondary oogonia. These are small cells of 5–7 μ in diameter, with a relatively large oval nucleus containing chromatin in large, irregular strands against a background of fine fibrils of low electron density. There is one round nucleolus adjacent to the nuclear envelope, with a dense periphery made

Circle 2 surrounds an oogonium on the left and an oocyte at the first transition stage on the right (approx. × 140). (B) Details of accessory cells showing at least four types of yolk-like inclusions, lipid droplets, and glycogen. Note absence of typical mitochondria. X indicates an unidentified inclusion (× 4,000). (C) Details of the relationship between an accessory cell and two oocytes (OA and OB). There is no indication of pinocytosis along the oocyte plasma membrane. Compare the glycogen of the accessory cell to the ribosomes of the oocytes and note the differences in morphology and staining characteristics (× 23,500). Abbreviations: A, annulus; AC, accessory cell; AL, annulate lamella; CG, cortical granule; CS, cross section; ER, endoplasmic reticulum; Gly, glycogen; G, Golgi complex; HB, heavy body; J, jelly; Li, lipid; M, mitochondria; MV, microvillus; N, nucleus; NE, nuclear envelope; Nu, nucleolus; OA, oocyte A; OB, oocyte B; PV, pigment vacuole; R, ribosomes; RV, rough-surfaced vesicle; TS, tangential section; X, unidentified inclusion; Y, yolk; YN, yolk nucleus. Asterisks, arrows, numbers, and circles are used to point out specific structures which are described in the appropriate plate caption. Magnification lines designate 1 μ unless otherwise indicated. (From Verhey and Moyer, 1967.)

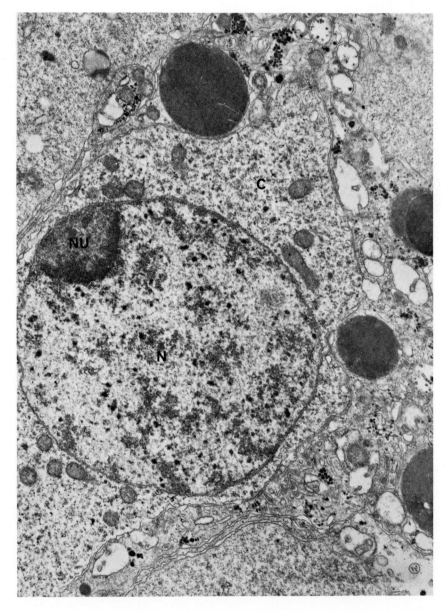

Fig. 2.2. A secondary oogonium of *Arbacia lixula* (× 15,000). Abbreviations: N, nucleus; NU, nucleolus; C, cytoplasm. (From Millonig *et al.*, 1968.)

by granules of 15–20 nm and a light core (Fig. 2.2). The cytoplasm contains mitochondria, cisternae, and the ergastoplasmic reticulum, Golgi elements, and short chains of polysomes. Some peculiar structures are already observable in the cytoplasm, termed by Millonig as "aggregates type I." These consist of a dense spherical body of about 1 μ, frequently surrounded by a crescent of material with the aspect of a nucleolonema. This structure seems to contain RNA since it can be stained with toluidine blue.

The secondary oogonium differentiates into the oocyte. This undergoes two periods of growth, the previtellogenic and the vitellogenic growth stages.

1. PREVITELLOGENIC GROWTH STAGE

The diameter of the oocyte increases gradually, to about 50 μ. The nucleus, almost spherical, reaches 10 μ in diameter and contains chromosomes which are now radially oriented toward the nucleolus (Fig. 2.3). They appear in a "lampbrush" state when observed by phase-contrast microscopy. The nucleolus, now in the central part of the nucleus, acquires a spherical shape and begins to show ribosomelike particles. These are at first confined to the cortical part, while the internal part of the nucleolus is represented by a fibrillar nucleolonema. Eventually, they will cover the entire area of the nucleolar sections. The nucleolus of the final stage is about 6 μ in diameter. In the cytoplasm, besides the described structures, another type of aggregate appears, named by Millonig "aggregates type II" (Fig. 2.4). These are made up of granules of about 30 nm, in a ground substance slightly denser than the cytoplasm.

2. VITELLOGENIC STAGE

The nucleus has grown to a diameter of about 30 μ, while no visible modifications of the karyoplasm occur; its envelope is perforated by pores, which are already visible in the previous stage. In the description of Millonig, which agrees with the views of Afzelius (1955a), the pores are represented by cylinders that extend from the inner to the outer membrane of the nucleus, filled with an electron-dense material. Actually, the cylinder seems to be transversally divided into two shorter cylinders, one on each side of the nuclear envelope. The extranuclear annulus is about 20 nm long with an outer diameter of about 100 nm; the intranuclear annulus is about 60 nm long and has a diameter of about 50 nm. Ribosomelike particles are seen adjacent to the external annulus but not to the internal one (Fig. 2.5) which militates against the transport of ribosomes as such from the nucleus to the cytoplasm.

Dramatic changes are observed in the nucleolus. Toward the end of the preceding period, the nucleolus assumes a fairly compact, granular

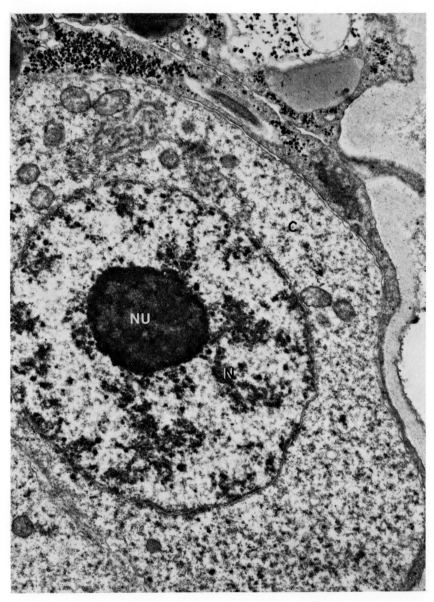

Fig. 2.3. An oocyte of *Arbacia lixula* in the early previtellogenetic growth stage (×
16,000). Abbreviations: N, nucleus, NU, nucleolus; C, cytoplasm. (Courtesy of Dr.
Millonig.)

appearance. Now one (Fig. 2.6) and occasionally more (Fig. 2.7) vacuoles
of a density similar to that of the nucleoplasm appear in its center. These
vacuoli appear to merge into each other, as already observed by Afzelius

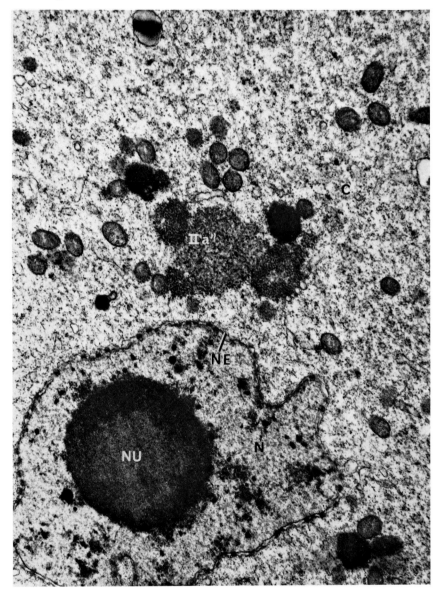

Fig. 2.4. The nucleus and part of the cytoplasm of an oocyte of *Arbacia lixula* in the pre-vitellogenic growth stage (× 16,000). Abbreviations: II a″, aggregate type II″; NE, nuclear envelope; N, nucleus; NU, nucleolus; C, cytoplasm. (Courtesy of Dr. Millonig.)

(1957a), and eventually the nucleolus disappears shortly before the break-down of the germinal vesicle (see also Esper, 1965). In the meantime several dense spherical bodies appear in the nucleoplasm, which have

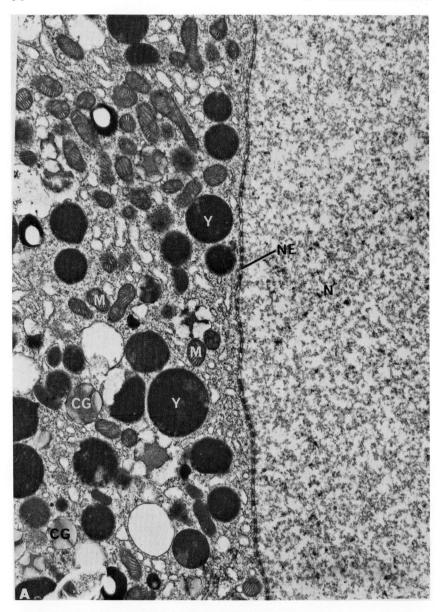

Fig. 2.5. (A) Part of nucleus and cytoplasm of an *Arbacia lixula* oocyte in the vitellogenic stage to show the nuclear pores (× 16,000). Abbreviations: Y, yolk; NE, nuclear envelope; M, mitochondria; N, nucleus. (Courtesy of Dr. Millonig.) (B) Nuclear envelope of an oocyte which has been isolated from its surrounding protoplasm by mechanical damage during fixation. The picture shows that both annuli, one toward the cytoplasm (bottom) and one toward the nucleus B (top), adhere to the pore. Ribosomes appear to adhere to the cytoplasmic annulus (× 43,000). (From Millonig *et al.*, 1968).

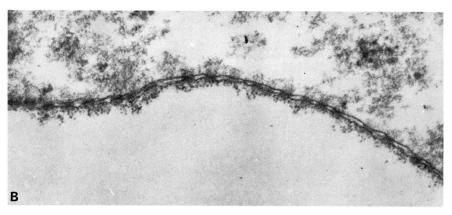

B

been called by Afzelius, after *in vivo* observations, "minor nucleoli."
In general, there is one major nucleolus per nucleus, but in some species
a few more can be observed (Cannata, 1970).

During the vitellogenetic period, the cytoplasm becomes filled with
mitochondria, lipid droplets, yolk, pigment vesicles (particularly evident
in the case of *Arbacia*), smooth- and rough-surfaced vesicles, Golgi
elements, and cortical granules. The cytoplasm sometimes contains
"yolk bodies" of spherical or ovoidal shape, consisting of ergastoplasmic
lamellae surrounding various cytoplasmic elements such as mitochondria,
rough-surfaced vesicles, yolk, or cortical granules. One occasionally
observes the so-called "heavy bodies" described by Afzelius (1957a),
who counted up to 1000 of them per egg in *Psammechinus miliaris* and
Echinus esculentus. They are basophilic particles which, at the electron
microscopic level, contain granules of about 15 nm, enclosed in a double
membrane resembling the nuclear envelope. Conway and Metz (1970)
have demonstrated, by means of cytochemical techniques, the presence
of RNA in the heavy body particles.

A more detailed description of some of the cytoplasmic structures
of the oocyte has been presented by other authors.

Afzelius (1956a) has described a kind of fragmentation of the Golgi
apparatus. He has also made an estimate of the amount of yolk granules,
which represent about 27% of the total mature egg volume. These granules are spherical, usually from 0.3 to 1 μ in diameter. They consist of
an internal mass, which is believed to be made up of inert storage nutrient
material, surrounded by a membrane about 6.5 nm thick. Malkin *et al.*
(1965) have extracted from the cytoplasmic granules (presumably yolk)
of eggs and embryos a crystalline protein with a sedimentation coefficient
of 27 S. According to Verhey and Moyer (1967), during the vitellogenic
period a tubular endoplasmic reticulum appears in the oocyte, and the
yolk granules appear to be bounded by ribosomes bearing membranes,

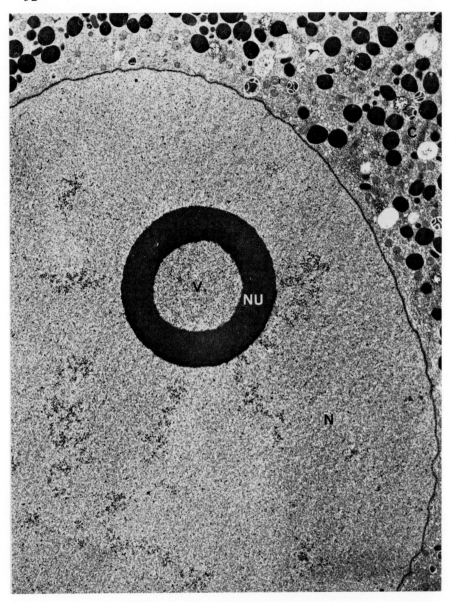

Fig. 2.6. Part of the nucleus, and the nucleolus containing one vacuole of an oocyte of *Arbacia lixula* in the vitellogenetic growth stage (× 4,500). Abbreviations: N, nucleus; NU, nucleolus; V, vacuole; C, cytoplasm. (Courtesy of Dr. Millonig.)

suggesting that the yolk may be synthesized in the cisternae of the endoplasmic reticulum. These authors have described structures in the cytoplasm called "annulate lamellae," i.e., membranes that bear the annuli

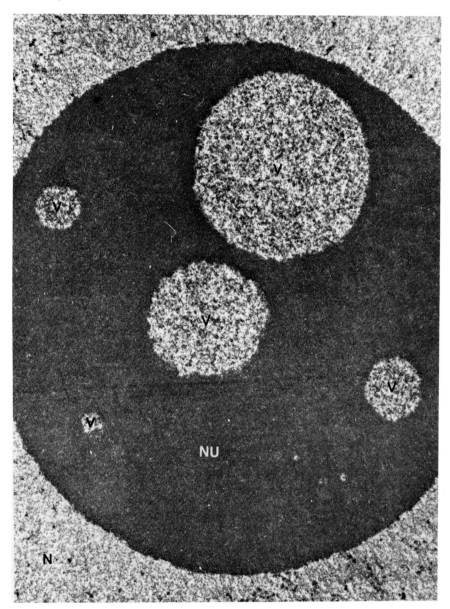

Fig. 2.7. A nucleolus with 5 vacuoles of an oocyte of *Arbacia lixula* in the vitellogenetic growth stage (× 16,000). Abbreviations: N, nucleoplasm; NU, nucleolus; V, vacuoles.

characteristic of the nuclear envelope, and which may therefore be supposed to have derived from the nuclear membrane (Bal *et al.,* 1968; Kessel, 1968; Merriam, 1959).

A thorough study of the pigment vacuoles was undertaken by Mc-Culloch (1951, 1952a,b). Their pigment content dissolves in some fixatives, but remains as osmiophilic material inside the vacuoli of *Echinus esculentus* and *Echinocardium*.

Oil droplets: These structures have been so termed because of their histochemical properties, and especially because of their behavior after centrifugation of the egg. They accumulate at the centripetal pole, where they coalesce (Harvey, 1932, 1956a; Lyon, 1906, 1907) because they have no limiting membrane. Their average diameter is 0.4–1 μ.

Cortical granules: They were first studied under the electron microscope by McCulloch (1952a), but their most recent description in oogenesis belongs to E. Anderson (1968), who considers that they originate from vesicles of the Golgi apparatus. Since these structures are directly involved in the fertilization reaction, we shall describe them in detail in the next section.

3. OOCYTE MATURATION

After vitellogenesis, the oocyte undergoes maturation. The germinal vesicle breaks down and polar bodies are extruded before the egg is shed. Shortly before the breakdown of the germinal vesicle, the nucleolus, as previously mentioned, gradually fades away. About 2 hours later the first polar body is extruded; about 1.5 hours after that, the second one is also thrust out. Fertilization of the egg, followed by normal development, is possible only about 5 hours after extrusion of the second polar body (Harvey, 1956a; Paspaleff, 1927; Runnström and Monné, 1945; Runnström, 1948a). It should be noted that, according to Verhey and Moyer, it is only after the maturation divisions that structures such as annulatae lamellae and heavy bodies appear in the cytoplasm.

In concluding the description of the fine structure of oocytes, it is tempting to correlate some facts: for example, the evolution of the nucleolar structure which parallels the appearance of nuclear pores, the presence of heavy bodies which appear to contain sequestered ribosomes, and the low rate of protein synthesis (Harris, 1967a) of the mature egg. Formation of the aggregate types I and II, containing RNA and proteins, is intriguing in view of the possibility, to be presented later, that masked messages, consisting of mRNA coupled to proteins, are accumulated during oogenesis in the cytoplasm of the unfertilized egg. None of the above correlations, however, has been the object of direct tests.

B. The Developing Embryo

Study of the fine structure of the mature egg concerns mainly the egg cortex and will, therefore, be described separately in the chapter dealing with the cortical reaction and fertilization process.

A systematic study of the ultrastructure of the developmental stages up to the pluteus is absent. We have available, however, several electron microscopic observations of various stages that emphasize the nucleolar structure (Millonig, 1966), the intercellular adhesion (Balinsky, 1959; Millonig and Giudice, 1967; Goodenough *et al.*, 1968; Vacquier, 1968; Wolpert and Mercer, 1963), and the differentiation of mitochondria (Berg and Long, 1964).

Changes of the intracellular structures that have been described during development, apart from the cortical reaction, are: (1) disappearance of the heavy bodies at the streak stage (Harris, 1967a); (2) a differential size distribution of the mitochondria, which become larger in the primary mesenchyme and endoderm cells than in other parts of the embryo (Berg and Long, 1964); (3) a progressive reduction in volume and number of the yolk granules; (4) changes in state of aggregation of ribosomes following fertilization (Schäfer, 1966); and (5) changes of the nucleolar structure.

1. THE NUCLEOLUS

One of the most thorough studies has been made by Millonig *et al.* (1968). In the mature egg, the nucleoli appear as small bodies of 1 μ, adhering to the inner aspect of the nucleolar membrane; they stain with toluidine blue, and under the electron microscope appear to be made up of loose fibrils of less than 8 nm. A few minutes after fusion of the pronuclei, several agranular nucleoli of about 5 μ are formed, which are often seen to protrude from the nucleus, while still being lined by the nuclear envelope (see also Harris, 1967b). Interestingly enough, they seem to bud off from the nucleus and pass to the cytoplasm. Indeed, some of them can be seen free in the cytoplasm still surrounded by the nuclear envelope. It seems that through this process most of the nucleoli are extruded from the nucleus, while a few may be seen close to the equatorial plate of the first metaphase. At the anaphase, when the chromosomes move toward the poles, these nucleoli remain close to the equator. At the late anaphase, when the single chromosomes become surrounded by an envelope, they display a great number of vesicles which, in the late telophase, coalesce to produce 20 or more agranular nucleoli per nucleus. These agranular nucleoli (i.e., those that do not contain a granular component under electron microscopy) disappear again at the next prophase, and the process is repeated at each cleavage up to the blastula stage.

The formation of these chromosomal vesicles and their transfer to the cytoplasm is certainly of great interest. However, the name "nucleoli" does not seem appropriate for these formatio s, if we are to reserve this denomination for the site of synthesis of ribosomal RNA. From what is known for other animal cells, it seems improbable, indeed, that this site is found in many chromosomes (Huberman and Attardi, 1967; Ritossa and Spiegelman, 1965). It is known, moreover, that little or no synthesis of ribosomal RNA is detected in sea urchin embryos up to the blastula stage (see Chapter 10). At a stage closely following hatching, concurrent with the onset of rRNA synthesis, 1 or 2 spherical nucleoli, about 1 μ in diameter, containing granules of about 15 nm, are formed anew. Their granular component now prevails over the fibrillar part. This morphology does not change up to the pluteus stage.

2. THE MICROTUBULES

A careful electron microscopic study of the stage of mesenchyme blastula has recently been presented by Gibbins et al. (1969) and Tilney and Gibbins (1969a,b). These authors emphasize the role of microtubules in shaping embryonic cells.

A good correlation has been shown between orientation of microtubules and cell shape. The microtubules of the presumptive mesenchyme cells are oriented, before migration of these cells into the blastocoel, parallel to the cell's longitudinal axis. They diverge from structures close to the basal body of the cilium and run parallel to the lateral cell walls. As the mesenchyme cells lose their cilia and migrate inside the blastocoel they round up, while the microtubules diverge radially from a centriole close to the center of the cells. These latter then develop pseudopodia that fuse with similar pseudopodia of other mesenchyme cells to form the cellular support wherein the organic matrix of the skeleton will be formed and the $CaCO_3$ deposited (K. Okazaki, 1956a, 1960, 1961, 1962, 1965; Okazaki et al., 1962). The microtubules are now parallel to the pseudopodial long axes (Fig. 2.8). Since the shape of the skeleton will be determined by the shape of the pseudopodial "cable," the role of microtubules in morphogenesis appears of major importance. One might argue, however, whether it is the microtubules that follow the shape of the cells or vice versa.

To substantiate their hypothesis, Tilney and Gibbins (1969b) treated the embryos with agents such as colchicine or hydrostatic pressure, which are known to disrupt microtubules. In both cases, development of the mesenchyme cells is disturbed. These latter, but not the ectodermal cells, tend to spherulate. It should be noted that many inhibitory treatments produce this effect on mesenchyme cells. However, treatment with D_2O (heavy water), which is known to preserve and stabilize microtubules, stops development, but no alteration of cell shape is observed, the cells

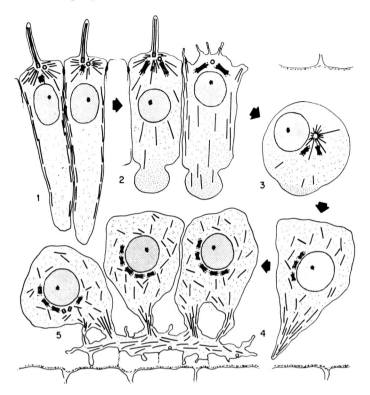

Fig. 2.8. The distribution of microtubules is depicted at each stage of formation and differentiation of the primary mesenchyme. (1) Epithelial cells of the vegetal pole of a swimming blastula; (2) these cells start to bud into the blastocoel; (3) a primary mesenchyme cell which has just migrated into the blastocoel; (4) the mesenchyme cell emits a pseudopodium which in (5) fuses with the pseudopodia of other mesenchyme cells. (From Gibbins *et al.,* 1969.)

appearing frozen in their original shape. The hypothesis of the morphological role of microtubules, even if not yet definitively proved still seems a very interesting possibility.

One question that remains to be answered is the mechanism of assembly of microtubules inside the cells. Tilney and Goddard (1970) have suggested that they are originated at three "nucleating sites" in each cell, which are represented by three cytoplasmic foci associated with the basal body of the cilium (Fig. 2.9). This suggestion is based on the observation that microtubules can be seen to be connected at one end with these nucleating sites, in sections that show these sites and the microtubules together. In sections far from the nucleating sites, orientation of the microtubules is such that their connection with the nucleating sites is possible. Moreover, if microtubules are experimentally disassembled by

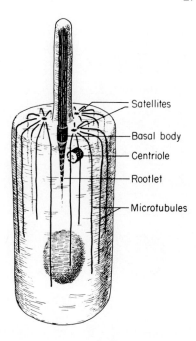

Fig. 2.9. Drawing summarizing the distribution of microtubules in an ectodermal cell. Note the three satellites. (From Tilney and Goddard, 1970.)

low temperatures, and then allowed to reappear by warming, they make their first appearance in proximity to the nucleating sites, resuming the same orientation as before.

3.   THE "BASEMENT MEMBRANE"

As will be described in detail when discussing the cortical layer of the egg, several membranes envelope the sea urchin egg. We will describe here another membrane that, as shown by Okazaki and Niijma (1964), lines the inner surface of the ectodermal wall of the embryos. According to these authors, after staining with Hale's reagent, a layer can be noted by observing the figures of the early works of Immers (1956, 1961a) and Motomura (1960a). Okazaki and Niijma succeeded with embryos of several species of sea urchins in clearly staining this basement membrane with the Hale reagent. By treating the embryos with distilled water, Okazaki was able to cause swelling of the basement membrane and to isolate it; the membrane was dissolved by pancreatin. This fact, together with the positive Hale reaction, suggests its mucopolysaccharidic nature. At the electron microscopic level of observation, the basement membrane appears as a distinct, thin, membranous structure about 10 nm thick.

Preliminary electron microscopic observations were performed by Endo and Uno (1960) and Wolpert and Mercer (1963). Okazaki and Niijma have suggested that the basement membrane may play a role in the regulation of permeability of the embryos to sugars since it is formed concomitantly with the drop of this permeability (Moore, 1940, K. Dan, 1952).

C. The Centrifuged Egg

A number of observations on the fine structure of the sea urchin egg preceded the use of electron microcopy. Many of these were concerned with the study of the cortical layer of the egg. We will mention here only a few of the latest ones among the preelectron microscopic observations. In fact, the significance of the earlier findings has considerably dropped in the light of the more detailed knowledge brought about by the use of the electron microscope and of the techniques of cell fractionation. A complete list of these early works can be found in Harvey's review (1956a).

The techniques by which the structure of the sea urchin egg has been studied have made use of the staining properties of the cell organelles and of the stratification of the latter after centrifuging the entire egg. The two techniques have very often been combined. The genus *Arbacia* is probably the most studied one from the point of view of centrifugation experiments (Sanzo, 1904; Lyon, 1906; Morgan, 1909; E. B. Harvey, 1932, 1933a,b, 1934, 1935a,b,c, 1936, 1938, 1940a,b,c, 1941, 1943, 1945, 1946, 1949, 1951, 1956a; Harvey and Hollaender, 1937; Harvey and Lavin, 1944, 1951). The typical distribution of the layers after centrifugation is shown in Fig. 2.10. The order of stratification beginning at the light (centripetal) pole is (1) oil; (2) clear cytoplasm, containing the nucleus in its lightest part; (3) mitochondria; (4) yolk; (5) pigment. Variations of this order of stratification have been found in other species. The mitochondrial layer is heavier than the yolk in *Echinaracnius parma, Echinocardium cordatum, Lytechinus variegatus, Paracentrotus lividus, Psammechinus microtuberculatus, Psammechinus miliaris, Strongylocentrotus dröbachiensis, Strongylocentrotus franciscanus, Strongylocentrotus purpuratus,* and *Tripneustes esculentus* (Callan, 1949; Lindahl, 1932b; Holter and Linderstrøm-Lang, 1940; Runnström and Kriszat, 1950). Less variability is found regarding the position of the clear cytoplasm. The nucleus is always found closest to the oil cap, with the exception of the *Echinocardium* and *Temnopleurus* spp. eggs, where it has been described as being the centrifugal pole (Monné, 1944; Motomura, 1935).

The stainability of these layers with vital dyes has been thoroughly studied by Harvey (1956a).

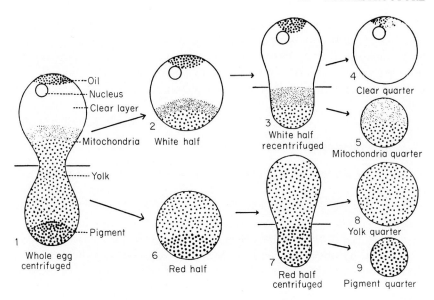

Fig. 2.10. The unfertilized egg of *Arbacia punctulata,* stratified by centrifugal force (about 3 minutes at 10,000 *g*), and the halves and quarters into which it breaks. The drawings are from camera lucida sketches and photographs, made as accurately as possible to scale (approx. × 450). The clear area in No. 7 at the centripetal pole is due to further packing of the granules with longer centrifuging. (From E. B. Harvey, 1956a, Fig. 12, p. 124. Reprinted by permission of Princeton Univ. Press.)

Immers (1960b), by means of histochemical methods, has found that mucopolysaccharides esterified with sulfate are localized not only in the cortex after centrifugation at 15,000 *g*, but also within granules scattered in the cytoplasm (these are, however, absent in *Paracentrotus*).

Ultrastructural analyses of the centrifuged eggs have been performed (Pasteels *et al.,* 1958; Gross *et al.,* 1960), most recently by E. Anderson (1969, 1970). This author reports that the layers that can be obtained in *Arbacia* eggs are the following ones, moving toward the centrifugal pole: lipids, pronucleus within a clear zone (made up of cisternae, annulate lamellae, heavy bodies, Golgi complexes, rod-containing vacuoles) mitochondria, yolk, and pigment. When the centrifugation is prolonged so as to break the egg into two halves, the breakage line passes through the mitochondrial layer. If quarters are obtained, the lightest one contains lipids, pronucleus, Golgi apparatus, some mitochondria, and annulatae lamellae; the second contains several mitochondria and various other organelles; the third contains mostly yolk but also some mitochondria and endoplasmic reticulum; the heaviest contains pigment yolk, some mitochondria, and rod-containing vacuoles.

Cortical granules are present in all the quarters at the cortex level, not being dislodged by a centrifugation at 10,000 g for 30 minutes unless the eggs have been treated with urethane. Other structures that are not moved by this kind of centrifugation are the ribosomes. Thus, while fundamentally confirming the earliest conclusions about egg stratification reached by optical microscopic observations, Anderson stresses the fact that each layer also contains part of the elements mostly accumulated in another layer. The same applies to the egg divided into quarters.

D. The Metachromatic Granules

Among the innumerable studies on the staining properties of the egg cell particulate, we shall mention here the observation that mitochondria stain vitally with difficulty with Janus Green B (Gustafson and Lenicque, 1952; Shaver, 1955).

It is worth mentioning that Pasteels discovered in the cytoplasm of the egg two groups of granules, α and β, that stain metachromatically, identity of which has not yet been established in any of the electron microscopic studies (Pasteels, 1955, 1958; Pasteels and Mulnard, 1957). The α-granules are uniformly scattered throughout the cytoplasm and can be stained with metachromatic dyes (toluidine blue, brilliant cresyl blue, azur B). The β-granules are lighter in the centrifugation experiments and stain more intensely with metachromatic dyes, but, according to Pasteels, they can only take up the dye through the mediation of the α-granules. They become stained at the moment of the first mitosis, when the egg has been previously stained in its α-granules with metachromatic dyes. If the α-granules have been stained with neutral red, the color is never passed on to the β-granules. At metaphase, these latter are located preferentially around the equatorial plate.

After centrifugation at 30,000 g, the α-granules are located in the most centrifugal part of the yolk zone, just above the mitochondria. Under the electron microscope, this zone does not show any characteristic structure besides the yolk platelets.

The β-granules accumulate in the most centripetal part of the yolk layer. The structures revealed by the electron microscope in this zone are Golgi vesicles. It is of interest that the β-granules exhibit a strong acid phosphatase activity and contain a very acidic mucopolysaccharide. Their identity with lysosomes has, therefore, been suggested. This would tally with the observation that the β-granules seem to undergo modifications following fertilization. For an explanation of the possible mechanism of staining of the α-granules, see Vercauteren (1958). To our knowledge, the most recent work on this subject is that of Mulnard *et al.* (1960), who described α- and β-granules with similar characteristics in *Arbacia punctulata*. A thorough description of the cytochemical properties of the egg particulate can be found in the papers by Monné and Slautterback (1950a,b).

Chapter 3

Cortical Layer of the Egg and Physiology of Fertilization

As previously stated, it is impossible to describe the cortical layer structure of the egg separately from the physiology of sperm penetration. Indeed its particular structure will acquire a meaning when seen in the light of its function.

A. The Egg Envelopes

In describing the cortical layer of the egg one should mention that the egg itself is surrounded by a layer of a gelatinous substance, the so-called jelly coat.

The nature of the jelly coat, its role in fertilization, and its relationship to the fertilizin will be discussed together with the process of sperm penetration.

As revealed by studies with the electron microscope (Afzelius, 1956b; Motomura, 1960b; Endo, 1961a; Wolpert and Mercer, 1961; Mercer and Wolpert, 1962), the surface of the unfertilized egg consists of two distinct layers: the external so-called vitelline envelope, and the internal plasma membrane. The question of the existence of these two distinct layers has long been debated (for reviews, see Moser, 1939a; Runn-ström, 1966b). In the opinion of Lönning (1967a,b,c) and Millonig (1969), the vitelline envelope is a fluffy amorphous layer 3.5 nm (Lönning) or 10 nm (Millonig) thick, which surrounds the plasma membrane. Balinsky (1961), on the contrary, finds no vitelline membrane in either fertilized or unfertilized eggs of *Tripneustes gratilla* and *Toxopneustes pileolus*. Pasteels (1965) has not been able to show a vitelline membrane in the unfertilized egg.

The question assumes particular importance when the theory of Endo (1961a) is accepted, according to which the vitelline membrane plays a fundamental role in the formation of the fertilization membrane. This theory, however, has been questioned by Balinsky (1961) and, more recently, by Millonig (1969).

The plasma membrane has the usual lipoprotein constitution. It is about 8 nm thick according to Millonig, and about 6 nm according to Lönning. It protrudes in the oocyte into many microvilli which become short in the mature egg and are revealed only by the electron microscope. Tyler and Tyler (1966) have suggested that the microvilli protrude through the vitelline membrane. This idea has mostly originated by extrapolation to sea urchins of observations in other materials. Direct observations by Lönning (1967a,b,c) and immunoelectron microscopic studies by Baxandall *et al.* (1964a) have established that they are covered with the vitelline membrane. Aketa (1967b) has presented a method, based on the treatment of the eggs with diluted NaOH, which allows the isolation of a membranous fraction, that the author suggests represents the plasma membranes.

B. The Cortical Granules

The most important structures that lie beneath the plasma membrane are the so-called cortical granules. They are spherical bodies about 1 μ in diameter, distributed in a single row. They were first described in the *Arbacia* egg by Harvey (1911), "as minute granules unmoved by centrifuging, which disappear on fertilization and whose substance helps to form the fertilization membrane." These words still express practically all that we know about the mechanism through which they act, even if a mass of morphological data has accumulated since then. They were later described in the *Echinus esculentus* egg by Gray (1924) and the *Lytechinus* egg by Hendee (1931). It is only after the studies of Moser (1939a,b, 1940) that we find a systematic study of the cortical granules. A great deal of work on this subject is linked to the name of Runnström and others of the Swedish school (see Runnström, 1966b, for review).

A cytochemical study by Monné and Härde (1951) has shown that the cortical granules contain an acid mucopolysaccharide associated with proteins. The same authors described how the cortical granules appear scattered in the cytoplasm of the oocyte and migrate to the periphery only upon its maturation.

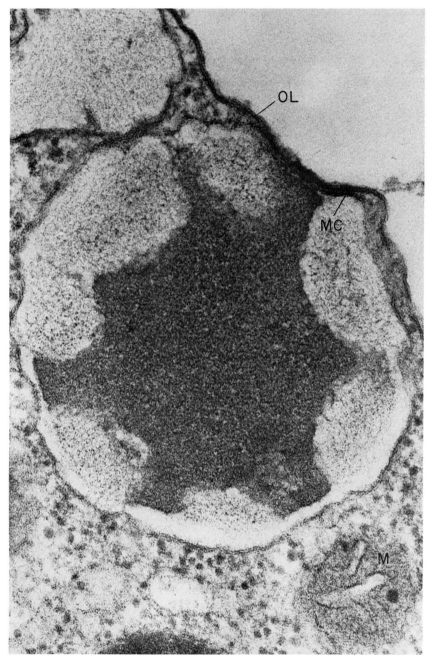

Fig. 3.1. A section through a mature cortical granule of an *Arbacia punctulata* egg. MC, membrane of the cortical granule; OL, oolemma; M, mitochondrion. (From Anderson, 1968.)

Electron microscopic study of the cortical granules by McCulloch (1952a,b) and Lansing *et al.* (1952) has been followed by more recent investigations by Afzelius (1956b), Takashima (1960), Endo (1961a,b), Wolpert and Mercer (1961), Franklin (1965), Lönning (1967a), E. Anderson (1968), Millonig (1969), and Sachs and Anderson (1969, 1970). It has been found that the ultrastructure of cortical granules changes with the species.

In Fig. 3.1, one of the most frequent appearances of the granules is depicted. A spherical body, limited by a membrane 20–30 nm thick, encloses an electron-dense core. A number of less electron-dense granules hang from the internal surface of the limiting membrane. In *Hemicentrotus pulcherrimus* the cortical granules are made up of concentrically arranged lamellar structures, whereas in *Temnopleurus toreumaticus* the matrix is granular and homogeneous (Takashima, 1960).

These cortical structures of the egg undergo characteristic changes following fertilization or parthenogenetic activation, which lead to the formation of the fertilization membrane. How this membrane is formed has been the subject of a series of studies and is still being discussed. Three main theories have been proposed in the last ten years, and will be briefly described.

First: Balinsky (1961) in *Tripneustes gratilla* and *Toxopneustes pileolus* describes the swelling and interfusion of the cortical granules

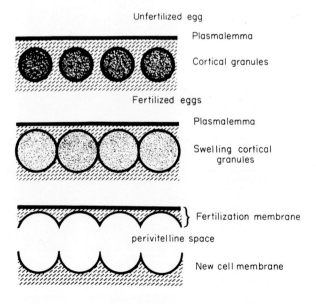

Fig. 3.2. Cortical granules reaction at fertilization, according to Balinsky. (From Balinsky, 1961.)

at fertilization. Thus a perivitelline space is formed and the external half of the cortical granules, together with the plasmalemma (plasma membrane) and the most peripheral layer of the cytoplasm, is lifted from the egg to form the fertilization membrane (see Fig. 3.2). As mentioned above, this author asserts that there is no vitelline membrane in sea urchin eggs.

Second: The theory of Endo (1961a,b) proposes that the cortical granules are initially attached to the plasma membrane, a view that has been accepted by many authors (Fig. 3.3A). At fertilization, the plasma

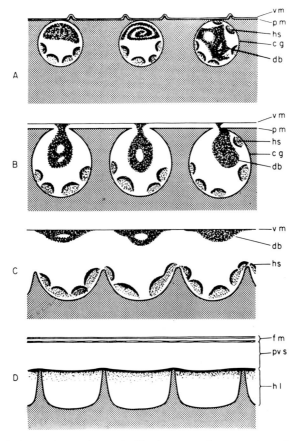

Fig. 3.3. Cortical granule reaction at fertilization, according to Endo, and the formation of the fertilization membrane in the sea urchin egg. (A) Surface of the unfertilized egg; (B) explosion of the cortical granules (cg); the vitelline membrane (vm) begins to be lifted up while the dark bodies (db) are extruded and the egg plasma membrane (pm) has become continuous with the membrane bounding the cortical granules; (C) the dark bodies have joined the vitelline membrane; the hemispheric globules (hs) begin to build up a layer over the new egg surface; this will then become the hyaline layer (hl) as indicated in (D); (D) the dark bodies have become fused with the vitelline membrane, thus giving rise to the definitive fertilization membrane (fm); pvs, perivitelline space. (From Endo, 1961a.)

membrane breaks at the points of contact with the cortical granules, whose limiting membrane becomes continuous with the plasma membrane (Fig. 3.3B). The central mass contained in the granules is extruded at this time and becomes attached to the inner surface of the vitelline membrane, which is lifted up, with the consequent formation of the perivitelline space. This term, as proposed by Millonig (1969), should be abandoned because it generates confusion. There is general agreement that the vitelline membrane is external to this space. The name derives from the old mammalian embryologists who had termed the mammalian egg "vitellum." The term "fertilization space" proposed by Millonig seems more adequate. According to Endo's theory, the fertilization membrane is made up of the material extruded from the cortical granules, together with the vitelline membrane (Fig. 3.3C and D). The internal surface of the limiting membrane of the granules, together with the plasma membrane, becomes the external surface of the fertilized egg. Meantime, the hemispheric globules hanging from the membrane of the granules have joined to build up a continuous layer covering the entire egg surface. This is the hyaline layer, which will adhere to the surface of the egg and, which presumably, helps in holding together the blastomeres during cleavage. It seems that in the cases where such globules do not exist, it is always some material contained in the cortical granules that makes up the hyaline layer. The inhibition of cortical granule breakdown, which can be obtained by treatment with urethane or by mild treatment with butyric or lactic acid, brings about impairment of the hyaline layer formation (Osanai, 1960; Longo and Anderson, 1970b,c) (also see Chapter 6, p. 158, for a discussion on the hyaline layer function and composition).

Third: Endo's views had resisted criticism for 8 years, till 1969, when Millonig proposed a modification of his theory. Millonig has investigated very carefully the question on the initial attachment of the cortical granules to the plasma membrane. He claims that on closer examination one can find a clear space of about 5–8 nm between the cortical granules and the inner cell surface in the unfertilized egg. However, such a narrow space is visible only in sections that perpendicularly cut the granule and egg membranes. That the section is really perpendicular would be true should the section show all three layers of the lipoprotein membrane in both membranes. Under such conditions, no figures of fusion are observed in the unfertilized egg of *Arbacia lixula* and *Arbacia punctulata* (Fig. 3.4A).

According to Millonig, therefore, the very first event of fertilization is the fusion at multiple points between the plasma membrane of the egg and the membrane of the cortical granules (Fig. 3.4B). This is attributed by Millonig to a change in the potential of this membrane,

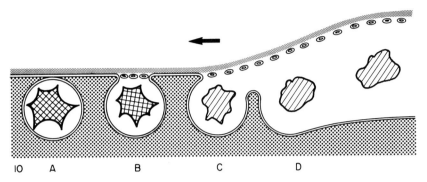

Fig. 3.4. Cortical granule reaction at fertilization in *Arbacia* eggs, according to Millonig. The arrow indicates the direction of the fertilization wave. (A) Unreacted cortical granule. Its membrane has, like the egg plasmalemma a trilaminar structure. A space of 50 to 80 Å separates the granule from the plasmalemma. The egg surface is covered by the amorphous vitelline membrane. (B) Multiple fusions between the cortical granule membrane and the plasmalemma produce several openings between the interior of the granule and the vitelline membrane. Vesiculation of the membranes. (C) Immediate diffusion of seawater through the vitelline membrane and through the openings, transformation of the granule into a vesicle, and dissolution of the peripheral lens-shaped bodies. (D) Formation of a fertilization space at the level of the cortical granule layer and elevation of the vitelline membrane together with the vesicles which are remnants of the cortical granule and plasma membranes. Transformation of the vitelline membrane into fertilization membrane. (From Millonig, 1969.)

which precedes elevation of the fertilization membrane (Hiramoto, 1959), since similar fusion between these membranes can be experimentally provoked by electric stimulation.

The second event is the swelling of the cortical granules due to the uptake of seawater. Indeed, the vitelline membrane does not contain polar-oriented lipid groups that can prevent the uptake of seawater and ions from the mucopolysaccharides contained in the cortical granules (Monroy, 1949) (Fig. 3.4C). From this point on, the scheme proceeds as described by Endo.

C. The Fertilization Membrane

The fertilization membrane was first described by Derbès (1847). It is found about 20 seconds after the sperm makes contact with the egg surface. Its thickness varies from 10 nm (Mitchison, 1953c) to 30 nm (Hillier *et al.*, 1952) in *Arbacia punctulata*, to about 1 μ in *Psammechinus miliaris* (Runnström *et al.*, 1946). In a few minutes, it becomes harder and thicker. In this hardening process, oxidation of the SH groups may occur, since the process is sensitive to thioglycholate. It has been suggested (Monroy and Runnström, 1948; Monroy, 1949) that a process similar to that of keratinization may take place. Lallier (1970) found that the hardening of the fertilization membrane is disturbed by glycine ethyl ester, an inhibitor of cross-linking of fibrinogen, and suggested that the formation of esterlike bonds is involved in this process. Motomura (1950b, 1957) isolated a basic factor, which he has called "colleterin," that is apparently contained in vesicles of the cortical region, different from the cortical granules, and catalyzes the hardening of the fertilization membrane. Under optical microscopy, the fertilization membrane appears much thicker because the real membrane lies separate from the egg surface at a variable distance in the different species. Its function is not yet clear; it probably helps in preventing polyspermy. The fertilization membrane seems to be of a proteic nature; it contains no lipids, according to old observations of its solubility characteristics (E. N. Harvey, 1910; Loeb, 1913; Heilbrunn, 1915; Kopac, 1940; 1941; Chambers, 1942, 1944; A. R. Moore, 1949; Monroy and Runnström, 1948). According to Lansing and Rosenthal (1948) and Bal et al. (1967) it contains RNA. Using the electron microscope, Ito et al. (1967) described the fertilization membrane as made up of three layers, which together are 50 nm thick. Two of these layers are made up of tubular structures running antiparallel to each other and enclosing the third layer, which is amorphous. Inoué et al. have isolated and examined under the electron microscope the fertilization membrane before (1970b) and after (1967) complete fusion of the cortical granule content with the lifted vitelline membrane, which should allow distinguishing between the fertilization membrane material derived from the vitelline membrane and that contributed by the cortical granules. From this work, it was suggested that "tight rolls of an elongated sheet, which has a crossed-grid network of about 15×24 nm mesh," migrate from the cortical granules to unroll and adhere to the inner surface of the lifted vitelline membrane through S — S bridges. Bryan (1970) reports having isolated the cortical granule content by removing the vitelline membrane with dithiothreitol, activating the eggs with butyric acid, and thus causing the cortical granule content to be extruded into the surrounding seawater. It has thus been possible to isolate from the cortical granule content a hyaline component that gelates in the presence of divalent cations, and that, because of its sedimentation properties, closely resembles the Ca-precipitable protein of Kane and Hersh (1959) (see Chapter 5) that Kane (1969) isolated from cortical granules with an approach very similar to that of Bryan. Another crystalline component also has been isolated; it appears to contain three proteins, sedimentable at 6, 8.5, and 13 S, respectively. Under the electron microscope, the crystalline component again has the appearance of cylinder sheets of 15–20 nm in diameter (see

Chapter 4 for a discussion on the cortical granule content). Bryan and Gilula (1970) draw attention to the fact that periodic networks of microdomains are present on both the inner and outer surfaces of the fertilization membrane. Recently Inoué *et al.* (1971) have extracted from *Strongylocentrotus purpuratus* sperms some "lysins" active on the egg membranes, that cause the eggs to lose their content into the surrounding medium. Some egg "ghosts" are left following a treatment with such "lysins." The authors believe these ghosts to be represented by the vitelline membranes, since no ghosts are obtained if the vitelline membranes had been previously removed by trypsin.

The latest description of the ultrastructure of the isolated fertilization membranes of *Strongylocentrotus purpuratus* eggs was performed by Inoué and Hardy (1971), who confirmed their trilaminated nature. The central layer is thought to derive from the vitelline membrane, while the other two are organized from the crystalline material extruded by the cortical granules. These two external layers are in turn trilaminated. Their central lamina is made up by filaments 4–5 nm thick and their outer laminae are made up by fibrils 7.5 nm thick, that intersect the filaments at 75°.

Several methods have been described for removing the fertilization membrane. They will be mentioned here because of their practical use, when one wants to allow the embryos to develop without this membrane, for example, in the study of egg permeability.

Mechanical treatments lasting from 30 seconds to 2 minutes after sperm addition, i.e., immediately after elevation of the fertilization membrane: these mechanical treatments may be represented by violent shaking (McClendon, 1910; and many others, reviewed by Harvey, 1956a); staining through bolting cloth (Just, 1939; Lindahl and Lundin, 1948); drawing through a fine pipette (Glough, 1927; Harvey, 1932), or forcing through a fine syringe needle. Of course, the success of such methods depends upon the intensity of the treatment; if too energetic, it may cause egg breakage, and if too mild, failure of the membrane removal. Other methods involve chemical treatments of the eggs while elevating the membranes with isosmotic KCl or 1.0 *M* urea (Kopac, 1940, 1943; Chambers, 1940, 1942, 1944; Moser, 1940; Moore, 1930), or with dithiothreitol (Epel *et al.,* 1970). Lastly, the membrane can be removed by enzymatic treatments: with seawater where hatching blastulae are cultured, which contains the "hatching" enzyme (Kopac, 1941), or with solutions of crystalline trypsin (Runnström, 1948b; Moore, 1951; Minganti, 1953; Epel, 1970) or of papain (Tyler and Spiegel, 1956). The last description of the trypsin method, in *Strongylocentrotus purpuratus,* involves incubation of the unfertilized eggs in 0.25 mg% of 2 × crystallized

(Worthington) trypsin of unfertilized eggs. Every 2 minutes, samples are removed to check when fertilization is no longer accompanied by eleva- tion of a membrane (Epel, 1970). The treatment with papain, which has been used with excellent results in *Strongylocentrotus purpuratus* and *Lytechinus pictus* (Tyler and Spiegel, 1956), involves either pretreatment of the unfertilized eggs or fertilization of the eggs in a 0.02–0.04% solu- tion of papain in seawater. In this latter case, a fertilization membrane will form, which will then shrink and apparently fuse with the egg plasma membrane. The development that follows is normal.

The effect of pretreatment of the unfertilized eggs has been attributed to action on the vitelline membrane. A thorough discussion of this subject is reported by Runnström (1966b).

D. The Egg Cortex

We have so far spoken of the cortical layer of the egg to indicate the membranes and peripheral part of the cytoplasm containing the cortical granules. The term cortex, however, has been used in the past to indicate a peripheral layer of the cytoplasm of the egg that has become differenti- ated for certain characteristics from the rest of the cytoplasm. Cham- bers (1917, 1938) was the first to observe that the cortical layer of the egg is denser than its interior and to suggest that it consists of an extensible gel. The thickness of this cortex has been estimated to be $1-2\ \mu$ by centri- fugation experiments (Mitchison, 1956), and $3-4\ \mu$ by experiments in which the cortical layer is mechanically deformed by pushing it with a fine needle and measuring the thickness of the cortex pushed out at the opposite side (Hiramoto, 1957). Other authors (Brown, 1934; Marsland, 1939; Marsland and Landau, 1954; Moser, 1939a,b) have inferred the existence of a rigid cortex because of the behavior of the pigment and cortical granules during centrifugation of the egg. The cortical granules are not displaced from the peripheral layer of the egg by centrifugation up to 10,000 g.

It should be noted, however, that recently many authors, have held that the cortical granules are attached to the plasma membrane. This would explain why they are not easily displaced by centrifugation without the need to postulate a gelatinous cortex. Moreover, Millonig (1969), who has shown that the cortical granules are not bound to the plasma mem- brane, has proved that they are movable by centrifugal forces higher than 10,000 g. An electron microscopic analysis by Wolpert and Mercer (1961) and Mercer and Wolpert (1962) failed to reveal any particular structure of the cortical layer of the cytoplasm, apart from the presence of the cortical granules. The idea that the ground cytoplasm of the egg periphery enjoys a special physical state has, however, been shared by many authors, Runnström, in particular, has devoted considerable attention to this problem, which is reviewed by the author in "Advances in Morphogenesis" (1966b). The same author (1969) recently reported an electron microscopic investigation of the membranous vesicles present in the outer cytoplasm of the egg before and after fertilization. The appearance of some of these vesicles in the egg cortex upon fertilization is described, among other observations. A movement of small vesicles toward the egg cortex during the first 30 minutes following fertilization has also been reported by Harris (1968), who has shown that fine fibril bundles project into the cortex from the microvilli remaining at the egg surface to mark the interval between the open cortical granules. Kimoto (1964) has reported that histological staining specific for the connective tissue reveals a three-layered cortex different from the endoplasm.

Recent experiments by Wolpert *et al.* (1971) are in contrast with the idea that a gelatinous structure of the cortex, if it exists, plays a role in the mechanism of surface contraction during cell division. In fact, the mechanical properties of the egg surface, as measured by the possibility of compressing the egg with a coverslip, do not change when the egg is subjected to high hydrostatic pressure, which is known to solate gellike structures, and to disassemble microtubules (see Chapter 5).

Attempts have also been made to isolate the egg cortex. The first approach belongs to Motomura (1954), who lysed the egg in slightly acidified distilled water and separated a portion of the cytoplasm containing the cortical granules. Since Heilbrunn (1956) has observed that rigidity of the cortex increases with calcium concentration, methods have been developed whereby homogenization in a high concentration of divalent cations causes gelification of the peripheral layer of the egg cytoplasm. This allows the separation of this layer from the fluid cytoplasm. Sakai (1960a) was the first to isolate the cortex by centrifugation after homogenization in $0.1\ M$ $MgCl_2$. Kane and Hersh (1959) succeeded in isolating from eggs a protein fraction that gelifies after homogenization in $0.02\ M$ $CaCl_2$.

Hence, the question has been asked if this protein is also located at the periphery of the egg and if it is identifiable with the cortical protein of Sakai. A thorough analysis by Kane and Stephens (1969) has established that, in some species, homogenization in $CaCl_2$ brings about the formation of a cortical hull, which contains the fraction of Kane and Hersh. This fraction is also contained in the cortices obtained by homogenization in $0.01\ M$ $MgCl_2$. In other species, however, the $CaCl_2$ gelating protein is not preferentially located in the cortical layer.

Sakai has studied extensively the content in SH groups of cortices, prepared according to his procedure, and their changes during first cleavage (see Chapter 5) (Sakai, 1960b, 1962a,b, 1963, 1965; Sakai and Dan, 1959). According to Yazaki (1968), the calcium gelating protein of Kane and Hersh may be one of the components of the cortex isolated by Sakai's method, and would be contained in the cortical granules of the unfertilized egg and hyaline layer of the fertilized egg. This view is shared by Kane and Stephens, on the basis of electron microscopic observations which show a good correlation in the various species between the gel protein content and the thickness of the hyaline layer. The latter would appear as a "dense meshwork between the fertilization membrane and the cell surface." They conclude, however, that more definitive proof is needed so as to establish that their protein is entirely contained in the cortical granules. Should this view prove correct, we should have a satisfactory explanation for the presence of a gelating substance in the cortical layer of the egg. One might tentatively speculate that this proteic complex, coming into contact with the calcium contained in seawater at fertilization, may, according to Millonig's theory, contribute to the formation of the fertilization membrane or, at least, of the hyaline layer [see also the already discussed work of Inoué et al. (1970b) and of Bryan (1970)]. Ultracentrifugal analysis of the protein of Kane and Hersh has been presented (Kane and Stephens, 1969). It would be desirable, however, that more criteria be adopted to ascertain the purity of the isolated fraction, considering that the sea urchin egg does contain hundreds, probably thousands, of different proteins (Giudice and Mutolo, unpublished).

E. Sperm–Egg Interaction

1. FERTILIZIN AND JELLY COAT

The sea urchin egg is enveloped, as already described, by the "jelly coat." We identify this gelatinous envelope with the substance Lillie (1914) has called "fertilizin."

This layer had first been observed by Derbès (1847) in *Echinus esculentus*. It is not visible under the light microscope in seawater, but can be demonstrated by India ink (Boveri, 1901a). This method also shows a micropyle, i.e., a funnel-shaped tunnel, formerly believed to be used by the spermatozoon to reach the egg surface. Presence of the jelly coat is indicated by the observation that the eggs lie spaced from each other when observed in a drop of seawater. If the jelly coat is removed, the eggs tend to stick to each other. Removal of the jelly coat is routinely performed by washing the eggs, at a concentration of about 30,000/ml, with $2 \times 10^{-3}\ M$ HCl in seawater. Removal is also possible by other methods: washing with isosmotic (0.54 M) NaCl (Lillie, 1921; Kopac, 1940), or with isosmotic (0.53 *M*) KCl (Harvey, 1956a), or with NH_4Cl (Kopac, 1948). Mechanical treatments such as straining through bolting silk (Just, 1928a), shaking and repeated washings (McClendon, 1914; Lillie, 1914; E. N. Harvey, 1914), have been reported to be equally effective in jelly coat removal. Lastly, we must remember that the jelly coat can be removed by proteolytic enzymes and by physical treatments such as X rays (E. B. Harvey, 1941, 1956a; Evans *et al.,* 1941) and UV irradiation (Harvey, 1956a).

This layer, as already mentioned, is laid down during the last phases of oogenesis. Its origin is still unknown. As seen under the electron microscope, it is easily damaged by the fixation procedure. Some pictures are, however, available (Motomura, 1960b; Balinsky, 1961; Takashima, 1963; Lönning, 1967a). It appears to be made up of a granular or fibrous material, which is reinforced at the external and internal boundaries. At the internal boundary, in particular, it seems to form a kind of membrane, which has been identified by Runnström with the vitelline membrane (1966b). In Tyler and Tyler's (1966) opinion, the jelly coat is part of the plasmamembrane. The latter protrudes through the surrounding vitelline membrane with microvilli, from which the jelly coat transudes. Vasseur (1952a) and Lönning (1967b) suggest, however, that the jelly coat always lies separate from the egg surface.

Upon ultracentrifugation and electrophoresis (Runnström *et al.,* 1942; Tyler, 1949, 1956; Tyler *et al.,* 1954), the jelly coat shows a homogeneous band. Among the earliest attempts to purify it, we shall mention the work by Tyler and Fox (1940). It appears constituted by long glycoprotein molecules of about 300,000 molecular weight, with a strongly acidic behavior owing to esterification of carbohydrates with SO_4 groups (Tyler, 1949; Vasseur, 1947a, 1949, 1950, 1952b; Vasseur and Immers, 1949; Bishop and Metz, 1952; Nakano and Ohashi, 1954; Minganti, 1958; Minganti and Vasseur, 1959). The carbohydrate composition varies in different species, suggesting that this may be responsible for the species specificity of fertilization. As observed by Monroy (1965), however, the relative distribution of the monosaccharide and amino acid residues in the molecule may give rise to a far greater variety of specific combinations. There is so far no direct proof that the jelly coat plays a role in such a specificity. Isaka *et al.* (1969, 1970) have fractionated, by hydroxylapatite columns, the jelly coat of *Anthocidaris crassispina* and *Pseudocentrotus depressus* and found that each fraction can be considered as a sialopolysaccharide, rich in sialic acid, poor in protein and sulfate. The amino acid composition of the different fractions has been found to be the same. Perlmann *et al.* (1959) were the first to describe the presence of sialic acid in sea urchin gametes.

What, then, is the function of the jelly coat? The old observation by
Lillie (1914), from which the "fertilizin" theory arose, is that the jelly
coat, dissolved in seawater, is able to cause a transitory activation of
sperm motility; furthermore, it interacts with sperms thus causing their
agglutination. Lillie's idea was that "fertilizin" might be the molecule
that, since it can bind the sperm surface from one side and the egg surface from the other, causes sperm egg interaction (see Fig. 3.5). All we

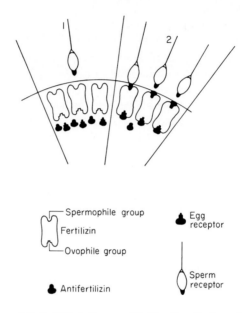

Spermophile group

Fertilizin

Ovophile group

Antifertilizin

Egg
receptor

Sperm
receptor

Fig. 3.5. Illustration of F. R. Lillie's theory of fertilization. In the unfertilized egg, fertilizin molecules are present in the cortical layer of the egg. Each one of them bears an ovophile
and a spermophile group (sector 1). Upon fertilization (sector 2), the sperm receptors of the
spermatozoon combine with the spermophile groups of a group of fertilizin molecules (for
the sake of simplicity, one sperm receptor per spermatozoon is indicated in the diagram).
This reaction activates the fertilizin molecules and they propagate over the egg surface. As a
result, molecules of antifertilizin rapidly block all the spermophile groups of the fertilizin
molecules, thus preventing reaction with other spermatozoa; this is Lillie's hypothesis concerning the mechanism of prevention of polyspermy. Another result of the activation of the
fertilizin molecules is the reaction of all ovophile groups each with one egg receptor: this
is the hypothetical mechanism of the activation of the egg. (Adapted from Lillie, 1914; from
Monroy, 1965.)

know today is that the jelly coat can actually bind the sperm, as shown
by experiments performed with ^{35}S-labeled jelly coat (Tyler and Hathaway, 1958; Hathaway, 1959; Hathaway and Metz, 1961). In favor of the
supposed function in the species specificity of fertilization must be mentioned the fact that sperm agglutination is largely species specific; Tyler
(1949) has found a close parallel between cross-agglutination and cross-

fertilization. The jelly coat appears to cause in the sperm the so-called "acrosomal reaction," a phenomenon of greatest importance in fertilization which we shall describe later. The transitory agglutination of sperm is not, in fact, a phenomenon that in nature plays a role in fertilization. This fact has been usefully exploited, however, as a test for jelly coat activity. In experimental conditions, and because of interaction of the sperm with the egg specific receptor, it would occur far from the egg surface. Actually, the sperm that have been treated with fertilizin lose some of their fertilization power; the magnitude of this loss varies with the species. Attempts at fertilizing eggs deprived of the jelly coat have brought about a marked percent decrease of fertilized eggs in *Strongylocentrotus purpuratus,* but only a slight decrease in *Arbacia punctulata* (Tyler and Metz, 1955). It has been noted, however, that such eggs can still be agglutinated by sperm extracts, which are able to react with fertilizin, and that the gradual loss of agglutinability, by progressive trypsin treatments, parallels loss of fertilizability. This suggests that fertilizin is present not only as a jelly coat (or as part of it) but also as part of the egg membrane, where it plays a fundamental role in fertilization.

Hagström (1956a) found that removal of the jelly coat increases the rate of fertilization, i.e., decreases the time required for fertilization to take place after sperm addition. This result led Hagström to conclude that the jelly coat does not favor fertilization; in fact, it is a barrier to polyspermy. This view is not shared by Metz, who attributes the slowing down of fertilization by the jelly coat to its viscosity, which causes a relative delay in sperm progression, and to the particular experimental conditions, which may cause some inhibition of the fertilizing capacity of the sperms (Metz, 1967).

Perlmann (1957) has shown that antijelly sera cause precipitation of the jelly around the egg but have little effect on fertilization. On the other hand, antiegg serum homogenate does inhibit fertilization. This would again speak against a fundamental role of the jelly coat in fertilization. Metz (1967), observes that such sera might interact with an antigenic site of the fertilizin different from that for interaction with the sperm. It should be mentioned that the antijelly sera do produce certain effects on the eggs — increase in surface tension, precipitation of the hyaline layer, delay in cleavage (Tyler and Brookbank, 1956a,b) — which suggest the presence of jelly antigens in the eggs.

Ishihara and Dan (1970) have oxidized with H_2O_2 and sodium periodate, or digested with trypsin and pronase the jelly coat of *Hemicentrotus pulcherrimus*. The capacity of such treated jelly preparations to cause sperm agglutination and acrosomal reaction were then studied with the aim of understanding the role of the glycidic and proteic moieties in these functions.

The results stress the importance of sialic acid for both sperm agglutination and acrosomal reaction; the former being more sensitive to mild
H_2O_2 oxidation. On the other hand, both activities were still present,
although at a lesser degree, after proteolytic treatments sufficient to
remove 80% of the amino acids.

2. ANTIFERTILIZIN

To complete the picture of the fertilizin effect on sperm, we shall mention some observations which will be of help for a better understanding of its action mechanism. In sea urchins, but not in other forms,
sperm agglutination caused by fertilizin reverses spontaneously after a
short time and the sperm become nonagglutinable by further addition of
fertilizin. They show, however, a reduced fertilizing ability. This has
been interpreted as meaning that the sperm are now coated with some
univalent fertilizin, which prevents the further binding of the agglutinating divalent fertilizin (Tyler, 1941; Metz, 1942). Since sperm extracts
are able to neutralize the agglutinating effect of fertilizin and to precipitate
the jelly coat, it has been supposed that they may contain the sperm
receptor of fertilizin, the so-called antifertilizin. Tyler and O'Melveny
(1941) have tried to remove the antifertilizin by treatment of the sperm
with acid. Treatments that are effective in removing some antifertilizin
but do not affect the respiration rate, lower the fertilizing power of
sperm.

Metz (1961a) has observed that the effect of extracts supposedly containing antifertilizin on sperm is not very specific. The possibility
exists that such an effect may be caused by some different inhibitors. The
chemistry of antifertilizin has been studied in sperm extracts. A heat-
stable acidic protein, of an average molecular weight under 10,000, was
tentatively proposed as antifertilizin in earlier studies (Runnström et al.,
1942; Metz, 1957; Tyler, 1948), although Hultin (1947, 1949b) implicated a basic protein.

More recently Metz and Köhler (1960) by freeze-thawing sperm have
isolated a jelly precipitating fraction that is sedimented at 30,000 g,
probably particulated, and that contains four or more antigens.

3. THE FERTILIZATION PRODUCT

The question of whether some fertilizin is contained in the egg membrane (Lillie, 1914) had received a negative answer (Tyler and Fox,
1940). It was postulated later (Motomura, 1950a, 1953a,b; Hagström,
1956a; Runnström et al., 1959; Gregg, 1966; Gregg and Metz, 1966) that
a sperm-agglutinating activity is found in the seawater of fertilized eggs
whose jelly has been removed by a variety of methods. Motomura called

the product responsible for this sperm agglutination "cytofertilizin." Ishihara (1964) proposed the name of "fertilization product." The identity of this with jelly fertilizin has not been definitively proved (Ishihara, 1964, 1968a,b; Gregg, 1966, 1969; Gregg and Metz, 1966). They appear to react with the same receptor site of the sperm. Chemical and immunological differences as well as similarities between the two products have been reported. The significance of these results cannot, however, shed much light on the identity of the two products as long as each of them remains unavailable in a pure form. The question of the fertilization product will be discussed again in Chapter 4.

It should be recalled that some authors also extend the term "fertilization product" to other macromolecules that are extruded from the egg into the surrounding seawater at fertilization. Among these are a β-1,3-glucanohydrolase (Epel *et al.*, 1969) and a trypsinlike protease (Vacquier *et al.*, 1972). Both of these proteins seem to be correlated functionally with the process of elevation of the fertilization membrane.

4. MOVEMENT OF THE SPERM TOWARD THE EGG

What is the mechanism by which the sperm approaches and reaches the egg surface? The possibility of a chemotactic mechanism, which has been demonstrated in plant gametes but not definitively proved in animal ones, has been suggested for sea urchins (Hartmann and Schartau, 1939; Hartmann *et al.*, 1939, 1940). These authors have indicated that the naphthoquinone echinochrome contained in *Arbacia lixula*, in combination with some substance of the jelly coat, would be responsible for sperm activation and agglutination. These experiments have not been confirmed by other authors (Tyler, 1939; Cornman, 1941; Bielig and Dohrn, 1950). It still remains, therefore, to be demonstrated that in sea urchins the sperm direct themselves toward the eggs. They have a good chance of reaching the egg surface even after a randomly oriented motion, because of the exceedingly high number of sperm shed by one male as compared to the number of eggs shed by a female (usually in the order of millions).

Yet, once the egg surface has been reached, a mechanism is needed for the specific attachment of the sperm. We have seen how tenuous is the evidence today that fertilizin may actually play the fundamental role that Lillie ascribed to it.

5. THE MECHANISM OF ATTACHMENT OF THE SPERM TO THE EGG SURFACE

In an effort to obtain information on the mechanism of specific interaction of sperm and egg, studies on the molecular constituents of the gamete surface have long been undertaken. One of the main approaches has been the immunological study of the gamete surfaces. The strategy of this kind of experiment has been the following: First, to recognize the different surface antigens of the gametes; second, to treat the gametes with antibodies against single antigens in order to see which antibody is able to inhibit fertilization and, therefore, which antigen is involved in such a process.

The sperm antigens have been extensively studied (Tyler and O'Melveny, 1941; Tyler, 1949; Köhler and Metz, 1960; Flake and Metz, 1962; Kloetzel and Metz, 1963; Baxandall, 1964; Metz and Köhler, 1960; Metz *et al.,* 1964), and many sperm surface antigens have been identified. Some of them are localized in the tail, some in the head, some others in both. The ones of the tail are usually easily extractable; those of the head are not. The jelly coat is able to neutralize some soluble sperm antigen, in agreement with the theory of antifertilizin. The effect of sperm treatment with antibodies against such antigens must, first of all, circumvent the difficulty that multivalent antibodies agglutinate sperms. This would reduce drastically the ability of sperm to fertilize even if the antibodies have reacted with antigens not directly involved in fertilization.

Hence, antibodies are rendered nonagglutinating by photooxidation (Tyler, 1946) or univalent by partial digestion with papain (Metz *et al.,* 1964). Metz and co-workers have found that treatment with univalent antibodies again strongly reduces the sperm fertilizing capacity. The antigens involved appear to be partially species specific by cross-absorption agglutination tests. They also seem to be surface antigens since the antibodies, at least the multivalent ones, do not diffuse into the sperm. An attempt to further characterize the fertilization antigens in *Arbacia* has shown that it is readily sedimentable at 30,000 g. It should be recalled that because a block of sperm antigen inhibits fertilization does not represent definitive proof that this antigen is directly involved in fertilization. Its block might in principle cause damage to some other sperm mechanism which is, in turn, essential for fertilization.

The egg antigens related to fertilization have also been extensively studied (Perlmann, 1957, 1959; Metz, 1961a,b; Tyler, 1957, 1959). One would expect that such a complex object as an egg might in principle contain thousands of different antigens. This is actually suggested by experiments of DEAE fractionation followed by acrylamide gel electrophoresis, which show at least one hundred different protein fractions (Giudice *et al.,* unpublished). A random search for antigens in total egg homogenates, with the ultimate goal of recognizing those involved in fertilization, seems almost hopeless today. The effect of antibodies on fertilization was first studied by Perlmann (1954). This author reported that antibody-treated eggs fail to fertilize. The antigen involved in this inhibition, called by Perlmann and Perlmann (1957a,b) F or fertilization antigen, is not contained in the jelly. Metz and co-workers have shown that papain-digested — i.e., univalent and, therefore, nonagglutinating or precipitating — rabbit antiegg antibodies do not inhibit fertilization. If such serum-reacted eggs are treated with antirabbit γ-globulin sheep serum (Coombs test), then fertilization is inhibited (Metz and Thompson, 1967; Graziano and Metz, 1967). This suggests that antibodies do not simply block a specific site for the sperm, but rather act through their cross-linking effect on the egg surface. Papain digestion of antijelly antibodies also eliminates their inhibitory effect on fertilization (Metz and Thompson, 1967).

The fertilization-inhibiting action of antibodies has been correlated with an electron-dense egg surface layer (Baxandall *et al.,* 1964a,b; Metz *et al.,* 1968).

Other effects of antiegg serum have been described by Perlmann and co-workers, but these are not obtained with univalent antibodies (Metz and Thompson, 1967):

(a) An effect on the egg cortex, which the authors attribute to an interaction with a C antigen of the cortical granules (Perlmann and Perlmann, 1957b; Perlmann, 1959).

(b) A parthenogenetic activation of the egg with antiegg homogenate serum (Perlmann, 1954, 1956, 1957; Baxandall *et al.,* 1964a,b), which the authors ascribe to an interaction with the so-called A antigen. This fact is highly interesting in view of the possibility that this antiserum may impinge upon a triggering mechanism by removing some specific protein factor that might hold the egg in the inactive conditions characteristic of the unfertilized egg. Other authors, however, have cast some doubt on the ability of serum treatment to induce parthenogenesis (Tyler, 1959; Brookbank, 1964). Still the main difficulty to such an approach is the tremendous variety of stimuli that are able to cause parthenogenetic activation. We wish to repeat here our idea of the unfertilized egg: An unstable system which almost any kind of nonspecific stimulus may precipitate into the more stable condition of activation, but which in nature awaits a very specific stimulus to become fertilized. It may be compared to a closed room with a thin, locked door, normally opened by a very specific key, but which any violent kick can smash down. Now, once we have identified one of the many stimuli that can start activation, we are at the beginning of the arduous course of exploring how much this stimulus resembles the one that, in nature, is responsible for egg activation.

Consequently, as pointed out by Metz (1967), experiments performed with fertilization-inhibiting agents nonrelated to gametes offer little hope toward understanding the fertilization process. Such agents have been studied in the past. The "dermal secretion" of *Arbacia,* a yellow fluid that can leak out from the damaged segment of the animal, has been intensely studied (Oshima, 1921; Pequegnat, 1948; Metz, 1960); for the same purpose some "polyphenols" from plants have been carefully studied (Harding, 1951; Runnström and Hagström, 1955; Esping, 1957a,b; Branham and Metz, 1960).

A direct approach to the study of a sperm receptor of the egg surface was performed by Aketa and co-workers (Aketa, 1967a; Aketa and Tsuzuki, 1968; Aketa *et al.*, 1968; Tsuzuki and Aketa, 1969; Aketa and Onitake, 1969). These authors isolated from the vitelline membrane a glycoprotein that is able to bind the sperm. Treatment of the eggs with an antiserum against this glycoprotein inhibits sperm attachment. Antisera against the same protein isolated from different species are not effective on sperm attachment, but are able to prevent the progression of the sperm within the egg. The protein has a sedimentation coefficient of 2.3 S. The amino acid, glycidic, and lipidic composition of this protein has also been analyzed. Destroying the glycidic moiety with periodate does not alter the sperm-binding properties, which are lost following treatment with SH-reducing agents or trypsin.

6.   ULTRASTRUCTURE OF THE SPERM AND ACROSOMAL REACTION

The structure of the sperm: The sea urchin sperm has the usual structure as that of most animal species. It is schematically made up of a conical head containing the nucleus, a middle piece consisting of a single large mitochondrion, and a tail characteristically containing the $9 + 2$ set of microtubular structures with the fibrils that run parallel to the sperm tail. The question has long been debated as to the number of sperm centrioles (Wilson, 1928). It is now agreed that the sperm has two centrioles (Franklin, 1965; Longo and Anderson, 1968, 1969): the distal, which is located between the base of the nucleus and the mito-chondrion and is associated with a bundle of fibers; and the proximal, which lies in the so-called "centriolar fossa" (Figs. 3.6 and 3.9b). The concept that the sperm contributes to the egg centriolus has been fought by Dirksen (1961) who has demonstrated that parthenogenetically activated eggs show normal centrioles. On the other hand, disturbance of the diaster formation caused by experimental removal of the male or female pronucleus has been described by Hiramoto (1962b): When the male pronucleus is removed, the egg undergoes a series of monaster cycles; if, instead, the female pronucleus is removed before or after sperm penetration, diaster figures can be observed. This has been interpreted by Hiramoto to mean that it is the spermatozoon that provides a pair of astral centers, thus permitting the formation of dicentric mitotic figures.

The most recent discussion on this subject can be found in Sachs and Anderson (1970), who have performed an electron microscopic analysis

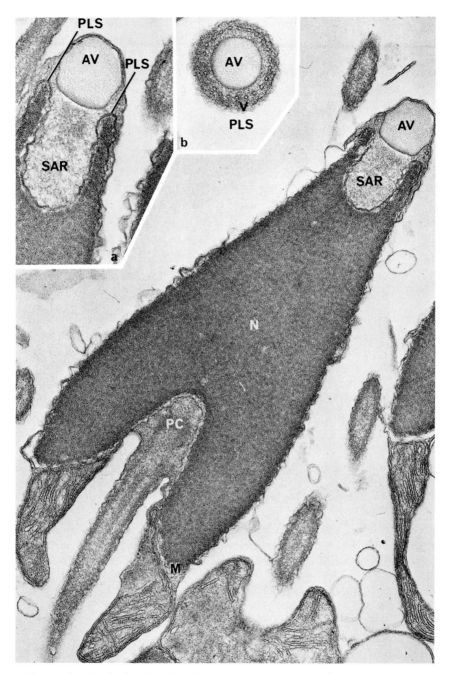

Fig. 3.6. Longitudinal section through a spermatozoon of *Strongylocentrotus purpuratus*. N, nucleus; M, mitochondrion; PC, proximal centriole; SAR, subacrosomal region; AV, acrosomal vesicle; F, flagellum (× 36,000). Insets a and b; Longitudinal (inset a) and cross (inset b) sections of the acrosomal vesicle (AV), subacrosomal region (SAR) and peglike structures (× 73,000). (From Longo and Anderson, 1969.)

of the parthenogenetically activated *Arbacia* eggs. The conclusion is that, although it has been described (Longo and Anderson, 1968) that the sperm pronucleus provides both centrioles for the formation of the diaster, and although it is confirmed (Sachs and Anderson, 1970) that the unfertilized egg does not contain centrioles, the latter are formed after parthenogenetic activation. The length of the head, middle piece and tail is, respectively, 3.25 μ, 0.75 μ, and 45.0 μ in *Arbacia* (Harvey and Anderson, 1943). Slight variations of these sizes usually parallel size variations of the corresponding eggs.

Earlier studies on sperm morphology (Pictet, 1891; Field, 1895; Retzius, 1910; Popa, 1927; Vasseur, 1947b), were followed by electron microscopic investigation (Tyler, 1949; Afzelius, 1955b, 1957b, Afzelius and Murray, 1957; Inoué *et al.,* 1970a; Anderson, 1968a,b,c). The study on the acrosome in these works is of major interest for a better understanding of the sperm activation and penetration process. The structure of the acrosomal region of the sea urchin sperm is illustrated in Fig. 3.7A, re-drawn from Colwin and Colwin (1967) with slight modifications. The entire scheme is based on the electron microscopic observations of various sea urchin species by several authors (Afzelius, 1955a, 1956b; Afzelius and Murray, 1957; Takashima and Takashima, 1960; Bernstein, 1961, 1962; J. C. Dan *et al.,* 1962, 1964; Franklin, 1965).

A fine electron microscopic investigation by Longo and Anderson (1969) on sperm differentiation in *Arbacia punctulata* and *Strongylocentrotus purpuratus* has provided accurate details of the sperm structure.

It must be noted here that our knowledge of the scheme of acrosomal reaction and the process of sperm penetration is mainly the result of the comparison of these processes with what has been thoroughly observed by Colwin and Colwin (1967) in *Hydroides* and *Saccoglossus*. As shown in Figs. 3.7A and 3.6, the apical part of the sperm head contains a granule made up of some electron-dense material, the so-called acrosomal granule. The acrosomal granule is bounded by a membrane, the acrosomal membrane, on whose internal face are attached small patches of electron-dense material. The tip of the sperm nucleus shows, in correspondence with the acrosomal granule, an indentation in which some fibrous material is lodged. Both the sperm nucleus and acrosomal granules, being structures originally enclosed in the sperm cytoplasm, are, therefore, still externally bounded by the sperm plasma membrane. This bounds an apical vesicle at the tip of the sperm.

7. ACROSOMAL REACTION

Popa (1927) first observed in sea urchins that the acrosomal region of a sperm undergoes some modification before the sperm gets attached to the egg surface. Thanks to the work of J. C. Dan (1952, 1954, 1956, 1960, 1967) on echinoderms, the importance of the acrosomal reaction in fertilization has been recognized.

When in the presence of the so-called egg water, i.e., a jelly coat solution in seawater, the sea urchin spermatozoa undergo a kind of activation called acrosomal reaction. The first sign of it is the fusion of the plasma membrane with the apical part of the acrosomal membrane, with concomitant disappearance of the apical vesicle. The two membranes break and the contents of the acrosomal vesicle is extruded from the sperm (Fig. 3.7B and C). It is believed that these granules contain some lytic agent that helps the sperm make its way through the egg envelope (Monroy and Ruffo, 1947; Krauss, 1950a,b; Messina, 1954; Brookbank, 1958; Hathaway and Metz, 1961; 1967; Isaka *et al.,* 1966; Hathaway and Warren, 1961). This notion is also based on the analogy with the finding in other animal species (for recent reviews, see Monroy, 1965; Metz and Monroy, 1967; Austin, 1968; Dan, 1970). The plasma membrane zone, corresponding to the former acrosomal membrane, now evaginates in the form of a short tubule containing the fibrous material already lodged within the nuclear indentation, consisting of fibrils oriented in a line parallel to the axis of the tubule. The acrosomal reaction is over, and the sperm is ready to contact the egg surface (Fig. 3.7D). A detailed description of this process in sea urchins is given by Dan (1967).

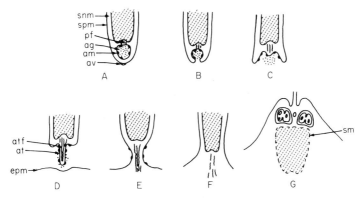

Fig. 3.7. Diagram illustrating the mechanism of sperm penetration (see text for explanation). Abbreviations: snm, sperm nuclear membrane; spm, sperm plasma membrane; pf, precursors of the acrosomal tubule fibrils; ag, acrosomal granule; am, acrosomal membrane; av, apical vesicle; atf, acrosomal tubule fibrils; at, acrosomal tubule; epm, egg plasma membrane; sm, sperm nuclear membrane.

8. Sperm–Egg Fusion

The sperm makes contact with the egg surface by means of the acrosomal tubule, which fuses with the plasma membrane of the egg (Fig.

3.7E); this undergoes the cortical changes already described earlier in this chapter. At this time, the fibrils of the acrosomal tubule seem to form a bridge between the sperm nucleus and the egg cytoplasm. The possibility has been suggested (Colwin and Colwin, 1967) that their contraction might help the sperm nucleus and the middle piece inside the egg cytoplasm (Fig. 3.7F and G). Once inside the egg cytoplasm the sperm nucleus loses its membrane. The egg cytoplasm is raised at the point of sperm entrance in the so-called fertilization cone.

Of particular significance is the interaction between sperm surface and egg cortical layer. This is indeed a unique moment in the life of an animal, when the cytoplasmic barrier is opened and fusion between the genetic patrimonies of two cells takes place. In fact, if viable sperm are introduced into the egg cytoplasm by microinjection, they remain inert inside the egg and no fertilization occurs (Hiramoto, 1962a). Giudice and Millonig (unpublished) have observed that if a suspension of dissociated gastrula cells of *Paracentrotus* is placed in contact with sperm previously treated with egg water, it is frequently noted that sperm have penetrated into the egg cytoplasm. An electron microscopic study shows that the sperm membrane is not lost and fusion between sperm and egg nuclei never takes place. The key of the process that allows nuclear fusion seems to lie in the specific interaction between gamete surfaces.

9. FORMATION AND FUSION OF THE PRONUCLEI

Once penetrated, the sperm nucleus quickly rotates 180° and starts moving toward the center of the egg, with the centriole in the front (Flemming, 1881; Boveri, 1888). Meanwhile the sperm has swollen and the sperm aster has formed (about 8 minutes from the moment of sperm attachment). At the same time the female pronucleus has started moving to meet the sperm pronucleus. This movement was thoroughly studied in the past (for review, see Wilson, 1928; Chambers, 1939). According to Chambers, the female pronucleus is attracted by the male pronucleus, as shown by the pathway of its movement toward the male pronucleus (Fig. 3.8). However, it has been observed that in parthenogenetically activated eggs, where there is no male pronucleus, the female nucleus also moves toward the center of the egg. The male pronucleus would, on the other hand, simply move toward the center of the egg, pushed on by the growing fibers of the sperm aster that press against the internal surface of the egg from the side of sperm penetration. Only one unrepeated experiment by Wilson (1902) stands against this hypothesis. In this experiment the suppression of aster development by treatment with ether had not affected the movement of the sperm. Other authors have, on the contrary, stressed the importance of microtubuli in sperm movement. Microtubular

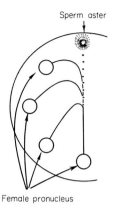

Fig. 3.8. Path of male pronucleus from periphery of egg. Four alternative paths of female pronucleus to center of egg, according to original position in the fertilized egg, are also shown. (From E. L. Chambers, 1939, *J. Exp. Biol.* **16**, 409.)

damage produced by colcemid or high pressure (Zimmerman and Silberman, 1964; Zimmerman and Zimmerman, 1967) impairs the movement of the male pronucleus. Microtubules are thought to be an important part of the sperm aster. This would consist of the centrioles and the region of the centrosphere, containing vesicles and microtubules and radially surrounded by a series of microtubules and lamellae (Longo and Anderson, 1968; Harris, 1965). Observations by Brachet (1910) and Allen (1954) of the movement of sperm pronuclei in polyspermic eggs or in eggs fertilized in a capillary tube suggest that the pronucleus movement is oriented and caused by the astral growth.

While moving toward the egg pronucleus, the sperm nucleus undergoes the changes that transform it into a "pronucleus." These, together with the process of zygote formation—i.e., fusion of the two pronuclei—have recently been the object of an accurate electron microscopic investigation by Longo and Anderson (1968, 1970a,c). The events that operate the transformation of the sperm nucleus into male pronucleus are the following: degeneration of the nuclear membrane through a process of vesiculation (followed by progressive dispersion of the chromatin) (Fig. 3.9). Meanwhile, a new nuclear envelope is formed by confluence of a series of smooth-surfaced cytoplasmic vesicles. The male pronucleus after going through a heart-shaped stage attains a spherical form (Fig. 3.10). These processes are accompanied by formation of the sperm aster and migration of the male pronucleus toward the female one, led by the sperm aster and accompanied by the sperm mitochondrion and flagellum. The envelope surface of the female pronucleus, facing the approaching male pronucleus, becomes flattened and highly convoluted as the latter comes close. At this time, the male pronucleus surface flattens at the side facing

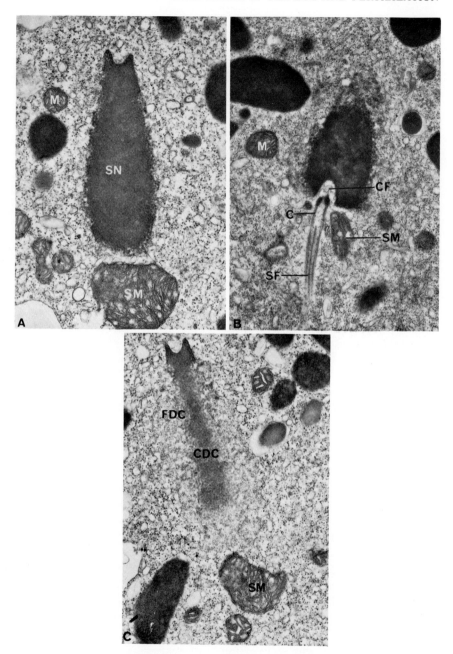

Fig. 3.9. The process of degeneration of the sperm nuclear membrane and of sperm chromatin dispersion at fertilization. (A) Rotated spermatozoon near the completion of nuclear envelope degeneration and the beginning of chromatin dispersion. Vesicles are

the female one, but without convolution. The "centriolar" fossa, with the proximal centriole, the mitochondria, and the flagellum, move aside, and the membranes of the two pronuclei make contact and fuse at a narrow zone. A plasmatic bridge between the two pronuclei is thus established, narrow at first, then becoming enlarged. The two chromatins intermix. For a short while, the male chromatin is still visible inside the zygote; then it disappears. The fusion is complete (Fig. 3.11). All the mechanisms that underlie this fascinating process are still unclear, and nothing but the ultrastructural details are available at present.

10. REFERTILIZATION

The earliest observation, widely confirmed later, that the sea urchin egg cannot be fertilized twice, are attributed to Loeb (1916). Treatment of fertilized eggs of *Paracentrotus lividus* or *Echinus microtuberculatus* at low temperatures (0°C) (Bury, 1913), however, allows refertilization. A subsequent discovery records that mechanical removal of the fertilization membrane, followed by treatment with calcium- and magnesium-free sea-water, allows refertilization of the egg of *Strongylocentrotus pulcherrimus* (Sugiyama, 1951) up to the two blastomere stage or later. An irregular cleavage is thereafter produced. Parthenogenetically activated eggs can also be refertilized by the method of Sugiyama (Ishida and Nakano, 1950; Nakano, 1954). For the purpose of refertilization the fertilization membrane can also be removed by trypsin treatment (Hagström and Hagström, 1954a,b). According to Tyler *et al.* (1956a), refertilization is possible without any particular treatment of the egg, provided it is performed within 30 minutes after the first fertilization, i.e., before the hyaline layer has formed.

11. BLOCK TO POLYSPERMY

Even if under abnormal conditions, which generally bring about a damage of the egg envelopes, it is possible to refertilize the sea urchin eggs, normally only one sperm succeeds in penetrating the egg. What actually blocks the entrance to further sperm?

---

present along the surface of the sperm nucleus (× 13,000). (B) A further stage in the dispersal of the sperm chromatin. The nuclear envelope at the centriolar fossa is intact (× 13,600). (C) Advanced stage in the dispersion of the sperm chromatin. Vesicles are evident along the junction of finely dispersed chromatin (FDC) and the ooplasm. The nuclear envelope surrounding the anterior region of the sperm nucleus (asterisk) is intact. The more medial portion of the sperm nucleus is composed of coarse aggregates of chromatin (CDC) (× 13,000). Abbreviations: SN, sperm nucleus; SM, sperm mitochondrion; M, egg mitochondrion; SF, sperm flagellum; CF, centriolar fossa; C, centriole. (From Longo and Anderson, 1968.)

Rothschild and Swann (1949, 1950, 1951a,b, 1952) were the first to assert that two changes occur in the sea urchin surface at fertilization: a quick one (about 2 seconds), which greatly reduces the ability to allow penetration of further sperm; and a slow one (about 1 minute), which completely abolishes it. Only this second one has been confirmed by Ginsburg (1963) in *Strongylocentrotus dröbachiensis*.

Monroy (1965) made an attempt to correlate these two steps in the establishment of the block to polyspermy with physiological changes of the egg surface at fertilization. The quick change corresponds to the color change of the egg observed with dark ground illumination (Runnström, 1928c) and to the disappearance of birefringence (Monroy, 1947). The slow change corresponds to the breakdown of the cortical granules, membrane elevation, transient change in the membrane potential (Tyler *et al.*, 1956b; Hiramoto, 1959), and increase in the rate of K^+ exchange (Tyler and Monroy, 1959), described in Chapter 4.

Actually, factors that are able to inhibit the breakdown of cortical granules and membrane elevation, such as uncouplers of oxidative phosphorylation (R. Okazaki, 1956) and high hydrostatic pressure (Whiteley and Chambers, 1960), also cause polyspermy.

The role in protecting the egg from polyspermy is attributed to the SH groups by Runnström (Runnström and Kriszat, 1953; Kriszat and Runnström, 1952; Runnström, 1957; Runnström *et al.*, 1959; Runnström and Manelli, 1964). No details are available on the exact mechanism through which the SH groups act in this respect, except for what has been discussed on the hardening of the fertilization membrane.

12. PARTHENOGENETIC ACTIVATION

Hertwig (1895, 1896) was the first to show that artificial activation of eggs of *Paracentrotus lividus* can be induced by chloroform. Soon after, Morgan (1899) obtained parthenogenetic plutei by treating *Arbacia* eggs with NaCl, KCl, or $MgCl_2$ in seawater.

Since the earliest investigations it has been understood that there is not one specific substance that may mimic the natural effect of sperm, but rather that the unfertilized egg can be considered an unstable system which a variety of stimuli may throw into conditions of activation.

A list of physical and chemical stimuli that are able to cause parthenogenetic activation of the sea urchin sperm is reported by Harvey (1956a). Among the physical stimuli: simple puncturing of the egg, heating up to around 32°C or cooling down to 0°–10°C, irradiation, electric stimulation; among the chemical stimuli: a variety of inorganic salts, weak acids, alkalis, and amines, fat solvents, ethers, narcotics, detergents, glycosides, alkaloids, proteins, enzymes, organ extracts, decrease in oxygen tension,

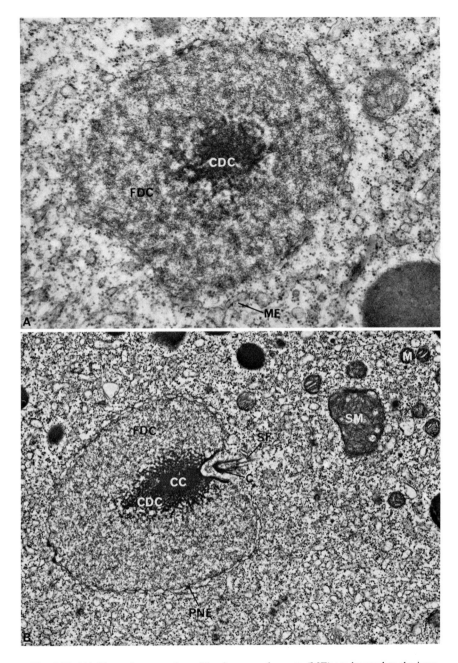

Fig. 3.10. (A) The male pronucleus. Membranous elements (ME) are located to the junction of the finely dispersed chromatin (FDC) and ooplasm; CDC, coarse aggregates of sperm chromatin (× 20,000). (B) Heart-shaped male pronucleus delimited by a pronuclear envelope (PNE) perforated by pores. FDC, finely dispersed chromatin; CDC, coarsely dispersed chromatin; CC, condensed chromatin; SM, sperm mitochondrion; C, centriole; SF, sperm flagellum; M, mitochondria of the egg (× 15,000).

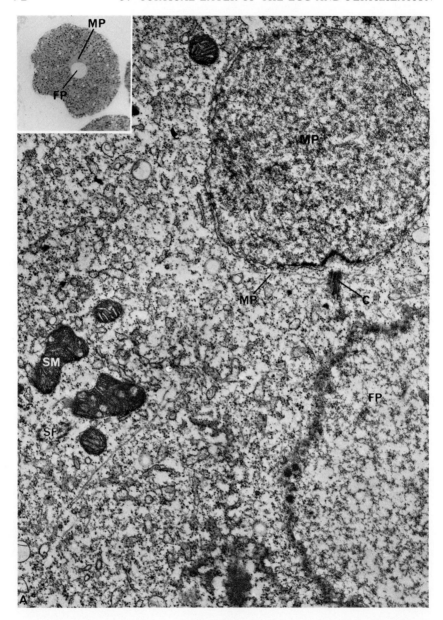

Fig. 3.11. Five different stages of fusion of the pronuclei. MP, male pronucleus; FP, female pronucleus. (A) Male and female pronuclei prior to their fusion. The centriole (C) and associated microtubules (MT) are still located between the pronuclei. The sperm mitochondrion (SM) and a portion of the sperm flagellum (SF) are to one side of the pronuclei (× 15,000; inset, × 350). (B) Initial stage of fusion of the pronuclei (× 13,000). Inset: The outer laminae have fused and the inner laminae are parallel to each other

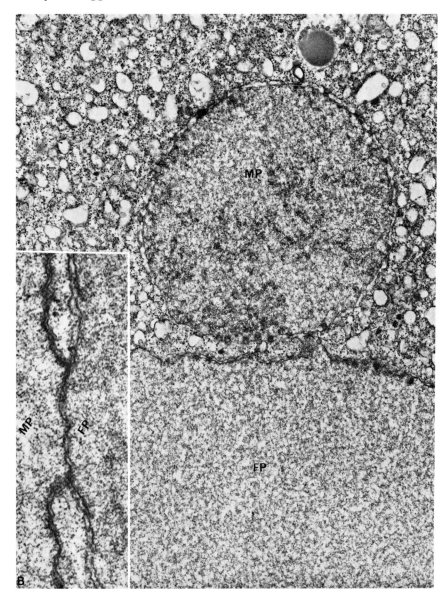

(× 21,000). (C) Completion of coalescence of the inner and outer laminae of the male and female pronuclear envelope. An internuclear bridge connects the two pronuclei (× 18,000). (D) Portion of the zygote nucleus containing a protuberance that was formerly the male pronucleus. The perforated zygote nuclear envelope is continuous (× 14,000). (F) Zygote nucleus containing a dense complement of paternal chromatin (PC) (× 7,500). (From Longo and Anderson, 1968.) (See Figs. 3.11C, 3.11D and 3.11E following.)

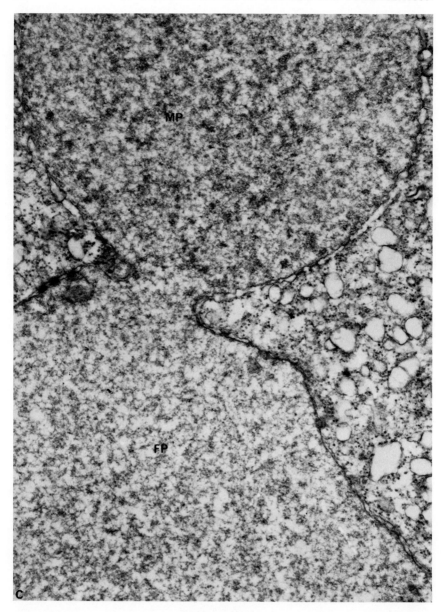

Fig. 3.11C

hypotonic seawater, and still many other stimuli. To complete the picture, suffice it to say that after prolonged stay in seawater, sea urchin eggs may show a spontaneous tendency to parthenogenetic activation. Most of the above methods, however, are not always satisfactory when an experi-

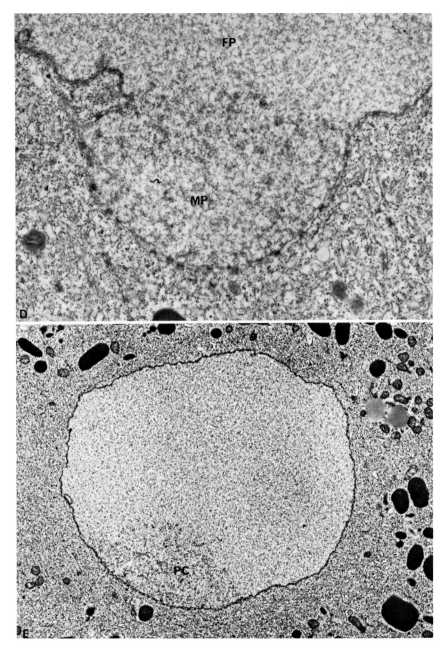

Figs. 3.11D and E

mental parthenogenetic activation is needed. Two methods are currently employed to this end: (1) Treatment for 20 minutes in seawater rendered hypertonic either by boiling to half its volume or by adding 30 gm of NaCl per liter (Hunter, 1901, 1903; Greeley, 1903; McClendon, 1909; Glaser, 1913; Just, 1928b; Harvey, 1936, 1940c); (2) treatment with $4 \times 10^{-3} N$ butyric acid in seawater for 2–4 minutes, followed by a treatment of 10–15 minutes in normal seawater, and 17.5–22.5 minutes in hypertonic seawater (Loeb, 1913, 1916). A slight modification of this method has been suggested by Heilbrunn (1915): 0.5-minute treatment with 5.6 $\times 10^{-3} N$ butyric, directly followed by exposure to hypertonic seawater. Treatment with butyric acid alone causes egg activation followed by a series of unsuccessful attempts of the egg to cleave, resulting in an incomplete blastomerization of the cytoplasm.

We found it important to neutralize carefully the butyric acid after the 2-minute treatment.

Parthenogenetic plutei have been raised experimentally through metamorphosis (Shearer and Lloyd, 1913) and two young adults of *Paracentrotus lividus* have been obtained (Delage, 1909). One of these reached sexual maturity; it was a male, in agreement with the views of other authors who have reported (see Chapter 5) that the male is digametic in sea urchins (Tennent, 1911, 1912a,b,c; Baltzer, 1913). On the other hand, it has been observed that, at least up to early cleavage, the number of somatic chromosomes of parthenogenetic embryos is haploid (Harvey, 1940c; Wilson, 1901; Hindle, 1910).

Chapter 4

Some Other Physiological Changes That Occur at Fertilization

We have already described the moment of fertilization as a time when dramatic changes occur which profoundly modify the egg at the morphological as well as the molecular level.

In Chapter 3 we described the process of modification of the egg surface, with the dramatic phenomenon of elevation of the fertilization membrane. We shall discuss the activation of respiration, nucleic acid and protein synthesis, and several more enzymatic activities, in the relevant chapters.

Other physiological changes take place at fertilization. Although probably related to the ones already mentioned, these will, for the sake of clarity, be described separately in this chapter.

A. Changes in Permeability

It had already been observed by Lillie (1909) and confirmed by Hobson (1932) that permeability of eggs to water increases at fertilization. Permeability to ethylene glycol had also been found to increase at fertilization (Stewart and Jacobs, 1932). Many other authors have confirmed these observations and extended them to other fluids. Ishikawa (1954) studied in detail the changes in the egg's permeability to water, and found that it increases until about 3 minutes after fertilization. A sudden drop follows to the level of the unfertilized egg; then in about 15 minutes a second rise occurs. Most of the earlier works on permeability were not performed with the aid of labeled tracers, several times the permeability measure being cytolysis and plasmolysis, which is not a very direct and unequivocal criterion. For a list of earlier papers, we refer the reader to

Harvey's review (1956a) and limit ourselves to some of the most significant studies performed more recently.

1. PERMEABILITY TO AMINO ACIDS AND NUCLEOSIDES

That permeability of the sea urchin egg to amino acids and nucleosides increases after fertilization has been observed by many authors (Hultin, 1953c; Giudice *et al.,* 1962; Nemer, 1962a) but it was Piatigorsky and Whiteley (1965) and Mitchison and Cummins (1966) who addressed their attention more directly to the problem of changes in permeability to these metabolites at fertilization and to the mechanism underlying the regulation of permeability. It should be stressed that the egg as well as the developing embryo obviously possesses mechanisms apt to selectively regulate at least the ionic influx. Indeed, they live in a medium of a very high Na^+ and a very low K^+ concentration while maintaining a fairly high intracellular content of K^+ and a very low content of Na^+.

Piatigorsky and Whiteley have confirmed that an increase in permeability to [^{14}C]uridine follows fertilization. The existence of an active mechanism for the uridine uptake has been proved by the following facts:

1. After fertilization, the exogenous labeled uridine is concentrated until complete depletion in the external medium.

2. Washing the eggs does not remove the isotope taken up.

3. Metabolic inhibition obtained through 2,4-dinitrophenol, or simply through lowering the temperature to $-3°C$ strongly inhibits uridine uptake. The authors tentatively propose that the uptake mechanism might take place through a phosphorylation of the nucleoside at the cell surface, since most of the uridine taken up is found in phosphorylated form primarily as triphosphate. Without denying validity to this hypothesis, we should observe that because the main use of uridine is to form RNA, the egg needs to phosphorylate it to UTP. The fact of finding it phosphorylated might be independent of the uptake mechanism.

The penetration kinetics of [^{14}C]valine and [^{3}H]cytidine have been carefully studied by Mitchison and Cummins (1966). For both these metabolites the uptake rate rises sharply after fertilization (Figs. 4.1 and 4.2) and then, at least for valine, remains constant up to pluteus (Fig. 4.3). Here again it is suggested that the penetration is due to a specific transport mechanism and not to a simple diffusion, because of the following facts:

1. Metabolic inhibitors such as 2,4-dinitrophenol and sodium azide strongly inhibit the uptake.

2. Valine and cytidine are concentrated from the external medium and variations of their external initial concentration affect the rate of uptake according to Michaelis–Menten kinetics.

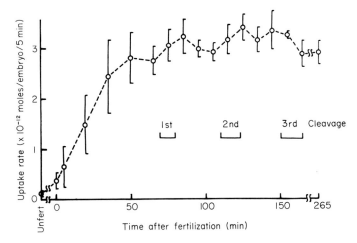

Fig. 4.1. Rate of total uptake of valine during the first 4.5 hours after fertilization. Aliquots of embryos taken at times indicated, treated with [^{14}C]valine (16.7 μg/ml) for 5 minutes, filtered off, washed, and counted. Means and standard errors from four experiments. The four experiments were normalized by equalizing the sum of all values beyond 65 minutes for each experiment. (From Mitchison and Cummins, 1966.)

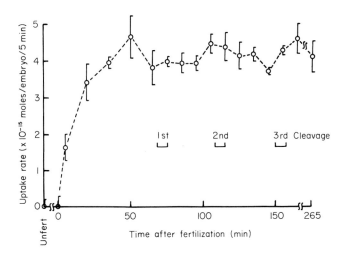

Fig. 4.2. Rate of total uptake of cytidine during the first 4.5 hours after fertilization. Aliquots of embryos taken at times indicated, treated with [^{3}H]cytidine (0.1 μg/ml) for 5 minutes, filtered off, washed, and counted. Means and standard errors from five experiments. The five experiments were normalized by equalizing the sum of all values beyond 65 minutes for each experiment. (From Mitchison and Cummins, 1966.)

3. The uptake is inhibited by competitors, i.e., by molecules that sterically resemble the used metabolite. This observation was confirmed by Tyler *et al.* (1966), who found that amino acids belonging to the same group (i.e., acidic, alkaline, and neutral) compete among themselves for uptake. Piatigorsky and Tyler (1968) observed that pretreatment of the egg with a mixture of all of the amino acids of a single group (i.e., acidic, basic, or neutral) but one increases incorporation of the amino acid omitted when this is administered later on. The interpretation is that the amino acid mixture displaces the missing amino acid from the pool. The subsequent administration of that amino acid, radioactively labeled, results in a lower dilution of the latter in the internal pool and, consequently, in a higher degree of incorporation of the isotope. Experiments performed by preloading the egg with [^{14}C]valine and subsequent treatment with cold neutral amino acids result in an efflux of [^{14}C]valine from the egg, in agreement with the hypothesis. Analogous experiments with other amino acids do not, however, provide an unequivocal answer.

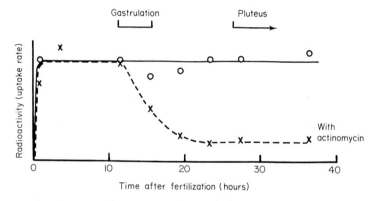

Fig. 4.3. Rate of total uptake of valine during the first 36 hours after fertilization. Same procedure as in Fig. 4.1. The continuous line is for embryos in seawater. The dashed line is for embryos in actinomycin D (25 μg/ml) in seawater 30 minutes before fertilization. In both cases, bactericidal agents were added (penicillin, 23 μg/ml; streptomycin sulfate, 33 μg/ml; sulfadiazine, saturated). (From J. M. Mitchison and J. E. Cummins, 1966, *J. Cell Sci.* **1**, 35.)

One interesting point raised by Mitchison and Cummins (1966) is that the increase in exposed cell surface that takes place during cleavage does not affect the uptake rate. This implies that the permeability increase that follows fertilization is not due to the higher availability of cellular surface. Actually, if specific carriers at cell surface are involved in the mechanism of transport, as suggested above, their number must remain constant throughout development, since no further increase in the uptake rate takes place following the initial one. Because of the increase in cell surface, the number of carriers per unit surface must, therefore, be in decrease. The burst of uptake does not seem to result from the sudden synthesis of carriers, at least of proteic nature, because it is not inhibited by addition of puromycin. The authors suggest that these carriers are synthesized during oogenesis, when they serve the purpose of taking up precursors from the surroundings. The carriers are inactivated when the egg is mature and no longer synthesized, because they would be useless in the egg developing in seawater. This argument, however, does not take into consideration the activation of permability coupled with fertilization.

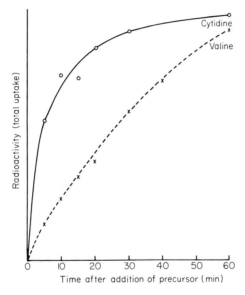

Fig. 4.4. Continuous labeling with valine and cytidine. Precursors ([^{14}C]valine, 16.7 μg/ml; [^{3}H]cytidine; 0.1 μg/ml) added to eggs 45 minutes after fertilization. Aliquots taken at times indicated, filtered off, washed, and counted. Continuous line for cytidine; dashed line for valine. (From J. M. Mitchison and J. E. Cummins, 1966, *J. Cell Sci.* **1**, 35.)

The kinetics of cytidine uptake shows how a plateau is reached before depletion of the external medium, provided the initial external concentration of the precursors is adequately high (Fig. 4.4). It seems that the level reached by the precursor in the internal pool may influence the uptake rate. In our opinion, this point deserves special attention. It is of practical importance in the evaluation of data on the rate of macromolecular synthesis obtained by external supply of labeled precursor. In fact, when we see that a precursor is both taken up at a very poor rate and scarcely incorporated into macromolecules, we can believe, if adequate information on the internal pool is not available, that the precursor is scarcely incorporated only because little of it penetrates into the egg, which, on the other hand, actively synthesizes the considered macromolecule. We have to take into account the possibility that the low uptake is a consequence of the low macromolecular synthesis rate, which causes an accumulation of the internal precursor pool. The latter, in view of what is discussed above, might depress the rate of uptake. Berg (1965, 1968c) has suggested that the internal pool is not an obligatory intermediate for the incorporation of exogenous amino acids into proteins. In fact, at high concentrations of exogenous amino acids, the pool is by-passed and the external precursors are directly incorporated into proteins. It is only at low exogenous amino acid concentrations that precursors are partially derived from the pool.

This theory has not been confirmed by Fry and Gross (1970a,b) in embryos of *Arbacia punctulata* and *Strongylocentrotus purpuratus*. These authors performed very accurate direct measurements of the pool size for various amino acids during early development. They concluded that the internal pool can be expanded severalfold by the addition of exogenous amino acids. The incorporation of exogenous [^{14}C]leucine is reduced according to the prediction made, assuming that all of it passes through the internal pool (and not according to Berg's model), by the previous or contemporary expansion of the pool with [^{12}C]leucine.

More recently, Berg (1970; Berg and Mertes, 1970) reviewed his own data and, on the basis of new experiments, reached the same conclusion as Fry and Gross. Berg's latest experiment is essentially as follows: Early gastrulae of *Lytechinus anamsesus* are treated with [^{14}C]valine; 10 minutes later, an excess of [^{12}C]valine is added, which proves to dilute the incorporation of ^{14}C. If this were due to preferential utilization of the external valine, radioactivity incorporation should now increase again following removal of the [^{12}C]valine from the medium. If the [^{12}C]valine were, on the other hand, to act by entering the embryos and expanding their pool, no relief from the dilution effect should be observed after removal of the external [^{12}C]valine. The latter case has been proved to be the correct one. Our personal experience of *Paracentrotus lividus* embryos agrees with the latter hypothesis.

2. PERMEABILITY TO SOME IONS

a. Permeability to PO_4^{3-}

The accumulation of phosphate in sea urchin embryos has been the object of many studies in the past. It is, however, only since 1943 (Brooks, 1943) that the use of ^{32}P has permitted a more accurate analysis of the permeability of embryos to phosphate. It had soon been discovered that the unfertilized egg is almost impermeable to phosphate, while a sharp increase in permeability immediately follows fertilization (Abelson, 1947; Brooks and Chambers, 1948, 1954; Whiteley, 1949; E. L. Chambers and White, 1954). Lindberg (1948, 1950) proposed that the unfertilized egg, although not incorporating ^{32}P from the external medium, is able to catalyze at its surface an incorporation of ^{32}P into ATP. After fertilization, the ATP, labeled at the surface, would be able to penetrate the egg. It has been confirmed by many authors that the ^{32}P incorporated by the fertilized eggs and developing embryos is found largely as acid-soluble phosphate compounds (Abelson, 1947; Chambers *et al.,* 1948; Chambers and White, 1949, 1954; Bolst and Whiteley, 1957; Giudice, 1958; Sconzo *et al.,* 1970a).

The question has also been asked whether the ^{32}P penetration represents a mere diffusion phenomenon or an active uptake mechanism. The latter hypothesis seems the correct one, since the ^{32}P uptake is inhibited by lowering the temperature (Abelson, 1947; Villee and Villee, 1952; Litchfield and Whiteley, 1959), and by metabolic inhibitors such as 4,5-dinitro-*o*-cresol (Abelson, 1947) or cyanide (Brooks and Chambers, 1948). E. L. Chambers and Mende (1953a) have observed that since the internal concentration of the free inorganic orthophosphate in the fertilized egg of *Strongylocentrotus dröbachiensis* is very low, the influx, at least in this case, might still be due to a simple diffusion gradient. The permability activation at fertilization might be due to an observed decrease of the internal inorganic phosphate (Chambers and White, 1949). The entire question of ^{32}P accumulation in the fertilized egg has been carefully examined by Litchfield and Whiteley (1959) and by Whiteley and Chambers (1960) by means of continuous recording of ^{32}P accumulation by eggs kept in a perfusion chamber mounted over a Geiger–Müller counter. The conclusions of such a study are that the uptake rate of ^{32}P is close to zero in the unfertilized egg, and increases sharply 7–30 minutes after fertilization or parthenogenetic activation (even in the absence of cleavage) to reach a maximum at 22–60 minutes after fertilization. 10^{-4} *M* 2,4-dinitrophenol inhibits this increase provided it is administered to the eggs within the lag period, i.e., the first 7–30 minutes following fertilization. 10^{-4} *M* arsenate strongly inhibits the ^{32}P uptake whenever administered after fertilization. The latter result is of interest since no visible effect on development is observed, thus leaving open the possibility that arsenate might produce a rather specific effect on a phosphate transport mechanism. These authors have also demonstrated that ATP does not penetrate the cleaving eggs, at least not to a sensible level, nor is it hydrolyzed by an ATPase at their surfaces. This notion is often forgotten in attempts at studying the effect of ATP on various functions. More recent studies by the same authors (E. L. Chambers and Whiteley,

1966; Whiteley and Chambers, 1966) confirm the earlier suggestion that at fertilization a phosphate transport system is synthesized by means of energy-requiring processes. The phosphate transport itself, on the other hand, does not depend directly on metabolic energy, but involves a surface-located carrier. In the latter experiments, the rate of phosphate transport has been carefully measured under several conditions. It has been found that its value is of 2×10^{-9} μ/egg/minute at 15°C at an external concentration of 2 μM, for the fertilized eggs of *Strongylocentrotus purpuratus*. The optimum pH for transport is 8.8–8.9, thus suggesting that phosphate enters the eggs as HPO_4^{2-} ion.

Again it is found that metabolic inhibitors, such as cyanide, azide, or anaerobiosis, block the rise in phosphate uptake when administered during the lag phase. The carrier system seems to be surface located and probably of a proteic nature, since it is inhibited by *p*-chloromercuribenzoate, under conditions where cleavage is permitted, thus suggesting that this reagent does not penetrate the cell. The carrier shows a good specificity toward the phosphate ions, since their transport can be competed by the similar arsenate ions only at concentrations higher than the latter ones. Phosphate is released by the carrier only inside the cell, since the ^{32}P taken up cannot be washed out. Ca^{2+} or Mg^{2+} ions are required for phosphate transport and the presence of Na^+ is essential, thus suggesting the formation of a complex phosphate–Na carrier.

b. Permeability to K^+

Changes in permeability to K^+ ions following fertilization have been thoroughly studied, because it has been thought that the activation process of the unfertilized egg may bear some similarity to that of nerve stimulation. Attempts were made to measure the electrical properties of the egg membrane and their possible changes at fertilization. The use of microelectrodes in sea urchin eggs has proved particularly difficult because of the remarkable extensibility of the egg cortex, which forms a sleeve around the electrode when one tries to force it into the egg (Tyler and Monroy, 1955). This difficulty has, however, been overcome and it can be shown that an electrical potential difference exists across the egg surface; it is positive outside and negative inside. Moreover, this difference undergoes a temporary decrease upon fertilization (Tyler *et al.,* 1956b) (Fig. 4.5). This change in the electrical potential of the echinoderm egg upon fertilization has been confirmed by Hiramoto (1959).

Steinhardt *et al.* (1971) have devised a new method to hold the eggs in place while inserting the electrode: It consists of covering the bottom of a plastic petri dish with a solution of 1% protamine sulfate. The electronegatively charged surface of the egg is attracted by such a positively charged surface.

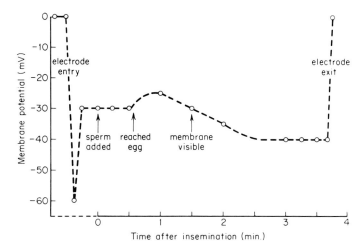

Fig. 4.5. Membrane potential of *Asterias* egg and its changes on fertilization. Upon successful insertion of the electrode a transient potential difference of 60 mV (inside negative) is recorded; then the membrane potential is stabilized at about −30 mV. Within 30 seconds after addition of sperm, the potential decreased by about 5 mV. Subsequently the potential increased again and remained steady at −40 mV. (From Tyler *et al.*, 1956b.)

By this method Steinhardt *et al.* were able to record several measurements of membrane potential action during fertilization or parthenogenetic activation of eggs of *Lytechinus pictus* or *Dendraster excentricus*. Three phases were described in *Lytechinus*: First, a rise of the membrane potential from − 8 mV (inside) to + 10 mV, within 5 seconds after the addition of sperm, followed by a fall to about −12 within 150 seconds. Second, a pause of about 3–4 minutes. Third, a further depolarization to values of about −60 mV 15–25 minutes after fertilization.

Essentially similar results were obtained with *Dendraster* eggs. This analogy with the process of nerve stimulation has prompted a search for a temporary increased efflux of K^+ from the egg. Earlier attempts to measure the K^+ content of seawater after fertilization by methods not involving the use of radioactive tracers had produced conflicting results: Shapiro and Dawson (1941) had found no appreciable change; Malm and Wachmeister (1950) a slight decrease, and Monroy-Oddo and Esposito (1951) an increase. It was, therefore, appropriate to reinvestigate the question by the use of ^{42}K (Tyler and Monroy, 1956, 1959; Tyler, 1958). These authors preloaded the eggs with ^{42}K and studied its release into seawater from unfertilized and fertilized control eggs. The results showed unequivocally that within the first minute after fertilization a great increase in the release rate of ^{42}K takes place. Experiments in which the influx of ^{42}K into unfertilized or fertilized eggs have been measured have shown that the influx of ^{42}K increases following fertilization. The data point to the conclusion that a large fraction of the K^+ of the egg becomes readily exchangeable only at fertilization. Thus the earlier observation of R. Chambers and Chambers (1949) is confirmed and extended to the first few minutes following fertilization of a continuous increase in the ^{42}K content of eggs exposed to the isotope following fertilization, which contrasts with the very low uptake of the unfertilized eggs exposed for the same period, i.e., from 30 to 1500 minutes.

The conclusions of E. L. Chambers (1949) on the increased efflux of ^{42}K from eggs following fertilization are also confirmed by the above experiments.

The balance between the internal and external K^+ concentration remains however unchanged for a few minutes according to measurements performed by Steinhardt et al. (1971) by means of a K^+ ion selective electrode. These authors conclude that only the final depolarization of -60 mV is attributable to the development of a K^+ conductance.

The first action potential at fertilization seems to depend upon a Na^+ influx.

In an effort to suggest causal relationship between metabolic activation and membrane changes at fertilization, Steinhardt et al. (1971) recall that the timing of these events can be ordered in the following way:

1. Development of the action potential, within 3 seconds after fertilization.
2. Increase of respiration, at 10–20 seconds (Nakazawa et al., 1970).
3. Cortical reaction, at 40–60 seconds (Paul and Epel, 1971).
4. Activation of protein synthesis.

c. Permeability to Na^+

The first evidence that the ^{24}Na uptake from unfertilized eggs is very low, while it increases dramatically following fertilization, is credited to E. L. Chambers and Chambers (1949).

From measurements of the K^+ and Na^+ content of the egg before and after fertilization and of the rate of ^{24}Na and ^{42}K influx and efflux, Chambers concluded that there is a transient drop in the K^+ content within 10 minutes after fertilization, followed by a slow increase, while reciprocal changes are shown by Na^+. The author suggests that the increased permeability to these ions at fertilization causes a diffusion in the direction of their electrochemical gradients. (The K^+ concentration in the eggs is 0.2 mole/liter and the Na^+ concentration is 0.02 mole/liter, i.e., respectively higher and lower than in seawater.) The reversal of this ion movement, which is observed after the first few minutes, might be due to activation of a Na–K pump. Hori (1965) observed an increase of the Na and K ions following fertilization of *Hemicentrotus pulcherrimus* eggs, of 135 and 72%, respectively. In Chambers' opinion (personal communication), such an increase would bring the concentration of these ions to 152 μmoles of K + Na/ml eggs, a value which is too high not to cause an osmotic swelling of the egg.

d. Permeability to Ca^{2+} and Mg^{2+}

A dramatic increase of the influx–efflux of ^{45}Ca has been reported (Azarnia and Chambers, 1969; E. L. Chambers *et al.*, 1970).

Azarnia and Chambers (1970) have also found that the Ca^{2+} concentration of the unfertilized egg is 2.98 ± 0.04 mmole/liter. Fertilization results in a transient increase (15% after 3 min), followed by a reversal to the normal values. The Mg^{2+} concentration (21.9 ± 0.3 mmole/liter) seems to show only a slow late decrease following fertilization to values 25% lower than those of the unfertilized eggs.

B. Production of Acid at Fertilization

In 1929, Ashbel reported that upon fertilization of *Arbacia lixula* eggs, a CO_2 evolution was observed by manometric techniques. It was, however, Runnström (1930a, 1933) who undertook a careful study of the phenomenon in eggs of *Paracentrotus lividus*. This author reported that the liberation of CO_2 was due to the production of some acid by the eggs following fertilization, which in turn caused the liberation of CO_2 from the bicarbonate contained in the surrounding seawater, which normally acts as a buffer, maintaining the pH at around 8.0. These data have been confirmed by many authors (Borei, 1933; Örström, 1935; Laser and Rothchild, 1939; Allen *et al.*, 1958). Since then, many experiments have been carried out aimed at understanding the nature of the acid produced at fertilization (Monné and Härde, 1951; Runnström and Immers, 1956; Immers, 1961a,b; Mehl and Swann, 1961; Aketa, 1961a,b, 1962, 1963; Gregg and Metz, 1967). According to Ishihara (1968a,b), the release of an acid polysaccharide is responsible for the production of 60% of the fertilization acid, which at fertilization would be extruded by the cortical granules into the perivitelline space where it would be partially released into the seawater. The results of Ishihara, who has been able to recover this glycoprotein from seawater, are at variance with those by Aketa (1963), who has reported that it is only the sulfate, deriving from the mucopolysaccharide released from the cortical granules, that is extruded from the eggs. Ishihara has analyzed the composition of such a polysaccharide in eggs of *Hemicentrotus pulcherrimus* and of *Arbacia punctulata*. In both species it has been found to contain fucose, mannose, glucose, galactose, hexosamine sulfate, some cations, and 16 or 17 amino acids, respectively, in the proportions indicated in Table 4.1.

TABLE 4.1

CHEMICAL COMPOSITIONS OF JELLY AND FERTILIZATION PRODUCT[a,b]

Constituent	Jelly	TFP[e]	FP
Amino acid	14.3	78.6	44.7
Hexose	37.8	9.7	10.1
Fucose	36.5	3.4	3.2
Mannose	+[c]	1.5	+
Glucose	0	1.6	+
Galactose	1.3	3.2	+
Hexosamine	2.6	9.2	10.0
SO_4^{2-}	19.0	5.0	6.4
Inorganic cations	1.7	1.3	−[d]
Ca^{2+}	0.6	0.7	−
Na^+	0.8	0.4	−
K^+	0.3	0.2	−
Total	75.4	103.8	71.2

[a] From Ishihara (1968a).
[b] In percentages of total dry weight.
[c] +, detected by paper chromatography but not estimated quantitatively.
[d] −, not determined.
[e] FP = Fertilization product; TFP = FP from eggs deprived of their vitelline membrane by treatment with trypsin.

According to Ishihara, these glycoproteins differ from those of the respective jelly coats, although Gregg and Metz (1966) and Metz (1967) have found some immunological similarities between the two. The notion that this glycoproteins might be contained in the cortical granules derives mainly from experiments by Aketa (1961a,b, 1962, 1963) where acid production has been observed following activation by means of reagents such as sodium choleinate. Monogen, or Lipon, which are known to cause breakdown of the cortical granules without propagation of the fertilization wave (Sugiyama, 1953). Acid production is also observed following treatment with urea which, according to Motomura (1941a), causes disappearance of the cortical granules without membrane elevation. Acid production also takes place from dejellied eggs. Furthermore, several metabolic inhibitors, such as iodoacetoamide, sodium arsenate, sodium malonate, sodium azide, phloridzin, eserine, diisopropylfluorophosphate, do not inhibit acid production. These results speak against a function in acid production of the elevation of the fertilization membrane, propagation of the fertilization wave, dissolution of the jelly coat, and many metabolic processes which are activated at fertilization. On the other hand, inhibition of the cortical granule breakdown by pretreatment of the eggs with butyric acid (Motomura, 1934) or with urethane (Sugiyama, 1956), although permitting sperm penetration, markedly inhibits acid production. Finally it should be recalled that the cortical granules contain mucopolysaccharides (Monné and Härde, 1951; Aketa, 1962). Allen *et al.* (1958) have cast some doubt on the correlation between the cortical granule breakdown and acid production since the latter phenomenon proceeds slower than the former one. Even if the causal relationship between the two phenomena still awaits definitive proof, there is, however, much more evidence in its favor than against it. The significance of the extrusion of this acid mucopolysaccharide at fertilization is still a matter of speculation. Ishihara (1968b) stresses the fact suggested by Immers (1958) and Runnström (1966b) that acid polysaccharides are bound to proteins to inhibit their biological activity before fertilization. As an example of this concept, the findings of Bäckström (1966a) indicate that a complex of basic proteins with an acid polysaccharide is dissolved at fertilization. It has been suggested that the release of fertilization acid plays a role in the prevention of polyspermy (Rothschild, 1956). It has already been mentioned how treatments that inhibit acid production also lead to polyspermy.

Among the other explanations proposed in the past for acid production is the suggestion by Mehl and Swann (1961) of an increased ionization of the egg surface proteins, and the release of protons by DPNH at fertilization (Fujii and Ohnishi, 1962). The lack of effect of the mentioned metabolic inhibitors does not speak in favor of this hypothesis. The same would apply to an earlier suggestion by Aketa (1957) of a role played by the accumulation of lactic acid. This suggestion, however, has now been withdrawn by the same author on the basis of the data by Rothschild (1958), who was unable to detect any lactic acid accumulation in eggs of *Echinus esculentus,* where there is acid production at fertilization.

Chapter 5

The Mechanism of Cleavage

We shall describe this event in some detail since cleavage of the sea urchin egg has long been regarded as a model for a general study of the process of cell division for the following reasons: First, the transparency of the egg, which allows observation in the living cell of the processes whereby cell division is brought about; second, the very good synchrony of at least the first of the sea urchin egg cleavages, which permits study of the different phases of mitosis on a bulk amount of material; and third, the high frequency at which cell divisions take place following fertilization.

We have described how the sperm penetrates the egg; soon after fusion of the pronuclei, the first spindle starts to form for the first cell division. This appears to divide the egg cytoplasm along a straight line. This is the "streak stage," which occurs about 30 minutes after sperm attachment. The nuclear membrane breaks down immediately thereafter and prophase starts. At metaphase (about 40 minutes) the chromosomes lie in an ordered array at the equator. The number of chromosomes of the sea urchin has been the subject of numerous studies, but it is a difficult task because they are extremely small and crowded. Reviews of the reported values are given by E. B. Harvey (1920), Grimpe (1930), MacClung (1939), Makino (1951), and von Ubisch (1961). The most frequently encountered number is 36–38 chromosomes for the diploid embryonic cells. The chromosomes of *Arbacia* have a spherical or rodlike shape with an average volume of about 0.268 μ^3 (Tennent, 1912a; Matsui, 1924; E. B. Harvey, 1940c). The male is heterogenetic (XO or XY), at least in

Paracentrotus lividus, Psammechinus microtuberculatus, Lytechinus variegatus, Tripneustes esculentus, Cidaris tribuloides, Hipponoe esculenta, Clypeaster rosaceus, according to Makino (1951) and E. B. Harvey (1956b); and also in *Arbacia lixula,* according to Gray (1921) but not according to Harvey (1956b). This question has been recently re-investigated by German (1964) on *Arbacia punctulata* blastomeres. The conclusions are that the diploid chromosome number is 44. Only 4 of them are large enough to allow a detailed study and no sex chromosomes have been identified by this author. The metaphase is followed by anaphase and telophase, which complete the first cleavage within 1 hour.

First cleavage of the sea urchin egg has been investigated to study the following problems: (1) formation mechanism of the furrow; (2) study of the composition of the mitotic apparatus; (3) effect of physical and chemical agents on the process of cell division. These problems will be briefly treated here.

A. Formation Mechanism of the First Furrow

The earlier theories have been reviewed by Swann and Mitchison (1958) and by Wolpert (1960). The large number of experiments and theories developed on this subject exists because the sea urchin egg has been held as the most convenient model for the study of cellular cleavage in general. The sea urchin egg is also the only living material in which the mitotic apparatus has been isolated in bulk amount (Mazia and Dan, 1952), with only a few exceptions (Siskens *et al.,* 1967).

The main conclusion of earlier work has been that the egg "cortex" itself (see Chapter 3) possesses the cleavage property without any help from the internal part of the egg, particularly the mitotic apparatus. In experiments where the mitotic apparatus has been damaged (Beams and Evans, 1940; Swann and Mitchison, 1953) or removed (Hiramoto, 1956), cleavage proceeds normally. One of the most dramatic pieces of evidence comes from the experiment of Hiramoto (1965) where the central part of the egg of *Clypeaster japonicus* is replaced by seawater and cleavage still occurs almost normally. It should be noted, however, that these experiments are successful only when the mitotic apparatus is removed after metaphase–anaphase. It is only from that stage on that the egg cortex seems to receive the information on how to cleave or, at least, that it has to initiate cleavage. This agrees with earlier work by Hiramoto (1956), in which he has shown that displacement of the mitotic apparatus before anaphase causes a corresponding change in the position of the furrow. If, on the other hand, the mitotic apparatus is displaced thereafter the furrow will occur at a position defined by the former position of the spindle. The latest approach of Hiramoto (1971) to this question has been the micro-surgical removal of the following parts of a dividing *Clypeaster japonicus* egg: one aster; two asters; the nucleus; the nucleus and one aster; the spindle; the entire mitotic apparatus. Most of the results are still consistent with the idea that the aster is formed around the centriole and that the furrow is formed because of cortex contraction after the inducing stimuli have left the tips of the aster rays.

In a series of papers, Rappaport (1961, 1964, 1965, 1967, 1968, 1969a,b; Rappaport and Ebstein, 1965; Rappaport and Ratner, 1967) tried to establish to which part of the egg cortex the asters signal that it has to undergo constriction in order to make the furrow, and how this signal is conveyed.

The main technique that this author has used has been that of flattening the eggs, thus altering the distance between the asters from each other and from various parts of the cortex, and that of perforating the eggs at different points between the asters and the cortex [see also Dan (1943a) and Scott (1960a) for earlier perforation experiments]. He concludes that the position of the furrow becomes fixed only when the asters have grown maximally. Before that stage, the position of the furrow can be varied by changing the position of the asters with respect to the egg cortex. Normally, the furrow forms at the equator of the egg because the effects of the two opposite asters meet there and become stronger. In fact, perforations made between the poles and the asters have little effect on the formation of the furrow, while perforations between the equator and the asters are much more effective. Moreover, the effect of the asters is weakened when the two asters are experimentally shifted apart from each other. Finally, these experiments suggest that the stimulating activity of the aster travels along straight lines and, therefore, is not mediated by any freely diffusible substance. The idea of a stimulus traveling from the aster to the cortex is also supported by some experiments of Timourian and Watchmaker (1971), showing that if the asters are moved closer to the cortex by inducing a tetrapolar mitosis by polyspermy and mercapto-ethanol treatment, the cleavage is accelerated.

We can now reformulate the question of the formation of the furrow and ask how the egg cortex cleaves.

Two main theories have been elaborated and are still a matter of discussion: The first one calls for an active expansion of the polar regions of the egg, in contrast to a stiffness of the equator, which would, therefore, be forced to invaginate passively; the second holds that there is an active constriction of the equatorial region (Marsland and Landau, 1954; Lewis, 1942). The latter theory is best supported by the recent experiments of Rappaport (1969a), who has microsurgically excised the furrowing region or a fragment of it from cleaving eggs of *Echinaracnius parma* and other marine eggs. These isolated regions completed their furrowing in the absence of the polar regions of the egg, thereby confirming similar observations by Scott (1960a). A morphological support for theories involving an active furrow contraction is provided by the presence of a dense layer below the cell membrane, especially at the level of the furrow (Mercer and Wolpert, 1958; Weinstein and Herbst, 1964), and by the finding of Tilney and Marsland (1969), who described the presence of filaments of 5 nm, similar to those described in many contractile cells, which appear at the level of the furrow during cleavage of the sea urchin egg.

The role of a contractile protein of the egg cortex is thoroughly discussed by Sakai (1968). This author has proposed a theory on the mechanism by which the egg cortex would receive a signal to divide. For the sake of brevity, we shall first outline the theory in its most far-reaching conclusions, and then report the simple facts.

The signal to the cortex would be conveyed by the mitotic apparatus, whose precursor is a monomer protein-rich in SH groups. The latter would oxidate (thus starting the assembly of polymeric units of the mitotic apparatus) at the expense of the S—S groups of a protein contained in the cortex, which thereby acquires its maximum contractility culminating at the metaanaphase. At this point, the cortical protein would start to contract, thus decreasing its SH content in favor of the S—S bridges.

Now for the facts: First of all, we shall mention that variations of the SH groups have long been correlated with cleavage (Rapkine, 1931; Bolognari, 1952; Mazia, 1954) and attributed to an equilibrium between oxidized and reduced glutathione. It has been observed that decrease in the reduced glutathione content are not matched by corresponding increases in oxidized glutathione (Infantellina and La Grutta, 1948; Bolognari, 1952). Mazia (1954, 1955) has, therefore, proposed that the oxidized glutathione binds to the proteins of the spindle causing the formation of intermolecular S—S bridges and, consequently, the gelation of the spindle. Kawamura (1960) has detected changes during the cleavage of the protein-bound SH groups. Wolfson and Wilbur (1960) have correlated the effect of cleavage inhibitor to a reaction with the SH groups, and many other authors, as will be discussed later, have described that substances that reduce the S—S bridges interfere with cleavage. Kojima (1960a,b) has attributed the appearance of clear spots in the cytoplasm of a cleaving egg, following treatments with ether, methane, and hypertonic solutions, to the cyclic increase of SH-containing materials.

Finally Sakai (1960a,b, 1963) measured the changes in the SH groups of the cortical proteins and found that they increase till metaanaphase. The egg contains a KCl-soluble protein, located mostly in the cortex, which is able to undergo reversible contraction in the presence of oxidants of the SH groups (Sakai and Dan, 1959; Sakai, 1960a,b, 1962a,b, 1963). The contractility of this protein is proportional to its content in the SH groups; during cleavage it undergoes the same variations as described for the entire cortex. The total thiol content of the egg proteins remains constant through division. The egg actually contains a water-extractable, calcium-insoluble fraction also rich in thiol groups. The reduction state of these groups also undergoes cyclical variations, which are reciprocal of those of the cortical KCl-soluble contractile protein. These two fractions *in vitro* undergo a thiol–disulfide exchange reaction when in the presence of glutathione, calcium ions, and a fraction that precipitates at pH 5 from the water extract after removal of the calcium-insoluble proteins (Sakai, 1965, 1967).

The reaction between the two fractions can be formulated as follows:

$$2 \text{ RSH} + \text{R'SSR'} \rightleftarrows \text{RSSR} + 2 \text{ R'SH}$$

The direction and reaction rate will depend mostly on the initial ratio of the SH content of the two proteins. Also the proteins of the isolated mitotic apparatus undergo *in vitro* the same thiol–disulfide reaction with the cortical contractile protein (Sakai, 1966).

The calcium-insoluble protein might be a precursor of the microtubules of the mitotic apparatus. This possibility will be discussed in the next section together with a description of the mitotic apparatus.

Finally, treatment with ether blocks equally the *in vitro* exchange reaction, the increase in SH content of the cortical protein and cleavage (Sakai, 1968; Wilson, 1902), while it does not affect nuclear division. Ikeda (1965) has noted that blockage of cleavage by heat treatment also blocks the SH cycle of the KCl-soluble protein. As noted at the beginning of this brief discussion on Sakai's findings, we acknowledge that any excess of extrapolation from his data is due only to our interest in providing a schematism in such an intricate matter, rather than to Sakai's rigorous description of his own data. We can safely state in conclusion that mechanisms do exist in the egg cortex that might ensure its contraction and, therefore, an active furrow constriction at the egg equator. More experimental evidence would, however, be welcome to prove further that they are really at work in the process of cell cleavage.

The fact that an active mechanism of furrow constriction seems to be operating does not exclude that polar relaxation or expansion normally plays a role in cell division. For example, one might assume that a gradient of cytoplasmic stiffness exists from the equator toward the poles, which would not at all be contradictory with the experiments of cleavage of isolated furrowing regions. Wolpert (1966) has indeed suggested that "astral relaxation" (i.e., relaxation of the region of the membrane closest to the asters) cooperates with a contraction of the furrow region for cleavage. His theory is based mainly on measurement of the mechanical properties of the egg membrane by means of the cell elastimeter designed by Mitchison and Swann (1954a,b). It has been found that resistance to deformation during cleavage increases in the furrow region while decreasing in the polar regions. The increase would be due both to an increase of Young's modulus × thickness and the development of a tension of about 1 dyne/cm. The stimulus exerted by the aster on the polar membrane would, however, follow a geometrical pattern which, in Rappaport's opinion, is not consistent with the geometrical analysis of the stimulation process (Rappaport, 1965, 1969a).

The conditions for the furrow formation would, according to Kinoshita, be brought about by a special mechanism, different from those mentioned thus far. In brief, his theory holds that the furrowing cortical region would cyclically "gelate" with development of a local tension, while the polar region would at the same time "solate" with development of a local relaxation. The sol and gel states would be regulated by a periodic local increase of a heparinlike polysaccharide.

The steps that have led Kinoshita to formulate his theory are the following: The author first described in chick fibroblasts the presence of particulate fractions sedimenting at 70,000 g, which he named "relaxation grana"; these would contain a material responsible for the relaxation of the polar region during division (Kinoshita *et al.,* 1964). A similar particulate had been isolated and partially purified from glycerinated eggs of *Pseudocentrotus depressus* and *Clypeaster japonicus.* In these eggs it had been possible to show, by immunofluorescence, a migration of the grana toward the poles during anaphase (Kinoshita and Yazaki, 1967). It had been known that centrifuged eggs can be stimulated to cleave by treatment with hypertonic seawater. In this case, the plane of the furrow is perpendicular to the axis of the centrifugal force (E. B. Harvey, 1960). Kinoshita (1968) had later found in such treated eggs, by means of fluorescent antibodies, a marked decrease in the concentration of the relaxing "granules" (now he uses this better term) in one of the egg layers obtained after centrifugation. Furrowing had invariably taken place at the level of this layer. Interestingly enough, the microinjection of a preparation of the granules into the cytoplasm of a living ameba had been without effect, but the injection of an extract of the granules had caused a profound modification of the gel state of the ameba cytoplasm. These facts had prompted the hypothesis that centrifugation of the egg causes an accumulation of the granules in the polar regions of the egg and that subsequent treatment with hypertonic seawater frees the relaxing principle from the granules.

Finally, Kinoshita (1969) found that heparinlike substance, identified by paper chromatography (and routinely assayed for its hexosamine content), is contained free in the cytoplasm or associated with the relaxing granules in eggs of *Clypeaster japonicus* and *Hemicentrotus pulcherrimus*. The respective amounts of free and granular heparin undergo cyclic and reciprocal variations during the cell cycle: When the cytoplasm is closer to the gel state the amount of free heparin decreases, to increase in the periods when the cytoplasm is closer to the sol state. The isolated granules can be induced to free the heparinlike agents, by an increase of over 0.5 M of the KCl concentration, and by agents able to oxidize the SH groups. It is tempting to speculate on an interaction between the SH-rich proteins of Sakai and these granules. It should be recalled, however, that an activation of permeability, as will be described later, takes place at fertilization, in particular with a transitory increase of permeability to K^+ ions, which might be implicated in the release of heparin from the granules. More difficult, of course, is to correlate these changes in permeability with the cleavages following the first one.

It is worth noting that Zimmerman and Marsland, who were able to elicit the formation of a furrow in *Arbacia punctulata* eggs by centrifugation and pressure, attributed the fact to the release of a cytoplasmic factor (besides a nuclear one) associated with the metachromatic β-granules (see Chapter 2), which becomes free following the breakage of cytoplasmic material (Zimmerman and Marsland, 1956, 1960; Marsland, 1956; Zimmerman *et al.,* 1957; 1968; Marsland *et al.,* 1960). Also Kojima (1959) had proposed a relationship between vitally stainable granules and cleavage activity in sea urchin and *Urechis* eggs.

More recently, Marsland's findings have been reinvestigated at an ultrastructural level (Tilney and Marsland, 1969). Both in spontaneously cleaving eggs and in eggs induced to cleave ahead of time by high pressure or by centrifugation, it has been found that the most dramatic ultrastructural change is the disappearance of the nuclear membrane and the annulate lamellae; the Golgi complex becomes "curled into round bodies" while there is no important change in the vacuoli. The authors stress the importance of the dissolution of such structures for both a mechanism of polar relaxation and the formation of a fibrillar material found in the cortex of the furrow, which might be responsible for an active contraction.

Zimmerman *et al.* (1968) find little effect of different metabolic and mitotic inhibitors on the induction of furrow by centrifugation and pressure. These results might also be explained in terms of the above theory but do not necessarily imply that none of the inhibited metabolic processes is involved in furrow establishment under normal conditions (see also Zimmerman, 1971, for a review on the effect of high pressure).

The observations by Wolpert *et al.* (1971), discussed in Chapter 2, deserve mention here. They do not favor the idea that a gelatinous structure of the cortex plays a role in the mechanical properties of the egg surface, since these are unchanged in conditions such as under high hydrostatic pressure, which are known to solate the gels and disassemble microtubules. Still, as the authors point out, the 5-nm filaments described by Tilney and Marsland (1969) might have remained unaffected by the high pressure treatment.

Among the various theories favoring an active role of the poles, it is worth mentioning that of the "membrane expansion." This has been suggested by Schechtman (1937), Lehmann (1946), and Hüber (1946), and fully developed by Mitchison and Swann (Mitchison, 1952, 1953a,b, 1956; Mitchison and Swann, 1952, 1954a,b, 1955; Swann, 1953, 1955, 1957; Swann and Mitchison, 1953, 1958). The theory proposes an active expansion of the membrane at the poles caused by a configurational and orientational change of its proteins, triggered by a supposed substance that diffuses from the chromosome groups.

The theory originated mainly from the observed changes in the birefringent power of the egg surface following fertilization. This theory has been criticized by the proponents of the active role of the furrow, and also by Wolpert (1966), especially on the basis of his reinvestigation of the elastimetric data of the membrane during cleavage.

The movements of the egg cortex during cleavage have been studied by Dan and Ono (1954), K. Dan (1954), Hiramoto (1958), Ishizaka (1958), and Scott (1960b) by following the movement of natural or artificially attached markers. These experiments show that the polar regions of the egg surface expand considerably for the first three-quarters of the cleavage, while there is a contraction of the area of the furrow at the beginning followed by an increase in surface, as documented by an electron microscopic analysis (Wolpert and Gustafson, 1961b).

The geometry of the effect of spindle elongation on surface deformation has been calculated and discussed by K. Dan (1963). Dan reports some theoretical considerations by Ishizaka (1958) on the forces that should be involved in the process of cleavage. It is concluded, on the basis of direct measurements of the spindle elongation in eggs cleaving under calibrated pressure (Yoneda, 1960), that "the contracting power of the equatorial ring . . . is not adequate to explain the changes in polar length under compression." The same author, however, recalls how eggs also have been shown to divide in the absence of mitotic apparatus.

Moreover, Hiramoto (1969a,b) has developed a method by which the viscosity of different regions of the egg protoplasm can be estimated by measuring the forces needed to move magnetic particles introduced into the egg. With this method it has not been possible to decide whether the astral rays are liquid channels surrounded by solid granular cytoplasm, as claimed by R. Chambers and Chambers (1961), or solid cylinders surrounded by fluid cytoplasm with suspended particles, as claimed by K. Dan (1943b). It has, however, been found that the spindle disintegrates during the late anaphase or telophase, which again rules out the possibility of a role of the spindle in the late phases of furrowing.

In conclusion, any of the existing theories involves contraction at the equator and expansion at the poles, and the differences lie where one of these is thought to be the active process. A very critical test would be to see whether the internal "hydrostatic" pressure rises or falls during cleavage, but this has not been done and would be difficult to do. A more subtle point which is not often made is that it is not a simple contraction at the equator. Let us consider a square area of the cortex deep down in a half-completed furrow. As the furrow moves inward, this area will change shape and become a rectangle by contracting in the direction at right angles to the plane containing the center of this area and the two astral centers, and by expanding in the direction parallel to this plane. Since the surface does not wrinkle up in the furrow, there must be this change in shape which involves both contraction in one direction and expansion in the other. The contracting ring theory emphasizes the contraction. In their review in 1958, Swann and Mitchison emphasized the expansion element in the furrow region as well as expansion at the poles. It is, we think, likely that the active region of the surface in cleavage is in the furrow, but this may involve active expansion as well as (or as an alternative to) contraction.

B. The Mitotic Apparatus

The modern approach to the study of the mitotic apparatus of the sea urchin egg starts with the development of a method for isolating it in bulk amounts (Mazia and Dan, 1952) from eggs at metaphase. In the past, the study of the mitotic apparatus had only been carried out on the entire egg by classic cytological methods, by polarized light, or by the effect of hydrostatic pressure, except for a brief report from Danielli (1950) on the isolation of mitotic apparatus.

A review of these works can be found in Hughes (1952). Although constituted by chromosomes, spindles, asters, and centrioles, the mitotic apparatus (for an ultrastructural description, see Harris, 1961, 1962) is in Mazia and Dan's opinion a single "physical entity," as proved by the fact that it can be isolated as such (Fig. 5.1).

The original methods of isolation consisted in fixation of the eggs (of *Strongylocentrotus franciscanus* and *Strongylocentrotus purpuratus*) with 30% ethanol at $-10°C$; treatment with H_2O_2, which had been supposed to oxidize the SH groups, thus hardening the mitotic apparatus,

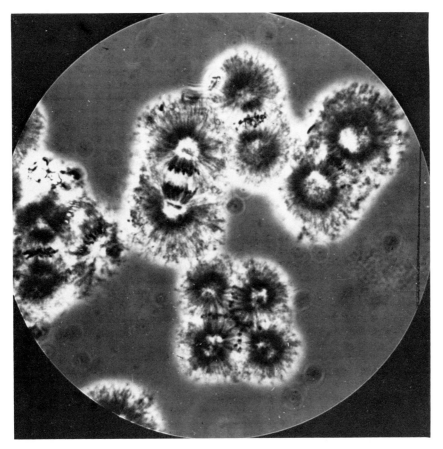

Fig. 5.1.   Isolated sea urchin mitotic apparatus. (Courtesy of Dr. Mazia.)

while damaging the surrounding cytoplasm; followed by cytolysis by means of the detergent sodium lauryl sulfate. This method has undergone several modifications (Dan and Nakajima, 1956; Kane, 1962a,b; Mazia, 1955; Mazia *et al.*, 1961; Mazia and Zimmerman, 1958; Miki, 1963; Zimmerman, 1960). The main modification has been the introduction of dithioglycol by Mazia *et al.* (1961) for the one-step fixation and oxidation treatment, followed by EDTA.

Kane (1965a), however, has denied the importance of the sulfur groups and has substituted dithioglycol by a number of nonsulfur-containing, six-carbon glycols. Moreover, he claims that the only necessary step is osmotic lysis of the egg at low pH (5.5–5.6). This has the disadvantage of coagulating other cytoplasmic proteins. Hexanediol would act through a rise of the pH to 6.2–6.4, thus avoiding this secondary effect. Hexanediol can, therefore, be substituted by number of other nonelectrolytes. Kane and Forer (1965) have also studied the possibility of storing the isolated mitotic apparatus without alteration and have encountered a breakdown of the microtubules of the spindle during prolonged storage. In discussing the stabilization of the isolated mitotic apparatus, Cohen (1968) has reported that this exhibits polyelectrolyte properties, since it shrinks to minimal size at pH's close to its isoelectric point, i.e., at about 4.5, or in the presence of ions that charge opposite to the net charge of the mitotic apparatus.

The main proteic component of the mitotic apparatus is expected to be the proteins of the spindle fibers. All the investigations reported here, aimed at studying the proteins of the mitotic apparatus, are to be considered as investigations on the proteins of the spindle. The hypothesis around which most of the recent reports tend to gather is that the main constituent of the mitotic apparatus is a protein of about 2.5 S, which would correspond to the monomeric globular subunit of about 3.3 nm in diameter, a constituent of the microtubules of the spindle fibers. The main steps through which this conclusion has been reached represent the work of several laboratories and can be briefly summarized as follows: Zimmerman (1960, 1963a) found that the protein of the mitotic apparatus, isolated by the digitonin method, sediments as two main peaks of 3.7 and 8.6 S. Miki-Nomura (1965, 1968) isolated and extensively purified from the fibrillar component of the mitotic apparatus a 2.3 S component. Inoué et al. (1965), Kane (1965b, 1967), and Stephens (1965, 1967) have drawn attention to a 22 S protein as a major component of the mitotic apparatus isolated by Kane's method. It has been found (Stephens, 1967; Miki-Nomura, 1968; Sakai, 1968) that this can be split into 8 subunits by 105,000–120,000 M.W. and 2.6 S. As will be noted later, however, the view that the 22 S protein might be an aggregated form of the 2.6 S protein described by Sakai is not supported by the most recent evidence (Stephens, 1968a,b; Bibring and Baxandall, 1968, 1969). This matter has been considerably clarified by the work of Sakai, who has isolated the mitotic apparatus by dithiopropanol, digitonin, and by hexanediol (Sakai, 1966, 1968). With the first method he has been able to isolate one major 3.2–3.5 S component and two minor 11–13 S and 21–22 S components. The 3.2 S is a dimer which by sulfite or dithiothreitol treatment can be reversibly split into two 2.5 S subunits of 34,700 M.W. and about 3.4 nm in diameter. The 11–13 S can be partly split into 2.5 S subunits. These results are fundamentally confirmed with the two other methods of isolation. As first shown by de Harven and Bernard (1956), the spindle fibers are composed of microtubules. Kiefer et al. (1966) have examined under the electron microscope the mitotic apparatus isolated by dithiopropanol, spread on an air–water interface and stained with uranyl acetate. They have clearly shown its microtubular structure. The microtubules are made up of about 13 fibrils. These latter are constituted by a pile of globular particles of about 3.3 nm in diameter. The suggestion has hence been made that these particles correspond to the 2.5-S monomeric subunit. This view is shared by Sakai (1968) and Miki-Nomura (1968).

Cohen and Gottlieb (1971) have also observed in isolated mitotic spindles of *Arbacia punctulata* eggs, some microtubules whose cross section appears as a C, instead of an O. They are more frequent in the interzonal regions of anaphase spindles and in the metaphase chromosome "plate," and might represent a stage of microtubule assembly.

Bibring and Baxandall (1968) extracted by mild (pH 3) HCl treatment about 10% of the proteins of the mitotic apparatus isolated with the hexylene glycol procedure. Under these conditions, a selective disappearance of the microtubules is observed under the electron microscope. The extracted proteins consist of a minor component of 22 S, which shows immunological analogies with Stephen's protein, and of a slowly sedimenting material of 4 S or less, representing about 80–95% of the extracted proteins, provided the acid treatment had not been protracted for much longer. This slow-sedimenting material has similarities to the monomeric unit of Sakai, as shown by its insolubility in calcium. It also has solubility similarities to a microtubular protein extractable from sperm flagella by the same procedure.

Moreover, Bibring and Baxandall (1969) have studied with immunochemical methods the 22 S protein extracted by the mitotic apparatus isolated by Kane's procedure. They have concluded, by electron microscopic localization of labeled antibodies, that the 22 S protein is not particularly concentrated at microtubular level; rather it appears ubiquitous in the cytoplasm of eggs at metaphase and does not exist in lighter microtubular material extracted with mild acid, or in the sperm flagella. The conclusion of the authors, therefore, is that the 22 S protein is not a candidate for microtubular protein and is distinct from the fractions of lower sedimentation coefficient, which are supposed to be the microtubular monomers.

The same authors (Bibring and Baxandall, 1971) have more recently succeeded into selectively extracting the microtubular proteins from isolated mitotic apparatuses of *Strongylocentrotus purpuratus* eggs by use of meralluride sodium. The conclusions from this work are that the microtubular proteins represent about 10% of the total mitotic apparatus proteins. They are made by subunits of 52,000 molecular weight. They look very similar to the microtubular proteins of the outer doublet of the sperm tail because of the following properties: precipitability with calcium ions or with vinblastine, electrophoretic and immunological behavior, amino acid composition, molecular weight.

Borisy and Taylor (1967a,b) have shown that colchicine binds a protein of about 6 S, believed to be made up of microtubular subunits. It is also possible to purify partially the microtubular proteins by specific precipitation with vinblastine. Wilson *et al.* (1970), however, draw attention to the fact that other proteins, precipitable by calcium ions, also are precipitated by vinblastine. Studies of amino acid composition of the microtubules constituting the outer fibers of the sea urchin sperm flagella (Stephens, 1968a) have revealed a good similarity to the muscle and plasmodial actin, and to the mitotic apparatus 2.5-S subunit of Sakai (1968). In this work, Stephens expresses the opinion that the Sakai 2.5-S particle may be considered the monomeric unit of microtubules, and that the 22 S of Kane (1967) and Stephens (1967) "is at present considered to be a matrix or tubule-associated component of the mitotic apparatus but definitely not a microtubule subunit or precursor."

It is pertinent to recall that Hatano *et al.* (1969) and Miki-Nomura and Osawa (1969) have isolated and purified from the acetone powder of *Pseudocentrotus depressus* eggs a protein closely resembling the muscular G actin, which is able to combine with myosin A from rabbit muscle to give actomyosin. Other authors (Mohri, 1968; Yanagisawa *et al.*, 1968), who have analyzed the chemical composition of the proteins isolated from microtubules of the sea urchin sperm flagella, have concluded that, despite the great similarity in amino acid composition between the muscular actin and the flagellar protein, they cannot be considered identical, mainly because the microtubular protein is associated with guanosine mono-, di-, and triphosphate, whereas the muscular actin contains adenosine mono-, di-, and triphosphate (see also Stephens *et al.*, 1967). The name "tubulin" was tentatively proposed for the microtubular protein.*

Optical rotatory dispersion analysis of the isolated mitotic apparatus (Kolodny and Roslansky, 1966) has produced results consistent with the possibility of the presence of a protein very similar to the muscular actin G. X-ray diffraction analyses of the sperm flagellar protein have also been attempted, with no conclusive results so far (Forslind *et al.*, 1968). The most recent one was performed by C. Cohen *et al.* (1971) on microtubules extracted from sperm tails of *Strongylocentrotus droe-*

---

*This name is currently used to indicate the proteins of microtubules, irrespective of their localization. But it has to be remembered that tubulins contained in the cilia, mitotic apparatus, cytoplasm, and sperm flagella are not necessarily equal to each other (Behnke and Forer, 1967). The best analyzed among them are probably the tubulins of sea urchin sperm flagella (see Stephens, 1970; Feit *et al.*, 1971; Summers and Gibbons, 1971). The conclusion of an immunological study of Fulton *et al.* (1971) is that the tubulins of different origin are similar but not identical to each other.

bachiensis. The results suggest a structure of 12–13 strand made up of subunits with a 4–5 nm packing diameter, alternatively half-staggered parallel to the tubule axis.

As to the identity of the calcium-insoluble protein of the egg-water extract described by Kane and Hersh (1959), the following considerations are reported by Sakai (1968). This fraction contains three main components of 2.6, 3.4, and 5.0 S and two minor ones of 7 and 22 S; it contains at least one antigen in common with the mitotic apparatus (Went, 1959). On the basis of acrylamide gel electrophoretic analyses and of the response to calcium and to sulfite, it is proposed that the 2.6 S component of the calcium-insoluble fraction is a precursor of the microtubule unit protein of the mitotic apparatus, already present in the unfertilized egg. The 3.4 S and the 5 S might, respectively, be dimer and tetramer of the 2.6-S fraction.

It should be recalled, however, that it has been proposed (see Chapter 3) that the Kane and Hersch protein is contained in the cortical granules. If this is the case, it is difficult to conceive how it can contain precursors of the spindle proteins. In fact, the cortical granule content is thought to be extruded from the egg at fertilization, to contribute to the formation of the hyaline layer.

A discussion of the mitotic apparatus protein synthesis is reported in Chapter 11.

Another interesting approach aimed at understanding the function of the mitotic apparatus fibers, namely, their contractility, has been that of finding out whether or not there is an ATPase associated with the mitotic apparatus. The question has long been investigated, but the results have not been unequivocal. Besides negative results, in which no ATPase activity has been found in the isolated mitotic apparatus (Mazia, 1955; Stephens, 1967), data exist where the mitotic apparatus, isolated with milder procedures, has clearly shown an ATPase activity (Mazia *et al.,* 1961; Miki, 1963; Weisenberg and Taylor, 1968). Weisenberg and Taylor, however, have pointed out that the mitotic apparatus-associated activity is not distinguishable from that isolable in a soluble form from the rest of the cytoplasm. Both migrate with a sedimentation coefficient of about 13 ($\pm$1) S when centrifuged in a sucrose gradient, and resemble the ciliary ATPase dynein. In these authors experience, ATPase is not particularly concentrated in the isolated mitotic apparatus. In their opinion, therefore, it is not possible to decide whether the ATPase is found there because it accomplishes a specific task, or simply as a cytoplasmic contaminant.

Miki (1964) has also reported the presence of an ATPase activity in the isolated egg cortex, which increases during metaphase.

Finally, the question of the birefringence of the isolated sea urchin mitotic apparatus has been reinvestigated by means of light and electron microscopy by Goldman and Rebhun (1969). These authors provide an accurate review of the work by which microtubules have been identified as the constituents of the mitotic apparatus, and the real presence of birefringent fibers in it has been acknowledged. They find some ribosome-like particles associated with the microtubules (see also Hartman and Zimmerman, 1968) and oriented parallel to the axis of the microtubules. Conditions that cause disappearance of the microtubules in the isolated mitotic apparatus cause disappearance of the birefringence. Orientation of the ribosomelike particles under these conditions, however, is also lost. In the authors' opinion, it is not legitimate, therefore, to conclude that all the birefringence of the isolated mitotic apparatus arises solely from the microtubules, since other structures oriented parallel to them might be responsible for at least part of it.

C.   Chemical and Physical Agents That Interfere with Cleavage

To get an idea of the amount of work performed in this field suffice it to mention that E. B. Harvey (1956a) lists 113 different chemical or physical treatments, along with a much higher number of references, that have been studied in connection with cleavage. The conclusion is prompted to the reader that such a delicate process as that of cleavage must be sensitive to a variety of different environmental conditions. Moreover, due to the complexity of cell division, conditions that affect the most different aspects of metabolism are expected to disturb cleavage. Actually, cleavage may be affected by disturbances of protein synthesis (Hultin, 1961a; Palincsar, 1960; Hogan and Gross, 1971) and energetic metabolism. The older literature in this latter field is reviewed by Harvey (1956a). Among subsequent works, we should mention the papers by Ishikawa (1957), Kitasume (1959), Kojima (1960c), and Hagström and Lönning (1966). Lastly, Sawada and Rebhun (1969) have concluded that the structural integrity of the mitotic apparatus may depend on the ATP intracellular level. Epel (1963) has correlated the ATP level and rate of mitotic activity. On the other hand, the correlation between oxygen consumption rate and mitotic activity during development has been repeatedly noted, as will be described later. Particular attention must be given to some treatments that interfere with the nucleic acid metabolism, or that are known to interact specifically with the spindle proteins. As for the nucleic acid metabolism, we shall mention here that treatments supposed to block DNA synthesis in the fertilized egg almost invariably block cell division at the 8-blastomere stage. Inhibition of RNA synthesis, on the other hand, does not in itself appreciably affect cleavage (Gross and Cousineau, 1964). These aspects of nucleic acid synthesis, however, will be treated in greater detail in the respective chapters.

We have to consider here the effect of treatments known to act through a damage of the fibrillar part of the mitotic apparatus. As noted by Marsland (1968) there is good evidence that three different agents, namely, colchicine, high pressure, and low temperature, interfere with cleavage by damaging the mitotic spindle. Actually, high pressure (Shimamura, 1939; Zimmerman and Marsland, 1964) and low temperature cause a change toward the sol condition of the mitotic apparatus gelated structures. Because of that an increase in the pressure or a decrease in the temperature is able to counteract the effect of the heavy water (Marsland, 1956, 1957, 1965; Marsland and Asterita, 1966), which is believed to produce a hypergelation of the spindle-aster structure.

The effect of colchicine on sea urchin egg has been thoroughly studied (see Eigisti *et al.*, 1949, for the older literature; Ludford, 1936; Zeuthen, 1951; Inoué, 1952, 1964; Taylor, 1965; Borisy and Taylor, 1967a,b). The most important conclusion reached by Borisy and Taylor is that the mechanism through which colchicine blocks the cells at metaphase would be a direct binding of the drug to a 6 S protein extractable from the mitotic apparatus under conditions leading to the disappearance of the microtubules, and which is, therefore, supposed to be a protein subunit of microtubules. This conclusion is based on the analysis of the binding of ^{3}H-labeled colchicine to the mitotic apparatus both *in vivo* and *in vitro*.

Marsland and Hecht (1968) have also studied the effect of combined treatments of sea urchin eggs with colchicine and D_2O. An antagonism had been expected, since colchicine is believed to act by interfering with the polymerization of the microtubular proteins, and the D_2O by favoring the dispersal of the H_2O shell around the microtubular protein subunits as a preliminary step for polymerization, thus bringing about an over-gelation of the microtubular proteins. The experimental results have revealed an antagonism only over a low range of D_2O concentration (25–35%), but a synergism for higher D_2O concentration (55–65%), and synergism or antagonism, depending on the colchicine dosage, at intermediate D_2O concentration, which does not make the interpretation of such findings very easy.

Correlated with the role of SH groups in the assembly of the mitotic apparatus, as already discussed, is the observation by Lallier (1962e) that thiosorbitol and thioglycerol block cleavage by causing disassembly of the mitotic apparatus. Mazia (1958b), Mazia and Zimmerman (1958), Bucher and Mazia (1960), Zimmerman (1964), and lastly Yuyama (1971) have described a period of sensitivity to 2-mercaptoethanol treatment. In the opinion of Yuyama, the mercaptoethanol-sensitive event occurs just before metaphase and lasts about 5 minutes, i.e., it takes place after synthesis completion of the protein(s) required for cell division. It is pertinent to recall that cleavage inhibition of sea urchin embryos has been used as a test for the toxicity of a variety of oxidation products of biogenic monoamines (Markova and Buznikov, 1970).

Zotin (1969) has found that cleavage-inhibiting thermolabile substances are contained in the eggs of *Strongylocentrotus intermedius* and *Strongylocentrotus droebachiensis*. Since their concentrations fluctuate within the cell cycle, being maximal at the stage of contact of the pronuclei and at the following prophase and anaphase, Zotin suggests that these substances play a role in the normal elicitation of furrow formation.

Reports of cleavage stimulation are also numerous, but often of not too clear significance. Kuno-Kojima (1967a,b, 1969a,b) has made the point that subliminal stimuli, which fail to activate the unfertilized egg, are able to accelerate cleavage when the egg is subsequently fertilized.

Earlier reports of cleavage stimulation by external administration of DNA fragments (Butros, 1959) or by vital staining (Kojima, 1961), appear too difficult to be interpreted and will not, therefore, be described in detail. No further attention, to our knowledge, has been given to the theory presented by Menkin (1959) of the presence in the ovaries of *Arbacia punctulata* of a dinucleotide that causes cleavage delay and of a polynucleotide that accelerates it.

A special word must be expressed on the effect of irradiations on cleavage.

D. Irradiation

X-ray irradiation and UV irradiation of sea urchin gametes or embryos have been used to investigate a series of problems. X-ray irradiation of embryos at different developmental stages has been employed by Neifakh as a tool for measuring nuclear activity at different developmental stages and will be discussed in Chapter 10 on RNA synthesis. Here we are primarily concerned with the effect of irradiation of sperm or eggs separately, or of fertilized eggs at different periods of the mitotic cycle. This subject has recently been reviewed by Rustad (1971).

1. IRRADIATION OF THE SPERM

a. UV Irradiation

This irradiation causes surface alteration of the sperm, which agglutinate and lose motility and ability to fertilize (Hinrichs, 1927; Evans, 1947).

Nuclear damage from UV irradiation does not seem to be photoreactivated within the sperm itself (Marshak, 1949; Blum *et al.*, 1951), whereas photoreactivation can take place once the sperm has penetrated the egg (Marshak, 1949). Fertilization with UV-irradiated sperm causes a mitotic delay.

b. X Irradiation

Again decrease of motility and ability to fertilize (Hinrichs, 1927; Evans, 1947) can be observed. Fertilization with X-irradiated sperm causes a mitotic delay proportional to the logarithm of the dose (Henshaw, 1940a; Lea, 1946; Rustad, 1970, 1971). Here again some recovery seems to take place only after the sperm has penetrated the egg (Failla, 1961, 1962b). Fertilization with heavily irradiated sperm may cause the development of gynogenic haploids (Hertwig, 1912). Rustad (1969) has observed that these divide at the same time as normal eggs, while androgenic haploids, obtained by fertilization of enucleated eggs with normal sperms, exhibit a delay in the first mitotic division, probably because the male pronucleus has to decondense in an unbalanced condition (Rustad, 1970).

2. IRRADIATION OF THE UNFERTILIZED EGG

a. UV Irradiation

Little effect is obtained on the surface of the egg, which does not change its permeability (Reed, 1948; Lucké *et al.*, 1951), and it is only with large doses that the jelly coat of the eggs is damaged or lost.

As observed for the sperm, irradiation of the egg brings about a mitotic delay proportional to the logarithm of the dose (Rustad, 1971). But, differently from the sperms, the eggs can be photoreactivated before fertilization (Wells and Giese, 1950; Blum *et al.*, 1951; Rustad *et al.*, 1966).

The large cytoplasm of the egg absorbs a great part of the UV irradiation so that the cytoplasm close to the directly irradiated surface suffers more than that of the other side. Unilateral disturbances of membrane elevation and hyaline layer formation can, therefore, be obtained (Rustad, 1959a).

Parthenogenic activation from UV has been described (Hollaender, 1938; Harvey and Hollaender, 1938).

b. X Irradiation

The same effects as UV irradiation can be obtained on the egg surface. Mitotic delay is also observed. The relationship between dose and mitotic delay is not easily measurable (Henshaw *et al.*, 1933; Henshaw and Francis, 1936; Miwa *et al.*, 1939, 1941; Rao, 1963; Nachtwey, 1965).

Partial recovery from the effect of ionizing radiations can also be observed before fertilization (Henshaw, 1932, 1940c; Miwa *et al.*, 1939; Failla, 1962a).

Rustad *et al.* (1971) have recently reinvestigated the effect of irradiating nonnucleated halves on the time of occurrence of the first cleavage. Previous experiments of this kind (Rustad, 1961) had been performed on nonnucleated halves obtained by centrifugation, which also causes dislocation of subcellular structures and per se a mitotic delay. The latest experiments, therefore, were performed on nonnucleated halves obtained by microsurgery. The experimental plan was the following: First, microsurgery of the egg dividing it into a nucleated and a nonnucleated half; second, irradiation of the two halves and of a nonoperated egg; third, fertilization of the halves and of the egg. The result was a marked mitotic delay of the diploid half; a medium delay of the entire egg; a little delay of the haploid half. This was interpreted by the authors as suggesting that the cytoplasm is somewhat damaged by the irradiation (delay of the haploid half), but that it can well contribute to the repair process (higher delay of the diploid half with respect to the entire egg).

3. IRRADIATION OF THE FERTILIZED EGG

a. UV Irradiation

The interesting point about this kind of investigation is that fertilized eggs exhibit a different sensitivity to irradiation during different phases of the mitotic cycle, the reason being that some of the events that take place in the interval between fertilization and the first cleavage are more sensitive to irradiation than others.

UV irradiation of fertilized eggs induces a mitotic delay. Sensitivity of the egg in this respect is maximal at fertilization, then decreases by a factor of 3, to attain a plateau at about 15 minutes following fertilization. A second sensitivity decrease is observed at 30 minutes, with a drop to zero by 40 minutes (Rustad, 1960a).

It is to be observed that cells irradiated during the "insensitive" period complete the first cleavage at the same time as the controls, indicating that the sensitive processes regarding the first division had already ended at the time of irradiation; but the second cleavage is delayed.

Insensitivity to UV starts, therefore, just before the streak stage, i.e., when the early prophase starts, when centrioles separate, after completion of DNA synthesis (Hinegardner *et al.*, 1964; Zeitz *et al.*, 1968, 1969, 1970), and before chromosome condensation (Rao, 1963).

Actually, the rate of DNA synthesis itself or the time when it is initiated, does not appear to be influenced by UV irradiation (Rao and Hinegardner, 1965; Zeitz *et al.,* 1968), although it seems that DNA itself is the target of UV, as appears from the fact that administration of 5'-bromodeoxyuridine to the egg, which presumably is incorporated into DNA, makes it more sensitive to UV (Cook, 1968). Incorporation of 5'-bromodeoxyuridine into egg DNA does actually bring about an almost complete suppression of photoreactivation in the sea urchin egg (Blum and Price, 1950; Cook and Rieck, 1962; Cook and Setlow, 1966; Cook and McGrath, 1967).

Obviously, the following round of DNA synthesis is delayed with respect to the controls because of the delay of the first cleavage.

The stages of the first mitotic cycle, which appear to be prolonged following irradiation, are the centriole separation and migration and chromosome condensation (Henshaw, 1940b; Yamashita *et al.,* 1940), whereas pronuclear fusion occurs at the normal time (Rustad, 1971).

The mechanism by which DNA damage brings about the disturbance of centriole migration and chromosome condensation is not known yet (Rustad, 1960b, 1964, 1971; Rustad *et al.,* 1964).

The cyclic variations of SH groups, believed to play a role during cleavage, remain normal following UV irradiation (Ikeda, 1965).

What has been described for the delay of the first mitotic division applies also to the following ones, at least up to the time when cleavage takes place synchronously in all cells.

It has been observed that high doses of UV may cause unequal cell division (Rustad, 1959a), while low doses may cause appearance of micromeres at the 8-cell stage, i.e., at the same time after fertilization, when they would appear in the untreated eggs (Ikeda, 1965).

b. X Irradiation

X irradiation during the first division time also brings about a mitotic delay. Here again there are phases of higher sensitivity (Yamashita *et al.,* 1939; Henshaw and Cohen, 1940; Rao, 1963; Failla, 1969; Rustad, 1964, 1970). The curve of sensitivity to ionizing radiations versus time following fertilization is biphasic. To a first increase from fertilization up to about 20 minutes later, follows a drop to the initial values, and then, between 35 and 45 minutes, i.e., at about the same time as in the case of UV irradiation, the sensitivity drops to zero. It should be recalled that while the first division is not affected by irradiation during the insensitive period, the following division will be delayed, and the same rules apply to the subsequent first cleavages.

In this case, chromosome condensation is the process that, like centriole separation, seems especially affected by X irradiation (Rustad, 1959b).

The target of X irradiation seems again to be the nucleus, since sperm, which contain little cytoplasm, are as sensitive as eggs, which are endowed with an enormous cytoplasm (Henshaw and Francis, 1936; Speidel and Cheney, 1960).

Ionizing radiations bring about a more severe alteration of the cleavage pattern than UV irradiations, with the formation of multipolar divisions. These cannot be explained by polyspermy since eggs, fixed and stained, have been shown to contain only one male pronucleus (Henshaw, 1940e); moreover, they occur also when eggs have been fertilized with very dilute sperm suspension (Rustad, 1959c).

What is important is the phenomenon observed here, more marked than with UV irradiation, that micromeres can be formed at the same time as in the untreated eggs, i.e., when the irradiated eggs are still at the 4- or even 2-cell stage (Rustad, 1960c), which suggests that the formation mechanism of this special furrow is not dependent on anything that can be affected by irradiation and therefore is probably not dependent on nuclear control.

A striking effect of X irradiation is the continuous growth of the nucleus during the mitotic delay, accompanied by size increase of the nucleolus-like bodies.

A similar enlargement of the nucleoluslike bodies has been observed during the mitotic delay induced by fluorodeoxyuridine (Emerson and Humphreys, 1971). It is not known whether these bodies represent true nucleoli, i.e., sites for ribosomal RNA genes.

Postfertilization recovery from X irradiation has been studied by Failla (1962a,b, 1965), who finds that it can take place under block conditions of the mitotic cycle experimentally induced by anoxia obtained through N_2 bubbling into the seawater. Puromycin (Rustad and Failla, 1969) or low temperatures (Henshaw, 1940d), but not actinomycin D (Rustad and Burchill, 1966), completely inhibit this recovery, thus suggesting that protein synthesis on preexisting templates is needed for recovery.

Respiration inhibition by various means or agents that affect microtubule formation, such as Colcemid or D_2O or EDTA, does not inhibit recovery. Anoxia or calcium chelation can in fact reduce sensitivity to X ray (Failla, 1969).

Chapter 6

Cell Dissociation and Reaggregation

A. Introduction

Cell dissociation and reaggregation in sea urchins have been used for understanding the relevance of cell interactions in morphogenesis. Study has been devoted also to the role of such interactions in the appearance of new metabolic patterns in development.

The first analysis of cell dissociation and reaggregation in sea urchin embryos is credited to Herbst (1900). This author's discovery relates to the importance of calcium ions in cell adhesion. Cell contact is loosened by calcium-free seawater treatment of embryos within the fertilization membrane. This brings about a mixing of the blastomeres among themselves. When brought back to normal seawater, these embryos somehow readjust themselves and develop into abnormal embryos. Herbst concludes that cells need at least one "point contact" to be able to readjust themselves so as to continue development when returned to normal seawater. If this point contact is lost, the cells can never reaggregate again, even after prolonged treatment with seawater.

Giudice (1962a) has developed a method by which sea urchin embryos can be completely dissociated into single cells, which are able to reaggregate and to differentiate into structures closely resembling normal larvae. This represents the first example in embryology of restitution of entire embryos from dissociated cells. The failure of Herbst to produce such a result probably stems from his method of dissociation, which is based on very long exposure to calcium-free seawater and which, as will be shown below, causes cell damage. The study of cell dissociation and reaggregation in sea urchin embryos from the blastula stage on has been performed almost entirely by Giudice and co-workers, who recently reviewed the subject (Giudice and Mutolo, 1970). This chapter mainly refers to their work, which, when not otherwise specified, was performed on *Paracentrotus lividus*.

B. Methods

1. EMBRYO DISSOCIATION

The procedure originally developed by Giudice (1962a) involves a preliminary washing of the embryos with calcium-free seawater, followed by suspension of the embryos in a solution containing 0.44 M sucrose, 0.05 M citrate, and 0.001 M ethylenediaminetetraacetate (EDTA), pH 8.0.

A later finding (Giudice and Mutolo, 1970) has shown that a solution of 0.5 M sucrose in 0.01 M Tris buffer pH 8.0 gives better results. The dispersion of the cells is achieved by a few strokes of the Teflon plunger in a glass homogenizer, under periodic microscopic control.

This procedure has proved satisfactory for stages of development from hatched blastulae to plutei. Earlier stages are easier to dissociate by simple washings with calcium-free seawater, after removal of the fertilization membrane.

The embryonic species tested by Giudice and collaborators for the disaggregation–reaggregation procedures have been *Paracentrotus lividus* and to a lesser extent *Arbacia punctulata, Arbacia lixula,* and *Sphaerechinus granularis*.

2. CELL VIABILITY TESTS

Three main criteria have been used to test the viability of the dissociated cells: the first is the ability of these cells to reaggregate and to differentiate into larval structures; the second is the rate of oxygen consumption; the third is the rate of amino acid incorporation into proteins.

Table 6.1 illustrates the levels of exogenous amino acid incorporation when the cells are incubated in different media. The requirement for K^+ ions is evident, while no exogenous Mg^{2+} seems to be necessary. The importance of the pH is also noted, which must be above 7.0. A good incorporation is observed in normal seawater. Higher values are, however, obtained in calcium-free seawater. Since calcium-free seawater has been used as a medium to dissociate cells and to prevent them from reaggregating, its effect on amino acid incorporation has been studied in greater detail. Figure 6.1 shows that, while there is a momentary stimula-

TABLE 6.1

LEVELS OF AMINO ACID INCORPORATION IN CELLS INCUBATED IN DIFFERENT MEDIA[a]

Incubation medium	Specific activity (counts/ min/mg protein)
0.4 M sucrose in 0.05 M citrate buffer pH 7.8 + 0.001 M EDTA	13
0.4 M sucrose in 0.05 M citrate buffer pH 7.8 + 0.001 M EDTA + 0.2 M KCl	1670
0.4 M sucrose in 0.035 M Tris buffer pH 7.8	12
0.4 M sucrose in 0.035 M Tris buffer pH 7.8 + 0.005 M MgCl$_2$	12
0.4 M sucrose in 0.035 M Tris buffer pH 7.8 + 0.005 M MgCl$_2$ + 0.1 M KCl	968
0.4 M sucrose in 0.035 M Tris buffer pH 7.8 + 0.005 M MgCl$_2$ + 0.2 M KCl	1334
0.4 M sucrose in 0.035 M Tris buffer pH 7.8 + 0.005 M MgCl$_2$ + 0.4 M KCl	2205
0.4 M sucrose in 0.035 M Tris buffer pH 7.8 + 0.005 M MgCl$_2$ + 0.2 M KCl	1818
0.4 M sucrose in 0.035 M Tris buffer pH 7.0 + 0.005 M MgCl$_2$ + 0.2 M KCl	235
0.4 M sucrose in 0.035 M Tris buffer pH 6.5 + 0.005 M MgCl$_2$ + 0.2 M KCl	195
Normal seawater	954
Ca-free artificial seawater	2232

[a] From Giudice (1962b).

tion of the rate of amino acid incorporation in calcium-free seawater as compared to normal seawater, upon prolonged permanence in calcium-free seawater the cells undergo a marked drop in their ability to incorporate amino acids into proteins.

The ability of these cells to reaggregate also drops after prolonged exposure to calcium-free seawater: after 2.5 hours there is a marked delay in the initiation of the reaggregation process when the cells are brought back to normal seawater, and the aggregates obtained thereafter show various defects in differentiation. After 6 hours of permanence in calcium-free seawater, the ability to reaggregate is almost completely lost.

3. CELL REAGGREGATION PROCEDURE

Two procedures have been used to reaggregate the dissociated cells. One has been called "self-aggregation" and the other "rotation-mediated aggregation." In the first case, the cells are allowed to lie in a monolayer at the bottom of a Syracuse dish in 4 ml of seawater; in the second, the cells, suspended in seawater at a concentration of 1.5×10^6 cells/ml, are gently stirred by a propeller rotating at about 40 rpm. In both cases, the temperature is about 18°–20°C, and antibiotics and a sulfamidic are added to the seawater. In the rotation-mediated aggregation it is more practical to dissociate the cells from an embryo suspension con-

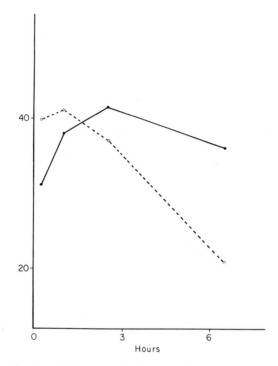

Fig. 6.1. Rate of amino acid incorporation into proteins by cells dissociated from mesenchyme blastulae. On the ordinate the rate of incorporation is given as percent incorporation into proteins of the total uptake after exposure to [³H]leucine for 20 minutes; on the abscissa durations of preincubation in normal seawater (filled-in circles) or in calcium-free seawater (open circles) are shown. (Experiments of Mutolo, Giudice, Cognetti, and Pirrone, reported by Giudice and Mutolo, 1970.)

taining 5000 embryos/ml and to suspend them in a volume of seawater equal to 1/4 the initial one. After roughly 5 hours of rotation, i.e., when aggregates of the average size of an embryo have developed, the volume of the seawater is raised about 12 times to prevent the formation of gigantic aggregates.

C. Morphology of Reaggregation

1. LIGHT MICROSCOPE OBSERVATIONS

a. Rotation-Mediated Aggregation

Freshly dissociated cells appear spherical and animated by an actively rotating pseudopodium. In some instances they still show a motile cilium (Fig. 6.2A–C). Intercellular adhesion in rotated seawater starts almost instantaneously, and solid clumps are formed which, by the addition of new cells, reach the average volume of a normal embryo in about 5 hours.

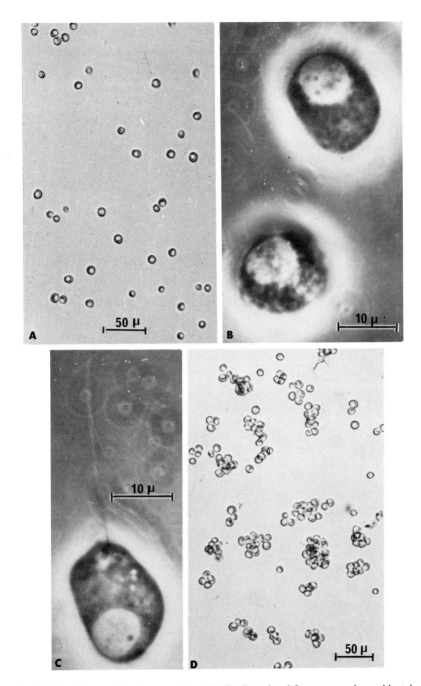

Fig. 6.2. Rotation-mediated aggregation of cells dissociated from mesenchyme blastulae of *Paracentrotus lividus*. (A–C) freshly dissociated cells; (D) after 1 hour of aggregation; (E) after 6 hours of aggregation; (F) after 9 hours of aggregation; (G) after 3 days of aggregation; (H) after 5 days of aggregation; (I) pluteuslike larva and a smaller aggregate flattened to show details of skeleton. (A–H, from Giudice and Mutolo, 1970; I, from Giudice, 1962a.)

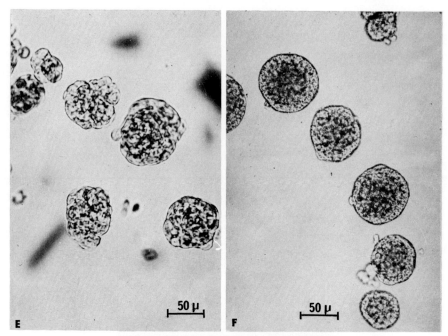

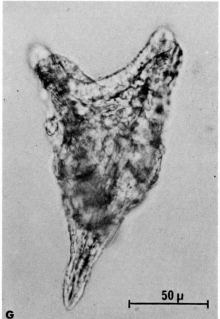

Fig. 6.2E–G

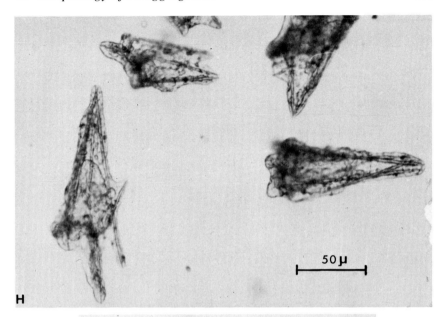

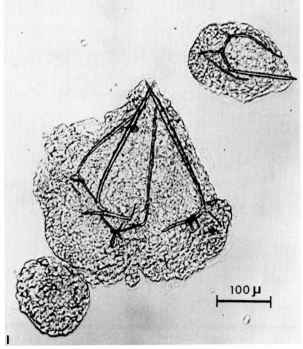

Fig. 6.2H,I

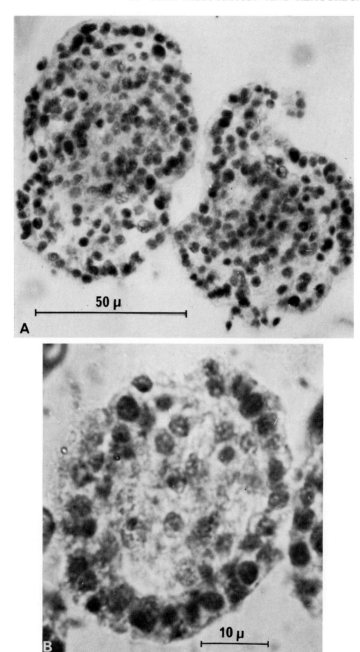

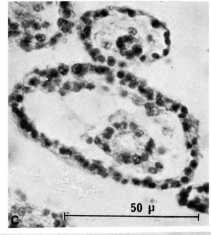

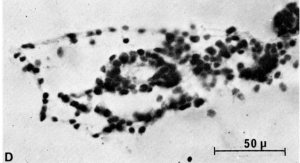

Fig. 6.3. Histological section of reaggregates deriving from cells dissociated from mesenchyme blastulae of *Paracentrotus lividus* (A and D) and *Arbacia lixula* (B and C). (A) after 12 hours of aggregation; (B) after 20 hours of aggregation; (C) after 30 hours of aggregation; (D) after 3 days of aggregation. (From Giudice, 1962a.)

Meanwhile, their edges become more and more regular to form a sharp boundary. After about 9 hours from the beginning of reaggregation, a ciliated epithelium starts to form. At 12 hours, the aggregates look very much like ciliated blastulae, which show very active rotatory movements, especially evident under the stimulus of a slight rise in temperature (Figs. 6.2D–F and 6.3A and B).

An intestinallike cavity is then formed (Fig. 6.3C) probably not through a process of invagination since unequivocal images of invagination have never been observed in histological sections.

The further evolution of the aggregates depends upon the developmental stage of the embryos at the time when disaggregation is performed. The following description applies to cells dissociated from embryos at stages from hatching to early gastrula.

A skeleton appears as the next step in differentiation, in the form of a variable number of irregularly scattered triradiated spiculae, which then elongate to armlike structures. Pigment cells also appear at this time and finally the aggregates closely resemble plutei, though with various abnormalities (Figs. 6.2G–I and 6.3D). These pluteuslike larvae are fed with monocellular algae and kept alive for 2 weeks. Whether or not they are able to undergo metamorphosis still remains to be studied. When cells have been dissociated from embryos at stages from late gastrula up to early prism, the skeleton usually fails to elongate to form armlike structures.

If cells have been dissociated from embryos at stages from late prism to early pluteus, no skeleton is formed by the aggregates.

The size of the aggregates varies with the conditions of aggregation, and gigantic aggregates which form pluteuslike structures of about 1 mm in diameter have been obtained. At first these large aggregates show a polyembryonic appearance, i.e., they contain a lot of intestinal cavities and pieces of skeleton. Eventually, however, they tend to become more regular and originate a truly gigantic larva. The efficiency of cell reaggregation can be close to 100% under optimal conditions, but a certain degree of variability can be noticed with different batches.

b. Self-Aggregation

This method is especially useful for continuous observation of the first phases of reaggregation. Figure 6.4A–H represents photographs of the same field of self-reaggregating cells during the early phases of the process. It can be seen that cell contact involves an increasingly higher number of cells, so that a network of cellular clumps is created. The cellular groups become more and more compact and, as a result, the cellular network breaks up at random points and individual groups are formed of variable sizes and shapes. They will again develop an external ciliated epithelial layer and follow the same differentiation pattern as the rotation-mediated aggregation. The size of these aggregates depends strictly on cell concentration. In a very thick suspension as, for example, at a concentration of about 5×10^6/ml, in an ordinary Syracuse dish, cells reaggregate to form a continuous monolayer, which covers the entire surface of the dish. This aggregate differentiates an external epithelial ciliated border, and if scratches are produced within the context of the aggregate, they will also be lined with ciliated epithelium (Fig. 6.5). This finding suggests that the differentiation of cells toward the ciliated epithelium depends on which side of their surface is not in contact with other cells.

These exceedingly large aggregates will degenerate before undergoing any further differentiation.

2. ELECTRON MICROSCOPIC OBSERVATIONS

As shown in Fig. 6.6, the freshly dissociated cells lose their epithelial appearance and become spherical.

A few minutes after the start of reaggregation, the cells approach each other by means of a flattened portion of their surfaces. Microvilli have never been observed in this process. The portion of the cell surfaces in contact increases with time and, as a result, compact, smooth-surfaced aggregates are formed (Fig. 6.7).

Later, cavities start to appear inside the cytoplasm of the inner cells, while the external ones again acquire an epithelial shape, i.e., their shape becomes cylindrical, the nucleus moves to the basal part of the cell, and microvilli and cilia appear on the external surface, while terminal bars join the outermost part of the adjacent cells. This latter type of junction has been described as one of the three types of intercellular connection of blastulae or gastrulae of *Tripneustes gratilla, Toxopneustes pileolus,* and *Salmacis color,* the other two types being flat surfaces in opposition at 14-nm intervals and interdigitation of cell processes (Balinsky, 1959). By the merging of cytoplasmic cavities of the internal cells, a blastocoel-like cavity is formed again. Some internal cells become arranged to form one or more tubular structures, which will later on open outside and form the intestine (Figs. 6.8 and 6.9) (for details, see Millonig and Giudice (1967) and Giudice and Mutolo (1970).

D. Mechanism of Cell Adhesion

No direct study on the production of extracellular factors for aggregation is available in sea urchin embryos.

An indirect approach has been to block RNA and protein synthesis and to study reaggregation under such conditions (Giudice, 1965). Cells dissociated from mesenchyme blastulae reaggregate as usual in the presence of actinomycin or of puromycin for about 6 hours and 1 hour, respectively. At that time protein synthesis drops to low values and cells spontaneously disaggregate. Unfortunately, the rate of oxygen consumption also drops at the same time, so that it is not possible to draw from these experiments any conclusion about the relevance of protein synthesis in cell adhesion. It was found, however, that upon addition of ethionine (a methionine analog), protein synthesis immediately drops to very low values, while the oxygen consumption declines only slightly in the first 5 hours. Cell reaggregation under these conditions occurs as usual

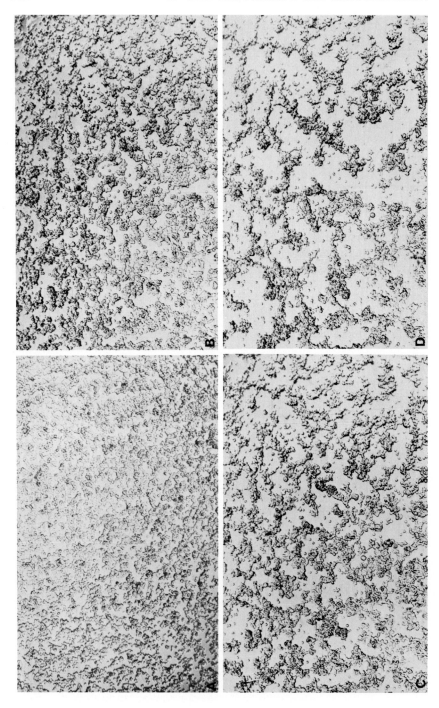

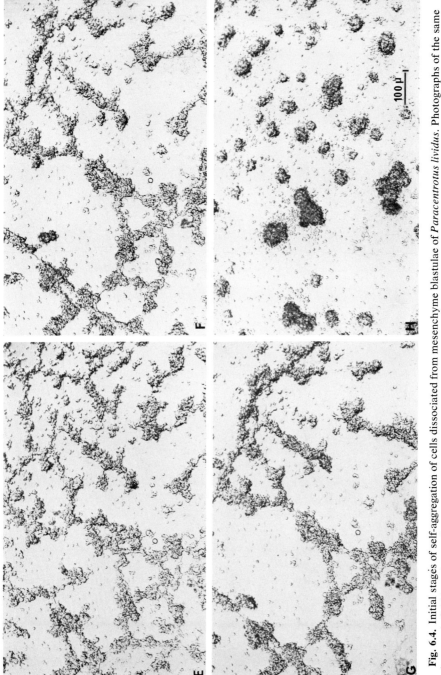

100 µ

Fig. 6.4. Initial stages of self-aggregation of cells dissociated from mesenchyme blastulae of *Paracentrotus lividus*. Photographs of the same microscopic field have been taken at 8-minute intervals starting from 32 minutes after suspension in normal seawater (A–G); H, after 2.5 hours. (From Giudice and Mutolo, 1970.)

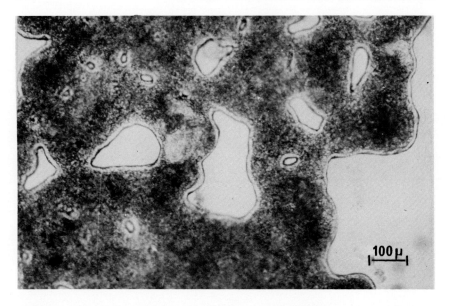

Fig. 6.5. Highly concentrated cells after 20 hours of self-aggregation. (From Giudice and Mutolo, 1970.)

for at least 5 hours. Then disaggregation occurs but, at about the same time, the oxygen consumption also drops.

This latter experiment suggests that the first phases of aggregation may take place also in the absence of protein synthesis in sea urchins. In all the above experiments, controls for permeability to exogenous precursors have not been performed. Since sea urchin cells do not reaggregate in the cold and since reaggregation is blocked by many metabolic inhibitors, the general conclusion can be drawn that reaggregation of embryonic sea urchin cells is a metabolism-dependent process.

The question of cell reaggregation specificity has been investigated only in what concerns species specificity. When the light-yellow cells of embryos of *Paracentrotus lividus* are mixed with the bright-red cells of *Arbacia lixula,* a random aggregation seems to take place at first, but a few hours later the cells from the two sources are sorted out and entirely yellow or entirely red aggregates are formed (Giudice, 1962a).

The problem of organ specificity in reaggregation of sea urchin cells has not been directly approached because of the lack of reliable criteria to distinguish from each other cells dissociated from different territories of an embryo. It is, however, known (see Chapter 1) that the different territories of an embryo are endowed with different protentialities. The question therefore arises as to how cells belonging to different embryonic territories will behave when brought in contact. Will these cells adhere

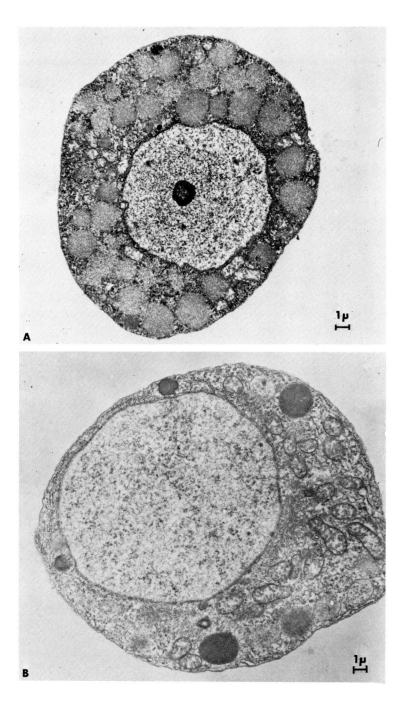

Fig. 6.6. Electron micrographs of freshly dissociated cells from mesenchyme blastulae of *Paracentrotus lividus*. (From Millonig and Giudice, reported by Giudice and Mutolo, 1970.)

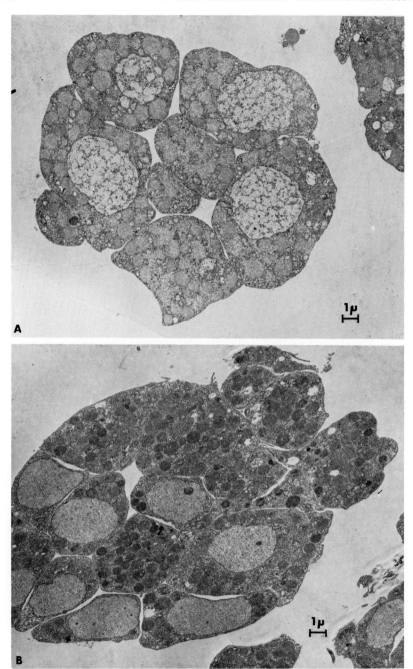

Fig. 6.7. Electron micrographs of cells after 30 minutes (A), and 2 hours (B) of aggregation. (From Millonig and Giudice, reported by Giudice and Mutolo, 1970.)

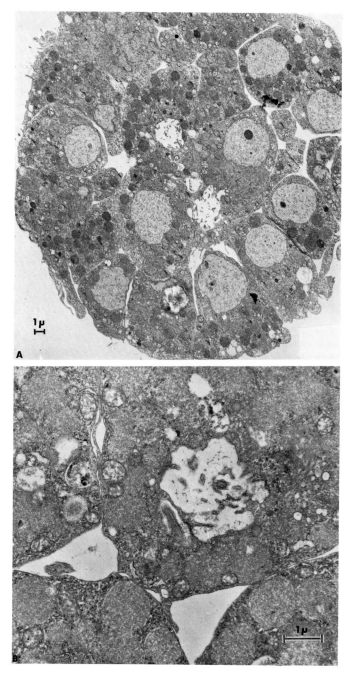

Fig. 6.8. Electron micrographs of aggregates at 7 hours; (B) detail of an intracellular cavity. (From Millonig and Giudice, reported by Giudice and Mutolo, 1970.)

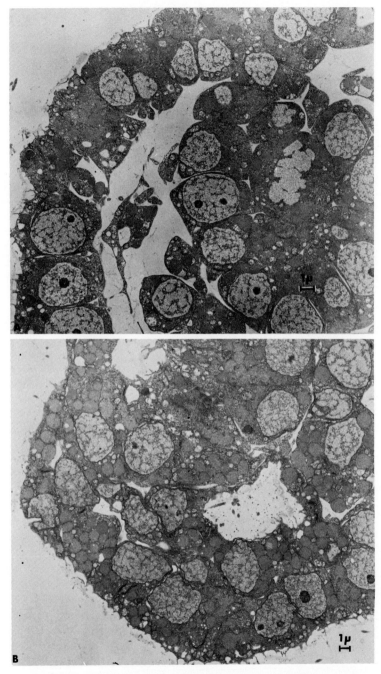

Fig. 6.9. Electron micrographs of aggregates showing successive stages of intestine formation; (D) detail of the intestinal lumen. (From Millonig and Giudice, reported by Giudice and Mutolo, 1970.)

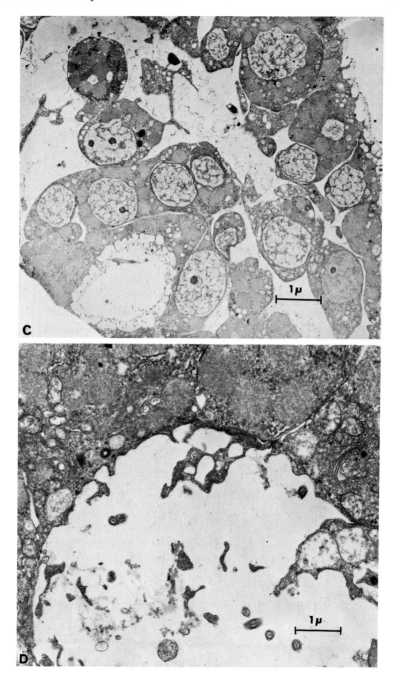

only selectively according to their territorial origin or will they adhere nonspecifically? No definitive answer to this question is available; Giudice (1963) has, however, made the following observations:

1. If embryos have been pretreated with animalizing or vegetalizing agents and then dissociated into cells, either at the blastula stage or when animalization or vegetalization has already been expressed, aggregates are obtained that still retain characteristics of animalization or vegetalization. In the first case, they form hollow spheres with long cilia; in the second, solid spheres with no ectoderm. This shows that at least these chemically induced potentialities are not lost through the disaggregation–reaggregation process.

2. If cells are dissociated from late gastrulae, and then reaggregated, the pigmented cells and skeleton appear in the aggregates earlier than if cells are dissociated from blastulae (Giudice, 1962a). This suggests lack of dedifferentiation during disaggregation–reaggregation.

3. Cells from blastulae, labeled with [³H]thymidine, reaggregate randomly with cells from unlabeled prisms, as clearly shown by autoradiography (Giudice et al., 1969).

These results can be interpreted either by assuming that cells dedifferentiate during disaggregation and reaggregation, or that no strict stage specificity of cell surface arises between the stages of blastula and prism.

E. Metabolic Properties of Reaggregating Cells

The relevance of cell interactions in the appearance of new metabolic patterns during development has been studied in sea urchins by means of dissociation and reaggregation experiments. Several aspects of metabolism have been considered in this respect.

1. PROTEIN SYNTHESIS

As described in Chapter 11, it is well established that the rate of exogenous amino acid incorporation into embryonic proteins of sea urchins undergoes variations during development. A rise has been observed at the mesenchyme blastula stage with a peak around the mid-gastrula stage.

The incorporation curve of freshly dissociated cells, as against the stages at which dissociation is performed, superimposes quite fully the incorporation curve of entire embryos at the different stages (although, under the conditions used, the incorporation rate of the cells is constantly 50% lower than that of the embryos). These results have been interpreted by us as meaning that the cells maintain the incorporation rate characteristic of the stage, through the dissociation process, and therefore do not dedifferentiate in this respect. The overall depression of the incorporation curve of the cells in respect to the embryos may possibly be due to the fact that, in the reported experiment, embryos are dissociated in the presence of citrate and EDTA, which, as found later (Giudice and Mutolo, 1970), somewhat lowers the ability of cells to incorporate amino acids into proteins.

At this point, it is of interest to recall the importance of cell contact in the regeneration of cilia. As discussed in Chapter 11 on protein synthesis, it is experimentally possible to deprive the swimming embryos of their cilia and to obtain cilia regeneration.

Amemiya (1971) has observed that if cells disaggregated from deciliated blastulae are allowed to reaggregate, cilia regeneration takes place. If, on the other hand, the cells are prevented from reaggregating by excessive dilution, no cilia regeneration takes place.

It should be recalled, however, that cilia regeneration does not necessarily imply synthesis of ciliary proteins (see Chapter 11 on protein synthesis).

2. Nucleic Acid Synthesis

a. RNA

As described in Chapter 10, RNA synthesis also undergoes characteristic developmental variations, which render it suitable as a marker for the study of the relevance of cell interaction to the pattern of RNA synthesis.

Since no purified classes of mRNA have been isolated in sea urchin embryos, with the recent possible exception of the mRNA's coding for histones, Giudice and co-workers have focused their attention on the variation in the synthesis rate of ribosomal RNA (rRNA).

The synthesis rate of this RNA has been found to be much higher in stages following the blastula than in earlier stages. The question has been whether or not cells deprived of their normal interaction before the blastula stage are able to undergo an increase in the rRNA synthesis rate at the same time as the control embryos. Two sets of experiments have been performed. In one, embryos are dissociated into cells which are allowed to reaggregate so that they soon regain intercellular contact (but are in the absence of a normal embryonic architecture, still many hours ahead). In the other set, the embryos are dissociated and cells prevented from reaggregating by keeping them overdiluted. In both cases conditions have been used that overcome difficulties caused by possible changes in pool size and permeability to external precursors. It has been found that the permeability of isolated cells to ^{32}P is different when cells are dissociated from different stages (Giudice *et al.*, 1967; Sconzo *et al.*,

1970a,b). The embryos are, therefore, preloaded with ^{32}P up to the moment of dissociation. It has been observed that cell disaggregation does not cause nucleotide leakage from the internal pool, whose specific activity, calculated on the basis of the α-phosphate radioactivity, remains constant and equal to that of the embryos throughout the experiment. Ribosomal RNA synthesis has, therefore, been studied by measuring the time course increase of the specific activity of the 26 S rRNA, under conditions where this latter has previously been shown not to be contaminated with nonribosomal RNA's.

Under such conditions, it has been shown that cells dissociated from hatching blastula and allowed to reaggregate synthesize the same amount of rRNA as the control embryos in the following 14 hours (Fig. 6.10). If cells dissociated at the same stage are prevented from reaggregating, they synthesize somewhat less rRNA than the control embryos, but it can be calculated that they have undergone the same change in the rRNA synthetic rate as the embryos.

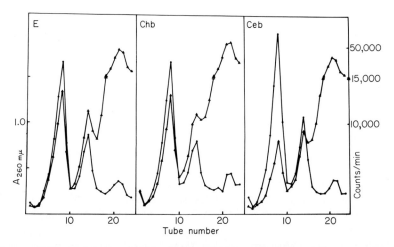

Fig. 6.10. Sucrose density gradient profiles of ribosomal RNA from embryos and re-aggregating cells. The embryos were exposed to ^{32}P from fertilization to 7 hours, then divided into three batches: one was allowed to develop normally (E), the second was immediately dissociated into cells (Chb), and the third was dissociated into cells at the hatching blastula (Ceb). Cell reaggregation was allowed to proceed and, at 24 hours after fertilization, the RNA was extracted from all three batches and the radioactivity accumulated into ribosomal RNA measured (triangles). (Derived from data of Sconzo *et al.,* 1970b.)

These results suggest that no cell interactions, at least from hatching on, are needed for the change in the rRNA synthesis rate to take place. Interestingly enough, when the cells are prevented from reaggregating, their

DNA synthesis stops completely. Even then the variation in the rRNA synthesis rate takes place as usual.

The next question has been whether, during development, cell interaction is ever needed for the acceleration of rRNA synthesis to take place. Embryos have been dissociated into cells at early blastula (3 hours before hatching). The results have not been clear-cut: If cells are allowed to reaggregate, rRNA synthesis increases, but somewhat less than in control embryos (Fig. 6.10). If cells are prevented from reaggregating, little or no rRNA synthesis takes place, but then also protein synthesis is halted.

Shiokawa and Yamana (1967a,b) have reported that cells dissociated from blastulae of *Xenopus laevis* embryos, when reaggregated together with cells from neurulae, are able to inhibit rRNA synthesis in the latter. We have never been able to reproduce a similar phenomenon in sea urchins.

b. DNA

When cells are dissociated at the mesenchyme blastula stage and then allowed to reaggregate, DNA synthesis takes place even if at a lower rate. Judging from the DNA content of embryos and reaggregating cells, it can be calculated that, on the average, 94% of the cells divide in the embryos and 70% in the aggregates over the considered period.

If, on the other hand, cells dissociated from hatching blastulae are prevented from reaggregating by excessive dilution, their DNA synthesis stops completely, as shown by the constancy of their DNA content (Fig. 6.11) and the lack of [^{3}H]thymidine incorporation (Fig. 6.12). We recall here that under these circumstances the cells show plurilobation but are still alive, since they have been shown at least to be able to increase their rRNA synthesis. These observations may be of relevance for the understanding of regulation of DNA synthesis in development through some signal starting from the cell membrane. Experiments in progress by Giudice and co-workers show that if cells dissociated at hatching are kept diluted, their DNA synthesis, as mentioned, is halted. If, however, a treatment with proteolytic agents is performed, aimed at altering the cell membrane, DNA synthesis is resumed.

3. ENZYMATIC ACTIVITY

Various enzymatic activity changes have been described during sea urchin development (see Chapter 12). One of the most striking is the increase in alkaline phosphatase activity. This takes place at the early pluteus stage in *Arbacia punctulata*. The question has been asked as to the importance of cell interaction for this change to take place. As shown

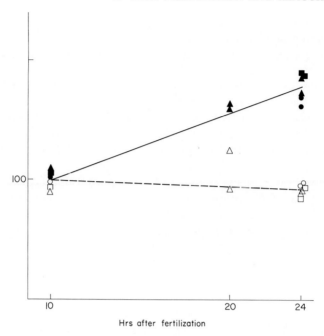

100 ⊢

| | | |
| 10 | 20 | 24 |

Hrs after fertilization

Fig. 6.11. Relative DNA content of normally developing embryos (filled-in symbols) and cells dissociated at the hatching blastula stage and prevented from reaggregating by over-dilution. Each symbol represents a different experiment. (From Sconzo *et al.,* 1970b.)

in Fig. 6.13, if embryos are disaggregated at the turning point of enzyme activity, the reaggregating cells show the same increase in alkaline phosphatase; if, on the other hand, the embryos are disaggregated much earlier, i.e., at the mesenchyme blastula stage, then no increase in enzymatic activity is shown by the aggregating cells when the embryos are late plutei. Only many hours later, when the reaggregating cells have differentiated into pluteuslike structures, does the increase in activity again take place, which, as shown by electron microscopic observations of Millonig and Giudice (unpublished), is mainly localized in the intestinal lumen as well as in the control plutei.

These results have been interpreted by us to mean that some time between the mesenchyme blastula and the early pluteus stage the cells, through a process involving cell interactions, become committed to the increase in alkaline phosphatase activity. If cell interactions are disturbed after the commitment has occurred, then the increase in enzymatic activity takes place as usual. If, on the other hand, cell interactions are interrupted before the commitment has taken place, then increase in alkaline phosphatase activity is temporarily halted, to be resumed when,

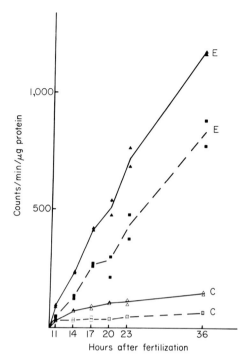

Fig. 6.12. Time course of [³H]thymidine incorporation into DNA of normally developing embryos (filled-in symbols) or cells dissociated at the hatching blastula stage and prevented from reaggregating by overdilution. Triangles, total uptake; squares, incorporation into DNA. (From data of Sconzo *et al.,* 1970b.)

through the process of cell reaggregation, normal cell interactions have been reestablished. The importance of cell interaction in the activity changes of deoxycytidylate aminohydrolase is discussed in Chapter 10.

4. RESPIRATION

The only experiments so far available on cell interaction and respiration are the measurements of the rate of oxygen consumption by Giudice (1965). Figure 6.14 shows that the rate of oxygen consumption of cells freshly dissociated from mesenchyme blastulae does not express a major difference from that of the control embryos, for at least a few hours. Whether or not the changes in the respiratory curve (see Chapter 8) are correlated with cell interactions has not yet been investigated.

Appendix

We have up to now described experiments where dissociation has been performed on embryos at stages from blastula on. In fact, as already

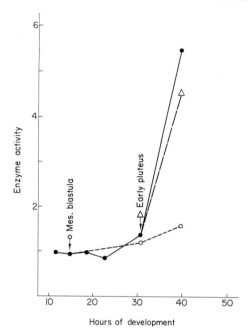

Fig. 6.13. Alkaline phosphatase activity of normal embryos and reaggregating cells. The values have been normalized assuming as 1.0 the value for the swimming blastulae. Control embryos (filled-in circles); cells dissociated from mesenchyme blastulae (open circles); cells dissociated from early plutei (open triangles). The arrows point to the moment of cell dissociation. (From Pfohl and Giudice, 1967.)

mentioned, dissociation methods involving squeezing of the embryos cannot be employed before that stage because the cells are still in the form of relatively large fragile blastomeres which would easily break as a result.

Cell dissociation can, however, be performed in these stages by preliminary removal of the fertilization membrane and stirring of the embryos in calcium-free seawater.

A few words must be said here about the nature of the intracellular contact at stages earlier than blastula.

It has long been proposed that the early blastomeres of sea urchins are joined by thin cytoplasmic threads (Andrews, 1897a,b). This idea has been criticized (Dan and Ono, 1952; K. Dan, 1960). Also Motomura (1941b) has observed that if eggs of *Strongylocentrotus pulcherrimus* are allowed to cleave in calcium-free seawater, they originate two blastomeres which cleave independently, but can still be seen connected by what the author has interpreted as a loose protoplasmic bridge. More recently, however, Vacquier (1968) has presented light and electron microscopic

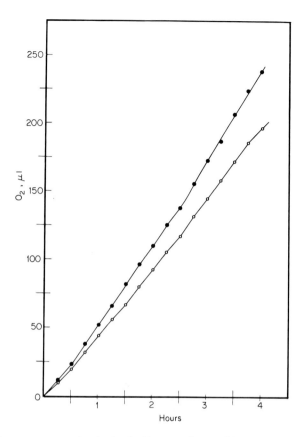

Fig. 6.14. Oxygen consumption by 3 ml of intact embryos (filled-in circles) or of isolated cells (open circles); concentration of protein, 3 mg/ml; temperature, 21°C. (From Giudice, 1965.)

evidence for the presence of filopodia which interconnect the early blastomeres of *Lytechinus anamnesus*. These filopodia are about 17 nm wide, are bounded by unit membranes, and exhibit movements of extension, retraction, and branching, as seen in time-lapse cinematography. No cytoplasmic organelles are found in their context.

The formation of intercellular junctions between blastomeres after telophase has also been described in *Arbacia punctulata* by Goodenough *et al.* (1968). Electrical measurements performed on cleaving *Asterias* and *Echinaracnius* eggs leave it doubtful whether some cytoplasmic continuity is maintained after the first cleavage (Loewenstein, 1967).

On the basis of electron microscope observations, Hagström and Lönning (1969) hold that the micromeres of *Paracentrotus lividus*, *Echinocianus pusillus*, *Psammechinus microtuberculatus*, *Psammechinus miliaris*, and *Strongylocentrotus droebachiensis* fuse with each other during interphase and also form syncytia with the macromeres. They have also declared that micromeres artificially implanted onto macromeres or mesomeres form syncytia with the host cells.

In view of the important implications that these observations might have on the mechanism of embryonic induction brought about by micromeres (see Chapter 1), it would be desirable, even if the pictures presented by Hagström and Lönning seem convincing, that other authors should confirm these observations.

Should they prove correct, we should have to admit that the procedures that lead to micromere isolation involve a breakage of these relatively large cytoplasmic interconnections, followed by an immediate healing of the cell surfaces.

Chemical treatments that interfere with the intercellular connections after the first or second cleavage have been described as leading to the formation of twins or quadruplets (see Chapter 1). To obtain this latter result, however, it is also necessary to alter the hyaline layer which, as stressed by K. Dan (1960) and by Vacquier and Mazia (1968b), has the function of pressing the blastomeres together. This can be achieved by treatment with calcium-free seawater or with proteolytic enzymes. Not very much is known about the chemical composition of this layer, which seems to derive from the cortical granule content (see Chapter 2). It has been suggested that this is constituted by a calcium proteinate (A. R. Moore, 1928, 1949). Vacquier (1969) claims to have isolated the hyaline layer, of which he has performed a preliminary analysis. Citkowitz (1971) has also described a method that yields very clean preparations of hyaline layers from eggs and embryos of *Strongylocentrotus purpuratus, Lytechinus pictus, Arbacia punctulata,* and *Echinaracnius.* It is interesting that the hyaline layers isolated from the gastrula stage clearly show an invagination corresponding to the intestine. This author also reports that the embryos incorporate amino acids into the proteins of the hyaline layer. This incorporation is inhibited by puromycin and, to a much lesser extent, by actinomycin D.

Twins have been obtained (E. B. Harvey, 1940a) by exposing the eggs, soon after the first cleavage, to hypertonic seawater or to a variety of SH-reducing agents such as 0.1 M mercaptoethanol, during spindle formation (Mazia, 1958a, Yuyama, 1971) or to dithiothreitol at 0.05–0.067 M for 10–14 minutes (Vacquier and Mazia, 1968a,b). This latter treatment acts by inhibiting the retraction of filopodia which, together with the external pressure of the hyaline layer, would be the factors that bring the blastomeres into close contact after the cleavage has been completed.

Osanai (1960) has obtained development of eggs of *Hemicentrotus pulcherrimus* or *Glyptocidaris crenularis* parthenogenetically activated but without breakdown of the cortical granules and, therefore, without formation of the hyaline layer. The lack of this latter layer causes an apparent random movement of the blastomeres, with formation of various structures ranging from nondifferentiated cellular masses to fused gigantic plutei.

Methods to isolate micromeres in bulk amounts have been repeatedly described (Lindahl and Kiessling, 1950; Spiegel and Tyler, 1966; Pucci-Minafra *et al.*, 1968; Hynes and Gross, 1970). The method by Hynes and Gross, which allows a good separation of micromeres, mesomeres, and macromeres at the 16-cell stage in *Arbacia punctulata* and *Strongylocentrotus purputatus,* will be briefly described here.

It involves removal of the fertilization membrane according to Tyler and Spiegel (1956) (see Chapter 3); two washings of the embryos at the 16-cell stage with calcium–magnesium-free seawater (CMFSW), and one with CMFSW + 2 mM EDTA; disaggregation in about 10–20 volumes of this latter medium by shaking in the cold for about 30 minutes; layering of 2–5 ml on top of 30 ml of 5–15% linear density gradient of Ficoll in CMFSW, and centrifugation at 250 g for 1 minute. Three bands are obtained, which correspond to micromeres, mesomeres, and macromeres, respectively, from the top. This fractionation procedure can be used up to the morula stage. Experiments of reaggregation of isolated micromeres after isolation in bulk amounts (Pucci-Minafra *et al.*, 1968) have yielded results fundamentally in agreement with those reported by Hörstadius, after manual experiments involving manual isolation. The micromeres reaggregate and cleave to originate solid, roundish masses which do not differentiate the skeleton or external epithelium, at least with the characteristics described by Millonig and Giudice (1967) for aggregates of cells deriving from entire embryos. Interestingly enough, their appearance greatly resembles that reported by Giudice for the reaggregates obtained from chemically vegetalized embryos. Intercellular fusions have been described at the electron microscope level.

In 1947, Dan (reported by K. Dan in 1960) observed that blastomeres, isolated from morulae, reaggregated together to form irregular swimmers. No further investigation of these aggregates was carried out.

Chapter 7

Hybrids

A great deal of work has been carried out on interspecific and inter-genetic hybrids of the sea urchin. Table 7.1 contains an incomplete list of the hybrids found in nature or produced experimentally. Some of them are able to reach larval stage bearing a variable amount of maternal and paternal characters, and even to undergo metamorphosis. Others, known as lethal hybrids, are arrested at an earlier developmental stage.

TABLE 7.1

Hᴀʙʀɪᴅs Fᴏᴜɴᴅ ɪɴ Nᴀᴛᴜʀᴇ ᴏʀ Pʀᴏᴅᴜᴄᴇᴅ Exᴘᴇʀɪᴍᴇɴᴛᴀʟʟʏ

Arbacia lixula ♀ × *Paracentrotus lividus* ♂ = pluteus (1)[a]

Arbacia punctulata ♀ × *Echinaracnius parma* ♂ = pluteus (2,3); × *Lytechinus variegatus* ♂ = pluteus (4); × *Mellita pentafora* ♂ = pluteus (5); × *Moira atropos* ♂ = pluteus (5); × *Strongylocentrotus dröbachiensis* ♂ = pluteus (2)

Asterias forbesii ♀ × *Arbacia punctulata* ♂ = a few gastrulae (6)

Cidaris tribuloides ♀ × *Lytechinus variegatus* ♂ = gastrula (7); × *Tripneustes esculentus* ♂ = gastrula (7)

Echinaracnius parma ♀ × *Arbacia punctulata* ♂ = pluteus (2,3); × *Strongylocentrotus dröbachiensis* ♂ = pluteus (2)

Echinometra mathaei ♀ × *Comatula pectinata* ♂ = blastula (24); × *Comatula purpurea* ♂ = blastula (24)

Echinus acutus ♀ × *Echinus esculentus* ♂ = pluteus (8); × *Psammechinus miliaris* ♂ = pluteus (8)

Hybrids

TABLE 7.1 *(Continued)*

Echinus esculentus ♀ × *Echinus acutus* ♂ = pluteus (8); × *Psammechinus miliaris* ♂ = pluteus (8)

Lytechinus (Toxopneustes) variegatus ♀ × *Arbacia punctulata* ♂ = pluteus (4); × *Mellita pentafora* ♂ = pluteus (5); × *Moira atropos* ♂ = pluteus (5); × *Tripneustes (Hipponoe) esculentus* ♂ = pluteus (5)

Mellita pentafora ♀ × *Moira atropos* ♂ = pluteus (5)

Moira atropos ♀ × *Tripneustes esculentus* ♂ = pluteus (5)

Paracentrotus lividus ♀ × *Arbacia lixula* ♂ = gastrula (9–12,25,26); × *Psammechinus microtuberculatus* ♂ = pluteus (1); × *Sphaerechinus granularis* ♂ = pluteus (9, 13)

Psammechinus microtuberculatus ♀ × *Arbacia lixula* ♂ = gastrula (9); × *Paracentrotus lividus* ♂ = pluteus (25)

Psammechinus miliaris ♀ *Arbacia lixula* ♂ = gastrula (12); × *Echinus acutus* ♂ = pluteus (8); × *Echinus esculentus* ♂ = pluteus (8)

Sphaerechinus granularis ♀ × *Paracentrotus lividus* ♂ = pluteus (13,14)

Strongylocentrotus franciscanus ♀ × *Asterias ochracea* ♂ = pluteus (15); × *Strongylocentrotus purpuratus* ♂ = pluteus (15–19)

Strongylocentrotus pallidus ♀ × *Strongylocentrotus dröbachiensis* ♂ (or vice versa) = pluteus (20)

Strongylocentrotus purpuratus ♀ × *Asterias ochracea* ♂ = pluteus (15); × *Dendraster excentricus* ♂ = pluteus (21,22); × *Strongylocentrotus franciscanus* ♂ = pluteus (2, 16–19,23)

Tripneustes (Hipponoë) esculentus ♀ × *Lytechinus variegatus* ♂ = pluteus (5)

---

[a] Key: (1) Baltzer *et al.* (1961); (2) E. B. Harvey (1942); (3) Matsui (1924); (4) Tennent (1912b,c); (5) Tennent (1910); (6) Morgan (1893; questioned by Mathews, 1901); (7) Tennent (1922); (8) Shearer *et al.* (1913); (9) Whiteley and Baltzer (1958); Baltzer *et al.* 1954, 1959); Baltzer and Bernhard (1955); Baltzer and Chen (1960); Chen and Baltzer (1962); (10) Ficq and Brachet (1963); (11) Hagström (1959); (12) S. Denis (1968); H. Denis and Brachet (1969a,b); (13) Vernon (1900); (14) Steinbruck (1902); (15) Hagedorn (1909); (16) Swan (1953); (17) J. Loeb *et al.* (1910); (18) Barrett and Angelo (1969); (19) Chafee and Mazia (1963); (20) Vasseur (1952c); (21) Flickinger (1957); (22) Moore (1957); (23) Moore (1943); (24) Tennent (1929); (25) Harding and Harding (1952a,b); Harding *et al.* (1954, 1955); (26) Geuskens (1968a).

The inheritance of paternal or maternal morphological characters in the hybrids of sea urchin embryos has long been the object of experimental investigation and controversies (see, for example, Boveri, 1889, 1903; Vernon, 1900; Hagedorn, 1909; Baltzer, 1910; Loeb *et al.*, 1910; Tennent, 1910, 1911, 1912a,b,c, 1913, 1922, 1929; Shearer *et al.*, 1913; Matsui, 1924; E. B. Harvey, 1942; Moore, 1957; Chaffee and Mazia, 1963).

Generally speaking, in some combinations hybrids reach pluteic stage with a maternal appearance, on the basis of morphological observations (e.g., crosses between *Strongylocentrotus purpuratus* and *Strongylocentrotus franciscanus;* Harvey, 1942). In other combinations, however, the morphological characters are intermediate (Hörstadius, 1936b; Moore, 1943).

A. Cross-Fertilization

Experimental cross-fertilization offers some difficulties. It has, however, been successfully performed in several cases. Table 7.2 reports one

TABLE 7.2

SUCCESSFUL ECHINODERM CROSS-FERTILIZATIONS[a]

Arbacia punctulata ♀
 × *Mellita pentapora* ♂ (Tennent)
 × *Moira atropos* ♂ (Tennent)

Arbacia pustulosa ♀
 × *Dorocidaris* ♂ (Vernon)
 × *Echinocardium* ♂ (Stassano)
 × *Echinus* ♂ (Driesch, Stassano, Vernon)
 × *Sphaerechinus* ♂ (Driesch, Hertwig, Stassano)
 × *Strongylocentrotus* ♂ (Driesch, Hertwig, Vernon)

Asteracanthion berylinus ♀
 × *Asteracanthion pallidus* ♂ (Agassiz)

Asterias forbesii ♀
 × *Arbacia pustulata* ♂ (Morgan)

Dorocidaris ♀
 × *Strongylocentrotus* ♂ (Vernon)

Echinocardium cordatum ♀
 × *Arbacia pustulosa* ♂ (Stassano, Vernon)
 × *Echinus* ♂ (Vernon)
 × *Sphaerechinus* ♂ (Stassano, Vernon)
 × *Strongylocentrotus* ♂ (Vernon)

Echinocardium mediterraneum ♀
 × *Echinus* ♂ (Vernon)
 × *Sphaerechinus* ♂ (Vernon)
 × *Strongylocentrotus* ♂ (Vernon)

Echinus acutus ♀
 × *Arbacia* ♂ (Vernon)
 × *Sphaerechinus* ♂ (Vernon)

Echinus microtuberculatus ♀
 × *Arbacia* ♂ (Driesch, Vernon)
 × *Echinocardium* ♂ (Stassano, Vernon)
 × *Echinus acutus* ♂ (Vernon)
 × *Strongylocentrotus* ♂ (Driesch, Hertwig. Vernon)
 × *Sphaerechinus* ♂ (Driesch. Morgan. Vernon)

Hipponoē ♀ (= *Tripneustes*)
 × *Cidaris* ♂ (Tennent)
 × *Ophiocoma* ♂ (Tennent)
 × *Pentaceros* ♂ (Tennent)
 × *Toxopneustes* ♂ (Tennent)

Mellita ♀
 × *Moira* ♂ (Tennent)

Moira ♀
 × *Arbacia* ♂ (Tennent)
 × *Mellita* ♂ (Tennent)
 × *Toxopneustes* ♂ (Tennent)

TABLE 7.2 *(Continued)*

Psammechinus miliaris ♀ × *Asterias rubens* ♂ (Giard)	× *Dorocidaris* ♂ (Köhler, Vernon) × *Echinus* ♂ (Driesch, Vernon) × *Psammechinus* ♂ (Köhler)

Psammechinus (pulchellus) ♀
  × *Spatangus* ♂ (Köhler)
  × *Sphaerechinus* ♂ (Köhler)
  × *Strongylocentrotus* ♂ (Köhler)
	× *Spatangus* ♂ (Köhler)
	× *Sphaerechinus* ♂ (Hertwig, Köhler,
	  Morgan, Vernon)

Spatangus ♀
  × *Strongylocentrotus* ♂ (Köhler)
  × *Psammechinus* ♂ (Köhler)
	Strongylocentrotus purpuratus ♀
	  × *Asterias capitata* ♂ (Loeb)
	  × *Asterias ochracea* ♂ (Hagedorn,
	  Loeb)

Sphaerechinus ♀
  × *Echinus* ♂ (Driesch, Hertwig,
  Morgan, Vernon)
  × *Psammechinus* ♂ (Stassano)
  × *Strongylocentrotus* ♂ (Driesch,
  Hertwig, Marion, Morgan, Stein-
  brück, Vernon)
  × *Antedon* ♂ (Godlewski)
	× *Asterina* ♂ (Loeb)
	× *Chlorostoma* ♂ (Loeb)
	× *Mytilus* ♂ (Kupelwieser)
	× *Pycnopodia* ♂ (Loeb)

	Toxopneustes ♀
	  × *Echinaster* ♂ (Tennent)
	  × *Hipponoë* ♂ (Tennent)
	  × *Holothuria floridana* ♂ (Tennent)
	  × *Mellita* ♂ (Tennent)
	  × *Moira* ♂ (Tennent)

Strongylocentrotus lividus ♀ × *Arbacia* ♂ (Driesch, Vernon)	

[a] From Tennent (1910).

of the earliest lists of cross-fertilization, compiled by Tennent. We have discussed in Chapter 3 the role of the egg envelopes and egg surface in the maintenance of the species specificity of fertilization. Several attempts have been made to force the species barrier in order to obtain cross-fertilization. One of such approaches has been that of altering the egg surface or the egg coats by treatment with proteolytic enzymes (Hultin, 1948a,b; Bohus-Jensen, 1953; Tyler and Metz, 1955). Other attempts have consisted in the removal of the jelly coat (Harding and Harding, 1952b; Hagström, 1956b,c); modification of the egg surface by addition of bovine serum albumin or amino acids (Runnström *et al.*, 1946); pretreatment of the eggs with egg water of the heterologous species either alone or in combination with other treatments, i.e., with glycine or sodium periodate (Hultin, 1948b; Harding and Harding, 1952b). A review of the old literature on the subject is given by Elster (1935). Among the most recent works attempting to clarify the nature of the barrier to heterologous spermatozoa, we mention that of Hagström (1956a,b,c, 1959). In the opinion of most of the authors, as already discussed (Chapter 3), enzy-

matic treatments would produce their effect by removing the vitelline
membrane. Hagström, on the other hand, stresses the fact that, at least in
some species, the jelly coat already represents a first obstacle to a
heterologous spermatozoon. He also criticizes the idea that the vitelline
membrane is the site of action where trypsin destroys the species specificity of fertilization, on the basis of the observation that the concentrations of crystalline trypsin needed to increase cross-fertilization are far
above the level of those needed to destroy the vitelline membrane, i.e.,
above those needed to impair the elevation of the fertilization membrane
and to permit polyspermy. He also points out that some treatments involving alkalinization to increase cross-fertilization (Tennent, 1910,
1923; Loeb, 1913, 1915; Baltzer and Bernhard, 1955) might act merely
on sperm, whose ability to cross-fertilize is increased up to pH 9.5. The
main conclusion from Hagström's work is that "a rather deep going
destruction of the egg surface is a prerequisite to an increased capacity
for cross fertilization." In our opinion, the only conclusion that can
safely be drawn from this work cannot go farther than the vague state-
ment of Hagström that "the protecting mechanism to hybridation may
depend upon specific properties of both egg and sperm in an inability of
the sperm to induce a cortical reaction in the surface of the heterologous
egg."

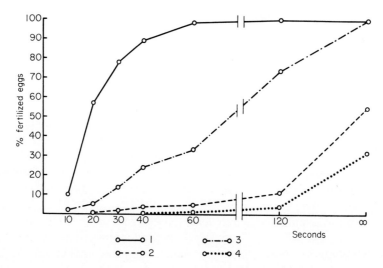

Fig. 7.1. An example of "easy" cross-fertilization between jelly-free eggs of *Psam-mechinus microtuberculatus* and sperm (at 5×10^5/ml) of *Paracentrotus lividus*. 1. Control, *Psammechinus* ♀ × *Psammechinus* ♂; 2. the eggs were pretreated for 10 minutes in 0.001% trypsin, *Psammechinus* ♀ × *Psammechinus* ♂; 3. *Psammechinus* ♀ × *Paracentrotus* ♂; 4. the eggs were pretreated for 10 minutes in 0.001% trypsin, *Psammechinus* ♀ × *Para-centrotus* ♂. (From Hagström, 1959.)

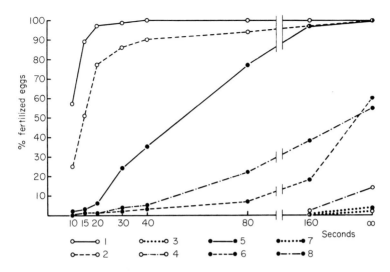

Fig. 7.2. Examples of "difficult" cross-fertilizations between jelly-free eggs from *Paracentrotus lividus* and *Sphaerechinus granularis*. The concentration of sperm was 6.6 × 10⁵/ml. 1. *Paracentrotus* × *Paracentrotus;* 2. eggs from *Paracentrotus* pretreated for 10 minutes in 0.001% trypsin, insemination with sperm from *Paracentrotus;* 3. *Paracentrotus* × *Sphaerechinus* male; 4. eggs from *Paracentrotus* pretreated for 10 minutes in 0.001% trypsin, insemination with sperm from *Sphaerechinus;* 5. *Sphaerechinus* × *Sphaerechinus;* 6. eggs from *Sphaerechinus* pretreated for 10 minutes in 0.001% trypsin, insemination with sperm from *Sphaerechinus;* 7. *Sphaerechinus* × *Paracentrotus* male; 8. eggs from *Sphaerechinus* pretreated for 10 minutes in 0.001% trypsin, insemination with sperm from *Paracentrotus.* (From Hagström, 1959.)

Electron microscopic demonstration of the fusion of the egg plasma membrane with the sperm plasma membrane (see Chapter 3) provides the anatomical basis of a phenomenon for which a specific interaction with a specific matching at the molecular level may be needed. Rothschild (1956) has compared the plasma membrane of egg and sperm to a three-dimensional "jig-saw puzzle, made of rubber and containing very weak magnets." The magnets may be represented by a variety of physicochemical forces (van der Waals forces, electric charges, hydrogen bonds). One effect of trypsin or of other treatments aiming at increasing cross-fertilization might be envisaged as that of a flame melting part of the surface of the jigsaw puzzle, thus permitting less accurate, but less specific matching of surfaces.

We do not wish to close this introduction by leaving the reader with the impression that cross-fertilization with the above means is always an easy task to accomplish. In our experience, it may undergo remarkable variability; very often it leaves a more or less important percent of unfertilized eggs. As an example, the success of cross-fertilization in a so-called "easy" crossing and two "difficult" crossings is reported in Figs. 7.1 and 7.2.

B.   Some Interesting Features of the Physiology of Hybrids

1. DEVELOPMENT

Among the most thorough studies on the physiology of hybrids, that of Whiteley and Baltzer (1958) is worth mentioning.

These authors provide a very careful description of the morphology of the hybrid *Paracentrotus lividus* ♀ × *Arbacia lixula* ♂. These hybrids develop almost normally until the formation of the primary mesenchyme. Thereafter, severe disturbances are observed and gastrulation as a rule is not accomplished. Part of the embryos, however, remain viable even if their development has halted, and can be purified by decanting, or sucking with a large pipette the ones that are able to swim toward the surface. A few embryos succeed in developing up to a prism or pluteus stage, even if with defects. They show a morphology which, mainly from the characteristics of the skeleton, can be judged as intermediate between those of the parental species.

The authors stress the importance of the stage of gastrulation as a turning point of development. This consideration goes back to the experiments of Boveri (1918) in which the merogonic hybrid *Sphaerechinus* ♀ × *Paracentrotus* ♂ also stops developing at gastrulation (see also von Ubisch, 1954). Boveri's comment that up to this stage the eggs are able to develop with any kind of nucleus fits in with our current views on the need for the synthesis of new RNA after fertilization for development to proceed beyond the mesenchyme blastula stage (see Chapter 10). It seems that these old observations can now be expressed in modern terms by stating that any disturbance of RNA synthesis in the period between fertilization and the gastrula stage brings about, as a first sign of developmental abnormalities, an alteration of the process of mesenchyme formation and the arrest of gastrulation.

An ultrastructural study of the same hybrids (Geuskens, 1968a) has revealed a delay in the formation of a typical ergastoplasm and in the appearance of projections of the nuclear membrane bearing attached ribosomes.

2. RESPIRATION

Respiration is the second aspect of the physiology of the *Paracentrotus* × *Arbacia* (PA) hybrid studied by Baltzer and his colleagues. The rate of oxygen consumption in the *Paracentrotus* × *Paracentrotus* (PP) embryos shows a rather continuous increase from early cleavage to pluteus, with the exception of a period when the respiration rate is steady, i.e., at hatching (see also Chapter 8). The same increase in respiration rate is observed during the development of the *Arbacia* × *Arbacia* (AA) embryos, at corresponding stages, except that the overall rate is about 50% lower than that of the PP embryos. The PA hybrids show values close to the maternal ones during 8 hours, i.e., shortly before hatching, and then reach a level that, in the surviving hybrids, stays halfway between the parental ones (Fig. 7.3). This observation is in close agreement with the results by Giudice *et al.* (1968), who found that an inhibition of RNA synthesis does not affect the respiration rate till hatching, but then prevents the rise in respiration rate that accompanies gastrulation (see Chapter 8).

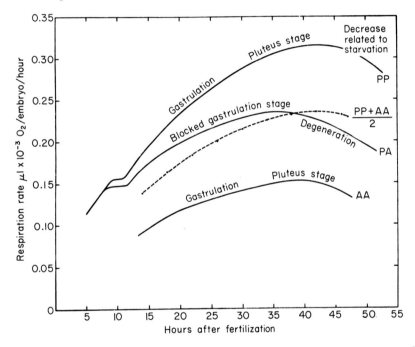

Fig. 7.3. Comparison of theoretical and actual respiratory rates of *Paracentrotus* ♀ × *Arbacia* ♂ hybrids. In addition to the actual respiratory rates for PP, PA, and AA, a curve of the average of PP and AA rates, representing the rate expected from a theoretical hybrid receiving equal contributions from each parent, is indicated by the broken line. (From Whiteley and Baltzer, 1958.)

Here again the need for gene expression becomes apparent only at the moment of mesenchyme formation. Nothing is known about the mechanisms by which the collaboration of the two parental genomes results in an "averaged" effect on the respiration rate. It is worth noting that both parental chromosomal haploid sets are retained by the PA hybrids throughout development (Baltzer *et al.,* 1954; Chen *et al.,* 1961; Baltzer and Bernhard, 1955).

Whiteley and Baltzer (1958) observe that since the rate of development is much slower in the PA hybrids than in either of the parental embryos, it follows that the amount of oxygen used by the hybrids to cover a certain developmental period is higher than that of either parents. The authors make the generic suggestion that this might reflect the "incompatibility between nucleus and cytoplasm" in the hybrid.

3. DNA

The last parameter studied by Whiteley and Baltzer (1958) on these hybrids has been DNA synthesis. This proceeds in the AA embryos at a lower rate than in the PP embryos between the gastrula and prism stages, so that each AA pluteus contains 44% of the DNA of a PP pluteus of corresponding age. The *Paracentrotus* ♀ × *Arbacia* ♂ embryos show intermediate values at the gastrula stage.

In another hybrid, *Paracentrotus lividus* ♀ × *Sphaerechinus granularis* ♂, in the period between 15 and 35 hours after fertilization, i.e., when the hybrid is a stereoblastula or a stereogastrula and the controls go from early gastrulae to plutei, the DNA content is about 50–62% that of the PP control (Chen *et al.,* 1961). A decrease in DNA content of the hybrids is to be expected since all but 3 to 4 of the paternal chromosomes are eliminated by the fourth cleavage (Baltzer, 1910).

The crosses reciprocal to the described ones show different behavior with respect to DNA synthesis: In the combination *Arbacia lixula* ♀ × *Paracentrotus lividus* ♂, the DNA content is at first similar to the maternal one, but after 25 hours it is only 50% that of the AA embryos. In the combination *Sphaerechinus* ♀ × *Paracentrotus* ♂, on the other hand, the DNA content remains normal throughout development (Chen and Baltzer, 1962). In disagreement with earlier cytological observations on the constancy of the paternal chromosomes throughout the development of the hybrid *Paracentrotus lividus* ♀ × *Arbacia lixula* ♂ (Baltzer, 1910), are the observations by Denis and Brachet (1969a,b) that the hybrids arrested at the blastula stage contain 2.5 more maternal than paternal DNA. This conclusion is drawn from the fact that the hybrid DNA reanneals at an efficiency of 1.7 times higher with *Paracentrotus* DNA than with *Arbacia* DNA: it is known that PP DNA reanneals 7 times more efficiently with homologous than with heterologous DNA, while AA DNA reanneals 10 times more efficiently with homologous than with heterologous DNA.

This discrepancy might be only an apparent one. Actually, Baltzer himself has suggested that some of the hybrids may lose some of the paternal chromosomes between the blastula and gastrula stage (Baltzer, 1910). As Denis and Brachet point out, the DNA–DNA reannealing under the conditions used is probably restricted to the repetitive sequences of DNA. There is, however, no reason to believe that such sequences might be preferentially replicated in either genome. Brachet and Hulin (1970), by cytochemical methods and cytophotometric analysis of *Paracentrotus* ♀ × *Arbacia* ♂ embryos, have concluded that nuclear abnormalities, including chromosome elimination, take place after hatching, so that the resulting aneuploidy could be considered the initial cause of lethality. In addition, the autoradiographic studies of Ficq and Brachet (1963) show some abnormalities in the incorporation of labeled thymidine in the nuclei of the hybrids *Arbacia lixula* ♀ × *Paracentrotus lividus* ♂ which, in the author's opinion, are consistent with the hypothesis of some chromatin elimination into the cytoplasm. The label accumulated in the nuclei of the hybrids is, in fact, less stable than that incorporated in the DNA of the controls. Furthermore, after a pulse with thymidine, part of the label is found in the cytoplasm; this never happens in the controls. Nothing is known about the mechanism(s) that bring about the disturbance of DNA synthesis in the PA hybrid. As shown by S. Denis (1968), the hypothesis of a defect of NADPH production after gastrulation, which in the hybrids might impair the reduction of the ribose to deoxyribose, should be discarded. Determinations performed by this author show that 8 hours after gastrulation the NADPH level is higher in the PA hybrid than in the PP control. The most recent study on DNA synthesis in the hybrid *Strongylocentrotus purpuratus* ♀ × *Dendraster excentricus* ♂ was done by Brookbank (1970). The time of S_1 is different for the two parental species. The behavior of thymidine incorporation in the hybrid is such as to lead the author to suggest that each chromosomal set initiates the first round of DNA synthesis according to its parental characteristic, i.e., before the fusion of the pronuclei (*Dendraster*) or after their fusion (*Strongylocentrotus*). Later on, the timing of DNA synthesis would be dictated by the cytoplasm. It seems desirable, however, that such a favorable theory be supported by a higher number of experimental observations than those produced by the author.

4. RNA

It was noted long ago that in both the *Paracentrotus* × *Arbacia* and *Paracentrotus* × *Sphaerechinus* hybrids, the RNA content remains equal to the maternal one, despite the fact that as development proceeds the DNA content of the hybrids becomes lower than that of the controls (Chen *et al.,* 1961). The earlier attempts to explain this fact in terms of rate of RNA synthesis (Chen and Baltzer, 1962) now have chiefly a historical value. The explanation of this constancy appears to us very simple nowadays if one considers that: (1) As has long been known, the total RNA content of the embryo does not vary appreciably from fertilization through pluteus stage (Chen *et al.,* 1961); (2) most cellular RNA in sea urchins is represented by ribosomal RNA; (3) the latter is stored in the egg during oogenesis and the amount of it that is synthesized thereafter is, at least till the prism stage, no more than 10% of the preexisting one (Sconzo *et al.,* 1970a). An arrest of RNA synthesis would, therefore, not bring about any appreciable reduction in the total amount of RNA per embryo, at least until the prism stage. Actually, in the pioneering work of Chen and Baltzer (1962) and of Markman (1961b), a certain decrease of the rate of incorporation of labeled nucleosides in the total RNA is reported. We believe that those results are open to the interpretation that postgastrular RNA synthesis is strongly reduced in the lethal hybrids and that the incorporation mainly represents the very active terminal turnover of transfer RNA.

The cytological observation (Brachet and Hulin, 1970) that larger and more stainable nucleoli appear in the lethal hybrids than in the controls might also be interpreted as an impairment of the nucleolar processing of ribosomal RNA.

Some direct information on RNA synthesis in the hybrid *Arbacia lixula* ♀ × *Paracentrotus lividus* ♂ comes from the work of Denis and Brachet (1969b). These authors have analyzed with MAK columns the RNA extracted by SDS and phenol, at room temperature, from embryos that had been exposed for variable periods of time to 100 μCi/ml of either [³H]uridine or ³²P. The authors' conclusion is that after the gastrula stage, as one would expect, there is an impairment in the overall RNA synthesis rate in the hybrids with respect to the controls; before the gastrula stage, on the other hand, the RNA synthesis rate is similar for the hybrids and the controls. A close examination, however, of the data presented suggests to us that also before the gastrula stage the hybrids show a diminished rate of incorporation of precursors into RNA. In any case, before these data can be definitively accepted as a measure of the RNA synthesis rate, data on permeability and pool size are needed. In an attempt to investigate the nature of the genetic product of the hybrids, Denis and Brachet have studied the efficiency of hybridization of the RNA synthesized by these embryos with either paternal or maternal DNA. The results have shown that the RNA of the hybrid, especially the class(es) of high molecular weight and with a high rate of labeling, hybridize better with the paternal DNA. This is apparently in contrast with the observation of the same authors that the hybrid contains more maternal DNA. The explanations proposed are two: (1) The paternal DNA, even if less represented, is transcribed more extensively or more rapidly; (2) the labeled RNA of maternal type becomes diluted in the cold preexisting RNA of the egg. This does not happen to the RNA of paternal type. The latter hypothesis seems to us the more probable since it has been proved (Glisin *et al.,* 1966; Whiteley *et al.,* 1966, 1970) that part of the RNA synthesized during development is homologous to the one that the egg has accumulated during oogenesis. This hypothesis, however, is rejected by the authors with the argument that such a dilution effect should affect relatively more the level of the plateau of DNA saturation than the hybridization level at lower RNA input.

An interesting feature of RNA metabolism in the lethal hybrid *Arbacia lixula* ♀ × *Paracentrotus lividus* ♂ has been revealed by the autoradiographic studies of Ficq and Brachet (1963). The label by [³H]uridine is accumulated mainly in the nuclei by the control embryos at stages from 4 blastomeres to blastula. At this stage, a cytoplasmic labeling also becomes prominent. While the nuclear labeling appears normal in the hybrids, labeling of the cytoplasm at the blastula stage is never observed. Moreover, if a chase at the blastula stage is performed in the control embryos, some radioactivity is lost by the nuclei in favor of the cytoplasm. If such a chase is performed in the hybrid blastulae, the only effect observed is a further accumulation of radioactivity in the nuclei without any cytoplasmic labeling. The suggestion of the authors is that the hybrids may fail to transfer their RNA from nuclei to cytoplasm.

5. PROTEINS

The concept already expressed that new RNA is needed after the mesenchyme blastula stage, is supported, among other things, by experiments concerning the apperance of antigens of paternal type in the hybrids. Harding *et al.* (1954) have shown that paternal antigens appear in the hybrid *Paracentrotus lividus* ♀ × *Psammechinus microtuberculatus* ♂ by late mesenchyme blastula stage. Moreover, it should be noted that even a normal embryo translates messages different from the maternal ones (i.e., the ones already contained in the unfertilized egg) at the gastrula stage. This is also supported by the finding that new antigens appear in sea urchin embryos after gastrulation (Perlmann and Gustafson, 1948; Perlmann, 1953; Ishida and Yasumasu, 1957).

Of course, as noted in Chapter 11, this does not necessarily mean that no new protein species are synthesized before the gastrula stage. It is interesting to mention here the work of Badman and Brookbank (1970), who have found that in both the intergeneric hybrid *Lytechinus variegatus* ♀ × *Tripneustes esculentus* ♂ and the interordinal hybrid *Strongylocentrotus purpuratus* ♀ × *Dendraster excentricus* ♂, the paternal influence is demonstrable because of the developmental rate and morphological features. The authors have, however, failed to show any major new class of antigen arising during development of the normal embryos or any paternal antigen in the hybrids, in spite of the very sensitive tests effected, such as the Outcherlony analysis, immunoelectrophoresis, and passive cutaneous anaphylaxis. This fact has led the authors to conclude (in agreement with what is discussed in Chapter 11 on protein synthesis) that the amount of new protein species synthesized during development must be rather small with respect to the bulk proteins continuously synthesized. The question, therefore, arises: Are these few new proteins really of primary importance in the regulation of differentiation, or are other mechanisms, not involving the appearance of new protein species, more relevant in that respect? It should be recalled that the lack of appearance of new protein species does not imply that gene control is not operating during differentiation. Besides the consideration that small amounts of new proteins might play a key regulatory role, it might well be that the switching on of one gene to synthesize more of a certain protein, already present in the cytoplasm, is of primary importance for the regulation of differentiation. Moreover, Ševaljević et al. (1971; Ševaljević and Ruzdijic, 1971) have observed that only 3–6% of the cytoplasmic proteins of *Arbacia lixula* embryos is precipitated by homologous antisera, and that the soluble cytoplasm contains only a minor fraction of the radioactive amino acids incorporated during embryogenesis. If these data are accepted, instead of those by Westin et al. (1967), who reported that 50% of the cytoplasmic newly synthesized proteins is immunoprecipitable, then it follows that experiments performed with antibodies tell us only about a very minor fraction of the protein synthetic activity of the embryo.

The only available data on the rate of protein synthesis in hybrids are those of Ficq and Brachet (1963) on the lethal hybrid *Paracentrotus lividus* ♀ × *Arbacia lixula* ♂. The results suggest a lower rate of incorporation of amino acids into proteins in the hybrids than in the controls. They are, however, based only on autoradiographic observations. Unpublished work of O'Dell (personal communication) shows that the hybrid (PA) synthesizes paternal antigens at the same rate as *Arbacia* haploids and at half the rate of the *Arbacia* diploids.

Among the criteria used to judge the paternal or maternal inheritance in the hybrid are those of the amino acid and peptide pools. These have been shown to differ characteristically among the species (Chen and Baltzer, 1958; Chen, 1958). This pattern has been found entirely of maternal type in the combinations *Paracentrotus* ♀ × *Arbacia* ♂ and *Sphaerechinus* ♀ × *Paracentrotus* ♂.

It might be supposed that such a pool is in any case provided by the cytoplasm of the egg and not by the sperm. It is, however, subjected to continuous renewal, for it is rapidly incorporated into proteins and re-furnished presumably by the yolk.

6. ENZYMATIC ACTIVITIES

As already observed for the respiratory rate, the enzymatic activities too can show in hybrid embryos an "average" expression of the parental genomes: The enzymatic activity of the alkaline phosphatase in the hybrid *Strongylocentrotus purpuratus* ♀ × *Dendraster excentricus* ♂ shows, at the prism stage, values intermediate between the parental ones (Flickinger, 1957) (Fig. 7.4). It seems that the study of the regulation of such enzymatic activity might provide an opportunity for understanding the mechanism of genetic control far better than that of respiration. This enzymatic activity is in fact brought about by a single protein, while the respiratory rate results from a series of metabolic reactions.

Fedecka-Brunner and Epel (1969) have reported that, in the hybrid *Allocentrotus fragilis* × *Strongylocentrotus purpuratus,* the enzymatic activity of the arylsulfatase reaches values intermediate between the paternal and maternal ones (see Chapter 12). An electrophoretic analysis

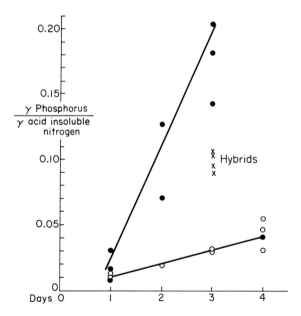

Fig. 7.4. Alkaline phosphatase activity of *Strongylocentrotus purpuratus, Dendraster excentricus,* and *Strongylocentrotus purpuratus* ♀ × *Dendraster excentricus* ♂ hybrids. Expressed as the ratio of micrograms phosphorus released in a 2-hour period per microgram of acid-insoluble nitrogen. Solid dots indicate determinations upon *Dendraster,* open circles are for *Strongylocentrotus purpuratus* and × indicates determinations upon the hybrids. (From Flickinger, 1957.)

shows that the enzyme of the hybrid has a mobility intermediate to that of the parents (Fedecka-Bruner *et al.,* 1971).

Lastly, Barrett and Angelo (1969) have reported that the hatching enzyme of the hybrid *Strongylocentrotus franciscanus* ♀ × *Strongylocentrotus purpuratus* ♂ has maternal characteristics, i.e., it is more sensitive to the inhibition by Mn^{2+} ions. The reciprocal cross used as a control does not show this sensitivity to Mn^{2+}, which rules out the possibility that the maternal character also is expressed in the presence of the paternal template. This speaks in favor of the idea that this enzyme is synthesized on templates already present in the cytoplasm of the egg. Most experiments of inhibition of RNA synthesis during early development lead to the same conclusion. In this case, too, the embryos are able to hatch (see Chapter 10).

PART II

METABOLISM

Introduction

A general description of the metabolism of developing sea urchin embryos should aim at establishing certain correlations between metabolic activities and defined stages of development, rather than listing papers that confirm metabolic patterns in sea urchin embryos already described in other systems. It is in this light that our review should be considered.

Such a criterion, where strictly observed, would of course too strongly reduce the amount of information provided here, and would probably suffer from some too subjective interpretation. Moreover, in some cases the study of certain metabolic activities in sea urchin embryos has provided a first hint of a general metabolic problem for which a solution has not yet been found.

The reader will soon realize that we have tried to keep a balance between the criterion of a "complete list of the literature" and a critical choice of the most significative experiments.

It is hoped that this balance will succeed in expressing a thorough review with particular stress on the main steps for the acquisition of man's present knowledge in the field.

Chapter 8

Energetic Metabolism

A. Oxygen Uptake

The first important variation in the respiratory activity of the sea urchin egg takes place at fertilization. Warburg's finding (1908, 1910, 1915), by the manometric method, that oxygen consumption undergoes a sharp increase following fertilization in the *Arbacia lixula* eggs was confirmed by many authors in other sea urchin species (Runnström, 1930b; Tang, 1931; Tang and Gerard, 1949; Whitaker, 1933a,b; Rubenstein and Gerard, 1934; J. Loeb, 1910; Loeb and Wasteneys, 1911; McClendon and Mitchel, 1912; Shearer, 1922a,b; Shapiro, 1935, 1939; Clowes and Krahl, 1936; Tyler and Humason, 1939; Korr, 1937; Ballentine, 1940; Robbie, 1946; Keltch and Clowes, 1947; Gonse, 1960). These data have been reviewed by Ballentine (1940), Krahl (1950), and E. B. Harvey (1956a). Lindahl and Holter (1941) have noted that the oocyte of *Paracentrotus lividus* has a higher rate of oxygen consumption than the mature egg. As an interpretation for a similar finding in oocytes of *Asterias* and eggs of *Psammechinus miliaris,* Borei (1948) proposes that the respiratory increase following fertilization in sea urchins is only an apparent one. The oxygen consumption rate in fact undergoes a progressive decrease during maturation of the oocyte. This decline becomes particularly evident following the shedding of the egg. Fertilization serves merely in restoring the rate of respiration proper of the newly shed eggs. This hypothesis is not supported by more recent experiments performed on different species, in which no decline in the oxygen consumption rate was detected up to at least 5 hours after shedding (Yasumasu and Nakano, 1963). According to these experiments, whenever fertilization is performed after spawning, it never fails to produce an immediate increase in the oxygen consumption rate.

Ohnishi and Sugiyama (1963) confirmed the respiratory increase at fertilization by means of the polarographic method. This appears especially important since the respiratory increase following fertilization is accompanied by a burst of CO_2 production, due also to CO_2 displacement from the seawater following liberation of a fertilization acid, according to Laser and Rothschild (1939). This CO_2 might not be promptly absorbed by the CO_2 traps used in the manometric methods, thus giving a false result. It should be added that the use of a CO_2 trap in the manometric flasks brings about a reduction in the bicarbonate content of seawater, which in turn decreases the oxygen consumption rate of the egg (Rothschild, 1956).

The respiratory increase described by Ohnishi and Sugiyama reaches values about 15 times those of the unfertilized egg within 2 minutes following fertilization, to become stabilized at a level only 4 times that of the unfertilized egg in the succeeding minutes. A fundamentally similar curve was reported by Epel (1964b) for *Strongylocentrotus purpuratus*. A somewhat lower increase has been found by Horwitz (1965) in *Arbacia punctulata,* again, however, with a similar overall shape of the respiratory curve. Nakazawa *et al.* (1970) measured, by means of the oxygen electrode, a burst of oxygen consumption within 1 minute following addition of the sperm to the unfertilized eggs. These authors studied the correlation between the increase in oxygen uptake and the phenomena of acid ejection, calcium uptake, and membrane elevation (see Chapter 4), which occur simultaneously at fertilization.

The facts reported by the authors are that (a) treatment with trypsin, which prevents membrane elevation, does not prevent the other three phenomena; (b) ejection of H^+ ions is prevented by chemical removal of calcium from the medium; (c) addition of calcium to homogenates stimulates oxygen consumption. This may suggest a role played by the calcium influx in the respiratory increase (see Section B,12).

This first rapid increase in the oxygen consumption rate is followed by other much slower changes in the respiratory activity, which give rise to a characteristic S-shaped curve during development. As shown in Fig. 8.1, there is general agreement on the overall shape of this curve: The initial plateau is followed by an increase that lasts from about the 16-cell stage up to early blastula; a second plateau follows up to the hatching stage. After this, i.e., during migration of the primary mesenchyme, the respiration rate starts to rise again more or less steadily up to the pluteus stage. Fundamentally similar curves have been obtained by Gray (1926) in *Psammechinus,* by Whitely and Baltzer (1958) in *Paracentrotus* and

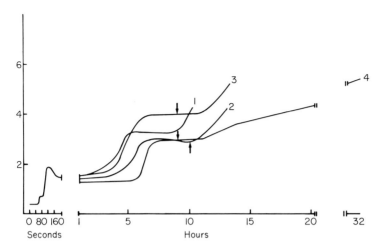

Seconds   Hours

Fig. 8.1. Rate of oxygen uptake by developing sea urchin embryos. The curves are re-drawn from the data of several authors: 1: From Lindahl, 1939; 2: from Giudice *et al.,* 1968; 3: from Borei, 1948; 4: from Immers and Runnström, 1960. The curve relative to the first 200 seconds following fertilization is redrawn from Epel (1964b). The arrows point to the moment of hatching.

Arbacia, and more recently by Isono and Yasumasu (1968) in *Pseudocentrotus depressus.* These S-shaped curves, with the exception of that of Borei, who used the Cartesian diver balance, were obtained by manometric methods. Other authors, by use of more refined diver balances, described finer details of this curve. In *Psammechinus miliaris, Strongylocentrotus franciscanus,* and *Dendraster excentricus* Zeuthen (1949, 1950, 1951, 1955, 1960; Frydenberg and Zeuthen, 1960; Holter and Zeuthen, 1957) was the first to show a fine cyclic variation of the oxygen consumption rate up to the hatching stage, which he correlates to the mitotic rhythm, supposedly synchronous enough up to at least that stage. The respiratory rate would increase in the interphases to reach a maximum in the prophase. A decrease would follow, reaching a minimum at telophase. Similar results have been reported by Tang (1948) by the Warburg method in *Arbacia punctulata.*

The existence of cycling and its relationship to the mitotic rhythm have been questioned. Scholander *et al.* (1952) have found, by a micromanometric method, that single eggs of *Strongylocentrotus franciscanus* may undergo cell division without cycling of oxygen consumption. In a subsequent paper, Scholander *et al.* (1958) state that mitotic respiratory cycling is not a constant phenomenon in *Psammechinus miliaris;* on the other hand, if cycling occurred there would be a correlation between cytoplasmic cleavage and increase in oxygen consumption. These discrepancies have aroused a debate on the instrumentation of microrespiration (Scholander *et al.,* 1958; Zeuthen, 1960).*

The question was recently reinvestigated by Løvtrup and Iverson (1969) in *Lytechinus variegatus* by means of a new automatic diver balance. A number of oscillations in the respiratory curve up to 10 hours of development have been confirmed and statistically evaluated (Fig. 8.2) in such a way as to distinguish roughly one phase per hour. The conclusion is reached that it is not possible to correlate such phases with the mitotic activity; their significance remains to be clarified.

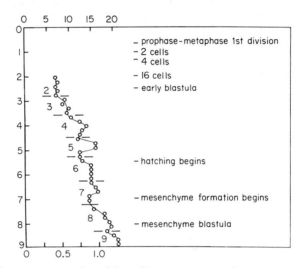

Fig. 8.2. Oxygen consumption of *Lytechinus variegatus* embryos as measured with the automatic diver balance. *Ordinate:* Time (hours); *abscissa* (upper): mm per 50 embryos and 10 minutes; *abscissa* (lower): mμl/embryo and hour. (From Løvtrup and Iverson, 1969.)

The problem of respiratory activity cycling gains new aspects from the observations that in several organisms mitochondria multiplication is either out of phase from the cell mitotic cycle or it takes place continuously. The apparent respiratory activity (due to mitochondria) measured as oxygen uptake is most probably dependent on multiple factors, some of them not directly governed by the nuclear cycle.

While the significance of the fine cycles remains to be settled, it appears

* It is not our purpose here to go into technical details, and even less into a historical description of the evolution of this technique, since, as reported by Claff (1953), the first account of the so-called "Cartesian Diver" can be traced back to 1648, when Raffaele Magiotti, a pupil of Galileo, published the paper "Very certain resistance of water to compression explained with various tricks in occasion of other curious problems" (Rome through Francesca Moneta, 1648, with permission of the Superiors to the Most Serene Prince Don Lorenzo Medici).

clear that the overall S-shaped curve superimposes quite satisfactorily to the curve of the number of cells per embryo, as pointed out by Monroy and Maggio (Fig. 8.3). It does not seem too simplistic to assume that the developmental increase in respiratory activity reflects the fact that higher number of cells, even with the same total mass as an egg, may show higher metabolic activity and, therefore, higher energetic requirement than a single egg.

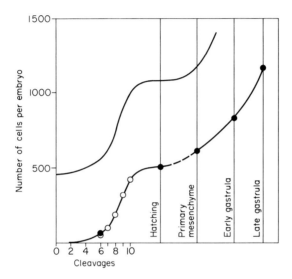

Fig. 8.3. The upper curve indicates the rate of oxygen consumption and the lower curve the number of cells in the sea urchin embryos at the indicated stages of development. The lower curve has been drawn from the combined data of Köhler (1912) for *Paracentrotus lividus* (●) and Zeuthen (1953) for *Psammechinus microtuberculatus* (○). (From Monroy and Maggio, 1963.)

It is appropriate at this point to recall that Gustafson and Lenicque (1955) have described an increase in the number of mitochondria per embryo that is in fair agreement with the overall changes of the respiratory curve. On the other hand, Matsumoto and Pikò (1971) have been unable to find any incorporation of labeled thymidine into mitochondrial DNA during cleavage, nor was any increase in mitochondrial malic dehydrogenase activity found up to the early pluteus stage of *Paracentrotus lividus* by Michejda and Hryniewiecka (personal communication).

The regulation of the gross shape of this curve might, with a high degree of probability, depend primarily upon the mechanism that regulate the increase in cell number of the embryo. Experiments by Giudice *et al.* (1968) have indeed proved that under conditions in which gene expression is blocked, but cell division is only slightly affected for at least 10 hours, i.e., in the presence of actinomycin D, the respiratory curve undergoes normal variations during the first 10 hours, after which it remains at a constant value (Fig. 8.4). The embryos actually survive but do not show any further differentiation or, presumably, any further cell division.

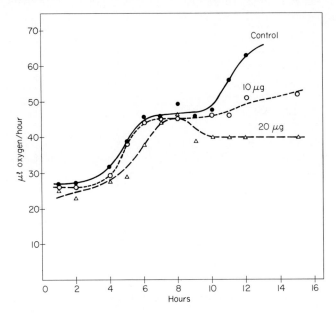

Fig. 8.4. Effect of actinomycin D on the rate of oxygen uptake of *Paracentrotus lividus*. Continuous line, control embryos; dashed lines, embryos kept in two different concentration of actinomycin, starting 15 minutes before fertilization. (From Giudice *et al.,* 1968.)

Much more difficult to explain is the rapid initial increase in respiration. We shall describe its significance in greater detail, because it represents a fine example of metabolic control.

The respiratory activation is part of the physiological changes that take place at fertilization. Its study is of value in the understanding of the role played by the single metabolic activations in the general physiological changes occurring at fertilization. The question of the first respiratory increase has indeed long been the object of several studies.

What is the mechanism that underlies this respiratory increase? To try to provide an answer to this question, we first must determine which are the oxidative pathways followed by the developing sea urchin embryos.

As a first question, the nature of the energetic substrate may be proposed. One straight answer to this could be the study of the respiratory quotient. Unfortunately, this presents particular difficulties in sea urchins because of unstable bicarbonate in seawater. Hence, the results have been conflicting (for a review, see Monroy and Maggio, 1963; Rothschild, 1956). The respiratory quotient of the unfertilized egg has been found to be higher than 1 (Ashbel, 1929; Borei, 1933; Laser and Rothschild, 1939), which only means that the excess of CO_2 developed from seawater has not been readily absorbed. A drop of this quotient has been reported immediately following fertilization: Laser and Rothschild (1939) have calculated that the average value for the first 30 minutes after fertilization is about 0.84.

Changes in the respiratory quotient during later development have first been investigated by Ephrussi (1933) and Borei (1933), who have reported a persistence of the low quotient for longer periods after fertilization. Lindahl and Öhman (1938) and Öhman (1940) have found that the respiratory quotient is 0.73 during early cleavage, thus indicating the utilization of fats up to the initiation of the first major rise in the respiratory curve (see Fig. 8.1). It should be recognized, however, that Hutchens *et al.* (1942) have cast some doubt on the significance of the above data when analyzed statistically. Furthermore, in the opinion of Hayes (1938) and Isono (1963a), there would be a preferential utilization of carbohydrates from fertilization up to hatching and a switch to amino acid (Hayes) or to lipid (Isono) utilization thereafter. Data on the total amount of lipids in developing embryos (Mohri, 1964) seem in agreement with the changes in the respiratory quotient reported by Isono.

B. Carbohydrate Metabolism

However one wants to consider the data on the respiratory quotient, it is clear from the sum of the evidence that we are about to list that the carbohydrate metabolism plays an essential role in the production of energy in sea urchin embryos. We shall, therefore, treat primarily the problem of the respiratory activation at fertilization with a description of the pathways for carbohydrate utilization.

It has long been known that the chemical glycolytic pathway, followed by the tricarboxylic acid cycle, operates in sea urchin embryos. Moreover, the pentose phosphate cycle has proved to be very active. In order to provide the reader with a reasonably complete bibliography, it is pertinent to mention the work that has provided evidence for the existence of such pathways. For a more detailed review of earlier work, Rothschild (1951, 1956) should be consulted.

1. GLYCOGEN

Örström and Lindberg (1940) measured the glycogen content of unfertilized eggs of *Paracentrotus lividus* and noted a decrease from 25 mg/100 mg N to 20.3 mg/100 mg N 10 minutes after fertilization. Similar values of glycogen content in the unfertilized egg of *Arbacia punctulata* were observed by Blanchard (1935), and later confirmed by Hutchens *et al.* (1942).

In addition to glycogen, the latter authors revealed in the egg an equal amount of an unknown acid-hydrolyzable carbohydrate. Measurements of the total carbohydrate content during development, reported by these authors, should be integrated with information on carbohydrate resyn-thesis, to be interpreted in terms of metabolic utilization. It is actually known, for example, that exogenous glucose is very actively incorporated into glycogen. Lindberg (1945) has suggested that glycogen might be coupled to a protein to be oxidized following fertilization. The presence of glycogen in the sea urchin egg has finally been confirmed by Cleland and Rothschild (1952a), who have found somewhat lower levels in eggs of *Echinus esculentus*.

A study of polysaccharides of *Arbacia lixula* and *Echinus esculentus* can be found in the paper by Immers (1960a).

2. GLYCOGEN PHOSPHORYLASE

This enzyme has recently been studied by Bergami *et al.* (1968) in eggs of *Sphaerechinus granularis* and *Paracentrotus lividus*. This study was undertaken with the hope of finding an increase in the activity of this enzyme. Since this enzyme is known to be a rate-limiting one among those that catalyze the breakdown of glycogen into glucose 6-phosphate, its activation at fertilization might have represented a triggering event for the physiological activation of respiration. The activity has, however, been found to be at the same level in homogenates of unfertilized or fertilized eggs and embryos. Interestingly enough, the enzyme is released, following fertilization, from a particulate fraction into the 20,000 *g* supernatant. The possibility still remains, therefore, that the enzyme is held in a cellular compartment before fertilization, to be released at the moment when its activity is needed, i.e., at fertilization.

3. HEXOSE MONOPHOSPHATES

After unsuccessful attempts by Lindberg (1943) to detect carbohydrate phosphate esters in sea urchin eggs, the level of these compounds has been studied and directly measured by enzymatic assay by Aketa *et al.* (1964) in search of a step limiting respiration of the unfertilized eggs. The level of glucose 1-phosphate, glucose 6-phosphate, fructose 1,6-diphosphate, triose phosphate, and pyruvate has been measured before and immediately after fertilization. As shown in Table 8.1, there is a sharp increase, following fertilization, in the level of glucose 6-phosphate as well as in those of fructose diphosphate and triose phosphate, which are very low in the unfertilized egg. These results have been interpreted by the authors in terms of a possible activation of glycogen phosphorylase at fertilization. Several authors have reported a decrease in the polysaccharide content of the egg following fertilization: Örström and Lindberg (1940), as mentioned above, have found a decrease in glycogen; Aketa (1957) in an acid-hydrolyzable carbohydrate; Ishihara (1964) in an acid-soluble polysaccharide, and Monroy and Vittorelli (1960) in a glycoprotein. The direct measurements of this enzyme (see above) have, however, only pointed to a change in its intracellular location.

4. GLYCOLYSIS

Cleland and Rothschild (1952a) found that the addition of glycolytic intermediates to a homogenate of *Echinus esculentus* stimulates the production of pyruvate or lactate more than the addition of glycogen or starch. The substrates tested have been glycogen, starch, glucose, fructose, glucose 1-phosphate, glucose 6-phosphate, fructose 6-phosphate, hexose diphosphate, and phosphoglyceric acid. These experiments provide indirect evidence for the existence of the enzymes and cofactors required for the glycolytic utilization of the above substrates. Some of these have, however, been directly assayed, as will also be mentioned later. For example, Krahl *et al.* (1954) assayed the hexokinase activity in homogenates from several stages of *Arbacia punctulata* and found a slight increase from fertilization up to early pluteus, followed by a steeper increase at the late pluteus stage. DPN and ATP were equally used by the homogenate.

The amount of lactic acid produced from eggs and embryos was measured and correlated to the amount of NH_3 produced and to the total carbohydrate content by Hutchens *et al.* (1942). As already discussed, the conclusion of these authors that little carbohydrate might be used for respiration in the first 6 hours of development has been questioned.

5. TRICARBOXYLIC ACID CYCLE

Lindberg (1943) has described a stimulatory effect on oxygen consumption in egg homogenates of *Echinocardium* upon addition of malate or fumarate. Crane and Keltch (1949) have shown that intermediates of this cycle, such as oxalate, succinate, α-ketoglutarate, glutamate and citrate, are rapidly oxidized by homogenates of *Arbacia punctulata* eggs. This oxidation is accompanied by orthophosphate esterification (Keltch *et al.*, 1950). Cleland and Rothschild (1952b) have also shown the stimulation

TABLE 8.1

Concentrations of Main Glycolytic Substrates in Unfertilized and Fertilized Sea Urchin Eggs[a,b]

Animal	Stage	Glucose 6-phosphate	Glucose 1-phosphate	Fructose diphosphate	Triose phosphate	Pyruvate
Arbacia	U	0.053	Undetectable			Undetectable
	F_5	0.260	Undetectable			Undetectable
	U	0.046	Undetectable			
	F_5	0.200	Undetectable			
	U			0.021	0.003	Undetectable
	F_6			0.046	0.030	Undetectable
	U	0.076		0.003	0.007	
	F_{10}	0.166		0.014	0.023	
	U	0.140			Undetectable	Undetectable
	F_{10}	0.431			0.021	Undetectable
	U	0.055				
	F_{10}	0.470				

Paracentrotus					
U			Undetectable	Undetectable	Undetectable
F_5			0.046	0.039	Undetectable
U			0.002	0.002	
F_5			0.039	0.043	
U			Undetectable	Undetectable	Undetectable
F_6			0.032	Undetectable	Undetectable
U	0.068	Undetectable			
F_8	0.456	Undetectable			
U	0.040	Undetectable			
F_{10}	0.177	Undetectable			
U	0.154	Undetectable			
F_{10}	0.308	Undetectable			
U	0.063				Undetectable
F_{12}	0.408				Undetectable
U	0.068				
F_{30}	0.381				

[a] From Aketa *et al.* (1964).

[b] Results expressed in μmoles per 100 mg total N of eggs; U and F_x represent unfertilized eggs and fertilized eggs at x minutes after fertilization.

of oxygen consumption in egg homogenates by the addition of citrate, ketoglutarate, succinate, fumarate, malate, glutamate and pyruvate. (For a direct demonstration of the malate dehydrogenase activity, see Chapter 12.) Similar results have been reported by Ycas (1950, 1954) on *Strongylocentrotus purpuratus*. Evidence for complete oxidation of pyruvate to CO_2 and H_2O has been provided by Krahl *et al.* (1942), Goldinger and Barrón (1946), and by Cleland and Rothschild (1952b). More recently, evidence has been repeatedly furnished that isolated sea urchin mitochondria are able to carry out oxidative phosphorylation (Aketa and Tomita, 1958; Aiello and Maggio, 1961; Giudice, 1960).

6. PENTOSE PHOSPHATE CYCLE

That this pathway of carbohydrate breakdown predominates in sea urchin eggs was first suggested by Örström and Lindberg (1940; Lindberg, 1943, 1945) and clearly demonstrated by Krahl *et al.* (1954, 1955; Krahl, 1956). The latter authors have shown that: (1) eggs of *Arbacia punctulata* contain glucose-6-phosphate dehydrogenase and phosphogluconate dehydrogenase; (2) egg homogenates reduce TPN at the expenses of glucose 6-phosphate 15–30 times more actively than they reduce DPN at the expenses of fructose 1,6-diphosphate; (3) more $^{14}CO_2$ is obtained *in vivo* from eggs to which [1-^{14}C]glucose has been administered than from eggs to which [6-^{14}C]glucose has been given.

This result was confirmed by Bäckström *et al.* (1960) in *Psammechinus miliaris,* and by Isono and Yasumasu (1968) in *Pseudocentrotus depressus.* These authors also measured the relative importance of the glycolysis and the pentose phosphate cycle during different developmental stages. They both agree that an enhancement of the pentose cycle activity occurs at fertilization and through early cleavage, so that this pathway predominates over the other one during the first part of development (up to gastrulation according to Isono and Yasumasu, and slightly earlier according to Bäckström *et al.*). Later, glycolysis and the tricarboxylic acid cycle prevail (Fig. 8.5). Bäckström *et al.* correlate the increase in the pentose phosphate cycle activity to an increase in the activity of glucose 6-phosphate and 6-phosphogluconate dehydrogenases during cleavage (Bäckström, 1959, 1963). Broyles and Strittmatter (1971), on the other hand, have not detected significant variation of either enzymatic activity throughout the development of *Arbacia punctulata.* Isono (1962) failed to find important variations of the activity of these two enzymes, at least up to mesenchyme blastula, in *Hemicentrotus, Pseudocentrotus,* and *Anthocidaris.* Following fertilization, however, the glucose-6-phosphate dehydrogenase is released from a particulate cell fraction into the cytoplasm (Isono, 1963b). This release from the particu-

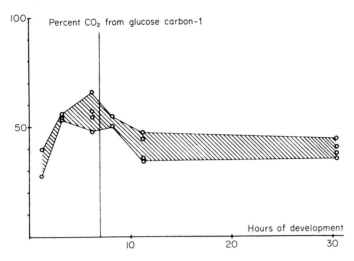

Fig. 8.5. Radioactive CO_2 expired from [1-^{14}C]glucose in percent of that from [^{14}C]glu-cose-U. Hatching is indicated by the vertical line. (From Bäckström *et al.*, 1960.)

late can be artificially brought about in homogenates of unfertilized eggs by increasing the ionic strength of the medium (Isono *et al.*, 1963). Since it is known that important changes of permeability occur at fertilization, with a remarkable increase of the rate of ionic influx followed by a rapid efflux (see Chapter 4), it may be speculated that such a mechanism nor-mally operates to activate this enzyme at fertilization. Michejda and Hryniewcka (1969) have found in *Paracentrotus lividus* and *Arbacia lixula* a very low level of lactate dehydrogenase and α-glycerophosphate dehydrogenase, at least up to the pluteus stage.

The lantern mussels of the adult animal, on the other hand, do show a good lactate dehydrogenase activity. The same authors confirm that throughout development glucose-6-phosphate dehydrogenase and 6-phosphate gluconate dehydrogenase are very active in both species. These results are again in favor of the importance of the pentose phos-phate shunt during early development; they would, however, deny any glycolytic activity at least up to the pluteus stage.

Ishihara (1957, 1958a,b, 1963) has demonstrated aldolase activity in the sea urchin egg. He suggests that this enzyme is bound in an inactive form to a cellular component, probably the cell surface, in the unfertilized egg. Following fertilization, or parthenogenetic activation, the enzyme is released into the soluble cytoplasm.

7. DPN AND TPN

Jandorf and Krahl (1942) estimated manometrically that eggs of *Arbacia punctulata* contain 250–500 μg of DPN per gram wet weight.

Somewhat lower values (about 110 μg/ml of packed eggs) have been re-ported by more recent determinations performed with the fluorimetric method of Krane and Crane (1960). These authors have also reported a 3- to 7-fold increase in the concentration of TPNH following fertilization. Since no parallel decrease of TPN is observed, the concentration of which remained more or less constant, the net synthesis of TPN is suggested at the expense of DPN, by means of a DPN-kinase. The transformation of DPN into TPN is correlated to the activity increase of the pentose phosphate pathway.

These results have been confirmed in *Strongylocentrotus purpuratus* by Epel (1964a,b). This author has found an immediate increase of TPNH at fertilization which is the very first detectable change in the respiratory events that follow fertilization (Fig. 8.6).

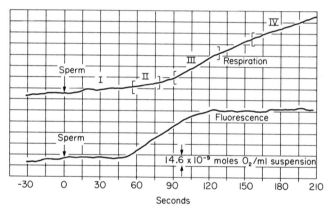

Fig. 8.6. Synchronized recorder tracings of fluorescence and respiration of *Strongy-locentrotus* eggs. Egg concentration was 121,000 eggs/ml in a 6-ml volume. (From Epel, 1964b.)

The DPNH level remains practically constant during the first minutes following fertilization, while DPN and TPN show symmetrical variations (Figs. 8.7 and 8.8). These results again support the idea of a synthesis of TPN from DPN, paralleled by a quick reduction of TPN. Already Krane and Crane (1958) had measured the DPN-kinase activity of homogenates of unfertilized and fertilized eggs of *Arbacia* in an attempt to find varia-tions that might justify the above results. This activity does not appear to change following fertilization; nor have variations in the intracellular distribution of the enzyme been observed (Epel and Iverson, 1965).

Blomquist (1969) has pointed out the extreme lability of DPN-kinase in extracts from unfertilized eggs: The activity is completely lost by in-cubation in Tris buffer pH 7.5 for 112 minutes at 30°C, or by dialysis

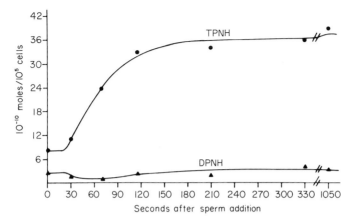

Fig. 8.7. Results of enzymatic analysis of reduced pyridine nucleotides in *Strongylocentrotus* eggs. (From Epel, 1964a.)

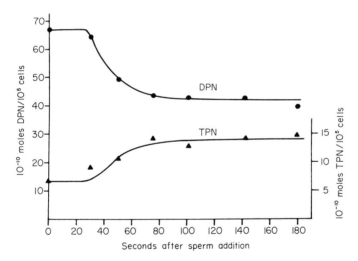

Fig. 8.8. Results of enzymatic analysis of oxidized pyridine nucleotides of *Strongylocentrotus* eggs. (From Epel, 1964a.)

against diluted buffer. It can be completely recovered by incubation with DPN or dithiothreitol. The ease with which the egg might regulate the activity of this enzyme is, therefore, stressed.

The level of TPN and TPNH at various developmental stages has also been studied by S. Denis (1968) in embryos of *Paracentrotus lividus* and the lethal hybrid *Paracentrotus lividus* ♀ × *Arbacia lixula* ♂ in order to find out whether or not the lack of DNA synthesis at gastrulation in the hybrid might be attributable to a disturbance of the production of TPNH, needed for the transformation of ribose into deoxyribose. The experiments have proved that this is not the case. However, the data on the TPNH increase up to the gastrula stage have been confirmed in both *Paracentrotus* and *Arbacia* embryos and, interestingly enough, the TPNH decrease at gastrulation, which is attributed to the shift of glucose catabolism toward glycolysis, has failed to take place in the lethal hybrids, which did not undergo gastrulation. This interesting correlation between gastrulation and regulation of TPNH level, which is in line with the data of Bäckström *et al.* (1960), deserves a more detailed dosage curve than that available up to now from Denis's data.

8. FLAVIN ADENINE DINUCLEOTIDE

The first direct assay is credited to Krahl *et al.* (1940).

9. UBIQUINONE

It has been purified from sea urchin sperm and eggs by Caserta and Ghiretti (1962, 1963).

10. CYTOCHROMES

The existence of cytochromes in sea urchin eggs had first been suggested by Runnström (1928d, 1930b) on the basis of the effect of carbon monoxide on respiration. The concept had been held for quite a while by earlier investigators that such a system did not operate before fertilization. The theory had also been held that cytochrome was "thrown into circulation" after fertilization. These old ideas, which were based mainly on observations of the effect of inhibitors of respiration, and are reviewed by Rothschild (1949), have been proved wrong by Krahl *et al.* (1941), who have shown that the sea urchin egg contains a normal amount of cytochrome oxidase. These authors, on the other hand, have failed to show the presence of any cytochrome c.

Rothschild (1949) concluded that respiration is mediated through the cytochrome system before and after fertilization, and identified spectroscopically cytochromes a and b_1 in the unfertilized egg of *Psammechinus miliaris*. Borei and Bjorklund (1953) also admitted that a series of experiments performed by studying the oxidation of many reductants of the phenylenediamine type strongly suggests that the cytochrome c system operates in sea urchins both before and after fertilization.

Maggio and Ghiretti-Magaldi (1958), taking advantage of the development of a method to purify mitochondria from sea urchin eggs (Monroy, 1957a), gave the first clear demonstration that isolated mitochondria of eggs of *Paracentrotus lividus* and *Sphaerechinus granularis* contain a complete and functional cytochrome system, consisting of cytochromes a, a_3, b, and c. These cytochromes have been studied both manometrically and spectrophotometrically and found similar in all respects to those of mammals and yeast.

It had also been observed that the cytochrome oxidase activity is entirely associated with the mitochondrial fraction and, more precisely, with that part of it which, on a sucrose density gradient, bands together with the pigment. These authors found the amount of cytochrome c too low for a direct estimate. Its presence, however, had been indirectly proved by the appearance of reduced bands of cytochrome a and a_3 in the presence of succinate. These results have been confirmed by Ghiretti *et al.* (1958).

With the acquisition of this more exact knowledge on the cytochrome system in the sea urchin egg, the question of the mechanism of the respiratory activation at fertilization has been reinvestigated. Maggio (1959) measured the cytochrome oxidase activity in isolated mitochondria of *Paracentrotus lividus* eggs and found that following fertilization an increase of only about 25% is observed, which persists through the blastula stage. This increase seemed to the author too low to be re-

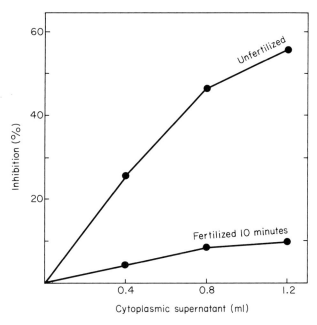

Fig. 8.9. Inhibitory effect of the cytoplasmic supernatant of unfertilized and fertilized eggs of *Paracentrotus lividus* on the cytochrome oxidase activity of mouse liver mitochondria. (From Maggio and Monroy, 1959.)

sponsible for the respiratory activation; a search has, therefore, been started for an extramitochondrial inhibitor of cytochrome oxidase activity in the unfertilized egg. It has indeed been found that the 105,000 *g* supernatant of a homogenate of jelly-free unfertilized eggs of *Paracentrotus lividus* inhibits the cytochrome oxidase activity of mitochondria isolated from sea urchin eggs or from mouse liver (Maggio and Monroy, 1959). A similar supernatant prepared from eggs fertilized 10 minutes before has shown very little inhibitory activity (Fig. 8.9). The inhibitory activity practically disappears from the egg cytoplasm 1 hour after fertilization.

An attempt at purifying this inhibitor has given the following results: It is a heat-labile, dialyzable compound that does not contain nitrogen. It becomes inactivated in the alkaline range of pH, while it is stable in the acidic range. If inactivated through the purification steps, it can be reactivated by treatment with reduced glutathione or cysteine (Maggio *et al.*, 1960). No further progress has been made in the identification of such an inhibitor, nor has definite proof been provided that it actually plays a role *in vivo* in the regulation of the respiratory activity.

11. ATP AND RELATED COMPOUNDS

A number of authors have measured the ATP level in sea urchin eggs. (Chambers and Mende, 1953b; Lindberg, 1954; Nilsson, 1961; Taguchi, 1962; Taguchi *et al.*, 1963; Epel, 1963; Epel and Iverson, 1965; Zotin *et al.*, 1965, 1967; Estabrook and Maitra, 1962; Mazia, 1963). The emphasis of many of these experiments has not focused on the correlation between ATP level and respiratory changes at fertilization, but between inhibition of ATP synthesis and inhibition of mitosis.

Table 8.2 shows the levels of ATP, ADP, and AMP as well as of other nucleotides in eggs and embryos of *Pseudocentrotus depressus,* according to Yanagisawa and Isono (1966). It has usually been reported that the ATP level (1.5 μg 10^3 eggs in *Strongylocentrotus dröbachiensis,* according to Zotin *et al.*, 1965) does not change after fertilization (Chambers and Mende, 1953b; Rothschild, 1956; Yanagisawa and Isono, 1966; Zotin *et al.*, 1967). The only claims for a decrease of ATP following fertilization are those of Hultin (1957) and Aiello *et al.* (reported by Monroy and Maggio, 1963). The latter authors, however, have so far never published their data. More recently, Epel (1969) has confirmed that there is no change in the levels of ATP, ADP, and AMP either immediately after fertilization or later on, at least up to 3 hours, in *Strongylocentrotus purpuratus,* as detected by means of the fluorimetric assay. Mackintosh and Bell (1969c) report that the amount of ATP, as well as of

TABLE 8.2

CHANGES IN THE AMOUNTS OF ACID-SOLUBLE NUCLEOTIDES DURING THE DEVELOPMENT OF *Pseudocentrotus* EGG[a,b]

	Unfertilized egg		Fertilized egg		64-cell stage		Early blastula stage		Mesenchyme blastula stage		Late gastrula stage		Pluteus stage	
	μ moles	mole %	μ moles	mole %	μ moles	mole %	μ moles	mole %	μ moles	mole %	μ moles	mole %	μ moles	mole %
CMP	3.70	14.2	1.00	3.9	1.30	6.3	1.10	6.0	1.30	7.2	3.50	19.9	6.80	35.7
AMP	0.16	0.6	0.23	0.9	0.52	2.5	0.51	2.8	0.65	3.6	1.15	6.5	2.22	11.7
G. UMP[c]	0.27	1.0	0.37	1.5	0.47	2.3	0.44	2.4	0.61	3.4	1.09	6.2	1.80	9.4
ADP	0.49	1.9	1.09	4.3	2.28	11.1	1.52	8.3	1.92	10.7	2.12	12.0	2.07	10.9
UDP-sugar	3.40	13.1	3.00	11.9	3.70	17.9	3.70	20.4	2.70	15.0	1.40	7.9	1.10	5.8
CTP + G. UDP[c]	0.76	2.9	1.16	4.5	1.76	8.5	1.22	6.7	0.78	4.3	1.32	7.5	1.62	8.5
ATP	13.90	53.5	13.80	54.9	7.50	36.3	7.00	38.4	6.40	35.6	4.80	27.3	2.70	14.2
GTP	1.39	5.3	2.15	8.5	1.24	6.0	1.14	6.2	1.39	7.7	1.14	6.5	0.74	3.8
UTP	1.95	7.5	2.43	9.6	1.87	9.1	1.61	8.8	2.26	12.5	1.10	6.2		
Sum	26.02	100	25.23	100	20.64	100	18.24	100	18.01	100	17.62	100	19.05	100

[a] From Yanagisawa and Isono (1966).
[b] Figures are μmoles per 10[7] eggs or embryos.
[c] G. UMP = GMP + UMP; G. UDP = GDP + UDP.

GTP, remains constant before and after fertilization of *Strongylocentrotus purpuratus* and *Arbacia lixula* eggs.

The only measurement of the ATP level during oogenesis is, to our knowledge, that of Ozernyuk (1970), who claims that during oocyte maturation there is a drop of about 50% in oxygen consumption, with a parallel doubling of the ATP content.

Connors and Scheer (1947) and Mullins (1949) claim that the ATPase activity increases after fertilization. Both of these authors, working on

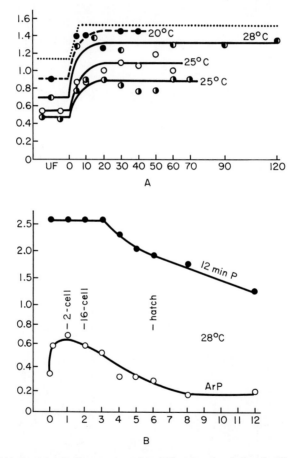

Fig. 8.10. (A) Increase in the amount of arginine phosphate after fertilization. ●----● *Pseudocentrotus;* ○, ◑, ◒, *Anthocidaris* (3 experiments); ·····, *Strongylocentrotus* (per 0.5 ml of eggs). (Redrawn by Yanagisawa, 1968, from data of Chambers and Mende, 1953a.) Abscissa: minutes after fertilization; ordinate: μmole of arginine phosphate/10^6 eggs. (B) Changes in the amount of arginine phosphate and 12 min. P during the development of *Authocidaris* embryos. Abscissa: hours after fertilization; ordinate: μmoles of arginine phosphate and 12 min. P/10^6 embryos. (From Yanagisawa, 1968.)

egg extracts and lyophilized eggs, respectively, have reported that the sea urchin ATPase is Ca^{2+} activated. Monroy (1957b), working on isolated mitochondria of *Paracentrotus lividus,* has described a Mg^{2+}-activated ATPase, whose activity undergoes only a slight increase following fertilization. More work on ATPase in sea urchin is again concerned with the role of this enzyme in the contraction of the mitotic spindle (see Chapter 5).

Mende and Chambers (1953) and Yanagisawa (1959, 1968) have reported that sea urchin egg contains a considerable amount of arginine phosphate. Yanagisawa (1968) studied the metabolism of ATP and of arginine phosphate in eggs of *Anthocidaris crassispina, Pseudocentrotus depressus* and *Hemicentrotus pulcherrimus.* He found that the amount of arginine phosphate is doubled 10 minutes following fertilization. From the 16-cell stage on, this amount decreases up to the gastrula stage (Fig. 8.10). The importance of arginine phosphate as energy reserve is stressed by the author, chiefly in connection with the problem of the effect of metabolic inhibitors on mitosis.

In a comparative study on the distribution of phosphoarginine and phosphocreatine in marine invertebrates (1971), Rockstein described the presence of slight amounts of them in the eggs of *Lytechinus variegatus* and of trace amounts in the eggs of *Arbacia punctulata.*

12.   INHIBITORS OF CARBOHYDRATE METABOLISM

Among the various metabolic inhibitors, DNP at uncoupling doses is one of the most used chemicals, the purpose being that of revealing the maximum of electron transport capacity of the sea urchin embryo respiratory system at different developmental stages.

After earlier works (Clowes and Krahl, 1936; Krahl and Clowes, 1935, 1936; Clowes *et al.,* 1950; Krahl, 1950) on the effect of nitro- and halophenols on the respiratory rate and on cell division of *Arbacia* eggs, Immers and Runnström (1960) studied the "respiratory control ratios," at different stages of development – the ratio being that between the respiration released by DNP and normal respiration. This should always be higher the more "controlled" the respiration is.* A high "respiratory control" is observed in the newly fertilized eggs of *Paracentrotus lividus* and *Psammechinus miliaris.* A drop of this value follows up to the mesenchyme blastula stage, when the value of the respiratory control seems to be stabilized at a comparatively low level. A rather wide scattering of the data does not allow a more precise curve.

---

* It should be observed that DNP might in itself stimulate the electron transport over the physiological maximum and that a low respiratory control ratio does not necessarily mean the lack of metabolic control but possibly a high turnover of ATP.

The authors suggest that the decrease of the respiratory control ratio might be attributed to an increased demand for energy and, therefore, to higher availability of phosphate acceptors. As we have seen, there is no definitive agreement on the amount of nucleotides mono-, di-, and triphosphates during development. De Vincentis *et al.* (1966) measured the respiratory control ratio during the early cleavage and at the mesenchyme blastula stage of isolated animal and vegetal halves of *Paracentrotus lividus*. The main conclusion of these experiments is that there is higher respiratory control ratio in the animal halves at both stages. At the mesenchyme blastula stage, the animal halves show the highest respiratory rate under conditions of release.

As already mentioned, DNP, cyanide, CO, NaF, Na-azide, iodoacetate phenylmercuric nitrate, phloridzin, phenylurethane, dithiooxalate, diphenylthiocarbazone, isonitrosoacetophenone, and malonate have been used to study the effect on cell division (Isihara, 1958a; Barnett, 1953; Kriszat, 1954; Epel, 1963; Mazia, 1963; Yanagisawa, 1968; Krahl and Clowes, 1940; Clowes and Krahl, 1940; Cleland and Rothschild, 1952a,b). The question has been debated as to whether or not the inhibition of cleavage is due to a lowering of the ATP level. In favor of this hypothesis is that the addition of ATP to eggs treated with metabolic poisons could counterbalance the effect on cleavage (Barnett, 1953; Kriszat, 1954), even if penetration of ATP in the cells is not proved. Furthermore, a decrease in the amount of ATP has been directly observed following treatments that inhibit cleavage (Epel, 1963; Amoore, 1963; Krahl, 1950; Mazia, 1963; Zotin *et al.*, 1965). Yanagisawa (1968), on the other hand, has proved that, in the presence of metabolic inhibitors such as DNP, azide, and cyanide, it is possible to obtain an effect on cleavage at concentrations that while not yet affecting the ATP level lower the content in arginine phosphate.

Without going into the details of this question, we wish to point out here that the action mechanism itself of these drugs seems of little interest. What one really wants to know is whether or not ATP plays a key role in cleavage. That ATP does not participate in an energy-requiring process like that of cleavage seems inconceivable nowadays; furthermore, there is now reasonable evidence that an actinelike protein is involved in the contraction of the mitotic spindle (see Chapter 5). The use of inhibitors in elucidating the metabolic pathways of carbohydrate utilization is now only of historical value. Consequently it will not be reported in detail here.

Finally, it will be recalled that Ca^{2+} ions have been found to cause a temporary increase in the oxygen uptake rate from egg homogenates obtained in Ca^{2+}-free media (Hultin, 1949a, 1950a). Hypertonicity has the same effect. To our knowledge no progress has been made since then in the interpretation of these data. Aiello and Maggio (1961) have found

that addition of a small amount of seawater to a suspension of rat liver
mitochondria strongly inhibits the oxidative phosphorylation, and has a
minor effect on the cytochrome oxidase activity. This effect is due to the
presence of Ca^{2+} ions in the seawater. These data are of practical value
for the evaluation of results obtained from sea urchin homogenates in
which seawater is present.

As reported in Section A, Nakazawa *et al.* (1970) have suggested the
possibility that the calcium influx that occurs at fertilization might play
a role in the respiratory increase.

To sum up, all the above data suggest the possibility of a multiple
mechanism that switches on the respiratory activity at fertilization. Isono
and Yasumasu (1968) have grouped the main data on this subject in an
outline that, even if not the only one possible, is not contradictory with
any of the available evidence and enjoys the merit of providing the reader
with a prompt synopsis of the question of respiratory activation (see
Fig. 8.11).

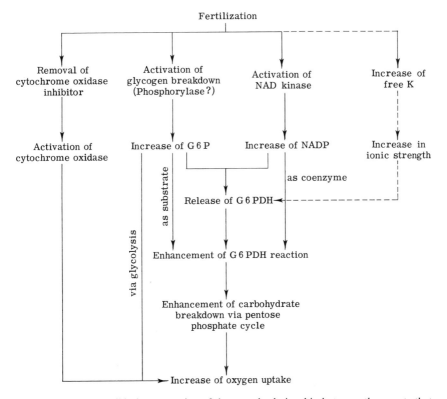

Fig. 8.11. One possible interpretation of the causal relationship between the events that
lead to the respiratory activation following fertilization in sea urchin eggs. (From Isono and
Yasumasu, 1968.)

Chapter 9

Deoxyribonucleic Acid

A. The DNA of the Unfertilized Egg

One debated problem in the past has been that of the DNA content of the sea urchin egg. In 1954 Hoff-Jørgensen, with the aid of the microbiological assay, had reached the conclusion that the amount of DNA in the egg of *Paracentrotus lividus* is about 20 times that of the haploid sperm nucleus. This value is in fair agreement with the finding that it is 25 times that of the sperm nucleus in *Arbacia lixula,* as reported by Baltus *et al.* (1965) following microfluorimetric assays, and by Bibring *et al.* (1965) following ultracentrifugation. Sugino *et al.* (1960) have reported it to be 37 times the haploid nucleus, following determination of the thymidine content of eggs of *Hemicentrotus lividus.* At the other extreme, we find the report by Marshak and Marshak (1953) who, by measurement of isotope dilution, have evaluated the DNA content of the *Arbacia punctulata* egg at 3–4 times the amount of the sperm nucleus. Owing to their failure to stain the nuclei with the Feulgen reaction, they had thought that the unfertilized egg nucleus did not contain DNA (see, also, Immers, 1957). Different evidence had been produced by others. Agrell (1958) had shown DNA by cytochemical techniques in the pronucleus of unfertilized eggs of *Psammechinus miliaris;* a similar conclusion had been reached by Burgos (1955) and Brachet and Ficq (1956) by means of histochemical techniques, and by Hinegardner (1961), who had assayed DNA on isolated nuclei of eggs of *Echinometra mathaei.* The question of the DNA content of the unfertilized egg and of its location within the cell has been thoroughly investigated recently by Pikò, Tyler, and Vinograd (Pikò and Tyler, 1965; Pikò *et al.,* 1967, 1968).

We shall, therefore, not insist on recalling the previous works on this subject since this would only carry a historical value.

The difficulties met in trying to determine the exact amount of DNA in the sea urchin egg are explained by the high cytoplasmic nuclear ratio of the egg. Besides, as shown by Pikò *et al.* (1967), the egg contains some compounds that interfere with the DNA assays. These authors have solved the problem of DNA extraction and purification by homogenizing the eggs in 4% sodium dodecyl sulfate, 0.08 M ethylenediaminetetraacetate (EDTA), pH 7.8. The homogenate was added to a CsCl solution of 1.70 gm/cm^3 and centrifuged in a SW-39 Spinco rotor for 50 hours at 35,000 rpm. This led to the separation of the DNA on a band which was clearly located by the addition of a marker ^{14}C-labeled DNA.

The fraction of the gradient where DNA is located still contains a polysaccharide material which interferes with the diphenylamine reaction and the OD measurements. In fact, the spectral absorption color curve obtained with nonpurified DNA is shifted toward the lower wavelengths (maximum at about 530 nm) while, after α-amylase treatment, the color curve of the DNA preparations is that typical for deoxyribose (maximum at 600 nm). Hence, the DNA-containing fractions were alcohol precipitated, treated with α-amylase, and purified twice more through buoyant density centrifugation.

According to the diphenylamine determinations after this purification, the DNA content of the unfertilized eggs is 8.0 pg/egg for *Lytechinus pictus* and 3.6 pg/egg for *Strongylocentrotus purpuratus*. Elson *et al.* (1954) had shown that the diphenylamine reaction on nonpurified sea urchin egg DNA gives rise to spurious colors. If whole homogenates of *Lytechinus* and *Strongylocentrotus* eggs are assayed for DNA with diphenylamine without proper purification of the nucleic acid, values of 90–150 times those of the sperm nucleus are obtained, owing to polysaccharide interference.

When DNA is assayed after this purification by measuring the absorption at 260 nm, the values obtained are 8.26 ± 0.30 pg/egg for *Lytechinus,* and of 3.30 ± 0.25 pg/egg for *Strongylocentrotus,* which closely agree with those obtained by the diphenylamine reaction. To show that no DNA losses occur during the purification procedure, the authors performed the following experiment: Females of *Lytechinus* were injected twice with 200 μCi of [^{3}H]thymidine (6 Ci/μmole) and the eggs collected 2 months later (shorter incubation periods fail to give DNA labeling, according to Esper, 1962a). They contained labeled DNA. All the radioactivity bound to DNA was recovered in the purified final DNA fraction of the CsCl gradient. Since the DNA content of the haploid sperm nucleus is 0.77 pg/sperm for *Strongylocentrotus* and 0.87 pg/sperm for *Lytechinus* (on the basis of two determinations), the DNA content of the respective eggs is 4.3 and 9.5 times that of the sperm nucleus.

Where is this extra amount of DNA located in the egg? To solve this problem, Pikò *et al.* performed a cell fractionation by homogenizing the eggs in 0.3 *M* sucrose, 0.36 *M* KCl in 0.03 *M* Tris–HCl pH 7.6, and, after low speed centrifugation to remove nuclei and debris, obtained a 18,000 *g* sediment, containing mitochondria and yolk granules. This fraction held at least 65% of the total egg DNA. In preliminary experiments where mitochondria were separated from yolk by sucrose gradient centrifugation, it appeared that most of the DNA was contained in the mitochondrial fraction even if, owing to the exceedingly higher number of mitochondria than of yolk granules, either particle contained the same amount of DNA. The cytoplasmic localization of this extra amount of

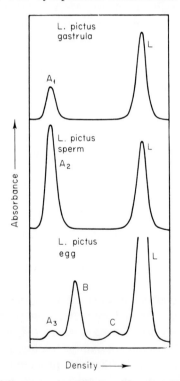

Fig. 9.1. Tracings of direct scans at 265 mμ of buoyant density bands (in CsCl) of preparations of DNA of *Lytechinus pictus* after 25 hours of centrifugation at 44,770 rpm in the Beckman model E centrifuge. L: density marker DNA (1.731 gm/cm^3) of *Micrococcus lysodeikticus;* A$_1$, A$_2$, and A$_3$: DNA's identified as nuclear in the three preparations and with similar buoyant density of 1.693; B: DNA identified as derived from mitochondria and yolk and with a buoyant density of 1.703; C: unidentified nucleic acid band of buoyant density 1.719. (From Pikò *et al.,* 1967.)

DNA explains why *Strongylocentrotus* eggs, having a lower volume, contain less DNA than *Lytechinus* eggs. If this extra amount of DNA is mitochondrial, one would expect it to have a base composition different from that of the bulk DNA. This was confirmed by Pikò *et al.* (1967, 1968) by means of buoyant density centrifugation and determination of the melting temperature. If the DNA is centrifuged in an analytical centrifuge, three bands of buoyant density are observed: 1.693, 1.703 and 1.719 gm/cm³, in the relative proportion of 1 : 7 : 1 (see Fig. 9.1). As shown by a marker sperm DNA the first peak corresponds to the nuclear DNA, the second to the mitochondrial DNA, and the third one to an unknown DNA. This latter, however, is not observed in further analyses (Fig. 9.2). At the gastrula stage, as is expected because of the enormous increase of the number of nuclei per embryo, not paralleled by any cytoplasmic growth, the nuclear fraction overwhelms the mitochondrial one.

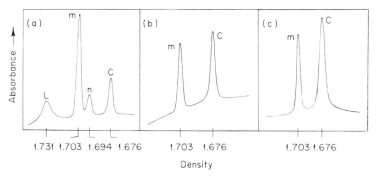

Fig. 9.2. Distribution of DNA in a buoyant density experiment in CsCl, 0.01 *M* Tris, pH 8. The DNA samples were obtained by dye-buoyant density centrifugation: (a) DNA from upper band; (b) DNA from lower band; and (c) DNA from middle band. L, DNA from *Micrococcus lysodeikticus;* C, crab dAT; m, mitochondrial DNA; n, nuclear DNA; (a) and (b) were centrifuged in the same rotor at 39,400 rpm for 43 hours, 25°C. (From Pikò *et al.,* 1968.)

The buoyant density suggests a guanine + cytosine content of 44% for the mitochondrial DNA and of 34% for the nuclear DNA. These values are in good agreement with those of 42 and 35%, respectively, obtained from the T_m determinations (Fig. 9.3). In a further analysis of the mitochondrial DNA, a preliminary CsCl centrifugation of the egg homogenates is followed by a centrifugation in CsCl with the addition of ethidium bromide. This causes the DNA to sediment into three distinct fluorescent bands, free from polysaccharide contamination. Ultracentrifugal analysis of the DNA of the three bands is shown in Fig. 9.2. All of them contain mitochondrial DNA. In addition the upper one contains some nuclear DNA. Electron microscope study of the mitochondrial DNA reveals that at least 95% of it is formed of circular molecules about 5 μ in average

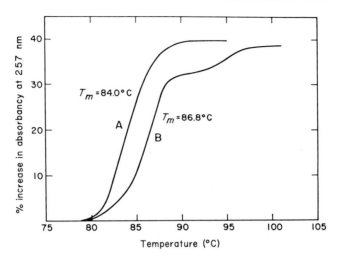

Fig. 9.3. Melting profiles of DNA's (in 0.15 M NaCl–0.015 M sodium citrate, pH 7) from *Lytechinus pictus.* Curve A: DNA from sperm and from gastrulae; curve B: DNA from whole unfertilized eggs. (From Pikò *et al.,* 1967.)

contour. About 11% of the circles are concatenate in the form of dimers, 1% in the form of trimers, and 0.3% of tetramers. The three CsCl ethidium bromide fractions contain different proportions of these oligomeres. The closed circular forms of DNA have an S value of 38 in 2.85 M CsCl and 1 M NaCl. Recent findings by Hartman *et al.* (1971) show that the density of purified mitochondrial DNA of *Lytechinus variegatus* is 1.693 gm/cm^3, i.e., identical to that of nuclear, or sperm, DNA. In this species, therefore, nuclear and mitochondrial DNA are not distinguishable from each other by CsCl gradient centrifugation.

By measuring the mean contour of mitochondrial DNA preparations under the electron microscope (5.4 μ), Hartman *et al.* (1971) have calculated that the molecular weight of mitochondrial DNA in *Lytechinus variegatus* is about 10.4 × 10^6 daltons.

B. Sperm DNA

Analysis of egg DNA, with the discovery of mitochondrial DNA, (whose implications in development will be discussed in Chapter 10) reached a meaningful level only recently, thanks to the modern techniques of macromolecular analysis. The study of DNA from sea urchin sperm, on the other hand, dates back at least to 1897 (Mathews, 1897). Here in fact we are met with the opposite situation to that of the egg, i.e., a very large nucleus with a very small cytoplasm. This makes the sperm a very suitable subject for DNA studies. We shall mention in this respect that the base ratio analysis of sea urchin DNA have provided part of the evidence that served Chargaff to establish his rules on the equivalence of A + G and T + C. Table 9.1, derived from data quoted by Chargaff and Davidson (1955), reports the base composition of sperm DNA from several species of sea urchins. It appears that sea urchin DNA has a particularly high A + T content, of the order of about 64% of the sum of the four bases. This value is in fair agreement with the CsCl gradient analyses and the melting profiles (Pikò *et al.*, 1967; Enea and Mutolo, unpublished; Kedes and Birnstiel, 1971; Carden *et al.*, 1965; Bibring *et al.*, 1965; Slater and Spiegelman, 1966b).

A method has been described by Solari (1967) that allows extraction of native DNA from sperm of *Strongylocentrotus purpuratus,* with very little shearing. Electron microscopic examination of the DNA strands isolated in this way reveal fibers longer than 100 μ, and 2.1–2.5 nm high. This means that, if one accepts the figures of 10^{-12} gm as DNA content of one sperm and of 20 as its chromosome number, the DNA of each chromosome may be made up at most of 20 distinct DNA segments. Pikò *et al.* (1967, 1968) have reported the occasional occurrence of a

TABLE 9.1

PURINE AND PYRIMIDINE CONTENTS OF SODIUM DEOXYPENTOSE NUCLEATES OF VARIOUS SEA URCHIN SPERM[a,b]

Animal	Adenine	Guanine	Cytosine	5-Methyl-cytosine	Thymine	A+T/G+C+MC	Actual recovery	Ref.[c]
Arbacia punctulata	28.4	19.5	19.3		32.8	1.58	93.9	(a)
Arbacia lixula	31.2	19.1	19.2		30.5	1.61	94.2	(b)
Echinus esculentus	30.9	19.4	18.4	1.8	29.4	1.52	92	(c)
Echino-cardium cordatum	32.9	17.0	17.9		32.2	1.86	96.4	(b)
Psamme-chinus miliaris	32.6	17.8	17.8		31.9	1.81	94.0	(b)
Paracen-trotus lividus	32.8	17.7	17.3	(1.1)	32.1	1.85	94.7	(b)

[a]Proportions in moles of nitrogenous constituent per 100 gram-atoms of P in hydrolyzate, corrected for a 100% recovery.

[b]Data derived from Chargaff and Davidson (1955).

[c](a) Daly *et al.* (1950); (b) Chargaff *et al.* (1952); (c) Wyatt (1951).

satellite band, of 1.719 gm/cm³ buoyant density, upon CsCl centrifugation of the sperm DNA of *Lytechinus pictus*. A similar band has been
observed in *Lytechinus variegatus* by Stafford and Guild (1969), of 1.722
gm/cm³ buoyant density. The authors suggest that this band represents
the cistrons for the ribosomal RNA. It constitutes 0.5% of the total
DNA and, at least under the conditions of extraction employed, is made
up of strands which, upon analytical ultracentrifugation, give a result of
22×10^6 daltons, i.e., about 10 times the lengths of the two subunits of
ribosomal RNA (a figure of 1×10^7 daltons is given by Patterson and
Stafford, 1970). In a first attempt at purifying these cistrons in bulk
amount, about 30 mg of DNA was loaded by these authors on a column
of hydroxylapatite. An elution with phosphate buffer at two ionic strengths
and at three different temperatures indicated that a fraction of high G + C
content, which is not eluted at least up to 91°C, is enriched. This hybridized better than the bulk DNA with ribosomal RNA. Finer details
of the results reported by the authors need, in our opinion, more hybridization experiments performed with ribosomal RNA of much higher
specific activity to obtain a safe interpretation. In a second paper, Patterson and Stafford (1970) describe a new attempt at purifying the ribosomal cistrons by a different approach. The total DNA was heated at
79°C with the aim of denaturing all of it except the sequences of high
G + C. The denatured sequences were then separated from those remaining still native by virtue of their different partition coefficient in a
polyethylene glycol dextran two-phase system. Ultracentrifugation
analysis of the DNA so purified showed that the satellite DNA, under
such conditions, was enriched by a factor of 700, with a recovery of 45%
of the total amount. A hybridization experiment, even if still performed
with a low number of hybridizable counts and without a study of the
kinetics of hybridization, shows clearly enough that the satellite band, so
purified, is able to hybridize homologous ribosomal RNA, while the
remaining bulk DNA is not. No control is reported of the ability of the
entire bulk DNA (i.e., that which is recuperated from the main band of
a CsCl gradient, with no prior loss of most of its sequences by polyethylene glycol-dextran) to hybridize ribosomal RNA.

In a third paper Patterson and Stafford (1971) have finally proved,
by hybridization experiments with rRNA of adequate specific activity,
that all of the satellite DNA of *Lytechinus variegatus* sperms represents
rRNA cistrons. A detailed study of the denaturation and renaturation
kinetics allows the authors to conclude that the satellite DNA is composed of two nearly equal parts of 59.5% G + C and 62.5% G + C. It
behaves as a single family of ribosomal genes of 5.2×10^6 daltons repeated about 260-fold in a haploid genome. It can be estimated from these
data that rRNA in sea urchins can be synthesized in the form of a precursor of 2.6×10^6 daltons, which is in excellent agreement with the

figures of 2.58×10^6 daltons reported by Sconzo *et al.* (1971) (see Chapter 10), after direct measurement of the rRNA precursor size.

The experiments of Patterson and Stafford also provide a valid suggestion that a situation of linkage of the genes for ribosomal RNA exists in sea urchin similar to that described in amphibians (Birnstiel *et al.*, 1969; Brown and Weber, 1968).

Besides the repetitious sequences for ribosomal RNA (Mutolo and Giudice, 1967; Patterson and Stafford, 1970, 1971) other repetitious sequences must exist in sea urchin DNA. On the basis of the pattern of reannealing of denatured DNA at different concentrations and for different lengths of time, Britten and Kone (1968) have calculated that the incidence of repetitious sequences in sea urchin sperm DNA is intermediate between that of calf or mouse satellite DNA, on the one hand, and that of plant DNA, on the other (Fig. 9.4). More recent calculations (Britten, personal communication) suggest that 60% of sea urchin DNA is made up of nonrepetitious sequences. The remaining 40% contains sequences repeated a variable number of times (from about 20 up to 10,000).

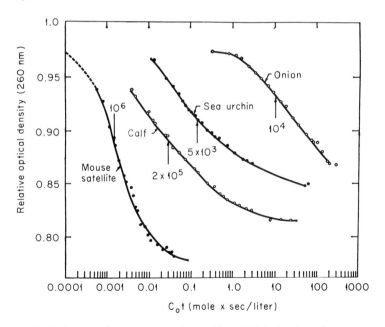

Fig. 9.4. Optical reassociation curves of repetitious DNA fractions from various organisms. All of the fractions were purified on hydroxyapatite with only minor modifications in the procedure for each different DNA. The left scale gives the ratio of the optical density at 60°C to the initial value measured at 98°C. All of the fractions except that from onion were reassociated in 0.08 *M* phosphate buffer at 60°C; the onion DNA was reassociated in 0.24 *M* phosphate buffer at 60°C. (From Britten and Kone, 1968. Copyright 1968 by the American Association for the Advancement of Science.)

Whiteley *et al.* (1970) have measured the extent of homology among repetitious sequences in the DNA's of echinoderm sperms of the genera *Strongylocentrotus, Dendraster,* and *Pisaster.* DNA–DNA annealing was performed under conditions that practically permitted only annealing of the repetitious sequences. To control the fidelity of base pairing in the heteroduplexes, the hybrids between DNA's of different genera were heated and the T_m compared to that of the homologous DNA–DNA duplexes. Under the conditions used, a decrease of only 0°–4°C of the T_m of the heteroduplexes, with respect to that of the homologous pairs, was found and taken as indicative of 0–2.8% of mismatch.

Homology of 70% was found between the DNA's of different species belonging to the same genus; 10% between the sand dollar and Strongylocentotides, and 7% between asteroids and echinoids.

Kedes and Birnstiel (1971) have elegantly demonstrated that purified 9 S RNA, believed to represent messenger RNA for histones (see Chapter 11), hybridizes specifically with sequences of DNA that self-anneal at an average of Cot ½ of 15–40. This means that the sequences for histone mRNA are highly repetitive. It is also shown that the 9 S RNA hybridizes preferentially with sequences of DNA which, after shearing into fragments of 5×10^5 daltons, sediment in CsCl gradients at 1.711 gm/cm^3, i.e., with a high $G + C$ content as would be expected from the amino acid composition of histones.

C. DNA Synthesis during Development

DNA synthesis is one of the most important anabolic phenomena of the developing sea urchin. Although there is no net mass increase of the embryo up to the prism stage, a marked increase of the DNA content per embryo is readily observable (see Figs. 9.5, 9.6, and 6.11). The embryo increases the number of its nuclei by a factor of about 2000 by the prism stage.

It is an old observation that this increase in the nuclear number is paralleled by a decrease in the nuclear volume and in the volume of the single chromosomes (Erdmann, 1908; Conklin, 1912; Whiteley and Baltzer, 1958). Is there a variation of the DNA content of the single nucleus during development? An affirmative answer is given by earlier microspectrophotometrical work (Lison and Pasteels, 1951); but McMaster (1952, 1955) by the same method, and Elson *et al.* (1954) and Whiteley and Baltzer (1958) by chemical assays have established that there is no variation of the total DNA per nucleus, at least from the 32-cell stage up to pluteus. The calculations in stages prior to the 32-cell stage are rendered difficult because of the reasons reported in the previous section.

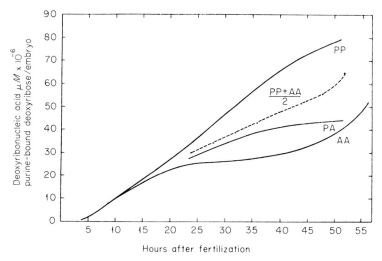

Fig. 9.5. Increase in DNA content during the development of *Paracentrotus lividus* (PP). *Arbacia lixula* (AA) or of the hybrid *Paracentrotus* ♀ × *Arbacia* ♂. In addition to the actual DNA values of PP, PA, and AA, a curve of the average of PP and AA values, representing the amounts expected in a theoretical hybrid receiving equal contributions from each parent, is indicated by the dotted line. (From Whiteley and Baltzer, 1958.)

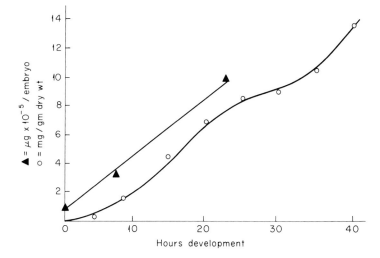

Fig. 9.6. The DNA content of sea urchin embryos in the course of early development. Open circles (O) represent data of Brachet (1933) on embryos of *Paracentrotus lividus*, given as mg DNA/gm dry embryo. Triangles (▲) represent data of Schmidt *et al.* (1948) on *Arbacia punctulata*, given as μg DNA phosphorus ($\times 10^{-5}$) per embryo. (From Mazia, 1949a.)

An approximate measure of DNA synthesis rate is given by pulse experiments where 5-iododeoxyuridine was incorporated into the acid-insoluble fraction of *Arbacia punctulata* at various developmental stages (Wheeler *et al.,* 1964). Permeability factors and pool variations, however, render an exact measure of the synthesis rate from these data rather difficult.

Data on the DNA content of sperms or blastula nuclei of different sea urchin species have recently been reported by Villiger *et al.* (1970). Assuming 1 as the DNA content in *Paracentrotus lividus,* the following values have been found in other species: *Sphaerechinus granularis,* 1.61; *Stylocidaris affinis,* 1.71; *Echinocardium cordatum,* 1.65; *Arbacia lixula,* 0.74.

How long after fertilization does synthesis of the new DNA start? Simmel and Karnofsky (1961) had shown that pronuclei of the sand dollar fertilized egg incorporate thymidine even before their fusion. This has been autoradiographically confirmed quite recently by Brookbank (1970) for *Dendraster excentricus,* but not for *Strongylocentrotus purpuratus.*

The same results have been obtained by W. A. Anderson (1969), by electron microscope autoradiographic study of *Paracentrotus lividus* eggs.

From the results of incorporation of labeled [2-¹⁴C]deoxyuridine, [2-¹⁴C]thymidine, and [2-¹⁴C]cytidine into DNA (Nemer, 1962a), it might be inferred that some DNA synthesis also takes place in *Paracentrotus lividus* eggs before fusion of the pronuclei. Nemer (1962a) has

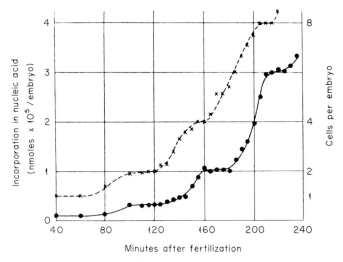

Fig. 9.7. Incorporation of [2-¹⁴C]deoxyuridine into nucleic acid of synchronously dividing embryos of *Paracentrotus lividus.* Initial concentration, 160 mμmoles of [2-¹⁴C]deoxyuridine/10⁵ embryos/20 ml, at 18°C. These data are single determinations from one of two similar experiments, ●———●, incorporation in total trichloroacetic acid precipitate; ×---×, cells/embryo. (From Nemer, 1962a.)

detailed the timing of DNA synthesis during the first divisions up to the
the 16-cell stage (Figs. 9.7–9.9). These experiments take advantage of
the synchrony of cell division of early cleavage. It appears that about
one half of DNA is synthesized around 5 minutes after half the cell has
divided. The possibility that the incorporation pattern reported in Fig.
9.7 is due to permeability variations to the isotope during the cell cycle
is disproved by the experiments shown in Figs. 9.8 and 9.9, where the
eggs had been preloaded for 2 hours, with [2-¹⁴C]thymidine and [2-¹⁴C]-
cytidine, respectively, after which the kinetics of incorporation into
DNA of the isotope accumulated in the pool was studied.

These results are in fair agreement with the conclusions reached by
Lison and Pasteels (1951) by the use of microspectrophotometry, and by
Ficq *et al.* (1963) and Zimmerman (1963a,b) by means of radioautog-

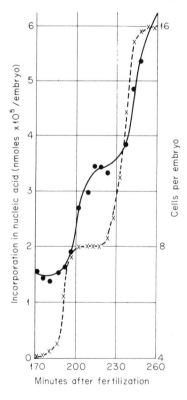

Fig. 9.8. Incorporation of [2-¹⁴C]thymidine into nucleic acid of synchronously dividing
embryos of *Paracentrotus lividus.* Initial concentration, 72 nmoles of [2-¹⁴C]thymidine/10⁵
embryos/20 ml, incubated at 18°C for 2 hours. Embryos were resuspended in fresh seawater,
after 2 washes, then again incubated, with samples taken every 5 minutes. These data are
single determinations from one of two similar experiments. ●——●, incorporation in total
trichloroacetic acid precipitate; ×---×, cells/embryo. (From Nemer, 1962a).

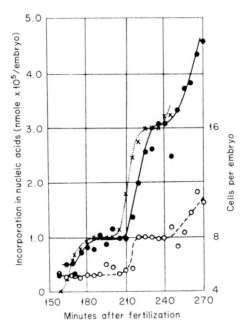

Fig. 9.9. Incorporation of [2-¹⁴C]cytidine into deoxyribonucleic acid and ribonucleic acid of synchronously dividing embryos of *Paracentrotus lividus*. Initial concentration of 34 nmoles of [2-¹⁴C]cytidine/10⁵ embryos/20 ml, incubated for 2 hours at 18°C. Embryos were washed twice and resuspended in fresh seawater, with samples then taken every 5 minutes. These data are single determinations from one of two similar experiments. ●——●, incorporation in DNA; O---O, incorporation in RNA; ×---×, cells/embryo. (From Nemer, 1962a.)

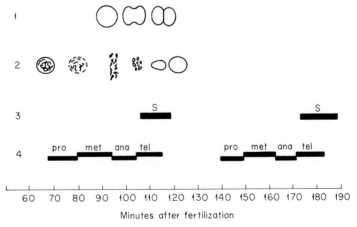

Fig. 9.10. Summary of experimental results: (1) Appearance of the egg at the time of DNA synthesis; (2) appearance of the nucleus and chromosomes at the beginning of each mitotic phase; (3) time and duration of DNA synthesis; (4) time and duration of each mitotic phase. (From Hinegardner *et al.,* 1964.)

raphy. No comparison is possible with the data of Hirshfield *et al.* (1961) because of the lack of details in the latter report.

The DNA synthetic period in the first two divisions, together with the morphological changes at chromosomal level, has been accurately studied by Hinegardner *et al.* (1964) in *Strongylocentrotus purpuratus.* A statistical evaluation results in the conclusions schematically reported in Fig. 9.10. According to these authors, DNA synthesis starts at the end of telophase and lasts for about 13 minutes (at 15°C), i.e., up to the beginning of interphase. Relative to the chromosomal morphological behavior, this means that DNA synthesis starts when the formation of vesicles including the chromosomes has taken place and ends when these vesicles have fused to form a spherical nucleus. A further confirmation of these findings comes from the thymidine incorporation experiments by Fansler and Loeb (1969). The timing of DNA synthesis during the first three cleavages has also been studied by Nagano and Mano (1958), by pulse labeling with ^{32}P or with [2-^{14}C]thymidine, in *Hemicentrotus pulcherrimus.* The curves for both isotopes representing the rate of incorporation into DNA show three distinct peaks, two corresponding to the early interphase after the first and second divisions, while the first peak precedes the first cell division. These results also show the periodicity of DNA synthesis and are roughly in agreement with the previous ones. A stepwise curve of thymidine incorporation into DNA of cleaving eggs of *Psammechinus miliaris* and *Paracentrotus lividus* has been reported by Czihak and Pohl (1970), who suggest that an active transport mechanism for thymidine is switched on at fertilization. Finally, Zeitz *et al.* (1969, 1970) have found that bromodeoxyuridine and iododeoxyuridine are immediately incorporated into the DNA of fertilized eggs of *Strongylocentrotus purpuratus* or *Arbacia punctulata,* while thymidine and deoxyuridine are incorporated after a lag of about 20 minutes. The authors suggest that DNA synthesis starts immediately after fertilization, as proved by the experiments with the first two precursors, and that the delayed incorporation of thymidine or deoxyuridine might be explained by a transitory inhibition of their phosphorylation because of the presence of a pool of deoxythymidine triphosphate (see following pages).

A recent study of DNA synthesis during embryogenesis of *Strongylocentrotus purpuratus* has been presented by Baker (1971), who, by pulse and chase experiments followed by analysis of the DNA on sucrose gradient and hydroxyapatite columns, found that single- and double-stranded DNA of about 8–16 S is labeled at morula. While radioactivity disappears from the single-stranded DNA molecules following the chase, it accumulates in the double-stranded ones, which are only much later incorporated into heavier (16–70 S) DNA molecules. It is proposed that the single-strand DNA labeling represents the semiconservative synthesis of short DNA strands which are then joined by the ligase, while the double-stranded DNA labeling is representative of an amplification phenomenon. Direct proofs of these suggestions would, of course, be most welcome.

J. Brachet (1933, 1937) long ago made the suggestion that the rapid increase of DNA during early development might occur at the expense of an RNA storage. This idea has been disproved by chemical assays of DNA and RNA in developing sea urchins by Schmidt *et al.* (1948) and by experiments of incorporation of labeled precursors into DNA (Villee *et al.*, 1949; Abrams, 1951; Scarano and Kalckar, 1953). These authors have shown that the dramatic DNA increase during early development is not paralleled by any decrease of RNA, whose gross amount actually stays constant up to pluteus stage. On the other hand, when incorporation of ^{32}P (Villee *et al.*, 1949), [1-^{14}C]acetate and [1-^{14}C]glycine (Abrams, 1951; Scarano and Kalckar, 1953). [8-^{14}C]-adenine (Scarano and Kalckar, 1953), or [2-^{14}C]cytidine (Nemer, 1962a), is followed during the early development, the specific activity attained by DNA is always much higher than that attained by RNA. This excludes the possibility that the RNA is quickly synthesized, disassembled, and fed into DNA.

1. PRECURSOR POOL

DNA appears to be made at the expense of a low-molecular-weight precursor pool. To have an idea of the nature of this precursor pool and its turnover, it is interesting to follow the experiments on the incorporation kinetics of exogenously fed, labeled precursors. The sea urchin egg is a closed system which ordinarily does not receive exogenous nucleotides to make its own nucleic acids; nonetheless, as already seen, it allows exogenously administered nucleosides and lower molecular weight precursors to penetrate its pool for incorporation into nucleic acid. As shown by Abrams (1951), Hultin (1953a), and Scarano and Kalckar (1953), acetate and glycine can be used to build the purine ring. The radioactivity from [1-^{14}C]glycine administered at fertilization to *Arbacia lixula* is equally shared at the 64-cell stage by adenine and guanine in RNA and DNA. Scarano and Kalckar have also shown that, at the swimming blastula stage of *Paracentrotus lividus* and *Sphaerechinus granularis,* [8-^{14}C]adenine is incorporated as such into nucleic acid and only one tenth is converted into guanine. The degree of this conversion is somewhat higher at later stages. Nemer (1962a) has shown that although unfertilized eggs of *Paracentrotus lividus* take up very little cytidine, uridine, thymidine, deoxyuridine, thymidylic acid, and deoxyuridylic

TABLE 9.2

INCORPORATION OF NUCLEOSIDES AND NUCLEOTIDES IN ACID-SOLUBLE AND ACID-INSOLUBLE COMPONENTS OF EARLY CLEAVAGE STAGE EMBRYOS[a, b]

Labeled compound	Millimicromoles $\times$ 10[5]/embryo			
	Amount incubated	Acid-soluble	Acid-precipitate	Total uptake
Cytidine	72	33	2.2	35.2
Uridine	118	27	0.8	27.8
Thymidine	101	6.5	4.6	11.1
Deoxyuridine	128	4.5	2.9	7.4
Thymidylic acid	134	2.5	3.2	5.7
Deoxyuridylic acid	38	0.5	0.9	1.4

[a]From Nemer (1962a).
[b]Incubations of 10[5] embryos/20 ml were performed for 3 hours. Embryos developed from the 1- to approximately the 8-blastomere stage. Amounts of exogenous incorporation were calculated with appropriate self-absorption corrections for acid-soluble material and precipitates on Millipore filters. These data are averages of duplicate determinations of $\pm$ 10% precision.

acid, fertilized eggs very actively take up all of these compounds (Table 9.2). Incorporation of the ribonucleosides into the acid-soluble pool is more active than that of the deoxyribonucleosides: 5000 fertilized eggs/ml are able to clear the seawater of all cytidine at 2×10^{-6} M, and 50% of uridine at 4×10^{-6} M, in 2 hours. Deoxyribonucleosides are more actively utilized for nucleic acid synthesis in early cleavage than the corresponding ribonucleosides. This may be due to the higher rate of DNA synthesis, and also, in principle, to a different dilution of the exogenous precursors in the internal pools, whose size has not been measured in these experiments. The lack of knowledge of the internal pool should not allow expression of the results of Fig. 9.11 in terms of micromoles incorporated.

Uridine is utilized more than twice as much for DNA synthesis as for RNA synthesis in the just fertilized eggs. On the other hand, at pluteus stage uridine is equally shared between DNA and RNA. This again may, in principle, be explained by the higher rate of RNA synthesis as compared to DNA synthesis in the later stages (see Chapter 10) or by variations in the internal pool or in the activity of enzymes, which convert uridine into deoxycytidine or thymidine. This latter possibility, however, is disproved by the effect of addition of unlabeled cytidine on uridine incorporation and vice versa, which is the same in early and later stages. That such interconversions are very active in the sea urchin embryo is also shown by the effect of addition of unlabeled cytidine on the incor-

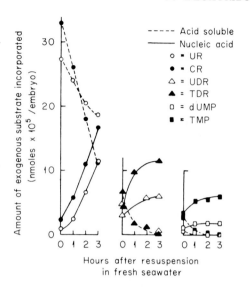

Fig. 9.11. Utilization of acid-soluble components derived from exogenously supplied nucleosides and nucleotides. These incubations followed resuspension in fresh seawater of embryos which had been preincubated for 3 hours with the given compounds, as described in Table 9.2. UR, uridine; CR, cytidine; UDR, deoxyuridine; TDR, deoxythymidine. (From Nemer, 1962a.)

poration of labeled uridine and vice versa (Table 9.3). It will be shown later that exogenous supplied uridine is very actively utilized for the terminal turnover of the cytidine of the transfer RNA during early cleavage (see Chapter 10). The incorporation values of [2-¹⁴C]deoxyuridine, [2-¹⁴C]thymidine, and [2-¹⁴C]cytidine in Figs. 9.7–9.9 are reported in terms of millimicromoles without considering the possible dilution of labeled nucleosides in the internal pool.

From the theoretical amount of DNA synthesized per cell division and calculated on the basis of the DNA content of the sperm nucleus (Elson *et al.,* 1954; Chargaff *et al.,* 1952), Nemer (1962a) has estimated that under the conditions used, most of the thymidine for DNA synthesis from 4 to 8 cells is derived from exogenous thymidine or deoxyuridine, while about 45% of cytidine for DNA synthesis from 8 to 16 cells is derived from the exogenous source which apparently is met with about as much of an endogenous pool, i.e., with about 4×10^{-4} nmoles per egg. The preferential utilization of exogenous thymidine may indicate a small endogenous pool and possibly a feedback mechanism on the endogenous synthesis of thymidine. The fact that the endogenous pool of thymidine is not very large is confirmed by the finding that fluorodeoxyuridine blocks development at the 8-blastomere stage. This nucleoside acts by blocking

TABLE 9.3

INCORPORATION IN RNA AND DNA IN PRESENCE AND ABSENCE OF UNLABELED
NUCLEOSIDES[a,b]

Labeled compound	Unlabeled compound	Ratio of unlabeled to labeled compound	Radioactivity incorporated/10^5 embryos (cpm)		Ratio of incorporation DNA/RNA
			DNA	RNA	
		Embryo at 1 hour			
Cytidine	None		4,570	592	7.7
	Uridine	5:1	745	118	6.3
Uridine	None		1,390	624	2.2
	Cytidine	1:1	352	314	1.1
		Embryo at 24 hours			
Cytidine	None		10,500	5,780	1.8
	Uridine	5:1	2,500	1,460	1.7
Uridine	None		21,100	18,300	1.1
	Cytidine	1:1	11,400	7,600	1.5

[a] From Nemer (1962a).
[b] Embryos were incubated for 5 hours in presence of [2-^{14}C]cytidine at 32 nmoles/10^5 embryos/20 ml or [2-^{14}C]uridine at 200 nmoles/10^5 embryos/20 ml. The 1-hour embryos developed from the 1- to the 32-blastomere stage; the 24-hour embryos were gastrulae. Values of $\pm20\%$ precision represent one of two similar experiments.

the conversion of 5-deoxyuridylic acid to 5-thymidylic acid. Actually, as shown by Nemer, it is possible to reverse its effect with thymidine (and also with 5-methyldeoxycytidine or with 5-iododeoxyuridine). Hence it is suggested that the reserve of endogenous thymidine in the egg is just enough to support DNA synthesis up to the 8-cell stage. This value is in fair agreement with that reported by Kavanau (1956) by means of a microbiological assay of free thymidine; 4.6×10^{-5} nmoles per egg, i.e., enough to support DNA synthesis up to the 16-cell stage. J. Brachet (1967), using hydroxyurea, a drug that interferes with the reduction of ribonucleotides to deoxyribonucleotides, has obtained exactly the same effect: arrest of development at 8 blastomeres of the *Paracentrotus* egg. The effect is only partially reversible by exogenous thymidine at a low concentration of hydroxyurea. Identical results have been obtained with *Paracentrotus* by Giudice (unpublished); the only difference is that exogenous nucleosides or nucleotides are found completely unable to reverse the hydroxyurea effect. Interestingly enough, the eggs thus blocked show a normal rate of oxygen consumption for several hours. They fail, however, to show a respiratory increase at blastula. A different result has been obtained by Karnofsky and Basch (1960) with *Echinaracninus parma*. Actually in this species the 5-fluorodeoxyuridine blocks development only at blastula stage. In addition, Karnofsky and Bevelander (1958) have shown that 6-diazo-5-oxo-L-norleucine and azaserine, two antagonists of glutamine, whose effect is counteracted by hypoxanthine and guanosine, allow the embryos to develop over a longer period than fluorodeoxyuridine, thus suggesting that the purine reserve in these embryos may be larger than that of pyrimidines.

D. Enzymes Involved in the Metabolism of Nucleotides

Apart from the indirect evidence for the metabolic pathways of nucleotides produced above, some direct measurements of enzymatic activities have been performed.

1. ADENOSINE DEAMINASE

This enzyme has been assayed on homogenates of *Psammechinus miliaris* eggs by Gustafson and Hasselberg (1951). The optimum pH is around 6.0. The activity remains constant throughout development, and is not affected by Li treatment of the embryos.

2. THYMIDINE KINASE AND THYMIDYLATE KINASE

These two enzymes might play a key role in the regulation of DNA synthesis. Nagano and Mano (1968) found that their activities, when assayed on homogenates or crude extracts of *Hemicentrotus pulcherrimus,* show cyclic variations, with maximal activity roughly coincident with the peaks of DNA synthesis. The first drop in activity is especially evident only for thymidylate kinase and takes place about 50 minutes following fertilization. What is the mechanism that regulates these enzymatic activities? That both puromycin and ethionine *in vivo* inhibit the thymidine kinase activity has led the authors to suggest the possibility that enzyme synthesis may be at least in part responsible for the cyclic increases. It should not be forgotten, however, that the severe inhibition of protein synthesis brought about by these drugs might produce other cell damages, such as block of mitosis (Hultin, 1961a) or inhibition of respiration (Giudice, 1965), which, in turn, might act upon this enzymatic activity. Alternatively, the authors propose that the activity changes of thymidine kinase might be brought about by reciprocal variations in the concentration of the substrate (thymidine) and of the terminal derivative of the product, i.e., thymidine triphosphate. As is known for other living materials, these two compounds are found, respectively, to stabilize and to inhibit the enzymatic activity. The following cycle might, therefore, be imagined: (1) Thymidine is exhausted due to thymidine monophosphate synthesis, and thymidine triphosphate is thereafter produced. (2) The thymidine kinase activity drops. (3) Thymidine triphosphate is used up for DNA synthesis, more thymidine is produced, and the thymidine kinase activity is permitted to rise again.

All four deoxyribonucleotide kinases have been directly assayed by Fansler and Loeb (1969) in *Strongylocentrotus purpuratus*. Their activity was not found to undergo important variations when unfertilized eggs, 2-cell and 100-cell stages were compared. These enzymes appeared to be present in both nucleus and cytoplasm of the unfertilized egg.

3. DEOXYCYTIDYLATE AMINOHYDROLASE

This enzymatic activity was first discovered by Scarano on homogenates or acetone powders of unfertilized eggs and embryos of *Paracentrotus lividus* and *Sphaerechinus granularis* (Scarano, 1958a–f; Scarano and Maggio, 1959a,b; Scarano *et al.*, 1960). This enzyme is able to convert 5′-deoxycytidylic acid to 5′-deoxyuridylic acid, and 5′-methyl-deoxycytidylic acid to 5′-thymidylic acid. The enzyme can, therefore, be defined as a 6-aminopyrimidine deoxyribonucleotide deaminase. Scarano and his co-workers have thoroughly studied the characteristics of this enzyme (which was first discovered in sea urchins) by extracting it from more suitable materials, e.g., from donkey spleen. Briefly, it is ascertained that compounds with a methyl, a hydroxymethyl, a fluorine, a bromine, or an iodine in the 5-position of the pyrimidine ring are also deaminated by the enzyme. The catalyzed reaction is at a branching point of the pathway for the production of deoxycytidine triphosphate (dTTP), i.e., the most immediate precursors of DNA synthesis (Scarano *et al.*, 1963). Using a homogeneous preparation of the enzyme, it is shown that deoxycytidylate aminohydrolase is a typical allosteric enzyme, activated by dCTP-Mg and inhibited by dTTP-Mg. Changes in the affinity of the catalytic sites of the enzyme for the substrates or for substrate competitors are caused by the allosteric effectors. By filtration on Sephadex G-25, it is seen that each enzyme molecule binds 4 molecules of dCTP-Mg or of dTTP-Mg. The enzyme cannot bind, at the same time, both activator and inhibitor. On the basis of the SH group content, it seems that the enzyme occurs in at least three conformational isomeres (Scarano *et al.*, 1964a, 1967a,b; Geraci *et al.*, 1967; Rossi *et al.*, 1967). Can this enzyme play a role in differentiation? A study of this kind is tempting because of the already reported detailed knowledge of its characteristics. Scarano and Maggio (1959b) have measured the enzymatic activity during development and found that it decreases during development with a more pronounced drop at gastrulation. Interestingly enough, if RNA synthesis is disturbed with doses of actinomycin, that are known to give a degree of inhibition of at least 70% in sea urchins, then the decrease in enzymatic activity does not take place. On the contrary, a paradoxical effect is observed in the case of highest doses of actinomycin, which yield an enzyme activity higher in the later stages than in the unfertilized eggs (Fig. 9.12) (Scarano *et al.*, 1964b). The sensitive period for actinomycin is from fertilization up to 16 hours later, thus suggesting that the decrease of such an enzymatic activity is under a positive control, i.e., dependent on the synthesis of some RNA. It should be noted that the embryos under such conditions do not gastrulate and remain arrested at the blastula stage for about 1 day. It is, therefore, possible that the arrest of RNA synthesis exerts its effect on the enzyme activity only in an indirect way, i.e., through the arrest of development.

The same authors (Scarano *et al.*, 1964c) have found that if the embryos are dissociated into single cells according to the method of Giudice (1962a) while the enzymatic activity is decreasing, then the activity de-

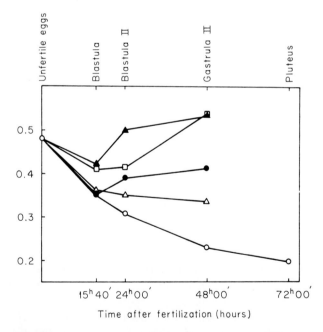

Fig. 9.12. Action of actinomycin C on dCMP aminohydrolase activity during the early embryonic development of *Sphaerechinus granularis*. On the ordinate are plotted the μM of dCMP deaminated per mg of proteins and per 10 minutes. Incubation mixture: 2 mM dCMP, 100 mM phosphate buffer (pH 7.3). The treated embryos remained at blastula stage. O, controls; $\triangle$, embryos grown in 5 mg/liter of actinomycin C; $\bullet$, embryos grown in 10 mg/liter of actinomycin C; $\square$, embryos grown in 20 mg/liter of actinomycin C; $\blacktriangle$ embryos grown in 40 mg/liter of actinomycin C. (From Scarano *et al.*, 1964b.)

crease is halted and the enzymatic level remains constant for at least 32 hours more. These findings would favor a role of cell interactions in the regulation of such enzymatic activity. Moreover, if the embryos are grown in Ca-free seawater, after removal of the fertilization membrane, which causes cell disaggregation, the drop in enzymatic activity is never observed. It should be noted that the embryonic cells were kept after dissociation in Ca^{2+}-free seawater. In our experience (Giudice and Mutolo, 1970) this causes a marked metabolic impairment, as revealed by a drop in the rate of protein synthesis, which might in turn affect the enzymatic activity.

4. DNA POLYMERASE

This enzymatic activity has been studied in sea urchins by Mazia and co-workers (Mazia and Hinegardner, 1963; Loeb *et al.,* 1967, 1969; Fansler and Loeb, 1969). The enzyme was first assayed on nuclei of *Strongylocentrotus purpuratus,* isolated by the method of Hinegardner (1962). The enzymatic activity of the isolated nuclei largely depends on the addition of exogenous primer DNA. Native DNA is a better primer than the denatured one. A slight treatment of the added DNA with pancreatic DNase increases its priming ability. The base composition of the product appears to depend on that of the primer. The presence of Mg^{2+} or Mn^{2+} is required. The external addition of all four deoxyribonucleotides is not strictly necessary, probably because of an endogenous pool, which may also be refurnished by the coupled activity of DNase and deoxyribonucleotide kinase. The pH optimum is around 7.3.

The enzymatic activity of total homogenates of *Strongylocentrotus purpuratus* or *Strongylocentrotus franciscanus* does not undergo variations with the phases of the cell cycle, i.e., at moments when the rate of DNA synthesis changes considerably. Nor are variations of enzyme activity found throughout development. There is only a slight increase from the time preceding fertilization up to gastrula stage.

What appears to change as development proceeds is the intracellular localization of the enzyme; from cytoplasmic, in the unfertilized egg, it becomes progressively more and more nuclear. L. A. Loeb and Fansler (1970) have provided indirect evidence that this is not due to breakdown of the cytoplasmic enzyme and synthesis of a nuclear one, but to a transfer of the enzyme from cytoplasm to the nucleus. This conclusion is based on studies of amino acid incorporation into the purified enzyme of *Strongylocentrotus purpuratus* embryos. They show that the rate of synthesis and turnover of the enzyme is not higher than that of the bulk proteins and, therefore, do not justify an active enzyme breakdown and resynthesis. To make their point, a careful method of cell fractionation has been devised by the authors. It should be noted that the test for the lack of nuclear damage reported refers only to the hatched blastulae; the danger for nuclear breakage appears greater at earlier stages when the nuclei are more fragile, probably because of their larger volume. The authors elegantly demonstrate the cytoplasmic localization of the polymerase in the unfertilized eggs by dividing them in nucleated and nonnucleated halves, by means of centrifugation through a continuous sucrose gradient according to a modification of Harvey's (1956a) technique. Considering the enormous increase in the number of nuclei throughout development, these results suggest that the egg has stored in its cytoplasm an amount of polymerase sufficient to synthesize hundreds of times the DNA of the egg nucleus at one time, e.g., in the lapse of one cell division at gastrula stage. It appears possible that the decrease of mitotic activity after hatching is somewhat correlated with the depletion of the cytoplasmic reserve of DNA polymerase.

The problem of the presence of a cytoplasmic deoxyribonuclease activity has been partially circumvented by the addition of high amounts of DNA and deoxyribonucleotide triphosphates and by the use of short incubation periods. It is also shown that when nuclei are rendered artificially diploid by means of estradiol treatment (Agrell, 1954) their polymerase content is increased.

Loeb (1969) has purified the sea urchin DNA polymerase to the point where it exhibits only one distinct band after polyacrylamide gel electrophoresis; the author concludes that most, if not all, of the proteins in the most purified enzyme fraction is DNA polymerase. On this basis, Loeb has been able to calculate the number of enzyme molecules per unit of activity. This has been followed by determination of the DNA polymerase activity of the chromatin from nuclei of *Strongylocentrotus purpuratus* and *Strongylocentrotus franciscanus* hatching blastulae (Loeb, 1970). The conclusion is that chromatin brings 1 molecule of DNA polymerase every 2000–3000 nucleotide pair. It can be calculated that at this stage, on the average, 15% of the nuclei are making DNA at any given moment.

Homogenous DNA polymerase preparations contain about 4 gm atoms Zn per enzyme mole according to Slater *et al.* (1971). On the basis of the effect of chelating substances, these authors suggest that Zn plays a role in the binding of the enzyme to DNA.

An interesting approach to the problem of the regulation of DNA replication is that used by Slater and Loeb (1970). These authors have observed that the treatment of isolated sperm chromatin with exonuclease III renders it active as template for DNA synthesis.

5. DEOXYRIBONUCLEASE

Study of this enzyme in sea urchins was done by Mazia (1941, 1949a,b; Mazia *et al.,* 1948). Similar to what has been described for DNA polymerase, the total deoxyribonuclease activity does not vary appreciably either after fertilization or throughout development. It is suggested, on the other hand, that the enzyme is progressively transferred from cytoplasm to nuclei, since the activity becomes more and more sedimentable at 20,000 *g* as development proceeds. Here again, and possibly more strongly (because of the lack of precautions during homogenization), the argument applies that nuclei become less and less fragile during development. Also here, however, the technique of splitting the egg into nucleated and nonnucleated halves make it certain that at least in the unfertilized egg the localization of the enzyme is largely cytoplasmic.

E. Methylation of DNA

Scarano has proposed a model on the chemical bases of cell differentiation (Scarano and Augusti-Tocco, 1967; Scarano *et al.,* 1967c; Scarano, 1969, 1971). The basic idea is that cell differentiation follows nuclear DNA modifications brought about by highly specific DNA-modifying enzymes. The author's hypothesis is that nucleocytoplasmic interactions are explained by allosteric properties of the DNA-modifying enzymes. The model would account for the program of differentiation being coded into DNA and how this is effected by the spontaneous sequential synthesis of DNA-modifying enzymes. Scarano has also proposed that mutation in the loci for the DNA-modifying enzymes might explain the action of lethal genes in embryos and of some of the so-called pleiotropic effects of genetics. For instance, he points out that the normal alleles of the eyeless locus in *Drosophila* and all the normal alleles of the organless mutants might code for the DNA-modifying enzyme responsible for the steps toward the differentiation of the eye and lacking organ, respectively. The loci for the DNA-modifying enzymes might be indicated as "Development Programing Genes."

The specific DNA modifications that Scarano and co-workers have investigated is the methylation of DNA cytosine to 5-methylcytosine and the subsequent deamination to thymine. On DNA replication, base transition GC to AT would occur (Fig. 9.13). In Scarano's laboratory a series of studies has been conducted with different approaches, in order to investigate DNA base changes occurring during cell differentiation. First, the ability of embryos of *Paracentrotus lividus* and *Sphaerechinus*

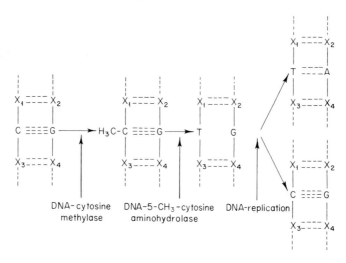

Fig. 9.13. Mechanism of the hypothetical base pair change in DNA underlying cell differentiation. (From Scarano *et al.*, 1967c.)

granularis to take up labeled methionine at different developmental stages was measured (Scarano *et al.*, 1965; Grippo *et al.*, 1968). The results (as expected from the studies on amino acid incorporation; see Chapter 11) show an initial sharp increase at fertilization, followed by a plateau during blastula stage and by a second increase at gastrulation. The second step was to look at the incorporation of radioactivity from the methyl group of methionine into the DNA bases. It was found that the only methylated minor base of DNA in sea urchin was methylcytosine. This base becomes labeled after administration of radioactive methyl-labeled methionine. Radioactivity from the methyl group of methionine was also incorporated into the methyl group of thymine and into the purine ring of adenine and guanine by its oxidation to intermediates of the 1-carbon metabolism (Grippo *et al.*, 1968; Scarano *et al.*, 1967c). It was proved that in DNA only 5-methylcytosine and probably also a small fraction of DNA thymine were labeled through a direct transfer of the labeled methyl group from methionine, while the label of the other bases always arose through the 1-carbon pool. This demonstration was achieved by administering to the developing embryos a mixture of L-methionine-[^{14}C]methyl and L-methionine-[^{3}H]methyl. The label from the methyl group of methionine, which by oxidation goes into the 1-carbon pool, loses some ^{3}H. Therefore, only if one class of bases of DNA incorporates methyl groups with the same ^{3}H/^{14}C ratio as in the initial methionine, it can be assumed that the incorporation occurs through a direct transfer of the methyl group. Table 9.4 shows that the initial ratio ^{3}H/^{14}C was main-

TABLE 9.4

RATIO $^3H/^{14}C$ IN BASES OF SEA URCHIN EMBRYO DNA[a]

Exp.	5-Methylcytosine	Thymine	Adenine	Guanine
1	2.9	1.8	1.7	0.4
2	2.8	1.7	1.4	0.5
3	3.1	1.5	1.3	0.6
4	2.8	1.9	1.3	0.6

[a] From Scarano (1969).

tained only for the methyl groups incorporated into 5-CH_3-cytosine. This point was again and more directly proved by administering to the embryos methionine whose methyl group contained 3 deuterium atoms in place of the 3 hydrogen atoms. It was possible to recover from the embryos' DNA 5'-methylcytosine whose mass spectra analyses indicated the presence of all three deuterium atoms. Some deuterium would have been lost if the methyl group had come through the 1-carbon pool (Scarano *et al.,* 1965; Grippo *et al.,* 1968).

The possibility still remained that the cytosine might have first been methylated and then incorporated into DNA. If so, one would expect a random distribution of the 5-methylcytosine through the DNA molecule. The DNA polymerase in fact would oppose the guanine of the parental strand cytosine or methylcytosine randomly picked up from a common pool (Grippo *et al.,* 1968).

To disprove this, Scarano's group carried out the following experiment. DNA extracted from embryos that had been cultured in the presence of methyl-labeled L-methionine was hydrolyzed with 3% diphenylamine in formic acid to yield the pyrimidine isostichs, i.e., fragments made only by pyrimidine sequences. The pyrimidine isostichs were then separated according to size and the distribution of 5'-methylcytosine among the isostichs measured from the label incorporation. Figures 9.14 and 9.15 show that 5'-methylcytosine is not randomly distributed throughout DNA but accumulates in the monopyrimidine isostichs, thus favoring the hypothesis of methylation of cytidine at specific points of DNA. At this point, Scarano tested the hypothesis that specific 5'-methylcytosines of DNA might be deaminated to thymine. This requires that following administration of CD_3-methionine, DNA thymine — containing a methyl group — should accumulate with all three hydrogen atoms substituted by deuterium. The experiments with deuterium-labeled methionine confirm and extend previous experiments by Scarano and co-workers (1967c) in which ^{14}C- and ^3H-labeled methionine was used. Six such experiments confirm this. It is suggested that about 1 out of 1000

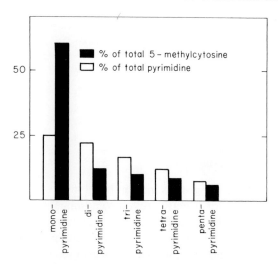

Fig. 9.14. Percentage distribution of 5-methylcytosine and of total pyrimidine deoxy-nucleosides in DNA pyrimidine isostichs of *Sphaerechinus granularis* embryos. *Sphaerechinus granularis* embryos at blastula stage cultured in the presence of 1 mCi of L-([14C]-methyl)methionine (13.9 mCi/mmole) for 7 hours. The embryo DNA was extracted and hydrolyzed with 3% diphenylamine in formic acid. The pyrimidine isostichs were separated and each isostich fraction was hydrolyzed to deoxynucleosides. 5-Methyldeoxycytidine was purified by paper chromatography. (From Grippo *et al.*, 1968.)

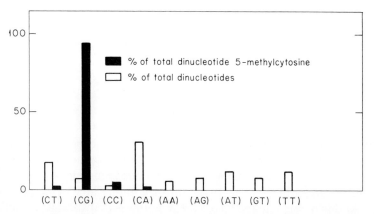

Fig. 9.15. Percentage distribution of 5-methylcytosine and of the four major bases in the dinucleotides from a DNase digest of *Sphaerechinus granularis* embryo DNA. *Sphaerechinus granularis* embryos at the blastula stage incubated for 7 hours with 1 mCi of L-([14C]-methyl)methionine (11.7 mCi/mmole). DNA and dinucleotides were prepared and separated as described by Grippo *et al.* (1968). Each dinucleotide was hydrolyzed with snake venom, and deoxynucleosides were separated by paper chromatography. 5-Methyldeoxycytidine spots were eluted and the radioactivity measured. The percentage of each dinucleotide was measured by UV spectrophotometry. Dinucleotide (GG) was not measurable. (From Grippo *et al.*, 1968.)

thymines of DNA in sea urchin embryos arises at the DNA level by methylation of cytosine followed by deamination. In addition, the same experiments indicate that not only has this thymine, which they name "minor thymine," a specific distribution on DNA but that this specific distribution changes with development (Grippo *et al.,* 1970). The consequence is that, following such an event, an originary cytosine of DNA is transformed into thymine. Then, as the new DNA replication takes place, two daughter molecules will originate: one, copied on the modified strand, that brings a TA pair in the place of a CG one, and the other equal to the parental molecule. Scarano suggests that such DNA modifications play a key role in differentiation. They would make available for transcription or for potential transcription entire specific sections of DNA, involved in specific differentiation steps.

Here we evidently face two problems: First, the validity of the experimental data and, second, the impact that such an event as DNA methylation might have on development. As for the first problem, more experiments would certainly be welcome to definitively prove the point, although the quality of the data at hand is undoubtedly excellent, in our opinion. As regards the second problem, while it is entirely possible theoretically that DNA base transitions might be able to profoundly affect and possible direct differentiation, no direct proofs that it actually does so are available, nor does any easy method come to our mind to test it.

Certainly Scarano's hypothesis would provide a means to yield at cell division a differentiated cell (in which cytosine has been substituted for thymidine) and a stem cell (in which DNA has arisen from the other strand). But are we willing to devolve differentiation to DNA modifications? Let us consider what we do know about the constancy of DNA during differentiation. The proofs thereof mainly consist in the constancy of the chromosome number in different organs and of the DNA content and base composition (Chargaff, 1963; Kit, 1960a,b, 1961). Moreover, DNA's from different organs have the same nearest neighbor frequencies (Swartz *et al.,* 1962; Skalka *et al.,* 1966) and look the same in tests of molecular hybridization (McCarthy and Hoyer, 1964; Denis, 1966a,b). None of the above criteria would, however, detect such small changes as those proposed by Scarano. Besides, there are exceptions to the above rules, where it is clear that gross DNA modifications accompany differentiation, even if it cannot be stated that they determine it, as, for example, the loss of chromosomes in *Ascaris* (Boveri, 1910) or in *Sciara* (C. W. Metz, 1938), or the loss of nucleus of human erythrocytes. Experiments on the totipotentiality of nuclei, namely, those of nuclear transplantation into amphibian eggs, might also be used in favor of Scarano's theory. While in fact they tend to emphasize that nuclei do not lose their genetic properties with development, they show, on the other hand, that there is a gradual loss of this totipotentiality as development proceeds (Briggs and King, 1960; Di Berardino and King, 1967; Fischberg et al., 1958; Gurdon, 1960; Laskey and Gurdon, 1970). Moreover, the extreme cases of apparent dedifferentiation of nuclei might be explained by Scarano's theory as due to the presence of stem cells among the differentiated ones. In conclusion, Scarano's theory remains, in our opinion, entirely possible even if not proved as yet.

F. Experiments of Inhibition of DNA Synthesis

DNA synthesis in sea urchin embryos has been experimentally inhibited in a number of ways. The interest of such experiments lies in the search for correlations between DNA synthesis and other metabolic activities, as well as with the process of cell division.

The inhibition of DNA synthesis might theoretically be brought about by agents that act directly on the primer DNA or on its precursors. It has long been known that agents that modify the parental DNA cause a disturbance of RNA synthesis and little or no effect on DNA synthesis itself. Among the agents that modify DNA, alkylating agents (Fox et al., 1963; Roguski, 1960; Levy and Weis, 1960), X ray (Neifakh, 1963, 1964; Neifakh and Dontsova, 1962; Neifakh and Krigsgaber, 1968; see also Chapter 5), and UV irradiation (Cook, 1968; see also Chapter 5) have been studied. The fertilization of eggs with sperm treated with nitrogen mustard causes disturbances of cleavage and arrest of development at blastula. The arrest of development at blastula, similar to the effect of X-ray irradiation, can well be explained by the effect on RNA synthesis (this topic will be extensively discussed in Chapter 10).

UV irradiation of Echinaracnius parma causes a delay of the first prophase. The target of the UV appear to be DNA: The administration of 5'-bromodeoxyuridine, which is mainly incorporated into DNA, actually increases UV sensitivity and decreases photoreactivability. Moreover, the target appears to be the unreplicated DNA since the sensitivity to UV irradiation drops after S_1. It does not seem, however, that UV affects DNA synthesis because, if it were so, UV irradiation would prolong the period where in DNA is not yet replicated and, therefore, the period of UV sensitivity, which is not the case. Hence it remains to be established on which DNA-dependent process of prophase the UV irradiation acts. Paul et al. (1970) have irradiated with laser eggs of Arbacia punctulata (3.2 mJ/cm^2 for 500 μsec). The result shows, besides severe developmental abnormalities, a delay in the first cleavages and DNA synthesis, so that after 4-cell division the treated eggs lagged one S period behind the controls.

The effect of altering the precursor pool of DNA has been studied by several authors. Markman (1963) has tried to overload the internal nucleotide pool by adding to seawater uridine $10^{-3} M$ or thymidine $10^{-4} M$, without any apparent effect on development. Some alterations of mesenchyme formation are obtained with adenine $10^{-5} M$.

Bamberger *et al.* (1963) have found that the administration of 8-azaguanine causes a slight inhibition of DNA synthesis in embryos of *Strongylocentrotus purpuratus*. The analog is, however, incorporated into RNA, causing the arrest of development at blastula stage. Here again, just as observed when using iododeoxyuridine (Nemer, 1962a), we are confronted with the effect of the disturbance of RNA synthesis during cleavage (for which we refer the reader to Chapter 10). Other modified bases that interfere with nucleic acid synthesis and block cleavage are folic acid antagonists (Stearns *et al.*, 1962) and 2-piperidino-8-mercaptoadenine (Young *et al.*, 1970).

The most interesting observation about the inhibition of DNA synthesis through disturbance of the reduction of ribonucleosides to deoxyribonucleosides, is the arrest at 8 blastomeres brought about by the use either of fluorodeoxyuridine or hydroxyurea. In this latter case some correlations with other metabolic events have been studied and demonstration made that, in the absence of DNA synthesis, the respiratory curve remains at the level characteristic of the stage at which cell division is stopped (Giudice and Donatuti, unpublished, see Chapter 8), and histone synthesis seems to be halted as well (see Chapter 11). An ultrastructural description of the effect of hydroxyurea has been reported by Geuskens (1968a). Crkvenjakov *et al.* (1970) have recently found that 5-azacytidine, a potent inhibitor of DNA synthesis in *Paracentrotus lividus,* also allows normal cell division only up to the 8-blastomere stage.

The effect of bromodeoxyuridine has been studied on eggs of *Dendraster excentricus* by Mazia and Gontcharoff (1964). They observed a cleavage delay and a disordered division bringing about the formation of embryos that are arrested at the stage of irregular morulae. This effect, which is in agreement with previous observations by Karnofsky and Simmel (1963) on *Echinaracnius parma,* is attributed by the authors to impairment of the separation of the sister chromosomes at anaphase, with consequent formation of nuclear bridges and irregular distribution of the chromosomes. No such alterations are produced by the same concentrations of bromodeoxyuridine on *Strongylcentrotus purpuratus* or *Lytechinus pictus* eggs. Thus, sand dollars appear to differ in this respect from sea urchins. DNA synthesis also has been inhibited by drugs that interfere primarily with protein synthesis such as puromycin and cycloheximide (Hultin, 1961a; Brachet *et al.,* 1963a; Rustad and Burchill, 1966; Black *et al.,* 1967). These drugs severely impair cell division. The inhibition of thymidine incorporation by puromycin is very low for S_1 in *Arbacia punctulata* or *Strongylocentrotus purpuratus*, but evident for S_2. As suggested by experiments where the embryos are preloaded with labeled thymidine before puromycin treatment, part of the drug effect is not exerted directly on the process of DNA synthesis but possibly on earlier steps of the process of thymidine uptake and processing to thymidine triphosphate. Bellemare *et al.* (1968) have demonstrated that hexahomoserine (δ-amino-ε-hydrocaproic acid), known to be an inhibitor of protein synthesis, when tested on embryos of *Strongylocentrotus purpuratus* inhibits the incorporation of both exogenous-labeled leucine and thymidine. However, when the uptake of these radioactive precursors is measured, one finds that it is strongly reduced, thus leaving still open the question of whether the effect of hexahomoserine is on both rate of nucleic acid (or protein) synthesis and on embryo permeability, or only on the latter. It is, however, very probable that at least puromycin does actually inhibit protein synthesis. Still, the results of the inhibition of DNA synthesis do not necessarily mean that the latter is directly dependent upon protein synthesis, since these drugs cause a profound alteration of metabolism in the cells. It has been directly demonstrated that in dissociated sea urchin cells puromycin causes a drop in respiration (Giudice, 1965). More recently, Young *et al.* (1969) have reported that in the presence of 1 μg/ml of cycloheximide, amino acid incorporation is reduced by 95% in the fertilized eggs of *Echinaracnius parma*. DNA synthesis is normal in S_1 but not thereafter, with consequent arrest of cleavage. The administration of cycloheximide at various periods allows some of the events of the cell cycle to proceed but not others. On the basis of these data, the authors suggest that proteins are synthesized during the cell cycle for (a) DNA synthesis; (b) karyokinesis; and (c) cleavage. Their synthesis proceeds in that order. The lack of protein synthesis, in the authors' opinion, somehow affects the DNA itself thus making it unavailable for replication. This is suggested by the observation that introduction of new sperm into eggs whose DNA synthesis is blocked, causes one wave of DNA synthesis.

According to Augusti-Tocco *et al.* (1969), amantadine is a compound that causes some inhibition of exogenous thymidine incorporation into DNA in *Paracentrotus lividus* and *Sphaerechinus granularis* embryos, probably through an effect on cell membranes. Other metabolic activities are also affected. Morphologically, the embryos show exogastrulation. Some disturbance of thymidine incorporation into cleaving eggs by amantadine has been autoradiographically demonstrated by Soupart *et al.* (1969); these authors report cleavage inhibition.

As a correlation of the inhibition of DNA synthesis with the inhibition of cell division, the latter always follows the former in all of the known cases. It is interesting to note that some of the mitotic events, on the other hand, can be inhibited with no consequence on DNA synthesis. Bucher and Mazia (1960), by treatment with β-mercaptoethanol, have inhibited the centriole duplication in sea urchin eggs, with no effect on DNA synthesis, as far as can be detected by an autoradiographic study of thymidine incorporation. Inhibition of the mitotic cycle, brought about by high hydrostatic pressures, does not impair thymidine incorporation into DNA.

Cleavage disturbances have been obtained by Rosenkranz *et al.* (1964) with purine- and pyrimidine-specific antibodies. Little is known about the specificity of such an effect.

Further, little is known of the effect of hormones in sea urchin development in general. Chestukhin (1969) has observed that cortisone disturbs cleavage and arrests development at the mesenchyme blastula stage in *Strongylocentrotus nudus;* this is probably because cortisone inhibits DNA synthesis in this embryo. On the other hand, cortisone has little effect on RNA synthesis.

Lack of correlation has been found by Sconzo *et al.* (1970b) between DNA synthesis and the activation of ribosomal RNA synthesis in dissociated cells of *Paracentrotus lividus* embryos (see Chapter 6).

Chapter 10

Ribonucleic Acid

A. Oogenesis

The importance of the oogenetic period for RNA synthesis will become apparent in the study of embryonic development, with the conclusion that most of the ribosomal RNA (rRNA) the sea urchin uses up to the pluteus stage, as well as a good deal of the messenger RNA (mRNA), is initially stored in the cytoplasm of the unfertilized egg, i.e., must have been synthesized during oogenesis.

Little literature has accumulated concerning a direct study of RNA synthesis in sea urchin oocytes, because of a series of technical difficulties. If it is easy indeed to label developing embryos by the simple addition of radioactive precursors to the beaker of seawater in which they are cultured, until recently it was necessary to inject entire animals kept in proper aquaria in order to get labeled oocytes. Moreover, oocyte development is not synchronous; therefore we label at the same time oocytes at different stages of maturation.

Nevertheless, some direct studies on RNA synthesis during oogenesis have been reported. Apart from the earlier cytochemical data on the increase of nucleolar and cytoplasmic RNA synthesis during the growth of *Lytechinus variegatus* oocytes (Cowden, 1962) and the more recent histochemical work on *Strongylocentrotus purpuratus* (Chatlynne, 1969), the available results fundamentally derive from long-term labeling experiments (Gross *et al.,* 1965a; Piatigorsky and Tyler, 1967, 1970). In the first experiments by Piatigorsky and Tyler, females of *Lytechinus pictus* were induced to spawn by KCl injection, with the double aim of stimulating a wave of oogenesis and of rendering it more synchronous. Then, a single injection of 10–100 μCi of [^{3}H]uridine was given. Each animal was then kept in 1.5 l of seawater in the presence of green algae and light, with continuous aeration. Under these conditions, the oocyte RNA reaches its maximum radioactivity after 1 month. By then up to 95% of the injected isotope had been taken up by the animal. Less satisfactory results were obtained by the same authors when the same method of oocyte labeling was applied to *Strongylocentrotus purpuratus*. The mature eggs were collected and the RNA extracted by SDS and cold phenol. A sucrose gradient analysis indicated that at least 80–90% of the radioactivity had been incorporated into the mature ribosomal RNA (rRNA) and into the 4 S RNA. It should be noted that had higher temperatures been used in the extraction procedure, higher amounts of nonribosomal and non-4 S RNA might have been obtained (Rinaldi, personal communication).

It is, however, clear that the main type of RNA labeled under the conditions of long-term labeling experiments is of ribosomal and transfer type. This is readily explainable if one thinks of the enormous storage of ribosomes in the egg cytoplasm, which occurs during oogenesis. These ribosomes, as mentioned, suffice for the embryos to reach at least the blastula and, perhaps, the pluteus stage.

These experiments do not provide direct evidence as to whether this rRNA is synthesized by the oocyte itself or whether it is synthesized outside the oocyte and then incorporated into the oocyte. No evidence exists for this second hypothesis, while dramatic changes in the nucleolar ultrastructure observed during oogenesis (see Chapter 2) may be connected with rRNA synthesis.

The existence of pinosomes and surface projections on the surface of growing oocytes of *Hemicentrotus pulcherrimus* (Tsukahara and Sugiyama, 1969) seems to be connected with yolk storage in the oocyte.

No ultrastructural evidence for the phenomenon of "amplification," as described in amphibian oocytes, has been reported in sea urchins. Nor has any attempt been made to measure the content of ribosomal cistrons in sea urchin oocytes. Judging from the data obtained in *Asterias* oocytes (Vincent *et al.,* 1968, 1969), one would expect the sea urchin oocyte, being mononucleolate, not to show the phenomenon of ribosomal gene amplification, which, according to these authors, seems to be restricted to the polynucleolated oocytes.

In their more recent experiments, Piatigorsky and Tyler (1970) have found that some polydispersely sedimenting RNA is synthesized during oogenesis. When unfertilized or just fertilized eggs of *Lytechinus* are subjected to cell fractionation and analyzed by sucrose gradient, the polydisperse RNA is found in the zone of particles lighter than the monoribosomes, which, as will be discussed later, corresponds to the informosome region. The same authors acknowledge that the low K^+ ion concentration used in the homogenization medium might have caused some polysome breakdown and, therefore, some release of mRNA from polysomes. This would, however, be disproved by the low amount of radioactivity found at the monoribosomal level after *in vivo* labeling with radioactive amino acids.

Similar results had previously been obtained by Gross *et al.* (1965a). In their experiments, females of *Arbacia punctulata* were induced to spawn by electrical stimulation and then injected with [^{3}H]uridine. One week later, an autoradiographic study showed a vast incorporation into the oogonia, uniform labeling of the little oocytes, and a gradient of radioactivity decreasing toward the lumen of the ovary, i.e., toward the mature eggs; the latter showed only a few cytoplasmic traces. The RNA was then extracted from the mature eggs by SDS and phenol at 5°C and analyzed by sucrose gradient; it was again found that most of the radioactivity had been incorporated into ribosomal and 4 S RNA. The ratio between the radioactivity and optical density in the zone between the peaks of rRNA subunits was higher than the same ratio in the ribosomal RNA zones — thus suggesting the synthesis of some nonribosomal RNA. Moreover, analysis by MAK column chromatography of this RNA showed that the ratio between radioactivity and optical density was higher out of the peak of rRNA. The presence of nonribosomal RNA in these zones was also suggested by experiments of hybridization DNA–RNA, in which the RNA is only partially competed by rRNA for hybridization.

A disturbance of RNA synthesis during oogenesis can be caused by injecting actinomycin D into the females. This, as shown autoradiographically (Sanchez, 1968), mainly causes an inhibition of the active uridine incorporation at the level of the nucleoli of the young oocytes (see, also, Ficq, 1964). This is consistent with the current notion of the particular sensitivity of rRNA synthesis to actinomycin. When 100 μg of actinomycin is injected into females of *Paracentrotus lividus* and the eggs are collected a few hours later, they can normally be fertilized and develop up to the start of gastrulation. Such an experiment allows the drug to act only on the later phases of oogenesis for the eggs whose development was then studied. No direct analysis of the effect of the drug on RNA synthesis is available except for the autoradiographic study, which shows a partial inhibition of [^{3}H]orotic acid incorporation into the large oocytes 48 hours after the actinomycin treatment. The main aim of such experiments is to block at different points of oogenesis the synthesis of particular classes of RNA, and to try to find a correlation between these and some of the morphological and biochemical events of embryogenesis; in particular it might be hoped to find a correlation between the suppression of RNA synthesis at certain periods and that of certain cytoplasmic localizations. The technical tools available, however, render such a project too ambitious at present.

It will be seen later that suppressing RNA synthesis from fertilization on has an effect on development, i.e., an arrest of gastrulation, similar to that of suppression of RNA synthesis during oogenesis. It should be noted, however, that gastrulation appears to be one of the most sensitive features of early morphogenesis, which can be disturbed by a variety of experimental treatments.

Another way to approach the problem of the synthesis of RNA during oogenesis is the one followed by Piatigorsky *et al.* (1967), who, by repeated stimulations to spawn *Lytechinus pictus* females, obtained egg populations with a very high percentage of oocytes (up to 60%). Incorporation of [¹⁴C]valine or [³H]uridine increased with the proportion of oocytes. As shown autoradiographically, the incorporation of [³H]-uridine was almost entirely restricted to the oocytes, with a preferential localization in the nucleolar region. Actinomycin inhibited the incorporation of uridine, but not that of valine, thus proving the presence of some long-lived mRNA in the oocytes.

More recently, Giudice and co-workers (Giudice *et al.*, 1972b; Sconzo *et al.*, 1972) have been able to isolate oocytes from the ovaries of *Paracentrotus lividus* by mild pronase treatment. The oocytes, purified according to size by Ficoll gradients, proved viable for at least 24 hours and very active in the uptake of labeled precursors of nucleic acids and proteins. It was possible for the first time to study directly the RNA-synthesizing ability of purified oocytes. It was again found that most of the radioactive uridine is incorporated at nucleolar level in the form of the heaviest precursor of ribosomal RNA (see farther on in this chapter). This is processed at a much slower rate than at the gastrula stage, suggesting that the rate of maturation is a step by which rRNA synthesis can be regulated. That maturation can proceed slowly during oogenesis is not surprising if one considers how long it takes the oocyte to grow and produce its rRNA.

It was found by autoradiography and cell fractionation that only a little amount of the newly synthesized RNA passes to the cytoplasm after 6 hours of labeling.

Other classes of RNA, besides the ribosomal one, were also labeled. They are at present under investigation, with the hope of identifying some specific mRNA class among the many that are stored in the cytoplasm of the unfertilized egg.

Among the most recent electrophoretic analyses of RNA's stored in the unfertilized egg, that of Dubois *et al.* (1971) is worth mentioning. These authors have identified on polyacrylamide gels the following

RNA classes, which are quantitatively represented in the reported order: 26 S and 18 S (mature rRNA); 4 S (transfer RNA); 5 S; 12 S; 9 S; and 23 S (presumably mitochondrial). An interesting point is that the 12 S and 9 S fractions appear to be localized almost entirely in the yolk (or at least cosediment with a reasonably pure yolk fraction). The amount of these two classes decreases as development proceeds in a parallel fashion with the yolk. What is their function? This is at present unknown. It is worth recalling, however, that, as will be discussed in Chapter 11, RNA's of such lengths are thought to be responsible for histone synthesis during embryogenesis in sea urchins.

B. Evidence That the Unfertilized Egg Contains Stored mRNA

The first series of evidence is represented by experiments in which RNA synthesis is either inhibited or altered in such a way as to lead to the formation of nonfunctional RNA. This has been achieved in a number of ways:

1. INCORPORATION OF ANALOGS

As already described in Chapter 9 on DNA synthesis, the effect of analogs that somehow interfere with RNA synthesis is the arrest of development at the blastula stage. This happens when 5-iododeoxyuridine (Nemer, 1962a) or 8-azaguanine (Bamberger et al., 1963) is given to the embryos from fertilization on. Crkvenjakov et al. (1970) have also reported that 5-azacytidine, at a concentration that brings about a 65–95% inhibition of [^{3}H]uridine incorporation, does not affect protein synthesis of Arbacia lixula eggs up to the blastula stage.

2. X-RAY IRRADIATION

Neifakh (1960, 1964; Neifakh and Krigsgaber, 1968) has found that irradiation of eggs of Strongylocentrotus droebachiensis or Strongylocentrotus nudus causes the arrest of development at the blastula stage. In the opinion of Kafiani et al. (1966), X-ray irradiation does not alter the rate of RNA synthesis but brings about the production of a nonfunctional RNA.

3. DEVELOPMENT OF ANUCLEATE FRAGMENTS

Harvey (1936) and Hiramoto (1956) have shown that cleavage is allowed to proceed in the absence of nucleus, even if a blastula is usually not formed. The nonnucleated halves undergo a normal rate increase of protein synthesis following parthenogenetic activation (Denny and

Tyler, 1964; Tyler, 1966; Brachet *et al.,* 1963b); polysome formation appears normal in the nonnucleated fragments (Burny *et al.,* 1965). Finally, the anucleate halves synthesize the microtubular proteins normally, while their cytoplasmic polysomes do not bind newly formed (probably mitochondrial) RNA (Raff *et al.,* 1972).

4. ARTIFICIAL PRODUCTION OF LETHAL HYBRIDS

As discussed in Chapter 7, development in these embryos is usually permitted until the blastula stage. Little is known about the nature and quantity of RNA synthesized by these embryos. The only direct recent data available are those of Denis and Brachet (1969b), which are actually interpreted by the authors as suggesting that a drop in the rate of RNA synthesis in the hybrids takes place only after the gastrula stage. It has already been pointed out (Chapter 7) that this conclusion cannot be considered definitive as yet.

5. DEUTERIUM PARTHENOGENESIS

Gross *et al.* (1963) have shown that activation of protein synthesis takes place normally in eggs of *Arbacia* parthenogenetically activated by D_2O, which blocks RNA synthesis. More recently, Pinard *et al.* (1969) have shown that the rate of protein synthesis is identical for the first 8 hours after fertilization in embryos reared in the presence of D_2O and in controls. Under these conditions, DNA synthesis is arrested at the eighth hour.

6. TREATMENT OF THE EGG WITH ACTINOMYCIN D

Probably the first use of actinomycin on sea urchin embryos was made by Wolsky and de Issekutz Wolsky (1961), who reported that pretreatment of *Arbacia punctulata* eggs with this drug produces a slight cleavage delay and arrest of development before the gastrula stage. The same conclusion was reached by Lallier on *Paracentrotus lividus* (1963b). It was Gross and co-workers who, in a series of papers, proved directly that actinomycin does effectively halt RNA synthesis in the egg under conditions that still allow protein synthesis to be activated following fertilization, and to proceed at an apparently normal rate up to the blastula stage. At this point, it was found that development was halted. It is worthwhile to comment briefly about the details of such experiments, on which is based the evidence for the storage in the cytoplasm of the egg of template RNA. Gross and Cousineau (1963a) provided the first evidence that *Arbacia punctulata* eggs, on actinomycin treatment (doses from 1.4 to 24 μg/ml) starting 10 minutes before fertilization, undergo a 74–94% drop of incorporation of exogenous [^{14}C]uracil into a TCA-insoluble form, while incorporation of exogenous valine into TCA-insoluble form remains practically unaffected. Development proceeds up to blastula for the low actinomycin doses, and to morula for the highest ones. Essentially similar data are reported in greater detail by Gross and Cousineau in a second paper (1964). The authors again note and express in more quantitative terms the correlation between actinomycin concentration and cleavage delay, with differentiation alterations, in *Arbacia punctulata* embryos. In summary, with concentrations of actino-mycin of 6 μg/ml that are given 10–30 minutes before fertilization, blastulae are produced (only slightly retarded with respect to the controls), and a few of them hatch. With concentrations of 20 μg/ml or higher, no blastulae are produced but only irregular cell masses. It is helpful to mention these earlier results since they may be misleading to a reader unfamiliar with the subject. In another paper, Gross (1964) established that blastulae are formed when 20 μg/ml of actinomycin is given several hours before fertilization; about 50% hatch. Gross and others report that the use of higher doses of actinomycin, which has a toxic effect on the embryos, does not bring about a higher effect on RNA synthesis. A large part of the RNA precursor incorporation resistant to the actinomycin, is actually due to synthesis and terminal turnover of transfer RNA (Gross *et al.*, 1964). Figures 10.1 and 10.2 show the effect on RNA synthesis of a 3-hour treatment with actinomycin D at 20 μg/ml started before fertilization. Practically all the residual synthesis is restricted to the 4 S zone. When the RNA synthesized under these conditions is hydrolyzed to nucleotides and the interconversion of uridine to cytidine measured, almost half of the label from [^{3}H]uridine is found to be recovered in the cytidine, thus suggesting that part of the 4 S labeling is due to turnover of the terminal CCA sequence. The authors calculate that at least an 85% inhibition of RNA synthesis can be obtained in *Strongylocentrotus* by a concentration of 20 μg/ml of actinomycin added 1 hour before fertilization. Consideration of the effect of the drug on RNA synthesis similar to that illustrated in Figs. 10.1 and 10.2 has been reported for *Arbacia* eggs. Giudice *et al.* (1968) have found a similar behavior in *Paracentrotus* eggs (Fig. 10.3); in other words, here again the resistant portion of RNA synthesis is localized in the 4 S region. A certain aliquot of radioactivity remains in the heavier zone of the sucrose gradient; when the incorporation of [^{3}H]uridine into the total RNA is calculated by recovering the labeled UMP after RNA hydrolysis, about 70% inhibition is obtained. It should be noted that here the timing of actinomycin administration is somewhat different from that of Gross *et al.* In fact, while with Gross the drug was already present before fertilization, with Giudice it was given to the eggs a few minutes after fertilization for a period of 5 hours, after which the eggs were tested for RNA synthesis. These embryos usually reach the stage of swimming

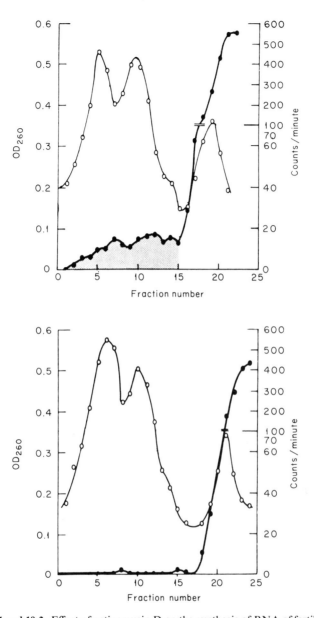

Figs. 10.1 and 10.2. Effect of actinomycin D on the synthesis of RNA of fertilized eggs of *Lytechinus pictus*. Figure 10.1 (upper), controls; Fig. 10.2 (lower), eggs treated with actinomycin D beginning 200 minutes before fertilization. RNA label: [^{14}C]uridine, 0.5 μCi and 4.0 μg/ml in artificial seawater from fertilization to 60 minutes later. Centrifugation of the RNA, extracted with SDS-phenol, at 37,000 rpm: 5 hours. OD peaks (open circles) correspond, on the basis of previous experience, to (approx.) 28 S, 18 S, and 4 S, with sedimentation toward lower fraction numbers. The filled circles give counts/minute of each fraction in 15 ml Bray's solution. At least 3000 counts were accumulated per sample. Shaded area in Fig. 10.1 represents newly synthesized non-4 S RNA. Each fraction comprised 3 drops from a 4.7-ml gradient. (From Gross *et al.,* 1964.)

239

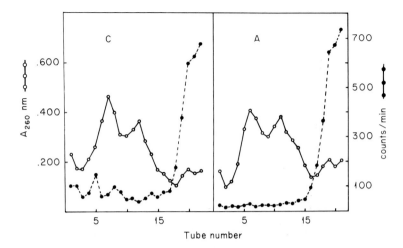

Fig. 10.3. Effect of 20 μg/ml of actinomycin D on RNA synthesis in *Paracentrotus lividus*. The drug was added at fertilization and 5 hours later the embryos were pulsed with [5-^{3}H]uridine. The RNA was analyzed by centrifugation on sucrose density gradient (5–20%). C, control; A, actinomycin. (From Giudice *et al.*, 1968.)

blastulae, more or less stuffed with what appear to be degenerated mesenchyme cells.

A direct test of the rate of protein synthesis with this kind of treatment is shown in Fig. 10.4. It is readily seen that the rate of amino acid incorporation remains normal up to the blastula stage. This ability to carry

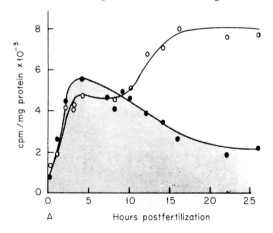

Fig. 10.4. Effect of actinomycin D on protein synthesis in three different sea urchin genera. A. Rates of incorporation of [^{14}C]L-valine in fertilized eggs of *Arbacia*, with and without actinomycin D (20 μg/ml). Filled circles: 20-minute pulse incorporations for embryos in actinomycin, pretreated with actinomycin for 3 hours before fertilization. Open circles: controls in normal, artificial seawater. (From Gross *et al.*, 1964.) B. Effect of

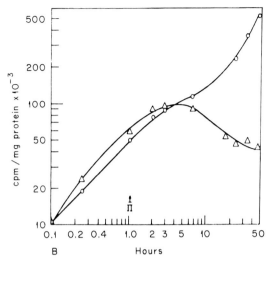

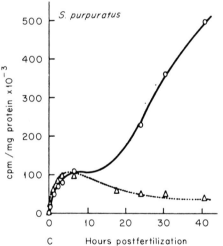

actinomycin treatment on rates of incorporation of [^{14}C]L-leucine into protein by fertilized eggs of *Strongylocentrotus purpuratus*. Ordinate: specific activity attained by total cell protein during a 15-minute exposure to the labeled precursor. Abcissa: time after fertilization. Log-log plot. Large triangles: eggs in the presence of actinomycin D, 20 μg/ml, from 1 hour before fertilization. Circles: controls. Penicillin and streptomycin at 1 mg/ml each present from fertilization. (From Malkin *et al.,* 1964.) C. Rates of incorporation of [^{14}C]L-valine in fertilized eggs of *Strongylocentrotus purpuratus*. Circles: controls. Triangles: embryos exposed continuously to 20 μg/ml actinomycin D, from before fertilization. The second rise in rate in the controls begins after hatching of the blastula, and it does not occur in actinomycin. Rates in actinomycin are slightly higher for the first 2–3 hours than in the controls. (From Gross, 1964.)

on protein synthesis at a normal rate is retained up to the blastula stage by cell-free systems from *Lytechinus* and *Strongylocentrotus,* with actinomycin treatment starting prior to fertilization (Stavy and Gross, 1969a,b). This is in agreement with the finding, to be discussed later, that even in the presence of 25 μg/ml of actinomycin D, heavy polyribosomes are formed during cleavage (Infante and Nemer, 1967; Kedes and Gross, 1969a; Nemer and Lindsay, 1969; Kedes *et al.,* 1969).

All the above evidence strongly suggests that the RNA accumulated in the egg cytoplasm during oogenesis permits the embryo to reach the blastula stage. The rate of protein synthesis of embryos that are prevented from synthesizing new RNA from fertilization on is comparable to that of normal embryos up to the blastula stage.

It has been argued that, as proved by experiments of incorporation of labeled actinomycin, embryo permeability to this drug is very low up to the early blastula stage (Ellis, 1969; Thaler *et al.,* 1969a). This cannot be the only explanation for the fact that the embryos reach the blastula stage when in the presence of actinomycin from the beginning of development, because whatever the amount of actinomycin penetrated, its effect on RNA synthesis usually has been directly tested (Villee and Gross, 1969).

Recently, Greenhouse *et al.* (1971) carefully measured the penetration of actinomycin D into the egg nucleus and cytoplasm, and demonstrated both the permeability to the drug and, once again, the effectiveness of the latter in inhibiting RNA synthesis from the beginning of development.

Surprisingly, to our knowledge, no one has directly checked the possible effects of actinomycin on permeability to RNA precursors or on the size of the RNA precursor pool in the sea urchin egg. That the effect of inhibition of RNA synthesis is an apparent one, due only to variations of permeability or of pool size, seems extremely unlikely. For example, while uridine incorporation into the heavy RNA is almost suppressed, no effect is observed at the level of the 4 S RNA (Figs. 10.1–10.3). No inhibitory effect is observed on permeability to amino acids. Finally, the effects of actinomycin coincide well with those of other forms of inhibition of RNA synthesis. It should be added that the degree of inhibition of the synthesis of heterodisperse RNA heavier than 4 S has always been calculated after relatively long periods of labeling, which might have allowed some RNA classes to undergo turnover, so that the real value of inhibition might in theory have been higher.

The problem of permeability variations to radioactive precursors always remains important in itself. For example, Raff *et al.* (1970) reported that 5-azacytidine brings about a severe impairment of labeled nucleoside incorporation into both RNA and DNA. Under such conditions, cell division progresses until blastula. Using ^{32}P, it is seen that the inhibition of DNA synthesis is only an apparent one and caused by the nonutilization of exogenous labeled nucleosides.

7. INHIBITION OF RNA SYNTHESIS BY ETHIDIUM BROMIDE

As will be discussed later in this chapter, it has been suggested that cytoplasmic RNA synthesis may play an important role in protein synthesis during the early phases of development, possibly on mitochondrial DNA template. It is known that actinomycin may fail to inhibit mitochondrial RNA synthesis. Craig and Piatigorsky (1971) examined the electrophoretical profile of proteins synthesized by nonnucleate fragments in which about 97% of cytoplasmic RNA synthesis is inhibited by ethidium bromide. The profile of the radioactivity incorporated into proteins under such conditions is very similar to that on untreated nonnucleate fragments, even if lower by a factor of 4. This shows that all the template RNA's for these proteins are already present in the egg cytoplasm. Factors of permeability and pool size should be considered before evaluating the significance of the lower incorporation of radioactive amino acids into the treated fragments.

Ethidium bromide has also been used in combination with actinomycin D to completely inhibit the egg RNA synthesis. Under these conditions the synthesis of tubulin has been shown to proceed normally following fertilization (Raff *et al.*, 1972).

Another direct proof of the presence of template RNA in the unfertilized egg is the ability of RNA extracted from unfertilized eggs to stimulate amino acid incorporation in a cell-free system from rat liver (Maggio *et al.*, 1964) or from *Escherichia coli* (Slater and Spiegelman, 1966a, 1968). According to the latter authors, 4.3% of the RNA of *Lytechinus pictus* eggs is mRNA. The calculation is made on the basis of the stimulation effect of amino acid incorporation in a 30 S of *E. coli*, in comparison with the effect of MS2 RNA, considered as pure mRNA.

Such a calculation method is, however, based on several assumptions:

1. The *E. coli* system should contain in nonlimiting amount all of the tRNA's required for the preferred triplet coding for the single amino acids in the sea urchin messenger.

2. All of the MS2 RNA be considered pure template, including in the calculation the possible zones that have initiation or other function.

3. That no RNA's other than mRNA could stimulate amino acid incorporation *in vitro*.

Of course it is entirely possible that most of, if not all, these conditions are actually fulfilled, within a negligible margin of error. In any case, these experiments make the point that mRNA is present in the unfertilized egg.

Finally, experiments of molecular hybridization have demonstrated that RNA contained in unfertilized eggs is a good competitor, for hybridization with DNA, of nonribosomal and nontransfer RNA synthesized at the stages of hatching blastulae (Glisin *et al.*, 1966) or prism (Whiteley *et al.*, 1966, 1970). The unfertilized egg RNA labeled *in vitro* with [^{3}H]dimethyl sulfate hybridizes at least 3% of the homologous DNA (Hynes and Gross, 1972), i.e., much more than would be expected from the hybridization of ribosomal and transfer RNA. Obviously the fact that an RNA is neither ribosomal nor transfer does not allow to conclude that it is messenger.

C. Synthesis of RNA during Development

1. GENERAL CONSIDERATIONS

Much work has accumulated in recent years on this subject. We shall only mention the earlier work that started the ball rolling in this field of study (Zimmerman and Zimmerman, 1960; Markman, 1961a,c, 1966, 1967; Markman and Runnström, 1963; Tocco *et al.*, 1963; Ficq and Brachet, 1963; Ficq *et al.*, 1963; Brachet *et al.*, 1963a; Chen and Baltzer, 1962; Olsson, 1965). We do not propose to go into the details of those studies where incorporation of labeled precursors into the "total" RNA has been followed, since their significance is strongly diminished by the fact that this incorporation includes the important aliquot due to the terminal turnover of tRNA. Moreover, it is known that several hundreds of classes of proteins and presumably of different RNA types are being synthesized during embryogenesis. For the experiment to contribute to the understanding of the significance of RNA synthesis, today it is desirable at least to distinguish between incorporations into the two classes of known RNA's, i.e., ribosomal and transfer, and others. Since most of the experiments performed are based on the external administration of labeled presursors to the eggs, some preliminary considerations should be made before examining the significance of the results. The amount of isotope incorporated will depend not merely upon the rate of RNA synthesis but also upon the permeability to the precursors and upon the dilution that these undergo owing to the presence of an internal pool; in addition, when different stages of development are compared, it should be remembered that these factors may undergo variations; moreover, when no specially characterized classes of RNA are studied, it is always probable that one is dealing with a complex mixture of RNA's. Hence, when one finds that the RNA has incorporated a high amount of isotope, it is theoretically possible, at one extreme, that only one class of RNA, representing only one variety of molecules, because of a very high synthesis rate, is responsible for the entire incorporation. At the other extreme, it is possible that hundreds of classes of RNA, of a very slow synthesis rate, have equally shared the entire incorporation. Of course, it is in principle possible to imagine all the intermediate situations. Corrections of the data for permeability and pool have been done infrequently (Sconzo *et al.,* 1970a,b; Kijima and Wilt, 1969; Wilt, 1970; Emerson and Humphreys, 1971).

We have already described (Chapter 4) the variations of permeability to RNA precursors that take place at fertilization. At this point, there is indeed a sharp increase of permeability which must always be taken into account when the synthesis rate of unfertilized eggs is compared with that of postfertilization stages. The rate of nucleoside uptake then stays constant up to pluteus. It seems of practical interest to recall that when labeled [^{3}H]uridine (specific activity 20 Ci/mmole) is administered in the amount of 200 μCi/ml to *Paracentrotus lividus* swimming blastulae at a concentration of 5000 embryos/ml, 66% of the isotope is taken up by the embryos in less than 1 minute at 20°C (Enea and Mutolo, personal communication). Similar observations have been reported by Nemer (1962a) (Chapter 9), and by Aronson and Wilt (1969). On the other hand, when 0.5 μCi/ml of [^{32}P]orthophosphate (specific activity 40 Ci/mg P) is given to *Paracentrotus lividus* blastulae, at the same concentration and temperature, the uptake increases linearly, at least up to 4 hours. After 7 hours about 20% of the isotope has been taken up (Pirrone and Giudice, unpublished).

Some direct measurements of the nucleotide pool size are available (Nilsson, 1959, 1961; Hultin, 1957; Sugino, 1960; Taguchi, 1962; Isono and Yanagisawa, 1966; Yanagisawa and Isono, 1966). The most detailed results are those of Yanagisawa and Isono, which are in fair agreement with the data obtained by Hultin on *Psammechinus miliaris.* Part of the quantitative data of the Japanese authors, who have worked on *Hemicentrotus pulcherrimus* and *Pseudocentrotus depressus,* is reported in Table 8.2. It is readily seen, as expected, that ATP is the main nucleotide of the acid-soluble pool (50 μmoles %), followed by UDP sugar (13 μmoles %). The other nucleoside phosphates are, however, also represented. During early development, i.e., from fertilization to early blastula, a remarkable decrease of triphosphates is observed, while monophosphates show a certain increase from mesenchyme blastula on. It is interesting to note that the value of cytidine is close to that calculated by Nemer through the effect of isotope dilution (see Chapter 9).

2. SYNTHESIS OF RNA BEFORE THE MESENCHYME BLASTULA STAGE

That embryos can reach the blastula stage in the absence of RNA synthesis does not imply that no RNA is normally synthesized in the period between fertilization and blastula. We shall describe a series of experiments that directly prove that RNA synthesis does occur in this period.

The earliest evidence that the synthesis of some messengerlike RNA takes place during early embryogenesis is attributed to Wilt and Nemer (Wilt, 1963, 1964; Nemer, 1963). In a preliminary analysis, Wilt showed that eggs of *Strongylocentrotus purpuratus,* exposed to [^{14}C]uridine for 40 minutes shortly after fertilization, incorporate the radioactivity mostly into the 4 S zone, and also into an RNA that sediments rather polydispersely in a sucrose gradient, with two broad peaks in the zones of about 20 and 18 S. After a 3-hour chase the 20 S peak disappears, while another one, between 18 and 4 S, becomes visible. In a second paper, the authors reported the total uptake and incorporation of [^{3}H]uridine into unfertilized eggs and eggs from 30 to 120 minutes after fertilization. As expected, both the rates of uptake and incorporation increase up to 60 and 90 minutes following fertilization, respectively. The RNA synthesized during cleavage was again characterized by sucrose gradient and its polydisperse nature confirmed. A tendency to form plateaus or peaks was reported in the zones of 42, 34, 28, 21, and 12–14 S. Again the extensive incorporation into the 4–6 S zone was observed. This is the first evidence that the newly synthesized RNA becomes associated with ribosomes, and is extractable from the light polyribosomes in a higher amount than from the heavy ones. At the same time, Nemer demonstrated that the pulse-labeled RNA of *Strongylocentrotus* embryos extracted with SDS and phenol at 60°C, shows a polydisperse pattern of sedimentation during cleavage and blastula. If a chase is set up, the radioactivity sediments in a broad peak of about 10 S in the pregastrular stages while it accumulates into rRNA in the postgastrular stages. Here again, the very high labeling of the 4 S zone is noted. Figure 10.5 shows the rate of labeling and the polydisperse nature of the rápidly labeled RNA synthesized in three different developmental stages.

Attempts by the same author to analyze the RNA labeled in the unfertilized eggs or shortly after fertilization are not reported here because the low amount of radioactivity incorporated might have been caused by bacterial contamination. This danger was stressed by Glisin and Glisin (1964) who demonstrated that the use of antibiotics strongly reduces but does not abolish the incorporation of radioactive precursors into the rRNA of bacteria, which are contributed mainly by sperm. To overcome this difficulty, the authors suggest collection of the eggs by filtra-

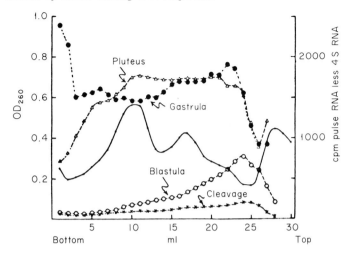

Fig. 10.5. A comparison of the sedimentation characteristics of non-4 S RNA labeled after a 10-minute pulse of [³H]uridine (3.5 μM) at various embryonic stages. The radioactivity of the 4 S zone has not been plotted. (From Nemer, 1963.)

tion through Miracloth tissue. This procedure removes the excess sperm and bacteria that contaminate the *Lytechinus* eggs. It should be noted that eggs of other species, e.g., of *Paracentrotus lividus,* may get damaged by this filtration.

The same authors confirm the polydisperse nature of the RNA synthesized when the embryos are exposed to ³²P from fertilization up to the 32-cell or the blastula stage. Again, the very high labeling of the 4 S zone is observed. Analysis of the distribution of ³²P among the 4 nucleotides shows that the labeling of the 4 S up to the blastula stage can be attributed exclusively to the terminal turnover of the CCA up to the 4-cell stage, with the possible addition of a modest synthesis up to the blastula stage. The base composition of the polydisperse RNA was found to be of DNA type, i.e., 40% G + C. The authors failed to detect any RNA synthesis in the unfertilized eggs and before the 32-cell stage. This result may partly be attributed to the low rate of RNA synthesis in these stages but also to the very low permeability of the unfertilized eggs to ³²P (see Chapter 4).

It has already been mentioned that Gross and co-workers (1964) had observed that the RNA labeled during the first hour of development is polydispersed when sedimented through a sucrose gradient. In a subsequent paper, Gross *et al.* (1965b) described the distribution of ³²P among the four nucleotides of the RNA of *Arbacia punctulata* labeled by exposure of eggs to the isotope from fertilization up to hatching, under conditions devised to provide a better guarantee of sterility. The RNA is collected on sucrose gradient and the base ratio of the labeled RNA of four zones of the gradient analyzed. The results are reported in Table 10.1, where the fraction I corresponds to the 26 S zone, IV to the 4 S zone, and II and III to two intermediate zones. The agreement of these data with those of Glisin and Glisin (1964) is very good, in that they confirm (1) that the polydisperse RNA is DNA-like, and (2) that the incorporation into the 4 S RNA is mainly due to terminal turnover.

TABLE 10.1

BASE COMPOSITIONS (IN MOLES %) OF SEA URCHIN RNA[a]

Sample	A	U	G	C	G + C	Source
Fraction I	28.9	24.4	23.6	23.1	46.7	These experiments
Fraction II	28.1	27.4	21.8	22.8	44.6	These experiments
Fraction III	33.8	16.2	18.2	31.8	50.0	These experiments
Fraction IV	14.4	12.9	14.5	58.2	72.7	These experiments
28 S rRNA	22.4	18.8	32.8	26.0	58.8	These experiments
18 S rRNA	24.4	21.7	30.0	24.0	54.1	These experiments
Bulk RNA	22.3	20.7	29.6	27.4	57.0	Elson et al. (1954)
Sperm DNA	28.4	32.8(T)	19.5	19.3	38.8	Daly et al. (1950)

[a] From Gross et al. (1965b).

Nemer and Infante (1965) agree that pulse-labeled RNA of *Lytechinus pictus* embryos at the 16- to 32-cell stage is heterogeneous when extracted from a fraction operationally to be considered equivalent to nuclei: the so-called phenolic nuclei, i.e., the interphase of a cold phenol extraction. The sedimentation behavior of such RNA is polydisperse, with a broad peak of around 10 S. The RNA extracted from phenolic nuclei of embryos labeled around hatching time is similar, with a tendency to sediment in the heavier zones of the gradient, forming a broad peak heavier than 26 S. This RNA was deemed to be different from ribosomal and 4 S RNA because of its greater ability to hybridize with DNA. The criterion of measuring the proportion of "informational" RNA, on the basis of the "percentage" of counts hybridizable with DNA as used by the authors, is no longer tenable today. In fact we know that ribosomal and transfer RNA are also able to hybridize DNA.

Under the conditions set up, the rRNA was tested for hybridization at the same input as the unknown RNA on the basis of radioactivity but probably not on that of mole number. The authors added to the hybridization mixture the same number of counts per minute of either rRNA or unknown RNA. The specific activities of the two RNA's, however, are not reported to be the same, so that the lack of rRNA hybridization may be attributed to its low specific activity, while, in principle, the unknown RNA might have been represented by rRNA at a much higher specific activity. Moreover, today the concept has been abandoned that all non-ribosomal and nontransfer RNA is necessarily informational.

We want to make it clear, at this point, that we are convinced, from the reported evidence, that the RNA of the phenolic nuclei of the 32-cell stage, reported by Nemer, is nonribosomal. We only feel that the hybridization argument in favor of this idea has lost much of its value with the passing of time. A similar polydisperse sedimentation, with a broad peak around the 18 S zone and several minor peaks was reported by Siekevitz *et al.* (1966) by pulse-labeling early blastulae of *Sphaerechinus granularis* with a mixture of [³H]uridine and [³H]cytidine. These authors found that the unfertilized egg synthesizes some heterogeneous RNA. The lower amount of incorporation may be partially explained by the much lower permeability to the isotopes. The authors show that a good proportion of the isotope taken up is incorporated into RNA at all stages, including the unfertilized egg.

The heterogeneous nature of the RNA synthesized by *Paracentrotus lividus* embryos, labled with ³²P during the first 5 hours following fertilization, was confirmed by Giudice and Mutolo (1967) who stress the importance of the use of SDS and hot phenol so as to achieve a good extraction of this RNA, which clearly appears of DNA-like type (Fig. 10.6). The failure of Comb *et al.* (1965b) to show any RNA synthesis before the blastula stage in *Lytechinus variegatus* embryos might be explained by the very short ³²P-labeling period, which does not allow the precursor pool to reach a specific activity high enough to detect a relatively low rate of synthesis. The same authors reported the synthesis of DNA-like RNA at the swimming blastula stage, which is heterogeneous on MAK columns. More recently, Hartman and Comb (1969), by the use of [³H]uridine, detected RNA synthesis between the 64-cell stage and early blastula. The heterogeneous nature of the RNA synthesized from 4 blastomeres, or earlier, up to blastula has also been proved by acrylamide gel electrophoresis by Slater and Spiegelman (1970), who found that the complexity of the electrophoretic pattern increases with development within this period, leading toward the synthesis of higher molecular weight RNA's, in *Strongylocentrotus purpuratus*. Part of this RNA is conserved through gastrulation, as shown by pulse and chase experiments.

To sum up, there is good evidence that in the period from fertilization to hatching, in addition to a very fast terminal turnover of transfer RNA, synthesis of a heterogeneous RNA takes place; this latter RNA can be judged DNA-like by the criterion of its base ratio and its ability to hybridize with DNA. To acquire more information about this RNA, two

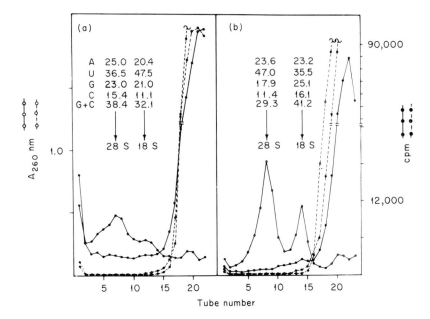

Fig. 10.6. Sucrose density gradient profiles labeled with ^{32}P (0.5 μCi/ml) between fertilization and 6 hours later, extracted with (a) SDS–hot phenol; and (b) cold phenol. The dotted lines indicate the absorbances and the radioactivities after treatment with ribonuclease. The base composition (as moles %) refers to the zones of the gradients indicated by the arrows. (From Giudice and Mutolo, 1967.)

lines of inquiry have been followed: First, that of investigating whether or not this RNA becomes engaged in polyribosomes and, possibly, if it can be correlated with the synthesis of some special class(es) of proteins; second, that of extracting it from the isolated nuclei in order to investigate the degree and rate of utilization of the nuclear RNA. The chief aim of such experiments is to learn about possible control mechanisms of RNA translation from a comparison of the nascent forms of nuclear RNA and cytoplasmic RNA's.

a. Study of Ribosome-Bound RNA Synthesized before the Mesenchyme Blastula Stage

Several authors have studied the sedimentation characteristics of the RNA extracted from polysomes after pulse-labeling with radioactive uridine. Figure 10.7A shows the sedimentation characteristics of such RNA extracted from light and heavy polyribosomes of *Strongylocentrotus purpuratus* embryos exposed to [^{3}H]uridine from fertilization up to 8-cell stage (Wilt, 1964).

Figure 10.7B shows polysomal RNA of *Lytechinus pictus* embryos labeled for 2 hours during the early cleavage stage. The nonribosomal

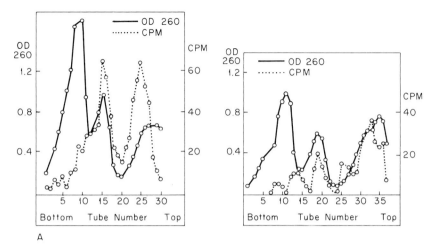

A

Fig. 10.7A. Sedimentation in sucrose gradient of radioactive RNA extracted from 70 S (left) and polyribosomes (right), after exposure of *Strongylocentrotus purpuratus* eggs to [³H]uridine from fertilization to the 8-cell stage. (From Wilt, 1964.)

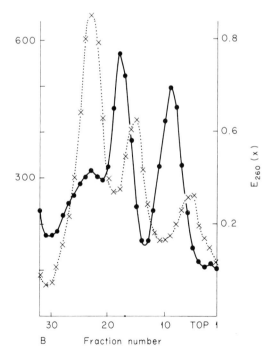

B Fraction number

Fig. 10.7B. Sedimentation in sucrose gradient of radioactive RNA extracted from polyribosomes of *Lytechinus pictus* embryos labeled with 1 μM [³H]uridine from 4 to 6 hours after fertilization. The dotted line indicates the absorbance of carrier ribosomal RNA. (From Nemer and Infante, 1965, copyright 1965 by the American Association for the Advancement of Science.)

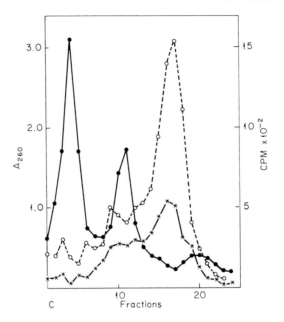

Fig. 10.7C. Sucrose gradient fractionation of labeled RNA extracted from light (dotted line and empty circles) and heavy (continuous line and stars) polyribosomes of 16-cell stage embryos labeled for 1 hour (i.e., from the 4 to 8-cell stage) with [5-³H]uridine (sp. act. 25 Ci/mM) 5 μCi/ml. Total RNA of *Paracentrotus* eggs was added as a carrier during the preparation and to provide a reference. (From Rinaldi and Monroy, 1969.)

and nontransfer nature of this RNA is confirmed by its lack of competition with these RNA's for DNA hybridization (Nemer and Infante, 1965). Figure 10.7C shows RNA extracted from heavy and light polysomes of *Paracentrotus lividus* embryos labeled for 1 hour with [³H]uridine from the 4- to 8-cell stage (Rinaldi and Monroy, 1969). Finally, Fig. 10.7D shows RNA extracted from heavy and light polysomes of *Arbacia punctulata* embryos labeled for 90 minutes with [³H]uridine at the indicated stages (Kedes and Gross, 1969a).

Despite differences in the species used and in the details of the labeling procedures (and although the techniques to prepare undegraded polysomes have become more and more sophisticated in recent years), we feel that some conclusions can be drawn that find support in all these experiments or, at least, are not contradictory with any of them. It is clear that newly synthesized RNA binds preferentially to light polysomes rather than to heavy ones (Fig. 10.7C and D) [see also Spirin and Nemer (1965) and other data by Wilt (1964)]. The finding (noted by Wilt and stressed by Nemer) that in contrast with the polydispersity of the total or nuclear RNA polysomal RNA can be classified into a few discrete-size classes appears less clear in the data of Kedes and Gross and of Rinaldi and Monroy. It should be recalled that the latter authors have prepared

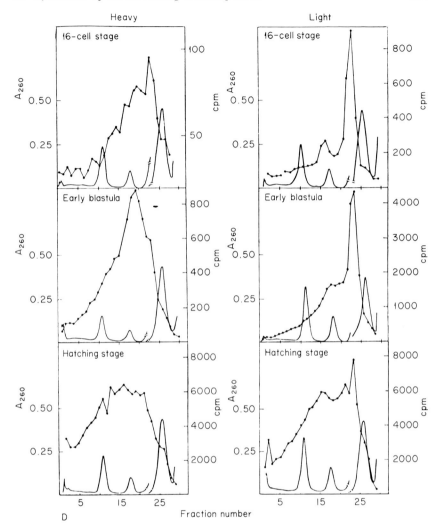

Fig. 10.7D. Sedimentation of radioactive RNA isolated from heavy and light polyribosomes at different developmental stages of *Arbacia punctulata,* exposed for 90 minutes to [5-^{3}H]uridine (26.6 Ci/mM) 100 μCi/ml. The lines closer to the abscissa indicate the optical densities. (From Kedes and Gross, 1969a).

the polysomes with a more modern approach. In all cases, however, a class of RNA sedimenting between the 18 S and the 4 S markers has been found that is clearly predominant in the light polyribosomes. This class has been further characterized by Kedes and Gross by means of polyacrylamide gel electrophoresis and resolved into three peaks. The authors have tentatively suggested that these represent three classes of mRNA's specific for the synthesis of histones. The arguments in favor of such a hypothesis will be discussed in Chapter 11. Additionally, Fromson and Nemer (1970) have recently shown that homogenization, by a few strokes of a Dounce homogenizer, of early blastulae of *Lytechinus pictus* brings about some nuclear breakage. In this case, a minor percentage of RNA cosedimenting with polysomes is caused by artificial nuclear leakage, as shown by the fact that it does not move to the light region of a sucrose gradient when polyribosomes are broken down by EDTA treatment. In a experiment to find out how much this may have affected the results reported in Fig. 10.7, Kedes and Gross observed that the labeled RNA, associated with their polysomes, is completely movable to the top of the gradient when polysomes are broken down by EDTA. Moreover, these authors do not find any polyribosomal label before a 15-minute exposure to [³H]uridine, while the nuclei have accumulated very highly labeled RNA by that time. So, at least in this case, nuclear leakage is unlikely to be responsible for the pattern observed. A similar conclusion may be valid for the experiments of Fig. 10.7C, because the method used for polyribosomal preparation is the same as that used by Kedes and Gross. In the other cases of Fig. 10.7, conditions of homogenization different from those reported by Fromson and Nemer have been used. In fact, 0.25 M sucrose was present in the homogenization medium, which might have prevented nuclear damage. In any case, the percentage of nonpolyribosomal RNA cosedimenting with polyribosomes does not seem very high, under the conditions set up by Fromson and Nemer. A study of the particle-bound RNA in the cytoplasm led Spirin and Nemer (1965) to the discovery in sea urchins of what Spirin names "informosome."

b. Informosomes

In 1964 Spirin and collaborators (Belitsina *et al.,* 1964; Spirin *et al.,* 1964) produced evidence that in the cytoplasm of developing embryos of the teleostean fish, *Misgurnus foxilis,* some messengerlike RNA could be recovered in association with proteins. Because of the labeling kinetics of these RNA and proteins it was believed that they had been newly synthesized. When analyzed by sucrose gradient, these ribonucleoproteins (RNP's) sedimented in the area of the subribosomal particles. The RNA extracted from the RNP's showed template activity when tested in a cell-free system. It was postulated that these RNP's represented the newly synthesized mRNA which was transferred to the cytoplasm associated with proteins of new synthesis. These RNP's were, therefore, named informosomes to mean that they represented the particulate form under which the genetic information was transferred from the nuclei to the cytoplasm.

The function of the proteins was not known. It was tentatively suggested that they might have served the purpose of protecting the fragile mRNA from the cytoplasmic RNases. The protein also might have played some role in regulating translation of the message (see Spirin, 1966, for review). The second example for the existence of informosomes was provided by Spirin and Nemer (1965) in sea urchin embryos: *Lytechinus pictus* embryos at the 4-cell stage were labeled for 2 hours with [³H]uridine, and for the last 2 minutes with [¹⁴C]leucine. The post-mitochondrial supernatant was then centrifuged in a sucrose gradient so as to expand the zone between 4 S and 70 S. Six peaks of radioactivity were observed with a parallel pattern of the ¹⁴C and ³H distribution. The RNA contained in these peaks was judged messenger because it hybridizes with DNA under conditions in which rRNA and 4 S RNA do not hybridize. Here again, the arguments previously exposed must be repeated. The most important is that the rRNA input and the supposed mRNA in the hybridization test were the same on the basis of the counts per minute, but not in terms of RNA micrograms. Under such conditions the "informosomal" RNA does not compete with cold rRNA and 4 S RNA for DNA hybridization.

When Spirin and Nemer analyzed the radioactivity distribution from [³H]uridine and [¹⁴C]leucine in the polyribosomal region of a sucrose gradient, they observed that while most of the radioactivity from uridine was found associated with the light polyribosomes, that from leucine was associated with the heavy ones. This result has been repeatedly confirmed. The interpretation given by the authors was that the light polysomes, formed at the expenses of the new mRNA were little active in protein synthesis, whereas the heavy polysomes containing mRNA preexisting in the egg, had a very high protein synthesis activity. The suggestion was also made that the little polysomes might have been rendered nonactive since their mRNA still contained part of the informosomal protein that impaired the ribosomal translocation along the messenger (see, also, Infante and Nemer, 1967). This interpretation was in agreement with the finding that the block of new mRNA synthesis by actinomycin from fertilization on did not affect the overall rate of amino acid incorporation. Kedes and Gross (1969a), although confirming these results, gave them a different interpretation: Assuming that the heavy polysomes contain longer mRNA (the validity of this assumption is based mainly on the results represented in Fig. 10.7D), one would actually expect to find the longer-growing peptide chains on the heavy polysomes, with a higher amount of radioactivity in them than in the light polysomes even if both synthesize protein at the same speed. The experimental data, in the author's opinion, match this theoretical expectation, without the need to assume that some of the light polysomes are inactive in protein synthesis (see Chapter 11).

Two more arguments are usually raised against the concept that the informosomes are real entities. The first is that they may represent nascent ribosomal subunits bringing some bound mRNA. This argument loses a good part of its value in sea urchins, where (as already shown and as will be proved in the following pages), there is little or no rRNA synthesis before the mesenchyme blastula stage. Moreover, Spirin has observed that the informosomes from several sources, when centrifuged in CsCl after fixation with formaldehyde, show a buoyant density different from that of the subribosomal particles.

Infante and Nemer (1968) reinvestigated the question of the informosomes on embryos of *Lytechinus* and *Strongylocentrotus*. They report that the zone of a sucrose gradient of a postmitochondrial supernatant between 70 and 20 S contains six peaks of radioactivity bound to RNA after a 15-minute exposure of cleavage embryos to [³H]uridine (Fig. 10.8). Up to 95% of this RNA is bound to proteins, as shown by the fact that it does not pass through Millipore filters. The RNA extracted from

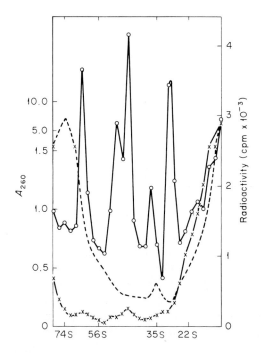

Fig. 10.8. Distribution in sucrose density gradient of subribosomal labeled RNA, retained by membrane filters. Eight-hour late cleavage embryos of *S. purpuratus* were incubated with [³H]uridine (100 μCi/ml.) for 15 minutes; the S 15 was prepared and centrifuged in a 15–30% sucrose gradient in the Spinco SW 39 rotor at 39,000 rpm for 4–5 hours. A_{260} was continuously monitored through a recording spectrophotometer. (From Nemer and Infante, 1968.)

these peaks sediments with broad peaks in the zone between 28 and 4 S. Again it was observed that it does not compete with cold rRNA and 4 S for hybridization with DNA. The same authors acknowledge that complexes of DNA-like RNA and 35 S ribosomal subunits, artificially prepared, display buoyant densities, after formaldehyde fixation (between 1.56 and 1.80), not easily distinguished from those of the informosomes. However, a mild treatment with RNase releases some RNA from the informosomes, causing a decrease in their buoyant density to values lower than those of the ribosomal subunits. The latter are not affected by the RNase treatment. This fact has led the authors to believe that the RNP's under investigation do not represent mRNA naturally or artificially bound to the ribosomal subunits, but some other form of ribonucleoprotein particles, possibly the informosomes.

The other main argument, and perhaps the most difficult to rule out, is that some mRNA may become artificially associated to basic cellular proteins following homogenization, thus generating artifactual RNP's (Girard and Baltimore, 1966). It can be argued, that if such artifactual complexes are so easily generated upon homogenization it seems improbable that the free RNA does not naturally bind to proteins within the cell. A binding factor of proteic nature has been described by Baltimore and Huang (1970) in HeLa cells, which is able to bind RNA. Huang and Baltimore (1970) have also recently found that the poliovirus RNA recovered from cellular polysomes is coated with a protein.

Finally, it must be mentioned that Hogan and Gross (1971) have reported that a 95% inhibition of protein synthesis does not inhibit for at least 1 hour the synthesis and the binding to polysomes of histone RNA. This suggests that, at least in this case, RNA does not need to be coupled to newly synthesized proteins to be transported from nuclei to polysomes.

Samarina *et al.* (1966, 1967, 1968) have found some nuclear nonribosomal RNA in rat liver, bound to proteins that they call "informofer" (Samarina *et al.*, 1966). Protein-bound nuclear RNA of a high synthesis rate has been described in sea urchins but variously interpreted (Roy and Giudice, 1967; Aronson and Wilt, 1969). Perry and Kelley (1966, 1968) found some polysome-bound mRNA still bearing attached proteins in mammalian cells. This result was recently confirmed by Yong Lee and Brawermann (1971), and similar observations are reported by Penman *et al.* (1968).

Are these RNA–protein complexes artifacts or are they real entities? If real, do they represent the form in which the information is sent from nuclei to cytoplasm?

This is certainly a most interesting field, and we believe that the problem is still open to solution.

c. Analysis of Nuclear RNA Synthesized before the
Mesenchyme Blastula Stage

It is known that most of the RNA synthesis takes place in the nucleus. It has been suggested that part of the nuclear RNA is not transferred to the cytoplasm. The selection of those copies of RNA that have to pass to the site of protein synthesis, i.e., the cytoplasmic ribosomes, might therefore represent a mechanism of transcription control that plays a key role in differentiation. Developing sea urchins have been used as a model for the study of such a problem, and analyses of nuclear RNA have been made.

Giudice and Mutolo (1969) modified for *Paracentrotus lividus* embryos the method used by Penman (1966) to isolate and purify nuclei from HeLa cells. Briefly, this involves cell lysis in a hypotonic buffer, sedimentation and washing of the nuclei by a mixture of Tween 40: DOC (2 : 1), which has the effect of removing the external nuclear membrane; the latter, in turn, as shown by Wartiowara and Branton (1970), brings forth attached ribosomes. Several other methods have been described to isolate nuclei from sea urchins (Hinegardner, 1961, 1962; Loeb *et al.,* 1967; Aronson and Wilt, 1969; Thaler *et al.,* 1969b; Kedes *et al.,* 1969; Roeder and Rutter, 1970b; Johnson and Hnlica, 1970). In our opinion, the method we have used provides operationally pure nuclei, in that they do not contain any 18 S rRNA and little 26 S rRNA. The RNA they do contain is in fact heterogeneous and sediments in a polydisperse fashion when analyzed in a sucrose gradient or by acrylamide gel electrophoresis. The stages examined were those of hatching blastula and of gastrula. We shall refer presently to the blastula stage.

If nuclear RNA is analyzed by gel electrophoresis after different intervals of exposure to [^{3}H]uridine of high specific activity (20 Ci/μmole), the picture displayed in Fig. 10.9 is obtained, showing an immediate labeling of RNA classes of very high molecular weight ($> \times 10^6$ daltons). The nuclear RNA becomes progressively less labeled after the first hour, probably because of isotope exhaustion, paralleled by the transfer of nuclear RNA to the cytoplasm and the trapping of radioactive precursors in the terminal nucleotides of the transfer RNA. The nuclear RNA optical density is polydisperse in this as in other stages. The possibility that part of this RNA is rapidly turning over with no transfer to the cytoplasm is not ruled out by this experiment; it will be discussed further in Section F of this chapter.

The finding of nuclear RNA heterogeneity and of its very large upper size is in agreement with the observation by Nemer and Infante (1965) on phenolic nucleic RNA.

Aronson and Wilt (1969) found that a good part of the RNA labeled

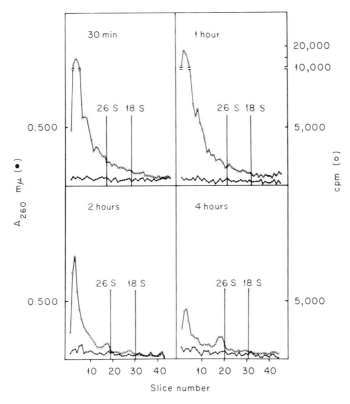

Fig. 10.9. Polyacrylamide gel electrophoresis of nuclear RNA of *Paracentrotus lividus* embryos, after various periods of *in vivo* exposure to [³H]uridine, beginning at the hatching blastula stage. The positions of the 26 S and 18 S peaks, as revealed by internal markers, are indicated by vertical lines. (From Giudice and Mutolo, 1969.)

with [³H]uridine from the 64-cell stage up to mesenchyme blastula of *Strongylocentrotus purpuratus* is associated with proteins within the nucleus. The authors provide evidence that this RNA is associated with nuclear "polysomes." The ribosomes sticking to the outer nuclear membrane form part of the "nuclear" preparation in these experiments. When extracted, this RNA sediments with a main peak at around 18 S. The question of the nuclear RNA size, especially in those stages where the synthesis of rRNA precursors does not yet complicate the picture, is an interesting one. If we admit that the giant RNA's shown in Fig. 10.9 are not an artifact due to aggregation or to residual contamination with proteins (as has been more recently suggested (Giudice *et al.,* 1972a), then we must consider the possibility that a polycistronic transcription takes place in sea urchin nuclei. About the genuineness of the RNA presented in these figures we can say that it does not arise from cytoplasmic contamination (a) because of the lack of absorbance in the 18 S region and (b) because the specific activity of the cytoplasmic RNA is lower by a factor of about 5. These giant RNA's look very fragile since they reach an S of about 18 when incubated at 37°C for 30 minutes. The presence of SDS in the incubation medium prevents this breakdown, suggesting that it might have been caused by nuclease action. The question still remains open to any solution at present.

d. RNA Synthesized before the Mesenchyme Blastula State and Extractable from the "Total Cytoplasm"

We have described the characteristics of nuclear RNA. For reasons of comparison, it is pertinent to take up the subject of cytoplasmic RNA. This might provide an answer as to how much nuclear RNA is transferred to the cytoplasm and if any processing of nuclear RNA takes place before its transfer to the cytoplasm, so that a control mechanism of protein synthesis might be envisaged. By "total cytoplasm" we mean the total homogenate minus the nuclear fraction purified, as described by Giudice and Mutolo (1969).

The major interest in analyzing this RNA lies in the fact that the giant RNA classes, as already described for the nucleus, are also detectable here (Fig. 10.10). Should it be possible to definitively prove that these very large RNA's are not artifacts, it might be proposed that polycistronic RNA's are transferred to the cytoplasm in sea urchins. The main point to emphasize is that these figures do not arise from nuclear contamination because of the different labeling kinetics of nuclei and cytoplasm (Giudice et al., 1972a). It is also interesting that Aronson (1972) found than an enzyme which cleaves the heterogeneous nuclear RNA is located in the cytoplasm in sea urchin embryos.

In conclusion, there is an active synthesis of RNA in the period between fertilization and the mesenchyme blastula stage, i.e., throughout that part of development which the embryo is able to perform, even when RNA synthesis has been inhibited.

This RNA is heterogeneous when extracted from entire embryos or from isolated nuclei. Its base ratio analysis and hybridization properties characterize it as nonribosomal. Part of this RNA can be recovered from the polyribosomes, especially the light ones. In this case, it sediments in sucrose gradient at more discrete peaks. One of them, of about 10 S, is predominant in the light polyribosome region and has been further resolved into three subclasses by electrophoresis. It has been tentatively identified with mRNA for histone synthesis (see Chapter 11).

Part of the RNA has been found bound to proteins between the 70 S

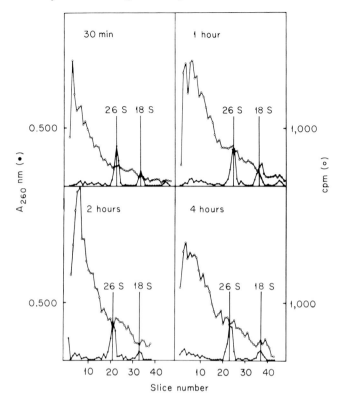

Fig. 10.10. Polyacrylamide gel electrophoresis of the RNA extracted with dodecyl-sulfate–hot phenol from the cytoplasm of the same embryos shown in Fig. 10.9 (i.e., blastulae). (From Giudice and Mutolo, 1969.)

and 20 S regions of a sucrose gradient and is presumed to be part of the "informosomes."

When the RNA extracted from the "total cytoplasm" is studied by acrylamide gel electrophoresis, classes of sizes ranging up to several millions are described; however, they still need further characterization.

Throughout this part of development, a very active terminal turnover of the transfer RNA occurs, to which some tRNA synthesis adds up in the last part of this period.

Since such an active RNA synthesis takes place, part of which is engaged in protein synthesis, a paradox arises: How do embryos reach the hatching blastula stage in the absence of this RNA synthesis, as happens, for example, in the presence of actinomycin? The answer is that the proteins synthesized on the new messengers are not needed for the embryos to reach the hatching stage. It has, however, been observed that cleavage is delayed by a variable factor in the presence of actinomycin. This might be attributed to the impairment of histone synthesis (Kedes *et al.,* 1969; Nemer and Lindsay, 1969). Moreover, Kiefer *et al.* (1969) have shown that in the presence of actinomycin at 20 μg/ml, about 5% of the mitoses show abnormalities consisting mainly of the formation of interchromosomal bridges in anaphase, which may persist so as to connect the nuclei of the daughter cells through the furrows. Is this also due to the disturbance of histone synthesis?

Furthermore, if actinomycin stops the synthesis of new proteins, such as histones, which represent (Kedes *et al.,* 1969) a good part of the proteins synthesized, why does the total rate of protein synthesis remain unaltered in the presence of actinomycin? Even if answers to this question can be given, no experimental proof for any of them has been provided as yet.

3. RNA SYNTHESIS IN THE PERIOD FROM MESENCHYME BLASTULA
   TO PLUTEUS

This period is characterized by the resumption of rRNA synthesis, which, while active during oogenesis, had ceased with egg maturation. The activation mechanism of this synthesis has been so interesting that most of the information available on the synthesis of RNA during this developmental period deals with rRNA. We shall, therefore, describe this synthesis first and then briefly review the fragmentary information available on the synthesis of other RNA's.

a. rRNA Synthesis

Nemer (1963) had shown that at the gastrula stage (but not before) it is possible to chase the radioactivity from a pulse exposure to [³H]uridine into the rRNA of *Strongylocentrotus purpuratus*. Comb *et al.* (1965b) had suggested that rRNA identifiable by MAK chromatography and base ratio analysis is synthesized only at the pluteus stage in *Lytechinus variegatus*.

In a series of experiments, Giudice and Mutolo have tried to establish the activation timing of this synthesis. When the development of *Paracentrotus lividus* is divided into four periods of 6 hours each and the embryos are treated with [³H]uridine during each of the periods, the results shown in Fig. 10.11 are obtained. In these experiments, the RNA is extracted only with cold phenol without addition of detergent. This procedure, as the authors have preliminarily shown, mainly extracts ribosomal and 4 S RNA, but fails to extract most of the heterogeneous RNA. Upon a first inspection, the figure shows that stage IV, i.e., from mid-gastrula to young prism, is more active in rRNA synthesis and that a

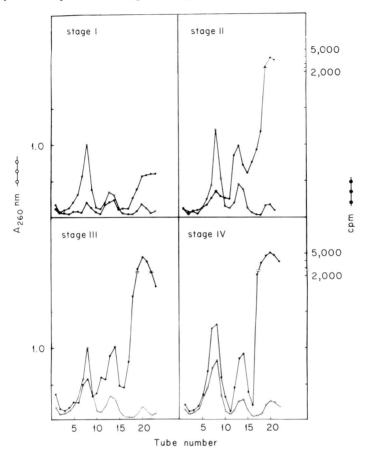

Fig. 10.11. Sucrose density gradient profiles of RNA extracted with cold phenol after 6 hours labeling with [³H]uridine during the following periods: Stage I, from 0 to 6 hours, i.e., from fertilization to very early blastula; stage II, from 6 to 12 hours, i.e., until the swimming blastula; stage III, from 12 to 18 hours, i.e., until the mid-gastrula; stage IV, from 18 to 24 hours, i.e., until the prism stage. (From Giudice and Mutolo, 1967.)

clear labeling of the 26 S rRNA* takes place only after the swimming blastula stage, even if a minor amount of radioactivity coincident with this peak is seen at every stage. On the other hand, the 18 S peak shows a much higher specific activity from the earliest stage. This fact is ascribed by the authors to synthesis of some nonribosomal RNA of about 18 S. The conclusion is based on the study of the ³²P distribution among the four nucleotides, following *in vivo* labeling, which shows that the 18 S labeling represents synthesis of nonribosomal RNA in stage II,

---

*S values of mature rRNA subunits are 26 and 18 in sea urchin embryos (see p. 278).

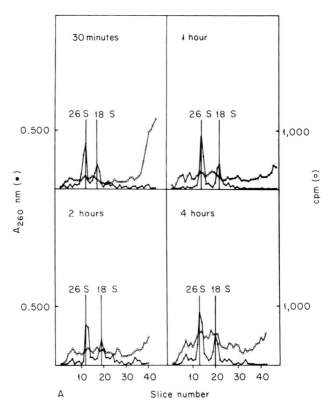

Fig. 10.12. A. Polyacrylamide gel electrophoresis of the RNA extracted with cold phenol from the cytoplasm of the same embryos shown in Fig. 10.9 (i.e., blastulae).

to which increasing amounts of true 18 S rRNA add up in stages III and IV. Labeling of the 26 S peak in stages III and IV is almost entirely due to rRNA synthesis. A better resolution of other RNA's from the true 18 S rRNA is obtained by acrylamide gel electrophoresis. Figure 10.12 shows that no radioactivity peak corresponding to the 18 S RNA is observed after a 4-hour exposure to [³H]uridine starting from hatching time. A clear rRNA labeling is observed, on the other hand, under the same conditions when the isotope is given at gastrula (see, also, Slater and Spiegelman, 1970).

These experiments have led to the conclusion that at some stage after swimming blastula, rRNA synthesis becomes activated and then further accelerated. The slow labeling kinetics of the 26 S rRNA has led Giudice and Mutolo (1967) to suggest the existence of a nuclear rRNA precursor. They have also attributed the failure of Comb *et al.* (1965b) to

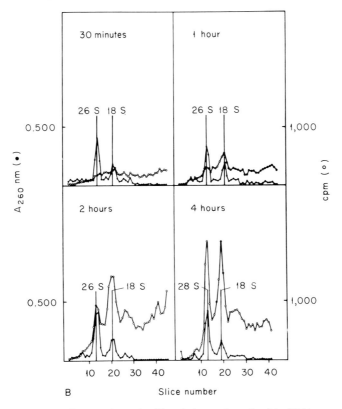

Fig. 10.12. (*continued*). B. Polyacrylamide gel electrophoresis of the RNA extracted with cold phenol from the cytoplasm of embryos after the same periods of exposure to [³H]uridine as in A, but beginning the treatment at the late mid-gastrula stage. (From Giudice and Mutolo, 1969.)

detect rRNA synthesis before the pluteus stage to too short a time of exposure to labeled precursors in the latter experiments.

The experiments reported so far do not take into account the changes in permeability and precursor pool, except for the observation by Giudice and Mutolo of an increased incorporation of [³H]uridine into the 26 S rRNA at gastrula compared to the incorporation into the "total" RNA. This increase in the rRNA synthesis rate after the swimming blastula stage is judged from the specific activity reached by the rRNA after exposure of the embryos to labeled precursors. Since the total RNA and rRNA per embryo remain practically unchanged, at least up to the prism stage (Sconzo *et al.*, 1970a; Schmidt *et al.*, 1948; Whitely, 1949; Elson *et al.*, 1954; Olsson, 1965; Chen, 1959; Chen *et al.*, 1961; Tocco *et al.*, 1963), it is possible to calculate the rRNA synthesis rate of each embryo. This is clearly found to increase after the swimming blastula stage. Since the number of cells and, therefore, that of nuclei are considerably increased with development, it might be thought that the increase of the rRNA synthesis rate of each embryo is due to the increased number of transcribing nuclei in each embryo. These arguments have been circumvented by experiments by Sconzo *et al.* (1970a) in which the nucleotidic pool is loaded with ^{32}P for 8 hours after fertilization. In this way, the specific activity of the α-phosphates of the nucleotidic pool remains constant at least for 24 hours. A quantitative measure of the rate of rRNA synthesis (and maturation) is obtainable by measuring the specific activity increase of the 26 S rRNA at various time intervals. As a correction for the increase in nuclei per embryo, these values can be referred to DNA units, assuming that the increase in nuclei is paralleled by an increase in DNA. The results of such an experiment are shown in Figs. 10.13 and 10.14. It is readily seen that there is little or no synthesis of rRNA in the stage between early blastula and swimming blastula. The synthesis becomes activated thereafter and then seems to be further accelerated.

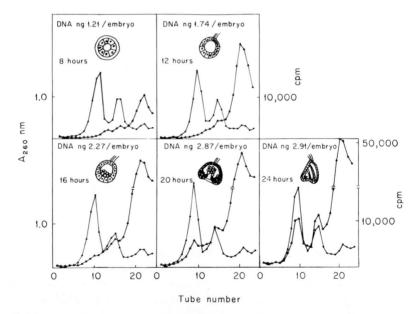

Fig. 10.13. Sucrose density gradient analysis of the RNA extracted at different developmental stages from embryos which have been prelabeled with ^{32}P from fertilization until 8 hours. The inserts show the developmental stages with the amount of DNA per embryo: 8 hours, early blastula; 12 hours, swimming blastula; 16 hours, late mesenchyme blastula; 20 hours, mid-gastrula; 24 hours, prism. ●——●, A_{260} nm; △——△, cpm. (From Sconzo *et al.,* 1970a.)

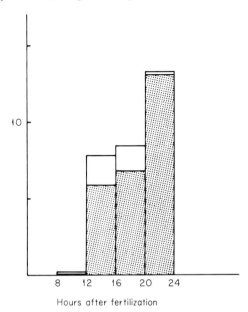

Hours after fertilization

Fig. 10.14. This diagram has been plotted by dividing the increase in specific activity of the 26 S peak during each 4-hour time interval by the DNA content at the beginning (whole length of the column) or at the end (dotted part of the column) of the same time interval. The data have been derived from the experiment reported in Fig. 10.13. (From Sconzo *et al.,* 1970a.)

Knowledge of the specific activity of the precursor pool permits an approximate calculation of the actual amount of rRNA synthesized during development, assuming that the specific activity of the α-phosphates in the nucleotide triphosphates is comparable to that of the α-phosphates of nucleotide monophosphates and nucleotide diphosphates (that this is the case is demonstrated by unpublished analyses of Giudice *et al.*). It is found that the amount of new rRNA synthesized up to the prism stage does not exceed 10% of that already present in the egg. This calculation is based on the data reported in Table 10.2, which are in good agreement with the measurements of the absolute size of nucleotidic pool reported by others (see above) and with those of the 26 S rRNA per embryo reported by Nemer and Infante (1967). This explains how it is possible for the total amount of RNA to remain practically unchanged up to the prism stage, without the need for a breakdown of rRNA synthesized during oogenesis.

Emerson and Humphreys (1970) have stressed the fact that, since the overall RNA synthesis is very active during cleavage, it might obscure the rRNA synthesis that might take place in the few nuclei present in the

TABLE 10.2

AMOUNTS OF COLD PHENOL-EXTRACTABLE RNA, 26 S rRNA, AND ACID-SOLUBLE
NUCLEOTIDE POOL IN EMBRYOS AT DIFFERENT DEVELOPMENTAL STAGES[a,b]

	Time after fertilization		
	12 hours (swimming blastula)	18–20 hours (mid-gastrula)	22–24 hours (prism)
μg RNA extracted with cold phenol from $1 \cdot 10^5$ embryos	132±18 (7)	–	143±1 (20)
Absorbance of 26 S RNA per 1 $A_{260\,nm}$ unit of the cold phenol RNA	0.517±0.026 (8)	–	0.487±0.017 (19)
ng 26 S RNA per embryo	0.58–0.84	–	0.62±0.77
ng acid-soluble nucleotides per embryo	3.48±0.79 (5)	2.50±0.59	2.89±0.50

[a] From Sconzo et al. (1970a).
[b] The values in parentheses are the number of experimental observations.

embryo at this stage. They have calculated that the amount of G + C-rich RNA, which becomes labeled after exposure to ^{32}P during the first 10 hours of development of *Strongylocentrotus purpuratus,* corresponds to the amount of rRNA that, in their opinion, should be labeled if the nuclei were synthesizing rRNA at the same rate as the pluteus nuclei (Emerson and Humphreys, 1971). These results do not agree with the conclusions by Sconzo et al. (1970a,b), in which comparison is made of the rRNA synthesis rate of two close stages of development, such as hatching blastula and early gastrula. Moreover, Sconzo and Giudice (1971) have recently found that ^{3}H from methyl-labeled methionine is not incorporated into rRNA at the hatching blastula stage, while an active incorporation takes place at the gastrula stage, under conditions of isotope utilization for RNA methylation that are comparable in the two stages, as shown by the fact that low-molecular-weight RNA's become equally labeled at blastula and gastrula.

Emerson and Humphreys (1971) have recently suggested that the agranular nucleoli observable during cleavage are actually precursors of the granular nucleoli that are seen following the blastula stage. This interpretation is based on the observation that if cleavage is blocked by fluorodeoxyuridine mixed with uridine, an enlargement of "cleavage nucleoli" is observed. They suggest, therefore, that during the normal cleavage period the nucleoli fail to enlarge and become similar to the gastrula stage nucleoli only because the interphase is too short. Brachet and his colleagues (1972) studied these enlarged cleavage nucleoli formed in the presence of fluorodeoxyuridine and uridine, and have concluded that there is no evidence at all that they contain RNA or play a role in rRNA synthesis. Hence, they suggest that cleavage agranular nucleoli are not precursors of gastrula granular nucleoli. This is also in agreement with the autoradiographic data by Karasaki (1968).

That the rRNA synthesized during oogenesis is stable throughout development has been demonstrated by Nemer and Infante (1967) by taking advantage of the fact that the maternal 18 S rRNA of *Strongylocentrotus purpuratus,* and not the newly synthesized 18-S rRNA, is broken down to 13 S by briefly heating at 60°C (other species of sea urchin do not display the same behavior). Consequently, the proportion of breakable and nonbreakable 18 S RNA was measured at different stages. At variance with our findings, however, some 20–50% of the maternal rRNA seemed to disappear by the prism stage, to be partially substituted by the new one. These last figures, however, might have been somewhat overestimated (Nemer, personal communication).

The question of the rRNA precursor has been thoroughly investigated by us. Preliminary analysis of the nuclear RNA undergoing active synthesis at gastrula as well as at hatching blastula (Giudice and Mutolo, 1969) had shown a number of peaks in the region of the heavy RNA's at both stages, i.e., also before rRNA synthesis was activated. This rendered it difficult to identify rRNA precursors among so many different heavy RNA's. The only class of nuclear RNA synthesized at a clearly higher rate during gastrula than during blastula was an RNA migrating slightly slower than the 26 S rRNA, which became, therefore, a candidate for a precursor of the 26 S rRNA. The possibility that some precursor synthesis not followed by maturation might take place at blastula, seemed unlikely because of the autoradiographic data by Karasaki (1968) indicating that no significant nucleolar labeling takes place before the mesenchyme blastula stage under conditions that clearly permit nucleoplasmic incorporation. One way to identify the rRNA precursor was that of isolating it from purified nucleoli. Sconzo *et al.* (1971) have tried a nucleolar purification, essentially according to the procedure by Vesco and Penman (1968) with the variation that the nuclei were lysed by forcing them through a French pressure cell, since, at least from the gastrula stage on, the nuclei of *Paracentrotus lividus* proved to be very resistant to other mechanical or enzymatic treatments. The nucleolar fraction so obtained contained a good part of the nuclear radioactivity after long-term *in vivo* labeling at the gastrula stage, which, as previously shown, resulted in a preferential accumulation of radioactivity into rRNA. A fraction obtained with the same procedure from blastulae labeled with [³H]-uridine contained little or no radioactivity. The nucleolar fraction of the gastrula stage accumulated, with respect to the rest of the nucleus, the RNA migrating in acrylamide slightly more slowly than 26 S rRNA. The nucleolar RNA was then analyzed after *in vivo* labeling with [³H]uridine or [³H]methylmethionine or with ³²P, by sucrose gradient and by acrylamide gel electrophoresis (Figs. 10.15 and 10.16). It was concluded that

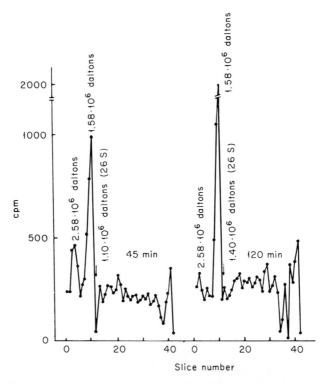

Fig. 10.15. Radioactivity profile of the acrylamide gel electrophoresis of nucleolar RNA from gastrulae exposed to [³H]L-methylmethionine for 45 or 120 minutes. The arrow points to the 26-S marker. (From Sconzo *et al.,* 1971.)

a precursor exists, having a sedimentation coefficient of 33 S and a molecular weight of 2.58×10^6 daltons, that this precursor cleaves to 18 S and 28 S, i.e., into two pieces by 0.68 and 1.5×10^6 daltons. The 18 S is immediately exported to the cytoplasm while the 28 S is slowly

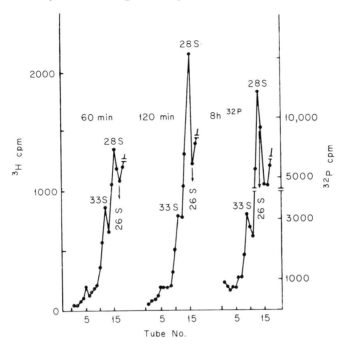

Fig. 10.16. Radioactivity profile of sucrose gradients of nucleolar RNA from gastrulae exposed to 0.5 μCi/ml of [5-^{3}H]uridine (21 Ci/mmole) for 60 or 120 minutes, or to 4 μCi/ml of carrier-free ^{32}P for 8 hours. The arrow points to the 26 S marker. (From Sconzo *et al.*, 1971.)

processed to 26 S, i.e., reduced to 1.4×10^6 daltons and then brought to the cytoplasm (Fig. 10.17). These calculations have been made by assuming 18 and 26 S as sedimentation coefficients, and 1.40×10^6 and 0.68 daltons as molecular weights of the two mature rRNA subunits, respectively (Sy and McCarty, 1968; McCarty *et al.*, 1968; Slater and Spiegelman, 1970; Loening, 1968). Processing of this rRNA precursor is in agreement with the labeling kinetics of the cytoplasmic rRNA (Fig. 10.12), and with the fact that an exhaustive labeling of the nucleolar RNA or an examination of the optical density reveals much more 28 S than 32 S.

The characterization of these classes as precursors of rRNA is based mainly on four facts: First, they accumulate in the nucleoli more than in the rest of the nucleus. Second, the base ratio of the 28 S is very close to that of the 26 S, and that of the 33 S is 50% G + C, while that of the DNA is about 35% G + C. Third, they are labeled with [^{3}H]methyl-methionine. Fourth, at least one of them, the 28 S, is shown to be labeled at a much higher rate in the whole nucleus of gastrulae than in that of hatching blastulae. The nucleotidic sequences, which are cut off during

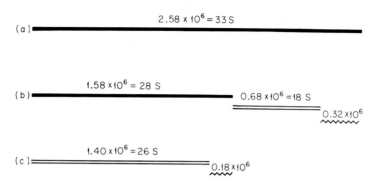

Fig. 10.17. Tentative scheme for processing of the precursor of rRNA. The solid line indicates the immature products; the double line the mature products; the zigzag line discarded fragments. (From Sconzo *et al.*, 1971.)

maturation, are of the molecular weight of about 0.5×10^6 daltons. They seem to contain a high amount of UMP.

These facts have been recently confirmed by Giudice and co-workers (Giudice *et al.*, 1972b; Sconzo *et al.*, 1972), by investigating the synthesis and maturation of rRNA during oogenesis; except that, as mentioned at the beginning of this chapter, the 33 S processing appears to be much slower during oogenesis.

Such a maturation pattern of rRNA places the sea urchin with the lower vertebrates, which lack the 45 S precursor proper of the vertebrates from reptiles on, and have as a 33 S RNA the largest precursor (Perry *et al.*, 1970). It is uncertain whether other intermediates between the 33 S and the mature forms, besides the 28 S, exist in sea urchin. Moreover, to absolutely negate that higher molecular weight precursors exist in sea urchins appears rather difficult because of the abundance of large classes of RNA and the danger of artificial aggregation or contamination with protein of what appears to be heavy RNA.

The figure of 2.58×10^6 daltons for the heaviest rRNA precursor is in excellent agreement with that of 2.6×10^6 daltons calculated from the analysis of the rDNA reported by Patterson and Stafford (1971) (see Chapter 9).

All these experiments on rRNA synthesis in sea urchin embryos can be considered preliminary in that their main value consists in stating the following problem: At mesenchyme blastula, there is an activation of gene transcription for RNA. How does this activation take place? The answer is, in our opinion, of primary interest in respect to the general problem of differentiation. Actually, differentiation can be viewed in molecular terms as the transcription of different parts of the genome in different cells. We do not mean that this is the only way by which differentiation is brought about, but it certainly might be one. If so, the problem is to find out how the transcription of different segments of the genome is regulated. To approach this problem, it is important to have a well-characterized gene product obtainable in fair amount and as homogeneous as possible. Otherwise, studies of synthesis rate would be impossible. In this respect, rRNA is so far the only class of RNA usable in sea urchins (as in almost all eukaryotes). Transfer RNA might play the same role, but it is much more difficult to break up into single classes. Only recently has the possibility come up of purifying mRNA for histones. Ribosomal RNA, moreover, offers the ideal condition of synthesizing at a very low rate, if any, up to mesenchyme blastula, and then undergoing the described activation of transcription. It is possible that the regulation of its transcription is a very special case, having little to do with differentiation. Ribosomal RNA is present in all cells, so that it cannot be considered like the RNA's transcribed only by certain differentiated cells. If so, however, the problem of the regulation of its transcription might become less important with respect to differentiation, but would not lose its general value, if only because of the general importance of rRNA.

We have initiated an approach to this problem from different angles: We have investigated the importance of morphogenesis in the activation of rRNA synthesis. To this end, we dissociated embryos of *Paracentrotus lividus* into single cells at stages before the activation of rRNA synthesis (see Chapter 6), and either kept them dissociated or allowed them to reaggregate. The answer to these experiments (Sconzo *et al.*, 1970b) was that when cells are dissociated from hatching blastula (10 hours of development), they undergo a normal activation of rRNA synthesis, whether when left dissociated or allowed to reaggregate. If disaggregated 3 hours before hatching (very early blastula), the cells still perform rRNA synthesis in time with the control embryos if permitted to reaggregate. If left disaggregated, they quickly degenerate. Hence, it seems that the normal morphology of embryos is not needed, at least from the 7-hour stage on, for the cells to undergo rRNA synthesis activation. Interestingly enough, cells dissociated from hatching blastulae, if prevented from reaggregating, immediately stop DNA synthesis; yet rRNA synthesis activation takes place punctually.

Another means of altering the morphogenesis is that of chemical animalization or vegetalization (see Chapter 1). This was performed (Pirrone *et al.*, 1970) by administration of $ZnSO_4$ or LiCl to embryos during the early phases of development. The amount of 26 S rRNA synthesized was scored after 48 hours. The method of preloading the pool with ^{32}P was used, thus avoiding problems of pool and permeability. The results obtained (Fig. 1.16) show that vegetalization does not affect the rRNA synthesis rate, whereas animalization severely impairs it. As already discussed in Chapter 1, it is too early to draw definitive conclusions from these experiments. It should be noted that this is true for the degrees of animalization and vegetalization shown in the figure, which are the highest obtained with little or no embryo degeneration. In lower degrees of animalization, an inhibition release is observed, whereas increasing the LiCl concentration provokes an inhibition, which seems to parallel embryonic degeneration. We must add that nothing is known about the possible side effects of such chemical treatment. The value of the above experiment lies mainly in contributing to accumulate experimental data, which might become useful only in connection with other information.

The regulation mechanism of rRNA synthesis may consist of a positive and/or a negative control. The positive control might be represented by the synthesis of an RNA polymerase, or part of it, specific for the translation of rDNA. Roeder and Rutter (1969, 1970b) extracted three chromatographically distinguishable forms of RNA polymerase from nuclei of *Strongylocentrotus purpuratus* gastrulae. All three are stimulated by Mn^{2+}. For only one of the three, termed polymerase I (because it is eluted with the first peak from the column), can Mn^{2+} be substituted with the same efficiency by Mg^{2+} (Fig. 10.18). The three enzymes also show a different behavior to variations of the ionic strength and to denaturation of the primer. Three similar forms of RNA polymerase have also been extracted by Roeder and Rutter (1969, 1970a) from rat liver (B of Fig. 10.18). One of these is concentrated in the nucleoli and is presumed to be specific for rRNA synthesis. This polymerase presents many analogies to one of the three polymerases extractable from sea urchin, i.e., to polymerase I. Because of this analogy of Mg^{2+} dependence and of the lack of sensitivity to the drug α-amanitine (Lindell *et al.,* 1970), the authors suggest that polymerase I of the sea urchin may be the nucleolar one. It is interesting to note that these authors found an increase of polymerase I at swimming blastula stage. When values of the RNA polymerase are calculated per nucleus, there is a decrease by a factor of about 3 from early blastula to late gastrula for polymerase II. On the other hand, polymerase I undergoes a 45% increase at the swimming blastula stage. Correction for the increase in cell number was made on the basis of data derived from other authors and not from the Roeder and Rutter experiments. It should be remembered that nucleoli have been found to be present in sea urchins even from the earliest phases of development; but they acquire granular and fibrillar components, characteristic of the functionally active nucleoli, only after the mesenchyme blastula stage (see Chapter 2). Moreover, we have not yet final proof that the intranuclear electron-dense body we see before the mesenchyme

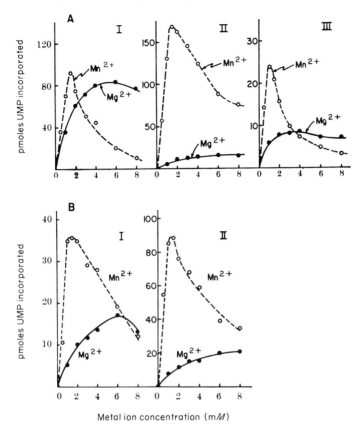

Fig. 10.18. Effect of divalent metal ion concentration on RNA polymerases, from sea urchin (A), or from rat liver (B). (From Roeder and Rutter, 1969.)

blastula stage actually represents nucleoli, i.e., the future sites of rRNA synthesis.

The findings of Roeder and Rutter do not seem to suggest that the regulation of rRNA synthesis is entirely mediated through the synthesis or activation of a specific RNA polymerase. It would seem that a good amount of polymerase I is contained in early blastulae. How the specificity for template is actuated is also unknown, because the isolated polymerases do not exhibit template specificity *in vitro*.

The possibility of a negative control is at present under investigation in our laboratory. We have recently defined the conditions for the study of RNA synthesis in nuclei isolated from embryos of *Paracentrotus lividus* at different developmental stages (Pirrone *et al.,* 1971). Since it is possible to stimulate the synthesis of DNA-like RNA or of rRNA from nuclei isolated from various sources by changing the ionic conditions of the incubation medium, we hope to find out whether nuclei of embryos in stages where rRNA synthesis is dormant can be induced to synthesize rRNA. This would represent a proof that the machinery for rRNA synthesis is already set up and that something is preventing it from functioning.

Roeder and Rutter (1970b) have recently published the results of the characteristics of incorporation of precursors into RNA by nuclei isolated from embryos of *Strongylocentrotus purpuratus* at various developmental stages. The system described by these authors very much resembles that of *Paracentrotus* in many respects. In both systems, however, it seems that the isolated nuclei synthesize little or no rRNA from any developmental stage and under any incubation conditions. As will be described later, the nuclei of younger stages seem to transcribe *in vivo* nonribosomal RNA at higher rates than those of later stages in the entire embryos. This property also seems to be carried over by the isolated nuclei under the *in vitro* conditions.

Shiokawa and Yamana (1967a,b, 1969) and Wada *et al.* (1968) have suggested that a kind of negative control of rRNA synthesis operates in amphibians; direct evidence for an inhibitor protein that regulates rRNA synthesis in amphibians has been provided by Crippa (1970). The approach by Shiokawa and Yamana is to reaggregate together cells from blastulae and neurulae of amphibians. The authors claim that the cells dissociated from blastula can specifically inhibit rRNA synthesis of cells dissociated from neurula, when the two-cell populations are reaggregated together. We have repeated these experiments with sea urchins, by reaggregating together cells dissociated from hatching blastula with cells dissociated from prisms. The nucleotidic pool of the two-cell population had been carefully brought to the same specific activity with respect to ^{32}P. The amount of rRNA synthesized after various times of reaggregation is exactly the sum of that synthesized by the two-cell populations when kept separate (Giudice and Pirrone, unpublished). Since this experiment is negative in sea urchins, it does not authorize extrapolations to amphibians.

An attempt to activate rRNA synthesis in stages before gastrulation was made by Barros and Giudice (1968), by administration of spermidine to embryos. A certain degree of stimulation was reported (Table 10.3), which was not due to variations of permeability to the radioactive precursors. The mechanism by which spermidine acts is not known, and the degree of activation is not so high to stimulate further research.

Finally, what advantage is there for the embryo to start forming new rRNA at the mesenchyme blastula stage? At first, we wondered whether the new rRNA or even the new ribosomal proteins were somehow different from the maternal ones (Mutolo and Giudice, 1967; Mutolo *et al.*,

TABLE 10.3

INCREASE OF SPECIFIC ACTIVITY OF 26 S rRNA
AFTER SPERMIDINE TREATMENT[a]

Labeling period (hours)[b]	Percentage increase[c]
^{32}P	
0–15	18
0–21	19
0–21	33
[^{3}H] uridine	
10–15	8
10–15	60
16–21	21
16–21	24

[a] From Barros and Giudice (1968).
[b] Expressed in hours after fertilization.
[c] Results are reported as percentage increase of specific activity over controls.

1967). The question appeared at that time more justified than it would today, in the light of our wider knowledge of ribosomal constituents. The homology of base sequence between the old and new rRNA was tested in the following way: Labeled rRNA synthesized at the prism stage was hybridized with homologous DNA at saturation level (0.03% of DNA for purified 26 S rRNA, in our hands), alone or in the presence of increasing amounts of unlabeled rRNA of the same stage or of two blastomeres. The competition curves for DNA hybridization of the cold RNA's from the two stages with the labeled RNA of the prism stage were practically superimposable, thus testifying to a lack of major differences in the sequences of the old and new rRNA as far as this technique can detect.

The ribosomal proteins of stages before the initiation of rRNA synthesis were also compared with the proteins of postgastrular stages by electrophoresis on polyacrylamide gel. The samples to be compared were run in the same gel column by the split gel technique. Again, no major differences were revealed between the ribosomal protein of the different stages. Davenport (1967) has reported lack of developmental changes of the electrophoretic pattern of ribosomal proteins. In this connection Mutolo *et al.* (1967) reported that some differences are detectable in the electrophoretic pattern of ribosomal proteins from two different genera, such as *Sphaerechinus* and *Paracentrotus*. The sea urchin material provides, to our knowledge, the first example of the species specificity of ribosomal proteins.

Apart from the mentioned difference in heat sensitivity, found by
Nemer in *Strongylocentrotus purpuratus,* the new rRNA and new ribosomes do not seem to differ altogether from the maternal ones. Why then
does the embryo form new ribosomal RNA? The question loses part of
its mystery when one considers the results of Sconzo *et al.* (1970a), who
measured the amount of rRNA synthesized from blastula to prism and
found that it does not exceed 10% of the maternal one. Hence, this
synthesis may represent only the beginning of what may be a more
massive synthesis at the pluteus stage, when the larva starts feeding and
undergoes a net increase in the cellular mass, and, therefore, needs to
form new ribosomes. This consideration might also explain the discrepancy of the result on the activation timing of rRNA synthesis. If this
represents only the beginning of a phenomenon that becomes more con-
spicuous later on, when real growth begins, it possibly starts with some
delay in species of slower development such as *Strongylocentrotus
purpuratus* than in those of faster development such as *Paracentrotus
lividus.*

Before concluding this section it is pertinent to report here some
characteristics of the mature sea urchin rRNA.

The sedimentation coefficient has been determined with reference to
markers of known S values by Slater and Spiegelman (1966b), who
measured the melting profile and the base ratio of the rRNA of *Arbacia*

TABLE 10.4

BASE COMPOSITION (IN MOLES %) OF SEA URCHIN MATURE rRNA

Lytechinus variegatus (total rRNA) from OD		*Arbacia punctulata*								*Paracentrotus lividus*	
		26 S				18 S				26 S	18 S
		From ³²P		From OD		From ³²P		From OD		From ³²P	
(1)		(2)	(3)	(3)	(3')	(4)	(2)	(3)	(4)	(5)	(5)
C	25.9	26.0	25.7	26.0	26.9	26.0	24.0	24.9	23.8	18.68	17.34
A	19.2	22.4	21.2	21.0	20.7	19.9	24.4	22.8	23.1	15.70	17.85
G	32.3	32.8	32.6	34.7	34.1	34.9	30.0	31.2	29.9	40.86	40.74
U	22.5	18.8	20.5	18.1	18.3	19.3	21.7	20.9	23.2	24.75	24.02
G+C	58.2	58.8	58.3	60.7	61.0	60.9	54.0	56.1	53.7	59.08	58.08

(1) From Comb *et al.* (1965b).
(2) From Gross *et al.* (1965b).
(3) From Sy and McCarty (1970).
(3') From Sy and McCarty (1970); after heating the 26 S.
(4) From Slater and Spiegelman (1966b).
(5) From Sconzo *et al.* (1971).

punctulata embryos. As one would expect, these authors report no variations of these parameters throughout development. The S values reported are 18 and 28. More recent studies, however, by means of iso-kinetic sucrose density gradient sedimentation, have provided values of 18 and 26 S (McCarty *et al.*, 1968; Sy and McCarty, 1968). The molecular weights calculated from migration in polyacrylamide gel electrophoresis are 0.68×10^6 and 1.40×10^6 for the small and large subunit, respectively (Loening, 1968). Base ratio analyses have been made by several investigators and are reported in Table 10.4.

b. RNA's Other than rRNA Synthesized at Stages Following Mesenchyme Blastula

Nemer (1963) noted that a short pulse of uridine at gastrula and pluteus of *Strongylocentrotus purpuratus* labels a heterogeneous RNA, whose

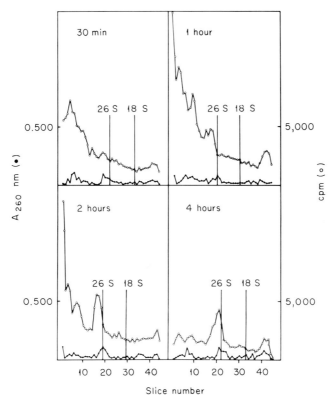

Fig. **10.19.** Polyacrylamide gel electrophoresis of nuclear RNA after various periods of *in vivo* exposure to [³H]uridine beginning at the stage of late mid-gastrula. The positions of the 26 S and 18 S peaks as revealed by internal markers are indicated by vertical lines. (From Giudice and Mutolo, 1969.)

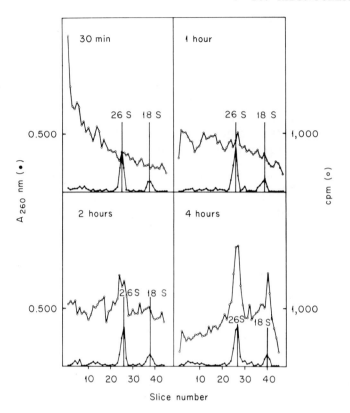

Fig. 10.20. Polyacrylamide gel electrophoresis of the RNA extracted with dodecylsulfate–hot phenol from the cytoplasm of the same embryos shown in Fig. 10.19 (i.e., gastrulae). (From Giudice and Mutolo, 1969.)

size, judged from the sedimentation coefficient, should range from 30,000 to several million daltons (Fig. 10.5). The heterogeneous nature of the pulse-labeled RNA of stages later than mesenchyme blastula has been repeatedly confirmed (Siekevitz *et al.,* 1966; Whiteley *et al.,* 1966; Slater and Spiegelman, 1970). These large RNA's also display a rather continuous pattern when analyzed by acrylamide gel electrophoresis (Giudice and Mutolo, 1969), and are recovered from the cytoplasm (Figs. 10.19 and 10.20). Obviously, not all of them can be considered as rRNA precursors. The same considerations should be made for those recovered from the gastrula cytoplasm as for those synthesized in the pregastrular stage: Should they prove not to be derived from artifacts it would probably mean that some giant (polycistronic?) RNA is transferred to the cytoplasm in sea urchins. We must stress again that there is no definitive proof that these RNA's do not derive from artificial aggregation. Here again the cytoplasmic RNA does not seem to derive from nuclear leakage because the labeling kinetics of nuclear and cytoplasmic RNA are not consistent with this hypothesis (Giudice *et al.*, 1972a).

The number of classes of nonribosomal RNA's synthesized after the gastrula stage seems to be smaller than before gastrulation (Slater and Spiegelman, 1970). No individual RNA classes besides the ribosomal and tRNA have been characterized as yet in these later developmental stages.

Daigneault *et al.* (1969, 1970) report that the general electrophoretic pattern of optical density of RNA derived from several developmental stages of *Strongylocentrotus purpuratus* is such that the S values extrapolated from the electrophoretic migration are of discrete classes (26, 23, 18, 16, 12, 9, 5, and 4 S).

D. The Small RNA's

Sea urchins were among the first materials in which 5 S RNA was described. Comb (1965; Comb *et al.*, 1965a) found in plutei of *Lytechinus variegatus* an RNA 105 nucleotides long, which does not accept amino acids. It is rapidly methylated and, once methylated, becomes indistinguishable from the tRNA, of which it was thought to be a precursor. This RNA, according to Comb (1965), starts to incorporate radioactivity from ^{32}P only after the gastrula stage.

Sy and McCarty (1970), by analyzing the low-molecular-weight RNA's of *Arbacia punctulata* embryos or eggs by acrylamide gel electrophoresis, report three main peaks of optical density corresponding to S values of 4, 5, and 5.8. The 5.8 S species, i.e., about 150 nucleotides long, is found associated with the 26 S rRNA, from which it can be reversibly detached by heating at 45°C in media of low ionic strength, or at 55°C in 0.1 M NaCl. The 5.8 S saturates 0.003–0.004% of the DNA in hybridization experiments, thus suggesting the presence of 300–400 sequences for it in DNA. The rRNA saturates 0.057% of the DNA (~ to 200 copies). The latter figure is in excellent agreement with the data by Mutolo and Giudice (1967), who report that purified 26 S rRNA saturates 0.03% of the sperm DNA in *Paracentrotus lividus*. A study of the methyl incorporation pattern, by administering [^{14}C]methylmethionine at the pluteus stage, revealed very little incorporation at the 5.8 and 5 S levels, while minor classes, unidentified by optical density, of the size of 210, 170, 140, and 100 nucleotides, become very actively labeled.

Sconzo *et. al.* (1971) observed that several small-sized classes of RNA become very actively labeled when RNA precursors or methyl-labeled methionine are given to *Paracentrotus lividus* gastrulae. These very rapidly labeled RNA's are recovered from nuclei and nucleoli. They certainly deserve further detailed analysis. The main difficulty one meets in such a study is distinguishing these small RNA's from possible break-down products resulting from the action of RNase on larger RNA's. Sy and McCarty (1971) recently studied the formation of a complex be-tween the 26 S and 5.8 S RNA *in vitro.* The complex formed under suitable experimental conditions is more correctly base paired than com-plexes artificially obtained between the 18 S and 5.8 S RNA. Bellemare *et al.* (1970) analyzed the 5 S RNA of *Strongylocentrotus purpuratus* by ultraviolet absorption spectra, optical rotatory dispersion, and circular dicroism, and concluded that 67% of the bases are hydrogen bonded and that its structure is more folded than that of the 5 S of *Escherichia coli.*

E. Nature of the RNA's Synthesized throughout Development as Analyzed by Molecular Hybridization Experiments

After exposing prisms of *Strongylocentrotus purpuratus* to ^{32}P for 1 hour, Whiteley *et al.* (1966) hybridized the RNA with sperm DNA trapped on agar, alone or in the presence of cold competitor RNA from different developmental stages. Under such labeling conditions, the radio-activity was bound to a heterogeneous RNA with a peak at the 4 S level. The results reported in Fig. 10.21 show that the cold RNA of the same stage is a good competitor, and that of the gastrula stage is more or less as good. On the other hand, cold RNA's from blastula or unfertilized eggs were about 50% less efficient as competitors than the cold RNA of prisms. The conclusion is that about 50% of the nonribosomal and nontransfer RNA synthesized after the blastula stage is different from that already existing up to this stage. No differences were detected by this method between the RNA's of blastulae and unfertilized eggs. Very similar con-clusions are reported by Glisin *et al.* (1966), who competed labeled RNA from hatching blastulae with cold RNA from the same or other stages by the technique of hybridization on filters. Recently, Whiteley *et al.* (1970) reinvestigated the question, using a more modern technical approach, with *Strongylocentrotus* and *Dendraster.* Hybridization experiments of the kind already described were repeated both by hybridization in com-petition or by preloading the DNA with the competitor cold RNA before the hybridization of the labeled prism RNA. Conditions of low RNA/DNA ratio and of high RNA/DNA ratio were used that, according to the authors, demonstrate the hybridization of repetitious and nonrepetitious sequences, respectively. Regarding the repetititious sequences, the previous findings were confirmed. As for the nonrepetitious ones, it was found that there is a more striking difference between the RNA synthesized at the prism stage (labeling with [³H]- or [¹⁴C]uridine for 1 hour) and the RNA present in the unfertilized egg, in that the unfertilized egg RNA competes with very little of the prism RNA for hybridization with DNA.

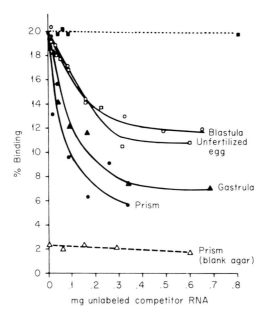

Fig. 10.21. Competition by unlabeled RNA from developmental stages in the binding of ³²P-labeled prism RNA to DNA–agar. Four μg ³²P-labeled *S. purpuratus* prism RNA, unlabeled competitor RNA as shown, 0.30 gm of *S. purpuratus* DNA–agar containing 110 μg DNA, or 0.30 gm agar lacking DNA (bottom curve); total volume, 0.475 ml, incubated at 60°C for 48 hours. (From Whiteley *et al.,* 1966.)

The authors have also found, with the same system, that the species differences are more striking for the nonrepetitious sequences than for the repetitious ones. This interesting result indicates that differentiation as well as evolution is linked to the nonrepeated segments of DNA, as one would expect if mutation has a role in evolution. Hence, in hybridization experiments to evaluate differences in the RNA's during development, conditions should preferably be devised that demonstrate the hybridization of the nonrepetitious sequences.

Hartman *et al.* (1971) have found by hybridization–competition experiments that total RNA from unfertilized eggs of *Lytechinus variegatus* is partially unable to compete with RNA synthesized at blastula and associated with ribosomes. This is at variance with the previous reports.

But since the previous observations were concerned only with the total RNA, and the fraction of it associated to ribosomes might be a very small one (Aronson and Wilt, 1969), some differences between stages might have escaped the earlier investigations. Hynes and Gross (1972), however, report that total RNA synthesized during the cleavage stage of *Arbacia punctulata* and *Strongylocentrotus purpuratus* eggs is only partially (30%) competed by the unfertilized egg RNA for DNA hybridization. Hartman *et al.* (1971) confirm the existence of some differences between blastula and gastrula in RNAs associated with polyribosomes (presumably messenger).

F. Rate of RNA Synthesis during Development

Preliminary indications that the overall rate of RNA synthesis increases with development can be found in most of the early investigations. According to a recent calculation by Timofeeva *et al.* (1969), the increase in the synthesis rate of high-molecular-weight RNA is lower than the increase in cell number during the first four hours of development in *Strongylocentrotus nudus*. Between the fourth and sixth hours of development the synthesis rate increases 1.5–2 times more than the cell number.

A correct approach to the problem that takes into proper account problems of permeability and pool size is found in the work of Kijima and Wilt (1969). These authors administered [³H]guanosine to embryos of *Strongylocentrotus purpuratus* at various developmental stages. The specific activity attained by the GTP in the pool and by the GMP in the RNA was then estimated. Table 10.5 shows the calculated RNA synthesis rate as compared to the increase in cell number per embryo. The increasing synthesis rate per embryo with development is confirmed. This increase is, however, overwhelmed by the increase in the number of nuclei per embryo so that the actual RNA synthesis rate per nucleus decreases with development. This idea is also supported by some autoradiographic data provided by the authors. The stability of the synthesized RNA is also calculated by comparing the labeling rate in the interval between 10 and 20 minutes after administering the isotope with that in the interval between 50 and 60 minutes or between 10 and 60 minutes. The values reported in Table 10.6 indicate that 0.2–0.5 of the newly formed RNA is degraded within 1 hour. Because each experimental point derives from the specific activity of nucleotides estimated by chromatography, the number of experimental points presented is not very high. More data of this kind would therefore be welcome to define the measurements provided.

TABLE 10.5

COMPARISON OF RATE OF RNA SYNTHESIS[a,b]

Stage	Time of development (hours)	Cells/embryo	RNA synthesis (% turnover in 10 minutes)
Mid-cleavage	12	140	0.71
Mesenchyme blastula	22	420	0.80
Late gastrula	46	700	1.23
Pluteus	74	1000	1.34

[a] From Kijima and Wilt (1969).

[b] The rate of RNA synthesis at different stages is compared by calculation of the turnover of total embryo RNA. The molar amount of radioactive $2',3'$-GMP that accumulates between 10 and 20 minutes after the addition of label is divided by the amount of total RNA and multiplied by 100. The total RNA/embryo is constant.

TABLE 10.6

STABILITY OF NEWLY SYNTHESIZED RNA[a]

Time of development (hours)	Accumulated label,[b] extrapolated accumulation	Rate of labeling[c] 50–60 min/10–20 min
12	0.53	0.15
18	0.79	0.53
48	0.83	0.42
72	0.68	0.35

[a] From Kijima and Wilt (1969).

[b] The amount of radioactivity that accumulated in $2',3'$-CMP of RNA in 1 hour is divided by the amount that would have accumulated in 1 hour if the initial rate (Δ 10–20 minutes) had been maintained.

[c] The slope of accumulation of $2',3'$-CMP into RNA between 50 and 60 minutes after addition of label is divided by the slope of accumulation between 10 and 20 minutes.

Wilt (1970) also established that RNA synthesis becomes appreciable only after the third cleavage, which is in agreement with earlier findings (see, for example, Glisin and Glisin, 1964).

Brandhorst and Humphreys (1971) described a method to measure the instantaneous rate of RNA synthesis and decay, involving analysis of the ATP pool's specific activity, following administration of [³H]-adenosine. The results show that the RNA synthesized at the blastula or pluteus stage by *Lytechinus pictus* can be divided into two categories. One, representing one third of the total, has a half-life of only 5–10 minutes. The other, representing the remaining two thirds, has a much longer half-life, i.e., 60–90 minutes. The synthesis rate is 9.7×10^{-15} gm of RNA/nucleus/minute at the blastula stage, and 3.1×10^{-15} gm of RNA/ nucleus/minute at the pluteus stage.

The conclusion regarding the above experiments seems to be that an overall activation of the RNA synthesis rate is observable throughout development, when the rate per embryo is measured; if, however, the increase in nuclei number is considered, one finds that the rate per nucleus decreases following the blastula stage. Of course, owing to the heterogeneity of RNA's synthesized it is not possible to know from these data how many kinds of molecules are involved in these measurements. It is possible, in principle, that nuclei that show a lower overall synthesis rate are synthesizing a higher number of RNA species than nuclei that show a higher overall synthesis rate and which, as far as we know, might be synthesizing only a few molecule species at a very high rate.

These considerations should be kept in mind when one examines the results of experiments aimed at measuring the template activity of the chromatin of different developmental stages *in vitro*. Marushige and Ozaki (1967) reported that chromatin of sea urchin embryos, isolated by homogenization in saline EDTA, can act as a template for RNA synthesis catalyzed by bacterial RNA polymerase. The chromatin isolated from pluteus was found to be twice as active than that isolated from blastulae. The authors suggest that at the pluteus stage, DNA is less repressed than at blastula. No differences are observed in the T_m of the chromatins of the two stages, and analysis of the histones gives an identical electrophoretic pattern.

Johnson and Hnilica (1970) studied the template activity of entire nuclei and of isolated chromatin from different developmental stages in the presence of bacterial RNA polymerase. This activity is reported to increase slightly up to the mesenchyme blastula stage. A relative decrease then takes place, followed by a new increase at the pluteus stage. The authors stress the point that if chromatin is treated with trypsin, so as to remove the histones, an increase in its template activity is obtained only if the treatment is effected after the blastula stage, in agreement with their previous findings that histones appear in sea urchin embryos only at the blastula stage.

Observations on histones in sea urchin embryos are often contradictory, as will be discussed in Chapter 11. In this respect, Benttinen and Comb (1971) observed that lysine-rich histones, supposed to condense chromatin (Mirsky *et al.,* 1968), are predominant in *Lytechinus variegatus* only after gastrulation, i.e., when the rate of RNA synthesis slows down.

Repsis (1967) reports differences in the electrophoretic pattern of the acid-soluble proteins of *Lytechinus variegatus* between eggs and blastulae but not between blastulae and plutei. According to Marushige and Ozaki

(1967), the chromatin of the pluteus stage contains twice as many proteins as that of the blastula stage. Ozaki (1971) compared the electrophoretic properties of the basic proteins of the chromatin from sperm and prisms of *Strongylocentrotus purpuratus*. Four main bands are described, two of which are shared by the two chromatins. The sperm chromatin contains less proteins than that of prism and, different from the latter, shows a biphasic melting curve. It has a template activity for RNA polymerase *in vitro* that is only 2% that of the purified DNA. Ozaki also reports that histones from both sperm and prisms have a high lysine content but that only those from sperm contain a high percentage of arginine.

Kinoshita (1971) suggested that heparin might play a role in the regulation of RNA synthesis in sea urchin development. However, the evidence produced so far is not adequate to make this hypothesis acceptable. Moreover, the author assumes that nuclear RNA synthesis becomes activated at the gastrula stage, which, within the limitations expressed above, seems to be the case only for ribosomal RNA.

A thorough analysis of *Strongylocentrotus purpuratus* embryonic chromatin was performed by Hill *et al.* (1971), who were able to resolve on acrylamide gel electrophoresis about 30 histones and 11 nonhistonic proteins. The migration pattern of the latter was found to present some quantitative differences arising between the blastula and the pluteus stages.

It has been proposed in other systems (Paul and Gilmour, 1968; Gilmour and Paul, 1969) that acidic proteins may play a role in the regulation of interactions between histones and DNA.

Cognetti *et al.* (1972), using the split gel technique, were able to detect some qualitative differences in the electrophoretic pattern of the chromosomal nonhistone proteins, arising between the 16-cell stage and pluteus in *Paracentrotus lividus*. There is no direct proof, however, that these changes are connected with changes in the RNA synthesis pattern.

It should be recalled that Immers *et al.* (1967) found that nuclei of sea urchin embryos become stainable with Hale's reagent only after the mesenchyme blastula stage. Before this stage, according to Runnström (1967a), a trypsin treatment renders stainable only the nuclei of blastulae, not those of earlier stages. This can also be interpreted to mean that the free phosphate groups of DNA are not available for the dye up to the gastrula stage, but that histones are not the protein responsible for blocking them up to the blastula stage (see Chapter 11).

An interesting approach for the purpose of isolating the active part of sea urchin chromatin was presented by Wilt and Ekenberg (1971). By treating purified nuclei of *Lytechinus pictus* blastulae with a mixture of Tween and DOC, a fraction is sedimented containing 98% of the nuclear DNP's and 90% of the pulse-labeled RNA, which is identified with chromatin. When treated with a mixture of the detergents DOC and Lubrol W in 0.5 M NaCl, and then subjected to isopycnic centrifugation in Cs_2SO_4, this fraction divides into a major band of rather pure DNA and into a smaller DNA peak associated to most of the pulse-labeled RNA, which, the authors suggest, represents the active part of the chromatin.

When the endogenous RNA polymerase activity is assayed on entire nuclei isolated from different stages, the results obtained (Roeder and Rutter, 1970b; Pirrone *et al.*, 1971) are in agreement with the overall rate decrease of RNA synthesis per nucleus, described in the *in vivo* experiments.

A decrease in the amount of RNA polymerase II extractable from each nucleus has been described by Roeder and Rutter (1970b), as discussed under Section C,3,a of this chapter.

An interesting point to be discussed in connection with the studies on the rate of RNA synthesis, as already mentioned under Section C,2,c of this chapter, is how much of the synthesized RNA leaves the nucleus for the cytoplasm. The first attempt to study this problem with a modern, thoughtful evaluation of the results was made by Singh (1968). The experimental design was to let the eggs of *Arbacia punctulata* develop from fertilization up to blastula in seawater containing nonlimiting amounts of [8-^{14}C]adenine, and to measure the specific activity attained at various developmental stages by the RNA purines. The RNA fractions examined were (a) RNA not extractable by cold phenol (considered nuclear), and (b) the cytoplasmic RNA insoluble in 1 M NaCl, i.e., deprived of the low-molecular-weight RNA's, including tRNA, whose terminal turnover would have disturbed the evaluation of the data. In another experiment, the isotope used was [2-^{14}C]uracil; labeling lasted from the late gastrula stage up to 150 minutes later. The results, reported in Fig. 10.22, were carefully elaborated by the author for measuring the flow rate of rapidly labeled RNA from the nucleus to the cytoplasm. It is apparent from a glance at A and B of Fig. 10.22 that this rate is much higher at gastrula than from cleavage up to blastula. It seems, however, that the measure of this flow rate is based on too many assumptions. The main difficulties for the exact evaluation of the results arise, in our opinion, mainly from the fact that nothing is known about the turnover rate of the cytoplasmic RNA at the different stages and, moreover, that the RNA population is heterogeneous. One might consequently envisage the following extreme situations: (a) All the counts might arise from a single very hot class of RNA, i.e., nondiluted by preexisting RNA classes of the same kind; (b) the counts might derive from the radioactivity distribution among all the RNA classes present. In the first case,

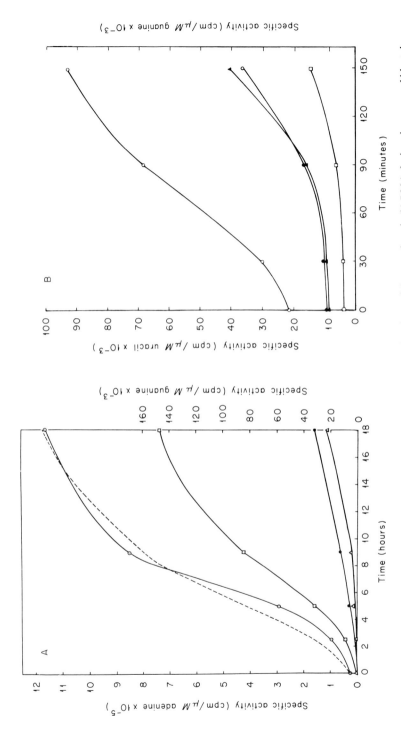

Fig. 10.22. A. Incorporation of [8-¹⁴C]adenine into nuclear (n) and high-molecular-weight cytoplasmic (h) RNA during cleavage and blastula stage. Labeled precursor added 10 minutes after fertilization. Zero time corresponds to 90 minutes after addition of [8-¹⁴C]adenine. Specific activity of adenine and guanine in nRNA and hRNA plotted against time. O, adenine (nRNA); □, guanine (nRNA); ●, adenine (hRNA); △, guanine (hRNA). The dotted curve represents increase in the number of cells with time. B. Incorporation of [2-¹⁴C]uracil into RNA in 36-hour-old embryos. O, uracil (nRNA); ●, uracil (hRNA); □, cytosine (nRNA); △, cytosine (hRNA). (From Singh, 1968.)

the flow of a certain number of counts from the nucleus to the cytoplasm may represent the flow of a limited number of RNA molecules; in the second, the flow of the same number of counts represents the flow of a much larger number of molecules. Actually, the specific activity is artifactual because it has been calculated by dividing the radioactivity presumably incorporated into messengerlike RNA by the optical density provided mostly by ribosomal RNA (at least as regards the cytoplastmic RNA).

Another estimate of the flow rate of nuclear RNA to the cytoplasm was made by Aronson and Wilt (1969). These authors continuously supplied [³H]uridine to hatching blastulae of *Strongylocentrotus purpuratus*. Under the conditions used, it was found that the specific activity of the nucleotidic precursor pool attains a plateau in about 10 minutes. The specific activity of the RNA of the nuclei (prepared according to Hine-gardner, 1962) attain a plateau in less than 20 minutes and remains constant for at least 3 hours (Fig. 10.23). Meanwhile, the specific activity of the cytoplasmic RNA undergoes a slow increase.

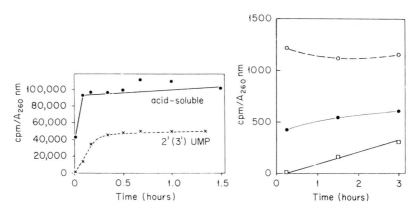

Fig. 10.23. Left. Kinetics of incorporation of [5-³H]uridine (1 μCi/ml) into hatched blastulae (23.5 hours). ●——●, cpm/A₂₆₀ nm in acid-soluble fraction; ×——×, cpm/A₂₆₀ nm of 2′,3′-UMP from hydrolyzed RNA. Right. Changes in specific activity with time of the RNA of various cell fractions; 24-hour embryos (hatched blastulae) incubated with 0.8 μCi/ml [5-³H]uridine, o——o, nuclei, ●——●, total extract;□——□, cytoplasm. (From Aronson and Wilt, 1969.)

The conclusion drawn by the authors is that nuclear RNA has a very high turnover and that only 6% of the RNA synthesized is transferred to the cytoplasm.

Because of the heterogeneity of nuclear RNA, it cannot be decided whether this 6% of radioactivity is referred to a few or to many classes of RNA.

Indications for a high turnover of nuclear RNA in sea urchin embryos were reported in a preliminary form by Brandhorst (1970), and confirmed for part of it by Brandhorst and Humphreys (1971) (see Section I of this chapter).

G. Effect of the Suppression of RNA Synthesis at Various Developmental Stages

This was first studied by experiments of nuclear inactivation following X-ray irradiation (Neifakh, 1960, 1964; Neifakh and Krigsgaber, 1968). Kafiani *et al.* (1966) found that X rays do not stop RNA synthesis in similar experiments performed on fish embryos, but probably act by causing the synthesis of an anomalous RNA.

The same kind of studies were then performed using actinomycin. In the first pages of this chapter we exhaustively reported the developmental and metabolic effect of actinomycin when given from fertilization on. Giudice *et al.* (1968) have observed the effect on development obtained by starting the actinomycin treatment at various stages during embryogenesis and for different time intervals. It is important to note that 5 hours of treatment at any of the stages studied, from fertilization on, causes about 70% inhibition of the total RNA synthesis, calculated by measuring the specific activity of the uridine 3'-monophosphate of the total RNA after 45 minutes of exposure to [³H]uridine. The results are reported in Table 10.7 and in Fig. 10.24. The main observations are: (a) inhibition of gastrulation is released when the treatment is started after the early mesenchyme blastula, thus suggesting that the synthesis of RNA's necessary for gastrulation is completed by that time. (b) Development of the skeleton improves the later the treatment is initiated from young gastrulae on, suggesting that part of the RNA(s) necessary for skeleton formation is already synthesized at the young gastrula stage, and continues to be synthesized thereafter. In this connection, we shall mention that a very low actinomycin concentration (0.5 μg/ml) causes a specific inhibition of skeleton formation, while development remains normal in other respects (Peltz and Giudice, 1967). Under such conditions, the Ca^{2+} uptake increase that precedes and accompanies skeleton formation is abolished and the synthesis of some RNA(s) smaller than 18 S seems to be depressed. Does this represent an effect of actinomycin on some specially sensitive genes important for skeleton formation? We note that many nonspecific adverse conditions, such as, a decrease of the seawater pH below 7.4, can also cause inhibition of skeleton formation in sea urchin embryos (Giudice, unpublished). On the other hand, De Vincentiis and Lancieri (1970) found that deaminoactinomycin C_3, an

TABLE 10.7

EFFECT ON DEVELOPMENT OF THE ADDITION OF ACTINOMYCIN D TO SEAWATER[a]

Beginning of the treatment (hours after fertilization)	Stage	Developmental stage attained 72 hours after fertilization
0.15	—	
3	16 blastomeres	
5	Morula	
6	Blastula with large cells	
7	—	Swimming blastulae more or less stuffed with degenerated cells[b]
8	—	
9	—	
11	Hatching	
12.5	—	
14	Early mesenchyme blastula	
15.5	Mesenchyme blastula	Gastrulae with small intestine, pigmented cells and stomadeum
17	Late mesenchyme blastula	Gastrulae
18		Prism without skeleton, and intestine divided into two cavities
19	Early gastrula	
20	—	Prism with triradiated spicules
21	Mid-gastrula	Prism with intestine divided into three cavities
22.15	Late gastrula	Prism with spicules which begin to elongate
23.45	Prism without skeleton	Prism with skeleton which surrounds the gut
25.55	Prism with spicules	Prism with the long skeleton branches which grow toward the apex
26.55	Prism with elongated spicules	Prism with skeleton which approaches the apex
27.55	Prism with skeleton which approaches the gut; pigmented cells	Prism with further evolution of the skeleton
28.55	Prism with skeleton near the apex	
31.25	Prism with beginning of arms elongation	Prism with skeleton which usually doesn't fully reach the apex; very beginning of arms formation

[a] 20 μg/ml. From Giudice et al. (1968).

[b] In some experiments an abortive gastrulation was observed, with a delay of 30 hours, with respect to controls. In these cases, the embryos acquired the transparency that is characteristic of the late pluteus stages.

antibiotic that shares the toxicity of actinomycin D, but does not inhibit RNA synthesis, allows development to proceed normally, with a normal skeleton formation. (c) An actinomycin treatment from fertilization up to

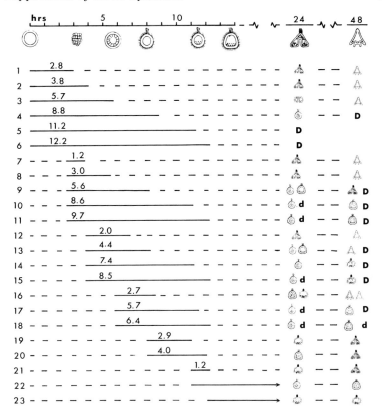

Fig. 10.24. Effect on development of pulse treatments with actinomycin D. Developmental stages of control embryos are indicated at the top. The continuous lines represent the period in which the drug was present, whose length is expressed in hours by the numbers above the lines. In the two last vertical columns the stages attained at 24 and 48 hours after fertilization are schematically represented; d indicates degeneration of minor fraction of the embryos; D, degeneration of a major fraction of the embryos. (From Giudice *et al.*, 1968.)

5 hours later is much less effective than a treatment from 6 to 11 hours after fertilization. This might be due to variations of permeability to the drug (even if after the 5-hour treatment the same degree of inhibition is attained in both instances), or more simply to the fact that RNA synthesis is much less active, at least on a per embryo basis, in the early cleavage period. This second hypothesis is in agreement with the data by Slater and Spiegelman (1970), based on the electrophoretic analysis of RNA's synthesized during these developmental periods, that show that some of the RNA's synthesized during the time of maximal sensitivity to actinomycin are normally retained throughout gastrulation.

We shall not repeat the observations on the criteria for measuring the rate of RNA synthesis, or on the specificity of the actinomycin effect, which have already been reported in these pages.

Lastly, we must mention the early attempts to study the RNA function during development by treating the entire eggs or embryos with RNase (Leone, 1960; Mateyko, 1961). Their value today, however, seems to be mostly historical.

H. RNA of Cytoplasmic Origin

The sea urchin egg represents a system particularly advantageous for the study of such a problem. Actually, only one nucleus dose of genome in the fertilized egg is confronted with the relatively high DNA content of the cytoplasm, which is due, at least in part, to mitochondrial DNA (see Chapter 9). The first study of cytoplasmic RNA synthesis in sea urchin was made by Chamberlain (1968). To be sure that the labeling from radioactive RNA precursors administered *in vivo* is not due to RNA synthesis in the nuclei followed by transfer to the cytoplasm is to divide the eggs in nucleated and nonnucleated halves upon centrifugation through a sucrose density gradient (see Chapter 2). When the nonnucleated halves of *Arbacia punctulata* eggs are parthenogenetically activated and then incubated with [³H]uridine under conditions free from bacterial contamination, there occurs incorporation of ³H into an RNA that sediments at about 14 S. Further studies (Chamberlain, 1970) have resolved this peak into two major ones, besides the 4 S RNA. In both nucleated and nonnucleated halves, fertilization stimulates RNA synthesis more than parthenogenetic activation. The characteristics of incorporation are similar to those of the normal embryos at 1- to 2-cell stage, thus inducing the author to conclude that at least up to this stage a large fraction of the RNA synthesized is not of nuclear origin. Chamberlain and Metz (1972) performed a cell fractionation of *Echinometra* eggs after *in vivo* exposure to [³H]uridine for 1 hour. A sucrose gradient centrifugation of the homogenate showed a good coincidence between the peak of incorporation into RNA and the peak of cytochromoxidase activity. This fact and the observation that this cellular fraction does not release radioactivity upon treatment with Triton X100 or RNase, but does release it upon DOC treatment, led the authors to suggest that the main site of RNA synthesis in these eggs is the mitochondria. The nuclear peak, identified by labeled thymidine incorporation into DNA, moves apart from the mitochondria in the sucrose gradient and shows little uridine incorporation.

These observations were fundamentally confirmed in a recent investigation by Craig (1970), who analyzed the RNA synthesized by nonnucleated activated halves of *Strongylocentrotus purpuratus* eggs by chromatography on benzoylated DEAE-cellulose and centrifugation in gradients of dimethyl sulfoxide to deuterated dimethyl sulfoxide. Most of the synthesized RNA has a molecular weight of $5-6 \times 10^5$. When DNA–RNA hybridization was performed under nonsaturating conditions, 32% of the radioactivity of RNA labeled in the nonnucleated fragment hybridized mitochondrial DNA, while only 4.5% of the radioactivity of the nucleated fragment hybridized mitochondrial DNA. Only 0.3% of the radioactivity in both cases hybridized sperm (i.e., nuclear) DNA. In view of the important implications of the latter findings, it seems appropriate to wait for a more extensive publication of the data before evaluating the results.

Selvig *et al.* (1970) found that parthenogenetically activated, non-nucleated halves of eggs of *Arbacia lixula* synthesize RNA that sediments at about 17 S and 4 S. The nucleated eggs synthesize similar RNA's with the addition of more 4 S and a small amount of classes heavier than 28 S. Moreover, the sensitivity to actinomycin is higher for the eggs than for the nonnucleated halves. Electron microscope autoradiography does not show any special intracellular localization of the traces. The authors stress that the length of the labeling period (2 hours) might have moved the radioactive RNA from its site of origin. Shorter labeling experiments, by the same authors, show that the cytoplasm is the site of synthesis of a significant portion of RNA in the fertilized eggs up to the 4-cell stage, whereas the nucleus becomes the predominant site of RNA synthesis from 8 cells on.

With respect to the relevance of cytoplasmic RNA synthesis for protein synthesis during early development, it has already been mentioned that inhibition of cytoplasmic RNA synthesis in nonnucleated fragments, obtained by ethidium bromide, does not qualitatively alter the electrophoretic pattern of the proteins synthesized during cleavage (Craig and Piatigorsky, 1971).

Finally, Vacquier and Claybrook (1969) found that treatment of *Paracentrotus lividus* embryos with ethidium bromide has an effect on early development similar to that of actinomycin. This is supported by the findings of Chamberlain and Metz (1972) that the drug not only acts preferentially on mitochondrial synthesis but also produces a severe inhibition of nuclear synthesis in this material.

Hartman *et al.* (1971) investigated the cytoplasmic origin of newly synthesized RNA during the early development of *Lytechinus variegatus* by the following method: Embryos at the 64-cell stage, and in one case also at gastrula, are labeled with [³H]uridine for about 1 hour, and then subjected to cell fractionation. Most of the radioactivity incorporated into RNA is associated with a cell fraction sedimenting between 600 and 22,000 g after homogenization in an Omni mixer. When this fraction is purified by a Urografin density gradient, about half the radioactivity is recovered in a fraction enriched in mitochondria. This fact and the observation that the radioactivity in this fraction is EDTA- and RNase-resistant, but becomes solubilized by DOC treatment of the fraction, led the authors to suggest a mitochondrial localization of a substantial portion of the newly synthesized RNA. This RNA anneals 50 times better to mitochondrial DNA than to nuclear DNA. The authors acknowledge, however, that the different sizes of the two genomes and the fact that their degree of complexity is not known do not allow any quantitative speculation about how much of this RNA is synthesized on mitochondrial template. The conclusion is that some part of it is complementary to mitochondrial DNA sequences. It is of interest that hybridization–competition experiments do not reveal differences between mitochondrial RNA synthesized at blastula and gastrula.

I. RNA Synthesis in Different Embryonic Territories

One speculation about an embryonic system is whether different RNA's are synthesized by the blastomeres that bear different embryological potentialities. Sea urchin embryos provide such a system in that they offer the possibility of separating such differentiated blastomeres as the micromeres from the mesomeres and macromeres. In spite of this, little progress has been made in this direction.

Czihak and co-workers (Czihak, 1965a,b, 1966; Czihak et al., 1967) found by autoradiography that labeled uridine, administered for about 20 minutes to embryos of *Paracentrotus lividus* at the 16-cell stage, is preferentially accumulated in acid-insoluble form in the nuclei of the micromeres during the interphase. Analysis by hydroxylapatite chromatography and electrophoresis of the alkaline hydrolyzate of the pulse-labeled RNA at this stage led the authors to conclude that it is neither ribosomal nor transfer and undergoes a rapid turnover. Under prolonged labeling, the radioactivity from the acid-soluble pool and breakdown products can be chased into other RNA's and the DNA of all the embryonic cells.

A disturbance of RNA synthesis at the 16-blastomere stage by nitro-orotic acid azauridine, or azaguanine, was found to bring about alterations in the development of the entodermal derivatives (Czihak, 1965b). From the last of a series of papers by Czihak on this subject, however, it was concluded that it is not possible to show that the RNA synthesized by the micromeres is transferred as such to other territories of the embryo.

More recently, Czihak and Hörstadius (1970) have shown that when micromeres of *Paracentrotus lividus* labeled with [¹⁴C]uridine are transplanted into unlabeled animal halves, a radioactivity transfer into the latter is observed. Since this transfer takes place also in the presence of nonlabeled uridine, the authors conclude that the radioactivity is transferred in a macromolecular form, i.e., RNA. Judging from the published values, the dilution by cold uridine does not seem to be enough to exclude the possibility that some low-molecular-weight RNA precursors have passed from the implanted micromeres into the animal halves. In support of their conclusion, the authors mention the observation by Hagström and Lönning (1969) that implanted micromeres soon fuse with the cells of the implantation site. Should the latter fact prove to be correct, not only might RNA be transferred from micromeres, but a free communication of cytoplasm between inducer and induced cells would take place.

Hynes and Gross (1970) have developed an accurate method to isolate micromeres from mesomeres and macromeres in bulk amount. They find a preferential labeling with [³H]uridine of micromeres of *Arbacia lixula* either before or after isolation. In their opinion, however, the difference in [³H]uridine incorporation is of a much lower order than that found by Czihak. Similar conclusions have been reached by Spiegel and Rubinstein (1972). Hynes and Gross also stress the point that it is not possible to extrapolate the rate of RNA synthesis from the incorporation data as long as measures of permeability and pool size are not available.

J. Enzymes of Polyribonucleotide Metabolism

We have already discussed RNA polymerase in Section C of this chapter; a few lines will be devoted here to the ATP polymerase and RNase of sea urchin embryos.

1. ATP POLYMERASE

Hyatt (1967a,b) found that nuclei of *Strongylocentrotus purpuratus* embryos (prepared according to Hinegardner, 1962) are able to incorporate [¹⁴C]AMP from labeled ATP into an acid-insoluble product characterized as polyadenylate. The other three nucleotide triphosphates are not incorporated and inhibit the reaction. Pyrophosphate, but not phosphate, is also inhibitory. Polyribonucleotides bringing free 3'-hydroxyl groups act as primer. No *ex novo* synthesis is started as demonstrated by the lack of [5'-¹⁴C]ATP in the alkaline hydrolyzate of the product.

It is tempting to speculate that this enzyme might play a role in adding some poly A sequences to the nuclear heterogeneous RNA that has to be transported to the cytoplasm (Darnell *et al.*, 1971).

2. RNase

A remarkable RNase activity has been found by Castañeda and Tyler (1968a) in the soluble cytoplasm of *Strongylocentrotus purpuratus* embryos. Very low activity was detected by the same technique in *Lytechinus pictus*. Sconzo (1967) searched for RNase activity in homogenates of eggs and embryos of *Paracentrotus lividus* and *Sphaerechinus granularis* under a variety of conditions, i.e., at different pH values, different ionic strengths, in homogenates obtained in the presence or absence of DOC and EDTA. In no case was RNase activity detected. Under the conditions used a high activity was detected from 2 ng of crystalline pancreatic RNase.

These negative results do not mean that no RNase exists in these two species, but they certainly emphasize that striking species differences may be met when the content of this enzyme is estimated. In addition, we must mention that Lindvall and Carsjö (1954) reported a release of acid-soluble phosphate upon prolonged incubation of *Paracentrotus lividus* homogenates at pH 5.2, which is attributed by the authors to the presence of a particulate-bound RNase. In our opinion, the apparent contradiction of these results with those by Sconzo is due to two facts. First, the incubation period for enzymatic assays in Sconzo's experiments does not exceed 30 minutes, at which time, in the experiments by Lindvall and Carsjö, no more than 20% of the acid-insoluble phosphate has been solubilized. In the latter experiments a plateau of phosphate solubilization is attained only after 24 hours of incubation. Second, the method used by Sconzo is more specific, in that the percent solubilization of a highly purified rRNA labeled with ^{32}P or ^{3}H at specific activities of more than 10^4 cpm/μg RNA, is measured with reference to the activity of 5 $\times$ crystalline pancreatic RNase.

Some RNase activity was also reported in *Paracentrotus lividus* by Molinaro and Hultin (1965). Also in this case, the assay is based on a less specific method and no more than 25% of the RNA used is hydrolyzed in 30 minutes.

Finally, Aronson (1972) recently discovered in the cytoplasm of sea urchin embryos a nuclease that shows the interesting property of cleaving the nuclear heterogeneous RNA into fragments of 4–5 S. The enzyme cleaves also poly U but not poly A or poly C. The cytoplasmic localization of this enzyme is intriguing and agrees with the observation (Giudice and Mutolo, 1969; Giudice *et al.*, 1972a) that at least part of the nuclear giant RNA is transferred as such to the cytoplasm in sea urchin embryos.

Chapter 11

Proteins

A. Introduction

The chapter on protein synthesis is probably the most fascinating in the history of the metabolic problems related to sea urchin development.

The mechanisms whereby the rate of protein synthesis can be regulated represent one of the key problems of molecular biology in general, and of the physiology of development in particular. The sea urchin egg offers a special attribute for the study of such a problem in that, from a state of very low synthetic activity before fertilization, it suddenly passes into a state of very high synthetic activity following fertilization or parthenogenetic activation.

A comparison between the respective protein-synthesizing machinery of the unfertilized and fertilized egg has proved very useful in the study of regulatory mechanisms in protein synthesis. In this chapter, we shall direct most of our attention to the problem of the activation of protein synthesis at fertilization.

Other problems that we shall examine here will deal mainly with the overall rate of protein synthesis during both development and mitotic cycle phases, and recognition of the synthesis of single species of proteins at specific developmental periods. Before going into these and other minor problems, it is necessary to set down some premises.

The total amount of proteins as well as that of nitrogen undergo but a slight variation throughout development up to the prism stage, i.e., before the embryo starts feeding (Ephrussi and Rapkine, 1928; Gustafson and

Hjelte, 1951; Nakano and Monroy, 1958a; Giudice, unpublished; Gold-schmidt, 1967; Fry and Gross, 1970b). The total amount of proteins of one embryo, calculated by the Lowry method, is about 40 ng for *Strongy-locentrotus purpuratus,* 36 ng for *Arbacia lixula* (Fry and Gross, 1970b), and 19.2 ± 4.4 ng for *Paracentrotus lividus* (Rinaldi, unpublished). We must mention that when the amount of a constituent is calculated per embryo it is extremely important to adopt a method that allows a good evaluation of the embryo number in a given suspension. The first pre-caution we recommend is a proper mixing of the embryo suspension. Eggs or embryos tend to distribute nonuniformly in a suspension and accumulate toward the tip of the pipette when blown out of it.

In our experience, the best method is that of filtering an embryo sus-pension, containing about 100 embryos in 5 ml, through a Millipore or Oxoid filter under gentle suction, drying, and counting the colored spots (representing the single embryos) under a dissecting microscope. For the species that contain little pigment, the embryos on the filters can be stained with amido Schwartz.

TABLE 11.1

FREE AMINO ACID POOLS IN SEA URCHIN EMBRYOS (AS PMOLES/EMBRYO)

Amino acid	*Arbacia punctulata*[a]	*Strongylocentrotus purpuratus*[a]	*Lytechinus variegatus*[b] Cleavage	Blastula	Mes. bla.	*Paracentrotus lividus*[c]
Taurine	1.210±10%	0.116±35%	—	—	—	—
Aspartic	0.201±23%	0.409±52%	0.21	0.22	0.19	4.48
Threonine	0.196±33%	0.399±28%	0.67	0.93	0.75	5.99
Serine	0.240±11%	0.883±38%	3.26	4.84	4.46	18.8
Glutamic	4.821± 6%	0.690±29%	0.67	1.21	1.06	7.48
Proline	0.457	0.058±12%	Trace	Trace	Trace	4.89
Glycine	0.664±10%	125.3	132	201	214	259
Alanine	0.300±20%	—	15.1	21.6	17.6	15.5
Valine	0.055±27%	0.129±31%	0.30	0.38	0.54	7.8
Cysteine	0.010	0.299	—	—	—	0.426
Methionine	0.011±21%	0.017± 9%	0.34	0.32	0.33	2.93
Isoleucine	0.022±23%	0.080±25%	0.24	0.30	0.36	7.92
Leucine	0.041±37%	0.123±50%	0.43	0.46	0.55	10.9
Tyrosine	0.174±29%	0.048±32%	—	—	—	1.24
Phenylalanine	0.022± 8%	0.059±19%	—	—	—	2.06
Lysine	2.555±10%	0.572±19%	1.87	1.96	1.76	7.39
Histidine	0.112±14%	0.061±34%	Trace	Trace	Trace	0.852
Arginine	2.640±11%	0.320±22%	1.40	1.56	1.61	6.43

[a]Data from Fry and Gross (1970b).
[b]Data from Silver and Comb (1966).
[c]Data from Kavanau (1954b).

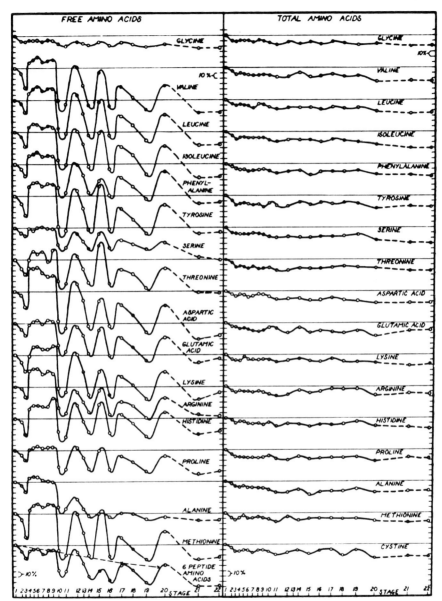

Fig. 11.1. Developmental changes in the free amino acids (and 6 peptide amino acids) and total amino acids of *Paracentrotus lividus* (the continuous horizontal gridlines are spaced at 60% intervals). (From Kavanau, 1954b.)

Returning to the problem of protein synthesis, we wish to emphasize that because of the constancy of the total protein content, the high rate of synthesis observed during development must necessarily be due to turn-over. Its significance should be looked for in a breakdown of reserve proteins (yolk) for the synthesis of cellular proteins, because of the very active cell division.

When a radioactive amino acid is administered to an embryo from the outside, it will become diluted into a pool flowing from the reserve pro-teins into the new ones. To obtain a measure of the rate of this flow we must consider two important parameters: First, the rate of penetration of the amino acid into the embryo; second, the degree of dilution by the internal pool. The dramatic increase of permeability to amino acids at fertilization has already been discussed in detail in Chapter 4, together with the theories on the dilution of exogenously supplied amino acids into the internal pool. Here we shall only describe briefly the available in-formation on the actual size of this pool for the single amino acids and in different developmental stages of various species.

The first analysis of the amino acid pool of sea urchin embryos was done by Berg (1950). Using chromatography of an alcoholic extract of *Strongylocentrotus purpuratus* eggs, he found that the glycine content is by far the highest, followed by alanine. A series of determinations of the amino acid composition of the pool, as well as that of the proteins, has been effected by paper chromatography (Kavanau, 1953) or by means of the microbiological assay (Kavanau, 1954a,b, 1956, 1958). More re-cently, determinations were made using the automatic amino acid analyzer (T. A. Evans *et al.*, 1962; Silver and Comb, 1967; Fry and Gross, 1970b). In Table 11.1 and in Fig. 11.1, some of these data are reported. There is fair agreement concerning the concentrations of these amino acids found by the different authors. The only disagreement is that Kavanau has re-peatedly demonstrated cyclic variations in the concentrations of the free amino acids in *Paracentrotus,* which have not been confirmed by Fry and Gross in *Strongylocentrotus purpuratus.* However, these authors have stressed the differences in pool composition among the different species. The possibility remains that cyclic fluctuations are observed in one species but not in another. It should be recalled that the question of cyclic metabolic variations through cell cycle is a debatable one in sea urchins with respect to several aspects of metabolism. We have already discussed this point in Chapter 8 and shall come back to it later on in this chapter.

B. Protein Synthesis during Oogenesis

That protein synthesis is active during oogenesis was first suggested by histoautoradiography experiments by Immers (1961b). The author injected ^{14}C-labeled amino acids into the body cavity of females of *Paracentrotus lividus, Psammechinus miliaris, Echinus esculentus,* and *Sphaerechinus granularis.* A lively incorporation took place in the oocytes: the less mature the oocyte the higher the incorporation. Essentially identical conclusions were reported by Monroy and Maggio (1963) with the same technique: Mature eggs incorporate very little radioactivity from [14C]D,L-alanine injected into the body cavity, whereas oocytes show a very active incorporation. An accumulation of tracks is seen at the level of the ovary walls, probably leading into the follicular cells. The authors do not think that this difference can be attributed to the low permeability of mature eggs, since they accumulate the injected amino acids in the soluble pool. A quantitative comparison, however, between the data obtained by autoradiography and those to be reported later, which were obtained by direct radioactivity measurements, is not possible. A concentration of tracks in the nucleolus of oocytes is evident. Immers suggests from the timing of labeling that some amino acids are first incorporated into the outer rim of the nucleolus, then they are transferred to the germinal vesicle, and then to the cytoplasm. From the cytochemical evidence Immers concluded that the incorporated amino acids are bound to a low-molecular-weight RNA, in the form of a complex with an excess of basic groups, probably representing amino acyl transfer RNA complexes. In the light of our present knowledge of ribosome synthesis, we are inclined to believe that the data of Immers are indicative of the synthesis of ribosomal proteins coupled with that of rRNA. That some low-molecular-weight RNA is also actively synthesized at nucleolar level has recently been demonstrated (Sconzo *et al.,* 1971), but knowledge of its coupling with proteins is still lacking. Finally, it should not be forgotten that at least part of the labeled precursors might have been utilized for purine synthesis and therefore incorporated directly into RNA. Actually, Immers reports that a treatment with RNase removes radioactivity.

Protein synthesis during oogenesis in *Paracentrotus* was confirmed by Ficq (1964). This author exposed fragments of ovaries to RNA precursors such as phenylalanine labeled with ^{14}C or ^{3}H and then studied the incorporation into RNA and proteins by autoradiography. She also demonstrated that puromycin strongly inhibits amino acid incorporation, while actinomycin does not.

These results suggest that protein synthesis is very active in oocytes and declines with maturation to reach very low levels in the unfertilized egg. Definitive proofs that the unfertilized egg performs little protein synthesis as compared to the fertilized egg follow.

It might be theoretically argued that the incorporation of amino acids into oocytes is caused by some synthetic activity of the follicular cells, which transfer their proteic products to the oocytes. Supporting this concept is the accumulation of radioactivity noticed along the ovarian walls; but against it is the precocious labeling of the oocyte nucleoli. Piatigorsky *et al.* (1967) found that suspensions of mature unfertilized eggs of *Lytechinus pictus,* mixed with variable amounts of oocytes, incorporate exogenous [^{14}C]valine into proteins in amounts proportional to the oocyte content of the suspension. Autoradiography confirms that the oocytes present in the suspension are almost exclusively responsible for the incorporation. Protein synthesis during oogenesis of *Arbacia punctulata* has also been illustrated by Esper (1962b) by injecting [^{14}C]glucose into adult females and observing the autoradiography of the gonads. Digestion with RNase, DNase, or treatment with hot TCA prove that the radioactivity observed was incorporated primarily into proteins.

Recently, Giudice and co-workers (1972b) developed a method allowing the preparation of a good amount of purified oocytes. Direct study of the synthetic ability of the isolated oocytes is at present being performed. It seems likely, from preliminary results, that the concept that oocytes are more active than mature eggs in protein synthesis might be reviewed.

C. Activation of Protein Synthesis at Fertilization

1. *In Vivo* LABELING EXPERIMENTS

The first evidence in favor of such activation comes from a series of experiments where labeled precursors are administered to unfertilized or fertilized eggs and their incorporation into proteins measured thereafter. Hultin (1950b) administered [^{15}N]H$_4$Cl to *Paracentrotus lividus* eggs and measured the amount of ^{15}N incorporation in a TCA-insoluble material, representing partially purified proteins. He found that the rate of ^{15}N incorporation into proteins was considerably higher in the fertilized than in the unfertilized eggs. This, however, was no proof of higher rate of overall protein synthesis in the fertilized egg, since the total ^{15}N uptake into the TCA-soluble fraction was also lower and, therefore, one might have argued that the lower concentration of isotope in the precursor pool of the unfertilized egg was responsible for the lower incorporation of ^{15}N into proteins.

In a subsequent series of papers Hultin essentially confirmed his first result by the use of more specific labeled precursors such as [^{15}N]glycine and [^{15}N]alanine, and of others such as [^{14}C]carbonate and [^{14}C]acetate. Also the eggs of *Psammechinus miliaris* behaved like those of *Paracentrotus* (Hultin, 1952, 1953a,b,d).

Increase of the incorporation of deuterium from heavy water into the egg proteins following fertilization was reported by Hoberman *et al.* (1952).

Nakano and Monroy (1957, 1958a,b; Monroy and Nakano, 1959) devised a way of getting around the problem of the different permeability to precursors of the unfertilized egg. They injected [^{35}S]methionine into the body cavity of adult females of *Paracentrotus,* and collected the eggs a few hours later. Most of the radioactivity was found in a TCA-soluble form in the cytoplasm of the egg. Part of it had been transformed into cysteine and incorporated into glutathione, and part was still in the form of methionine. The situation did not change appreciably for many hours when the eggs were left unfertilized. In the fertilized eggs, however, a rapid transfer of the radioactivity was observed from the TCA-soluble pool to the proteins of the microsomal and mitochondrial particulate and of the soluble cytoplasm (Giudice and Monroy, 1958; Monroy, 1960). Recent investigations have been performed by the use of more sensitive radioactivity detection techniques: Adult females of *Arbacia punctulata* were injected with a [^{14}C]amino acid mixture. At different intervals after injection, a portion of the eggs was collected by electrical stimulation of the animal. After 6 hours, all the mature eggs were collected and divided into two batches, one of which was fertilized. Samples were taken after different intervals. The amount of total ^{14}C uptake and of the incorporation into proteins was measured in each sample (Fig. 11.2).

It is clear that a certain incorporation of isotope into proteins takes place in the mature eggs within the ovary. After the egg is shed some further incorporation into proteins takes place at a slightly lower rate. (It should be noted that from that moment on the external supply of isotope is cut off.) If, however, the eggs are fertilized, a clear increase of the incorporation rate is immediately observed. The difference in incorporation rate between fertilized and unfertilized eggs should appear even higher if one considers that the TCA-soluble pool becomes progessively depleted of labeled precursors as they become incorporated into the proteins of the fertilized egg, while it is being replenished by unlabeled precursors deriving from the unlabeled reserve protein breakdown.

Such a measurement has been carefully performed by Epel (1967) (Fig. 11.3). The author calculated that the rate of increase of amino acid incorporation into proteins is 5- to 15-fold within 20 minutes after fertilization in *Lytechinus pictus.* The rate increase of amino acid incorporation into proteins following fertilization was also reported by Mackintosh and Bell (1967, 1969a), Tyler *et al.* (1968), and Humphreys (1969). The latter author exposed unfertilized and fertilized eggs of *Lytechinus pictus* to pulses of labeled amino acids for 0.5 and 1 minute, respectively, and measured the percentage of the isotope taken up, which is subsequently in-

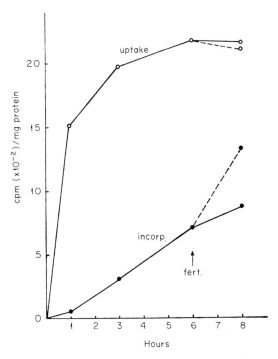

Fig. 11.2. A female *Arbacia punctulata* was injected with 10 μCi of [¹⁴C]algal protein hydrolyzate; after 1 and 3 hours eggs were obtained by electrical stimulation; 6 hours after injection, the animal was cut open and all the mature eggs were collected. One portion was allowed to stand in seawater as unfertilized eggs while the other was fertilized (------); 2 hours later both samples were collected. Each sample was analyzed for total uptake and for incorporation into total proteins. (From experiments of Giudice and Monroy, reported by Monroy, 1967.)

corporated into proteins. The rate increase of protein synthesis following fertilization found in this way is 14-fold. The short duration of the pulses makes it unlikely that the lower specific activity of the proteins of the unfertilized eggs is due to the higher rate of proteolysis. The sum of the above data can well be taken as good evidence of a sharp rate increase of protein synthesis at fertilization. Much attention has been given during the last 15 years to the mechanism whereby this activation can be brought about.

2.   EXPERIMENTS WITH CELL-FREE SYSTEMS

Since the discovery of the amino acid-activating enzyme and the use of cell-free systems for amino acid incorporation, much effort has been expended in finding an explanation for this activation of protein synthesis, at a molecular level, by analyzing the various steps of the process of

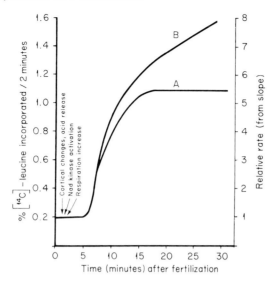

Fig. 11.3. Relative rates of protein synthesis of *Lytechinus pictus* eggs, analyzed by two alternative models. Curve A, derived from slope analysis of the cumulative formation of radioactive protein, would be valid if amino acid compartmentation existed, and if the pool involved in protein synthesis were small and essentially saturated by added [^{14}C]leucine. Curve B, calculated from the percentage of [^{14}C]leucine incorporated/2-minute interval, would be valid if [^{14}C]leucine were always in equilibrium with leucine utilized for protein synthesis (whether compartmentation existed or not). Temporal sequence of other changes determined in separate experiments. (From Epel, 1967).

protein synthesis in cell-free systems. The results of the work of several authors (see reference list), while fundamentally in agreement on many basic facts, differ from each other in many details and with respect to some important conclusions. Since differences in the methods used for the preparation of cell-free systems and subcellular fractions are believed to bring about important differences in the results, and since the choice of such methods is at times controversial, we shall provide the reader with a list of all the methods in the papers quoted in our review, so as to enable him to make a personal evaluation of the importance that each single experiment may have in the general context. This will not exempt us, however, from expressing our own point of view on the validity of these results, whenever we feel this to be of some value.

It is worth underlining here that the importance of high K$^+$ concentration for the preparation of cell-free systems for amino acid incorporation has been emphasized repeatedly (Hultin, 1961b; Ecker and Brookbank, 1963; Molinaro and Hultin, 1965; Cohen and Iverson, 1967). The most recent attempts at optimizing the conditions for cell-free amino acid incorporation and polysome preparation in sea urchin eggs and em-

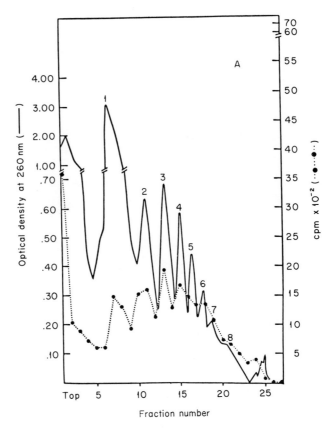

Fig. 11.4. Sucrose density-gradient centrifugation of 15,000 g supernatants extracted from 10-hour-old *Lytechinus variegatus* blastulae. Embryos were labeled with [^{14}C]L-phenylalanine for 3.5 minutes, washed, and then homogenized with more than 12 strokes of a motor-driven Teflon pestle and a Duall tube in 1–2 volumes of 0.01 M Tris–HCl, pH 7.8, containing 0.24 M KCl and 0.01 M MgCl$_2$ (A) or 0.43 M KCl and 0.018 M MgCl$_2$ (B).

bryos are those of Cohen and Iverson (1967), Castañeda and Tyler (1968a), Stavy and Gross (1969a), Humphreys (1969), and Fromson and Nemer (1970).

A thorough analysis of the requirements for a cell-free system for amino acid incorporation can be found in the work of Stavy and Gross (1969a). The importance of the procedure for obtaining a good polysome preparation was stressed by Cohen and Iverson (1967) (Fig. 11.4 and Table 11.2); they emphasize that a high KCl and MgCl$_2$ concentration is required to prevent polysomal damage. Fromson and Memer (1970) advise forcing embryos through a 20-gage hypodermic needle instead of homogenizing them by the Dounce homogenizer (see, also, Nemer and

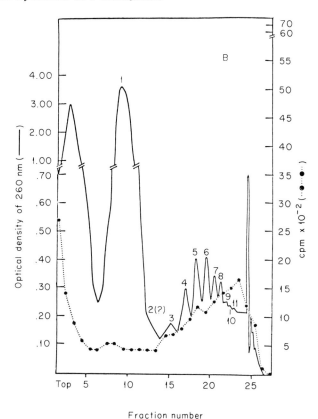

Fig. 11.4. (*continued*) About 28 OD_{260} units of S 15 were layered onto a 28-ml 17–50% (w/v) linear sucrose density gradient (in type B buffer) in a Beckman SW 25.1 rotor tube. The gradient was centrifuged at 24,000 rpm for 3.75 hours at 4°C. Absorption in fractions 24–25 marks interface of the displacing sucrose solution at the bottom of the gradient. Numbers assigned to peaks are arbitrary points of reference. (From Cohen and Iverson, 1967.)

Lindsay, 1969). These authors have shown that the second type of homogenization may cause nuclear leakage as judged by the appearance in the cytoplasm of DNA and RNA, which latter cosediments with polysomes, but is not bound to ribosomes, as shown by the fact this RNA does not move to the top of sucrose gradients when polyribosomes are broken by EDTA treatment. Moreover, both DNA and this RNA can be separated from the ribosomes by centrifugation in CsCl, after fixation in formaldehyde (Figs. 11.5–11.7).

Furthermore, Castañeda and Tyler (1968a) have shown that homogenates of *Strongylocentrotus purpuratus* embryos contain an active RNase, which causes the amino acid-incorporating activity to stop within 10

310

11. PROTEINS

TABLE 11.2

HOMOGENIZATION BUFFER WITH RESULTING SEDIMENTATION PATTERN[a,b]

Molarity		
KCl	MgCl₂	Pattern type[c]
0.01	0.0015 (RSB)	I
0.01	0.01	I
0.24	0.01 (buffer A)	II
0.24	0.0015	II
0.05	0.01	II
0.10	0.01	II
0.43	0.018 (buffer B)	II

[a]From Cohen and Iverson (1967).
[b]All buffers contained 0.01 M Tris–HCl, pH 7.8, at 25°C.
[c]Pattern types I and II refer respectively to parts A and B of Fig. 11.2.

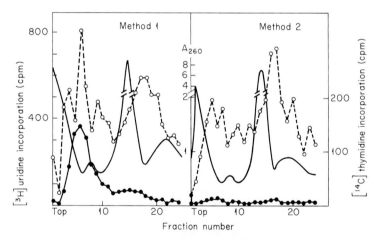

Fig. 11.5. Sedimentation diagrams of supernatants prepared by different methods of cell disruption. The fertilization membranes of *Lytechinus pictus* embryos were removed immediately after fertilization by passage through bolting silk (No. 16), and the embryos were developed at 18°C in artificial seawater. The embryos were incubated with [2-¹⁴C]thymidine (5 μCi/ml; 52.8 mCi/mmole) for 180 minutes and with [5-³H]uridine (50 μCi/ml; 23.7 Ci/mmole, New England Nuclear Corp.) for 45 minutes before the 9-hour stage of development. Equal aliquots of embryos in seawater were layered onto, then centrifuged through, ice-cold 1 M dextrose in distilled water. The pelleted embryos were resuspended in 5 volumes of TK medium (0.24 M KCl, 0.005 M MgCl₂, 0.01 M triethanolamine-HCl buffer, pH 7.8). The two aliquots were submitted to different methods of cell disruption. Method 1: Bentonite was added to a concentration of 0.2 mg/ml, and the embryos were quickly homogenized by four complete strokes in an all-glass Dounce homogenizer. Method 2: The same amount of bentonite was added, and the suspension was passed gently through a 20-gage hypodermic needle. In each case the cell lysate was centrifuged for 15 minutes at

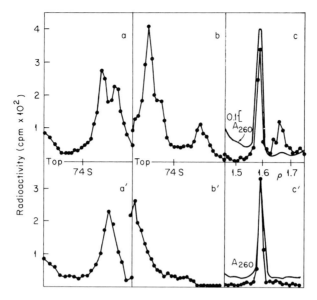

Fig. 11.6. Polyribosomes and cosedimenting RNA structures. Embryos of *Strongylocentrotus purpuratus* were developed and incubated with [³H]uridine, and S 15 extracts were prepared and sedimented as in Fig. 11.5. The material in the polyribosomal region was dialyzed against TK medium for 2 hours to remove sucrose and then divided into three portions for further processing. Resedimentation under conditions of Fig. 11.5 without further treatment (a,a′); resedimentation after addition of EDTA to a concentration of 0.1 M (b,b′); and fixation for 24 hours with 6% formaldehyde and centrifugation for 14 hours in CsCl gradients (c,c′). The series (a,b,c) was derived from extracts prepared by method 1; the series (a′,b′,c′) was derived by method 2. This experiment with embryos of *Lytechinus pictus* yielded the same results. (From Fromson and Nemer, 1970. Copyright 1970, American Association for the Advancement of Science.)

minutes. The addition of poly U can restore the incorporation. The use of bentonite is recommended by these authors and also by Infante and Graves (1971). The latter authors actually report that the high KCl concentration may act in *Strongylocentrotus purpuratus* by merely inhibiting the RNase. In fact, in the presence of bentonite, no polysome degradation is observed even at low KCl concentrations. It was found that homogenates of *Lytechinus pictus* embryos contain, on the other hand,

15,000 *g*, and the supernatant (S 15) was layered onto a 15–30% sucrose gradient in TK medium underlaid with 2 ml of 50% sucrose as a cushion. The gradients were centrifuged for 90 minutes in a Spinco rotor SW 50.1 at 50,000 rpm. The A_{260} (———) was continuously monitored by a recording spectrophotometer, and gradient fractions were collected for assay of [¹⁴C]thymidine (●) and [³H]uridine (○) incorporation in material adhering to membrane filters. Radioactivity was normalized to equal yields for each preparation. (From Fromson and Nemer, 1970. Copyright 1970, American Association for the Advancement of Science.)

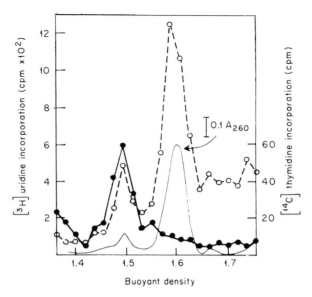

Fig. 11.7. Buoyant densities of labeled DNA and RNA cosedimenting with polyribosomes. The polyribosomal region (fractions No. 16–23) of a sucrose gradient parallel to that of Fig. 11.5 (method 1) was fixed with formaldehyde and centrifuged in a CsCl gradient as in Fig. 11.6c. All experiments were performed with both species of sea urchin, *S. purpuratus* and *L. pictus,* and the same results were obtained. [^{14}C]thymidine, ●; [^{3}H]uridine, ○. (From Fromson and Nemer, 1970. Copyright 1970, American Association for the Advancement of Science.)

low RNase activity (see Chapter 10). Stavy and Gross (1969a) confirmed that more reproducible results with cell-free systems can be obtained with *Lytechinus pictus* than with *Strongylocentrotus purpuratus* or *Arbacia puntulata,* because of the lower RNase activity of the former. Humphreys (1969), although acknowledging the superiority of high salt buffers over low salt buffers, denies that in *Lytechinus pictus* the high K$^+$ concentration in the homogenization medium has a beneficial effect on the maintenance of large-sized polysomes as reported by Cohen and Iverson (1967) for *Lytechinus variegatus.* Piatigorsky and Tyler (1970) claim to have obtained good polysome profiles by the use of low salt buffers, even if a direct comparison with profiles in high salt buffers is not reported by the latter authors.

a. List of the Methods Used in Preparing Cell-Free Systems for Amino Acid Incorporation and for Polysome Analyses

Hultin and Bergstrand (1960): Psammachinus miliaris: Homogenization of embryos with Potter all-glass in 0.005 *M* MgCl$_2$ in isotonic KCl, followed by addition of 0.5 volumes of 1 *M* sucrose, 1 *M* KCl, 0.175 *M* Tris (pH 7.8). *Incorporation system:* 10 μmoles PEP, 1 μmole ATP, 0.06 μmole of [^{14}C]leucine, 0.7 ml of homogenate in 1.7 ml final volume.

For the ribosomes: Homogenization in 1.5 ml of 0.15 *M* sucrose, 0.025 *M* KCl, 0.01 *M* MgCl$_2$ in 0.035 *M* Tris (pH 7.8). Addition during homogenization of 0.66 ml of 2.5 *M* KCl, 0.01 *M* MgCl$_2$, and 0.17 ml of 10% Lubrol W + 0.33 ml of 10% DOC. Layering over 0.3 *M* sucrose in 0.6 *M* KCl in 0.01 *M* MgCl$_2$ in Tris, pH 7.8. Centrifugation at 105,000 *g* for 1 hour.

Hultin (1961b): Paracentrotus lividus. Preliminary wash of the eggs to remove Ca^{2+} and some Na^{+}.

Homogenization in 0.25 *M* KCl, 0.01 *M* MgCl$_2$, 0.25 *M* sucrose, and 0.035 *M* Tris (pH 7.8). The 12,000 *g* supernatant is layered on top of 0.3 *M* sucrose and centrifuged at 70,000 *g* for 75 minutes. Pellet, microsomes; red layer, endoplasmic particles; bottom clear pellet, free ribosomes.

The "endoplasmic particles" treated with 0.5% Lubrol, 1% DOC in 0.5 *M* KCl yield the endoplasmic RNP. Incorporation system as above, with modifications: 0.24 *M* KCl, 3.6×10^{-3} *M* MgCl$_2$, 10 μmoles PEP, 1 μmole ATP, 0.75 μmole of [^{14}C]L-valine and homogenate to 0.6 ml final volume. Occasionally 0.2 μmoles of GTP and 50 μg of pyruvate kinase (whose effect is negligible). Composition of the above incubation media was occasionally slightly modified.

Wilt and Hultin (1962): Psammechinus miliaris. Essentially as by Hultin (1961b). Incubation medium 0.2 *M* KCl, 0.007 *M* MgCl$_2$, 0.15–0.25 *M* sucrose, 0.05 *M* Tris (pH 7.8), 10^{-3} *M* ATP, 10^{-2} *M* PEP, 0.051 m*M* [^{14}C]L-phenylalanine (9.8 Ci/mole) and about 8 mg/ml of homogenate protein.

Nemer (1962b): Arbacia punctulata. Microsomes prepared as by Hultin (1961b), in the presence of 5×10^{-3} *M* mercaptoethanol. Incubation medium of 0.9 ml: 4 mg microsomal protein, 0.5 mg yeast sRNA, 10 μg PEP kinase, 0.25 μCi of [^{14}C]L-leucine (13 μCi/μ*M*), and the following in μmoles: 5.0 PEP, 1 ATP, 0.06 GTP, 215 K^{+}, 10 MgCl$_2$, 6 mercaptoethanol, 10 of each amino acid except leucine, but 100 of serine and of leucine, or as otherwise specified.

Nemer and Bard (1963): Arbacia punctulata and *Lytechinus pictus.* Essentially as above.

Monroy and Tyler (1963): Paracentrotus lividus and *Lytechinus pictus.* Homogenization: washing with Ca^{2+}- and Mg^{2+}-free seawater. Homogenization in Potter with Teflon plunger motor-driven 1–2 minutes in 4 volumes of 0.05 *M* Tris succinate buffer (pH 7.6), 0.025 *M* KCl, 0.004 *M* MgCl$_2$, and 0.005 *M* mercaptoethanol. Polysome preparation: (a) *Paracentrotus:* addition of sucrose to 0.18 *M* final concentration to homogenates and centrifugation at 8,000 *g*. (b) *Lytechinus:* centrifugation at 2,000 *g*. The supernatants are supplemented with DOC to 0.5–1% final concentration, layered on top of 24 ml of a linear gradient of 15–30% sucrose and centrifuged at 25,000 rpm in an SW 25 Spinco L ultracentrifuge for 2 hours in the cold.

Tyler (1963): Strongylocentrotus purpuratus. Homogenization or sonication for assay of amino acid incorporation in 0.01 *M* Tris buffer, 0.01 *M* Mg acetate, 0.275 *M* KCl. Incubation system for amino acid incorporation: 0.225 ml of homogenate or sonicate and 0.025 ml of a reaction mixture containing 0.8 ml of 0.8 *M* PEP, 0.1 ml of 0.1 *M* ATP, and 0.1 ml of 0.0038 *M* [^{14}C]phenylalanine at 9.8 Ci/mole.

Ecker and Brookbank (1963): Mellita quinquiesperforata (sand dollar). Ribosome preparation for chemical and ultracentrifugal analysis: Homogenization by forcing the eggs through a 25-gage needle in 0.01 *M* Tris buffer (pH 7.5), containing either 0.2 *M* KCl or 0.01 *M* $MgCl_2$. The 25,000 *g* supernatant was centrifuged at 105,000 *g*.

Wilt (1964): Strongylocentrotus purpuratus. Homogenization in 3 volumes of 0.03 *M* Tris (pH 7.8), containing 0.15 *M* sucrose, 0.1 *M* KCl, 0.007 *M* Mg acetate, 0.006 *M* mercaptoethanol, 0.1% bentonite.

Polysomes: The homogenate was centrifuged at 10,000 *g* for 5 minutes. The supernatant to which DOC was added to 1% final concentration, was layered on top of a 15–30% sucrose gradient [in 0.03 *M* Tris (pH 7.8), 0.1 *M* KCl, 0.007 *M* $MgCl_2$] and centrifuged at 24,000 rpm in an SW 25 Spinco L rotor for 2 hours.

Stafford et al. (1964): Lytechinus variegatus: Polysomes: washing of the eggs in isotonic NaCl–KCl. Homogenization: with three strokes of a Teflon pestle in a Duall homogenizer in 0.01 *M* Tris (pH 7.6), containing 0.24 *M* KCl and 0.1% bentonite. The 10,000 *g* supernatant, containing 0.3% DOC, was layered on top of a linear 15–30% sucrose gradient and centrifuged for 2 hours at 25,000 rpm, in an SW 25 Spinco L rotor.

Malkin et al. (1964): Strongylocentrotus purpuratus. Polysomes: washing of the eggs with Ca^{2+}- and Mg^{2+}-free seawater. Homogenization for 1 minute with a motor-driven Teflon pestle of a glass homogenizer in 0.01 *M* Tris buffer (pH 7.4), containing 0.01 *M* KCl, 0.01 *M* $MgCl_2$, 0.001 *M* mercaptoethanol, and 0.1% bentonite. The 6,000 *g* supernatant, containing 0.5% DOC, was layered on top of a 15–30% linear sucrose gradient and centrifuged for 2 hours at 25,000 rpm in an SW 25 Spinco L rotor.

Brookbank and Yonge (1964): Lytechinus variegatus, Mellita quinquiesperforata, Arbacia punctulata. Preparation of ribosomes for immunological studies and analytical ultracentrifugation: Homogenization as by Ecker and Brookbank (1963) with both KCl and $MgCl_2$ present. The 12,000 rpm supernatant was centrifuged twice at 50,000 rpm for 30 minutes.

Hultin (1964): Paracentrotus lividus. Polysomes: Homogenization in 0.15 *M* sucrose, 0.05 *M* Tris buffer (pH 7.8), 0.1 *M* KCl, 0.009 *M* $MgCl_2$. The 12,000 *g* supernatant was provided with 1.3% DOC, layered on top of a 7.5–22.5% linear sucrose gradient (containing 0.1 *M* KCl, 0.005 *M* $MgCl_2$, 0.05 *M* Tris, and 0.1% bentonite) and centrifuged for 2.25 hours at 53,000 *g* in an SW 25 Spinco L rotor. Incubation system for amino acid incorporation: 8 mg of proteins of 12,000 *g* supernatant, 10 μmoles PEP, 1 μmole ATP, 0.2 μmole GTP, 0.5 μCi of [^{14}C]L-leucine (6.0 Ci/mole) or [^{14}C]L-phenylalanine (7.55 Ci/mole), 250 μmoles KCl, 7 μmoles $MgCl_2$ in 1 ml total volume.

Maggio et al. (1964): Paracentrotus lividus. Homogenization: with a Potter homogenizer in 0.05 *M* Tris–HCl (pH 7.6), containing 0.25 *M* sucrose, 0.25 *M* KCl; 0.004 *M* Mg acetate, 0.005 *M* mercaptoethanol. Ribosomes were sedimented from the 15,000 *g* supernatant. The incubation system for amino acid incorporation contained in 1 ml: Tris buffer (pH 7.6), 25 μmoles; Mg acetate, 4 μmoles; KCl, 50 μmoles; mercaptoethanol, 20 μmoles; creatine phosphate, 15 μmoles; creatine kinase, 10 μg; ATP, 4 μmoles; GTP, 1 μmole; radioactive amino acids, in a variable amount; ribosomes and cell sap.

Burny et al. (1965): Arbacia lixula. Polysomes: Homogenization with 5 strokes of a Teflon pestle in a Thomas glass homogenizer in 0.35 *M* sucrose, 0.1 *M* Tris buffer (pH 7.8),

0.1 *M* KCl, 0.001 *M* MgSO₄, 1% Lubrol. The 12,000 *g* supernatant was supplemented with 0.3% DOC, layered onto a 15–30% linear sucrose gradient, and centrifuged for 90 minutes at 37,000 rpm in an SW 25 Spinco L rotor.

Spirin and Nemer (1965): Lytechinus pictus. Polysomes: Homogenization with 2 strokes of a Dounce homogenizer in 0.25 *M* sucrose, 0.24 *M* NH₄Cl, 0.01 *M* MgCl₂, 0.01 *M* Tris buffer (pH 7.8). The 12,000 *g* supernatant was layered on top of a 15–30% linear sucrose gradient and centrifuged for 2–3 hours at 24,000 rpm in an SW 25.1 Spinco L rotor.

Molinaro and Hultin (1965): Paracentrotus lividus. Preparation of the 12,000 *g* supernatant: Preliminary washings of the eggs. Homogenization with a Dounce homogenizer in 0.15 *M* sucrose, 0.009 *M* MgCl₂ and 0.05 *M* Tris buffer. The 12,000 *g* supernatants were then tested for the KCl dependence of the amino acid-incorporating activity. Incubation system for amino acid incorporation: about 8 mg of proteins of 12,000 supernatant (or RNP particles and cell sap) 1 μmole ATP, 0.2 μmole GTP, 10 μmole PEP, 0.5 μCi of [¹⁴C]leucine (6 mCi/mole), 15 μg of pyruvate kinase, 0.15 mmole sucrose, 0.009 mmole MgCl₂, 0.05 mmoles Tris buffer, pH 7.8, and variable amounts of KCl, in 1.0 ml.

Monroy et al. (1965): Paracentrotus lividus. Preparation of ribosomes for amino acid incorporation assay: Homogenization in 0.35 *M* sucrose, 0.01 *M* Tris buffer (pH 7.6), 0.025 *M* KCl, 0.004 *M* Mg acetate, 0.005 *M* mercaptoethanol. The 10,000 *g* supernatant was centrifuged at 105,000 *g* for 1 hour. Incubation system for amino acid incorporation: ribosomal pellet corresponding to 0.2–0.5 mg proteins; 4 mg proteins of rat liver cell sap; 4 μmoles ATP, 0.5 μmoles GTP; 10 μmoles PEP; 10 μg PEP kinase; 50 μmoles KCl; 4 μmoles Mg acetate; 20 μmoles mercaptoethanol. Variable amounts of radioactive amino acids. Other variable additions.

Candelas and Iverson (1966): Lytechinus variegatus and *Echinometra lucunter.* Polysomes: washing of the eggs with homogenization medium. Homogenization with Duall homogenizer in 0.01 *M* Tris buffer (pH 7.6), 0.24 *M* KCl, 0.01 *M* MgCl₂. The 12,000 *g* supernatant was layered on top of a linear 15–30% sucrose gradient with a 5-ml cushion of 50% sucrose, and centrifuged for 2 hours at 24,000 rpm in an SW 25 Spinco L rotor. Ribosomes were prepared by pelleting the 12,000 *g* supernatant at 105,000 *g* for 2 hours. Incubation system for amino acid incorporation: as by Hultin (1961b).

Mano and Nagano (1966): Hemicentrotus pulcherrimus and *Pseudocentrotus depressus.* Preparation of ribosomes for the assay of the amino acid-incorporating activity: as by Hultin (1961b), but with the addition of 2 m*M* CaCl₂ at the homogenization and centrifugation of the first precipitate. Incubation mixture: 3 mg proteins of ribosomes; 3 mg pH 5 enzymes; 0.5 mg, 28,000 cpm [¹⁴C]aminoacyl tRNA; [¹⁴C]algal acid protein hydrolyzate; 5 μmole PEP; 1 μmole ATP; 0.2 μmole GTP; 0.2 unit crystalline pyruvate kinase; 180 μmoles sucrose; 10 μmoles MgCl₂; 120 μmoles KCl, and 60 μmoles Tris buffer (pH 7.8), in a total volume of 0.5 ml.

Mutolo et al. (1967). Paracentrotus lividus. Preparation of ribosomes for the analysis of ribosomal proteins. Homogenization in 0.3 *M* sucrose in 0.035 *M* Tris buffer (pH 7.6), containing 0.025 *M* KCl, 0.004 *M* Mg acetate and 0.005 *M* mercaptoethanol. The 15,000 *g* supernatant was centrifuged at 105,000 *g* for 90 minutes. The pellet was resuspended with 1% DOC in 0.01 *M* Tris buffer, pH 7.4, layered over 1.5 ml of 0.6 *M* sucrose in Tris buffer, and centrifuged at 105,000 *g* for 1 hour.

Stavy and Gross (1967): Lytechinus pictus. Preparation of microsomes and polysomes: washing with Ca^{2+}- and Mg^{2+}-free seawater, and with homogenization medium. Homogenization with a Potter homogenizer with a Teflon pestle in 0.035 M Tris buffer (pH 7.4), 0.25 M sucrose, 0.01 M KCl, 0.006 M MgCl$_2$, 0.006 M mercaptoethanol. Centrifugation at 5000 g and then at 24,000 g. The supernatant (S 24) was either centrifuged at 135,000 g for 90 minutes, to prepare the microsomes, or layered on top of a 15–30% linear sucrose gradient with a 1-ml cushion of 40% sucrose and centrifuged at 25,000 rpm for 2 hours in an SW 25 Spinco L rotor, in order to prepare the polysomes. Incubation system for amino acid incorporation: microsomes, cell sap, and pH 5 enzyme in various amounts, 17.5 μmoles Tris buffer (pH 7.4), 50 μmoles sucrose, 50 μmoles KCl, 3–4 μmoles MgCl$_2$ (except when the system was tested for Mg^{2+} dependence), 1 μmole ATP, 0.2 μmole GTP, 1.2 μmoles mercaptoethanol, 2 μmoles PEP, 0.015 μmole each of 20 L-amino acids minus either leucine or phenylalanine, [^{14}C]leucine, or [^{14}C]phenylalanine, in 0.5 ml.

Infante and Nemer (1967): Strongylocentrotus purpuratus. Polysomes: washing with homogenization medium. Homogenization with two strokes of a Dounce homogenizer in 0.25 M sucrose, 0.05 M triethanolamine–HCl, pH 7.8, 0.24 M KCl, 0.005 M MgCl$_2$, and 0.2% bentonite. The 15,000 g supernatant was layered onto a 15–30% linear sucrose gradient and centrifuged for 48 minutes at 39,000 rpm.

Cohen and Iverson (1967): Lytechinus variegatus. Polysomes: washing with isotonic NaCl–KCl. Homogenization with 5–12 or more strokes of a motor-driven Teflon pestle of a Duall homogenizer in either 0.01 M Tris (pH 7.8), 0.01 M KCl, and 0.0015 M MgCl$_2$, or in 0.01 M Tris buffer, pH 7.8, 0.24 M KCl, and 0.01 M MgCl$_2$. The 15,000 g supernatant was layered onto a 17–50% linear sucrose gradient in homogenization medium and centrifuged at 24,000 rpm in an SW 25.1 Spinco L rotor for 3.75 hours.

Infante and Nemer (1968): Strongylocentrotus purpuratus and Lytechinus pictus. Preparation of monoribosomes and subribosomal particles for analytical ultracentrifugation: Homogenization either as by Infante and Nemer (1967), or in 0.25 M sucrose in 0.05 M Tris buffer (pH 7.8), 0.24 M NH$_4$Cl, 0.005 M Mg^{2+}, and 0.2% bentonite. (The same results are obtained with either medium. Bentonite was not necessary for *Lytechinus*.) The 15,000 g supernatant was layered on top of a 15–30% linear sucrose gradient and centrifuged either at 39,000 rpm (SW 39 Spinco L rotor) or at 25,000 rpm (SW 25 Spinco L rotor) for 1, 2, and 4 hours or 2.5, 7, and 12 hours, respectively. Under these conditions the monoribosomes sediment at about 0.25, 0.50, and 0.85 fractional distance from top to bottom of the gradient.

Maggio et al. (1968): Paracentrotus lividus. Preparation of ribosomes: as by Monroy *et al.* (1965). Monosomes prepared by sedimentation through a 5–20% linear sucrose gradient for 90 minutes at 55,000 g.

Piatigorsky (1968): Lytechinus pictus: Polysomes: washing with 0.55 M KCl. Homogenization with 2 or 3 strokes in 0.05 M Tris buffer (pH 7.6), 0.025 M KCl, 0.004 M MgCl$_2$, 0.005 M mercaptoethanol. The 10,000 g supernatant was supplemented with 0.5% DOC, layered onto a 5–20% linear sucrose gradient, and centrifuged for 80 minutes at 27,500 rpm in an SW 39 Spinco L rotor.

Castañeda and Tyler (1968a): Strongylocentrotus purpuratus and Lytechinus pictus. Homogenate for test of amino acid incorporation and of RNase activity. Washing with 0.55 M KCl. Homogenization with 2 strokes of a Potter homogenizer with a tight fitting Teflon pestle in 0.05 M Tris buffer (pH 7.8), 0.2 M KCl, 0.005 M Mg acetate, 0.005 M

mercaptoethanol. Centrifugation at 12,000 g. Ribosomes for test of amino acid incorporation: Procedure A (Murthy and Rappaport, 1965): Homogenization in 0.2 M sucrose, 0.035 M Tris buffer, pH 7.8, 0.025 M KCl, and 0.01 M MgCl$_2$. Each 7.5 ml of the 12,000 g supernatant were supplemented with 1.5 ml of 2.5 M KCl and 0.01 M MgCl$_2$ and 2 ml of 10% DOC. The 20,000 g supernatant was layered over 20 ml of 0.4 M sucrose, 0.035 M Tris buffer (pH 7.8), 0.5 M KCl, and 0.01 M MgCl$_2$ and centrifuged at 78,500 g for 90 minutes. Procedure B (Murthy and Rappaport, 1965): Homogenization in 0.035 M Tris buffer, pH 7.8, 0.5 M KCl, 0.015 M MgCl$_2$, and 2% bentonite. Stepwise centrifugation at 400 g, 1,500 g, and 8,700 g. The final supernatant was made 1% with respect to DOC and centrifuged as in Procedure A. The pellet was resuspended once again in homogenization medium, the MgCl$_2$ concentration raised to 0.05 M, and the suspension centrifuged again at 20,000 g for 10 minutes. Incubation system for amino acid incorporation: 2.5 mg protein of homogenate (or 0.1 mg of ribosomes and 0.35 mg of rat liver, pH 5 fraction) in 125 μl of final volume containing in μmoles/ml: 100 KCl, 30 Tris (pH 7.6), 3.3 Mg acetate, 5 mercaptoethanol, 10 ATP, 0.5 GTP, 10 PEP, 0.8 μCi of [^{14}C]L-phenylalanine, and 25 μg of PEP-kinase.

Tyler et al. (1968): Lytechinus pictus. Polysomes: homogenization with 2 strokes of the pestle of a Potter homogenizer in 0.05 M Tris buffer (pH 7.4), 0.025 M KCl, 0.004 M MgCl$_2$, 0.005 M mercaptoethanol. The 10,000 g supernatant was made 0.3% with respect to DOC, layered on top of a 15–30% sucrose gradient with a 0.4-ml cushion of 60% sucrose, and centrifuged at 30,000 rpm for 100 minutes in an SW 39 Spinco L rotor.

Rinaldi and Monroy (1969): Paracentrotus lividus. Polysomes: washing with Ca^{2+}- and Mg^{2+}-free seawater. Homogenization with 5 gentle strokes in 0.05 M Tris buffer (pH 7.6), 0.4 M KCl, 0.018 M Mg acetate, 0.5% DOC, 0.5% Tween 40, and 0.1% bentonite. The 7,000 g supernatant was layered onto a 17–50% linear sucrose gradient with a 60% sucrose cushion and centrifuged at 52,000 g for 3.5 hours in an SW 25.1 Spinco L rotor.

Castañeda (1969): Strongylocentrotus purpuratus and *Lytechinus pictus.* Ribosomes prepared as by Castañeda and Tyler (1968a). Incubation system for amino acid incorporation (in μmoles/ml): 30 Tris (pH 7.6), 150 KCl, 7–10.5 Mg acetate, 5 mercaptoethanol, 0.5 ATP, 0.25 GTP, 10 PEP, 25 μg PEP kinase, 10–30 μg ribosomes (as RNA) 40–150 μg pH 5 fraction (as protein), 0.1 μCi of [^{14}C]L-phenylalanine (366 Ci/mole), in 0.1 ml final volume. Preparation and assay of transfer factors: homogenization in 0.05 M Tris buffer (pH 7.4), 0.01 M Mg acetate, 0.01 M NH$_4$ acetate, and 0.001 M dithiothreitol. The 117,000 g supernatant was precipitated with (NH$_4$)$_2$SO$_4$ at 35% saturation. The supernatant was brought to 65% of saturation and the precipitate suspended in homogenization buffer freed of the low-molecular-weight compounds by filtration on Sephadex G 25. The assay was based on the retention of GTP on a nitrocellulose filter.

Stavy and Gross (1969a): Lytechinus pictus (after selection, for the lowest RNase content as compared to *Strongylocentrotus purpuratus* and *Arbacia punctulata*). Homogenates for amino acid incorporation assay: Washing with Ca^{2+}- and Mg^{2+}-free seawater and then with homogenization medium. Homogenization with gentle strokes of a Potter homogenizer in 0.035 M Tris buffer (pH 7.4), 0.25 M sucrose, 0.1 M KCl, 0.006 M MgCl$_2$, 0.006 M mercaptoethanol. Centrifugation at 5,000 g and then at 21,000 g. The upper two thirds of the supernatant was called "crude extract." Microsomes: Centrifugation of the crude extract at 135,000 g for 90 minutes. Ribosomes: The microsomes were resuspended in homogenization medium containing 0.33% DOC, and sedimented at 135,000 g for 90 minutes. Incubation system for amino acid incorporation assay: in μmoles/0.5 ml: 17.5 Tris buffer (pH 7.4), 50 KCl, 2 MgCl$_2$, 1.2 mercaptoethanol, 1 ATP, 0.2 GTP, 50 sucrose,

2 PEP, 6–8 μg PEP kinase, 0.015 each of 20 L-amino acids minus L-leucine, 0.0021 [^{14}C]L-leucine or 0.0016 [^{14}C]L-phenylalanine. (These conditions were modified when the effect of modifying the concentration of each of the components was tested.)

Stavy and Gross (1969b): Strongylocentrotus purpuratus and Lytechinus pictus. Incubation system for amino acid incorporation assay: as by Stavy and Gross (1969a).

Kedes and Stavy (1969): Strongylocentrotus purpuratus. Homogenization of washed eggs or embryos in 0.4 M KCl, 0.01 M MgCl$_2$, 0.05 M Tris–HCl (pH 7.4). The homogenate was centrifuged at 10,000 g for 10 minutes and the supernatant sedimented through 2.0 M sucrose in homogenization medium at 164,000 g for 3–4 hours. The ribosomal pellet was resuspended in 0.1 M KCl, 0.006 M MgCl$_2$, 0.035 M Tris–HCl (pH 7.4), and cleared by centrifugation at 10,000 g for 15 minutes. Subunit separation was performed by treatment with 1 M KCl. Incubation system for amino acid incorporation: 1 ml containing: 4.4 OD ribosomes, 100 μmoles KCl; 8–10 μmoles MgCl$_2$, 40 μmoles Tris–HCl (pH 7.4), 10 μmoles mercaptoethanol; 100 μg poly U; 0.3 mg rat liver pH 5 enzyme fraction, 0.05 μCi of [^{14}C]L-phenylalanine (409 mCi/mmole); 2 μmoles of ATP, 0.4 μmole of GTP, 4 μmoles of PEP, and 12 μg of PEP–kinase. Incubation for 2 hours at 20°C.

Vittorelli et al. (1969): Paracentrotus lividus. Preparation of microsomes for assay of amino acid incorporation: Homogenization in 0.3 M sucrose, 0.05 M Tris buffer (pH 7.6), 0.025 M KCl, 0.004 M Mg acetate, 0.005 M mercaptoethanol. The 12,000 g supernatant was centrifuged at 105,000 g for 1 hour. Polysomes: The microsomal pellet was resuspended in homogenization medium layered on top of a 15–30% linear sucrose gradient and centrifuged at 55,000 g for 90 minutes. Incubation system for amino acid incorporation assay: In μmoles/ml: 25 Tris buffer (pH 7.6), 10 Mg acetate, 50 KCl, 20 mercaptoethanol, 4 ATP, 0.5 GTP, 10 PEP, 10 μg PEP kinase, about 300 μg microsomes (as protein), 1.5 mg of 105,000 g supernatant of rat liver (as protein), 0.1 μCi of [^{14}C]phenylalanine (155 μCi/μmole).

Nemer and Lindsay (1969): Strongylocentrotus purpuratus. Polysomes: Centrifugation through 1 M dextrose. Homogenization by one stroke of a Dounce homogenizer or by forcing the eggs through a 20 gage hypodermic needle, in triethanolamine-HCl (pH 7.8), 0.24 M KCl, 0.005 M MgCl$_2$. The 15,000 g supernatant was layered onto a 15–30% sucrose gradient in homogenization medium and centrifuged for 27 minutes at 50,000 rpm in an SW 50 Spinco L rotor (Fig. 11.1).

Mackintosh and Bell (1969a): Arbacia punctulata and Strongylocentrotus purpuratus. Polysomes: Homogenization of eggs washed in homogenization medium, by 10 strokes of tight-fitting Dounce homogenizer in 0.01 M Tris (pH 7.4) containing 0.24 M NH$_4$Cl and 0.01 M MgCl$_2$. Deoxycholate and Brij 58 to 0.5% each were added and the 1,000 g supernatant layered onto a linear 15–30% (w/w) sucrose gradient in homogenization medium. Centrifugation follows in an SW 25.1 or SW 41 Spinco L rotor for 6–7 hours at 24,000 rpm or 3 hours at 41,000 rpm, respectively.

Kedes and Gross (1969b): Arbacia punctulata. Polysomes: Washing with Ca^{2+}- and Mg^{2+}-free seawater. Homogenization in 0.05 M Tris buffer (pH 7.6), 0.4 M KCl, 0.01 M MgCl$_2$, 0.5% Tween 40, and 0.5% DOC. The 10,000 g supernatant was layered onto a 17–50% linear sucrose gradient in homogenization medium and centrifuged at 25,000 rpm for 3.5 hours in an SW 25 Spinco L rotor.

Kedes et al. (1969): Arbacia punctulata. Polysomes: As by Kedes and Gross (1969b).

Humphreys (1969): Lytechinus pictus. Polysomes: (a) Washing with homogenization medium. Homogenization with 3–6 strokes of a Dounce homogenizer in 0.01 M Tris buffer (pH 7.8), 0.25 M sucrose, 0.24 M NH_4Cl, 0.01 M $MgCl_2$, 0.5% Nonidet P-40. The homogenate was layered onto a 15–30% linear sucrose gradient in homogenization medium and centrifuged at 24,000 rpm for 3.5 hours in an SW 25.3 Spinco rotor. (b) Homogenization in 0.01 M Tris buffer (pH 7.8), 0.24 M sucrose, 0.01 M KCl; 0.0015 M $MgCl_2$, 0.5% Nonidet P-40. Centrifugation as in (a). It is reported that the higher salt concentration in this species has not the effect of increasing the size of polyribosomes as reported by Cohen and Iverson (1967) for *Lytechinus variegatus.*

Mano (1970): Hemicentrotus pulcherrimus, Pseudocentrotus depressus, Anthocidaris crassispina. Homogenization (for tests of amino acid incorporation in cell-free system) in Millipore-filtered seawater. Incubation system: 27–37 mg (as protein) of total homogenate or 6,000 g supernatant, 1 μCi of [^{14}C]amino acids. Ribosomes prepared according to Mano and Nagano (1966). Polysomes: the 12,000 g supernatant was layered onto a 15–30% linear sucrose gradient in 0.05 M Tris (pH 7.8) and 0.01 M Mg acetate, and centrifuged at 130,580 g for 150 minutes.

Mano and Nagano (1970): Homogenates for assay of amino acid incorporation and incubation system, essentially as by Mano (1970) with occasional variations.

Fromson and Nemer (1970): Strongylocentrotus purpuratus and *Lytechinus pictus.* Polysomes: Homogenization as by Nemer and Lindsay (1969), but with the addition of 0.02% bentonite. The 15,000 g supernatant was layered onto a 15–30% linear sucrose gradient in homogenization medium, with a 2-ml cushion of 50% sucrose, and centrifuged at 50,000 rpm in an SW 50.1 Spinco L rotor for 90 minutes.

Piatigorsky and Tyler (1970): Lytechinus pictus. Polysomes: Washing of the eggs with 0.55 M KCl. Homogenization with 1–3 strokes of a loose-fitting Teflon pestle, in 0.05 M Tris buffer (pH 7.6), 0.025 M KCl, 0.004 M $MgCl_2$, 0.005 M mercaptoethanol. Addition of DOC to 0.5% (a short time after low-speed centrifugation). Stepwise centrifugation at 5,000 rpm for 2 minutes in an SW 65 Spinco L rotor and at 15,000 rpm for 10 minutes. The two pellets, resuspended in homogenization medium or the supernatant, were layered onto a 15–30% linear sucrose gradient in homogenization medium and centrifuged for 85 minutes at 40,000 rpm in an SW 65 rotor. Ribosomes for the assay of amino acid incorporation: Homogenization as above, with the addition of 0.08% bentonite and 0.5% DOC. The 7,000 g supernatant was centrifuged at 100,000 g for 1 hour. The pellet, resuspended in homogenization medium, was cleared by centrifugation at 7,000 g. Incubation system: similar to that of Castañeda and Tyler (1968a).

Jenkins and Denny (1970): Lytechinus pictus. Homogenization of washed eggs by passing once through a 25-gage needle in 1 volume of 0.55 M KCl and 2 volumes of buffer [6.6 mM Mg acetate, 0.132 M sucrose, 66 mM Tris–HCl (pH 7.8)]. The 15,000 g supernatant was made 1% with Triton X 100, layered on 35 ml of a 15–30% (w/w) linear sucrose gradient and centrifuged at 20,000 rpm for 16 hours at 5°C in an SW 27 rotor.

Moav and Nemer (1971): Lytechinus pictus and *Strongylocentrotus purpuratus.* Polysome preparation: Lysis in 5 volumes of 240 mM KCl, 5 mM $MgCl_2$ and 50 mM triethylamine–HCl (pH 7.8), in the presence of bentonite at 1 mg/ml, by passing once through a 30- or 25-gage hypodermic needle. The 15,000 g supernatant was centrifuged onto a 15–30% sucrose gradient in the above medium at 50,000 rpm for 27 minutes in an SW 50 or SW 50.1 Spinco L rotor. Incubation of polysomes *in vitro:* 2 mg of polysomes, 15 mg of 100,000 g supernatant, 1 m*M* ATP, 5 m*M* PEP, 0.06 m*M* GTP, 5 m*M* mercaptoethanol, 5 μg/ml of PEP kinase, 240 m*M* KCl, 5 m*M* MgCl₂ and 50 m*M* triethanolamine–HCl buffer (pH 7.8) in a total of 15 ml with the addition of a mixture of 20 unlabeled amino acids, 1 m*M* each (the growing peptide chains having been prelabeled *in vivo*).

Infante and Krauss (1971; also see Infante and Graves, 1971; Infante and Baierlein, 1971): Strongylocentrotus purpuratus and *Arbacia lixula.* Ribosome preparation: Homogenization of washed eggs with 2–4 strokes of a Dounce homogenizer in 4–8 volumes of 0.05 *M* triethanolamine, 0.005 *M* MgCl₂ and concentration of KCl, NaCl, or NH₄Cl ranging from 0 to 0.80 *M*; 0.25 *M* sucrose (pH 7.8) (and for polysomes 1–2 mg/ml of bentonite). The 15,000 g supernatant was centrifuged at different speeds for varying periods in order to study polysomes, ribosomes, or subunits. Cell-free system for amino acid incorporation into protein as by Kedes and Stavy (1969).

b. Activation of the mRNA–Ribosome Interaction at Fertilization

Hultin and Bergstrand (1960) made the first attempt to demonstrate amino acid incorporation in a cell-free system of sea urchin embryos. They found that total homogenates of fertilized eggs of *Psammechinus miliaris* displayed the same rate increase of [¹⁴C]leucine incorporation *in vitro* with respect to homogenates of unfertilized eggs. They also showed that ribosomes from unfertilized eggs are almost unable to carry out amino acid incorporation in the presence of rat liver cell sap. On the other hand, ribosomes of fertilized eggs or later stages of development undergo amino acid incorporation to a clearly higher extent under the same conditions. This was the first suggestion that the low activity of the protein-synthesizing machinery in the unfertilized egg is due to some impairment at ribosomal level. In a subsequent paper Hultin (1961b) showed that the so-called "microsomes" of fertilized eggs of *Paracentrotus lividus* are equally stimulated to incorporate [¹⁴C]valine into proteins by a cell sap of either fertilized or unfertilized eggs. This represented the first evidence against the presence of an inhibitor of protein synthesis in the cell sap of unfertilized eggs. The cell sap of unfertilized eggs seemed to contain a normal amount of the factors capable of stimulating amino acid incorporation at ribosomal level. Further proof for the absence of inhibitors in the unfertilized egg was offered by Hultin by mixing homogenates of fertilized and unfertilized eggs, and checking the rate of amino acid incorporation *in vitro* (Tables 11.3 and 11.4) (Fig. 11.8). Again it seemed that the main reason for the impairment of protein synthesis in the unfertilized eggs might be found in the inactivity of ribosomes.

Attempts to activate ribosomes *in vitro* were made by Hultin; he treated the isolated ribosomes with a large series of different chemicals.

They all met with very little success. It is of interest to note here that the experimental conditions used by this author are in many respects not too far off from the more sophisticated ones very recently set up.

TABLE 11.3

ACTIVITY OF CELL SAP AND PARTICULATE FRACTIONS FROM UNFERTILIZED AND BUTYRIC ACID-ACTIVATED EGGS IN CELL-FREE INCORPORATION SYSTEMS[a,b]

	Cell sap from unfertilized eggs	Cell sap from butyric acid-activated eggs
Particles from unfertilized eggs		
12,000 g sediment	2.8	1.3
Microsomes	2.2	2.3
Particles from butyric acid-activated eggs		
12,000 g sediment	7.2	9.9
Microsomes	29.6	36.0

[a]From Hultin (1961b).
[b]Incubation of 0.2 ml of suspended particles and 0.6 ml of cell sap. Data expressed as $m\mu moles \times 10^3$ of [^{14}C]valine incorporated per mg total protein.

TABLE 11.4

INCORPORATION ACTIVITY OF RIBOSOMES AND ENDOPLASMIC PARTICLES FROM UNFERTILIZED AND FERTILIZED EGGS[a,b]

	RNA/protein ratio of particles	[^{14}C] valine incorporated	
		nmoles $\times 10^3$/mg particle–protein added	nmoles $\times 10^3$/mg particle–RNA added
Particles from unfertilized eggs			
Free ribosomes	0.78	2.0	2.6
Endoplasmic particles	0.26	0.7	2.5
Ribosomes from endoplasmic particles	0.70	4.7	6.7
Particles from fertilized eggs			
Free ribosomes	0.89	91.5	102.4
Endoplasmic particles	0.29	7.4	25.4
Ribosomes from endoplasmic particles	0.60	53.9	89.5

[a]From Hultin (1961b).
[b]The incubation system contained 0.55 ml cell sap from fertilized eggs (5.7 mg protein). Particles from unfertilized eggs or from eggs 30 minutes after fertilization were added at different concentrations. After incubation all samples were adjusted to equal protein content.

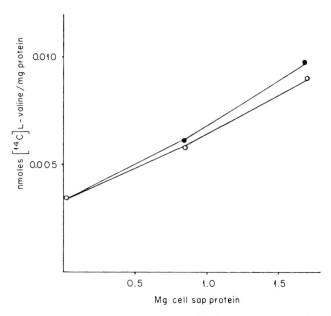

Fig. 11.8. Activity of cell sap from *Paracentrotus lividus* eggs in cell-free [^{14}C]L-valine-incorporating system. Incubation of whole microsomes from fertilized eggs (8 mg protein) and indicated amounts of cell sap from unfertilized eggs (O), or eggs 35 minutes after fertilization (●). After incubation all samples were adjusted to equal protein content. (From Hultin, 1961b.)

Hence, the question arose as to why these ribosomes are inactive. That was the time of the discovery of messenger RNA in bacterial systems. Investigations were begun, therefore, aimed at discovering whether or not ribosomes are inactive because of the lack of mRNA in the unfertilized egg. Nemer (1962b) demonstrated that "microsomes" of unfertilized eggs of *Arbacia punctulata* are stimulated by the addition of poly U in cell-free systems, to incorporate phenylalanine even to a higher extent than microsomes from fertilized eggs or developing embryos. Wilt and Hultin (1962) also showed that total homogenates or 12,000 *g* supernatants or microsomes plus cell sap of unfertilized eggs of *Psammechinus miliaris* are rendered active in the incorporation of phenylalanine by the addition of poly U. Similar conclusions were also reported by Nemer and Bard (1963), inducing these authors to suggest the lack of mRNA in the unfertilized egg as a possible mechanism for the block of protein synthesis before fertilization. It was soon evident, however, that this was not the case. Gross and Cousineau (1963a) demonstrated that protein synthesis becomes activated in sea urchins even under conditions that block RNA synthesis, such as in the presence of actinomycin D. We refer the reader to Chapter 10 for the numerous proofs that have accumulated since, confirming that mRNA is already present in the unfertilized egg. The finding however, that poly U can stimulate phenyl-alanine incorporation in cell-free systems from unfertilized eggs has repeatedly been confirmed (Tyler, 1963, 1967; Monroy *et al.*, 1965; Castañeda, 1969; Stavy and Gross, 1967, 1969b; Kedes and Stavy, 1969; Vittorelli *et al.*, 1969).*

Soon after the discovery of polyribosomes, work was started on check-ing whether or not the unfertilized eggs contain such an active form of ribosomes. Monroy and Tyler (1963) demonstrated that the polysome population is very low before fertilization and increases thereafter up to the blastula stage in *Lytechinus pictus* and *Paracentrotus lividus*. These earlier results have been more recently confirmed also by the use of more modern methods for polysome preparation (Humphreys, 1971; Rinaldi and Monroy, 1969; Hultin, 1964; Infante and Nemer, 1967; Wilt, 1964; Piatigorsky, 1968; Stafford *et al.*, 1964). (See Figs. 11.9 and 11.10.) Only

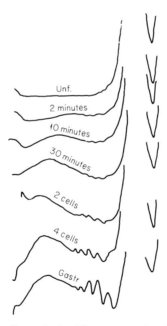

Fig. 11.9. Tracings of gradients obtained from eggs and embryos at the stages indicated. The gradients of unfertilized eggs and fertilized eggs up to the 2-cell stage were prepared from the same batch of eggs. The total optical densities assignable to ribosomes had the following values relative to that of the ribosomes from unfertilized eggs: 2 minutes after fertilization, 0.74; 10 minutes, 0.86; 30 minutes, 0.70; 2-cell stage, 0.80. (From Rinaldi and Monroy, 1969.)

---

*Stimulation of amino acid incorporation by poly U, added *in vivo* to the entire egg, has also been reported (Tyler, 1963, 1965). Since, however, stimulation was not only for phenyl-alanine but also for other amino acids, the mechanism whereby this was brought about still remains to be understood.

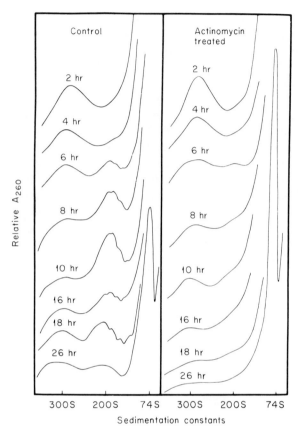

Fig. 11.10. Sedimentation profiles of polyribosomes from embryos of *S. purpuratus* developing in the presence and absence of actinomycin. The series of continuous tracings by the recording spectrophotometer has been drawn from a single batch of eggs. The controls were repeated five times with close agreement and the actinomycin treatment was studied three times. Variability in response to actinomycin was noted. Similar qualitative changes can be observed in the embryonic development of *Lytechinus pictus* and *Arbacia punctulata*. (From Infante and Nemer, 1967.)

Schäfer (1966), to our knowledge, has reported that a change in the ribosome aggregation is visible at the electron microscope. This author finds that whereas the ribosomes in the unfertilized egg lie free in the cytoplasm, they appear after fertilization to be grouped in rosettelike structures. The question then arises: If mRNA is present in the unfertilized egg, why do ribosomes not become attached to it to form active polysomes before fertilization? In formulating this question we have to warn the reader that for the sake of simplicity we continue to speak of the absence of polysomes before fertilization, while it is known (see, for example, Rinaldi and Monroy, 1969; Piatigorsky, 1968; Mackintosh and

Bell, 1969a,b; Humphreys, 1969) that a small amount of polysomes are at work even before fertilization. This agrees with the observations that some protein synthesis takes place in the unfertilized eggs, even if at a highly reduced rate. Going back to our question, Monroy *et al.* (1965) found that, while ribosomes of unfertilized eggs are able to respond to the stimulation by poly U, they are unable to respond to stimulatory effect of RNA from eggs of embryos. This RNA had been proved to be stimulatory to ribosomes of rat liver or of developing embryos (Maggio *et al.*, 1964). This result was taken as an indication of the presence of some factor(s) cosedimenting with ribosomes in the unfertilized egg which prevents the ribosomes from interacting with mRNA to form polyribosomes. Attempts to remove this factor(s) met with success. If the unfertilized egg ribosomes are first treated with trypsin, they are able to respond to stimulation by exogenous RNA. Moreover, they show endogenous amino acid-incorporating activity, thus suggesting the presence of some messenger RNA in the ribosomal fraction. Furthermore, the effect of poly U on unfertilized egg ribosomes appears more marked after fertilization (Table 11.5). Grossman *et al.* (1971) find that treatment of the unfertilized egg ribosomes with a proteolytic enzyme (tosylarginine methyl ester hydrolase) extracted from the egg, renders them active in protein synthesis (see Chapter 12). In agreement with the idea of the presence of inhibitory factors of proteic nature at ribosomal level, Maggio *et al.* (1968) found that ribosomes from unfertilized eggs of *Paracentrotus lividus* and *Sphaerechinus granularis* are more resistant to dissociation into subunits by dialysis against low Mg^{2+} concentrations than ribosomes from fertilized eggs. Pretreatment with trypsin rendered the unfertilized egg ribosomes readily dissociable, like those from fertilized eggs. Castañeda (1969) was unable to confirm this different sensitivity of ribosomes to low Mg^{2+} before and after fertilization. However, the conditions of dialysis used differed from those of Maggio *et al.* (1968). The data by Maggio *et al.* (1968) are indirectly supported by the finding of Jenkins and Denny (1970) that there is a pool of ribosomal subunits in unfertilized eggs of *Lytechinus pictus,* corresponding to 3% of the ribosomal population. Following fertilization there is a small but consistent increase of the subunit pool.

Infante and Graves (1971) confirmed the higher dissociation resistance at low Mg^{2+} concentrations of ribosomes from unfertilized eggs than those from blastulae of *Strongylocentrotus purpuratus*. However, if the monoribosomes from the two stages are prepared, not by pelleting them at 105,000 *g* but by a sucrose gradient purification, those from unfertilized eggs become as readily dissociable at low Mg^{2+} as those from blastulae. The authors suggest that some proteins might be contaminating the pelleted, unfertilized egg ribosomes and not those from blastulae,

TABLE 11.5

EFFECT OF TREATMENT WITH TRYPSIN ON THE ABILITY OF RIBOSOMES FROM
UNFERTILIZED EGGS TO INCORPORATE AMINO ACIDS INTO PROTEINS[a,b]

Expt. No.	Amino acid(s)	Addition	cpm/mg ribosomal RNA	
			Control	Trypsin-treated
1	Phenylalanine	None	0	122
	Phenylalanine	Poly U	270	340
2	Phenylalanine	None	0	72
	Phenylalanine	Poly U	360	2200
	AH	None	25	260
	AH	RNA blastula	0	475
3	AA	None	18	448
	AA	RNA unfert	9	644

[a]From Monroy *et al.* (1965).
[b]Incubation procedure: The incubation mixture contained in 1.0 ml 25 μM Tris buffer (pH 7.6); 4 μM Mg acetate; 50 μM KCl; 20 μM mercaptoethanol; 4 μM ATP; 0.5 μM GTP; 10 μM PEP; 10 μg PEP–kinase; about 4 mg (estimated as proteins) of rat liver cell sap. Additions: poly U, 1 mg; total RNA from blastula (RNA blastula), 1.3 mg; total RNA from unfertilized eggs (RNA unfert), 1.23 mg. Radioactive amino acids: [^{14}C]phenylalanine (7.8 μCi/μM), 1 μCi; [^{14}C]algal protein hydrolyzate (AH), 1 μCi; 1 μCi total of a mixture of [^{14}C]phenylalanine, lysine, valine, glycine, and glutamic acid (AA). In Expt. 1, 0.193 mg; in Expt. 2, 0.483 mg; and in Expt. 3, 0.327 mg of ribosomes were used. After 30 minutes at 30°C, the reaction was terminated by addition of 100 μM of phenylalanine or amino acid mixture and 0.4 ml of 50% TCA. The precipitate was extracted with cold and hot (90°C) 5% TCA, hot alcohol–ether, and ether; it was then dissolved in ammonia, dried in the vials, and counted. Trypsin treatment was with 100 μg/ml for 30 minutes. A sample of the ribosomal preparation was precipitated with 5% TCA and analyzed for RNA content, and this was used as a reference.

thus making the former more resistant to dialysis dissociation. We believe that before calling the different dissociability of unfertilized egg ribosomes artifactual, we should consider that an extensive purification might wash out some loosely adhering protein, which actually plays a role in somehow preventing ribosome dissociation. A comparison between unfertilized and just fertilized egg ribosomes would be useful in this respect. While comparing the dissociability of ribosomes from different developmental stages, Infante and co-workers made a number of useful observations on the sedimentation behavior of ribosomes from sea urchin embryos in different conditions of salinity—a very welcome addition to the only information available from the old studies by Allison and Clark (1960).

They observed that if unfertilized egg ribosomes are dissociated by increasing the KCl concentration, their behavior is superimposable over that of ribosomes from embryos. Ribosomes derived from polysomes are not dissociated into subunits by high concentration of KCl, unless the peptidyl tRNA has been stripped off (Infante and Graves, 1971). Subunits produced by treatment with 0.5 *M* KCl (but not with NaCl or NH₄Cl) are able to reassociate readily at lower ionic strengths and to translate poly U (Infante and Krauss, 1971). Finally, there is the interesting discovery that at moderate ionic strengths (0.24 *M* KCl), ribosomes can dissociate into subunits during centrifugation by effect of the gravitation field. The ribosome conformation is not altered during this process, which is also influenced by the concentration of ribosomes and the ionic conditions. The authors suggest that the hydrostatic pressure influences the equilibrium between free ribosomes and subunits (Infante and Krauss, 1971; Infante and Baierlein, 1971).

The earlier suggestion of the presence in the unfertilized egg ribosomes of a protein factor inhibiting mRNA ribosome interaction has received recent confirmation by the work of Metafora *et al.* (1971). These authors were able to isolate from ribosomes of unfertilized eggs of *Paracentrotus lividus* a protein factor that is absent in fertilized egg ribosomes. This factor was recovered from the 1 *M* NH₄Cl ribosomal wash, and is at present being further purified (Metafora, personal communication). If the 1 *M* NH₄Cl wash of unfertilized egg ribosomes is added to fertilized egg ribosomes, there results a marked inhibition of the ability of ribosomes to bind poly U and phenylalanyl-tRNA, so much so that their ability to synthesize polyphenylalanine is impaired, even if exogenous elongation factors T_1 and T_2 are added. The inhibitory effect of the 1 *M* NH₄Cl wash of unfertilized egg ribosomes is not species specific. Even prokaryote ribosomes can be inhibited by it.

Other theories have been proposed to explain the low level of protein synthesis in unfertilized eggs. At variance with what is reported above, Piatigorsky (1968) has suggested the presence of inactive polyribosomes in unfertilized eggs. Actually, if eggs of *Lytechinus pictus* are labeled with [³H]uridine during oogenesis and the polysomes are prepared, little of the radioactivity of the polysomal region is movable to the top of the sucrose gradient by RNase treatment. Pretreatment of the polysomes with trypsin, on the other hand, renders them sensitive to RNase treatment. Only a small aliquot of these polysomes becomes labeled after a 20-minute exposure of the egg to radioactive amino acids. This aliquot is completely sensitive to RNase. The author suggests that some polyribosomes are bound to some RNA-containing inhibitory protein, which prevents flowing of the ribosomes through the RNA chain. It seems to us that the possibility that some protein-bound RNA is cosedimenting with polysomes should be more thoroughly investigated. This argument would be ruled out by further data on the recovery in the monosomal peak of the radioactivity displaced by the double treatment, trypsin RNase. More recently, Piatigorsky and Tyler (1970) have shown that the bulk RNA labeled during oogenesis, extractable from the polyribosomal region, is mature ribosomal RNA. Some polydisperse RNA is recoverable only from the postribosomal region. Furthermore, it was shown that whereas the number of polysomes, as judged by the increase of radioactivity from [^{3}H]uridine in the polysomal region, only doubles following fertilization, the amount of radioactivity from amino acids taken up by these polysomes *in vitro* increases by a factor of 15 following fertilization. This is taken as a suggestion of the presence of nonactive polysomes in the unfertilized eggs.

Humphreys (1969) has suggested that more copies of mRNA are translated at fertilization. In fact, the other way of explaining the increased rate of protein synthesis would be either by a faster movement of each single ribosome through the mRNA or a crowding of the ribosomes along the mRNA, with consequent increase in the size of the polysomes. Neither of these two possibilities has proved to be true. The rate of ribosomal flow through mRNA was calculated by exposing eggs or embryos to radioactive amino acids and measuring how long it took for an amount of radioactivity equal to that present on the polysomes (as growing peptide chains) to be transferred to the soluble cytoplasm. The results of the calculation indicated that the growth rate of the average peptide chain was 0.61 minutes at 18°C for unfertilized eggs of *Lytechinus pictus* and 1.16 minutes for embryos. That there is no change (but actually a slight decrease) in the growth rate of the single peptide chain following fertilization was also reported by Mackintosh and Bell (1969a), even though the absolute numbers differ considerably — 6.1 minutes for unfertilized and 5.9 minutes for fertilized *Arbacia* eggs. Some increase in the size of polyribosomes, however, was observed in the data presented by Humphreys, and agrees with the observations of Rinaldi and Monroy on *Paracentrotus lividus* (Fig. 11.11). Since both Humphreys (1969, 1971) and Rinaldi and Monroy (1969) indicate that the average size of the growing peptide chain (as judged by gross sucrose gradient analysis) is unchanged following fertilization, a conclusion can be drawn that this is indicative of an increased crowding of the ribosomes along mRNA. This phenomenon, however, does not seem to account by itself for the total increase in the rate of protein synthesis, especially in the case of Humphrey's data. The increase in number of active polysomes might also be invoked. The question then arises: Is the difference in optical density between polysomes of fertilized and unfertilized eggs enough to account for the increased rate of protein synthesis after fertilization? One calculation of this kind, that of Piatigotsky and Tyler (1970), accepts the idea of the existence of nonactive polysomes in unfertilized eggs. A

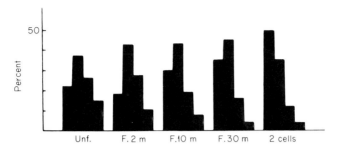

Fig. 11.11. This diagram has been obtained by dividing the polyribosome area of eggs and embryos of *Paracentrotus lividus* into four segments of five tubes each and computing the percent of the total radioactivity over the whole polyribosome area in each one of the four segments, after 10-minute pulse with [^{14}C]protein hydrolyzate. The heavy region of the gradient is on the left side. (From Rinaldi and Monroy, 1969.)

different calculation, performed by Humphreys (1971), shows that ribosomes (measured as 26 S rRNA) engaged in polysome increase 30-fold following fertilization. Mackintosh and Bell (1969a), report an increase of active polysomes after fertilization, which would account for all of the increase in the protein synthesis rate (Fig. 11.12). This calculation, based on the amount of radioactivity by exogenously labeled amino acids

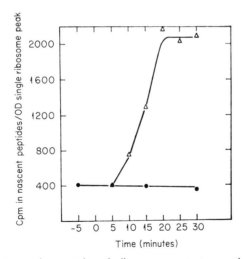

Fig. 11.12. Time course increase in polyribosomes content over the first 30 minutes following fertilization of *Arbacia punctulata* eggs. Eggs were labeled with 1 μCi [^{14}C]-amino acids/ml for 1.5 hours, washed, and a portion fertilized. The time of sperm addition is taken as time zero. Samples of eggs were taken from fertilized (Δ) and unfertilized (●) portions at the times indicated, homogenized, ribonuclease-treated, and analyzed on sucrose gradient. Each symbol represents the counts/minute, associated with the monomer ribosome peak in a sucrose gradient normalized to equal optical density in the monomer ribosome peak. (From Mackintosh and Bell, 1969a.)

movable to the monomer peak by RNase treatment, refers again to the number of active polysomes. The increase in the polysome number at fertilization is tentatively attributed by these authors to a step-up in the rate of chain initiation, on the basis of the observation that treatment with cycloheximide, which is known to slow down the movement rate of ribosomes along mRNA, causes a polysome increase in unfertilized eggs. The idea of a block of chain initiation in unfertilized eggs has also been indicated by Stavy and Gross (1969a) as the only possibility, if the impaired interaction between mRNA and ribosomes is due to ribosomal incompetence. In fact, repeated experiments (Stavy and Gross, 1967, 1969a; Kedes and Stavy, 1969) suggest that no difference in the responsiveness of fertilized or unfertilized egg ribosomes to poly U can be observed. Kedes and Stavy (1969) also dissociated the ribosomes into subunits by treatment with 1 M KCl. The reconstituted ribosomes deriving from light subunits of unfertilized eggs mixed with heavy subunits from embryos and vice versa, always show the same responsiveness to poly U, like entire ribosomes from either eggs or embryos. This is at variance with what was suggested by Monroy et al. (1965), Castañeda (1969), Nemer and Bard (1963), and Vittorelli et al. (1969). Vittorelli et al. (1969) found that ribosomes from embryos achieve a higher level of phenylalanine incorporation in the presence of poly U because of their greater content of polysomes. Actually, ribosomes derived from polysomes are, for some unknown reason, more responsive to poly U than those deriving from the monoribosomal peak. Responsiveness to poly U can be taken as an indication that the process of chain elongation can normally be functional in unfertilized eggs. It leaves open the possibility to impairment of the chain initiation process.

Several authors have been inclined to believe that the reason for the impaired interaction between mRNA and ribosomes has to be looked for in the fact that mRNA is scarcely available for translation before fertilization because it is somehow masked, probably by proteins:

1. Spirin and Nemer (1965), Nemer and Infante (1965), and Infante and Nemer (1968) have proposed a role for the informosomes in such a mechanism of regulation of protein synthesis (this has already been discussed in Chapter 10).

2. Kedes and Stavy (1969) failed to reproduce the trypsin activation of unfertilized egg ribosomes of *Arbacia punctulata, Lytechinus pictus,* and *Strongylocentrotus purpuratus*. They found no differences either between the electrophoretic pattern of the ribosomal proteins of unfertilized and fertilized eggs or between their ability to reform ribosomes responsive to poly U, after dissociation into subunits. Therefore they suggest that the lesion of protein synthesis may lie in the mRNA.

3. Mano and Nagano (1966, 1970) and Mano (1966) found in *Hemi-*

centrotus pulcherrimus and *Pseudocentrotus depressus* that template RNA, as judged by its ability to stimulate amino acid incorporation, is contained in all subcellular fractions. At fertilization, however, there is a movement of template RNA from a fraction sedimenting between 8,000 and 17,000 *g,* which is specially endowed with it, to the microsomes, which now become the fraction containing more template RNA. The treatment of the total homogenate with trypsin would produce the same effect as fertilization. These authors suggest a role of activation of a protease at fertilization releasing the mRNA from the proteins which had made it sediment as a particulate fraction, thus permitting its interaction with ribosomes. In support of this theory these authors submit an analysis of the protease activity at fertilization (see Chapter 12) and the following experiment: If the 15,000 *g* sediment is centrifuged through a stepwise sucrose density gradient, a peak of template RNA is found before fertilization. After fertilization this peak disappears, and in its place a peak of proteolytic activity becomes evident. These findings, because of their implications, certainly deserve further investigation. An electron microscopic study of such particles (Mano and Nagano, 1970) shows that they appear before fertilization, like rough endoplasmic reticulum vesicles which become smooth after fertilization or trypsin treatment. Significant changes of the proportion of rough ER in the living egg following fertilization have not, to our knowledge, been described by other authors.

The explanation given by Mano for the stimulability by trypsin of the isolated ribosomes reported by Monroy *et al.* (1965) is that ribosomes still contain the particles sedimentable between 8,000 and 15,000 *g*. This does not account for: (1) the increased sensitivity to stimulation by exogenous RNA of the trypsin-treated ribosomes; (2) the possibility (Monroy, personal communication) to stimulate by trypsin monoribosomes purified through a sucrose gradient; (3) Humphreys reports, differing from Rinaldi and Monroy (1969), that the increase in polysomes that occurs within 2 hours following fertilization is not accompanied by a progressive increase in their size. This, together with the constancy of the movement rate of ribosomes along mRNA and of the growing peptide chains length, is taken by the author as indicating that the mRNA is the limiting factor in the unfertilized egg. If, in fact, ribosomes were limiting, one would expect them to bind the available messenger as they became active and therefore there would be a progressive increase in polysome size. This argument rests on the assumption that ribosomes randomly attach to the mRNA molecules, without showing any selective binding to some of them. Second, it does not exclude, in our opinion, that besides mRNA, the ribosomes also are inactive in the unfertilized egg. In this work, Humphreys also makes a direct calculation of the amount of nonribosomal RNA synthesized during the first 2 hours following fertilization, and concludes that it is not enough to explain the increase in polysome number, thus confirming once more the existence of a store of mRNA in the unfertilized egg (see Chapter 10).

So far, we have directed our attention to the impaired interaction between mRNA and ribosomes as a cause for the reduced rate of protein synthesis before fertilization, the problem being whether the ribosomes or the messenger or both are responsible for this reduced interaction. The other steps leading to amino acid incorporation have also been taken into consideration. A brief account thereof will be given here.

c. Amino Acyl–tRNA Synthetase

It has already been shown that substituting pH 5 enzyme from rat liver for the cell sap of sea urchin does not change the difference in activity between homogenates or ribosomes from unfertilized or fertilized eggs (Hultin and Bergstrand, 1960). The absence of differences in the cell sap was also confirmed by the results of crossing the soluble cytoplasm of unfertilized and fertilized or butyric acid-activated eggs. Candelas and Iverson (1966) report that in similar experiments of reciprocal crossing of microsomes from unfertilized eggs with cell sap from fertilized eggs, not only the microsomes but also the cell sap is less functional before fertilization in *Echinometra lucunter* and *Lytechinus variegatus*. It should be noted that the cell sap in these experiments had not been dialyzed and, therefore, a difference in the endogenous pool might have influenced these data. On the other hand, Castañeda (1969) reported that the pH 5 fraction of *Strongylocentrotus purpuratus* and *Lytechinus pictus* is doubly more active after fertilization. He attributes this to the higher "transfer" activity of a factor partially purified by the $(NH_4)_2SO_4$ fractionation contained in the 100,000 g supernatant; the transfer activity of this factor was measured by its ability to bind GTP to nitrocellulose filters. This confirms older observations by Yasumasu and Koshihara (1963) who reported a marked difference in the activity of the transfer enzyme before and after fertilization in *Hemicentrotus pulcherrimus* and *Anthocidaris crassispina*. However, Stavy and Gross (1967, 1969a) failed to find any difference in the activity of the soluble factors (Kedes and Stavy, 1969) of unfertilized and fertilized eggs of *Lytechinus pictus*.

Direct tests for the activity of aminoacyl-tRNA synthetase and of the transfer RNA (tRNA) in eggs and embryos have also been carried out.

The first demonstration of the existence of aminoacyl-tRNA synthetase in the unfertilized sea urchin egg is credited to Scarano and Maggio (1957), who have also shown (1959c) that these eggs contain a system capable of activating the carboxylic group of the acetate leading to the formation of acetyl-CoA. Maggio and Catalano (1963) measured the amino acid-activated ATP-^{32}PP exchange in the soluble cytoplasm of *Paracentrotus lividus,* filtered through Sephadex G-25, and reported an increase of this enzymatic activity in the blastulae as compared to unfertilized eggs. The amino acids used were phenylalanine, leucine, histidine, glycine, serine, and isoleucine. It is difficult to judge from these results how relevant this increase is for the activation of protein synthesis at fertilization. (1) No comparison between unfertilized eggs and eggs immediately following fertilization were made; and (2) the degree of the reported increase was not calculated because of the very high endogenous activity of the extracts (i.e., in the absence of added amino acids), which made the estimation of the exact value of the samples at lower activity (unfertilized eggs) practically impossible. Such high endogenous reaction values were also reported by Molinaro and Hultin (1965), who measured the influence of K^+ concentration. Once again, no comparison was made between unfertilized eggs and developmental stages. The activity of aminoacyl–tRNA synthetase was also measured by Ceccarini *et al.* (1967) by challenging the 105,000 *g* supernatant, purified through Sephadex G-25, against a yeast tRNA preparation in the presence of a mixture of labeled amino acids. The charged tRNA was then purified by MAK column chromatography and the radioactivity profile along the effluent fluid studied. The following results were obtained when the crude enzyme from unfertilized eggs was compared to that from blastulae or plutei: The overall ability of the sea urchin aminoacyl–tRNA synthetase to charge the yeast tRNA is doubled in the blastulae with respect to the unfertilized eggs. A drop in activity is, on the other hand, observed at the pluteus stage. Also the specific activity profile shows modifications in the three stages (Figs. 11.13–11.15). Again no direct comparison between unfertilized and freshly fertilized eggs was made, so that we do not know whether the increase in synthetase activity observed at blastula also contributes to the rate increase of protein synthesis at the moment of fertilization. No overall differences in the ability to charge RNA between the synthetases of unfertilized eggs and blastulae of *Strongylocentrotus purpuratus* have been reported by Zeikus *et al.* (1969).

In a more elaborate series of experiments Ceccarini and Maggio (1969) thoroughly looked for possible differences among the single aminoacyl–tRNA synthetases throughout development of *Paracentrotus lividus.* The experimental design was the following: Preparation of crude enzymatic extracts by sonication of the cells in the presence of glycerol. Charging of yeast tRNA with one single amino acid labeled with ^{3}H, in the presence of the enzyme of one stage or with the same amino acid, but labeled with ^{14}C in the presence of the enzyme of another stage. Analysis of the radio-

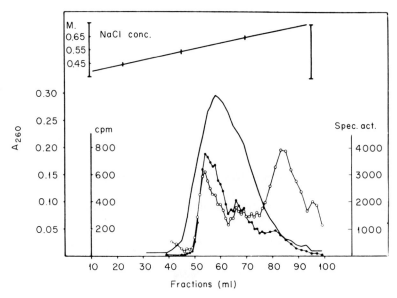

Fig. 11.13. Ability of synthetases from unfertilized eggs of *Paracentrotus lividus* to charge yeast tRNA. Yeast tRNA was charged with [^{14}C]labeled amino acids in an incubation mixture containing aminoacyl–tRNA synthetases from unfertilized eggs. The crude enzyme extract contained 1.2 mg of proteins. The tRNA was fractionated on a methylate albumin kieselguhr (MAK) column. Fractions of 1 ml were collected at a rate of 1 ml/minute and the optical density read at 260 nm. The tRNA was precipitated by adding carrier serum albumin and cold 10% TCA. The precipitate was placed on Millipore filters, washed with TCA, and counted at a 67% efficiency. Optical density, ———— ; counts per minute, ●——● ; specific activity ○——○. (From Ceccarini *et al.*, 1967.)

activity profile following chromatography of the two tRNA's on MAK column. No major differences for several of the tested amino acids were detected under such conditions, with the exception of lysine and methionine. In both cases the radioactivity profile displayed two symmetrical peaks at pluteus and at gastrula, whereas the second peak predominates in the blastula and unfertilized egg (Figs. 11.16 and 11.17). Having always used the same tRNA might level off developmental differences, not from changes in the aminoacyl–tRNA synthetases but in the tRNA itself. On the other hand, the use of a heterologous tRNA might mask the appearance of developmental differences in the synthetase, which might not show in these experiments because they were unmatched by corresponding changes in the tRNA.

d. Transfer RNA

The question of whether tRNA is responsible for the impaired synthesis of protein in the unfertilized egg has so far received a negative answer. The experiments of crossing of cell saps, already mentioned, on the

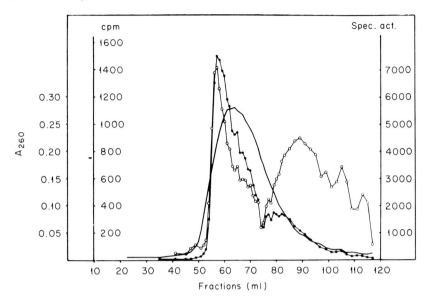

Fig. 11.14. Extracted yeast tRNA was charged with aminoacyl-tRNA synthetases from the early blastula stage. The conditions of incubation were the same as described in Fig. 11.13. Optical density, ————; counts per minute, ●——●; specific activity, ○——○. (From Ceccarini *et al.*, 1967.)

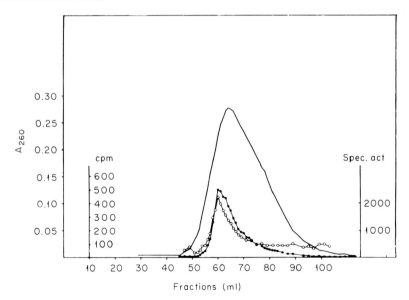

Fig. 11.15. Charging activity of aminoacyl–tRNA synthetases extracted from the pluteus stage on tRNA extracted from baker's yeast. The conditions of incubation and assay are the same as those described in Fig. 11.13. Optical density, ————; counts per minute ●——●; specific activity, ○——○. (From Ceccarini *et al.*, 1967.)

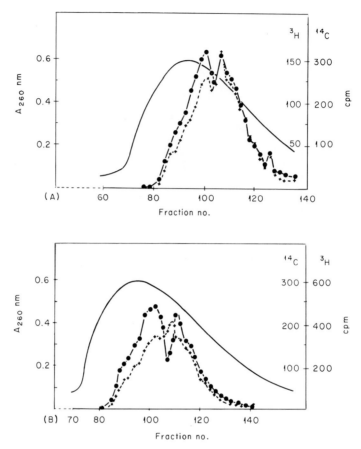

Fig. 11.16. A. Ability of activating enzyme preparations from unfertilized eggs and plutei to charge with lysine an identical preparation of yeast tRNA. ●——●; pluteus [¹⁴C]lysine; +--+, unfertilized egg [³H]lysine. B. Comparison between the ability of activating enzymes from blastulae and gastrulae to charge with lysine an identical preparation of yeast tRNA. ●——●, gastrula [¹⁴C]lysine; +--+, blastula [³H]lysine; ----, absorbances. At the end of the incubation period the charged tRNA was extracted with cold phenol, alcohol-precipitated, and chromatographed on a methylated albumin kieselguhr columns. The absorbance at 260 nm and the TCA-precipitable radioactivity were measured on 10-ml samples. (From Ceccarini and Maggio, 1969.)

whole militate against it. Questions have, however, been asked in this respect by many investigators: Nemer and Bard (1963) found that ribosomes from unfertilized eggs of *Lytechinus pictus,* in the presence of poly U, synthesized about 10 times more polyphenylalanine when exogenous tRNA was added. On the other hand, ribosomes from the zygote stage were stimulated 10-fold and those from the blastula stage were stimulated to synthesize polyphenylalanine almost 7-fold by

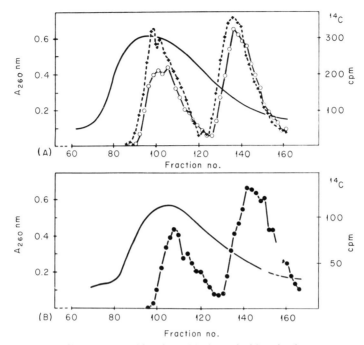

Fig. 11.17. A. Profile of yeast methionyl–tRNA charged with activating enzyme extracted from unfertilized eggs (+--+) and plutei (O———O) of *Paracentrotus lividus*. B. Enzyme extracted from blastulae (●———●); (———) absorbances. Experimental conditions as in Fig. 11.16. (From Ceccarini and Maggio. 1969.)

exogenous tRNA. Moreover, when ribosomes from *Arbacia punctulata* eggs were stimulated to incorporate leucine into proteins by the addition of poly UG, the effect of exogenous tRNA was less than a 2-fold stimulation on ribosomes from unfertilized eggs or zygote and practically zero on ribosomes from the blastula stage. These results suggest an increase of tRNA activity during early development; but, especially because of the lack of difference between the effect of exogenous tRNA on ribosomes from unfertilized eggs and zygote, seem to exclude that the 10- to 14-fold increase in the rate of protein synthesis, which takes place within 1 hour after fertilization, can be even partially attributed to changes in the tRNA activity. In the past this idea received some consideration on the basis of the observation that there is a very active terminal turnover of tRNA after fertilization and a rapid synthesis of tRNA during early development (see Chapter 10).

Finer analyses of the single tRNA classes during development have also been performed, aimed at understanding whether changes in the different classes of tRNA corresponding to different "codons" for the same amino acid can be operative during development in regulating gene

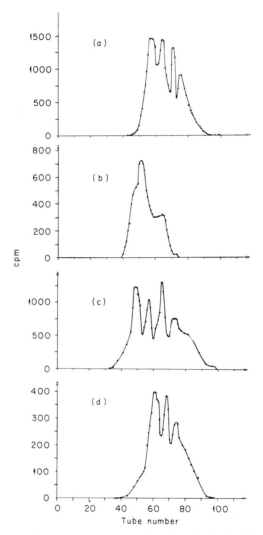

Fig. 11.18. Amino acid-accepting activity of tRNA from fertilized *Paracentrotus lividus* eggs chromatographed on benzoylated DEAE cellulose column and eluted with a linear 0.4–1.0 *M* NaCl gradient, containing 0.01 *M* MgCl$_2$, followed by 1 *M* NaCl in 0.01 *M* MgCl$_2$, containing 9% ethanol. Each fraction was tested for the ability to be charged *in vitro* with radioactive amino acids in the presence of sea urchin cell sap, cofactors and [^{3}H]L-leucine, 1 Ci/mmole (a); [^{14}C]L-tyrosine 50 mCi/mmole (b); [^{3}H]L-arginine, 300 mCi/mmole (c); [^{3}H]DL-serine, 157 mCi/mole (d). (From Molinaro and Mozzi, 1969.)

expression at a translational level. A preliminary analysis was presented by Molinaro and Mozzi (1969). Analysis of the radioactivity elution pattern of tRNA from fertilized egg of *Paracentrotus lividus,* charged with four different amino acids after chromatography on benzoylated

DEAE cellulose column, shows a complex pattern for each of them, suggesting an extensive codon degeneracy (Fig. 11.18). No striking differences were observed, however, when the elution pattern of leucyl–tRNA from the pluteus stage was compared to that of the fertilized eggs.

Zeikus *et al.* (1969) have reported differences in the elution profile from MAK columns between leucyl–tRNA (Fig. 11.19), seryl–tRNA (Fig. 11.20) and lysyl–tRNA (Fig. 11.21) of unfertilized eggs and blastulae of *Strongylocentrotus purpuratus.* The described differences were not altered by inverting the amino acid labeling or the synthetase employed. No differences were found for the elution profile of arginyl–, tyrosyl–, valyl–, phenylalanyl–, and aspartyl–tRNA's of the two studied stages.

It should be mentioned in this context that Yang and Comb (1968) reported a change in the intracellular distribution of the multiple forms of lysyl–tRNA in *Lytechinus variegatus* at the 2-cell stage with respect to the unfertilized eggs (Figs. 11.22 and 11.23). The main change consisted of a decrease of peak II from the 105,000 *g* supernatant following fertilization, accompanied by an increase of this peak in the 105,000 *g* sediment. The significance of this apparent movement is at present unknown, although the suggestion is tempting that this class of tRNA becomes engaged protein synthesis and, therefore, bound to ribosomes following fertilization. Finally, Sharma *et al.* (1971) detected changes in tRNA

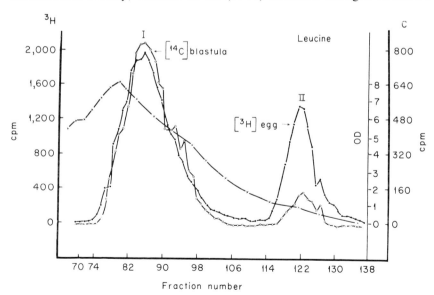

Fig. 11.19. MAK chromatography of [³H] egg and [¹⁴C] blastula leucyl–tRNA of *Strongylocentrotus purpuratus.* Egg tRNA (180 µg) and blastula tRNA (240 µg) were acylated by blastula synthetase, ×——×, OD at 253 nm; ●——●, [³H] egg; o——o, [¹⁴C] blastula. (From Zeikus *et al.,* 1969.)

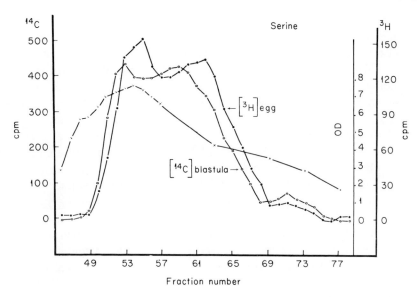

Fig. 11.20. MAK chromatography of [³H] egg and [¹⁴C] blastula seryl–tRNA of *Strongylocentrotus purpuratus*. Egg tRNA (180 μg) and blastula tRNA (240 μg) were acylated by blastula synthetase. ×——×, OD at 254 nm; ●——●, [³H] egg; ○——○, [¹⁴C] blastula. (From Zeikus *et al.*, 1969.)

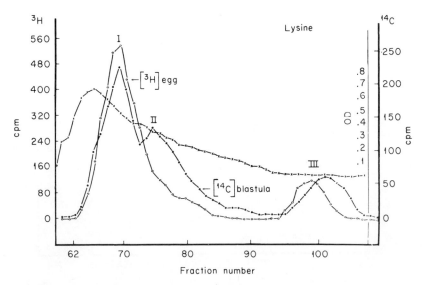

Fig. 11.21. MAK chromatography of [³H] egg and [¹⁴C] blastula lysyl–tRNA of *Strongylocentrotus purpuratus*. Egg tRNA (180 μg) and blastula tRNA (240 μg) were acylated by blastula synthetase. ×——×, OD at 254 nm; ○——○, [³H] egg; ●——●, [¹⁴C] blastula. (From Zeikus *et al.*, 1969.)

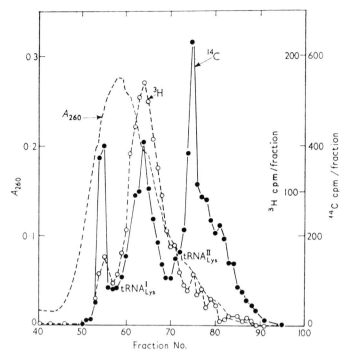

Fig. 11.22. MAK chromatography of [^{14}C]lysyl–tRNA from the soluble fraction (see text) of unfertilized eggs (●—●) of *Lytechinus variegatus* combined with [^{3}H]lysyl–tRNA from the soluble fraction of 2-celled cleavage embryos (O--O); (--), A$_{260}$. (From Yang and Comb, 1968.)

methylation following fertilization of *Strongylocentrotus purpuratus* eggs, namely, that the N$_2$-monomethylguanines decrease by a factor of 2, whereas the methylated uridylic acids increase 3-fold. Other minor changes of the methylated bases were observed throughout development. These changes were detected by *in vivo* labeling experiments with [^{3}H]methionine. The ability of crude enzyme preparations from *Strongylocentrotus* eggs and embryos to methylate bacterial tRNA was also tested. A decrease in enzyme activity following fertilization was observed, but its significance has so far remained unexplained.

To sum up, studies on the control of protein synthesis in unfertilized eggs at the subcellular level have produced the following conclusions: There is general agreement that unfertilized eggs contain less ribosomes actively engaged in protein synthesis in a polyribosomal form, and that the polyribosome content of the egg increases immediately following fertilization. Some authors propose that the impairment of ribosome formation is due to a ribosomal defect possibly affecting chain initiation.

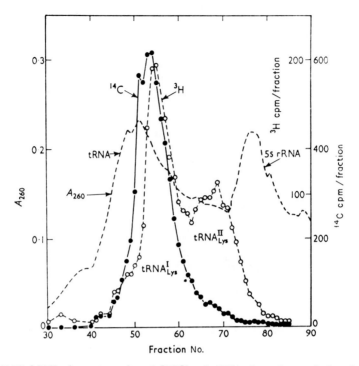

Fig. 11.23. MAK chromatography of [¹⁴C]lysyl–tRNA from the particulate fraction (see text) of unfertilized eggs (●———●) of *Lytechinus variegatus* combined with [³H]lysyl–tRNA from the particulate fraction of 2-celled embryos (O––O); (––), A_{260}. (From Yang and Comb, 1968.)

This idea is based mainly on the possibility of stimulating unfertilized egg ribosome to accept natural templates by trypsin, on the effect of cycloheximide, and finally on the direct demonstration of the presence of two proteins in the 1 M NH_4Cl wash of unfertilized egg ribosomes, which inhibit the attachment of ribosomes to artificial mRNA.

Other authors propose that mRNA is masked by proteins or somehow rendered nonusable by egg ribosomes. This idea is based on sporadic, direct experimental observations and on the lack of gross differences in sedimentation properties, the electrophoretic pattern of proteins, and sensitivity to poly U (controversial) between ribosomes from unfertilized and fertilized eggs.

It has also been claimed that the difference in the optical density profile of polysomes between unfertilized and fertilized eggs is not enough alone to account for the 14-fold increase in the rate of protein synthesis and that inactive polysomes exist in the unfertilized egg. It has been found that the average time for the growth of a single peptide chain does not change following fertilization. Increase in the activity of soluble factors following fertilization has been claimed by some, but denied by many authors. The transfer enzyme has been mentioned as one of the factors involved in such an increase. No differences between the amino-acyl–tRNA-synthetase activity and the tRNA content of unfertilized eggs and newly fertilized eggs have been reported, although such differences have been described between unfertilized eggs and later stages of development.

3. WHAT TRIGGERS PROTEIN SYNTHESIS ACTIVATION AT FERTILIZATION?

Whatever are the changes that bring about the increase of the protein synthesis rate at fertilization, we still do not know which of the events triggers these changes. The first thing to exclude is that the sperm itself may play a specific role in this triggering event. The same changes can be brought about by parthenogenetic activation (Nakano *et al.,* 1958; Giudice and Monroy, 1958; Hultin, 1961b; Gross *et al.,* 1963; Brachet *et al.,* 1963b; Denny and Tyler, 1964; Baltus *et al.,* 1965; Tyler, 1966).

Epel (1967) has asked: How soon does the increase of protein synthesis rate take place following fertilization with respect to other metabolic activities that increase at fertilization? The results of such an investigation can be listed in time-sequence order as follows: (1) cortical granule breakdown; (2) liberation of acid; (3) activation of NAD kinase and of oxygen consumption; (4) activation of protein synthesis [see also the work of Steinhardt *et al.* (1971) in Chapter 4, for a more detailed time-sequence order of these events]. It might be conceived that some energy-dependent process is involved in the mechanism of activation of protein synthesis at fertilization. Actually, Hultin (1964) has demonstrated that this activation is prevented by the administration of DNP, KCN, or chloramphenicol (in doses at which it may also act as an uncoupler). These substances exert their effect both *in vivo* and in cell-free systems. They have been shown to prevent the increase in polysomes *in vivo*.

It should be recalled that the first burst of oxygen consumption is coincident with the phenomenon of membrane elevation and hardening, for which it might be responsible. The slower second respiratory increase (see Chapter 8) partly coincides with the increase of the protein synthesis rate and partly follows it, as will be discussed later.

More recently, Timourian and Watchmaker (1970) reinvestigated the question of how soon the increase of the protein synthesis rate takes place after fertilization. They observed that the data of Rinaldi and Monroy (1969), which show an increase of the polysomal population within 2 minutes after fertilization, cannot be reconciled with the data of Epel (1967), which describe this increase as a relatively "late" phenomenon.

According to Timourian and Watchmaker, if radioactive amino acids are given to the eggs, a temporary loss of labeled proteins from the egg takes place immediately following fertilization. If such a phenomenon is taken into account and the data of incorporation of amino acids into proteins are corrected accordingly, it is found that the increase of the protein synthesis rate occurs within 2 minutes after fertilization.

As will be discussed in Chapter 12, many authors have reported an increase of proteolytic activities at fertilization. According to the theories that call for proteic inhibitors of protein synthesis at the level of ribosomes or mRNA, this protease activation might be responsible for removal of the inhibitor. Direct proof of this is lacking, except for the experiments by Mano and Nagano (1966, 1970; Mano, 1966), already discussed.

Hand (1971) reported that treatment of entire unfertilized eggs of *Lytechinus pictus* or *Dendraster excentricus* with trypsin brings about an activation of protein synthesis. The phenomenon can be explained by a simple parthenogenetic activation of the egg in the sand dollar, but not in the sea urchin. How much this treatment mimics what really happens at fertilization is difficult to establish.

It can be speculated that many of the physiological changes taking place at fertilization (see Chapter 4) are involved in the activation of protein synthesis. Among them, one of the most interesting candidates appears to be the dramatic change in permeability to K^+ ions, which brings about drastic changes in the intracellular ionic conditions, which may in turn be responsible for various metabolic changes. However, no direct evidence for such correlations are available as yet.

Finally, Mackintosh and Bell (1967, 1969a,b,c) have directed their attention to the mechanism by which the reduction of the protein synthesis rate is brought about in the unfertilized egg. In preliminary experiments, attempting to prevent the synthesis of a proteic inhibitor, these authors found that temporary treatment of unfertilized eggs (but not of oocytes or embryos; Mackintosh and Bell, 1970), of *Arbacia punctulata* with puromycin led to a subsequent doubling of the rate of protein synthesis of the unfertilized eggs. A similar effect was obtained by temporary exposure of the eggs to anaerobic conditions, by bubbling N_2 through seawater. Later, they succeeded in stimulating the protein synthesis rate of unfertilized eggs of *Arbacia punctulata* and *Strongylocentrotus purpuratus* to levels comparable to those of the fertilized eggs by removal of CO_2 from seawater. The authors claim that this treatment does not result in egg activation, as proved by the possibility to fertilize the eggs so treated. The authors do not suggest, however, that the accumulation of CO_2 in the eggs is to be considered as the actual cause of the block to protein synthesis in the unfertilized egg. In fact, they produced some direct evidence that GTP and ATP are present at the same level and equally available before and after fertilization. Whatever the inhibition mechanism may be, this approach makes the point that the phenomenon we are dealing with is, in all probability, not an increase in a normal rate of protein synthesis, but the release from an inhibition that was established during late maturation of the oocyte.

Harris (1967a) proposed that this block is brought about by sequestering the ribosomes in "heavy bodies" (see Chapter 2). Even if the appearance of such structures coincides with the time of establishment of the block, it does not seem likely that a simple sequestering of ribosomes would be responsible for such a block for the following reasons: (1) The number of ribosomes (if any) enclosed in heavy bodies is a small percentage of the total; (2) upon cell fractionation these should either sediment with the heavy particulate, thus depleting the postmitochondrial supernatant of a certain percentage of ribosomes, or be liberated and, therefore, available for protein synthesis in cell-free systems. Of course these two arguments do not disprove that heavy bodies may somehow be involved in the block of protein synthesis.

D. Rate of Protein Synthesis throughout Development

This study has been biased by the possibility of changes in permeability or in pool size. The first investigation by Giudice *et al.* (1962) fundamentally showed that both the rate of uptake and that of incorporation of amino acids into the proteins of *Paracentrotus lividus* undergo two phases of increase, one lasting from fertilization until about the 4- to 8-blastomere stage and the other one from mesenchyme blastula up to early gastrula stage (Fig. 11.24). When the increases in incorporation rates were corrected for the increases in uptake rates, the two curves shown in Fig. 11.25 resulted. In other words, the second increase in incorporation was still visible and the first only in the case of methionine. Both of them were, however, attenuated.

Subsequent experiments by Berg (1965) confirmed the existence of two major periods of acceleration in the rate of protein synthesis in *Lytechinus anamnesus*: the first from fertilization through cleavage and the second from hatching to early gastrula, i.e., roughly but not exactly coincident with those described by Giudice *et al.* (1962). A similar biphasic curve has been reported by several authors: Neifakh and Krigsgaber (1968) in *Strongylocentrotus nudus* found that a first increase of the incorporation rate up to mid-blastula is followed by a slight decrease, and by a second increase at the beginning of gastrulation. No data on the rate of uptake are reported. Ellis (1966) confirmed the two increase periods of incorporation rate in *Arbacia punctulata*: one after fertilization and a second one after

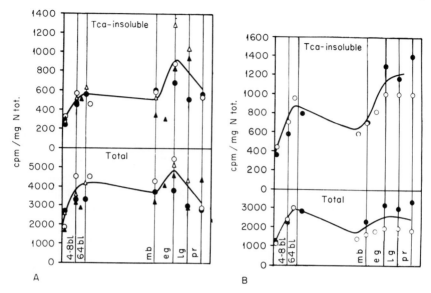

Fig. 11.24. Rate of uptake of [³⁵S]methionine (A) and [¹⁴C]leucine (B) in the total eggs and embryos and in the TCA-insoluble fraction of *Paracentrotus lividus*. Vertical lines indicate stages of development. 4–8 bl, 4–8-cell stage; 64 bl, 64-cell stage; mb, mesenchyme blastula; eg, early gastrula; lg, late gastrula; pr, prism; pl, pluteus. (From Giudice *et al.*, 1962.)

the mesenchyme blastula, but again with no data on total uptake. Bellemare *et al.* (1968) studied the rate of uptake and incorporation of radioactive leucine up to the blastula stage of *Strongylocentrotus purpuratus*. Their results agree fundamentally with those of Giudice *et al.* Berg also stresses the importance of more or less parallel variations in the rate of uptake, suggesting that the data should always be corrected for the variations in amino acid uptake. When this correction is made very little difference is seen between the incorporation rate of early blastulae and gastrulae. Moreover, this author draws attention to two facts: (1) The complexity of the curves of uptake and incorporation, which, besides the two major periods of acceleration, show many minor irregularities; and (2) the great variability of the results. Even if we agree with this latter observation, and acknowledge the great detail with which these curves have been built, we are inclined to believe that the use of a large amount of embryos (about 100/experimental point in Berg's data; 10⁶ in Giudice *et al.*'s), brings about a lower scattering of the results.

   The correction for the variations of uptake, however, does not account for errors deriving from possible variations in the internal pool. Direct measurements of the internal pool were performed by Fry and Gross (1970b). On the basis of the data on the rate of uptake and the size of the

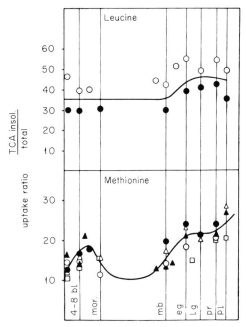

Fig. 11.25. Incorporation of radioactive amino acids into the TCA-insoluble fraction of *Paracentrotus lividus* embryos at various developmental stages as percent of the total uptake. Abbreviations as in Fig. 11.24; mor, morula. (From Giudice *et al.,* 1962.)

internal pool, these authors reached the following important conclusions: *Arbacia punctulata* embryo synthesize protein at a rate of 12×10^{-6} μg of proteins/embryo/minute during early cleavage, corresponding to a complete turnover of the endogenous pool (at least for leucine) in 5 minutes. If we assume that this rate is maintained constant over a 24-hour period, since there is no net increase in the protein mass of the embryos up to late prism, this would mean that about 45% of the yolk is broken down to be utilized, via the pool, for the synthesis of cellular proteins. These authors stress the variability of the experimental data, but are inclined to believe that, after the proper corrections are made, i.e., for the rate of uptake, there is essentially no difference in the protein synthesis rate between the 2-cell stage and blastula.

We have already mentioned that in his latest paper Berg (1970) has revised the interpretation of his own data on the kinetics of uptake and incorporation of exogenous amino acids added at different levels of concentration. This author has devised a method for measuring the actual protein synthesis rate in sea urchins. This is based on the consideration that at high exogenous amino acid levels the internal pool can be expanded to an upper level at which the author presumes the internal specific activity of

TABLE 11.6

AMOUNT OF PROTEIN SYNTHESIZED AT THE EARLY GASTRULA STAGE OF THE
SEA URCHIN *Lytechinus*[a,b]

Embryo batch	Stage	Amino acid	Incorporation rate of labeled amino acid 10^{-5} μg/ embryo/hour	Protein amino acid (average) 10^{-3} μg/ embryo	Amount of protein synthesized	
					10^{-4} μg/ embryo/hour	% of total protein/hour
a	Early gastrula	[^{14}C] Val	4.4	—	7.1	0.83
b	Early gastrula	[^{14}C] Val	4.7	—	7.6	0.89
c	Early gastrula	[^{14}C] Val	4.0	—	6.5	0.75
d	Mesenchyme blastula	[^{14}C] Val	4.0	—	6.5	0.75
d	Mesenchyme blastula	[^{14}C] Val	4.7	5.3	7.6	0.89
e	Mesenchyme blastula	[^{14}C] Pro	3.7	—	8.4	0.97
f	Early gastrula	[^{14}C] Pro	3.5	3.8	8.0	0.92
g	Early gastrula	[^{14}C] Ala	6.4	—	12.8	1.45
g	Early gastrula	[^{14}C] Ala	5.1	4.4	10.2	1.16
h	Early gastrula	[^{14}C] His	1.9	—	8.6	1.00
i	Early gastrula	[^{14}C] His	1.5	1.9	6.8	0.79
j	Early gastrula	[^{14}C] Phe	3.9	—	8.1	0.93
k	Early gastrula	[^{14}C] Phe	3.2	4.2	6.7	0.76
j	Early gastrula	[^{14}C] Thr	5.3	—	10.4	1.20
k	Early gastrula	[^{14}C] Thr	3.5	4.4	6.9	0.80

[a]From Berg and Mertes (1970).

[b]Incorporation rates from the amino acid pool were measured in embryos preloaded with labeled amino acids; protein amino acids were measured in hydrolyzates of the acid-insoluble fractions of embryos.

the labeled amino acid to be equal to that of the external medium. Embryos of *Lytechinus anamnesus* were preloaded with radioactive amino acids to full expansion of the internal pool and the increase in the specific activity of the proteins measured at brief intervals (Berg and Mertes, 1970). The results of such an experimental approach are not too far off from those reported by Fry and Gross (1970b) (Table 11.6). The amount of turnover of the newly synthesized protein, which might have complicated the calculation, was shown by the same authors to be very low (Table 11.7).

In conclusion, two clear phases of acceleration of protein synthesis are observed during sea urchin development: one from fertilization up to early cleavage and the second from about mesenchyme blastula up to early gastrula. However, they more or less disappear when the parallel increase of the rate of amino acid uptake is considered. On the other hand,

TABLE 11.7

Turnover of Labeled Proteins in Embryos of the Sea Urchin *Lytechinus* as Measured by the Decrease of Acid-Insoluble Label from Late Cleavage to the Early Pluteus Stage[a,b]

Expt No.	Acid-insoluble label at late cleavage stage (cpm/100 embryos)	Acid-insoluble label at mid-gastrula stage (cpm/100 embryos)	Acid-insoluble label at early pluteus stage (cpm/100 embryos)	% loss of label/hour during cleavage-gastrula interval	% loss of label/hour during gastrula-pluteus interval
1	469 ± 10	359 ± 13	302 ± 9	1.3	0.6
2	646 ± 19	573 ± 12	421 ± 10	0.7	0.9
3	518 ± 10	410 ± 12	357 ± 9	1.2	0.5
4	112 ± 2	94 ± 4	73 ± 3	0.8	1.0
5	738 ± 9	619 ± 13	—	0.9	—
6	373 ± 12	335 ± 9	—	0.6	—
7	—	1550 ± 43	1293 ± 27	—	0.7
8	—	1340 ± 27	1242 ± 42	—	0.4
9	—	2240 ± 68	1930 ± 62	—	0.7
10	—	717 ± 4	571 ± 19	—	1.0

[a] From Berg and Mertes (1970).
[b] Expts 1–6: Proteins were labeled with [14C]valine shortly after fertilization; expts 7–10: proteins labeled with [14C]valine at the mesenchyme blastula stage. Embryos were reared in [12C]valine after depletion of the pool label.

the question has arisen (Chapter 4) of considering the possibility that the machinery for amino acid uptake is set at a higher rate of work because of an increased rate of protein synthesis in certain developmental periods. It should be recalled that Hultin and Bergstrand (1960) found increasing ability for amino acid incorporation in cell-free systems, at least up to blastula; Giudice (1962b) found that the variations of rate of amino acid incorporation of embryos around the gastrula stage is retained by the corresponding total homogenates. However, Stavy and Gross (1969b) have not been able to detect differences in the amino acid-incorporating activity of cell-free systems from the 2-cell stage up to blastula. On the other hand, the continuous increase in the polysomal population at least up to the blastula stage has been repeatedly confirmed.

In our opinion, the question of the actual variation of the overall rate of protein synthesis throughout development still remains to be defined in certain fundamental aspects.

E. Rate of Protein Synthesis through the Cell Cycle

Sea urchin eggs have been used to study the rate of protein synthesis in the various phases of the cell cycle. In particular, the question has been asked if there is a slowdown of the protein synthesis rate during meta-phase, as observed for cultured mammalian cells.

Gross and Fry (1966) failed to observe any slowdown of the protein synthesis rate at the metaphase of the first two cleavages of *Strongy-locentrotus purpuratus* eggs; but Sofer *et al.* (1966) reported that the rate of incorporation of exogenous [^{14}C]leucine into the proteins of eggs of *Lytechinus variegatus* does increase from fertilization up to breakdown of the nuclear membrane for the first prophase; a plateau follows during metaphase and anaphase, which is then followed by a second increase. The same curve is obtained in the presence of colchicine, which inhibits cytokinesis. These authors reported that the cell-free system retains the same phasic properties.

Variable results were reported by Timourian (1966) for both *Ly-techinus pictus* and *Strongylocentrotus purpuratus*. This author em-phasizes that he was not able to decide between the two hypotheses after a long series of attempts alternatively pointing to both possibilities. More recently, Fry and Gross (1970a) acknowledged that eggs of *Arbacia lixula* and *Strongylocentrotus purpuratus* show a transitory decrease in the rate both of amino acid uptake and incorporation at metaphase but, differing from what appears to be the case in HeLa cells, this decrease does not exceed 15% of the previous rate. The decrease is not dependent on karyo-kinesis or cytokinesis; moreover, when the decrease of the protein syn-thesis rate is corrected for the decrease in the amino acid uptake rate, it completely disappears. On the other hand, Mano (1968) confirmed that eggs of *Pseudocentrotus depressus,* cultured at two different tempera-tures, show cyclic oscillations of the incorporation rate of amino acids into proteins for the first three cell divisions. The cycles persist in the presence of colchicine and of low doses of puromycin or cycloheximide, which cause a partial inhibition of protein synthesis. The addition of sodium fluoride blocks the variations of the incorporation rates. These differences in the protein synthesis rate would be retained by a cell-free system, which this author prepares in a very special way: homogenization in seawater. Mano (1970) has also reported that a 12,000 g supernatant of fertilized eggs of *Pseudocentrotus depressus, Anthocidaris crassispina,* and *Strongylocentrotus nudus* undergoes *in vitro* cyclic variations of its polysome content, to which specular variations of the protease activity correspond. Mano (1969) claimed that the 12,000 g supernatant of ferti-lized eggs of *Hemicentrotus pulcherrimus* and *Anthocidaris crassispina* contains a factor that, when added to the unfertilized egg 12,000 g super-natant, stimulates the latter to initiate protein synthesis at a rate that undergoes cyclic variations. This factor consists of a macromolecular part (replaceable by egg RNA) and of an unidentified micromolecular part. Moreover, the 12,000 g supernatant contains a KCl-soluble protein that undergoes ·cyclic variations in SH content and is responsible for the cyclic protein synthetic activity, spontaneous in the fertilized eggs or induced by the factors in the unfertilized egg supernatant. This SH-rich protein seems to influence the aminoacyl–tRNA synthetase reaction and the binding of aminoacyl–tRNA to ribosomes.

In view of these very unusual findings and their contrast with many of the other reports discussed, it would appear advisable to wait for confirmation of these results before expressing any opinion on them.

Meeker and Iverson (1971) have shown cyclic waves of synthesis of tubulin during cleavage, with a slowdown during metaphase. Moreover, the amount of tubulin detectable on polysomes by [^{3}H]colchicine binding, probably representing growing tubulin chains, also decreases during metaphase.

F. Synthesis of Specific Proteins during Sea Urchin Development

Up to now we have been dealing with the quantitative aspect of protein synthesis. Its interest lies chiefly in using it as a model for the study of regulatory mechanisms. In this respect, it seems more relevant to study the qualitative changes that take place in protein synthesis during development, with the hope that they may provide a model for the study of the molecular mechanisms of differentiation. It must not be forgotten, however, that what seems to be a qualitative change may turn out to be only a quantitative one upon finer analysis.

The earlier approaches to the problem of changes in the protein population of the developing sea urchin were made by Perlmann and Gustafson (1948), Perlmann (1953), Perlmann and Couffer-Kaltenbach (1964), Ranzi (1957), Ishida and Yasumasu (1957), and Couffer-Kaltenbach and Perlmann (1961). These authors demonstrated by means of serological methods that adult proteins appear in measurable amounts for the first time after the mesenchyme blastula stage. These earlier findings have recently been confirmed by Westin *et al.* (1967) and Westin (1969), who have shown that alterations of the pattern of protein synthesis, which they found at the mesenchyme blastula stage, is blocked by actinomycin D. We have already mentioned (Chapter 7) that Badman and Brookbank (1970), by means of a sensitive immunological test failed to detect any appearance of new antigens even after the gastrula stage. The importance of this finding lies in the fact that whatever the relevance of the synthesis of new protein is in the process of differentiation in the early development, as discussed in Chapter 7, the amount of newly arising different proteins certainly does not represent a high proportion of the total amount of protein being synthesized during early embryogenesis.

The search for the synthesis of a specific class of proteins in this developmental period has proceeded in an effort to find a model for the molecular approach to the study of differentiation, viewed as synthesis of specific proteins at specific times.

Good candidates for this purpose have appeared: (a) ciliary proteins, (b) mitotic apparatus proteins, (c) histones, (d) enzymatic proteins, and (e) skeleton matrix. Proteins of the mitotic apparatus and histones cannot be considered as specific for a differentiated kind of cell. However, their synthesis has been studied because it was thought that, owing to the great mitotic activity of the cleavage stage, their synthesis might be very active during this period, and also in view of the fact that very little is known today about the mechanism of regulation of the synthesis of a special class of proteins in general, and of the mechanism of synthesis of histones in particular.

1. CILIARY PROTEINS

Auclair and Siegel (1966a,b) reported that it is possible to remove the cilia of swimming embryos of *Paracentrotus lividus* by brief exposure to seawater made 2-fold osmolar by addition of 29.2 gm of NaCl to 1 liter of normal seawater. When returned to normal seawater the embryos quickly started to regenerate their cilia at a rate of elongation of about 1/5 μ/minute for 2–3 hours to their original length (24–25μ). Only the apical tuft was not regenerated to its original length. During the process of cilia regeneration there was an increase in the specific rate of amino acid incorporation into the proteins of the cilia, isolated after regeneration, with respect to the overall embryonic proteins. The addition of actinomycin D at 25 μg/ml did not affect either amino acid incorporation or cilia regeneration. This result is in agreement with those presented in Chapter 10 on the presence of long-lived messenger for the normal appearance of cilia during development. However, the addition of puromycin at 50 μg/ml strongly inhibited amino acid incorporation in both total proteins and ciliary proteins. In spite of this, cilia regeneration was normal. The authors conclude, therefore, that a large pool of ciliary proteins exists in the embryo, which can account for the possibility of cilia regeneration in the absence of protein synthesis. The embryos are able to regenerate cilia four times in the presence of puromycin. It would be useful, as a final control, to check the effect of puromycin on permeability to exogenous amino acids so as to exclude completely the possibility of masked synthesis of proteins unrevealed under the above conditions.

Iwaikawa (1967) confirms that embryos from blastula to pluteus of the sea urchins *Anthocidaris crassispina, Pseudocentrotus depressus, Hemicentrotus pulcherrimus,* and *Temnopleurus toreumaticus* can be stripped five times of their cilia by treatment with hypertonic seawater and their regeneration capacity remains unaffected. Auclair and Siegel suggest that the ciliary proteins may have much in common with the proteins of the mitotic apparatus, since colchicine at $10^{-4}\,M$ inhibits both ciliary growth and organization of the mitotic apparatus. Tilney and Gibbins (1968) found that colchicine or high hydrostatic pressure causes the disassembly of cytoplasmic microtubules of the gastrula cells, which might, at least in part, be related to the mitotic apparatus, but which do not affect the ciliar microtubules. The authors suggest, however, that the fundamental sub-units of the two kinds of microtubules are the same, but that the ciliar ones might be stabilized by the addition of some other material. Iverson (1971) found that polysomes of embryos of *Lytechinus variegatus* de-ciliated five times are engaged more actively in the synthesis of tubulin, as judged by the ability of colchicine to bind the peptide chains growing on polysomes. These observations lead us to the study of synthesis of the proteins of the mitotic apparatus.

2. MITOTIC APPARATUS PROTEINS

The attempts to identify and isolate the proteins representing the sub-units of the spindle have been described in detail in Chapter 5. We shall limit ourselves to the question of whether a substantial proportion of the proteins synthesized during early cleavage is represented by spindle pro-teins. Actually, as discussed by Mazia (1961), it seems that in the egg there is a reserve of spindle proteins (see, also, Rebhun and Sawada, 1969); one of the main arguments is the observation by Went (1959) that it is possible to detect, immunologically, proteins of the mitotic apparatus in the unfertilized egg. On the other hand, it has been shown that puro-mycin blocks cleavage (Hultin, 1961a). However, if the antibiotic is added 30 minutes after fertilization, first cleavage is allowed to proceed (Wilt *et al.,* 1967).

Earlier observations by Gross and Cousineau (1963b) provided histo-autoradiographic evidence for the concentration of radioactivity from exogenous-supplied [^{3}H]leucine in the mitotic apparatus during the first two cleavages of *Arbacia punctulata* eggs.

In subsequent work, Mangan *et al.* (1965) reported that electron-microscopical autoradiography reveals a certain accumulation of radio-activity from exogenously labeled amino acids in the fibrous part of the mitotic apparatus of *Arbacia punctulata* eggs. Analysis by filtration on Sephadex G-200 of the proteins of the mitotic apparatus dissolved by urea, shows four peaks of radioactivity.

Bibring and Cousineau (1964) confirmed that part of the radioactivity from labeled amino acids administered following fertilization can be re-covered in the isolated mitotic apparatus of *Paracentrotus lividus* eggs.

Stafford and Iverson (1964) reported similar findings upon auto-radiographic examination of the isolated mitotic apparatus of *Lytechinus variegatus* and *Echinometra lucunter* eggs. The latter authors also reported that the isolated mitotic apparatus is still able to incorporate [^{14}C]leucine into its proteins, probably because of the presence of ribosomes within the mitotic apparatus preparation. It should be recalled that Gross *et al.* (1958) described a concentration of ribosomes in areas where the perinuclear "prespindle" is observed at the electron microscope, and that Hartman and Zimmerman (1968) characterized, by sucrose gradient analysis, ribosomes extracted from mitotic apparatus preparations obtained by hexylene glycol. R. A. Rinaldi (1967) reported autoradiographic evidence for *in vivo* incorporation of labeled amino acids into the mitotic apparatus of cleaving eggs, even if no special concentration of the radioactive tracks over it was detected. Moreover, Wilt *et al.* (1967) found that [^{3}H]leucine administered to eggs of *Strongylocentrotus purpuratus* becomes incorporated into the proteins of the mitotic apparatus.

Bibring and Cousineau (1964) and Mangan *et al.* (1965) showed that 10% of the radioactivity incorporated into the fertilized egg proteins is due to synthesis of the spindle. Since it has been reported (Mazia and Roslansky, 1956) that the mitotic apparatus represents about 10% of the egg protein, these figures seem at a first glance to suggest an *ex novo* synthesis of the mitotic apparatus.

Two corrections have to be made: First, the figure given by Mazia and Roslansky refers to gross preparations of mitotic apparatus, which very probably include many other elements besides the spindle proteins. Indeed, Cohen and Rebhun (1970) estimated that the microtubular proteins of the spindle at first metaphase represent about 0.1% of the total egg proteins. Second, the amount of the overall proteins synthesized by the egg during one cleavage does not exceed 1% of the total proteins of the eggs (see Table 11.6).

Mangan *et al.* (1965) reported that the specific activity in the isolated mitotic apparatus proteins is about 3 times that of the average proteins.

Wilt *et al.* (1967) dissolved the isolated mitotic apparatus in 0.53 M KCl and analyzed the distribution of the incorporated radioactivity after centrifugation on a sucrose density gradient. The radioactivity was distributed rather uniformly throughout the gradient except for a slight peak at 22 S and a very clear peak at 3.5 S. The specific activity of the KCl-soluble proteins was equal to that of the average proteins. An insoluble residue, however, representing about 15% of the total mitotic apparatus, exhibited a much higher specific activity. The conclusion was that, while they agree with other authors that synthesis of the mitotic apparatus does not represent the major part of the proteins synthesized by the cleaving egg, probably some very important part of the mitotic apparatus is synthesized *ex novo*. Of course, to determine which parts of the mitotic apparatus need to be synthesized *ex novo* for cleavage to take place and to proceed, requires a complete purification of the proteins constituting such a complex structure, in order to be properly performed.

Recently, Meeker and Iverson (1971) isolated the "tubulin" from cleaving eggs pulse-labeled with radioactive amino acids. Tubulin purification was accomplished in two ways: by precipitation with vinblastine and by the method of Weisenberg *et al.* (1968); tubulin was then identified by its ability to bind colchicine. The results clearly show that tubulin is synthesized by the cleaving eggs. Raff *et al.* (1971) have found synthesis of microtubular proteins during cleavage, but stress the fact that there is a store of these proteins in the unfertilized egg. By acrylamide gel electrophoresis two major bands were identified in the preparation of microtubular proteins, which are identical to the A and B microtubular proteins from the cilia. The same authors (1972) also proved by means of different indirect criteria that the synthesis of microtubular proteins proceeds during cleavage on maternal templates. This synthesis becomes accelerated (even more than that of the other proteins) from fertilization to cleavage.

An interesting approach aimed at isolating tubulin in bulk amount from sea urchin eggs was presented by Bryan (1971), who succeeded in inducing the formation of crystalline bodies by vinblastine treatment in eggs of *Strongylocentrotus purpuratus*. The author has developed a procedure to purify these crystals, which are believed to represent microtubules because their induction is enhanced by heavy water and inhibited by extreme temperatures or mercaptoethanol.

It should finally be mentioned that—as expected from the fact that actinomycin D does not block cleavage—for the mitotic apparatus proteins to be synthesized, the template RNA's for their synthesis must already be present in the unfertilized egg. Experiments where RNA synthesis (but not protein synthesis) has been blocked by D_2O treatment (Gross and Spindel, 1960; Gross and Harding, 1961; Marsland and Zimmerman, 1963; Gross and Cousineau, 1963b) have shown that the eggs form a large number of cytasters, which, upon removal of D_2O, form several multipolar spindles in each blastomere.

3. HISTONES

Infante and Nemer (1967) stated that two main classes of polyribosomes appear following fertilization in *Strongylocentrotus purpuratus* (see Fig. 11.10): one class of about 300 S (r-polysomes), which increases during the first 2–3 hours following fertilization, then stays constant up to blastula, and finally increases again, and another class of smaller polysomes (s-polysomes) of about 200 S. The latter appear and increase between 4 and 10 hours following fertilization, then decrease again. If actinomycin D, at 25 μg/ml, is present from the time of fertilization, the large polysomes appear as usual and only fail to undergo the final increase, which follows the blastula stage in normal development. The small ones do not appear under such conditions. This is in agreement with the previous observations by the same authors and confirmed by others (see Chapter 10) that the large polysomes bind little of the new RNA, which is preferentially bound to the small ones. On the other hand, it had been observed that, when radioactive amino acids are given to the cleaving embryos, most of the incorporation takes place in the heavy polysomes (Spirin and Nemer, 1965). This had led these authors to believe that the small polysomes were little active in protein synthesis during cleavage, and to suggest that their low activity might have been due to the fact that their messenger was still partially in the form of informosome, i.e., still partially bound to some regulatory protein that prevented the ribosomal flow through the mRNA for translation.

Kedes and Gross (1969a) in *Arbacia punctulata* confirmed the results by Spirin and Nemer (1965) and Infante and Nemer (1967), but interpreted them differently. They observed that if one considers that the smaller polysomes bear shorter growing peptide chains than the larger ones, it can be expected, after *in vivo* pulses with radioactive amino acids, that the radioactivity on the small polysomes is lower than on the large ones. Actually, if one corrects the data for this factor, the results show (see Figs. 11.26 and 11.27) that all classes of polysomes are working at the same rate during cleavage. These calculations are based on the assumption that the smaller polysomes have shorter mRNA, which was directly proved (see Chapter 10). All the pulse-labeled RNA associated with polysomes at the morula stage, under the conditions set up by Kedes and Gross (1969a), was displaced to the top regions of the sucrose gradient by treatment with EDTA or with puromycin, while the polysomal optical density was moved to the subunits or monomere regions. The object of this procedure was to show that all of the RNA being studied could really be considered as engaged in protein synthesis as polysomal mRNA. Kedes and Gross (1969b) completed their observations by attributing a function to the new RNA, found in the light polysomal regions, i.e., those that fail to appear in the presence of actinomycin D. As described in Chapter 10, they isolated from these polysomal regions a 9 S RNA; by electrophoresis this was subdivided into three main classes, which, it was suggested, serve as template for histone synthesis. As proof, Kedes et al. (1969) provided the following observations:

    1. About 50% of the radioactivity from exogenous amino acids given

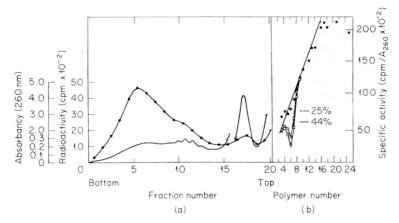

Fig. 11.26. Sucrose density gradient patterns of 15,000 g supernatant from amino acid-labeled 32- to 64-cell stage *Arbacia punctulata* embryos (a) and the relationship between specific activity and polyribosome polymer number (b). A. ———. Absorbancy at 260 nm; ●——●, protein radioactivity. Labeling was for 10 minutes with 1 μCi of [^{14}C]leucine/ml; 24% of the total ribosomal optical density sediments in the polyribosome region of the gradient. B. (●) Specific activities calculated from the polyribosome pattern. The solid line is the theoretical specific activity expected at each polymer number using the octamer as a standard; o--o and ▢——▢ are the expected deviations from the theoretical specific activity if two subpopulations of small polyribosomes (representing either 25% or 44% of the total from trimer to monomers) contributed optical density but not radioactivity to the polyribosome pattern. (From Kedes and Gross, 1969a.)

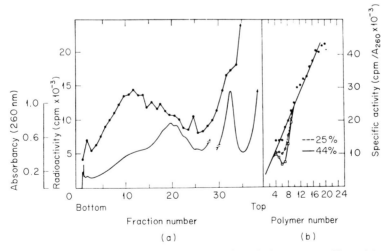

Fig. 11.27. Sucrose gradient pattern (a) and relationship between specific activity and polyribosome polymer number (b) of early swimming blastulae of *Arbacia punctulata*. Labeling for 10 minutes with 2 μCi of [^{14}C]amino acid mixture/ml; 40% of the ribosomes sediment as polyribosomes. Other details as in Fig. 11.26. (From Kedes and Gross, 1969a.)

during cleavage to *Arbacia punctulata* embryos is incorporated into nuclear proteins, as shown by electron microscope autoradiography and by study of the isolated nuclei.

2. If [³H]tryptophan and [¹⁴C]lysine are given to the embryos during cleavage the ratio of the two isotopes in the light polysome regions is more in favor of lysine than in other regions of the gradient (Fig. 11.28).

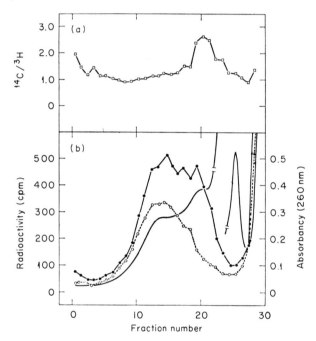

Fig. 11.28. Asymmetric distribution of lysine and tryptophan incorporation ratios. Embryos at 32- to 64-cell stage were concentrated in 4 volumes seawater and labeled for 10 minutes with [¹⁴C]lysine (2 μCi/ml) and [³H]tryptophan (10 μCi/ml). The embryos were washed twice with iced calcium magnesium-free seawater and polyribosomes prepared on sucrose density gradients as described previously (Kedes and Gross, 1969a). Final precipitation of proteins was with 10% trichloroacetic acid onto Millipore filters which were dried and counted in a Beckman liquid scintillation counter. Spillover of ¹⁴C into the ³H channel was 24% and appropriate corrections were made. The ¹⁴C/³H ratio of each fraction was calculated and normalized to the average ratio of fractions from the heavy polyribosome region (fractions 6 to 15). The normalized ratios are plotted in (a); (b) represents the polyribosomes and radioactivity distribution in the sucrose density gradient: (———) OD $_{260}$; (–●–●–), [¹⁴C]lysine cpm; (--o--o--), [³H]tryptophan cpm. (From Kedes *et al.,* 1969.)

3. When DNA synthesis is blocked by treatment with hydroxyurea (Fig. 11.29), the excess of lysine incorporated into the light polysome region markedly decreases.

4. In the presence of actinomycin, which suppresses appearance of the light polysomes, there is a reduction of 20–40% of the accumulation of

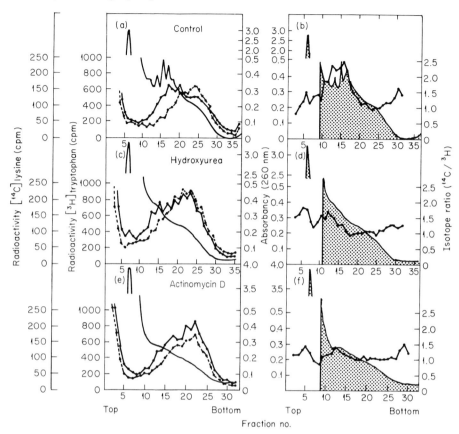

Fig. 11.29. Effect of hydroxyurea and actinomycin on the lysine/tryptophan ratios of nascent peptides on polyribosomes. One third of the eggs from a single female were fertilized after a 30-minute exposure to actinomycin (25 μg/ml) and cultured with the drug continuously. When the control culture reached 16- to 32-cell stage, half was made 1 mM in hydroxyurea. After 90 minutes the control and hydroxyurea-treated cultures were concentrated and labeled with [¹⁴C]lysine and [³H]tryptophan as described in the text and legend of Fig. 11.28. The actinomycin culture was labeled 1 hour later when it had reached a morphological stage comparable to the control. Polyribosomes were prepared by sucrose density gradient centrifugation and examined for optical density and radioactivity (left panels) as described in Fig. 11.28. The normalized isotope ratios are plotted in the right-hand panels superimposed on the optical density patterns of the polyribosomes (shaded areas) for reference. (From Kedes *et al.*, 1969.)

radioactivity at nuclear level. The latter observation is partially in agreement with the data reported by Lindsay (1969), which show that no inhibition of amino acid incorporation into histones by actinomycin is observed up to hatching, but a severe inhibition takes place after that stage in *Strongylocentrotus purpuratus*. The data by Lindsay (1969) and Thaler *et al.* (1970) also explain how, even if histone synthesis represents about 25% of the total protein synthesis during cleavage (Kedes *et al.*, 1969; Nemer and Lindsay, 1969), no inhibition of the overall rate of protein synthesis in the presence of actinomycin has ever been observed before hatching. According to Thaler *et al.* (1970), actinomycin D inhibits valine incorporation into the lysine-rich histones in *Arbacia* embryos between fertilization and the blastula stage, but at the same time stimulates incorporation into the arginine-rich histones. These authors suggest then that a mechanism might exist through which high rates of synthesis of some embryonic proteins are maintained, when the synthesis of others is inhibited because of the lack of new templates.

At the same time, and independently of Kedes and co-workers (1969), Nemer and Lindsay (1969) reported very similar observations and the same conclusions on *Strongylocentrotus purpuratus*. Here again, in the zone of small polyribosomes, the ratio of incorporation of [^{14}C]arginine to [^{3}H]tryptophan is about 3 times higher than in other polysomal fractions (Fig. 11.30), from which it was calculated that about 25% of the total proteins being synthesized at the morula stage is probably histones,

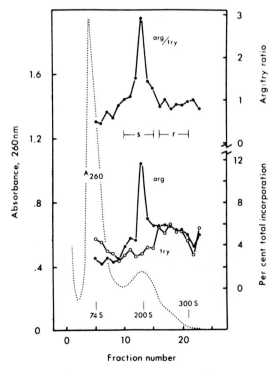

Fig. 11.30. Incorporation of [^{14}C]arginine and [^{3}H]tryptophan into polysomes of morulae of *Strongylocentrotus purpuratus* after a 5-minute pulse; S, slowly sedimenting polysomes; r, rapidly sedimenting polysomes. (From Nemer and Lindsay, 1969.)

and that their site of synthesis is the small polysomes. Hnilica and co-workers, after a thorough analysis of the nuclear proteins of *Strongylocentrotus purpuratus, Paracentrotus lividus,* and *Sphaerechinus granularis* embryos (Orengo and Hnilica, 1970; Hnilica and Johnson, 1970; Johnson and Hnilica, 1970), have argued that histones appear in the nuclei of sea urchin embryos only after the blastula stage.

It seems reasonable to assume that their synthesis starts somewhat earlier, i.e., in the period indicated by Nemer, Gross, and co-workers. This is actually what has been suggested by further experiments of Johnson and Hnilica (1971). These authors labeled with [^{14}C]amino acids eggs at the 32- to 64-cell stage or blastulae of *Strongylocentrotus purpuratus.* In both cases, it was possible to demonstrate labeling of basic proteins extractable from the cytoplasm with the same electrophoretic mobility as histones. It was only at the blastula stage that these proteins were recovered from the nuclei, with the exception of the F 3 fraction, which was recovered as a labeled protein from the nuclei even at the zygote stage. One can postulate that histones are being synthesized during early cleavage but held stored in the cytoplasm and transferred to the chromatin only at the blastula stage (with the exception of the F 3 fraction, which is transferred earlier). Since actinomycin D does not inhibit the appearance of the normal nuclear histone pattern at the blastula stage, it can be inferred that histones during early cleavage are synthesized on templates made during oogenesis and stored in the egg.

In this respect, it is interesting to note the observation of Dubois *et al.* (1970) that certain RNA classes of 9 and 12 S, detected by acrylamide gel electrophoresis in *Strongylocentrotus purpuratus* (see, also, Daigneault *et al.,* 1970), disappear at the late prism stage. It is tempting to suggest that these RNA's might be connected with histone synthesis, and decrease when the bulk of the histones has already been synthesized.

Silver and Comb (1967) reported the incorporation of radioactive amino acids into acid-soluble proteins of probable nuclear localization during development. Moreover, these authors noted differences between the amino acid composition of some of the labeled proteins and histones.

Electrophoretic analysis of the histones from different developmental stages of *Lytechinus variegatus* (Benttinen and Comb, 1971) also reveals that lysine-rich and arginine-rich histones become the major components only after gastrulation, whereas a slightly lysine-rich histone predominates at the 32-cell stage. Thaler *et al.* (1970) reported that electrophoretic and amino acid composition analysis of chromosomal proteins from sperm, eggs, and gastrulae of *Arbacia punctulata* shows a change during development from a lysine-rich to a relatively arginine-rich form. Here again we have acid-soluble proteins from egg chromatin that differ remarkably from mammalian histones, while those from gastrulae do not.

Analysis of histone synthesis in embryos of *Strongylocentrotus droe-bachiensis* was performed by Voroboyev (1969), who compared the amino acid composition and the electrophoretic pattern of blastulae and gastrulae. This author reports that gastrulae contain relatively less arginine-rich fractions than blastulae. Voroboyev also provides some data on the variations of amino acid incorporation into different histone fractions at different developmental stages and (Voroboyev *et al.,* 1969a,b) on the effects of addition of histones to cultured embryos. Analyses of sea urchin histones were also performed by Subirana (1970) and Subirana *et al.* (1970) (see also Chapter 10 under Section I, for more data on this subject).

Moav and Nemer (1971) recently characterized, by acid extraction, gel filtration, cation-exchange chromatography, and acrylamide gel electro-phoresis, the growing peptide chains on the small polysomes of 10-hour-old embryos of *Strongylocentrotus purpuratus,* which are supposed to synthesize histones. On the basis of all these criteria it is confirmed that these small polysomes are synthesizing histones. Analysis of the ratio between [^{3}H]tryptophan and [^{14}C]arginine and lysine incorporated at the small polysome level at different developmental stages, gives a meas-ure of the amount of histones being synthesized at these stages. It is concluded that the maximum histone synthesis is reached at the 200-cell stage, and that the rate of histone synthesis between 3 and 20 hours of development in *Strongylocentrotus* agrees well with the rate of DNA synthesis in the same embryos.

These results are of the highest importance: first, because they probably provide the first purifiable protein class whose messenger RNA has been characterized and partially isolated in sea urchins and, with a few excep-tions, in all eukaryotes; second, because they suggest a polysomal site of synthesis of histones, whose general mechanism of synthesis is still a matter of speculation.

Moreover, Kedes and Birnstiel (1971) have also provided evidence (see Chapter 9) that the mRNA's for histones are synthesized on repe-titious DNA sequences, which is the first instance where translation of such sequences has been observed.

A series of papers dealing with studies of the basic proteins of oocytes, eggs, and embryos of sea urchins, mainly from a cytochemical point of view, has been published by Bäckström (1965a,b, 1966a,b,c, 1968, 1969).

Little is known about the synthesis of ribosomal proteins during oogenesis and embryogenesis. A study of isotope-labeling of the acid-soluble proteins made by Silver and Comb (1967) had shown no incor-poration of exogenous amino acids into the acid-soluble microsomal proteins before the early pluteus stage.

Giudice and Mutolo (unpublished) have found that synthesis of ribosomal proteins does not represent a major part of the embryonic protein synthesis, at least up to the prism stage.

4. ENZYMATIC PROTEINS

We shall describe in Chapter 12 the attempts made to purify some enzymatic protein that might serve as a model for the study of the synthesis of a specific protein in sea urchin embryos. We shall report on the crystallization of the hatching enzyme and describe efforts made to purify alkaline phosphate, isozymes of malate dehydrogenase, as well as some other enzymes. Suffice it here to mention that none of the above attempts can be considered final as yet.

One interesting point to stress here is the possibility shown by Westin (1970) of the existence of enzymes in an inactive form stored in the egg, which can be activated at the pluteus stage.

5. SKELETON MATRIX

To our knowledge, most of the investigation of the "matrix" of spiculae has been done by K. Okazaki (1956a, 1960, 1961, 1962, 1965). This author has described how the primary mesenchyme cells aggregate in a triangular mass on each side of the larva. From each apex of these triangles one chain of cells will then proliferate to originate the ventral, anal, and body rods of the skeleton (see Chapter 1). These aggregates of mesenchymal cells form the skeleton matrix and the skelton itself by means of the following mechanism: They emit pseudopodia which fuse with those of the neighboring mesenchyme cells to form some hyaloplasmic masses; these, by further coalescence, will give rise to the so-called "organic matrix" of the skeleton, within which the calcium carbonate will be deposited (see, also, Gustafson and Wolpert, 1961c; Wolpert and Gustafson, 1961a; Prenant, 1926; von Ubisch, 1937; Nakano *et al.,* 1963; Millonig, 1970 and Chapter 1). We have already discussed some problems concerning calcium uptake (Chapter 4). We shall, therefore, deal here with the study of the organic matrix. Nothing is actually known about its nature, except that it is still possible, under phase contrast or by staining with Nile sulfate, to see "strands" of materials reproducing the shape of the spiculae when these have been dissolved by treatment with 10^{-2} M acetic acid or hydrochloric acid after isolation. Isolation of spiculae can be performed in a number of ways: (a) treatment with distilled water at pH 8.0, followed by digestion of the protoplasm with 0.2 M NaOH at 100°C for 30 minutes, and final repeated washings with distilled water at pH 8.0 (Okazaki, 1956a); (b) treatment with 5% sodium hypochlorite

(Ellis and Wintex, 1967); (c) dissolution of the cells by treatment with sodium deoxycholate (Giudice, unpublished); (d) digestion of the cells by trypsin treatment (Millonig, 1970).

It is tempting, however, to think that collagen synthesis may start in correlation with the synthesis of the skeleton organic matrix. Vanable (1961) has reported that embryos of *Strongylocentrotus droebachiensis* lack hydroxyproline in their proteins, as shown by column chromatography, while this amino acid is present in adult tissue proteins and in the free amino acid pool of both embryos and adults. Klein and Currey (1970) have found only a small amount of collagen in adult sea urchin tissue, localized as calcified collagen at the base of the spine. Ellis and Wintex (1967), on the other hand, reported incorporation of [³H] proline into the matrix proteins of *Arbacia punctulata,* and suggested that at the pluteus stage this embryo might be able to convert the proline into hydroxyproline.

Pucci-Minafra *et al.* (1972) have recently proved that *Paracentrotus lividus* embryos incorporate proline into the total proteins at similar rates in earlier and later stages of development, whereas, with the same amount of incorporated proline, a substantial portion is transformed into hydroxyproline in the stages from mesenchyme blastula on, but not in earlier stages. All the labeled hydroxyproline is recovered in a spiculae-bound protein fraction, which shows solubility properties characteristic of collagen.

The suggestion is therefore justified that collagen is a protein specifically synthesized for skeleton formation.

G.   Evidence of Translational Control of Protein Synthesis
during Early Development

We have mentioned that only a few new proteins, if any, can be detected after the gastrula stage. It is, therefore, conceivable that most of the proteins synthesized up to the pluteus stage, at least in terms of mass, even if not of number, mainly represent proteins belonging to the main cell constituents, such as histones, cell membranes, mitochondria, etc., so that one would not expect to detect major changes in their overall composition throughout development. Actually, it has been repeatedly proved that part of the proteins synthesized after fertilization is represented by mitocondrial proteins (Nakano and Monroy, 1958a; Nakano et al., 1958; Giudice and Monroy, 1958). It has also been suggested that mitochondria might be able to synthesize at least part of their own proteins, on the basis of results of incorporation of amino acids into isolated mitochondria (Giudice, 1960) and of *in vivo* kinetics of labeling (Tyler and Pikò, 1968).

The search for changes in the kind of proteins synthesized during the period between fertilization and blastula has attracted the attention of several workers for the following reasons: Since the embryo is able to reach the blastula stage even in the absence of RNA synthesis (see Chapter 10), and should the changes in the pattern of protein synthesis persist under these conditions, a mechanism of control of protein synthesis at translational level must be conceived.

The first experimental approach to this problem (after an earlier attempt by Monroy *et al.*, 1961) was made by Spiegel *et al.* (1965). These authors exposed *Strongylocentrotus purpuratus* embryos for 1 hour to [^{14}C]valine at the 8-cell stage or at the late blastula stage. The 100,000 *g* supernatant was then analyzed by acrylamide gel electrophoresis. Sixteen bands were resolved, all of which showed the same pattern of radioactivity at both stages. No changes in this profile were obtained in the presence of actinomycin. Nor were differences observed when control embryos were raised to the prism stage. Similar conclusions were reported by Mackintosh and Bell (1969b), who failed to observe differences between the electrophoretic pattern of the proteins synthesized from prefertilization up to gastrula, at which point changes were detected. These results are not surprising: The resolution method still seems too crude to reveal fine differences among thousands of minor proteins.

On the other hand, preliminary experiments by Terman and Gross (1965), by autoradiography of sliced acrylamide gel electrophoresis from gross protein extracts of *Arbacia puntulata* embryos labeled with radioactive amino acids at different stages, had suggested that some changes in the pattern of protein synthesis take place between fertilization and hatching, and that actinomycin D does not influence these changes. This was the first suggestion of a translational control of protein synthesis. As expected, further changes taking place after the hatching stage were inhibited by actinomycin D.

These results were essentially confirmed by Ellis (1966) who analyzed, by DEAE-Sephadex A-50 chromatography, the proteins of *Arbacia punctulata* embryos, soluble in 0.5 *M* NaCl, after labeling at different developmental stages. The results showed clear variations in the elution pattern as early as 8 hours after fertilization, which is surprising in view of the fact that only two major peaks were obtained. The change, however, consists of the prevalent synthesis of more negatively charged and possibly shorter protein chains at 8 hours than at 1 hour after fertilization. It is possible that this represents the synthesis of histones, even if it seems improbable that they would have been solubilized under the conditions set up by the author. Actinomycin only slightly inhibited these changes. It was again found to inhibit further changes taking place after gastrulation.

Analysis of the acid-soluble proteins throughout the development of *Arbacia punctulata* embryos has also led Spiegel *et al.* (1970) to conclude that a new electrophoretic band, among the 32 observed, appears at about the 4- to 8-cell stage.

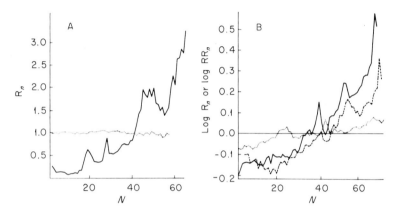

Fig. 11.31. Difference distribution plots of pairs of ³H- and ¹⁴C-labeled proteins. A. Dotted line: normal and dactinomycin-treated zygotes compared. Continuous line: normal hatched blastulae and normal zygotes compared (the normalized ratio of ³H/¹⁴C counts, R_n, is plotted versus fraction number, N). B. Solid line: normal hatched blastulae and normal zygotes compared. Dashed line: dactinomycin-treated hatched blastulae and dactinomycin-treated zygotes compared. Dotted line: normal hatched blastulae and dactinomycin-treated hatched blastulae compared (in order to retain graphic and experimental consistency when ³H or ¹⁴C is arbitrarily administered, the reciprocal of R_n, RR_n, is plotted on the same graph as R_n. Since log R_n and log RR_n are equally distant from the line log 1, and the linear representations are not, logs are plotted). (From Terman, 1970.)

More recently, Terman (1970) presented a detailed analysis of this problem, which essentially confirms his previous results. The experimental conditions had been carefully planned and the data analyzed by the aid of a computer: Embryos of *Arbacia punctulata* were pulse-labeled with [¹⁴C]leucine at one stage and with [³H]leucine at another. The 200,000 g supernatants were run together in acrylamide gel electrophoresis, and the ratio ³H:¹⁴C measured after slicing the gels. As shown in Fig. 11.31 and in Table 11.8, the incorporation profile changes between the zygote and hatching blastula. Again, these changes are little influenced by the presence of actinomycin. After the hatching stage, further changes take place which are inhibited by actinomycin.

The conclusion is, therefore, that a control of protein synthesis is operating at a translational level up to hatching, while a transcriptional control becomes more important thereafter.

Finally, it has been reported (Butros, 1969) that exogenously ad-

TABLE 11.8

DISTRIBUTION DIFFERENCE COEFFICIENTS: COMPARISON OF DISTRIBUTIONS OF
RADIOACTIVE PROTEINS FROM NORMAL AND DACTINOMYCIN-TREATED EMBRYOS[a,b]

Distributions compared	Experiment 1		Experiment 2	
	Run 1	Run 2	Run 1	Run 2
ZN,ZA	0.01[c]	0.71	0.11	0.58
MN,ZN	0.29		1.33	
MA,ZA	0.53		0.65	
MN,MA	0.17	0.43	0.25	
HN,ZN	8.28	9.91[c]	3.75[d]	
HA,ZA	5.24	5.92	3.44[d]	
HN,HA	3.30	4.50	0.65[d]	0.90[d]
EGN,ZN	2.65		3.60	
"EG"A,ZA	3.08		3.38	
EGN,"EG"A	0.86	0.96	0.61	
LGN,ZN	1.39	1.11	4.12	
"LG"A,ZA	1.29	1.34	4.67	
LGN,"LG"A	2.01	1.90	0.83	
PN,"P"A	2.52	2.46		

Significance levels

Hypothesis tested (coefficients compared)	Experiment 1			Experiment 2
	Run 1	Run 2	Average	
HN,ZN > HA,ZA	> 0.9999	> 0.9999	> 0.9999	0.76
HA,ZA > HN,HA	> 0.9999	> 0.9988	> 0.9999	> 0.9999
HA,ZA > HN,ZN − HA,ZA	0.9987	0.9868	> 0.9999	> 0.9999

[a]From Terman (1970).

[b]Newly synthesized proteins were labeled for 20 minutes at various stages with [^{3}H]- or [^{14}C]leucine, and the electrophoretic distributions of soluble proteins were compared in various combinations. Z, zygote; M, mid-cleavage; H, hatched blastula; EG, early gastrula; LG, late gastrula; P, prism; N, normal embryos; A, dactinomycin-treated embryos. A difference of 0.41% is not to be considered significant and has already been subtracted from these values. A difference of 6.5% has been found between mixtures of HeLa cells and sea urchin proteins.

[c]See Fig. 11.31A.

[d]See Fig. 11.31B.

ministered RNA is able to alter the pattern of protein synthesis of embryos of *Strongylocentrotus purpuratus* and *Lytechinus pictus*. In our opinion, however, the specificity of such an effect is not demonstrated by the produced evidence.

H. Effect of Inhibition of Protein Synthesis

We have repeatedly described the use of puromycin or cycloheximide to inhibit protein synthesis in sea urchin oocytes eggs and embryos. Since the most important effect observed is block of cleavage, these drugs have been used mainly to study the relationship between protein synthesis, DNA synthesis, and cleavage. We therefore refer the reader to Chapters 5 and 9 for detailed references.

It should be noted that Bosco and Monroy (1960) stated that the disturbance of protein synthesis in the first 2 hours following fertilization of *Paracentrotus lividus* eggs, by addition of the methionine analog, ethionine, at 10^{-3} M, causes block of development at the mesenchyme blastula stage. A recent investigation of the effect of ethionine on macromolecular synthesis of *Sphaerechinus granularis* eggs under the same conditions (Graziani *et al.,* 1970) has shown only a slight inhibition (about 30%) of amino acid incorporation. On the other hand, these authors reported that ethionine becomes incorporated into proteins. Hence, its developmental effect may, in principle, be brought about by (a) selective inhibition of the synthesis of a special class of proteins; (b) synthesis of nonfunctional proteins; (c) other side effects. Methylation of DNA is not apparently disturbed by ethionine.

What is of interest is that the ethionine experiments represent one of the earliest claims that disturbances of macromolecular synthesis may have a delayed effect on development.

Chapter 12

Enzymatic Activities

To conclude the description of metabolism, some of the enzymatic activities studied in the developing sea urchin will be described here. For those more directly concerned with nucleic acid and protein synthesis, as well as with respiration, the reader is referred to the relevant chapters.

The purpose of such a description, besides the obvious one of providing a useful list of the related bibliography, is that of establishing, whenever possible, specific correlations between developmental events and specific patterns of enzymatic activities.

A. Phosphatases

1. ALKALINE PHOSPHATASE

This is one of the most studied enzymes in sea urchin development. The first histochemical study was made by Krugelis (1947a,b) on oocytes of *Arbacia punctulata*. According to this author, the enzymatic activity is localized throughout the nuclear structures (nucleolus, nucleoplasm, and nuclear membrane), while it is low in the cytoplasm. In the mature egg (Krugelis, 1947b), the situation is reversed, and the cytoplasm is the major site of activity. During development, however, a second change gradually takes place, and the nuclei again become the major site of alkaline phosphatase.

Similar observations were reported by Wicklund (1948) on *Paracentrotus lividus*. The site of activity was reported to be the nucleolus and nuclear envelope in oocytes. When the egg is mature, the activity appears in the cortex of the cytoplasm and at the periphery of the nucleus. At fertilization, it is distributed throughout the cytoplasm in a matter of minutes.

No preferential localization in the nucleated halves of *Arbacia lixula* has been found by means of biochemical analysis (Mazia *et al.*, 1948).

Hsiao and Fujii (1963), by means of histochemical observations, reported a nucleolar localization of the alkaline phosphatase in oocytes of *Tripneustes gratilla* and *Colobocentrotus auratus*. No activity was detected in the nucleoplasm or in the cytoplasm. In the mature eggs of *Tripneustes gratilla,* a cytoplasmic and particularly a nuclear activity appear. These authors also performed a biochemical quantitative assay of the enzyme at different developmental stages. They report that the enzymatic activity doubles at gastrulation with respect to the unfertilized egg, and becomes 6 times higher at the pluteus stage.

These results superimpose quite well on the biochemical observations by Mazia *et al.* (1948) on *Arbacia punctulata,* subsequently confirmed by Pfohl and Monroy (1963), Pfohl (1965), and Pfohl and Giudice (1967). Gustafson and Hasselberg (1950) observed that the alkaline phosphatase activity is very low until the beginning of gastrulation and increases exponentially thereafter.

Flickinger (1957) found that the rise in activity of this enzyme after gastrulation follows a different pattern in *Dendraster excentricus* and in *Strongylocentrotus purpuratus*. In the latter the increase is much less dramatic than in the former. There is, however, general agreement that, even though it takes place differently in the different species, the enzymatic activity starts to increase at gastrulation, to become particularly high at the pluteus stage.

This increase, first shown again histochemically by Hsiao and Fujii (1963), correlates with the special localization of the enzymatic activity in the archenteron, in the primary mesenchyme cells, and in their descendants, the skeletogenic cells. In the ectodermal cells of the anterior border of the pluteus some enzyme accumulation also has been observed. These histochemical localizations of enzymatic activity in the gastrula and plutei are confirmed by the observations of Evola-Maltese (1957a) on *Paracentrotus lividus*.

The localization in the intestine may be connected with the development of the digestive function. Actually, the enzyme seems to accumulate in the intestinal lumen more than within the endodermal cells. In experimental exogastrulation, for example, the intestine appears devoid of alkaline phosphatase activity (Okazaki, 1956b). Localization at the mesenchyme level has been associated with skeletogenesis. It must be recalled, however, that the skeleton is made up of calcium carbonate and not of phosphate (Yasumasu, 1959). The hypothesis was proposed that the primitive triradiate spicules and developing rods are formed of calcium phosphate, which is later replaced by calcium carbonate (Evola-Maltese, 1957a). In support of this idea, the author states that the birefrigency in polarized light, characteristic of calcium carbonate, appears only late in skeletogenesis. In an attempt to correlate the function of alkaline phosphatase with differentiation, Evola-Maltese (1957b) treated the developing embryos of *Paracentrotus lividus* with beryllium, which may inhibit the enzymatic activity by substituting for the magnesium ions. This metal is also effective at relative low doses ($6-8 \times 10^{-4} M$) in suppressing the alkaline phosphatase activity in the developing sea urchin; under such conditions the embryo shows defects of intestine and skeleton formation. It is known that gastrulation and skeletogenesis are two processes that are inhibited in a great variety of abnormal conditions. A clear correlation between the inhibition of alkaline phosphatase and these developmental processes is not easy to establish, considering how many side effects may be exerted by an ion acknowledged to compete with divalent metals such as Mg^{2+} or Ca^{2+}.

Another attempt to correlate the rise in this enzymatic activity with development has been made by Pfohl and Giudice (1967). As described in Chapter 6, the destruction of the normal embryo architecture by cell dissociation halts the increase in enzymatic activity. Only when, because of reaggregation, the cells again form intestinallike structures does the rise in enzymatic activity take place. If, however, dissociation of the embryo is performed just before the turning point of enzymatic activity, i.e., at the early pluteus stage, the normal increase in enzymatic activity takes place in the dissociated cells at the same time as in the control embryos, thus demonstrating that the dissociated cells are already "committed" to such an increase in enzymatic activity.

Is the developmental increase of such an activity due to net synthesis of new enzyme or to an activation of a nonactive, preexisting form? A series of experiments aimed at answering this question was performed by Pfohl (Pfohl and Monroy, 1963; Pfohl, 1965). A Tris–glycine extract of *Arbacia punctulata* unfertilized eggs shows, upon electrophoresis on polyacrylamide gel, one single band of enzymatic activity; from the mesenchyme blastula stage on, a second band of activity appears.

Part of the enzyme activity is not displayed in the total homogenates of unfertilized eggs, and becomes detectable upon extraction and dialysis of the homogenate with butanol. At later stages, however, the homogenate activity equals that of the butanol extract. The author suggests that this may be indicative of a release from inhibition or of activation of a preexisting enzyme during early development. At the late pluteus stage there is such an increase in total activity and in the specific activity of the butanol extracts as to lead the author to suggest a net increase of the enzyme, which superimposes over the previous activation. To further elucidate this matter, Pfohl (personal communication) initiated a series of attempts to purify the enzyme in order to detect if it undergoes *de novo* synthesis, by the incorporation of labeled amino acids. Up to 500-fold purification of the enzyme was achieved by Pfohl from *Paracentrotus lividus* embryos. The alkaline phosphatase appears to fall into two categories, which elute from a Sephadex G-200 column with partition coefficients of Kav (I) $\simeq$ 0.010 and Kav (II) $\simeq$ 0.140. The first peak is generally predominant in the unfertilized egg. The enzyme from plutei is almost entirely of the second type. Enzyme I elutes from DEAE-cellulose columns at 0.4 M NaCl, while enzyme II elutes at 0.65–0.70 M NaCl. Acrylamide gel electrophoresis separates the two enzymes. The pH optimum is 9.5 for both of them. Preliminary experiments suggest a different substrate preference.

2. OTHER PHOSPHATE-SPLITTING ENZYMES

A thorough description of phosphate-splitting enzymes was made by Gustafson and Hasselberg (1951), who undertook one of the most extensive studies on enzymatic activities in sea urchin embryos.

a. Acid Phosphatase

This has been determined by the above authors on *Psammechinus miliaris* at pH 6.0, using phenylphosphate as substrate. The activity remains rather constant throughout development, similar to the finding by Mazia *et al.* (1948) on *Arbacia punctulata,* with glycerophosphate as substrate.

Doré and Cousineau (1967) studied the acid phosphatase activity of subcellular fractions of unfertilized eggs and blastulae of *Arbacia punctulata,* with the substrates glucose 6-phosphate, glucose 6-glycerophosphate and *p*-nitrophenylphosphate. Most of the activity is recovered in the yolk fraction. The activity of the total homogenate of blastulae is slightly higher than that of unfertilized eggs, but, interestingly, the activity of the blastula microsomes is much higher than that of the egg microsomes. Is that indicative of synthesis of acid phosphatases (as the authors suggest)? Or is it somehow related to the functional activation of ribosomes following fertilization (see Chapter 11)?

b. Apyrase

This name was used by Gustafson and Hasselberg to indicate an enzyme (or, perhaps, an enzymatic complex) that liberates orthophosphate when ATP is used as a substrate, with no distinction between true ATPase activity and ADPase.

This activity was checked on homogenates of *Paracentrotus lividus* obtained in several ionic conditions. No relevant differences were found between isotonic or hypotonic media and no effect of Ca^{2+} was reported (see, also, Connors and Scheer, 1947). The optimum pH was found at about 8.0. This activity is present prior to fertilization, but shows a very clear increase beginning at the formation of the primary mesenchyme and continuing up to the pluteus stage. This increase is less pronounced in Li^+-treated embryos. An early study of the intracellular distribution of apyrase is found in Mullins (1949).

c. Pyrophosphatase and Metaphosphatase

These two activities were measured by Gustafson and Hasselberg (1951) at pH 7.6 (their optimum pH was found to lie between 7.0 and 8.0) in homogenates of *Paracentrotus lividus*, by measuring the ability to liberate orthophosphate, using sodium pyrophosphate and sodium hexametaphosphate, respectively, as substrates. These activities were present and fairly constant throughout development.

The Li^+ treatment does not seem to have any effect. Again we note that whenever a metabolic activity changes in concomitance with an important morphological event, as in the case of the formation of mesenchyme and gastrulation, treatments that disturb these morphological events prevent the change in the metabolic activity. On the other hand, metabolic activities that show no changes during development are usually not affected by treatments that impair morphogenesis.

Furthermore, Dalcq and Pasteels (1963) have provided histochemical evidence that cytoplasmic granulations, differing from mitochondria in the eggs and embryos of *Psammechinus miliaris*, show a phosphate-splitting activity when nucleotides are used as substrates. The activity decreases according to the substrate used in the following order: adenosine 5'-triphosphate; adenosine 5'-diphosphate; adenosine 5'-phosphate. The activity remains constant throughout development up to the early gastrula stage, and drops at the young prism stage, being present only in the nuclei of mesenchyme cells. After fertilization, the two pronuclei, especially the paternal one, are intensely active. Interestingly enough, at the four blastomere stage, one or two of them are more active than the others. Has this a significance in the differentiation mechanism? The main suggestion that comes to one's mind, considering the preferential localization of such activities in the yolk granules, is that they are involved in yolk utilization.

Jackson and Black (1967) obtained from egg homogenates of *Arbacia lixula* a fraction consisting of large, not well identifiable granules. The granule fraction was separated into two distinct subfractions: one containing acid phosphatase and esterases; the other containing sulfatase, RNase, and nucleic acids.

It is of practical value to know that glucose 6-phosphatase, which is a microsomal enzyme in mammalian cells, is mainly localized within a large particulate sedimenting together with the yolk granules in sea urchins (Cousineau and Gross, 1960).

Finally, Vittorelli (1964) studied the phosphoprotein phosphatase activity of eggs and embryos of *Paracentrotus lividus* and *Arbacia lixula*. She found an optimum of pH between 5.5 and 6. The activity was stimulated by monovalent cations such as K^+ and Na^+ and inhibited by divalent ones such as Ca^{2+} and Mg^{2+}. It increased after fertilization to reach a steady level at 64 blastomeres.

B. Proteases

The most thorough research on proteolytic enzymes in sea urchin eggs and embryos was done by Lundblad (1949, 1950, 1952, 1954a,b,c; Lundblad and Lundblad, 1953; Lundblad and Runnström, 1962; Lundblad and Falksveden, 1964; Lundblad and Schilling, 1968; Lundblad et al., 1966, 1968). The work of this author extended to the gametes of several species, namely, *Paracentrotus lividus, Arbacia lixula, Psammechinus microtuberculatus, Echinus esculentus, Echinocardium cordatum,* and *Briossopsis lyrifera*. Up to 1954 the papers were devoted mainly to the study of enzymatic activities at different pH's on rather crude extracts. The methods used consisted of viscosimetrical assays, formol titration with gelatin as substrate, and the method of Schultz using 1-benzoylarginine amide as substrate.

An activity at pH 4.3 was found in all the investigated gametes. This was attributed to what was at that time called cathepsin II and is now known as cathepsin B. Enzyme activity was found at pH 6.7, 7, and 7.8. The enzymes supposedly responsible for those activities were named respectively EI, EII, and EIII. They were also differentiated from each other on the basis of the sensitivity to SH-reducing or SH-oxidating agents and to Ca^{2+} ions. On the basis of the activating effect of trypsin on the isolated ribosomes of unfertilized eggs (see Chapter 11), it is of interest to note the variations of such enzymatic activities in relation to fertilization. They are reported in Fig. 12.1.

A transitory increase of all these fractions is observed. The author noted no difference in cathepsin activity at fertilization.

From 1962 on, Lundblad attempted to purify these enzymatic fractions by the use of gel filtration and chromatography on DEAE-Sephadex (a

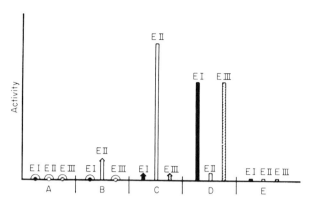

Fig. 12.1. A scheme showing the activity of proteolytic enzymes postulated in intact sea urchin eggs before and after fertilization. A, before fertilization; B, at fertilization; C, at membrane elevation; D, immediately after membrane elevation; E, 10 minutes or more after membrane elevation. (From Lundblad, 1954d.)

similar earlier attempt can be found in the paper by Porath and Flodin, 1959).

Cathepsin B was first purified 350 times by gel filtration on Sephadex G-100 from homogenates of oocytes of *Brissopsis lyrifera*. Its molecular weight was estimated to be between 50,000 and 60,000. By the use of Sephadex G-200 and G-100 superfine, Lundblad *et al.* (1966) recovered, in addition to cathepsin B, two more acidic proteases able to hydrolyze hemoglobin; they were classified as cathepsin D according to the definition by Press *et al.* (1960). Their optimum of activity was at pH 3.75; one of them was also able to hydrolyze gelatin. Two years later, Lundblad and Schilling (1968) showed that one of these two enzymes, called cathepsin D2, decreased gradually after fertilization and disappeared at the pluteus stage. The other one, called cathepsin D1, remained at a constant level throughout development. In further work (Lundblad *et al.*, 1968) the D1 and D2 cathepsins, isolated by gel filtration, were analyzed by isolectric focusing. Five peaks of activity were found for D1, and only one major and two minor ones for D2. In addition, two more peaks of catheptic activity of type D were found by gel filtration and called D0 and D3. This work gives us an idea of how complex can be the study of an enzyme with such a general function as proteolysis.

The work of other authors on proteolytic activity has been limited to the measurement of variations of activity on crude extracts.

There is general agreement on a rise in activity following fertilization. Maggio (1957) studied the proteolytic activity at pH 5.4–5.9 of mitochondria and postmitochondrial supernatant of *Paracentrotus lividus* eggs. She found a decrease of the former but an increase of the latter following fertilization. Mano (1966), in eggs of *Hemicentrotus pulcherrimus* and *Anthocidaris crassispina*, found three optima of activity at pH 4.3, 6.7, and 8.0. Only the enzyme with optimum at pH 8.0, according to the author, is transiently activated at fertilization. The author also describes the appearance of activity at fertilization in a particulate fraction sedimenting between 8,000 and 17,000 g. The relevance of this finding in the question of the activation of protein synthesis at fertilization is discussed in Chapter 11. Gustafson and Hasselberg (1951) have found that the catheptic activity type II (i.e., B) in *Paracentrotus lividus, Sphaerechinus granularis, Strongylocentrotus droebachiensis, Echinus esculentus,* and *Psammechinus miliaris* is very low up to the mesenchyme blastula stage, when it undergoes a very strong increase. Troll *et al.* (1968) observed in the sediment of sonicated embryos of *Arbacia punctulata* a proteolytic activity similar to that of trypsin. This similarity is based on the observation that both enzymes hydrolyze the synthetic substrates tosylarginine methyl ester and acetyllysine methyl ester at the same rate ratio, i.e., 8:1. This activity increases by a factor of 10 in the first 20 hours of development. The increase might be due to synthesis of new enzymes since it depends on RNA synthesis; no increase takes place in the presence of actinomycin. The analog tosyllysine chloromethyl inhibits the enzyme. Its effect on development is inhibition of gastrulation at low doses and inhibition of cleavage at higher doses. Of course, it is not possible to make direct correlations between these effects and enzymatic activity since nothing is known about the side effects that this analog might exert on metabolism.

Grossman *et al.* (1971) found that this enzyme before fertilization is located in a particulate sedimenting at 750 g and with a density of 1.120 in sucrose gradients. Following fertilization the enzyme moves to a less dense particulate (1.092). If the unfertilized egg ribosomes are treated with this enzyme they become active in protein synthesis (see Chapter 11).

Recently, Krischer and Chambers (1970) have assigned the bulk of proteolytic activity in the alkaline range of *Lytechinus variegatus* eggs to chymotrypsin. Two minor activities at pH 3.5 and 4.3 have also been described; they are attributed to an enzyme that can probably be classified as cathepsin D. Cathepsin B and cathepsin IV seem to be present.

The protease activities are almost entirely particulate bound, and sediment together with the yolk, from which the acid proteinases are easily released. In this behavior they resemble the lysosomal enzymes.

Krischer and Chambers, in contrast with previous reports in the literature, hold that no changes in the protease activity or intracellular distribution take place at fertilization.

C. Isozymes

MALIC DEHYDROGENASE

A series of papers has been devoted to this subject by Villee and co-workers (Moore and Villee, 1961, 1962, 1963; Billiar *et al.,* 1964, 1966; Patton *et al.,* 1967). In *Arbacia punctulata* this enzymatic activity shows but a slight increase from fertilization through pluteus. Changes were observed in the electrophoretic isozymatic pattern of the enzyme and in its intracellular distribution. The enzyme extracted from whole unfertilized eggs show 7 bands of activity upon acrylamide gel electrophoresis. Only 5 of these bands are present in the nonnucleated halves, while all 7 are represented in the nucleated halves. Upon fertilization, the number of the bands is reduced from 7 to 4 in the nucleated halves and from 5 to 3 in the nonnucleated ones. Of the 7 fractions, 5 are present in the cytoplasm and 4 in the particulate. Reduction of the total number of bands following fertilization appears to be due primarily to the soluble forms. It does not seem to depend upon genetic activity since it is observed, as mentioned, also in the nonnucleated halves and is not influenced by actinomycin or puromycin (even if a direct control of the effect of these drugs, under the experimental conditions used, was not carried out).

The sperm contains three bands of activity, only one of which corresponds to one of the unfertilized egg.

At the 64-cell stage, three bands were found in the small blastomeres and only two in the large ones.

Working on *Paracentrotus lividus,* Michejda and Hryniewiecka (1969) reported no variations of the total level of malic dehydrogenase activity throughout development and no signs of enzyme synthesis, as judged by attempts to incorporate [^{14}C]amino acids into the enzyme of the developing embryos. According to these authors the agar and starch electrophoretic pattern of the total malic dehydrogenase remains unchanged following fertilization and up to the early pluteus stage, provided the extraction conditions are adequate. Ultrasounds or sodium deoxycholate were successfully used to this end. Besides the band of the cytoplasmic isozyme, three bands of activity upon agar–gel microelectrophoresis were attributed to the mitochondrial enzyme regardless of the developmental stage. However, this pattern was found to be subjected to various changes in different batches of eggs or in different seasons. This finding led the authors to suggest that the different bands may represent only different conformational states of the same protein (Michejda, personal communication).

These results contrast with the earlier ones by Gustafson and Hasselberg (1951), who had reported more than a doubling of malate dehydrogenase activity following the mesenchyme blastula stage in *Psammechinus miliaris*. Michejda and Hryniewiecka find that the electrophoretic patterns of different species (*Paracentrotus lividus, Arbacia lixula* and *Sphaerechinus granularis*) show striking differences. Are the discrepancies between the results of the different authors due to the difference in species?

Recent work by Ozaki and Whiteley (1970) also emphasized the different electrophoretic pattern of this enzyme in different species. These authors find only two enzymatic forms in *Strongylocentrotus purpuratus* that are distinguished according to four criteria: (1) electrophoretic mobility; (2) chromatographic behavior on DEAE cellulose columns; (3) sensitivity to substrate inhibition; and (4) intracellular localization. The last mentioned criterion has been carefully established by a cell fractionation controlled at the electron microscope. The two enzymes appear to be localized in the mitochondria and in the soluble cytoplasm, respectively. Both enzymatic activities increase by a factor of 3 up to the pluteus stage. This increase does not seem to be due to the removal of an inhibitor, as suggested by mixing the homogenates of different stages. One main electrophoretic enzymatic band and two minor ones have been found by the same authors in *Dendraster excentricus*. An individual variability is also reported. The hybrids between *Strongylocentrotus* and *Dendraster* always show severe disturbance of gastrulation and never form enzymes of the paternal type.

D. Hatching Enzyme

To our knowledge, Ishida (1936) was the first to report that seawater, where embryos of the hatching blastula stage are suspended, is able to lyse the fertilization membrane of eggs or embryos at any stage before hatching. The author attribute this effect to a "hatching enzyme" secreted by the blastulae of the sea urchin *Strongylocentrotus pulcherrimus* at the time of hatching. These observations were confirmed on *Arbacia punctulata* by Kopac (1941). The work on *Strongylocentrotus pulcherrimus* was continued by Sugawara (1943), and on other Japanese sea urchins by Yasumasu (1958, 1960, 1963), who claims to have crystallized the enzyme.

Because this enzymatic activity rises at a special point of development and this would be the only crystalline enzyme available from sea urchins up-to-date, a test of the validity of the purification procedure in other species as well would be most welcome.

As discussed in Chapter 10, the ability of sea urchin embryos to hatch in the presence of actinomycin has been debated. It is our opinion that in the presence of actinomycin at the concentration of 20 $\mu g/ml$ seawater, from fertilization on, a good part of the embryos of *Paracentrotus lividus* and other species are able to hatch. Under these conditions, 50–70% of the RNA synthesis is inhibited. Increasing the concentration of actinomycin does not produce a greater effect on RNA synthesis but instead causes extensive cell degeneration. Similar conclusions can be drawn from the experiment of Gross *et al.* (1964) in which actinomycin administered 200 minutes before fertilization at the concentration of 20 $\mu g/ml$ (which, in *Lytechinus pictus,* completely inhibits the synthesis of RNA heavier than 4 S) allows one third of the embryos to hatch. According to Yasumasu (1963), a treatment with actinomycin during cleavage causes a 10% decrease in the percentage of hatching. No direct check of the effect on RNA synthesis is reported. When analogs such as 5-bromodeoxyuridine and 8-azaguanine at nonlethal concentrations are used, no inhibition of hatching is observed in *Strongylocentrotus purpuratus* (Mazia and Gontcharoff, 1964; Bamberger *et al., 1963*). Also the results of Barrett and Angelo (1969) speak in favor of a transcription of the messenger for the hatching enzyme during oogenesis. As discussed in Chapter 7, the latter authors were able to find differences in the sensitivity to Mn^{2+} of the enzymes from two different species (*Strongylocentrotus purpuratus* and *Strongylocentrotus franciscanus*). The reciprocal hybrids of the two species always showed a hatching enzyme that was entirely of a maternal type.

From the sum of the above evidence, we are inclined to believe that at least some of the templates for the synthesis of the hatching enzyme are already present in the unfertilized egg. It has also been suggested that the enzyme itself might be present in the unfertilized egg. Hallberg (1964) has in fact found that the 12,000 g supernatant of an unfertilized egg homogenate is not able to dissolve the fertilization membrane, but it acquires this property when filtered through Sephadex G-100 to remove the low-molecular-weight material. The author makes the suggestion that the hatching enzyme is present in the egg even before fertilization together with a low-molecular-weight inhibitor, which would be removed artificially by gel filtration and naturally by some unknown mechanism at the hatching blastula stage. Of course, before considering such a hypothesis, one would at least like to know whether a 12,000 g supernatant of a blastula homogenate has a hatching effect or not.

All of the experiments on the hatching enzyme, however, suffer from the limitation that no specific enzymatic reaction is available for the assay: first, the exact chemical nature of the substrate, the fertilization membrane, is not known; nor is it known on which chemical constituent of such a complex structure the enzyme is acting. It is, therefore, my opinion that the name hatching enzyme, which has come into current use, is not justified as yet. Nobody indeed knows what enzymatic reaction is being catalyzed. Since, as shown in Chapter 3, a number of various agents are able to dissolve the fertilization membrane, it would be more appropriate to speak about a hatching "factor" until such time as the terms of the enzymatic reaction(s) supposedly catalyzed have been clarified.

From the foregoing discussion, the difficulty to trace such an enzyme inside the embryo appears obvious. A number of proteases, for example, are able to dissolve the fertilization membrane, owing to its protein content. It is clear that the embryos do contain proteases. The question then arises: Is any of them really responsible for the hatching process in nature?

Crystallization of the enzyme from the seawater surrounding the hatching blastulae seems to be the only valid approach to this matter. It would hence be desirable to perform a chemical analysis of the substrate, i.e., the fertilization membrane, aiming at finding out on which one of its chemical constituents the enzyme acts. A step directed at standardizing the conditions of the substrate has been made by Barrett and Angelo (1969), who used a partially purified enzyme isolated from the seawater and membranes of prehatching embryos from a single batch previously stored frozen in ethanol. This treatment does not destroy the hatchability following enzymatic treatment over a period of months.

Barrett (1968) has reported that the "enzyme" has a pH optimum of 8; requires Ca^{2+} ions; is not dependent upon reduced SH groups; and does not show esterase activity.

E. Acetylcholinesterase

A list of the earlier works on this enzyme in invertebrates was reported by Augustinsson (1948). The same author studied the behavior of several esterases during the development of *Paracentrotus lividus*. The data summarized in Fig. 12.2 show a low activity during early development. In particular, the cholinesterase activity is practically zero in the unfertilized egg. A general rise takes place at about 20 hours of development, i.e., during late gastrulation. The activity then increases exponentially up to about 50 hours. Augustinsson and Gustafson (1949) suggested that the increase in cholinesterase activity during the development of *Paracentrotus lividus* might be correlated with the following morphological events: (a) a first rise, beginning at prehatching and ending at late gastrulation (15–18 hours), may be connected with the first ciliary activity; (b) a second rise (15–18 hours to 30–35 hours) may be connected with the development of the cilia along the arms and other ectodermal derivations; (c) a third rise may be correlated with the intestinal movements.

This suggestion is supported by the effect of Li^+. This ion does not

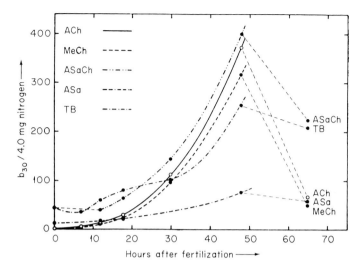

Fig. 12.2. Esterase activities of developing sea urchin eggs. Abbreviations for the various substrates: ACh, acetylcholine; MeCh, acetyl-β-methylcholine; ASaCh, acetylsalicyl-choline; ASa, acetylsalicylic acid; TB, tributyrin. Data are expressed as μl CO_2 liberated in 30 minutes. (From Augustinsson, 1948.)

affect the first increase, but, as would be expected from its effect on development, somehow impairs the other two rises. Recently, Gustafson and Toneby (1970) have reported that serotonin and acetylcholine play a role in the movements of the coelom–esophagus complex.

The significance of this enzymatic activity with respect to the development of a nervous system in the embryos is not well-understood. There is, in fact, no detailed information on the existence of nervous structures in sea urchin embryos. McBride (1903) found a dorsal ganglion in late plutei. Nerve cells have also been described in the oral region of the plutei by Mortensen (1920), who does not, however, provide any stainability criterion for their identification. Runnström (1917–1918) has inferred the existence of a system for the coordination of the movements of the early plutei.

These larvae are actually able to change coordinately the direction of the ciliary movement according to the availability of food in the medium (Strathmann, 1968). Mackie *et al.* (1969) measured the electrical activity associated with the ciliary movement reversal in larvae of *Strongylocentrotus droebachiensis*. They report the production of an electric monophasic potential of 20 μV at each reversal. Neither ciliary reversal nor electric potential is produced at high Mg^{2+} concentrations. These facts, which would speak in favor of the presence of a nervous conduction in the larvae, contrast with the failure of the same authors to detect histo-

logically any nervous structure following staining with methylene blue
and protargol.

Westin (1970) has suggested that the cholinesterase of sea urchins
should be classified as a pseudocholinesterase since it is inhibited by
diisopropyldiamidophosphofluoridate but not by 1,5-bis(4-allyldimethyl-
ammoniumphenyl)pentan-3-one dibromide.

The conduction mechanism of the motor stimuli in sea urchin embryos,
therefore, still remains an open question.

F. Lipase

The earlier literature is scanty and contradictory. Positive results have
been reported in very early work by Woodward (1918, 1921) and Glaser
(1921, 1922, 1923), but negative ones by Just (1929) and Runnström
(1949). The behavior of the tributyrin-splitting enzyme has already been
described in Section E. Lindvall (1948), following the observation by
Öhman (1944, 1947) that the lipoid composition of the egg surface
changes at fertilization, investigated this enzyme activity in the first
minutes following sperm penetration, and found a rise with a first major
peak at about 15 minutes. More recently, Mohri (1959) described the

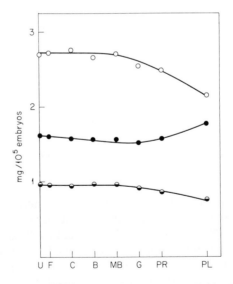

Fig. 12.3. Changes in the content of total lipid (O), phospholipids (◓), and total nitrogen
(●) during the early development of the sea urchin *Paracentrotus lividus*. U, unfertilized
egg; F, newly fertilized egg; C, cleavage (32–64 cells); B, blastula; MB, mesenchyme
blastula; G, gastrula; PR, prism; PL, pluteus. (From Mohri, 1964.)

ability of spermatozoa of *Anthocidaris crassispina* to hydrolyze lecithins and cephalins (see, also, Numanoi, 1959a,b,c). Indirect information concerning the enzymes of lipidic metabolism can be derived mainly from the work of Mohri (1964; Mohri and Monroy, 1963), who studied the incorporation of ^{14}C-labeled acetate and glycerol into lipids of developing *Paracentrotus lividus* embryos. The main findings of this work are: (1) the total lipids decrease slightly in the late development, about a third being represented by phospholipids (Fig. 12.3); (2) [1-^{14}C]acetate and, to a lesser extent, the [1-^{14}C]glycerol are incorporated into the cephalin fraction; (3) incorporation of the acetate is very low in the unfertilized eggs but starts to increase after fertilization to reach a maximum at the prism stage; (4) incorporation of the glycerol decreases slightly after fertilization, then starts to increase again, describing a curve with a peak at blastula and a maximum at the pluteus stage (Fig. 12.4). Mohri (1964) reports a chemical fractionation of the embryo lipids, which confirms the previous information on the lipidic composition of sea urchin embryos (Ephrussi and Rapkine, 1928; Hayes, 1938; Öhman, 1944). The lipidic composition of a *Paracentrotus* gastrula is, according to Mohri, 41.5% triglycerides, 27.4% phospholipids, and 8% free cholesterol.

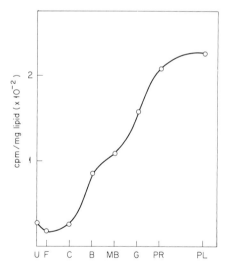

Fig. 12.4. Incorporation of [1-^{14}C]glycerol into the total lipid of sea urchin embryos during the early development. Abbreviations as in Fig. 12.3. (From Mohri, 1964.)

Marsh (1968) isolated from *Arbacia* eggs a lipoprotein of about 10^7 molecular weight, which contains 74% lipids. The author tentatively suggests that it might represent some storage material.

G. Other Esterases

Westin (1970) performed immunoelectrophoretic analysis of extracts of *Paracentrotus lividus* eggs and embryos. The precipitation bands so obtained were then stained for esterase activities. She reports that the unfertilized egg contains at least seven bands with β-carboxylesterase activity. Five of these are present till the pluteus stage. At this stage three more bands appear showing pseudocholinesterase activity (ability to use α-naphthyl esters as substrates).

What appears more interesting, from the point of view of the molecular mechanisms of differentiation, is that the antigens of these three latter enzymes are present even in the unfertilized eggs, in a form that is not yet enzymatically active.

H. Sulfatases

Lindahl (1936) was the first to demonstrate a phenolsulfatase activity in sea urchin eggs. This author made manometrical measurements of the CO_2 liberated from $CaCO_3$ by sulfuric acid. Gustafson and Hasselberg (1951) were the first to make a direct assay with a colorimetric method, using potassium *p*-nitrophenylsulfate as substrate, on *Paracentrotus lividus* homogenates. They reported a pH optimum at about 6.0. The activity remains at a constant level throughout development. On the other hand, Fedecka-Bruner and Epel (1969) have more recently studied the aryl sulfatase activity of the egg of *Strongylocentrotus purpuratus* and found that it increases slowly by a factor of 2 or 3 up to the hatching blastula stage, after which it shows a more rapid increase, by a factor of 30 or 40. Up to 90% of this activity is found to be localized in a particulate fraction of a lysosomal type. We have already mentioned in the section on phosphatases (see Section A,2,c) the granular localization of sulfatase (Jackson and Black, 1967). Administration of puromycin allows the enzyme to continue increasing for only one more hour. This would suggest that the activity increase is due to new enzyme synthesis. It is to be recalled, however, that the block of protein synthesis may in turn produce a severe general metabolic damage of the sea urchin cells (Giudice, 1965). Fedecka-Bruner *et al.* (1971) report that the increase in activity during the embryonic development of *Allocentrotus fragilis* is only 10-fold. In hybrids between *Strongylocentrotus* and *Allocentrotus,* the enzyme activity always reaches an intermediate value, thus suggesting once again that the activity is under nuclear control (see also Chapter 11).

I. Adenyl Cyclase

In view of the increasing interest in the regulatory role of the cyclic AMP in several biological systems, the search for such an enzyme in sea urchin embryos is well-justified. Castañeda and Tyler (1968b) have found that the 2000 *g* sediment of a homogenate of *Lytechinus pictus* eggs, if incubated with [¹⁴C]ATP, produces labeled cyclic AMP. The adenyl cyclase activity increases after fertilization to reach a plateau at about 30 minutes. (The investigation was not protracted beyond 60 minutes; the 2000 *g* supernatant was active to a lesser extent.)

Hand (1971) has tried administering cyclic AMP to unfertilized eggs. He reports no activation of protein synthesis or parthenogenesis under the conditions used.

J. Photoreactivating Enzyme

Cook and Setlow (1966) reported this activity in the 2000 *g* super-natant of a homogenate of *Arbacia punctulata* eggs (see also Chapter 5).

K. Glucosamine 6-Phosphate Kinase

Nicotra *et al.* (1967) have reported that eggs and embryos of *Paracen-trotus lividus* are able to phosphorylate glucosamine. The same authors (1968) have shown that glucosamine 6-phosphate can also be synthesized by *Paracentrotus lividus* homogenates by transamidation of glucose 6-phosphate. This activity starts to increase at around the mesenchyme blastula stage, to reach the pluteus stage with values about 7 times higher than those of the unfertilized eggs.

L. β-1,3-Glucanase

Epel *et al.* (1969) have shown this enzymatic activity in eggs of *Strongylocentrotus purpuratus*. Interestingly enough, the activity is particulate bound in the unfertilized egg. At fertilization, it is partly re-leased into the perivitelline space and the surrounding seawater, suggest-ing that it might also be involved in the cortical reaction through the glycoprotein transformations that bring about the hardening of the ferti-lization membrane (Fig. 12.5). This enzyme has been described by these authors as an exohydrolase specific for the β-1,3-glucosidic linkage.

The enzyme more recently was studied by Vacquier (1971a,b) on *Dendraster excentricus*. Here it undergoes a sharp increase at the time of gut differentiation at the pluteus stage. By partial purification of the guts of exogastrulating embryos, Vacquier was able to demonstrate a 1.5-fold concentration of the activity in the gut, suggesting a digestive role of the enzyme. The enzyme activity increase is completely, but reversibly, blocked by cycloheximide, and depressed by actinomycin D. This suggests that the increase is owing to synthesis of new enzyme. Interestingly enough, the catalysis product of the enzyme, glucose, is able to reduce the developmental increase of glucanase activity if added to seawater. This effect is reversible and specific, since other monosaccharides have proved ineffective in this respect.

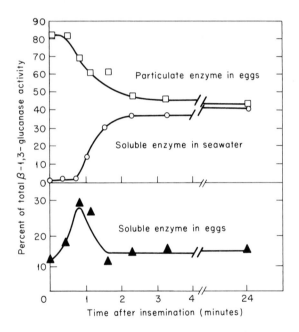

Fig. 12.5. Timing of release of β-1,3-glucanase from particles and its excretion into surrounding seawater after fertilization (14°C). Particulate enzyme represents all activity associated with particles sedimented by 28,000 g for 15 minutes; soluble enzyme in eggs represents activity remaining in the 28,000 g supernatant. (From Epel *et al.*, 1969, copyright, 1969 by the American Association for the Advancement of Science.)

Differences are noted between the larval enzyme and that isolated from adult animals. The former can be resolved by SDS–acrylamide gel electrophoresis into a main component of 50,000 and a minor one of 75,300 molecular weight. The latter shows only one component of 75,300 molecular weight.

M.   Benzidine Peroxidase

A microchemical detection of this reaction in eggs and embryos of *Psammechinus miliaris, Paracentrotus lividus,* and *Sphaerechinus granularis* was reported by Pitotti (1939). She showed that the reaction is lost by the cells that have differentiated into ectoderm.

N.   Glutaminase

This activity has been determined by Gustafson and Hasselberg (1951) by measuring the NH_3 liberated following incubation of glutamine with homogenates of *Psammechinus miliaris* and *Paracentrotus lividus.* The optimum pH is 8.7. The activity starts to increase at the formation of the primary mesenchyme. This increase is partially inhibited by a treatment with LiCl (Fig. 12.6).

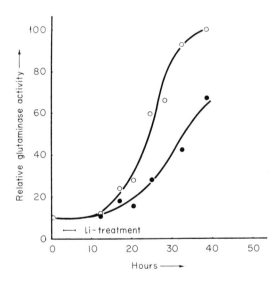

Fig. 12.6. Relative glutaminase activity in various normal (O) and Li-treated (●) developing stages of *Psammechinus miliaris.* (From Gustafson and Hasselberg, 1951.)

O.   Transaminase

Black (1964) has assayed the glutamic–aspartic transaminase and glutamic–alanine transaminase activity of homogenates of *Lytechinus variegatus* eggs and embryos. The activity is measured by following spectrophotometrically the DPNH oxidation by the keto acids produced in the transaminase reaction. Both these activities are present in the un-fertilized eggs, and they show only slight variations throughout development. In one assay performed on a particulate fraction, which contains most of the homogenate activity, it was again found that the trans-aminases remain constant throughout development, while the succinic dehydrogenase activity, parallelly tested, increases about 3-fold by the time the embryos reach the pluteus stage.

Botvinnik and Neifakh (1969) have described a doubling of aspartate–aminotransferase activity following fertilization in the eggs of *Strongy-locentrotus nudus*. The activity fluctuates then with a drop at the early blastula, followed by another rise and drop before hatching. The first increase is not sensitive to actinomycin or puromycin and seems to be attributable to activation of a preexisting enzyme through mechanisms that remain to be investigated.

P.   Phosphocholinetransferase (CDP-Choline: 1,2-Diglyceride Cholinephosphotransferase-E.C.2.7.8.2)

This enzyme has been studied by R. D. Ewing and K. Köhler (Fertiliza-tion and Gamete Physiology Training Program, 1970, M. B. L., Woods Hole, unpublished) and assayed by paper chromatography using [³H]CMP as substrate. Rapid synthesis of CDP-choline from CMP is observed in extracts of *Arbacia punctulata* eggs. The enzyme activity is almost entirely concentrated in a cell fraction sedimenting at 10,000 *g* or less.

The activity is entirely dependent upon Mg^{2+}, Mn^{2+}, or Co^{2+} and is not stimulated by the addition of egg lecithin.

CDP–choline formation occurs at a rate of 15.4 nmoles/minute/10^6 eggs. The enzyme activity decreases following fertilization and remains at low levels through the early blastula stage to attain a second peak during gastrulation, followed by a second decrease. Very low activity is found in the eggs.

Q.   α-Amylase

This enzyme has been recently studied by Vacquier *et al.* (1971). It appears to be connected with the development of the intestine in the plutei of *Dendraster excentricus*. It shows maltase activity. The larval enzyme can be resolved by SDS–acrylamide gel electrophoresis into two components of 52,000 and 76,000 molecular weight, whereas the enzyme from the intestine of the adult animal shows only one component of 57,000 molecular weight.

R.   Cytidine 5′-Monophosphosialic Acid Synthetase

In agreement with the findings in other animal cells, this enzyme is found largely in the nucleated halves of *Arbacia punctulata* or *Strongylocentrotus purpuratus* eggs (Kean and Bruner, 1971).

S.   β-Glucuronidase

This enzyme, which is usually considered characteristic of lysosomes, is found in the unfertilized eggs of *Arbacia punctulata,* in a particulate sedimenting between 1,000 and 15,000 g, from which it is released upon treatment with Triton X 100 at low pH. The glucuronidase-containing particulate is made up of two types of particles: the first consists of particles with a density of 1.065 and about 0.1 μm in diameter; the second of particles with a density of 1.120 and about 0.45 μm in diameter. The latter resemble the particles contained in the cortical granules. Following fertilization there is a redistribution of this enzyme activity, which becomes located in two types of particles with a density of 1.040 and 1.092, respectively (Weissman *et al.,* 1971).

Bibliography

Abelson, P. H. (1947). Permeability of eggs of *Arbacia punctulata* to radioactive phosphorus. *Biol. Bull.* **93**, 203.

Abrams, R. (1951). Synthesis of nucleic acid purines in the sea urchin embryo. *Exp. Cell Res.* **2**, 235.

Afzelius, B. A. (1955a). The ultrastructure of the nuclear membrane of the sea urchin oocyte as studied with the electron microscope. *Exp. Cell Res.* **8**, 147.

Afzelius, B. A. (1955b). The fine structure of the sea urchin spermatozoa as revealed by the electron microscope. *Z. Zellforsch. Mikrosk. Anat.* **42**, 134.

Afzelius, B. A. (1956a). Electron microscopy of Golgi elements in sea urchin eggs. *Exp. Cell Res.* **11**, 67.

Afzelius, B. A. (1956b). The ultrastructure of the cortical granules and their products in the sea urchin egg as studied with the electron microscope. *Exp. Cell Res.* **10**, 257.

Afzelius, B. A. (1957a). Electron microscopy on the basophilic structures of the sea urchin eggs. *Z. Zellforsch. Mikrosk. Anat.* **45**, 660.

Afzelius, B. A. (1957b). "Electron Microscopy on Sea Urchin Gametes." Almqvist & Wiksell, Stockholm.

Afzelius, B. A., and Murray, A. (1957). The acrosomal reaction of spermatozoa during fertilization or treatment with egg water. *Exp. Cell Res.* **12**, 325.

Agassiz, A. (1867). On the embryology of the echinoderms. *Mem. Amer. Acad. Arts & Sci.* **9**, 1.

Agrell, I. (1954). Oestradiol and testosterone propionate as mitotic inhibitors during embryogenesis. *Nature (London)* **173**, 172.

Agrell, I. (1958). Cytochemical indication of DNA in the pronucleus of the mature sea urchin egg. *Ark. Zool.* **11**, 457.

Aiello, F., and Maggio, R. (1961). The effect of sea water on cytochrome oxidase and oxidative phosphorylation. *Experientia* **17**, 390.

Aketa, K. (1957). Quantitative analyses of lactic acid and related compounds in sea urchin eggs at the time of fertilization. *Embryologia* **3**, 267.

Aketa, K. (1961a). Studies on the production of the fertilization acid in sea urchin eggs. I. Acid production at fertilization and activation, and the effect of some metabolic inhibitors. *Embryologia* **5**, 397.

Aketa, K. (1961b). Studies on the production of the fertilization acid in sea urchin eggs. II. Experimental analysis of the production mechanism. *Embryologia* **5**, 408.

Aketa, K. (1962). Studies on the production of the fertilization acid in sea urchin eggs. III. Cytochemical examination of the possible role of acid mucopolysaccharide components in the acid production. *Embryologia* **7**, 223.

Aketa, K. (1963). Studies on the acid production at fertilization of sea urchin eggs. *Exp. Cell Res.* **30,** 93.

Aketa, K. (1967a). On the sperm-egg bonding as the initial step of fertilization in the sea urchin. *Embryologia* **9,** 238.

Aketa, K. (1967b). Isolation of the plasma membrane from sea urchin egg. *Exp. Cell Res.* **68,** 222.

Aketa, K., and Onitake, K. (1969). Effect on fertilization of antiserum against sperm-binding protein from homo- and heterologous sea urchin egg surfaces. *Exp. Cell Res.* **56,** 84.

Aketa, K., and Tomita, H. (1958). Oxidative phosphorylation by a cell-free particulate system from unfertilized eggs of the sea urchin *Hemicentrotus pulcherrimus. Bull. Mar. Biol. Sta. Asamushi, Tohoku Univ.* **9,** 57.

Aketa, K., and Tsuzuki, H. (1968). Sperm-binding capacity of the S—S reduced protein of the vitelline membrane of the sea urchin egg. *Exp. Cell Res.* **50,** 675.

Aketa, K., Bianchetti, R., Marré, E., and Monroy, A. (1964). Hexose monophosphate level as a limiting factor for respiration in unfertilized sea urchin eggs. *Biochim. Biophys. Acta* **86,** 211.

Aketa, K., Tsuzuki, H., and Onitake, K. (1968). Characterization of the sperm-binding protein from sea urchin egg surface. *Exp. Cell Res.* **50,** 676.

Allen, R. D. (1954). Fertilization and activation of sea urchin eggs in glass capillaries. I. Membrane elevation and nuclear movements in totally and partially fertilized eggs. *Exp. Cell Res.* **6,** 403.

Allen, R. D., Markman, B., and Rowe, E. C. (1958). The time sequence of early events in the fertilization of the sea urchin eggs. II. The production of acid. *Exp. Cell Res.* **15,** 346.

Allison, W. S., and Clark, E. E. (1960). Observations on the ribosomes of sea urchins. *Biol. Bull.* **119,** 302.

Amemiya, S. (1971). Relationship between cilia formation and cell association in sea urchin embryos. *Exp. Cell Res.* **64,** 227.

Amoore, J. E. (1963). Non-identical mechanisms of mitotic arrest by respiratory inhibitors in pea root tips and sea urchin eggs. *J. Cell Biol.* **18,** 555.

Anderson, E. (1968). Oocyte differentiation in the sea urchin, *Arbacia punctulata,* with particular reference to the origin of cortical granules and their participation in the cortical reaction. *J. Cell Biol.* **37,** 514.

Anderson, E. (1969). An ultrastructural analysis of the centrifuged whole, half and quarter eggs of the sea urchin *Arbacia punctulata. J. Cell Biol.* **43,** 6a.

Anderson, E. (1970). A cytological study of the centrifuged whole, half and quarter eggs of the sea urchin *Arbacia punctulata. J. Cell Biol.* **47,** 711.

Anderson, W. A. (1968a). Structure and fate of the paternal mitochondrion during early embryogenesis of *Paracentrotus lividus. J. Ultrastruct. Res.* **24,** 311.

Anderson, W. A. (1968b). Cytochemistry of sea urchin gametes. I. Intramitochondrial localization of glycogen, glucose-6-phosphatase, and adenosinetriphosphatase activity in spermatozoa of *Paracentrotus lividus. J. Ultrastruct. Res.* **24,** 398.

Anderson, W. A. (1968c). Cytochemistry of sea urchin gametes. III. Acid and alkaline phosphatase activity of spermatozoa and fertilization. *J. Ultrastruct. Res.* **25,** 1.

Anderson, W. A. (1969). Nuclear and cytoplasmic DNA synthesis during early embryogenesis of *Paracentrotus lividus. J. Ultrastruct. Res.* **26,** 95.

Andrews, G. F. (1897a). Some spinning activities of protoplasm in starfish and sea urchin eggs. *J. Morphol.* **12,** 367.

Andrews, G. F. (1897b). The living substance as such and as organism. *J. Morphol.* **12,** Suppl. to Part 2, 1.

Aronson, A. I. (1972). Degradation products and a unique endonuclease in heterogeneous nuclear RNA in sea urchin embryos. *Nature (London) New Biol.* **235,** 40.

Aronson, A. I., and Wilt, F. H. (1969). Properties of nuclear RNA in sea urchin embryos. *Proc. Nat. Acad. Sci. U.S.* **62**, 186.

Ashbel, R. (1929). La glicolisi nelle uova di riccio di mare fecondate e non fecondate. *Boll. Soc. Ital. Biol. Sper.* **4**, 492.

Auclair, W., and Siegel, B. W. (1966a). Cilia regeneration in sea urchin embryo. *Biol. Bull.* **131**, 379.

Auclair, W., and Siegel, B. W. (1966b). Cilia regeneration in the sea urchin embryo: Evidence for a pool of ciliary proteins. *Science* **154**, 913.

Augustinsson, K.-B. (1948). Cholinesterases. A study in comparative emzymology. *Acta Physiol. Scand.* **15**, Suppl. 52, 1.

Augustinsson, K.-B., and Gustafson, T. (1949). Cholinesterase activity in developing sea urchin eggs. *J. Cell. Comp. Physiol.* **34**, 311.

Augusti-Tocco, G., De Petrocellis, B., and Scarano, E. (1969). Effects of amantadine on the early embryonic development of the sea urchin. *Develop. Biol.* **19**, 341.

Austin, C. R. (1968). "Ultrastructure of Fertilization." Holt, New York.

Azarnia, R., and Chambers, E. L. (1969). Effect of fertilization on the uptake and efflux of calcium-45 in the eggs of *Arbacia punctulata*. *Biol. Bull.* **137**, 391.

Azarnia, R., and Chambers, E. L. (1970). Effect of fertilization on the calcium and magnesium content of the eggs of *Arbacia punctulata*. *Biol. Bull.* **139**, 413.

Bäckström, S. (1959). Reduction of blue tetrazolium in developing sea urchin eggs after addition of various substrates and phosphopyridine nucleotides. *Exp. Cell Res.* **18**, 357.

Bäckström, S. (1963). 6-Phosphogluconate dehydrogenase in sea urchin embryos. *Exp. Cell Res.* **32**, 566.

Bäckström, S. (1965a). Basic proteins in the sea urchin embryo (*Paracentrotus lividus*). *Acta Embryol. Morphol. Exp.* **8**, 20.

Bäckström, S. (1965b). Basic proteins during sea urchin ovogenesis (*Psammechinus miliaris*). *Acta Embryol. Morphol. Exp.* **8**, 178.

Bäckström, S. (1966a). A complex between basic proteins and acid polysaccharides in sea urchin oocytes and eggs. *Acta Embryol. Morphol. Exp.* **9**, 37.

Bäckström, S. (1966b). Basic proteins in parthenogenetically activated sea urchin eggs. *Acta Embryol. Morphol. Exp.* **9**, 83.

Bäckström, S. (1966c). Distribution of basic proteins in centrifuged sea urchin eggs. *Exp. Cell Res.* **43**, 578.

Bäckström, S. (1968). Incorporation of tritium-labelled lysine in sea urchin oocytes. *Acta Embryol. Morphol. Exp.* **10**, 264.

Bäckström, S. (1969). Changes in protein-bound tritiated lysine after fertilization of the sea urchin eggs. *Acta Embryol. Morphol. Exp.* **10**, 275.

Bäckström, S., and Gustafson, T. (1953). Lithium sensitivity in the sea urchin in relation to the stage of development. *Ark. Zool.* **6**, 185.

Bäckström, S., Hultin, K., and Hultin, T. (1960). Pathways of glucose metabolism in early sea urchin development. *Exp. Cell Res.* **19**, 634.

Badman, W. S., and Brookbank, J. W. (1970). Serological studies of two hybrid sea urchins. *Develop. Biol.* **21**, 243.

Baker, R. F. (1971). Changing size pattern of newly synthesized nuclear DNA during early development of the sea urchin. *Biochem. Biophys. Res. Commun.* **43**, 1415.

Bal, A. K., Krupa, P. L., and Cousineau, G. H. (1967). Localization of RNA in the membrane systems of developing embryos of sea urchins. *J. Cell Biol.* **35**, 8A.

Bal, A. K., Jubinville, F., Cousineau, G. H., and Inoué, S. (1968). Origin and fate of annulate lamellae in *Arbacia punctulata* eggs. *J. Ultrastruct. Res.* **25**, 15.

Balinsky, B. I. (1959). An electron microscopic investigation of the mechanism of adhesion of the cells in a sea urchin blastula and gastrula. *Exp. Cell Res.* **16**, 429.

Balinsky, B. I. (1961). The role of cortical granules in the formation of the fertilization membrane and the surface membrane of fertilized sea urchin eggs. *Symp. Int. Inst. Embryol., 1960* p. 205.

Ballentine, R. (1940). Analysis of the changes in respiratory activity accompanying the fertilization of marine eggs. *J. Cell. Comp. Physiol.* **15,** 217.

Baltimore, D., and Huang, A. S. (1970). Interaction of HeLa cell proteins with RNA. *J. Mol. Biol.* **47,** 263.

Baltus, E., Quertier, J., Ficq, A., and Brachet, J. (1965). Biochemical studies of nucleate and anucleate fragments isolated from sea urchin eggs. A comparison between fertilization and parthenogenetic activation. *Biochim. Biophys. Acta* **95,** 408.

Baltzer, F. (1910). Über die Beziehung zwischen dem Chromatin und der Entwicklung und Verebungsrichtung bei Echinodermbastarden. *Arch. Zellforsch.* **5,** 497.

Baltzer, F. (1913). Über die Herkunft der Idiochromosomen bei Seeigeln. *Sitzungsber. Phys.-Med. Ges. Wurzburg* p. 90.

Baltzer, F., and Bernhard, M. (1955). Weitere Beobachtungen über Letalität und Verebungsrichtung beim Seeigelbastard *Paracentrotus* ♀ × *Arbacia* ♂. *Exp. Cell Res., Suppl.* **3,** 16.

Baltzer, F., and Chen, P. S. (1960). Cytological behaviour and the synthesis of nucleic acids in sea urchin hybrids *Paracentrotus* ♀ × *Arbacia* ♂ and *Paracentrotus* ♀ × *Sphaearechinus* ♂. *Rev. Suisse Zool.* **67,** 183.

Baltzer, F., Harding, C., Lehman, H. E., and Bopp, P. (1954). Über die Entwicklungshemmungen der Seeigelbastarde *Paracentrotus* ♀ × *Arbacia* ♂ und *Psammechinus* ♀ × *Arbacia* ♂. *Rev. Suisse Zool.* **61,** 402.

Baltzer, F., Chen, P. S., and Whiteley, A. H. (1959). Biochemical studies on sea urchin hybrids. *Exp. Cell Res., Suppl.* **6,** 192.

Baltzer, F., Chen, P. S., and Tardant, P. (1961). Embryonalentwicklung, DNS-synthese und Respiration des Bastards *Arbacia* ♀ × *Paracentrotus* ♂, mit Vergleichen zu anderen Seeigelbastarden. *Arch. Julius Klaus-Stift. Vererbungsforsch. Sozialanthropol. Russenhyg.* **36,** 126.

Bamberger, J. W., Martin, W. E., Stearns, L. W., and Jolley, W. B. (1963). Effect of 8-azaguanine on cleavage and nucleic acid metabolism in sea urchin, *Strongylocentrotus purpuratus,* embryos. *Exp. Cell Res.* **31,** 266.

Barber, M. L. (1971). Effects of mycostatin in sea urchin development. *Wilhelm Roux' Arch. Entwicklungsmech. Organismen* **166,** 226.

Barnett, R. C. (1953). Cell division inhibition of *Arbacia* and *Chaetopterus* eggs and its reversal by Krebs cycle intermediates and certain phosphate compounds. *Biol. Bull.* **104,** 263.

Barrett, D. (1968). Hatching enzyme of the sea urchin *Strongylocentrotus purpuratus.* *Amer. Zool.* **8,** 816.

Barrett, D., and Angelo, G. M. (1969). Maternal characteristics of hatching enzymes in hybrid sea urchin embryos. *Exp. Cell Res.* **57,** 159.

Barros, C., and Giudice, G. (1968). Effect of polyamines on ribosomal RNA synthesis during sea urchin development. *Exp. Cell Res.* **50,** 671.

Baxandall, J. (1964). Sperm antigens in sperm and fertilized eggs. *Proc. 3rd European Regional Conf. Electron Microscopy, B* pp. 463–464. Publishing House Czech. Acad. Sci., Prague.

Baxandall, J., Perlman, P., and Afzelius, B. A. (1964a). Immunoelectron microscope analysis of the surface layers of the unfertilized sea urchin egg. I. Effects of the antisera on the cell ultrastructure. *J. Cell. Biol.* **23,** 609.

Baxandall, J., Perlman, P., and Afzelius, B. A. (1964b). Immunoelectron microscope analysis of the surface layers of the unfertilized sea urchin egg. II. Localization of surface antigens. *J. Cell. Biol.* **23,** 629.

Beams, H. W., and Evans, T. C. (1940). Some effects of colchicine upon the first cleavage in *Arbacia punctulata. Biol. Bull.* **79,** 188.

Behnke, O., and Forer, A. (1967). Evidence for four classes of microtubules in individual cells. *J. Cell Sci.* **2,** 169.

Belitzina, N. V., Ajtkhozhin, M. A., Gavrilova, L. P., and Spirin, A. S. (1964). Informational ribonucleic acids of differentiating animal cells. *Biokhimiya* **29,** 363.

Bellemare, G., Pinard, J., Aubin, A., and Cousineau, G. H. (1968). Uptake and incorporation of leucine and thymidine in developing sea urchin eggs. The effects of hexahomoserine. *Exp. Cell Res.* **51,** 406.

Bellemare, G., Cedergren, R. J., Diagneault, R., and Cousineau, G. H. (1970). 5 S ribosomal RNA of sea urchin eggs analyzed by optical techniques. *J. Cell Biol.* **47,** 17a.

Benttinen, L. C., and Comb, D. G. (1971). Early and late histones during sea urchin development. *J. Mol. Biol.* **57,** 355.

Berg, W. E. (1950). Free amino acids in sea urchin eggs and embryos. *Proc. Soc. Exp. Biol. Med.* **75,** 30.

Berg, W. E. (1965). Rates of protein synthesis in whole and half embryos of the sea urchin. *Exp. Cell Res.* **40,** 469.

Berg, W. E. (1968a). Rates of protein and nucleic acid synthesis in half embryos of the sea urchin. *Exp. Cell Res.* **50,** 679.

Berg, W. E. (1968b). Effect of lithium on the rate of protein synthesis in the sea urchin embryo. *Exp. Cell Res.* **50,** 133.

Berg, W. E. (1968c). Kinetics of uptake and incorporation of valine in the sea urchin embryo. *Exp. Cell Res.* **49,** 379.

Berg, W. E. (1970). Further studies on the kinetics of incorporation of valine in the sea urchin embryo. *Exp. Cell Res.* **60,** 210.

Berg, W. E., and Akin, E. J. (1971). Inhibition of gastrulation by the blastocoelic fluid from the sea urchin embryo. *Develop. Biol.* **26,** 353.

Berg, W. E., and Chang, A. C. (1962). Tests for diffusible morphogenetic substance in the sea urchin embryo. *Acta Embryol. Morphol. Exp.* **5,** 167.

Berg, W. E., and Long, N. D. (1964). Regional differences of mitochondrial size in the sea urchin embryo. *Exp. Cell Res.* **33,** 422.

Berg, W. E., and Mertes, D. H. (1970). Rates of synthesis and degradation of protein in the sea urchin embryos. *Exp. Cell Res.* **60,** 218.

Berg, W. E., Taylor, D. A., and Humphreys, W. J. (1962). Distribution of mitochondria in echinoderm embryo as determined by electron microscopy. *Develop. Biol.* **4,** 165.

Bergami, M., Mansour, T. E., and Scarano, E. (1968). Properties of glycogen phosphorylase before and after fertilization in the sea urchin eggs. *Exp. Cell Res.* **49,** 650.

Bernstein, M. H. (1961). Electron microscopic observations on the effects of homologous egg water on echinoderm spermatozoa. *Biol. Bull.* **121,** 382.

Bernstein, M. H. (1962). Normal and reactive morphology of sea urchin spermatozoa. *Exp. Cell Res.* **27,** 197.

Bibring, T., and Baxandall, J. (1968). Mitotic apparatus: The selective extraction of protein with mild acid. *Science* **161,** 377.

Bibring, T., and Baxandall, J. (1969). Immunochemical studies of 22 S protein from isolated mitotic apparatus. *J. Cell Biol.* **41,** 577.

Bibring, T., and Baxandall, J. (1971). Selective extraction of isolated mitotic apparatus. Evidence that typical microtubule protein is extracted by organic mercurial. *J. Cell Biol.* **48,** 324.

Bibring, T., and Cousineau, G. H. (1964). Percentage incorporation of leucine labelled with carbon-14 into isolated mitotic apparatus during early development of sea urchin eggs. *Nature (London)* **204**, 805.

Bibring, T., Brachet, J., Gaeta, F. S., and Graziosi, F. (1965). Some physical properties of cytoplasmic DNA in unfertilized eggs of *Arbacia*. *Biochim. Biophys. Acta* **108**, 644.

Bielig, H. J., and Dohrn, P. (1950). Zur Frage der Wirkung von Echinochrome A und Gallerthüllensubstanz auf die Spermatozoen des Seeigels *Arbacia lixula*. *Z. Naturforsch. B* **5**, 316.

Billiar, R. B., Brungard, J. C., and Villee, C. A. (1964). D-Malate: Effects on activity of L-malate dehydrogenase in developing sea urchin embryos. *Science* **146**, 1464.

Billiar, R. B., Zalewski, L., and Villee, C. A. (1966). L-Malate dehydrogenase activity and protein synthesis in sea urchin embryos. *Develop. Biol.* **13**, 282.

Birnstiel, M., Grunstein, M., Speirs, J., and Hennig, W. (1969). Family of ribosomal genes of *Xenopus laevis*. *Nature (London)* **223**, 1265.

Bishop, D. W., and Metz, Ch. B. (1952). Fructose as carbohydrate constituent of fertilizin from the sand dollar, *Echinaracnius parma*. *Nature (London)* **169**, 548.

Black, R. E. (1964). Transaminase activity in homogenates of developing eggs of the sea urchin, *Lytechinus variegatus*. *Exp. Cell. Res.* **33**, 613.

Black, R. E., Baptist, E., and Piland, J. (1967). Puromycin and cycloheximide inhibition of thymidine incorporation into DNA of cleaving sea urchin eggs. *Exp. Cell Res.* **48**, 439.

Blanchard, K. C. (1935). The nucleic acid of the eggs of *Arbacia punctulata*. *J. Biol. Chem.* **108**, 251.

Blomquist, C. H. (1969). Reversible inactivation of nicotinamide adenine dinucleotide kinase in extracts of unfertilized sea urchin eggs. *Exp. Cell Res.* **56**, 172.

Blum, H. F., and Price, J. P. (1950). Delay of cleavage of the *Arbacia* egg by ultraviolet radiation. *J. Gen. Physiol.* **33**, 285.

Blum, H. F., Robinson, J. C., and Loos, G. M. (1951). The loci of action of ultraviolet and X-radiation and of photorecovery in the egg and sperm of the sea urchin *Arbacia punctulata*. *J. Gen. Physiol.* **35**, 323.

Bohus-Jensen, A. A. (1953). The effect of trypsin on the cross-fertilizability of sea urchin eggs. *Exp. Cell Res.* **5**, 325.

Bolognari, A. (1952). Variazioni quantitative del contenuto in glutatione nelle uova fecondate di *Paracentrotus lividus*. *Arch. Sci. Biol. (Bologna)* **36**, 40.

Bolst, A. L., and Whiteley, A. H. (1957). Studies of the metabolism of phosphorus in the development of the sea urchin, *Strongylocentrotus purpuratus*. *Biol. Bull.* **112**, 276.

Boolootian, R. A., ed. (1966). "Physiology of Echinodermata." Wiley (Interscience), New York.

Borei, H. (1933). Beitrage zur Kenntnis der Vorgänge bei der Befruchtung des Echinodermeneies. *Z. Vergl. Physiol.* **20**, 258.

Borei, H. (1948). Respiration of oocytes, unfertilized eggs and fertilized eggs from *Psammechinus* and *Asterias*. *Biol. Bull.* **95**, 124.

Borei, H. G., and Björklund, U. (1953). Oxidation through the cytochrome system of substituted phenylenediamines. *Biochem. J.* **54**, 357.

Borisy, G. G., and Taylor, E. W. (1967a). The mechnism of action of colchicine. Colchicine binding to sea urchin eggs and the mitotic apparatus. *J. Cell Biol.* **34**, 535.

Borisy, G. G., and Taylor, E. W. (1967b). The mechanism of action of colchicine. Binding of colchicine-H³ to cellular protein. *J. Cell Biol.* **34**, 525.

Bosco, M., and Monroy, A. (1960). Inhibition of the differentiation of the primary mesenchyme in the sea urchin embryo caused by ethionine. *Acta Embryol. Morphol. Exp.* **3**, 53.

Bosco, M., and Monroy, A. (1962). Differential incorporation of labelled amino acids in the territories of the sea urchin blastula. *Experientia* **18**, 124.

Botvinnik, N. M., and Neifakh, A. A. (1969). Changes of aspartate-amino-transferase activity in sea urchin early development and their independence from macromolecular synthesis. *Exp. Cell Res.* **54**, 287.

Boveri, T. (1888). Über partielle Befruchtung. *Ber. Naturforsch. Ges. Freiburg i. Br.* **4**, 64.

Boveri, T. (1889). Ein geschlechtlich erzeugte Organismus ohne mütterliche Eigenschaften. *Sitzungsber. Gesell. Morphol. Physiol. Muench* **5**, 73.

Boveri, T. (1901a). Die Polarität von Oocyte, Ei und Larve des *Strongylocentrotus lividus*. *Zool. Jahrb., Abt. Anat. Ontog. Tiere* **14**, 630.

Boveri, T. (1901b). Über die Polarität des Seeigeleis. *Verh. Phys.-Med. Ges. Wurzburg* [N.S.] **35**, 145.

Boveri, T. (1902). Über mehrpolige Mitosen als Mittel zur Analyse des Zellkerns. *Verh. Phys.-Med. Ges. Wurzburg* [N.S.] **35**, 67.

Boveri, T. (1903). Über den Einfluss der Samenzelle auf die Larvencharactere der Echiniden. *Arch. Entwicklungsmech. Organismen* **16**, 340.

Boveri, T. (1905). Zellenstudien. V. *Jena. Z. Naturwiss.* **39**, 445.

Boveri, T. (1907). Zellenstudien. VI. *Jena. Z. Naturwiss.* **43**, 1.

Boveri, T. (1910). *Festschr. von R. Hertwig 60. Geburstag* Vol. 3, p. 133.

Boveri, T. (1918). Zwei Fehlerquellen bei Merogonieversuchen und die Entwicklungsfähigkeit merogonischer und partiell-merogonischer Seeigelbastarde. *Arch. Entwicklungsmech. Organismen* **44**, 417.

Brachet, A. (1910). La polyspermie experimentale comme moyen d'analyse de la fécondation. *Arch. Entwicklungsmech. Organismen* **30**, 261.

Brachet, J. (1933). Recherches sur la synthèse de l'acide thymonucléique pendant le développement de l'oeuf d'oursin. *Arch. Biol.* **44**, 519.

Brachet, J. (1937). Remarques sur la formation de l'acide thymonucléique pendant le développement des oeufs à synthèse partielle. *Arch. Biol.* **48**, 529.

Brachet, J. (1967). Effects of hydroxyurea on development and regeneration. *Nature (London)* **214**, 1132.

Brachet, J., and Ficq, A. (1956). Remarques à propos du rôle biologique des acides nucléiques. *Arch. Biol.* **67**, 431.

Brachet, J., and Hulin, N. (1970). Observations sur les acides désoxyribonucléiques des hybrides létaux entre les oursins. *Exp. Cell Res.* **60**, 393.

Brachet, J., Decroly, M., Ficq, A., and Quertier, J. (1963a). RNA metabolism in unfertilized and fertilized sea urchin eggs. *Biochim. Biophys. Acta* **72**, 660.

Brachet, J., Ficq, A., and Tencer, R. (1963b). Amino acid incorporation into proteins of nucleate and anucleate fragments of sea urchin eggs: Effect of parthenogenetic activation. *Exp. Cell Res.* **32**, 168.

Brachet, J., O'Dell, D., Steinert, G., and Tencer, R. (1972). Cleavage nucleoli and ribosomal RNA synthesis in sea urchin eggs. *Exp. Cell Res.* **73**, 463.

Brandhorst, B. P. (1970). Kinetics of turnover of DNA-like RNA and its transport to the cytoplasm in sea urchin embryos. *J. Cell. Biol.* **47**, 23a.

Brandhorst, B. P., and Humphreys, T. (1971). Synthesis and decay rates of major classes of DNA-like RNA in sea urchin embryos. *Biochemistry* **10**, 877.

Branham, J. M. (1969). Comparative fertility of sea urchins. *Amer. Zool.* **9**, 598.

Branham, J. M., and Metz, C. B. (1960). Inhibition of fertilizin agglutination in *Arbacia* by *Fucus* extracts. *Biol. Bull.* **122**, 194.

Brice, M. (1959). Animalization and vegetalization in eggs of the sea urchin treated with metachromatic dyes. *Arch. Biol.* **70**, 127.

Briggs, R., and King, T. J. (1960). Nuclear transplantation studies on the early gastrula (*Rana pipiens*). *Develop. Biol.* **2**, 252.

Britten, R. J., and Kone, D. E. (1968). Repeated sequences in DNA. *Science* **161**, 529.

Brookbank, J. W. (1958). Dispersal of the gelatinous coat material of *Mellita quinquies-perforata* eggs by homologous sperm and sperm extracts. *Biol. Bull.* **115**, 74.

Brookbank, J. W. (1964). The effect of antisera against fertilizin on the uptake of ortho-phosphate by sea urchin eggs. *Biol. Bull.* **126**, 1.

Brookbank, J. W. (1970). DNA synthesis and development in reciprocal interordinal hybrids of a sea urchin and a sand dollar. *Develop. Biol.* **21**, 29.

Brookbank, J. W., and Yonge, J. G. (1964). Studies on the 85 S ribosome fraction of echinoid egg and embryos. *Acta Embryol. Morphol. Exp.* **7**, 296.

Brooks, S. C. (1943). Intake and loss of ions by living cells. I. Eggs and larvae of *Arbacia punctulata* and *Asterias forbesi* exposed to phosphate and sodium ions. *Biol. Bull.* **84**, 213.

Brooks, S. C., and Chambers, E. L. (1948). Penetration of radioactive phosphate into the eggs of *Strongylocentrotus purpuratus, Strongylocentrotus franciscanus* and *Urechis caupo*. *Biol. Bull.* **95**, 262.

Brooks, S. C., and Chambers, E. L. (1954). The penetration of radioactive phosphate into marine eggs. *Biol. Bull.* **106**, 279.

Brown, D. D., and Weber, C. S. (1968). Gene linkage by RNA–DNA hybridization. I. Unique DNA sequences homologous to 4 S RNA, 5 S RNA and rRNA. *J. Mol. Biol.* **34**, 661.

Brown, D. E. S. (1934). The pressure coefficient of "viscosity" in the eggs of *Arbacia punctulata*. *J. Cell Comp. Physiol.* **5**, 335.

Broyles, R. H., and Strittmatter, C. F. (1971). Hexose monophosphate shunt dehydrog-enases during sea urchin development. *Exp. Cell Res.* **67**, 471.

Bryan, J. (1970). The isolation of a major structural element of the sea urchin fertilization membrane. *J. Cell Biol.* **44**, 635.

Bryan, J. (1971). Vinblastine and microtubules. I. The induction and isolation of crystals from sea urchin oocytes. *Exp. Cell Res.* **66**, 129.

Bryan, J., and Gilula, N. B. (1970). Crystalline structure of the proteins from the fertiliza-tion membrane as revealed by freeze-etching. *J. Cell Biol.* **47**, 26a.

Bucher, N. L. R., and Mazia, D. (1960). DNA synthesis in relation to duplication of centers in dividing eggs of the sea urchin, *Strongylocentrotus purpuratus*. *J. Biophys. Biochem. Cytol.* **7**, 651.

Burgos, M. H. (1955). The Feulgen reaction in mature unfertilized sea urchin eggs. *Exp. Cell Res.* **9**, 360.

Burny, A., Marbaix, G., Quertier, J., and Brachet, J. (1965). Demonstration of functional polyribosomes in nucleate and anucleate fragments of sea urchin eggs following parthe-nogenetic activation. *Biochim. Biophys. Acta* **103**, 526.

Bury, J. (1913). Experimentelle Untersuchungen über die Einwirkung der Temperatur 0°C auf die Entwicklung der Echinideneier. *Arch. Entwicklungsmech. Organismen* **36**, 537.

Butros, J. M. (1959). Stimulation of cleavage in *Arbacia* eggs with DNA fractions. *Exp. Cell Res.* **18**, 318.

Butros, J. M. (1969). Entry and action of exogenous RNA on protein synthesis in the sea urchin. *Acta Embryol. Morphol. Exp.* p. 70.

Callan, H. G. (1949). Cleavage rate, oxygen consuption and ribose nucleic acid content of sea urchin eggs. *Biochim. Biophys. Acta* **3**, 92.

Candelas, G. C., and Inverson, R. M. (1966). Evidence for translational level control of protein synthesis in the development of sea urchin eggs. *Biochem. Biophys. Res. Commun.* **24**, 867.

Cannata, F. (1970). Esame strutturale e citochimico dell'apparato nucleolare degli ovociti in accrescimento di alcune specie di Echinodermi: *Astropecten aurantiacus* L.; *Dorocidaris papillata* Leske: *Ophiomyxa pentagona* Lamk; *Stichopus regalis* Cuvier. *Arch. Zool. Ital.* **55**, 13.

Carden, G. A., Rosenkranz, S., and Rosenkranz, H. S. (1965). Deoxyribonucleic acids of sperm, eggs and somatic cells of the sea urchin *Arbacia punctulata. Nature (London)* **205**, 1338.

Caserta, G., and Ghiretti, F. (1962). Crystalline ubiquinone (coenzyme Q 10) from sea urchin sperm. *Nature (London)* **193**, 4820.

Caserta, G., and Ghiretti, F. (1963). Distribuzione degli ubichinoni negli invertebrati marini. *Boll. Soc. Ital. Biol. Sper.* **39**, 2072.

Castañeda, M. (1969). The activity of ribosomes of sea urchin eggs in response to fertilization. *Biochim. Biophys. Acta* **179**, 381.

Castañeda, M., and Tyler, A. (1968a). The lability of *in vitro* amino acid incorporating systems of sea urchin eggs to nuclease release and other factors. *Biochim. Biophys. Acta* **166**, 741.

Castañeda, M., and Tyler, A. (1968b). Adenylcyclase in plasma membrane preparations of of sea urchin eggs and its increase in activity after fertilization. *Biochem. Biophys. Res. Commun.* **33**, 782.

Ceccarini, C., and Maggio, R. (1969). A study of aminoacyl tRNA synthetase by methylated albumin Kieselghur column chromatography in *Paracentrotus lividus. Biochim. Biophys. Acta* **190**, 556.

Ceccarini, C., Maggio, R., and Barbata, G. (1967). Aminoacyl-sRNA synthetases as possible regulators of protein synthesis in the embryo of the sea urchin *Paracentrotus lividus. Proc. Nat. Acad. Sci. U.S.* **58**, 2235.

Chaffee, R. R., and Mazia, D. (1963). Echinochrome synthesis in hybrid sea urchin embryos. *Develop. Biol.* **7**, 502.

Chamberlain, J. P. (1968). Extranuclear RNA synthesis in sea urchin embryos. *J. Cell Biol.* **38**, 23a.

Chamberlain, J. P. (1970). RNA synthesis in anucleate egg fragments and normal embryos of the sea urchin *Arbacia punctulata. Biochim. Biophys. Acta* **213**, 183.

Chamberlain, J. P., and Metz, C. B. (1972). Mitochondrial RNA synthesis in sea urchin embryos. *J. Mol. Biol.* **64**, 593.

Chambers, E. L. (1939). The movement of the egg nucleus in relation to the sperm aster in the echinoderm egg. *J. Exp. Biol.* **16**, 409.

Chambers, E. L. (1949). The uptake and loss of K^{42} in the unfertilized and fertilized eggs of *Strongylocentrotus purpuratus* and *Arbacia punctulata. Biol. Bull.* **97**, 251.

Chambers, E. L., and Chambers, R. (1949). Ion exchanges and fertilization in echinoderm eggs. *Amer. Natur.* **83**, 269.

Chambers, E. L., and Mende, J. T. (1953a). Alterations of the inorganic phosphate and arginine phosphate content in sea urchin eggs following fertilization. *Exp. Cell Res.* **5**, 508.

Chambers, E. L., and Mende, J. T. (1953b). The adenosine triphosphate content of the unfertilized and fertilized eggs of *Asterias forbesii* and *Strongylocentrotus dröbachiensis. Arch. Biochem. Biophys.* **44**, 46.

Chambers, E. L., and White, W. E. (1949). The accumulation of phosphate and evidence for the synthesis of adenosine triphosphate in fertilized sea urchin eggs. *Biol. Bull.* **97**, 225.

Chambers, E. L., and White, W. E. (1954). The accumulation of phosphate by fertilized sea urchin eggs. *Biol. Bull.* **106**, 297.

Chambers, E. L., and Whiteley, A. H. (1966). Phosphate transport in fertilized sea urchin eggs. I. Kinetics aspects. *J. Cell Physiol.* **68**, 289.

Chambers, E. L., Whiteley, A., Chambers, R., and Brooks, S. C. (1948). Distribution of radioactive phosphate in the eggs of the sea urchin *Lytechinus pictus. Biol. Bull.* **95**, 263.

Chambers, E. L., Azarnia, R., and McGowan, W. E. (1970). The effect of temperature on the efflux of ^{45}Ca from the eggs of *Arbacia punctulata. Biol. Bull.* **139**, 417.

Chambers, R. (1917). Microdissection studies. I. The visible structure of cell protoplasm and death changes. *Amer. J. Physiol.* **43**, 1.

Chambers, R. (1938). Structural and kinetics aspects of cell division. *J. Cell. Comp. Physiol.* **12**, 149.

Chambers, R. (1940). The relation of extraneous coats to the organization and permeability of cellular membranes. *Cold Spring Harbor Symp. Quant. Biol.* **8**, 144.

Chambers, R. (1942). The intrinsic expansibility of the fertilization membrane of echinoderm ova. *J. Cell Comp. Physiol.* **19**, 145.

Chambers, R. (1944). Some physical properties of protoplasm. *Colloid Chem.* **5**, 864.

Chambers, R., and Chambers, E. L. (1961). "Exploration into the Nature of the Living Cell." Harvard Univ. Press, Cambridge, Massachusetts.

Chargaff, E. (1963). "Essays on Nucleic Acids." Elsevier, Amsterdam.

Chargaff, E., and Davidson, J. N., eds. (1955). "The Nucleic Acids," Vol. 1, p. 357. Academic Press, New York.

Chargaff, E., Lipshitz, R., and Green, C. (1952). Composition of the desoxypentose nucleic acids of four genera of sea urchin. *J. Biol. Chem.* **195**, 155.

Chatlynne, L. G. (1969). A histochemical study of oogenesis in the sea urchin *Strongylocentrotus purpuratus. Biol. Bull.* **136**, 167.

Chen, P. S. (1958). Further studies on free amino acids and peptides in eggs and embryos of different sea urchin species and hybrids. *Experientia* **14**, 369.

Chen, P. S. (1959). Über den Nucleinsäure-und Proteinstoffwechsel der Frühentwicklung bei Seeigeln. *Vierteljahresschr. Naturforsch. Ges. Zuerich* **104**, 284.

Chen, P. S., and Baltzer, F. (1958). Species-specific differences in free amino acids and peptides in sea urchin eggs and embryos (pure species and hybrids). *Nature (London)* **181**, 98.

Chen, P. S., and Baltzer, F. (1962). Experiments concerning the incorporation of labelled adenine into ribonucleic acid in normal sea urchin embryos and in the hybrid *Paracentrotus* ♀ × *Arbacia* ♂. *Experientia* **18**, 522.

Chen, P. S., Baltzer, F., and Zeller, C. (1961). Changes in nucleic acids in early amphibian and sea urchin embryos (pure species, merogonic and hybrid combinations). *Symp. Int. Inst. Embryol., 1960* p. 506.

Chestukhin, A. V. (1969). Effect of cortisone on development of the sea urchin *Strongylocentrotus nudus* and loach *Misgurnus fossilis. Dokl. Biol. Sci.* **187**, 521.

Child, C. M. (1936). Differential reduction of vital dyes in the early development of echinoderms. *Roux'Arch. Entwicklungsmech. Organismen* **135**, 426.

Citkowitz, E. (1971). The hyaline layer: its isolation and role in echinoderm development. *Develop. Biol.* **24**, 348.

Claff, C. L. (1953). Respiratory studies on single cells. Methods instrumentation, observations. *Trans. N.Y. Acad. Sci.* [2] **15**, 281.

Cleland, K. W., and Rothschild, Lord. (1952a). The metabolism of the sea urchin egg. Anaerobic breakdown of carbohydrate. *J. Exp. Biol.* **29**, 285.

Cleland, K. W., and Rothschild, Lord. (1952b). The metabolism of the sea urchin egg. Oxidation of carbohydrate. *J. Exp. Biol.* **29**, 416.

Clowes, G. H. A., and Krahl, M. E. (1936). Studies on cell metabolism and cell division. I. On the relation between molecular structures, chemical properties, and biological activities of the nitrophenols. *J. Gen. Physiol.* **20**, 145.

Clowes, G. H. A., and Krahl, M. E. (1940). Studies on cell metabolism and cell division. III. Oxygen consumption and cell division of fertilized sea urchin eggs in the presence of respiratory inhibitors. *J. Gen. Physiol.* **23**, 401.

Clowes, G. H. A., Keltch, A. K., Strittmatter, C. F., and Walters, C. P. (1950). Action of nitro- and halophenols upon oxygen consumption and phosphorylation by a cell-free particulate system from *Arbacia* eggs. *J. Gen. Physiol.* **33**, 555.

Cognetti, G., Settineri, D., and Spinelli, G. (1972). Developmental changes of chromatin non-histone proteins in sea urchins. *Exp. Cell. Res.* **71**, 465.

Cohen, C., Harrison, S. C., and Stephens, R. E. (1971). X-ray diffraction from micro-tubules. *J. Mol. Biol.* **59**, 375.

Cohen, G. H., and Iverson, R. M. (1967). High-resolution density gradient analysis of sea urchin polysomes. *Biochem. Biophys. Res. Commun.* **29**, 349.

Cohen, W. D. (1968). Polyelectrolyte properties of the isolated mitotic apparatus. *Exp. Cell Res.* **51**, 221.

Cohen, W. D., and Gottlieb, T. (1971). C-microtubules in isolated mitotic spindles. *J. Cell Sci.* **9**, 603.

Cohen, W. D., and Rebhun, L. I. (1970). An estimate of the amount of microtubule protein in the isolated mitotic apparatus. *J. Cell. Sci.* **6**, 159.

Colwin, L. H., and Colwin, A. L. (1967). Membrane fusion in relation to the sperm-egg association. *In* "Fertilization: Comparative Morphology, Biochemistry and Immuno-logy" (C. B. Metz and A. Monroy, eds.), Vol. 1, pp. 295–367. Academic Press, New York.

Comb, D. G. (1965). Methylation of nucleic acids during sea urchin embryo development. *J. Mol. Biol.* **11**, 851.

Comb, D. G., Sarkar, N., De Vallet, J., and Pinzino, C. J. (1965a). Properties of transfer-like RNA associated with ribosomes. *J. Mol. Biol.* **12**, 509.

Comb, D. G., Katz, S., Branda, R., and Pinzino, C. J. (1965b). Characterization of RNA species synthesized during early development of sea urchins. *J. Mol. Biol.* **14**, 195.

Conklin, E. G. (1912). Cell size and nuclear size. *J. Exp. Zool.* **12**, 1.

Connors, W. M., and Scheer, B. T. (1947). Adenosinetriphosphatase in the sea urchin egg. *J. Cell Comp. Physiol.* **30**, 271.

Conway, C. M., and Metz, C. B. (1970). Cytochemical demonstration of RNA in heavy bodies of sea urchin eggs. *J. Cell Biol.* **47**, 40a.

Cook, J. S. (1968). On the role of DNA in the U.V. sensitivity of cell division in sand dollar zygotes. *Exp. Cell Res.* **50**, 627.

Cook, J. S., and McGrath, J. R. (1967). Photoreactivating-enzyme activity in metazoa. *Proc. Nat. Acad. Sci. U.S.* **58**, 1359.

Cook, J. S., and Rieck, A. F. (1962). Studies on photoreactivation in gametes and zygotes of the sand dollar, *Echinaracnius parma. J. Cell. Comp. Physiol.* **59**, 77.

Cook, J. S., and Setlow, K. (1966). Photoreactivating enzyme in the sea urchin egg. *Bio-chem. Biophys. Res. Commun.* **24**, 285.

Cornman, J. (1941). Sperm activation by *Arbacia* egg extracts, with special relation to echinochrome. *Biol. Bull.* **80**, 202.

Couffer-Kaltenbach, J., and Perlmann, P. (1961). Antigens in eggs and developmental stages of the sea urchin. I. Immunological and physicochemical properties. *J. Biophys. Biochem. Cytol.* **9**, 93.

Cousineau, G. H., and Gross, P. R. (1960). Distribution and substrate specificity of sea urchin egg phosphatases. *Biol. Bull.* **119**, 292.

Cowden, R. R. (1962). RNA and yolk synthesis in growing oocytes of the sea urchin. *Lytechinus variegatus. Exp. Cell Res.* **28**, 600.

Craig, S. P. (1970). Synthesis of RNA in non-nucleate fragments of sea urchin eggs. *J. Mol. Biol.* **47**, 615.

Craig, S. P., and Piatigorsky, J. (1971). Protein synthesis and development in the absence of cytoplasmic RNA synthesis in non-nucleate egg fragments and embryos of sea urchins: Effect of ehtidium bromide. *Develop. Biol.* **24**, 214.

Crane, R. K., and Keltch, A. K. (1949). Dinitrocresol and phosphate stimulation of the oxygen consumption of a cell-free oxidative system obtained from sea urchin eggs. *J. Gen. Physiol.* **32**, 503.

Crick, F. (1970). Diffusion in embryogenesis. *Nature (London)* **225**, 420.

Crippa, M. (1970). Regulatory factor for the transcription of the ribosomal genes in amphibian oocytes. *Nature (London)* **227**, 1138.

Crkvenjakov, R., Bajkovic, N., and Glisin, V. (1970). The effect of 5-azacytidine on development, nucleic acid and protein metabolism in sea urchin embryos. *Biochem. Biophys. Res. Commun.* **39**, 655.

Czihak, G. (1960). Untersuchungen über die Coelomanlagen und die Metamorphose des Pluteus von *Psammechinus miliaris* (Gmelin). *Zool. Jahrb., Abt. Anat. Ontog. Tiere* **78**, 235.

Czihak, G. (1961). Ein neuer Gradient in der Pluteusentiwicklung. *Wilhelm Roux' Arch. Entwicklungsmech. Organismen* **153**, 353.

Czihak, G. (1962). Entwicklungsphysiologische Untersuchungen an Echiniden (Topochemie der Blastula und Gastrula, Entwicklung der Bilateral-und Radiärsymmetrie under des Coelonidivertikel). *Wilhelm Roux' Arch. Entwicklungsmech. Organismen* **154**, 29.

Czihak, G. (1965a). Entwicklungsphysiologische Untersuchungen an Echiniden. *Wilhem Roux' Arch. Entwicklungsmech. Organismen.* **155**, 709.

Czihak, G. (1965b). Evidence for inductive properties of the micromere-RNA in sea urchin embryos. *Naturwissenchaften* **52**, 141.

Czihak, G. (1965c). Entwicklungsphysiologische Untersuchungen an Echiniden. *Wilhelm Roux' Arch. Entwicklungsmech. Organismen* **156**, 504.

Czihak, G. (1966). Entwicklungsphysiologische Untersuchungen an Echiniden Zerstörung der Micromeren durch UV-Bestrahlung ein Beitrag zum Problem der Induktion und Regulation. *Wilhelm Roux' Arch. Entwicklungsmech. Organismen* **157**, 211.

Czihak, G., and Hörstadius, S. (1970). Transplantation of RNA-labeled micromeres into animal halves of sea urchin embryos. A contribution to the problem of embryonic induction. *Develop. Biol.* **22**, 15.

Czihak, G., and Pohl, E. (1970). DNA synthesis in early cleavage stages of sea urchin embryos. *Z. Naturforsch. B* **25**, 1047.

Czihak, G., Wittman, H. G., and Hindennach, I. (1967). Uridineinbau in die Nucleinsäuren von Furchungsstadien der Eier des Seeigels *Paracentrotus lividus. Z. Naturforsch. B* **22**, 1176.

Daigneault, R., Bellemare, G., and Cousineau, G. H. (1969). A 12 S and 9 S RNA species in *Strongylocentrotus purpuratus* eggs. *J. Cell Biol.* **43**, 28a.

Daigneault, R., Bellemare, G., and Cousineau, G. H. (1970). A 12 S and a 9 S RNA species in *Strongylocentrotus purpuratus* eggs. *Biochim. Biophys. Acta* **224**, 256.

Dalcq, A. (1941). "L'oeuf et son dynamisme organisateur." Albin Michel, Paris.

Dalcq, A. M., and Pasteels, J. J. (1963). La localization d'enzymes de déphosphorylation dans les oeufs de quelques Invertébrés. *Develop. Biol.* **7**, 457.

Daly, M. M., Allfrey, V. G., and Mirsky, A. E. (1950). Purine and pyrimidine contents of some desoxypentose nucleic acids. *J. Gen. Physiol.* **33**, 497.

Dan, J. C. (1952). Studies on the acrosome. I. Reaction to egg water and other stimuli. *Biol. Bull.* **103**, 54.

Dan, J. C. (1954). Studies on the acrosome. II. Acrosome reaction in starfish spermatozoa. III. Effect of calcium deficiency. *Biol. Bull.* **107**, 203.

Dan, J. C. (1956). The acrosome reaction. *Int. Rev. Cytol.* **5**, 365.

Dan, J. C. (1960). Studies on the acrosome. VI. Fine structure of the starfish acrosome. *Exp. Cell Res.* **19**, 13.

Dan, J. C. (1967). Acrosome reaction and lysins. *In* "Fertilization: Comparative Morphology, Biochemistry and Immunology" (C. B. Metz and A. Monroy, eds.), Vol. 1, pp. 237–294. Academic Press, New York.

Dan, J. C. (1970). Morphogenetic aspects of acrosome formation and reaction. *Advan. Morphog.* **8**, 1.

Dan, J. C., Kusida, H., and Ohori, Y. (1962). Formation of the acrosomal process in echinoderm spermatozoa. *Electron Micros., Proc. Int. Congr., 5th, 1962,* Vol. 2, Art. YY-12.

Dan, J. C., Ohori, Y., and Kushida, H. (1964). Studies on the acrosome. VII. Formation of the acrosomal process in sea urchin spermatozoa. *J. Ultrastruct. Res.* **11**, 508.

Dan, K. (1943a). Behaviour of the cell surface during cleavage. V. Perforation experiments. *J. Fac. Sci., Imp. Univ. Tokyo, Sect. 4* **6**, 297.

Dan, K. (1943b). Behaviour of the cell surface during cleavage. VI. On the mechanism of cell division. *J. Fac. Sci., Imp. Univ. Tokyo, Sect. 4* **6**, 323.

Dan, K. (1952). Cytoembryological studies of sea urchins. II. Blastula stage. *Biol. Bull.* **102**, 74.

Dan, K. (1954). Further study on the formation of the "new membrane" in the eggs of the sea urchin *Hemicentrotus (Strongylocentrotus) pulcherrimus. Embryologia* **2**, 99.

Dan, K. (1960). Cytoembryology of echinoderms and amphibia. *Int. Rev. Cytol.* **9**, 321.

Dan, K. (1963). Force of cleavage of the dividing sea urchin egg. *Symp. Int. Soc. Cell Biol.* **2**, 261–276.

Dan, K., and Nakajima, T. (1956). On the morphology of the mitotic apparatus isolated from echinoderm eggs. *Embryologia* **3**, 187.

Dan, K., and Okazaki, K. (1956). Cytoembryological studies of sea urchins. III. Role of the secondary mesenchyme cells in the formation of the primitive gut in sea urchin larvae. *Biol. Bull.* **110**, 29.

Dan, K., and Ono, T. (1952). Cytoembryological studies of sea urchins. I. The means of fixation of the mutual positions among the blastomeres of sea urchin larvae. *Biol. Bull.* **102**, 58.

Dan, K., and Ono, T. (1954). A method of computation of the surface area of the cell. *Embryologia* **2**, 87.

Danielli, J. F. (1950). Studies on spindle material. *Biol. Bull.* **99**, 369.

Darnell, J. E., Wall, R., and Tushinski, R. J. (1971). An adenylic acid-rich sequence in messenger RNA of HeLa cells and its possible relationship to reiterated sites in DNA. *Proc. Nat. Acad. Sci. U.S.* **68**, 1321.

Davenport, R. (1967). An electrophoretic characterization of ribosomal and nuclear basic proteins in the sea urchin embryos. *Acta Embryol. Morphol. Exp.* **9**, 270.

Dawydoff, C. (1948). Embryologie des échinodermes. *In* "Traité de Zoologie" (P. P. Grassé, ed.), Vol. 11, pp. 277–363. Masson, Paris.

De Angelis, E., and Runnström, J. (1970). The effect of temporary treatment of animal half-embryos with lithium and the modification of this effect by simultaneous exposure to actinomycin D. *Wilhelm Roux' Arch. Entwicklungsmech. Organismen* **164**, 236.

de Harven, E., and Bernhard, W. (1956). Etude au microscope électronique de l'ultrastructure du centriole chez les Vertébrés. *Z. Zellforsch. Mikrosk. Anat.* **45**, 378.

Delage, Y. (1909). Le sexe chez les oursins issus de parthénogenèse expérimentale. *C. R. Acad. Sci.* **148,** 453.

Denis, H. (1966a). Gene expression in amphibian development. I. Validity of the model used: Interspecific and intraspecific hybridation between nucleic acids. Properties of messenger RNA synthesized by developing embryos. *J. Mol. Biol.* **22,** 269.

Denis, H. (1966b). Gene expression in amphibian development. II. Release of the genetic information in growing embryos. *J. Mol. Biol.* **22,** 284.

Denis, H., and Brachet, J. (1969a). Gene expression in interspecific hybrids. I. DNA synthesis in the lethal cross *Arbacia lixula* ♂ × *Paracentrotus lividus* ♀. *Proc. Nat. Acad. Sci. U.S.* **62,** 194.

Denis, H., and Brachet, J. (1969b). Gene expression in interspecific hybrids. II. RNA synthesis in the lethal cross *Arbacia lixula* ♂ × *Paracentrotus lividus* ♀. *Proc. Nat. Acad. Sci. U.S.* **62,** 438.

Denis, S. (1968). Changes in the level of triphosphopyridine nucleotides during development of sea urchin eggs (normal and letal hybrids). *Biochim. Biophys. Acta* **157,** 212.

Denny, P. C., and Tyler, A. (1964). Activation of protein biosynthesis in non-nucleate fragments of sea urchin eggs. *Biochem. Biophys. Res. Commun.* **14,** 245.

Derbès, M. (1847). Observations sur le méchanisme et les phénomènes qui accompagnent la formation de l'embryon chez l'oursin comestible. *Ann. Sci. Natur.: Zool.* [3] **8,** 80.

De Vincentiis, M., and Lancieri, M. (1970). Observations on the development of the sea urchin embryo in the presence of actinomycin. *Exp. Cell Res.* **59,** 479.

De Vincentiis, M. Hörstadius, S., and Runnström, J. (1966). Studies on controlled and released respiration in animal and vegetal halves of the embryo of the sea urchin *Paracentrotus lividus*. *Exp. Cell Res.* **41,** 535.

Di Berardino, M. A., and King, T. J. (1967). Development and cellular differentiation of neural nuclear transplants of known karyotype. *Develop. Biol.* **15,** 102.

Dirksen, E. R. (1961). The presence of centrioles in artificially activated sea urchin eggs. *J. Biophys. Biochem. Cytol.* **11,** 244.

Doré, D., and Cousineau, G. H. (1967). Acid phosphatase analysis in sea urchin eggs and blastulae. *Exp. Cell Res.* **48,** 179.

Driesch, H. (1891). Entwicklungsmechanische Studien. I–II. *Z. Wiss. Zool.* **53,** 160.

Driesch, H. (1892). Entwicklungsmechanische Studien. III–VI. *Z. Wiss. Zool.* **55,** 1.

Driesch, H. (1898). Ueber rein-mütterliche Charaktere an Bastardlarven von Echiniden. *Arch. Entwicklungsmech. Organismen* **7,** 65.

Driesch, H. (1900). Die isolirten Blastomeren des Echinidenkeimes. *Arch. Entwicklungsmech. Organismen* **10,** 361.

Driesch, H. (1902). Neue Ergänzungen zur Entwicklungsphysiologie des Echindenkeimes. *Arch. Entwicklungsmech. Organismen* **14,** 500.

Driesch, H. (1903). Drei Aphorismen zur Entwicklungsphysiologie jüngster Stadien. *Arch. Entwicklungsmech. Organismen* **17,** 41.

Dubois, R., Bellemare, G., and Cousineau, G. H. (1970). The 12 S and 9 S RNA species found in purple sea urchin eggs. *J. Cell Biol.* **47,** 53a.

Dubois, R., Dugré, M., Denker, I., Inoué, S., and Cousineau, G. H. (1971). 12 S and 9 S RNA species. Localization and fate during development of *Strongylocentrotus purpuratus* eggs. *Exp. Cell Res.* **68,** 197.

Ecker, R. E., and Brookbank, J. W. (1963). A ribosome fraction from sand dollar (*Mellita quinquiesperforata*) ovo. *Biochim. Biophys. Acta* **72,** 490.

Eigisti, O. J., Dustin, P., Jr., and Gay-Winn, N. (1949). On the discovery of the action of colchicine on mitosis in 1889. *Science* **110,** 692.

Ellis, C. H., Jr. (1966). The genetic control of sea urchin development: A chromatographic study of protein synthesis in the *Arbacia punctulata* embryo. *J. Exp. Zool.* **163,** 1.

Ellis, C. H., Jr. (1969). Permeability of the sea urchin embryo to dactinomycin: Measurement with tritiated dactinomycin. *Amer. Zool.* **9**, 600.

Ellis, C. H., Jr., and Wintex, R. J. (1967). Protein synthesis and skeletal spicule formation in the sea urchin larvae. *Amer. Zool.* **7**, 750 (abstr.).

Elson, D., Gustafson, T., and Chargaff, E. (1954). The nucleic acids of the sea urchin during embryonic development. *J. Biol. Chem.* **209**, 285.

Elster, H.-J. (1935). Experimentelle Beiträge zur Kenntnis der Physiologie der Befruchtung bei Echinoiden *Wilhelm Roux'Arch. Entwicklungsmech. Organismen* **133**, 1.

Emerson, C. P., Jr., and Humphreys, T. (1970). Regulation of DNA-like RNA and apparent activation of ribosomal RNA synthesis in sea urchin embryos: Quantitative measurements of newly synthesized RNA. *Develop. Biol.* **23**, 86.

Emerson, C. P., Jr., and Humphreys, T. (1971). Ribosomal RNA synthesis and the multiple, atypical nucleoli in cleaving embryos. *Science* **171**, 898.

Endo, Y. (1961a). Changes in the cortical layer of sea urchin eggs at fertilization as studied with the electron microscope. *Exp. Cell Res.* **25**, 383.

Endo, Y. (1961b). The role of the cortical granules in the formation of the fertilization membrane in the eggs of sea urchin. II. *Exp. Cell Res.* **25**, 518.

Endo, Y., and Uno, N. (1960). Intercellular bridges in sea urchin blastula. *Zool. Mag.* **69**, 8.

Epel, D. (1963). The effect of carbon monoxide inhibition on ATP level and the rate of mitosis in the sea urchin egg. *J. Cell. Biol.* **17**, 315.

Epel, D. (1964a). A primary metabolic change of fertilization: Interconversion of pyridine nucleotides. *Biochem. Biophys. Res. Commun.* **17**, 62.

Epel, D. (1964b). Simultaneous measurement of TPHN formation and respiration following fertilization of the sea urchin egg. *Biochem. Biophys. Res. Commun.* **17**, 69.

Epel, D. (1967). Protein synthesis in sea urchin eggs: A "late" response to fertilization. *Proc. Nat. Acad. Sci. U.S.* **57**, 899.

Epel, D. (1969). Does ADP regulate respiration following fertilization of sea urchin eggs? *Exp. Cell Res.* **58**, 312.

Epel, D. (1970). Methods for removal of the vitelline membrane of the sea urchin eggs. II. Controlled exposure to trypsin to eliminate post-fertilization clumping of the embryos. *Exp. Cell Res.* **61**, 69.

Epel, D., and Iverson, R. M. (1965). *In* "Control of Energy Metabolism" (B. Chance, R. W. Estabrook, and J. R. Williamson, eds.), p. 267. Academic Press, New York.

Epel, D., Weaver, A. M., Muchmore, A. V., and Schimke, R. T. (1969). β-1,3-glucanase of sea urchin eggs. Release from particles at fertilization. *Science* **163**, 294.

Epel, E., Weaver, A. M., and Mazia, D. (1970). Methods for removal of the vitelline membrane of sea urchin eggs. I. Use of dithiothreitol (Cleland reagent). *Exp. Cell Res.* **61**, 64.

Ephrussi, B. (1933). Contribution a l'analyse des premières stades du développement de l'oeuf. Action de la température. *Arch. Biol.* **44**, 1.

Ephrussi, B., and Rapkine, L. (1928). Composition chimique de l'oeuf d'oursin (*Paracentrotus lividus* L.K.) et ses variations au cours du développement. *Ann. Physiol. Physiochim. Biol.* **3**, 386.

Erdmann, R. H. (1908). Experimentelle Untersuchung der Massenverhältnisse von Plasma, Kern und Chromosomen in dem sich entwickelnden Seeigelei. *Arch. Zellforsch.* **2**, 76.

Esper, H. (1962a). Uptake of H^3-thymidine by eggs of *Arbacia punctulata*. *Biol. Bull.* **123**, 475.

Esper, H. (1962b). Incorporation of C^{14}-glucose into oocytes and ovarian eggs of *Arbacia punctulata*. *Biol. Bull.* **123**, 476.

Esper, H. (1965). Studies on the nucleolar vacuoles of *Arbacia punctulata*. *Exp. Cell Res.* **38**, 85.

Esping, V. (1957a). A factor inhibiting fertilization of sea urchin eggs from extracts of the alga, *Fucus vesciculosus*. I. The preparation of the factor inhibiting fertilization. *Ark. Kemi* **11**, 107.

Esping, V. (1957b). A factor inhibiting fertilization of sea urchin eggs from extracts of the alga, *Fucus vesciculosus*. II. The effect of the factor inhibiting fertilization on some enzymes. *Ark. Kemi* **11**, 117.

Estabrook, R. W., and Maitra, P. K. (1962). A fluorimetric method for the quantitative microanalysis of adenine and pyridine nucleotides. *An. Biochem.* **3**, 369.

Evans, T. A., Monroy, A., and Senft, A. (1962). Free amino acids and peptides in unfertilized and fertilized eggs of *Arbacia punctulata*. *Biol. Bull.* **123**, 476.

Evans, T. C. (1947). Effects of hydrogen peroxide produced in the medium by radiation on spermatozoa of *Arbacia punctulata*. *Biol. Bull.* **92**, 99.

Evans, T. C., Beams, H. W., and Smith, W. E. (1941). Effects of roentgen radiation on the jelly of the *Arbacia* egg. *Biol. Bull.* **80**, 363.

Evola-Maltese, C. (1957a). Histochemical localization of alkaline phosphatase in the sea urchin embryo. *Acta Embryol. Morphol. Exp.* **1**, 99.

Evola-Maltese, C. (1957b). Effects of beryllium on the development and alkaline phosphatase activity of *Paracentrotus lividus* embryos. *Acta Embryol. Morphol. Exp.* **1**, 143.

Failla, P. M. (1961). *In vivo* and *in vitro* recovery of irradiated gametes of *Arbacia punctulata*. *Biol. Bull.* **121**, 374.

Failla, P. M. (1962a). *In vivo* and *in vitro* recovery of irradiated gametes of *Arbacia punctulata*. *Radiat. Res.* **17**, 767.

Failla, P. M. (1962b). Recovery from radiation-induced delay of cleavage in gametes of *Arbacia punctulata*. *Science* **138**, 1341.

Failla, P. M. (1965). Recovery from division delay in irradiated gametes of *Arbacia punctulata*. *Radiat. Res.* **25**, 331.

Failla, P. M. (1969). Recovery and modifications of radiation-induced division delay in developing sea urchin eggs. *Radiology* **93**, 643.

Fansler, B., and Loeb, L. A. (1969). Sea urchin nuclear DNA polymerase. II. Changing localization during early development. *Exp. Cell Res.* **57**, 305.

Fedecka-Bruner, B., and Epel, D. (1969). Nuclear control of "lysosomal" acyl sulfatase activity in sea urchin embryos. *J. Cell. Biol.* **43**, 35a.

Fedecka-Bruner, B., Anderson, M., and Epel, D. (1971). Control of enzyme synthesis in early sea urchin development. Aryl sulfatase activity in normal and hybrid embryos. *Develop. Biol.* **25**, 655.

Feit, H., Slusarek, L., and Shelanski, M. L. (1971). Heterogeneity of tubulin subunits. *Proc. Nat. Acad. Sci. U.S.* **68**, 2028.

Fell, H. B. (1948). Echinoderm embryology and the origin of chordates. *Biol. Rev.* **23**, 81.

Fewkes, J. W. (1881). On the development of the pluteus of *Arbacia*. *Mem. Peabody Acad. Sci.* **1**, 1.

Ficq, A. (1964). Effets de l'actinomycine D et de la puromycine sur le métabolisme de l'oocyte en croissance. *Exp. Cell Res.* **34**, 581.

Ficq, A., and Brachet, J. (1963). Métabolisme des acides nucléiques et des protéines chez les embryons normaux et les hybrides létaux entre échinodermes. *Exp. Cell Res.* **32**, 90.

Ficq, A., Aiello, F., and Scarano, E. (1963). Métabolisme des acides nucléiques dans l'oeuf d'oursin en développement. *Exp. Cell Res.* **29**, 128.

Field, G. W. (1895). On the morphology and physiology of the echinoderm spermatozoon. *J. Morphol.* **11**, 235.

Fischberg, M., Gurdon, J. B., and Elsdale, T. R. (1958). Nuclear transfer in amphibia and the problem of the potentialities of the nuclei of differentiating tissues. *Exp. Cell Res., Suppl.* **6**, 161.

Flake, G. P., and Metz, C. B. (1962). Soluble surface and subsurface antigens of the *Arbacia* sperm. *Biol. Bull.* **123**, 472.

Flemming, W. (1881). Beiträge zur Kenntnis der Zelle und ihrer Lebenserscheinungen. 3. *Arch. Mikrosk. Anat.* **20**, 1.

Flickinger, R. A. (1957). Evidence from sea urchin sand dollar hybrid embryos for a nuclear control of alkaline phosphatase activity. *Biol. Bull.* **112**, 21.

Forslind, B., Swanbeck, G., and Mohri, H. (1968). The flagellar proteins of sea urchin spermatozoa *Pseudocentrotus depressus*. An X-ray diffraction study. *Exp. Cell Res.* **53**, 678.

Fox, B. W., Partington, M., and Jackson, H. (1963). Action of alkylating agents on sea urchin gametes. *Exp. Cell Res.* **29**, 137.

Franklin, L. E. (1965). Morphology of gamete membrane fusion and of sperm entry into oocytes of the sea urchin. *J. Cell Biol.* **25**, 81.

Fromson, D., and Nemer, M. (1970). Cytoplasmic extraction: Polyribosomes and heterogeneous ribonucleoproteins without associated DNA. *Science* **168**, 266.

Fry, B. J., and Gross, P. R. (1970a). Patterns and rates of protein synthesis in sea urchin embryos. I. Uptake and incorporation of amino acids during the first cleavage. *Develop. Biol.* **21**, 105.

Fry, B. J., and Gross, P. R. (1970b). Patterns and rates of protein synthesis in sea urchin embryos. II. The calculation of absolute rates. *Develop. Biol.* **21**, 125.

Frydenberg, O., and Zeuthen, E. (1960). Oxygen uptake and carbon dioxide output related to the mitotic rhythm in the cleaving eggs of *Dendraster excentricus* and *Urechis caupo*. *C. R. Trav. Lab. Carlsberg* **31**, 423.

Fudge, M. W. (1959). Vegetalization of sea urchin embryos by treatment with tyrosine. *Exp. Cell Res.* **18**, 401.

Fuji, A. (1960). Studies on the biology of the sea urchin. I. Superficial and histological gonadal changes in the gametogenic process of two sea urchins. *Strongylocentrotus nudus* and *Strongylocentrotus intermedius*. *Bull. Fac. Fish. Hokkaido Univ.* **11**, 1.

Fuji, T., and Ohnishi, T. (1962). Inhibition of acid production at fertilization by nicotinamide and other inhibitors of diphosphopyridine nucleotidase (DPNase) in the sea urchin. *J. Fac. Sci., Imp. Univ. Tokyo, Sect. 4* **9**, 333.

Fukuhushi, T. (1959). The presumptive position of the dorsal and ventral areas in the sea urchin egg, studied with local vital staining. *Bull. Mar. Biol. Sta. Asamushi, Tohoku Univ.* **9**, 127.

Fulton, C., Kane, R. E., and Stephens, R. E. (1971). Serological similarity of flagellar and mitotic microtubules. *J. Cell Biol.* **50**, 762.

Garbowsky, M. T. (1905). Über die Polarität des Seeigeleies. *Bull. Int. Acad. Cracovie* p. 599.

Garman, H., and Colton, B. P. (1883). Some notes on the development of *Arbacia punctulata* Lam. *Stud. Biol. Lab. Johns Hopkins Univ.* **2**, 247.

Geraci, G., Rossi, M., and Scarano, E. (1967). Deoxycytidylate aminohydrolase. I. Preparation and properties of the homogeneous enzyme. *Biochemistry* **6**, 183.

German, J. (1964). The chromosomal complement of blastomeres in *Arbacia punctulata*. *Biol. Bull.* **127**, 370.

Geuskens, M. (1968a). Etude ultrastructurale des embryons normaux et des hybrides létaux entre echinodermes. *Exp. Cell Res.* **49**, 477.

Geuskens, M. (1968b). Etude au microscope électronique de l'action de l'hydroxyurée sur les embryons. I. Embryons d'oursins. *Exp. Cell Res.* **52**, 608.

Ghiretti, F., Ghiretti-Magaldi, A., Rothschild, H. A., and Tosi, L. (1958). A study of the cytochromes of marine invertebrates. *Acta Physiol. Lat. Amer.* **8**, 239.

Gibbins, J. R., Tilney, L. G., and Porter, K. R. (1969). Mictotubules in the formation and development of the primary mesenchyme in *Arbacia punctulata*. I. The distribution of microtubules. *J. Cell Biol.* **41**, 201.

Gilmour, R. S., and Paul, J. (1969). RNA transcribed from reconstituted nucleoprotein is similar to natural RNA. *J. Mol. Biol.* **40**, 137.

Ginsburg, A. S. (1963). On the mechanism of egg protection against polyspermy in echinoderm. *Dokl. Akad. Nauk SSSR* **152**, 501.

Girard, M., and Baltimore, D. (1966). The effect of HeLa cell cytoplasm on the rate of sedimentation of RNA. *Proc. Nat. Acad. Sci. U.S.* **56**, 999.

Giudice, G. (1958). The distribution of P^{32} among some of the cell components in the course of development of *Paracentrotus lividus*. *Acta Embryol. Morphol. Exp.* **2**, 88.

Giudice, G. (1960). Incorporation of labelled amino acids into the proteins of the mitochondria isolated from the unfertilized eggs and developmental stages of *Paracentrotus lividus*. *Exp. Cell. Res.* **21**, 222.

Guidice, G. (1962a). Restitution of whole larvae from disaggregated cells of sea urchin embryos. *Develop. Biol.* **5**, 402.

Giudice, G. (1962b). Amino acid incorporation into the proteins of isolated cells and total homogenates of sea urchin embryos. *Arch. Biochem. Biophys.* **99**, 447.

Giudice, G. (1963). Aggregation of cells isolated from vegetalized and animalized sea urchin embryos. *Experientia* **19**, 83.

Giudice, G. (1965). The mechanism of aggregation of embryonic sea urchin cells; a biochemical approach. *Develop. Biol.* **12**, 233.

Giudice, G., and Hörstadius, S. (1965). Effect of actinomycin D on the segretation of animal and vegetal potentialities in the sea urchin egg. *Exp. Cell Res.* **39**, 117.

Giudice, G., and Monroy, A. (1958). Incorporation of S^{35}-methionine in the proteins of the mitochondria of developing and parthenogenetically activated sea urchin eggs. *Acta Embryol. Morphol. Exp.* **2**, 58.

Giudice, G., and Mutolo, V. (1967). Synthesis of ribosomal RNA during sea urchin development. *Biochim. Biophys. Acta* **138**, 276.

Giudice, G., and Mutolo, V. (1969). Synthesis of ribosomal RNA during sea urchin development. II. Electrophoretic analysis of nuclear and cytoplasmic RNA's. *Biochim. Biophys. Acta* **179**, 341.

Giudice, G., and Mutolo, V. (1970). Reaggregation of dissociated cells of sea urchin embryos. *Advan. Morphog.* **8**, 115.

Giudice, G., Vittorelli, M. L., and Monroy, A. (1962). Investigations on protein metabolism during the early development of the sea urchin. *Acta Embryol. Morphol. Exp.* **5**, 113.

Giudice, G., Mutolo, V., and Moscona, A. A. (1967). The role of cell interactions in the control of RNA synthesis. *Biochim. Biophys. Acta* **138**, 607.

Giudice, G., Mutolo, V., and Donatuti, G. (1968). Gene expression in sea urchin development. *Wilhelm Roux' Arch. Entwicklungsmech. Organismen* **161**, 118.

Giudice, G., Mutolo, V., Donatuti, G., and Bosco, M. (1969). Reaggregation of mixtures of cells from different developmental stages of sea urchin embryos. *Exp. Cell Res.* **54**, 279.

Giudice, G., Sconzo, G., Ramirez, F., and Albanese, I. (1972a). Giant RNA is also found in the cytoplasm in sea urchin embryos. *Biochim. Biophys. Acta* **262**, 401.

Giudice, G., Sconzo, G., Bono, A., and Albanese, I. (1972b). Studies on sea urchin oocytes. I. Purification and cell fractionation. *Exp. Cell Res.* **72**, 90.

Glaser, O. (1913). On inducing development in the sea urchin (*Arbacia punctulata*), together with considerations on the initiatory effect by fertilization. *Science* **38**, 446.

Glaser, O. (1921). The duality of egg secretion. *Amer. Natur.* **55**, 368.

Glaser, O. (1922). The hydrolysis of higher fats in egg secretion. *Biol. Bull.* **43**, 68.

Glaser, O. (1923). Copper, enzymes and fertilization. *Biol. Bull.* **44**, 79.

Glisin, V. R., and Glisin, M. V. (1964). RNA metabolism following fertilization in sea urchin eggs. *Proc. Nat. Acad. Sci. U.S.* **52,** 1548.

Glisin, V. R., Glisin, M. V., and Doty, P. (1966). The nature of messenger RNA in the early stages of sea urchin development. *Proc. Nat. Acad. Sci. U.S.* **56,** 285.

Goldinger, J. M., and Barrón, E. S. G. (1946). The pyruvate metabolism of sea urchin eggs during the process of cell division. *J. Gen. Physiol.* **30,** 73.

Goldman, R. D., and Rebhun, L. I. (1969). The structure and some properties of the isolated mitotic apparatus. *J. Cell Sci.* **4,** 179.

Goldschmidt, R. M. (1967). Protein content of sea urchin embryos, fractions, and particles. Master's Thesis, Massachusetts Institute of Technology, Cambridge, Massachusetts.

Gonse, P. H. (1960). Respiratory levels in mature sea urchin eggs. *J. Embryol. Exp. Morphol.* **8,** 73.

Goodenough, D. A., Ito, S., and Revel, J. P. (1968). Electron microscopy of early cleavage stages in *Arbacia punctulata. Biol. Bull.* **135,** 420 (A).

Grassé, P. P., ed. (1948). "Traité de Zoologie," Vol. 2, pp. 307–312. Masson, Paris.

Gray, J. (1921). Note on true and apparent hermaphroditism in sea urchins. *Proc. Cambridge Phil. Soc.* **20,** Part 4, 481.

Gray, J. (1924). The mechanism of cell division. I. The forces which control the form and cleavage of the eggs of *Echinus esculentus. Biol. Rev. Biol. Proc. Cambridge Phil. Soc.* **1,** 164.

Gray, J. (1926). The mechanism of cell division. III. The relationship between cell division and growth in segmenting eggs. *Brit. J. Exp. Biol.* **4,** 313.

Graziani, F., Parisi, E., and Scarano, E. (1970). Biochemical effects of ethionine on sea urchin embryo development. *Biochim. Biophys. Acta* **213,** 208.

Graziano, K. D., and Metz, C. B. (1967). Failure of papain digested antibody to inhibit fertilization of *Arbacia punctulata* eggs. *Exp. Cell Res.* **46,** 220.

Greeley, A. W. (1903). On the effect of variations in the temperature upon the process of artificial parthenogenesis. *Biol. Bull.* **4,** 129.

Greenhouse, G. A., Hynes, R. O., and Gross, P. R. (1971). Sea urchins are permeable to actinomycin. *Science* **171,** 686.

Gregg, K. W. (1966). A comparison of fertilizin and cytofertilizin from eggs of *Arbacia punctulata.* Master's Thesis. Emory University, Atlanta, Georgia.

Gregg, K. W. (1969). Cortical response antigens released at fertilization from sea urchin eggs and their relation to antigens of the jelly coat. *Biol. Bull.* **137,** 146.

Gregg, K. W., and Metz, C. B. (1966). A comparison of fertilizin and cytofertilizin from eggs of *Arbacia punctulata. Ass. Southeast. Biol. Bull.* **13,** 34.

Grimpe, G. (1930). Echinodermata (Stachelhäuter). *Tabulae Biol.* **6,** 490.

Grippo, P., Jaccarino, M., Parisi, E., and Scarano, E. (1968). Methylation of DNA in developing sea urchin embryos. *J. Mol. Biol.* **36,** 195.

Grippo, P., Parisi, E., Carestia, C., and Scarano, E. (1970). A novel origin of some deoxyribonucleic acid thymine and its nonrandom distribution. *Biochemistry* **9,** 3605.

Gross, P. R. (1964). The immediacy of genomic control during early development. *J. Exp. Zool.* **157,** 21.

Gross, P. R., and Cousineau, G. H. (1963a). Effect of actinomycin D on macromolecule synthesis and early development in sea urchin eggs. *Biochem. Biophys. Res. Commun.* **10,** 321.

Gross, P. R., and Cousineau, G. H. (1963b). Synthesis of spindle-associated proteins in early cleavage. *J. Cell Biol.* **19,** 260.

Gross, P. R., and Cousineau, G. H. (1964). Macromolecule synthesis and the influence of actinomycin on early development. *Exp. Cell Res.* **33,** 368.

Gross, P. R., and Fry, B. J. (1966). Continuity of protein synthesis through cleavage meta-phase. *Science* **153**, 749.

Gross, P. R., and Harding, C. V. (1961). Blockade of deoxyribonucleic acid synthesis by deuterium oxide. *Science* **133**, 1131.

Gross, P. R., and Spindel, W. (1960). Heavy water inhibition of cell division: An approach to mechanism. *Ann. N.Y. Acad. Sci.* **90**, 500.

Gross, P. R., Philpott, D. E., and Nass, S. (1958). The fine structure of the mitotic spindle in sea urchin eggs. *J. Ultrastruct. Res.* **2**, 55.

Gross, P. R., Philpott, D. E., and Nass, S. (1960). Electron microscopy of the centrifuged sea urchin egg, with a note on the structure of the ground cytoplasm. *J. Biophys. Biochem. Cytol.* **7**, 135.

Gross, P. R., Spindel, W., and Cousineau, G. H. (1963). Decoupling of protein and RNA synthesis during deuterium parthenogenesis in sea urchin eggs. *Biochem. Biophys. Res. Commun.* **13**, 405.

Gross, P. R., Malkin, L. I., and Moyer, W. A. (1964). Templates for the first proteins of embryonic development. *Proc. Nat. Acad. Sci. U.S.* **51**, 407

Gross, P. R., Malkin, L. I., and Hubbard, M. (1965a). Synthesis of RNA during oogenesis in the sea urchin. *J. Mol. Biol.* **13**, 463.

Gross, P. R., Kraemer, K., and Malkin, L. I. (1965b). Base composition of RNA syn-thesized during cleavage of the sea urchin embryo. *Biochem. Biophys. Res. Commun.* **18**, 569.

Grossman, A., Cagan, L., Levy, M., Troll, W., Weck, S., and Weissman, G. (1971). Is the redistribution of tosyl-arginine methyl ester hydrolase activity that follows fertilization of *Arbacia punctulata* eggs intimately related to embryogenesis? *Biol. Bull.* **141**, 387.

Gurdon, J. B. (1960). The developmental capacity of nuclei from differentiating endoderm cells of *Xenopus laevis. J. Embryol. Exp. Morphol.* **8**, 505.

Gustafson, T. (1963). Cellular mechanisms in the morphogenesis of the sea urchin embryo. *Exp. Cell Res.* **32**, 570.

Gustafson, T., and Hasselberg, I. (1950). Alkaline phosphatase activity in developing sea urchin. *Exp. Cell Res.* **1**, 642.

Gustafson, T., and Hasselberg, I. (1951). Studies of enzymes in the developing sea urchin. *Exp. Cell Res.* **2**, 642.

Gustafson, T., and Hjelte, M. B. (1951). The amino acid metabolism of developing sea urchin egg. *Exp. Cell Res.* **2**, 474.

Gustafson, T., and Hörstadius, S. (1955). Vegetalization and animalization in the sea urchin egg induced by antimetabolites. *Exp. Cell Res., Suppl.* **3**, 170.

Gustafson, T., and Hörstadius, S. (1956). 2-Thio-5-methyl-cytosine, an animalizing agent. *Zool. Anz.* **156**, 102.

Gustafson, T., and Hörstadius, S. (1957). Change in the determination of the sea urchin egg induced by amino acids. *Pubbl. Sta. Zool. Napoli* **29**, 407.

Gustafson, T., and Kinnander, H. (1956a). Gastrulation in the sea urchin larva studied by aid of time-lapse cinematography. *Exp. Cell Res.* **10**, 733.

Gustafson, T., and Kinnander, H. (1956b). Microaquaria for time-lapse cinematographic studies of morphogenesis in swimming larvae and observations on sea urchin gastrula-tion. *Exp. Cell Res.* **11**, 36.

Gustafson, T., and Kinnander, H. (1960). Cellular mechanism in morphogenesis of the sea urchin gastrula. *Exp. Cell Res.* **21**, 361.

Gustafson, T., and Lenicque, P. (1952). Studies on mitochondria in the developing sea urchin egg. *Exp. Cell Res.* **3**, 251.

Gustafson, T., and Lenicque, P. (1955). Studies on mitochondria in early cleavage stages of the sea urchin egg. *Exp. Cell Res.* **8**, 114.

Gustafson, T., and Sävhagen, R. (1949). Studies on the determination of the oral side of the sea urchin egg. I. The effect of some detergents on the development. *Ark. Zool.* **42,** 1.

Gustafson, T., and Toneby, M. (1970). On the role of serotonin and acetylcholine in sea urchin morphogenesis. *Exp. Cell Res.* **62,** 102.

Gustafson, T., and Wolpert, L. (1961a). Studies on the cellular basis of morphogenesis in the sea urchin embryo. *Exp. Cell Res.* **24,** 64.

Gustafson, T., and Wolpert, L. (1961b). Studies on the cellular basis of morphogenesis in the sea urchin embryo. *Exp. Cell. Res.* **22,** 437.

Gustafson, T., and Wolpert, L. (1961c). Cellular mechanisms in the morphogenesis of the sea urchin larva. *Exp. Cell Res.* **22,** 509.

Gustafson, T., and Wolpert, L. (1962). Cellular mechanisms in the morphogenesis of the sea urchin larva. *Exp. Cell Res.* **27,** 260.

Gustafson, T., and Wolpert, L. (1963a). Studies on the cellular basis of morphogenesis in the sea urchin embryo. Formation of the coelom, the mouth, and the primary pore-canal. *Exp. Cell Res.* **29,** 561.

Gustafson, T., and Wolpert, L. (1963b). The cellular basis of morphogenesis and sea urchin development. *Int. Rev. Cytol.* **15,** 139.

Gustafson, T., and Wolpert, L. (1967). Cellular movement and contact in sea urchin mor-phogenesis. *Biol. Rev.* **42,** 442.

Hagedorn, A. L. (1909). On the purely motherly character of the hybrids produced from the eggs of *Strongylocentrotus. Arch. Entwicklungsmech. Organismen* **27,** 1.

Hagström, B., and Hagström, B. E. (1954a). Refertilization of the sea urchin egg. *Exp. Cell Res.* **6,** 491.

Hagström, B., and Hagström, B. E. (1954b). The action of trypsin and chymotrypsin on the sea urchin egg. *Exp. Cell Res.* **6,** 532.

Hagström, B. E. (1956a). On "cytofertilizin" from sea urchins. *Exp. Cell Res.* **11,** 160.

Hagström, B. E. (1956b). The influence of the jelly coat *in situ* and in solution on cross-fertilization in sea urchins. *Exp. Cell Res.* **11,** 306.

Hagström, B. E. (1956c). Further studies on cross-fertilization in sea urchins. *Exp. Cell Res.* **11,** 507.

Hagström, B. E. (1959). Experiments on hybridization of sea urchins. *Ark. Zool.* **12,** 127.

Hagström, B. E., and Lönning, S. (1966). Analysis of the effect of an α-dinitrophenol on cleavage and development of the sea urchin embryo. *Protoplasma* **62,** 246.

Hagström, B. E., and Lönning, S. (1969). Time-lapse and electron microscopic studies of sea urchin micromeres. *Protoplasma* **68,** 271.

Hallberg, R. L. (1964). A qualitative study of the hatching enzyme in the sea urchin *Arbacia punctulata. Biol. Bull.* **127,** 372.

Hand, G. S., Jr. (1971). Stimulation of protein synthesis in unfertilized sea urchin and sand dollar eggs treated with trypsin. *Exp. Cell Res.* **64,** 204.

Harding, C. B. (1951). The action of polysaccharides on fertilization in sea urchins. *Exp. Cell Res.* **2,** 403.

Harding, C. V., and Harding, D. (1952a). The hybridization of *Echinocardium cordatum* and *Psammechinus miliaris. Ark. Zool.* **4,** 403.

Harding, C. V., and Harding, D. (1952b). Cross-fertilization with the sperm of *Arbacia lixula. Exp. Cell Res.* **3,** 475.

Harding, C. V., Harding, D., and Perlmann, P. (1954). Antigens in sea urchin hybrid em-bryos. *Exp. Cell Res.* **6,** 202.

Harding, C. V., Harding, D., and Bamberger, J. W. (1955). On cross-fertilization and the analysis of hybrid embryonic development in echinoderms. *Exp. Cell Res., Suppl.* **3,** 181.

Harris, P. (1961). Electron microscope study of mitosis in sea urchin blastomeres. *J. Biophys. Biochem. Cytol.* **11,** 419.

Harris, P. (1962). Some structural and functional aspects of the mitotic apparatus in sea urchin embryos. *J. Cell Biol.* **14,** 475.

Harris, P. (1965). Some observations concerning metakinesis in sea urchin eggs. *J. Cell Biol.* **25,** 73.

Harris, P. (1967a). Structural changes following fertilization in the sea urchin egg. Formation and dissolution of heavy bodies. *Exp. Cell Res.* **48,** 569.

Harris, P. (1967b). Nucleolus-like bodies in sea urchin eggs. *Amer. Zool.* **7,** 753.

Harris, P. (1968). Cortical fibers in fertilized eggs of the sea urchin *Strongylocentrotus purpuratus. Exp. Cell Res.* **52,** 677.

Hartman, J. F., and Comb, D. G. (1969). Transcription of nuclear and cytoplasmic genes during early development of sea urchin embryos. *J. Mol. Biol.* **41,** 155.

Hartman, J. F., and Zimmerman, A. M. (1968). The isolated mitotic apparatus. Studies on nucleoproteins. *Exp. Cell Res.* **50,** 403.

Hartman, J. F., Ziegler, M. M., and Comb, D. G. (1971). Sea urchin embryogenesis. I. RNA synthesis by cytoplasmic and nuclear genes during development. *Develop. Biol.* **25,** 209.

Hartmann, M., and Schartau, O. (1939). Untersuchungen über die Befruchtungsstoffe der Seeigel. 1. *Mitt. Biol. Zentralbl.* **59,** 571.

Hartmann, M., Schartau, O., Kuhn, R., and Wallenfels, K. (1939). Ueber die Sexualstoffe der Seeigel. *Naturwissenschaften* **27,** 433.

Hartmann, M., Schartau, O., and Wallenfels, K. (1940). Untersuchungen über die Befruchtungsstoffe der Seeigel. 2. *Mitt. Biol. Zentralbl.* **60,** 398.

Harvey, E. B. (1920). A review of the chromosome numbers in the Metazoa. Part II. *J. Morphol.* **34,** 1.

Harvey, E. B. (1932). The development of half and quarter eggs of *Arbacia punctulata* and of strongly centrifuged whole eggs. *Biol. Bull.* **62,** 155.

Harvey, E. B. (1933a). Development of the parts of sea urchin eggs separated by centrifugal force. *Biol. Bull.* **64,** 125.

Harvey, E. B. (1933b). Effects of centrifugal force on fertilized eggs of *Arbacia punctulata* as observed with the centrifuge–microscope. *Biol. Bull.* **65,** 389.

Harvey, E. B. (1934). Effects of centrifugal force on ectoplasmic layer and nuclei of fertilized sea urchin eggs. *Biol. Bull.* **66,** 228.

Harvey, E. B. (1935a). The mitotic figure and cleavage plane in the egg of *Parechinus microtuberculatus,* as influenced by centrifugal force. *Biol. Bull.* **69,** 287.

Harvey, E. B. (1935b). Some surface phenomena in the fertilized sea urchin egg as influenced by centrifugal force. *Biol. Bull.* **69,** 298.

Harvey, E. B. (1935c). Cleavage without nuclei. *Science* **82,** 277.

Harvey, E. B. (1936). Parthenogenic merogony or cleavage without nuclei in *Arbacia punctulata. Biol. Bull.* **71,** 101.

Harvey, E. B. (1938). Parthenogenetic merogony or development without nuclei of the eggs of sea urchins from Naples. *Biol. Bull.* **75,** 170.

Harvey, E. B. (1940a). A new method of producing twins, triplets and quadruplets in *Arbacia punctulata,* and their development. *Biol. Bull.* **78,** 202.

Harvey, E. B. (1940b). Development of half eggs of *Arbacia punctulata* obtained by centrifuging after fertilization, with special reference to parthenogenic merogony. *Biol. Bull.* **78,** 412.

Harvey, E. B. (1940c). A comparison of the development of nucleate and non-nucleate eggs of *Arbacia punctulata. Biol. Bull.* **79,** 166.

Harvey, E. B. (1941). Vital staining of the centrifuged *Arbacia punctulata* egg. *Biol. Bull.* **81,** 114.

Harvey, E. B. (1942). Maternal inheritance in echinoderm hybrids. *J. Exp. Zool.* **91,** 213.

Harvey, E. B. (1943). Rate of breaking and size of "halves" of the *Arbacia punctulata* egg when centrifuged in hypo- and hyper-tonic sea water. *Biol. Bull.* **85,** 141.

Harvey, E. B. (1945). Stratification and breaking of the *Arbacia punctulata* egg when centrifuged in single salt solutions. *Biol. Bull.* **89,** 72.

Harvey, E. B. (1946). Structure and development of the clear quarter of the *Arbacia punctulata* egg. *J. Exp. Zool.* **102,** 253.

Harvey, E. B. (1949). The growth and metamorphosis of the *Arbacia punctulata* pluteus, and late development of the white halves of centrifuged eggs. *Biol. Bull.* **97,** 287.

Harvey, E. B. (1951). Cleavage in centrifuged eggs and in parthenogenetic merogones. *Ann. N.Y. Acad. Sci.* **51,** 1336.

Harvey, E. B. (1956a). "The American *Arbacia* and Other Sea Urchins." Princeton Univ. Press, Princeton, New Jersey.

Harvey, E. B. (1956b). Sex in sea urchins. *Pubbl. Sta. Zool. Napoli* **28,** 127.

Harvey, E. B. (1960). Cleavage with nucleus intact in sea urchin eggs. *Biol. Bull.* **119,** 87.

Harvey, E. B., and Anderson, T. F. (1943). The spermatozoon and fertilization membrane of *Arbacia punctulata* as shown by the electron microscope. *Biol. Bull.* **85,** 151.

Harvey, E. B., and Hollaender, A. (1937). Activation of centrifuged whole eggs and their fractions by monochromatic ultraviolet radiation. *Biol. Bull.* **73,** 365.

Harvey, E. B., and Hollaender, A. (1938). Parthenogenetic development of the eggs and egg fractions of *Arbacia punctulata* caused by monochromatic ultraviolet radiation. *Biol. Bull.* **75,** 258.

Harvey, E. B., and Lavin, G. I. (1944). The chromatin in the living *Arbacia punctulata* egg and the cytoplasm of the centrifuged egg as photographed by ultraviolet light. *Biol. Bull.* **86,** 163.

Harvey, E. B., and Lavin, G. I. (1951). The eggs and half-eggs of *Arbacia punctulata* and the plutei as photographed by ultraviolet visible and infrared light. *Exp. Cell Res.* **2,** 393.

Harvey, E. N. (1910). The mechanism of membrane formation and other early changes in developing sea urchins eggs as bearing upon the problem of artificial parthenogenesis. *J. Exp. Zool.* **8,** 355.

Harvey, E. N. (1911). Studies on the permeability of cells. *J. Exp. Zool.* **10,** 507.

Harvey, E. N. (1914). Is the fertilization membrane of *Arbacia* eggs a precipitation membrane? *Biol. Bull.* **27,** 237.

Hatano, S., Kondo, H., and Miki-Nomura, T. (1969). Purification of sea urchin egg actin. *Exp. Cell Res.* **55,** 275.

Hathaway, R. R. (1959). The effect of sperm on ^{35}S-labelled *Arbacia* fertilizin. *Biol. Bull.* **117,** 395.

Hathaway, R. R., and Metz, C. B. (1961). Interaction between *Arbacia* sperm and S[35]-labelled fertilizin. *Biol. Bull.* **120,** 360.

Hathaway, R. R., and Warren, L. (1961). Further investigation of egg jelly dispersal by *Arbacia* sperm extract. *Biol. Bull.* **121,** 416.

Hayes, F. R. (1938). The relation of fat changes to the general chemical embryology of the sea urchin. *Biol. Bull.* **74,** 267.

Heilbrunn, L. V. (1915). Studies in artificial parthenogenesis. II. Physical changes in the egg of *Arbacia Biol. Bull.* **24,** 149.

Heilbrunn, L. V. (1956). "The Dynamics of Living Protoplasm." Academic Press, New York.

Hendee, E. C. (1931). Formed components and fertilization in the egg of the sea urchin *Lytechinus variegatus. Pap. Tortugas Lab.* **27**; *Carnegie Inst. Wash. Publ.* **413,** 99.

Hendey, N. I. (1954). Note on the Plymouth "Nitzschia" culture. *J. Mar. Biol. Ass. U.K.* **33**, 335.

Henshaw, P. S. (1932). Studies of the effect of Roentgen rays on the time of the first cleavage in some marine invertebrate eggs. I. Recovery from Roentgen ray effects in *Arbacia* eggs. *Amer. J. Roentgenol. Radium Ther.* [N.S.] **27**, 890.

Henshaw, P. S. (1940a). Further studies on the action of Roentgen rays on the gametes of *Arbacia punctulata*. I. Delay in cell division caused by exposure of sperm to Roentgen rays. *Amer. J. Roentgenol. Radium. Ther.* [N.S.] **43**, 899.

Henshaw, P. S. (1940b). Further studies on the action of Roentgen rays on the gametes of *Arbacia punctulata*. II. Modification of the mitotic time schedule in the eggs by exposure of the gametes to Roentgen rays. *Amer. J. Roentgenol. Radium Ther.* [N.S.] **43**, 907.

Henshaw, P. S. (1940c). Further studies on the action of Roentgen rays on the gametes of *Arbacia punctulata*. III. Fixation of irradiation effect by fertilization in the eggs. *Amer. J. Roentgenol. Radium Ther.* [N.S.] **43**, 913.

Henshaw, P. S. (1940d). Further studies on the action of Roentgen rays on the gametes of *Arbacia punctulata*. V. The influence of low temperature on recovery from Roentgen-ray effects in the eggs. *Amer. J. Roentgenol. Radium Ther.* [N.S.] **43**, 921.

Henshaw, P. S. (1940e). Further studies on the action of Roentgen rays on the gametes of *Arbacia punctulata*. VI. Production of multipolar cleavage in the eggs by exposure of the gametes to Roentgen rays. *Amer. J. Roentgenol. Radium Ther.* [N.S.] **43**, 923.

Henshaw, P. S., and Cohen, I. (1940). Further studies on the action of Roentgen rays on the gametes of *Arbacia punctulata*. IV. Changes in radiosensitivity during the first cleavage cycle. *Amer. J. Roentgenol. Radium Ther.* [N.S.] **43**, 917.

Henshaw, P. S., and Francis, D. S. (1936). The effects of X-rays on cleavage in *Arbacia* eggs: Evidence for nuclear control of division rate. *Biol. Bull.* **70**, 28.

Henshaw, P. S., Henshaw, C. T., and Francis, D. S. (1933). The effect of Roentgen rays on the time of the first cleavage in marine invertebrate eggs. *Radiology* **28**, 533.

Herbst, C. (1892). Experimentelle Untersuchungen über den Einfluss der veränderten chemischen Zusammensetzung des umgebenden Mediums auf die Entwicklung der Tiere. I. *Z. Wiss. Zool.* **55**, 446.

Herbst, C. (1893). Experimentelle Untersuchungen über den Einfluss der veränderten chemischen Zusammensetzung des umgebenden Mediums auf die Entwicklung der Tiere. II. *Mitt. Zool. Sta. Neapel* **11**, 136.

Herbst, C. (1895). Experimentelle Untersuchungen über den Einfluss der veränderten chemischen Zusammensetzung des umgebenden Mediums auf die Entwicklung der Tiere. V. *Arch. Entwicklungsmech. Organismen* **2**, 482.

Herbst, C. (1896). Experimentelle Untersuchungen über den Einfluss der veränderten chemischen Zusammensetzung des umgebenden Mediums auf die Entwicklung der Tiere. III. IV. *Arch. Entwicklungsmech. Organismen* **2**, 455.

Herbst, C. (1897). Ueber die zur Entwicklung der Seeigellarven notwendigen anorganischen Stoffe, ihre Rolle und ihre Vertretbarkeit. I. *Arch. Entwicklungsmech. Organismen* **5**, 649.

Herbst, C. (1900). Ueber das Auseinanderegenen im Furchungs- und Gewebe-zellen in kalkfreiem Medium. *Arch. Entwicklungsmech. Organismen* **9**, 424.

Herbst, C. (1901). Ueber die zur Entwicklung notwendigen anorganischen Stoffe, ihre Rolle und ihre Vertretbarkeit. Theil II. *Arch. Entwicklungsmech. Organismen* **11**, 617.

Herbst, C. (1904). Über die zur Entwicklung der Seeigellarven notwendigen anorganischen Stoffe, ihre Rolle und ihre Vertretbarkeit. III. *Arch. Entwicklungsmech. Organismen* **17**, 306.

Herbst, C. (1907). Vererbungsstudien V. *Arch. Entwicklungsmech. Organismen* **24,** 185.

Hertwig, R. (1895). Ueber Centrosoma und Centralspindel. *Sitzungsber. Ges. Morphol. Physiol. Muench.* **11,** 41.

Hertwig, R. (1896). Ueber die Entwicklung des unbefruchteten Seeigeleies. *Festschr. Gegenbaur* **II,** 21.

Hertwig, R. (1912). Das Schicksal des mit Radium bestrahlten Spermachromatins in Seeigelei. *Arch. Mikrosk. Anat.* **79,** 201.

Hill, R. J., Poccia, D. L., and Doty, P. (1971). Towards a total macromolecular analysis of sea urchin embryo chromatin. *J. Mol. Biol.* **61,** 445.

Hillier, J., Lansing, A. I., and Rosenthal, T. (1952). Electron microscopy of some marine egg surfaces. *Biol. Bull.* **103,** 293 (A).

Hindle, E. (1910). A cytological study of artificial parthenogenesis in *Strongylocentrotus purpuratus. Arch. Entwicklungsmech. Organismen* **31,** 145.

Hinegardner, R. T. (1961). The DNA content of isolated sea urchin egg nuclei. *Exp. Cell Res.* **24,** 341.

Hinegardner, R. T. (1962). The isolation of nuclei from eggs and embryos of the sea urchin. *J. Cell Biol.* **15,** 503.

Hinegardner, R. T. (1969). Growth and development of the laboratory-cultured sea urchin. *Biol. Bull.* **137,** 465.

Hinegardner, R. T., Rao, B., and Feldman, D. E. (1964). The DNA synthetic period during early development of the sea urchin egg. *Exp. Cell Res.* **36,** 53.

Hinrichs, M. A. (1927). Ultraviolet radiation and the fertilization reaction in *Arbacia punctulata. Biol. Bull.* **53,** 416.

Hiramoto, Y. (1956). Cell division without mitotic apparatus in sea urchin eggs. *Exp. Cell Res.* **11,** 630.

Hiramoto, Y. (1957). The thickness of the cortex and the refractive index of the protoplasm in sea urchin eggs. *Embryologia* **3,** 361.

Hiramoto, Y. (1958). A quantitative description of protoplasmic movement during cleavage in sea urchin egg. *J. Exp. Biol.* **35,** 407.

Hiramoto, Y. (1959). Change in electric properties upon fertilization in the sea urchin egg. *Exp. Cell Res.* **16,** 421.

Hiramoto, Y. (1962a). Microinjection of the live spermatozoa into sea urchin eggs. *Exp. Cell Res.* **27,** 416.

Hiramoto, Y. (1962b). An analysis of the mechanism of fertilization by means of enucleation of sea urchin eggs. *Exp. Cell Res.* **28,** 323.

Hiramoto, Y. (1965). Further studies on cell division without mitotic apparatus in sea urchin eggs. *J. Cell Biol.* **25,** 161.

Hiramoto, Y. (1969a). Mechanical properties of the protoplasm of the sea urchin egg. I. Unfertilized egg. *Exp. Cell Res.* **56,** 201.

Hiramoto, Y. (1969b). Mechanical properties of the protoplasm of the sea urchin egg. II. Fertilized egg. *Exp. Cell Res.* **56,** 209.

Hiramoto, Y. (1971). Analysis of cleavage stimulus by means of micromanipulation of sea urchin eggs. *Exp. Cell Res.* **68,** 291.

Hirshfield, H. I., Zimmerman, S. B., and Zimmerman, A. M. (1961). Nucleotide metabolism in developing *Arbacia. Biol. Bull.* **121,** 392.

Hnilica, L. S., and Johnson, A. W. (1970). Fractionation and analysis of nuclear proteins in sea urchin embryos. *Exp. Cell Res.* **63,** 261.

Hoberman, H. D., Metz, Ch. B., and Graff, J. (1952). Uptake of deuterium into proteins of fertilized and unfertilized *Arbacia* eggs suspended in heavy water. *J. Gen. Physiol.* **35,** 639.

Hobson, A. D. (1932). The effect of fertilization on the permeability to water and on certain other properties of the surface of the egg of *Psammechinus miliaris. J. Exp. Biol.* **9**, 69.

Hoff-Jørgensen, E. (1954). Deoxyribonucleic acid in some gametes and embryos. *Proc. Symp. Colston Res. Soc.* **7**, 79.

Hogan, B., and Gross, P. R. (1971). The effect of protein synthesis inhibition on the entry of mRNA into the cytoplasm of sea urchin embryos. *J. Cell Biol.* **49**, 692.

Hollaender, A. (1938). Monochromatic ultraviolet radiation as an activating agent for the eggs of *Arbacia punctulata. Biol. Bull.* **75**, 248.

Holland, N. D. (1967). Gametogenesis during the annual reproduction cycle in a cidaroid sea urchin *(Stylocidaris affinis). Biol. Bull.* **133**, 578.

Holland, N. D., and Giese, A. C. (1965). An autoradiographic investigation of the gonads of the purple sea urchin *(Strongylocentrotus purpuratus). Biol. Bull.* **128**, 241.

Holter, H., and Lindahl, P. E. (1940). Beiträge zur enzymatischen Histochemie. Die Atmung animaler und vegetativer Keimhälften von *Paracentrotus lividus. C. R. Trav. Lab. Carlsberg, Ser. Chim.* **23**, 257.

Holter, H., and Linderstrøm-Lang, K. (1940). Enzymatische Histochemie. *In* "Handbuch der Enzymologie" (F. F. Nord and R. Neidenhagen, eds.), p. 65. Akad. Verlagsges, Leipzig.

Holter, H., and Zeuthen, E. (1957). Dynamics of early echinoderm development, as observed by phase contrast microscopy and correlated with respiratory measurements. *Pubbl. Sta. Zool. Napoli* **29**, 285.

Hori, R. (1965). The sodium and potassium content in unfertilized and fertilized eggs of the sea urchin. *Embryologia* **9**, 34.

Hörstadius, S. (1928). Ueber die Determination des Keimes bei Echinodermen. *Acta Zool. (Stockholm)* **9**, 1.

Hörstadius, S. (1931). Ueber die Potenzverteilung im Verlaufe bei *Paracentrotus lividus* Lk. *Ark. Zool., B* **23**, No. 1.

Hörstadius, S. (1935). Ueber die Determination im Verlaufe der Eiachse bei Seeigeln. *Pubbl. Sta. Zool. Napoli* **14**, 251.

Hörstadius, S. (1936a). Weitere Studien über die Determination im Verlaufe der Eiachse bei Seeigeln. *Wilhelm Roux' Arch. Entwicklungsmech. Organismen* **135**, 40.

Hörstadius, S. (1936b). Studien über heterosperme Seeigelmerogone nebst Bemerkungen über einige Keimblattchimären. *Mem. Mus. Hist. Natur. Belg.* [2] No. **3**, p. 801.

Hörstadius, S. (1938). Schnüzungsversuche und Seeigelkeimen. *Wilhelm Roux' Arch. Entwicklungsmech. Organismen* **138**, 197.

Hörstadius, S. (1939). The mechanics of sea urchin development, studied by operative methods. *Biol. Rev.* **14**, 132.

Hörstadius, S. (1949). Experimental researches on the developmental physiology of the sea urchin. *Pubbl. Sta. Zool. Napoli* **21**, Suppl., 131.

Hörstadius, S. (1953). Vegetalization of the sea urchin egg by dinitrophenol and animalization by trypsin and ficin. *J. Embryol. Exp. Morphol.* **1**, 227.

Hörstadius, S. (1957). On the regulation of the bilateral symmetry in plutei with exchanged meridional halves and in giant plutei. *J. Embryol. Exp. Morphol.* **5**, 60.

Hörstadius, S. (1963). Vegetalization of sea urchin larvae by chloramphenicol. *Develop. Biol.* **7**, 144.

Hörstadius, S. (1965). Ueber die animalizierende Wirkung von Trypsin auf Seeigelkeine. *Zool. Jahrb., Abt. Allg. Zool. Physiol. Tiere* **71**, 245.

Hörstadius, S., and Gustafson, T. (1954). The effect of three antimetabolites on sea urchin development. *J. Embryol. Exp. Morphol.* **2**, 216.

Hörstadius, S., and Strömberg, S. (1940). Untersuchungen über Umdeterminierung von Fragmenten des Seeigeleis durch chemische Agentien. *Wilhelm Roux' Arch. Entwicklungsmech. Organismen* **140**, 409.

Hörstadius, S., and Wolsky, A. (1936). Studien über die Determination der Bilateralsymmetrie des Jungen Seeigelkeimes. *Wilhelm Roux' Arch. Entwicklungsmech. Organismen* **135**, 69.

Hörstadius, S., Lorch, I. J., and Danielli, J. F. (1950). Differentiation of the sea urchin egg following reduction of the interior cytoplasm in relation to the cortex. *Exp. Cell Res.* **1**, 188.

Hörstadius, S., Immers, J., and Runnström, J. (1966). The incorporation of $^{35}SO_4$ in whole embryos and meridional, animal and vegetal halves of the sea urchin *Paracentrotus lividus. Exp. Cell Res.* **43**, 441.

Hörstadius, S., Joseffsson, L., and Runnström, J. (1967). Morphogenetic agents from unfertilized eggs of the sea urchin *Paracentrotus lividus. Develop. Biol.* **16**, 189.

Horwitz, B. (1965). Rates of oxygen consumption of fertilized and unfertilized *Asterias, Arbacia* and *Spisula* eggs. *Exp. Cell Res.* **38**, 620.

Hsiao, S. C., and Fujii, W. K. (1963). Early ontogenetic changes in the concentration of alkaline phosphatase in Hawaiian sea urchins. *Exp. Cell Res.* **32**, 217.

Huang, A. S., and Baltimore, D. (1970). Initiation of polyribosome formation in poliovirus-infected HeLa cells. *J. Mol. Biol.* **47**, 275.

Hüber, W. (1946). Der normale Formwechsel des Mitose-apparates und der Zellrinde beim Ei von Tubifex. *Rev. Suisse Zool.* **53**, 468.

Huberman, J. A., and Attardi, G. (1967). Studies of fractionated HeLa cell metaphase chromosomes. I. The chromosomal distribution of DNA complementary to 28 S and 18 S ribosomal RNA and to cytoplasmic messenger RNA. *J. Mol. Biol.* **29**, 487.

Hughes, A. F. (1952). *In* "The Mitotic Cycle." Academic Press, New York.

Hughes, A. F., and Swann, M. M. (1948). Anaphase movements in the living cell. A study with phase contrast and polarized light on chick tissue cultures. *J. Exp. Biol.* **25**, 45.

Hultin, E., and Hagström, B. (1954). Sea urchin eggs survive deep-freezing. *Ark. Zool.* [2] **6**, 523.

Hultin, T. (1947). On the question of sperm antifertilizin. *Pubbl. Sta. Zool. Napoli* **21**, 153.

Hultin, T. (1948a). Species specificity in fertilization reaction. The role of the vitelline membrane of sea urchin eggs in species specificity. *Ark. Zool., A* **40**, No. 12, 1.

Hultin, T. (1948b). Species specificity in fertilization reaction. II. Influence of certain factors on the cross-fertilization capacity of *Arbacia lixula* (L.). *Ark. Zool., A* **40**, No. 20, 1.

Hultin, T. (1949a). The effect of calcium on respiration and acid formation in homogenates of sea urchin eggs. *Ark. Kemi, Mineral. Geol., A* **26**, No. 27, 1.

Hultin, T. (1949b). Agglutination of sea urchin eggs by nucleoproteins. *Ark. Kemi* **1**, 419.

Hultin, T. (1950a). On the oxygen uptake of *Paracentrotus lividus* egg homogenates after the addition of calcium. *Exp. Cell Res.* **1**, 159.

Hultin, T. (1950b). The protein metabolism of sea urchin eggs during early development studied by means of ^{15}N-labeled ammonia. *Exp. Cell Res.* **1**, 599.

Hultin, T. (1952). Incorporation of N^{15}-labeled glycine and alanine into the proteins of developing sea urchin eggs. *Exp. Cell Res.* **3**, 494.

Hultin, T. (1953a). Incorporation of C^{14}-labeled carbonate and acetate into sea urchin embryos. *Ark. Kemi* **6**, 195.

Hultin, T. (1953b). Incorporation of N^{15}-labeled ammonium chloride into pyrimidines and purines during the early sea urchin development. *Ark. Kemi* **5**, 267.

Hultin, T. (1953c). The amino acid metabolism of sea urchin embryos studied by means of N^{15}-labeled ammonium chloride and alanine. *Ark. Kemi* **5**, 543.

Hultin, T. (1953d). Incorporation of N^{15}-*dl*-alanine into protein fractions of sea urchin embryos. *Ark. Kemi* **5**, 559.

Hultin, T. (1957). Acid-soluble nucleotides in the early development of *Psammechinus miliaris*. *Exp. Cell Res.* **12**, 413.

Hultin, T. (1961a). The effect of puromycin on protein metabolism and cell division in fertilized sea urchin eggs. *Experientia* **17**, 410.

Hultin, T. (1961b). Activation of ribosomes in sea urchin eggs in response to fertilization. *Exp. Cell Res.* **25**, 405.

Hultin, T. (1964). Factors influencing polyribosome formation *in vivo*. *Exp. Cell Res.* **34**, 608.

Hultin, T., and Bergstrand, A. (1960). Incorporation of C^{14}-leucine into protein by cell-free systems from sea urchin embryos at different stages of development. *Develop. Biol.* **2**, 61.

Humphreys, T. (1969). Efficiency of translation of messenger RNA before and after fertilization in sea urchins. *Develop. Biol.* **20**, 435.

Humphreys, T. (1971). Measurements of messenger RNA entering polysomes upon fertilization of sea urchin eggs. *Develop. Biol.* **26**, 201.

Hunter, S. J. (1901). On the production of artificial parthenogenesis in *Arbacia* by the use of sea water concentrated by evaporation. *Amer. J. Physiol.* **6**, 177.

Hunter, S. J. (1903). On the conditions governing the production of artificial parthenogenesis in *Arbacia*. *Biol. Bull.* **5**, 143.

Hutchens, J. O., Keltch, A. K., Krahl, M. E., and Clowes, G. H. A. (1942). Studies on cell metabolism and cell division. VI. Observations on the glycogen content, carbohydrate consumption, lactic acid production and ammonia production of eggs of *Arbacia punctulata*. *J. Gen. Physiol.* **25**, 717.

Hyatt, E. A. (1967a). Polyriboadenylate synthesis by nuclei from developing sea urchin embryos. I. Characterization of the ATP polymerase reaction. *Biochim. Biophys. Acta* **142**, 246.

Hyatt, E. A. (1967b). Polyriboadenylate synthesis by nuclei from developing sea urchin embryos. II. Polyadenylic acid priming of ATP polymerase. *Biochim. Biophys. Acta* **142**, 254.

Hyman, L. H. (1955). "The Invertebrates. Echinodermata," Vol. IV. McGraw-Hill, New York.

Hynes, R. O., and Gross, P. R. (1970). A method for separating cells from early sea urchin embryos. *Develop. Biol.* **21**, 383.

Hynes, R. O., and Gross, P. R. (1972). Informational RNA sequences in early sea urchin embryos. *Biochim. Biophys. Acta* **259**, 104.

Ikeda, M. (1965). Behaviour of sulphydryl groups of sea urchin eggs under the blockage of cell division by UV and heat shock. *Exp. Cell Res.* **40**, 282.

Immers, J. (1956). Changes in acid mucopolysaccharides attending the fertilization and development of the sea urchin. *Ark. Zool.* [2] **9**, 367.

Immers, J. (1957). Cytochemical studies of fertilization and first mitosis of the sea urchin egg. *Exp. Cell Res.* **12**, 145.

Immers, J. (1958). Metabolism of glucosamine in the early sea urchin development. *Exp. Cell Res.* **15**, 595.

Immers, J. (1959). Autoradiographic studies on incorporation of ^{14}C-labelled algal protein hydrolysate in the early sea urchin development. *Exp. Cell Res.* **18**, 585.

Immers, J. (1960a). Carbohydrates with free reducing groups in unfertilized sea urchin eggs. *Ark. Kemi* **16**, 63.

Immers, J. (1960b). Studies on cytoplasmic components of sea urchin eggs stratified by centrifugation. *Exp. Cell Res.* **19**, 499.

Immers, J. (1961a). The occurrence of sulphates mucopolysaccharide in the perivitelline liquid of *Echinus esculentus. Ark. Zool.* [2] **13**, 299.

Immers, J. (1961b). Comparative study of the localization of incorporated ^{14}C-labeled amino acids and $^{35}SO_4$ in the sea urchin ovary, egg and embryo. *Exp. Cell Res.* **24**, 356.

Immers, J. (1965). Monoiodoacetate as an animalizing agent in experiments with embryos of the sea urchin, *Paracentrotus lividus. Acta Embryol. Morphol. Exp.* **8**, 205.

Immers, J., and Runnström, J. (1960). Release of respiratory control by 2,4-dinitrophenol in different stages of sea urchin development. *Develop. Biol.* **2**, 90.

Immers, J., and Runnström, J. (1965). Further studies on the effects of deprivation of sulfate in the early development of the sea urchin *Paracentrotus lividus. J. Embryol. Exp. Morphol.* **14**, 289.

Immers, J., Markman, B., and Runnström, J. (1967). Nuclear changes in the course of development of the sea urchin studied by means of Hale staining. *Exp. Cell Res.* **47**, 425.

Infante, A. A., and Baierlein, R. (1971). Pressure-induced dissociation of sedimenting ribosomes. Effect on sedimentation patterns. *Proc. Nat. Acad. Sci. U.S.* **68**, 1780.

Infante, A. A., and Graves, P. N. (1971). Stability of free ribosomes, derived ribosomes and polysomes of the sea urchin. *Biochim. Biophys. Acta* **246**, 100.

Infante, A. A., and Krauss, M. (1971). Dissociation of ribosomes induced by centrifugation. Evidence for doubting conformational changes in ribosomes. *Biochim. Biophys. Acta* **246**, 81.

Infante, A., and Nemer, M. (1967). Accumulation of newly synthesized RNA templates in a unique class of polyribosomes during embryogenesis. *Proc. Nat. Acad. Sci. U.S.* **58**, 681.

Infante, A., and Nemer, M. (1968). Heterogeneous RNP particles in the cytoplasm of sea urchin embryos. *J. Mol. Biol.* **32**, 543.

Infantellina, F., and La Grutta, G. (1948). Contenuto in glutatione nelle uova di *Paracentrotus lividus* e sue variazioni nelle varie fasi dello sviluppo. *Arch. Sci. Biol. (Bologna)* **32**, 85.

Inoué, A. (1952). The effect of colchicine on the microscopic and submicroscopic structure of the mitotic spindle. *Exp. Cell Res., Suppl.* **2**, 305.

Inoué, A. (1964). Organization and function of the mitotic spindle *In* "Primitive Motile Systems in Cell Biology" (R. D. Allen and N. Kamiya, eds.), p. 549. Academic Press, New York.

Inoué, S., and Hardy, J. P. (1971). Fine structure of the fertilization membranes of sea urchin embryos. *Exp. Cell Res.* **68**, 259.

Inoué, S., Sato, H., Kane, R. E., and Stephens, R. E. (1965). Dynamic structure of the living spindle. *J. Cell Biol.* **27**, Suppl., 115A.

Inoué, S., Hardy, J. P., Cousineau, G. H., and Bal, A. K. (1967). Fertilization membranes structure analysis with the surface replica method. *Exp. Cell Res.* **48**, 248.

Inoué, S., Buday, A., and Cousineau, G. H. (1970a). Observations of sea urchin spermatozoa with the surface replica method. *Exp. Cell Res.* **61**, 285.

Inoué, S., Buday, A., and Cousineau, G. H. (1970b). Developing fertilization membranes. *Exp. Cell Res.* **59**, 343.

Inoué, S., Preddie, E. C., Buday, A., and Cousineau, G. H. (1971). Use of egg membrane lysins in the preparation of sea urchin egg ghosts. *Exp. Cell Res.* **66**, 164.

Isaka, S., Kanatani, H., and Suzuki, N. (1966). Jelly dispersing enzyme obtained from spermatozoa of sea urchin, *Anthocidaris crassispina. Exp. Cell Res.* **44**, 66.

Isaka, S., Akino, M., Hotta, K., and Kurokana, M. (1969). Sperm isoagglutination and sialic acid content of the jelly coat of sea urchin eggs. *Exp. Cell Res.* **54**, 247.

Isaka, S., Hotta, K., and Kurokawa, M. (1970). Jelly coat substances of sea urchin eggs. I. Sperm isoagglutination and sialopolysaccharide in the jelly. *Exp. Cell Res.* **59**, 37.

Ishida, J. (1936). An enzyme dissolving the fertilization membrane of sea urchin eggs. *Annot. Zool. Jap.* **15**, 453.

Ishida, J., and Nakano, E. (1950). Fertilization of activated sea urchin eggs deprived of fertilization membrane by washing with Ca–Mg-free media. *Annot. Zool. Jap.* **23**, 43.

Ishida, J., and Yasumasu, I. (1957). Changes in protein specificity determined by protective enzyme tests during embryonic development of the sea urchin and the fresh-water fish. *J. Fac. Sci., Univ. Tokyo Sect. 4* **8**, 95.

Ishihara, K. (1957). Release and activation of aldolase at fertilization in sea urchin egg. *J. Fac. Sci., Univ. Tokyo, Sect. 4* **8**, 71.

Ishihara, K. (1958a). Compensatory respiration and pentose formation in sea urchin eggs by treatment with monoiodoacetate. *Sci. Rep. Saitama Univ., Ser. B* **3**, 1.

Ishihara, K. (1958b). Effect of butyric acid on aldolase complex in sea urchin eggs. *Sci. Rep. Saitama Univ., Ser. B* **3**, 11.

Ishihara, K. (1963). Isolation of aldolase complex in sea urchin egg. *Sci. Rep. Saitama Univ., Ser. B* **6**, 173.

Ishihara, K. (1964). Release of polysaccharides following fertilization of sea urchin eggs. *Exp. Cell Res.* **36**, 354.

Ishihara, K. (1968a). Chemical analysis of glycoproteins in the egg surface of the sea urchin, *Arbacia punctulata. Biol. Bull.* **134**, 425.

Ishihara, K. (1968b). An analysis of acid polysaccharides produced at fertilization of sea urchin. *Exp. Cell Res.* **51**, 473.

Ishihara, K., and Dan, J. C. (1970). Effects of chemical disruption on the biological activities of the sea urchin jelly. *Develop. Growth Differ.* **12**, No. 3, 179.

Ishikawa, M. (1954). Relation between the breakdown of the cortical granules and permeability to water in the sea urchin egg. *Embryologia* **2**, 57.

Ishikawa, M. (1957). Antagonistic effects of some chemicals on the induction of parthenogenetic development of the sea urchin egg by hypertonic treatment. *Embryologia* **3**, 261.

Ishizaka, S. (1958). Surface character of dividing cells. I. Stationary surface rings. *J. Exp. Biol.* **35**, 396.

Isono, N. (1962). Carbohydrate metabolism in sea urchin eggs. II. Pentose phosphate cycle in developing eggs. *J. Fac. Sci., Univ. Tokyo, Sect. 4* **9**, 369.

Isono, N. (1963a). Carbohydrate metabolism in sea urchin eggs. III. Changes in respiratory quotient during early embryonic development. *Annot. Zool. Jap.* **36**, 126.

Isono, N. (1963b). Carbohydrate metabolism in sea urchin eggs. IV. Intracellular localization of enzymes of pentose phosphate cycle in unfertilized and fertilized eggs. *J. Fac. Sci., Univ. Tokyo, Sect. 4* **10**, 37.

Isono, N., and Yanagisawa, T. (1966). Acid-soluble nucleotides in sea urchin egg. II. Uridine diphosphate sugars. *Embryologia* **9**, 184.

Isono, N., and Yasumasu, I. (1968). Pathways of carbohydrate breakdown in sea urchin eggs. *Exp. Cell Res.* **50**, 616.

Isono, N., Isusaka, A., and Nakano, E. (1963). Studies on glucose-6-phosphate dehydrogenase in sea urchin eggs. *J. Fac. Sci., Univ. Tokyo, Sect. 4* **10**, 55.

Ito, S., Revel, J. P., and Goodenough, D. A. (1967). Observations on the fine structure of the fertilization membrane of *Arbacia punctulata. Biol. Bull.* **133**, 471.

Iverson, R. M. (1971). Studies on deciliated sea urchin embryos. *Exp. Cell Res.* **66**, 197.

Iwaikawa, Y. (1967). Regeneration of cilia in the sea urchin embryo. *Embryologia* **9**, 287.

Jackson, C., and Black, R. E. (1967). The subcellular distribution of some hydrolytic enzymes in unfertilized eggs of the sea urchin, *Arbacia punctulata. Biol. Bull.* **132**, 1.

Jandorf, B. J., and Krahl, M. E. (1942). Studies on cell metabolism and cell division. VIII. The diphosphopyridine nucleotide (cozymase) content of eggs of *Arbacia punctulata*. *J. Gen. Physiol.* **25**, 749.

Jenkins, K. D., and Denny, P. C. (1970). Effect of fertilization on the ribosomal subunit pool of sea urchin eggs. *Biochim. Biophys. Acta* **217**, 206.

Jenkinson, J. W. (1911). On the origin of the polar and bilateral structure of the egg of the sea urchin. *Arch. Entwicklungsmech. Organismen* **32**, 699.

Johnson, A. W., and Hnilica, L. S. (1970). *In vitro* RNA synthesis and nuclear proteins of isolated sea urchin embryo nuclei. *Biochim. Biophys. Acta* **224**, 518.

Johnson, A. W., and Hnilica, L. S. (1971). Cytoplasmic and nuclear basic protein synthesis during early sea urchin development. *Biochim. Biophys. Acta* **246**, 141.

Josefsson, L., and Hörstadius, S. (1969). Morphogenetic substances from sea urchin eggs. Isolation of animalizing and vegetalizing substances from unfertilized eggs of *Paracentrotus lividus*. *Develop. Biol.* **20**, 481.

Just, E. E. (1928a). Initiation of development in *Arbacia*. IV. Some cortical reactions as criteria for optimum fertilization capacity and their significance for the physiology of development. *Protoplasma* **5**, 97.

Just, E. E. (1928b). Initiation of development in *Arbacia*. V. The effect of slowly evaporating sea water and its significance for the theory of auto-parthenogenesis. *Biol. Bull.* **55**, 358.

Just, E. E. (1929). Initiation of development in *Arbacia*. VI. The effect of sea water precipitates with special reference to the nature of lipolysin. *Biol. Bull.* **57**, 422.

Just, E. E. (1939). "Basic Methods for Experiments on Eggs of Marine Animals." McGraw-Hill (Blakiston), New York.

Kafiani, K. A., Timofeeva, M. Ya., Neifakh, A. A., Rachkus, J. A., and Melnikova, N. L. (1966). The effect of X-ray irradiation upon the synthesis of messenger RNA at the early stages of loach embryogenesis. *Biokhimiya* **31**, 365.

Kane, R. E. (1962a). The mitotic apparatus: Isolation by controlled pH. *J. Cell Biol.* **12**, 47.

Kane, R. E. (1962b). The mitotic apparatus: Fine structure of the isolated unit. *J. Cell Biol.* **15**, 279.

Kane, R. E. (1965a). The mitotic apparatus. Physical-chemical factors controlling stability. *J. Cell Biol.* **25**, 137.

Kane, R. E. (1965b). Identification and isolation of the mitotic apparatus protein. *Biol. Bull.* **129**, 396 (A).

Kane, R. E. (1967). The mitotic apparatus. Identification of the major soluble component of the glycol-isolated mitotic apparatus. *J. Cell Biol.* **32**, 243.

Kane, R. E. (1969). Investigations on the hyaline protein of the sea urchin egg. *J. Cell Biol.* **43**, 63a.

Kane, R. E., and Forer, A. (1965). The mitotic apparatus. Structural changes after isolation. *J. Cell Biol.* **25** No. 3, Part 2, 31.

Kane, R. E., and Hersh, R. T. (1959). Isolation and preliminary characterization of a major soluble protein of sea urchin egg. *Exp. Cell Res.* **16**, 59.

Kane, R. E., and Stephens, R. E. (1969). A comparative study of the isolation of the cortex and the role of the calcium-insoluble protein in several species of sea urchin egg. *J. Cell Biol.* **41**, 133.

Karasaki, S. (1968). The ultrastructure and RNA metabolism of nucleoli in early sea urchin embryos. *Exp. Cell Res.* **52**, 13.

Karnofsky, D. A., and Basch, R. S. (1960). Effects of 5-fluorodeoxyuridine and related halogenated pyrimidines on the sand-dollar embryo. *J. Biophys. Biochem. Cytol.* **7**, 61.

Karnofsky, D. A., and Bevelander, G. (1958). Effects of DON (6-diazo-5-oxo-L-norleucine) and azaserine on the sand-dollar embryo. *Proc. Soc. Exp. Biol. Med.* **97**, 32.

Karnofsky, D. A., and Simmel, E. (1963). Effects of growth-inhibiting chemicals on the sand-dollar embryo, *Echinarachinius parma*. *Progr. Exp. Tumor Res.* **3**, 254.

Kavanau, J. L. (1953). Metabolism of free amino acids, peptides and proteins in early sea urchin development. *J. Exp. Zool.* **122**, 285.

Kavanau, J. L. (1954a). Amino acid metabolism in developing sea urchin embryos. *Exp. Cell Res.* **6**, 563.

Kavanau, J. L. (1954b). Amino acid metabolism in the early development of the sea urchin *Paracentrotus lividus*. *Exp. Cell Res.* **7**, 530.

Kavanau, J. L. (1956). "Metabolic Patterns in the Sea Urchin Embryo," Develop. Biol. Conf. Ser. Univ. of Chicago Press, Chicago, Illinois.

Kavanau, J. L. (1958). Biochemical patterns and autolytic artifact. *In* "The Chemical Basis of Development" (W. D. McElroy and B. Glass, eds.), p. 433. Johns Hopkins Press, Baltimore, Maryland.

Kawamura, N. (1960). Cytochemical and quantitative study of protein-bound sulfhydryl and disulfide groups in eggs of *Arbacia* during the first cleavage. *Exp. Cell Res.* **20**, 127.

Kean, E. L., and Bruner, W. E. (1971). Cytidine 5'-monophosphosialic acid synthetase. *Exp. Cell Res.* **69**, 384.

Kedes, L. H., and Birnstiel, M. L. (1971). Reiteration and clustering of DNA sequences complementary to histone messenger RNA. *Nature (London), New Biol.* **230**, 165.

Kedes, L. H., and Gross, P. R. (1969a). Synthesis and function of messenger RNA during early embryonic development. *J. Mol. Biol.* **42**, 559.

Kedes, L. H., and Gross, P. R. (1969b). Identification in cleaving embryos of three RNA species serving as templates for the synthesis of nuclear proteins. *Nature (London)* **223**, 1335.

Kedes, L. H., and Stavy, L. (1969). Structural and functional identity of ribosomes from eggs and embryos of sea urchins. *J. Mol. Biol.* **43**, 337.

Kedes, L. H., Gross, P. R., Cognetti, G., and Hunter, A. L. (1969). Synthesis of nuclear and chromosomal proteins on light polyribosomes during cleavage in the sea urchin embryo. *J. Mol. Biol.* **45**, 337.

Keltch, A. K., and Clowes, G. H. A. (1947). On the relation between oxygen consumption, fertilization membrane formation, and cell division in artificially fertilized *Arbacia* eggs. *Biol. Bull.* **93**, 195.

Keltch, A. K., Strimatter, C. F., Walters, C. P., and Clowes, G. H. A. (1950). Oxidative phosphorylation by a cell-free particulate system from unfertilized *Arbacia* eggs. *J. Gen. Physiol.* **33**, 547.

Kessel, R. G. (1968). Fine structure of annulate lamellae. *J. Cell Biol.* **36**, 658.

Kiefer, B., Sakai, H., Solari, A. J., and Mazia, D. (1966). The molecular unit of the microtubules of the mitotic apparatus. *J. Mol. Biol.* **20**, 75.

Kiefer, B. I., Entelis, C. F., and Infante, A. A. (1969). Mitotic abnormalities in sea urchin embryos exposed to dactinomycin. *Proc. Nat. Acad. Sci. U.S.* **64**, 857.

Kijima, S., and Wilt, F. H. (1969). Rate of nuclear RNA turnover in sea urchin embryos. *J. Mol. Biol.* **40**, 235.

Kimoto, Y. (1964). Stratified structures in the cortical layer of dividing sea urchin eggs. I. Use of connective tissue staining including Mallory's. *Embryologia* **8**, 166.

Kinnander, H., and Gustafson, T. (1960). Further studies on the cellular basis of gastrulation in the sea urchin larva. *Exp. Cell Res.* **19**, 278.

Kinoshita, S. (1968). Relative deficiency of intracellular relaxing system observed in presumptive furrowing region in induced cleavage in the centrifuged sea urchin egg. *Exp. Cell Res.* **51**, 395.

Kinoshita, S. (1969). Periodical release of heparin-like polysaccharide within cytoplasm during cleavage of sea urchin egg. *Exp. Cell Res.* **56**, 39.

Kinoshita, S. (1971). Heparin as a possible inhibitor of genomic RNA synthesis in early development of sea urchin embryos. *Exp. Cell Res.* **64**, 403.

Kinoshita, S., and Yazaki, I. (1967). The behaviour and localization of intracellular relaxing system during cleavage in the sea urchin egg. *Exp. Cell Res.* **47**, 449.

Kinoshita, S., Andoh, B., and Hoffmann-Berling, H. (1964). Das Erschlaffungssystem von Fibroblastenzellen. *Biochim. Biophys. Acta* **79**, 88.

Kit, S. (1960a). Fractionation of deoxyribonucleic acid preparations on substituted cellulose anion exchangers. *Arch. Biochem. Biophys.* **87**, 318.

Kit, S. (1960b). Investigations of the DNA content, base composition and chromatography on ECTEOLA-cellulose of normal and tumor DNA preparations. *Arch. Biochem. Biophys.* **87**, 330.

Kit, S. (1961). Equilibrium sedimentation in density gradients of DNA preparations from animal tissues. *J. Mol. Biol.* **3**, 711.

Kitasume, Y. (1959). Effects of Na salicylate upon the cleavage of sea urchin eggs. *Mem. Coll. Sci., Univ. Kyoto* **26**, 15.

Klein, L., and Currey, J. D. (1970). Echinoid skeleton: Absence of a collagenous matrix. *Science* **169**, 1209.

Kloetzel, J. A., and Metz, C. B. (1963). Studies on the soluble antigens of the sperm of *Arbacia punctulata. Biol. Bull.* **125**, 363.

Köhler, K., and Metz, C. B. (1960). Antigens of the sea urchin sperm surface. *Biol. Bull.* **118**, 96.

Köhler, O. (1912). Über die Abhangigkeit der Kernplasmarelation von der Temperatur und von Reifezustand der Eier. Experimentelle Untersuchungen an *Strongylocentrotus lividus. Arch. Zellforsch.* **8**, 272.

Kojima, M. K. (1959). Relation between the vitally stained granules and cleavage activity in the sea urchin. *Experientia* **17**, 191.

Kojima, M. K. (1960a). Cyclic changes of the cortex and the cytoplasm of the fertilized and the activated sea urchin egg. I. Changes in the thickness of the hyaline layer. *Embryologia* **5**, 1.

Kojima, M. K. (1960b). Cyclic changes of the cortex and the cytoplasm of the fertilized and the activated sea urchin egg. II. The formation of clear spots by the hypertonicity, ether and urethane. *Embryologia* **5**, 178.

Kojima, M. K. (1960c). The effect of DNP and NaN_3 on fertilized eggs of the sea urchin with special reference to the induction of the abnormal cleavage. *Embryologia* **5**, 71.

Kojima, M. K. (1961) Acceleration of certain protoplasmic changes in activated sea urchin eggs by vital staining with neutral red. *Acta Embryol. Morphol. Exp.* **4**, 346.

Kolodny, G. M., and Roslansky, J. D. (1966). Optical rotatory dispersion of mitotic apparatus isolated from dividing eggs of *Strongylocentrotus drobachiensis. J. Mol. Biol.* **15**, 381.

Kopac, M. J. (1940). The physical properties of the extraneous coats of living cells. *Cold Spring Harbor Symp. Quant. Biol.* **8**, 154.

Kopac, M. J. (1941). Disintegration of the fertilization membrane of *Arbacia* by the action of an "enzyme." *J. Cell. Comp. Physiol.* **18**, 215.

Kopac, M. J. (1943). Micrurgical application of surface chemistry to the study of living cells. *In* "Micrurgical and Germ-Free Techniques" (J. A. Reyniers, ed.), pp. 26–71. Univ. of Notre Dame, Indiana.

Kopac, M. J. (1948). The action of NH_4Cl on the surface membranes of *Arbacia* eggs. *Biol. Bull.* **95**, 267.

Korr, I. M. (1937). Respiratory mechanisms in the unfertilized and fertilized sea urchin egg. A temperature analysis. *J. Cell. Comp. Physiol.* **10**, 461.

Krahl, M. E. (1950). Metabolic activity and cleavage of eggs of the sea urchin, *Arbacia punctulata*. A review. 1932. *Biol. Bull.* **98**, 175.

Krahl, M. E. (1956). Oxidative pathway for glucose in eggs of the sea urchin. *Biochim. Biophys. Acta* **20**, 27.

Krahl, M. E., and Clowes, G. H. A. (1935). Stimulation of oxygen consumption and suppression of cell division by dihalo- and trihalophenols. *Proc. Soc. Exp. Biol. Med.* **33**, 477.

Krahl, M. E., and Clowes, G. H. A. (1936). Studies on cell metabolism and cell division. II. Stimulation of cellular oxidation and reversible inhibition of cell division by dihalo- and trihalophenols. *J. Gen. Physiol.* **20**, 173.

Krahl, M. E., and Clowes, G. H. A. (1940). Studies on cell metabolism and cell division. IV. Combined action of substituted phenols, cyanide, carbon monoxide, and other respiratory inhibitors on respiration and cell division. *J. Gen. Physiol.* **23**, 413.

Krahl, M. E., Keltch, A. K., and Clowes, G. H. A. (1940). Flavindinucleotide in eggs of the sea urchin, *Arbacia punctulata*. *Proc. Soc. Exp. Biol. Med.* **45**, 719.

Krahl, M. E., Keltch, A. K., Neubeck, C. E., and Clowes, G. H. A. (1941). Studies on cell metabolism and cell division. V. Cytochrome oxidase activity in the eggs of *Arbacia punctulata*. *J. Gen. Physiol.* **24**, 597.

Krahl, M. E., Jandorf, B. J., and Clowes, G. H. A. (1942). Studies on cell metabolism and cell division. VII. Observations on the amount and possible function of diphosphothiamine (cocarboxylase) in eggs of *Arbacia punctulata*. *J. Gen. Physiol.* **25**, 733.

Krahl, M. E., Keltch, A. K., Walters, C. P., and Clowes, G. H. A. (1954). Hexokinase activity from eggs of the sea urchin *Arbacia punctulata*. *J. Gen. Physiol.* **38**, 31.

Krahl, M. E., Keltch, A. K., and Clowes, G. H. A. (1955). Glucose-6-phosphate and 6-phosphogluconate dehydrogenases from eggs of the sea urchin *Arbacia punctulata*. *J. Gen. Physiol.* **38**, 431.

Krane, S. M., and Crane, R. K. (1958). Changes in the levels of triphosphopyridine nucleotide in the eggs of *Arbacia punctulata* subsequent to fertilization: Presence of pyridine nucleotide transhydrogenase and diphosphopyridine nucleotide kinase. *Biol. Bull.* **115**, 355.

Krane, S. M., and Crane, R. K. (1960). Changes in levels of TPN in marine eggs subsequent to fertilization. *Biochim. Biophys. Acta* **43**, 369.

Krauss, M. (1950a). On the question of hyaluronidase in sea urchin spermatozoa. *Science* **112**, 759.

Krauss, M. (1950b). Lytic agents of the sperm of some marine animals. 2. Extraction of a hetero-egg membrane lysin from sea urchin sperm. *J. Exp. Zool.* **114**, 279.

Krischer, K. N., and Chambers, E. L. (1970). Proteolytic enzymes in sea urchin eggs: Characterization, localization and activity before and after fertilization. *J. Cell. Physiol.* **76**, 23.

Kriszat, G. (1953). Die Wirkung von Periodat auf den Zustand der Plasmamembran des Seeigeleis. *Exp. Cell Res.* **5**, 420.

Kriszat, G. (1954). Die Wirkung von Purinen, Nucleosiden, Nucleotiden und Adenosinetriphosphat auf die Teilung und Entwicklung des Seeigeleis bei Anwendung von Dinitrophenol. *Exp. Cell Res.* **6**, 425.

Kriszat, G., and Runnström, J. (1952). The effect of iodoacetamide on fertilization and division of the sea urchin egg. *Exp. Cell Res.* **3**, 500.

Krohn, A. (1849). "Beitrag zur Entwicklungsgeschichte der Seeigellarven." Heidelberg.

Krugelis, E. J. (1947a). Alkaline phosphatase activity in developmental stages of *Arbacia*. *Biol. Bull.* **93**, 209.

Krugelis, E. J. (1947b). Alkaline phosphatase activity in oocytes of various marine invertebrates. *Biol. Bull.* **93**, 209.

Kuno-Kojima, M. (1967a). Acceleration of the cleavage in sea urchin eggs by insufficient treatments with activating reagents before fertilization. *Embryologia* **10**, 75.

Kuno-Kojima, M. (1967b). Acceleration of the cleavage in sea urchin eggs by insufficient stimulation by spermatozoa before actual fertilization. *Embryologia* **10**, 83.

Kuno-Kojima, M. (1969a). Acceleration of cleavage in sea urchin eggs by repeated insufficient stimulations with various activating reagents and spermatozoa. *Embryologia* **10**, 323.

Kuno-Kojima, M. (1969b). Induction of nuclear changes and cleavage by repeated insufficient stimulation with activating reagents in the sea urchin egg. *Embryologia* **10**, 334.

Lallier, R. (1954). L'action des sels biliares sur le développement de l'oeuf de l'oursin *Paracentrotus lividus. Arch. Biol.* **66**, 75.

Lallier, R. (1955). Effets des ions zinc et cadmium sur le développement de l'oeuf de l'oursin *Paracentrotus lividus. Arch. Biol.* **66**, 75.

Lallier, R. (1957a). Perchlorate et détermination embryonnaire chez les Echinodermes. *C. R. Soc. Biol.* **151**, 471.

Lallier, R. (1957b), Recherches sur l'animalisation de l'oeuf d'oursin *Paracentrotus lividus* par les dérivés polysulfoniques (bleu Evans, bleu de ciel et Germanine). *Pubbl. Sta. Zool. Napoli* **30**, 185.

Lallier, R. (1957c). Animalisation de l'oeuf d'oursin *Paracentrotus lividus* par le poly-anétholsulfonate de sodium (Liquoide). *C. R. Soc. Biol.* **151**, 638.

Lallier, R. (1957d). Colorants acides et détermination embryonnaire chez les Echinodermes. *Experientia* **13**, 362.

Lallier, R. (1959). Studies on the animalization of sea urchin (*Paracentrotus lividus*) eggs by Zn ions. *J. Embryol. Exp. Morphol.* **7**, 540.

Lallier, R. (1960a). Recherches sur les effets des ions de métaux alcalins sur le développement embryonnaire de l'oeuf d'oursin. *Exp. Cell Res.* **21**, 556.

Lallier, R. (1960b). 2-Deoxy-*d*-glucose and sea urchin (*Paracentrotus lividus*) development. *C. R. Acad. Sci.* **250**, 3509.

Lallier, R. (1961). Protective action of adenosine against the effects of lithium ions in the development of the egg of the sea urchin *Paracentrotus lividus. C. R. Acad. Sci.* **252**, 182.

Lallier, R. (1962a). Recherches sur le contrôle de la différentiation de l'oeuf d'oursin par des inhibiteurs des synthèses protéiques. *C. R. Soc. Biol.* **156**, 1249.

Lallier, R. (1962b). Les effets du chloramphénicol sur le développement de l'oeuf d'oursin. *J. Embryol. Exp. Morphol.* **15**, 563.

Lallier, R. (1962c). Les effets de quelques analogues de purines, de pyrimidines et d'acides aminés sur le développement de l'oeuf d'oursin. *Acta Embryol. Morphol. Exp.* **5**, 179.

Lallier, R. (1962d). Végétalisation de l'oeuf de l'oursin *Paracentrotus lividus* par le CAP. *Experientia* **18**, 141.

Lallier, R. (1962e). Les effets du thiosorbitol et du thioglycérol sur la structure de l'appareil mitotique de l'oeuf de l'oursin *Paracentrotus lividus. J. Cell Biol.* **15**, 382.

Lallier, R. (1963a). Effets de substances polycationiques sur la détermination embryonnaire de l'oeuf de l'oursin *Paracentrotus lividus. C. R. Acad. Sci.* **256**, 5409.

Lallier, R. (1963b). Effets de l'actinomycine D sur le développement de l'ouef de l'oursin *Paracentrotus lividus. C. R. Acad. Sci.* **257**, 2159.

Lallier, R. (1963c). Effets de l'actinomycine D sur le développement normal et sur les modifications experimentales de la morphogenèse de l'oeuf de l'oursin *Paracentrotus lividus. Experientia* **19**, 572.

Lallier, R. (1963d). Effet inhibiteur de nucléosides sur les processus de la végétalisation chez l'oeuf d'oursin. *Exp. Cell Res.* **29**, 119.

Lallier, R. (1964a). Biochemical aspects of animalization and vegetalization in the sea urchin embryo. *Advan. Morphog.* **3,** 147.

Lallier, R. (1964b). Effet de l'acide thiazolidine-4-carboxylique sur le développement de l'oeuf de l'oursin *Paracentrotus lividus. C. R. Soc. Biol.* **158,** 2029.

Lallier, R. (1965a). Végétalisation de l'oeuf de l'oursin *Paracentrotus lividus* par l'hydrazide de l'acide isonicotinique (isoniazide). *Experientia* **21,** 453.

Lallier, R. (1965b). Acides mono- et diaminés; effets et antagonismes au cours du développement de l'oeuf de l'oursin *Paracentrotus lividus. C. R. Acad. Sci.* **260,** 4607.

Lallier, R. (1965c). Effets du 5-fluoro-uracile et de la 6-méthylpurine sur le développement de l'oeuf de l'oursin *Paracentrotus lividus. J. Embryol. Exp. Morphol.* **14,** 181.

Lallier, R. (1965d). Effets de substances sulfhydrilées (cysteine, homocystéine et pénicillamine) sur le développement de l'oeuf de l'oursin *Paracentrotus lividus* et action protectrice des acides aminés. *Acta Embryol. Morphol. Exp.* **8,** 12.

Lallier, R. (1965e). Effets de la *S*(1,2-dichlorovinyl)-L-cysteine sur la différentiation de l'oeuf de l'oursin *Paracentrotus lividus. C. R. Soc. Biol.* **159,** 603.

Lallier, R. (1966a). Recherches sur les effets de l'acide ribonucléique soluble sur la différentiation de l'oeuf de l'oursin *Paracentrotus lividus. C. R. Soc. Biol.* **160,** 269.

Lallier, R. (1966b). Relations entre la structure des polyamines et leur action, sur la différentiation de l'oeuf de l'oursin *Paracentrotus lividus. C. R. Acad. Sci.* **262,** 1460.

Lallier, R. (1966c). Glycoprotéines acides et différentiation de l'oeuf de l'oursin *Paracentrotus lividus. C. R. Acad. Sci.* **262,** 1871.

Lallier, R. (1966d). Relation entre la valence et l'activité de complexes cationiques sur la différentiation de l'oeuf de l'oursin *Paracentrotus lividus. C. R. Acad. Sci.* **263,** 386.

Lallier, R. (1966e). Morphogenetic effects of acidic glycopoteins on the development of sea urchin eggs. *Nature (London)* **211,** 99.

Lallier, R. (1966f). Effets de l'isoniazide et de substances apparentées sur la différentiation de l'oeuf d'oursin. *Life Sci.* **5,** 1761.

Lallier, R. (1966g). Effets d'analogues du chloramphenicol sur la différentiation de l'oeuf de l'oursin *Paracentrotus lividus. Experientia* **22,** 724.

Lallier, R. (1966h). Les modifications expérimentales de la morphogenèse chez la larve d'oursin. *Annee Biol.* [4] Nos. **5, 7–8,** 22.

Lallier, R. (1968). Relations entre la structure du chloramphénicol et ses effets végétalisants sur l'oeuf de l'oursin *Paracentrotus lividus. Acta Embryol. Morphol. Exp.* **10,** 280.

Lallier, R. (1970). Formation of fertilization membrane in sea urchin eggs. *Exp. Cell Res.* **63,** 460.

Lansing, A. I., and Rosenthal, T. B. (1949). Ribonucleic acid at cell surfaces and its possible significance. *Biol. Bull.* **97,** 263.

Lansing, A. I., Hillier, J., and Rosenthal, T. B. (1952). The relation between RNA and ionic transport across the cell surface. *J. Cell. Comp. Physiol.* **40,** 337.

Laser, H., and Rothschild Lord. (1939). The metabolism of the eggs of *Psammechinus miliaris* during fertilization reaction. *Proc. Roy. Soc., Ser. B* **126,** 539.

Laskey, R. A., and Gurdon, J. B. (1970). Genetic content of adult somatic cells tested by nuclear transplantation from cultured cells. *Nature (London)* **228,** 1332.

Lea, D. E. (1946). "Actions of Radiation on Living Cells." Cambridge Univ. Press, London and New York.

Lehmann, F. E. (1946). Mitoseablauf und Bewegungsvorgänge der Zellrinde bein zentrifugierten Keimen von Tubifex. *Rev. Suisse Zool.* **53,** 475.

Lenicque, P., Hörstadius, S., and Gustafson, I. (1953). Change of the distribution of mitochondria in animal halves of sea urchin eggs by the action of micromeres. *Exp. Cell Res.* **5,** 400.

Leone, V. (1960). Effetti del trattamento con RNAasi sullo sviluppo embrionale di *Arbacia punctulata* lam. *Acta Embryol. Morphol. Exp.* **3**, 146.

Levy, M., and Weis, P. (1960). Delayed cleavage of fertilized *Arbacia* eggs after treatment with a "nitrogen mustard" or with formaldehyde. *Biol. Bull.* **119**, 295.

Lewis, W. H. (1942). The relation of viscosity changes of protoplasm to amoeboid locomotion and cell division. *In* "The Structure of Protoplasm" (W. Seifriz, ed.), pp. 163–197. Iowa State Press, Ames.

Lillie, F. R. (1914). Studies of fertilization. VI. The mechanism of fertilization in *Arbacia. J. Exp. Zool.* **16**, 523.

Lillie, R. S. (1909). The general biological significance of changes in the permeability of the surface layer or plasma membrane of living cells. *Biol. Bull.* **17**, 188.

Lillie, R. S. (1921). A simple case of salt antagonism in starfish eggs. *J. Gen. Physiol.* **3**, 783.

Lindahl, P. E. (1932a). Zur Kenntnis des Ovarialeies bei dem Seeigel. *Wilhelm Roux'Archiv. Entwicklungsmech. Organismen* **126**, 373.

Lindahl, P. E. (1932b). Zur experimentellen Analyse der Determination der Dorsoventralachse beim Seeigelkeim. II. Versuche mit zentrifugierten Eier. *Wilhelm Roux'Arch. Entwicklungsmech. Organismen.* **127**, 323.

Lindahl, P. E. (1933). Ueber "animalisierte" und "vegetativisierte" Seeigellarven. *Wilhelm Roux'Arch. Entwicklungsmech. Organismen* **128**, 661.

Lindahl, P. E. (1936). Zur Kenntnis der physiologischen Grundlagen der Determination in Seeigelkeim. *Acta Zool. (Stockholm)* **17**, 179.

Lindahl, P. E. (1939). Zur Kenntnis der Entwicklungsphysiologie des Seeigeleies. *Z. Vergl. Physiol.* **27**, 233.

Lindahl, P. E. (1942). Contribution to the physiology of form generation in the sea urchin development. *Q. Rev. Biol.* **17**, 213.

Lindahl, P. E., and Holter, H. (1941). Über die Atmung der Ovozyten erster Ordnung von *Paracentrotus lividus* und ihre Veränderung während der Reifung. *C. R. Trav. Lab. Carlsberg, Ser. Chim.* **24**, 49.

Lindahl, P. E., and Kiessling, K. H. (1950). Separation of micromeres of the 16-cell stage of the sea urchin *Paracentrotus lividus. Experientia* **6**, 425.

Lindahl, P. E., and Lundin, J. (1948). Removal of the fertilization membranes from large quantities of sea urchin eggs. *Science* **108**, 481.

Lindahl, P. E., and Öhman, L. O. (1938). Weitere Studien über Stoffwechsel und Determination im Seeigelkeim. *Biol. Zentralbl.* **58**, 179.

Lindberg, O. (1943). Studien über das Problem des Kohlehydratabbaus und der Säurebildung bei der Befruchtung des Seeigels. *Ark. Kemi, Mineral. Geol., A* **16**, No. 15 1.

Lindberg, O. (1945). On the metabolism of glycogen in the fertilization of the sea urchin egg. *Ark. Kemi, Mineral. Geol., B* **20**, No. 15 1.

Lindberg, O. (1948). On the turnover of ATP in the sea urchin egg. *Ark. Kemi, Mineral. Geol., B* **26**, No. 13 1.

Lindberg, O. (1950). On surface reactions in the sea urchin egg. *Exp. Cell Res.* **1**, 105.

Lindberg, O. (1954). On the turnover of adenosine triphosphate in the sea urchin egg. *Biol. Bull.* **106**, 297.

Lindell, T. J., Weinberg, F., Morris, P. W., Roeder, R. G., and Rutter, W. J. (1970). Specific inhibition of nuclear RNA polymerase II by α-amanitin. *Science* **170**, 447.

Lindsay, D. T. (1969). Synthesis of chromosomal histones during development of the sea urchin. *Ann. Embryol. Morphol., Suppl.* **1**, 277.

Lindvall, S. (1948). Changes in activity of tributyrin-splitting enzyme during early sea-urchin egg development. *Ark. Kemi, Mineral. Geol., B* **26**, No. 9 1.

Lindvall, S., and Carsjö, A. (1954). The influence of calcium on the relative distribution of phosphate compounds and ribonuclease between the particulate compounds. *Ark. Kemi* **7**, 17.

Lison, L., and Pasteels, J. (1951). Etudes histophotométriques sur la teneur en acide désoxyribonucléique des noyaux au cours du développement embryonaire chez l'oursin *Paracentrotus lividus. Arch. Biol.* **62**, 1.

Litchfield, J. B., and Whiteley, A. H. (1959). Studies on the mechanism of phosphate accumulation by sea urchin embryos. *Biol. Bull.* **117**, 133.

Loeb, J. (1910). The prevention of the toxic action of various agencies upon the fertilized egg through the suppression of oxidation in the cell. *Science* **32**, 411.

Loeb, J. (1913). "Artificial Parthenogenesis and Fertilization." Univ. of Chicago Press, Chicago, Illinois (a translation from the German edition of 1909).

Loeb, J. (1915). On the nature of the conditions which determine or prevent the entrance of the spermatozoon into the egg. *Amer. Natur.* **49**, 257.

Loeb, J. (1916). "The Organism as a Whole," p. 85. Putnam, New York.

Loeb, J., and Wasteneis, H. (1911). Sind die Oxydationvorgänge die unabhängige Variable in den Lebenserscheinungen? *Biochem. Z.* **36**, 345.

Loeb, J., King, W. O. R., and Moore, A. R. (1910). Uber Dominauzerscheinungen bei den hybriden Pluteen des Seeigels. *Arch. Entwicklungsmech. Organismen* **29**, 354.

Loeb, L. A. (1969). Purification and properties of deoxyribonucleic acid polymerase from nuclei of sea urchin embryos. *J. Biol. Chem.* **244**, 1672.

Loeb, L. A. (1970). Molecular association of DNA polymerase with chromatin in sea urchin embryos. *Nature (London)* **226**, 448.

Loeb, L. A., and Fansler, B. (1970). Intracellular migration of DNA polymerase in early developing sea urchin embryos. *Biochim. Biophys. Acta* **217**, 50.

Loeb, L. A., Mazia, D., and Ruby, A. D. (1967). Priming of DNA polymerase in nuclei of sea urchin embryos by native DNA. *Proc. Nat. Acad. Sci. U.S.* **57**, 84.

Loeb, L. A., Fansler, B., Williams, R., and Mazia, D. (1969). Sea urchin nuclear DNA polymerase. I. Localization in nuclei during rapid DNA synthesis. *Exp. Cell Res.* **57**, 298.

Loening, U. E. (1968). Molecular weights of ribosomal RNA in relation to evolution. *J. Mol. Biol.* **38**, 355.

Loewenstein, W. R. (1967). Permeability of membrane junctions. *Ann. N.Y. Acad. Sci.* **137**, 441.

Longo, F. J., and Anderson, E. (1968). The fine structure of pronuclear development and fusion in the sea urchin *Arbacia punctulata. J. Cell. Biol.* **39**, 339.

Longo, F. J., and Anderson, E. (1969). Sperm differentiation in the sea urchin *Arbacia punctulata* and *Strongylocentrotus purpuratus. J. Ultrastruct. Res.* **27**, 486.

Longo, F. J., and Anderson, E. (1970a). The effects of nicotine on fertilization in the sea urchin *Arbacia punctulata. J. Cell Biol.* **46**, 308.

Longo, F. J., and Anderson, E. (1970b). The effect of urethane on the events of fertilization in the sea urchin *Arbacia punctulata. J. Cell Biol.* **47**, 125a.

Longo, F. J., and Anderson, E. (1970c). A cytological study of the relation of the cortical reaction to subsequent events of fertilization in urethan-treated eggs of the sea urchin *Arbacia punctulata. J. Cell Biol.* **47**, 646.

Lönning, S. (1967a). Studies of the ultrastructure of sea urchin eggs and the changes induced at insemination. *Sarsia* **30**, 31.

Lönning, S. (1967b). Experimental and electron microscopic studies of sea urchin oocytes and eggs and the changes following insemination. *Arbok Univ. Bergen, Mat.-Natur. Ser.* **8**, 1.

Lönning, S. (1967c). Electron microscopic studies on the block to polyspermy. The influence of trypsin, soy bean trypsin inhibitor and chloralhydrate. *Sarsia* **30**, 107.

Løvtrup, S., and Iverson, R. M. (1969). Respiratory phases during early sea urchin development measured with the automatic diver balance. *Exp. Cell Res.* **55**, 25.

Lucké, B., Ricca, R. A., and Parpart, A. K. (1951). Differential effects of Roentgen rays on cell permeability and on cell cleavage. Experiments with egg cells of *Arbacia punctulata*. *J. Nat. Cancer Inst.* **11**, 1007.

Ludford, R. J. (1936). The action of toxic substances upon the division of normal and malignant cells *in vitro* and *in vivo*. *Arch. Exp. Zellforsch. Besonders Gewebezuecht.* **18**, 411.

Lundblad, G. (1949). Proteolytic activity in eggs and sperms from sea urchins. *Nature (London)* **163**, 643.

Lundblad, G. (1950). Proteolytic activity in sea urchin gametes. I. Activity in untreated extracts. *Exp. Cell Res.* **1**, 264.

Lundblad, G. (1952). Proteolytic activity in sea urchin gametes. II. Activity of extracts and homogenates of the egg subjected to different treatments. *Ark. Kemi* **4**, 537.

Lundblad, G. (1954a). Proteolytic activity in sea urchin gametes. IV. Further investigations of the proteolytic enzymes of the egg. *Ark. Kemi* **7**, 127.

Lundblad, G. (1954b). Proteolytic activity in sea urchin gametes. V. The influence of RNase upon the proteolytic activity of egg extracts. *Ark. Kemi* **7**, 159.

Lundblad, G. (1954c). Proteolytic activity in sea urchin gametes. VI. A study of a proteolytic enzyme in extracts of spermatozoa. *Ark. Kemi* **7**, 169.

Lundblad, G. (1954d). "Proteolytic Activity in Sea Urchin Gametes." Almqvist & Wiksell, Stockholm.

Lundblad, G., and Falksveden, L. G. (1964). Purification of cathepsin B from oocytes and mature eggs of the sea urchin *Brissopsis lyrifera* by means of gel filtration. *Acta Chem. Scand.* **18**, 2044.

Lundblad, G., and Lundblad, I. (1953). Proteolytic activity in sea urchin gametes. III. A study of the proteolytic enzymes of the egg. *Ark. Kemi* **6**, 387.

Lundblad, G., and Runnström, J. (1962). Distribution of proteolytic enzymes in protein fractions from non-fertilized eggs of the sea urchin *Paracentrotus lividus*. *Exp. Cell Res.* **27**, 328.

Lundblad, G., and Schilling W. (1968). Changes in cathepsin D activity and concomitant studies of macromolecular components in early sea urchin development. *Ark. Kemi* **29**, 367.

Lundblad, G., Lundblad, M., Immers, J., and Schilling, W. (1966). Chromatographic analysis of the proteolytic enzymes of the sea urchin egg. II. Gel filtration of extracts from unfertilized and fertilized eggs and investigation of the catheptic activity. *Ark. Kemi* **25**, 395.

Lundblad, G., Schilling, W., and von Zeipel, E. (1968). Chromatographic analysis of the proteolytic enzymes of the sea urchin egg. III. Purification and study of cathepsin D1 and D2 in extracts from unfertilized *Paracentrotus* eggs. *Ark. Kemi* **30**, 247.

Lyon, E. P. (1906). Some results of centrifugalizing the eggs of *Arbacia*. *Amer. J. Physiol.* **15**, 301.

Lyon, E. P. (1907). Results of centrifugalizing eggs. *Arch. Entwicklungsmech. Organismen* **23**, 151.

McBride, E. W. (1903). On the development of *Echinus esculentus, Echinus miliaris* and *Echinus acutus. Phil. Trans. Roy. Soc. London, Ser. B* **195**, 302.

McBride, E. W. (1914a). "Text-Book of Embryology," Vol. I, pp. 456–567. Macmillan, New York.

McBride, E. W. (1914b). The development of *Echinocardium cordatum. Quart. J. Microsc. Sci.* **59**, 471.

McCarthy, B. J., and Hoyer, B. H. (1964). Identity of DNA and diversity of messenger RNA molecules in normal mouse tissues. *Proc. Nat. Acad. Sci. U.S.* **52**, 915.

McCarty, K. S., Stafford, D., and Brown, O. (1968). Resolution and fractionation of macromolecules by isokinetics sucrose density gradient sedimentation. *Anal. Biochem.* **24**, 314.

McClendon, J. F. (1909). On artificial parthenogenesis of the sea urchin egg. *Science* **30**, 454.

McClendon, J. F. (1910). On the dynamics of cell division. II. Changes in permeability of developing eggs to electrolytes. *Am. J. Physiol.* **27**, 240.

McClendon, J. F. (1914). On the nature and formation of the fertilization membrane of the echinoderm egg. *Int. Z. Phys.Chem. Biol.* **1**, 163.

McClendon, J. F., and Mitchell, P. H. (1912). How do isotonic sodium chloride solution and other parthenogenetic agents increase oxydation in the sea urchin egg? *J. Biol. Chem.* **10**, 459.

MacClung, C. E. (1939). Chromosome numbers in animals. *Tabulae Biol.* **18**, 1.

McCulloch, D. (1951). An electron and polarization microscopic study of the egg of *Arbacia punctulata.* Ph.D. Thesis, Biol. Dept., Massachusetts Institute of Technology, Cambridge, Massachusetts.

McCulloch, D. (1952a). Note on the origin of the cortical granules in *Arbacia punctulata* eggs. *Exp. Cell Res.* **3**, 605.

McCulloch, D. (1952b). Fibrous structures in the ground cytoplasm of the *Arbacia* egg. *J. Exp. Zool.* **119**, 47.

Mackie, G. O., Spencer, A. N., and Strathmann, R. (1969). Electrical activity associated with ciliary reversal in an echinoderm larva. *Nature (London)* **223**, 1384.

Mackintosh, F. R., and Bell, E. (1967). Stimulation of protein synthesis in unfertilized sea urchin eggs by prior metabolic inhibition. *Biochem. Biophys. Res. Commun.* **27**, 425.

Mackintosh, F. R., and Bell, E. (1969a). Regulation of protein synthesis in sea urchin eggs. *J. Mol. Biol.* **41**, 365.

Mackintosh, F. R., and Bell, E. (1969b). Proteins synthesized before and after fertilization in sea urchin eggs. *Science* **164**, 961.

Mackintosh, F. R., and Bell, E. (1969c). Labelling of nucleotide pools in sea urchin eggs. *Exp. Cell Res.* **57**, 71.

Mackintosh, F. R., and Bell, E. (1970). Reversible response to puromycin and some characteristics of the uptake and use of amino acids by unfertilized sea urchin eggs. *Biol. Bull.* **139**, 296.

McMaster, R. (1952). The deoxyribonucleic acid content of nuclei in the sea urchin, *Lytechinus variegatus,* during development. *Anat. Rec.* **113**, 542.

McMaster, R. (1955). Deoxyribose nucleic acid in cleavage and larval stages of the sea urchin. *J. Exp. Zool.* **130**, 1.

Maggio, R. (1957). Mitochondrial and cytoplasmic protease activity in sea urchin eggs. *J. Cell. Comp. Physiol.* **50**, 135.

Maggio, R. (1959). Cytochrome oxidase activity in the mitochondria of unfertilized and fertilized sea urchin eggs. *Exp. Cell Res.* **16**, 272.

Maggio, R., and Catalano, C. (1963). Activation of amino acids during sea urchin development. *Arch. Biochem. Biophys.* **103**, 164.

Maggio, R., and Ghiretti-Magaldi, A. (1958). The cytochrome system in mitochondria of unfertilized sea urchin eggs. *Exp. Cell Res.* **15**, 95.

Maggio, R., and Monroy, A. (1959). An inhibitor of cytochrome oxidase activity in the sea urchin egg. *Nature (London)* **184**, 68.

Maggio, R., Aiello, F., and Monroy, A. (1960). Inhibitor of the cytochrome oxidase of unfertilized sea urchin eggs. *Nature (London)* **188**, 1195.

Maggio, R., Vittorelli, M. L., Rinaldi, A. M., and Monroy, A. (1964). *In vitro* incorporation of amino acids into proteins stimulated by RNA from unfertilized eggs. *Biochem. Biophys. Res. Commun.* **15**, 436.

Maggio, R., Vittorelli, M. L., Caffarelli-Mormino, I., and Monroy, A. (1968). Dissociation of ribosomes of unfertilized eggs and embryos of sea urchin. *J. Mol. Biol.* **31**, 621.

Makino, S. (1951). "An Atlas of the Chromosome Numbers in Animals." Iowa State Coll. Press, Ames.

Malkin, L. L., Gross, P. R., and Romanoff, P. (1964). Polyribosomal protein synthesis in fertilized sea urchin eggs. The effect of actinomycin treatment. *Develop. Biol.* **10**, 378.

Malkin, L. L., Mangan, J., and Gross, P. R. (1965). A crystalline protein of high molecular weight from cytoplasmic granules in sea urchin eggs and embryos. *Develop. Biol.* **12**, 520.

Malm, M., and Wachmeister, L. (1950). A comparison between the potassium content of unfertilized and fertilized sea-urchin eggs. *Ark. Kemi* **2**, 443.

Mangan, J., Miki-Nomura, T., and Gross, P. R. (1965). Protein synthesis and the mitotic apparatus. *Science* **147**, 1575.

Mano, Y. (1966). Role of a trypsin-like protease in "informosomes" in a trigger mechanism of activation of protein synthesis by fertilization in sea urchin eggs. *Biochem. Biophys. Res. Commun.* **25**, 216.

Mano, Y. (1968). Regulation system of protein synthesis in early embryogenesis in the sea urchin. *Biochem. Biophys. Res. Commun.* **33**, 877.

Mano, Y. (1969). Factors involved in cyclic protein synthesis in sea urchin cells during early embryogenesis. *J. Biochem. (Tokyo)* **65**, 483.

Mano, Y. (1970). Cytoplasmic regulation and cyclic variation in protein synthesis in the early cleavage stage of the sea urchin embryo. *Develop. Biol.* **22**, 433.

Mano, Y., and Nagano, H. (1966). Release of maternal RNA from some particles as a mechanism of activation of protein synthesis by fertilization in sea urchin eggs. *Biochem. Biophys. Res. Commun.* **25**, 210.

Mano, Y., and Nagano, H. (1970). Mechanism of release of maternal messenger RNA induced by fertilization in sea urchin eggs. *J. Biochem. (Tokyo)* **67**, 611.

Markman, B. (1961a). Regional differences in isotopic labelling of nucleic acid and protein in early sea urchin development. *Exp. Cell Res.* **23**, 118.

Markman, B. (1961b). Differences in isotopic labelling of nucleic acid and protein in early sea urchin development. *Exp. Cell Res.* **23**, 197.

Markman, B. (1961c). Differences in isotopic labelling of nucleic acid and protein in sea urchin embryos developing from animal and vegetal egg halves. *Exp. Cell Res.* **25**, 224.

Markman, B. (1963). Morphogenetic effects of some nucleotide metabolites and antibiotics on early sea urchin development. *Ark. Zool.* [2] **16**, 207.

Markman, B. (1966). Histochemical and autoradiographic studies on the role of the nucleus in the early development of the sea urchin egg. *Yearb. Swed. Cancer Soc.* **4**, 488.

Markman, B. (1967). Isotopic labelling of nucleic acids in sea urchin embryos developing from animal halves in relation to protein and nucleic acid content. *Exp. Cell Res.* **46**, 1.

Markman, B., and Runnström, J. (1963). Animal and vegetal halves of sea urchin larvae subjected to temporary treatment with actinomycin C and mitomycin C. *Exp. Cell Res.* **31**, 615.

Markman, B., and Runnström, J. (1970). The removal by actinomycin D of the effect of endogenous or exogenous animalizing agents in sea urchin development. *Wilhelm Roux'Arch. Entwicklungsmech. Organismen* **165**, 1.

Markova, L. N., and Buznikov, G. A. (1970). Influence of products of enzymatic conversion of monoamines on cell division. *Dokl. Biol. Sci.* **192**, 295.

Marsh, J. B. (1968). Isolation and composition of a low density lipoprotein from the eggs of *Arbacia punctulata*. *Biol. Bull.* **135**, 193.

Marshak, A. (1949). Recovery from ultraviolet light-induced delay in cleavage of *Arbacia* eggs by irradiation with visible light. *Biol. Bull.* **97**, 315.

Marshak, A., and Marshak, C. (1953). Deoxyribonucleic acid in *Arbacia* eggs. *Exp. Cell Res.* **5**, 288.

Marsland, D. A. (1939). The mechanism of cell division. Hydrostatic pressure effects upon dividing egg cells. *J. Cell. Comp. Physiol.* **13**, 15.

Marsland, D. A. (1956). Protoplasmic contractility in relation to gel structure temperature–pressure experiments on cytokinesis and amoeboid movement. *Int. Rev. Cytol.* **5**, 199.

Marsland, D. A. (1957). Temperature–pressure studies on the role of sol–gel reactions in cell division. *In* "Influence of Temperature on Biological Systems" (F. H. Johnson, ed.), pp. 111–126. Amer. Physiol. Soc., Washington, D.C.

Marsland, D. A. (1965). Partial reversal of the antimitotic effects of heavy water by high hydrostatic pressure. An analysis of the first cleavage division in the eggs of *Strongylocentrotus purpuratus*. *Exp. Cell Res.* **38**, 592.

Marsland, D. A. (1968). Cell division-enhancement of the antimitotic effects of colchicine by low temperature and high pressure in the cleaving eggs of *Lytechinus variegatus*. *Exp. Cell Res.* **50**, 369.

Marsland, D. A., and Asterita, H. (1966). Counteraction of the antimitotic effects of D₂O in the dividing eggs of *Arbacia punctulata*: A temperature pressure analysis. *Exp. Cell Res.* **42**, 316.

Marsland, D. A., and Hecht, R. (1968). Cell division: Combined antimitotic effects of colchicine and heavy water on first cleavage in the eggs of *Arbacia punctulata*. *Exp. Cell Res.* **51**, 602.

Marsland, D. A., and Landau, J. V. (1954). The mechanism of cytokinesis: Temperature–pressure studies on the cortical gel system in various marine eggs. *J. Exp. Zool.* **125**, 507.

Marsland, D. A., and Zimmerman, A. M. (1963). Cell division: Differential effects of heavy water upon the mechanisms of cytokinesis and karyokinesis in the eggs of *Arbacia punctulata*. *Exp. Cell Res.* **30**, 23.

Marsland, D. A., Zimmerman, A. M., and Auclair, W. (1960). Cell division: Experimental induction of cleavage furrows in the eggs of *Arbacia punctulata*. *Exp. Cell Res.* **21**, 179.

Marushige, K., and Ozaki, H. (1967). Properties of isolated chromatin from sea urchin embryo. *Develop. Biol.* **16**, 474.

Mateyko, G. M. (1961). The effect of cobalt, RNA and RNase on the development of *Arbacia punctulata*. *Biol. Bull.* **121**, 397.

Mathews, A. P. (1897). Zur Chemie der Spermatozoen. *Hoppe-Seyler's Z. Physiol. Chem.* **23**, 399.

Mathews, A. P. (1901). The so-called cross-fertilization of *Asterias* by *Arbacia*. *Amer. J. Physiol.* **6**, 216.

Matsui, K. (1924). Studies on the hybridization among echinoderms with special reference to the behavior of chromosomes. *J. Coll. Agr., Tokyo Imp. Univ.* **7**, 211.

Matsumoto, L., and Pikò, L. (1971). *In vivo* radioactive labeling of mitochondrial DNA in *Arbacia punctulata* oocytes. *Biol. Bull.* **144**, 397(a).

Mazia, D. (1941). Enzyme studies on chromosomes. *Cold Spring Harbor Symp. Quant. Biol.* **9**, 40.

Mazia, D. (1949a). Deoxyribonucleic acid and deoxyribonuclease in development. *Growth* **9**, 5.

Mazia, D. (1949b). The distribution of deoxyribonuclease in the developing embryo (*Arbacia punctulata*). *J. Cell Comp. Physiol.* **34**, 17.

Mazia, D. (1954). SH and growth. *In* "Glutathione" (S. P. Colowick *et al.,* eds.), pp. 209–223. Academic Press, New York.

Mazia, D. (1955). The organization of the mitotic apparatus. *Symp. Soc. Exp. Biol.* **9**, 335.

Mazia, D. (1958a). The production of twin embryos in *Dendraster* by means of mercapto-ethanol. *Biol. Bull.* **114**, 247.

Mazia, D. (1958b). SH compounds in mitosis. I. The action of mercaptoethanol on the eggs of the sand dollar *Dendraster excentricus. Exp. Cell Res.* **14**, 486.

Mazia, D. (1961). Adenosinetriphosphatase in the mitotic apparatus. *Proc. Nat. Acad. Sci. U.S.* **47**, 788.

Mazia, D. (1963). Synthetic activities leading to mitosis. *J. Cell. Comp. Physiol.* **62**, Suppl. 1, 123.

Mazia, D., and Dan, K. (1952). The isolation and biochemical characterization of the mitotic apparatus of dividing cells. *Proc. Nat. Acad. Sci. U.S.* **38**, 826.

Mazia, D., and Gontcharoff, M. (1964). The mitotic behavior of chromosome in echino-derm eggs following incorporation of bromodeoxyuridine. *Exp. Cell Res.* **35**, 14.

Mazia, D., and Hinegardner, R. T. (1963). Enzymes of DNA synthesis in nuclei of sea urchin embryos. *Proc. Nat. Acad. Sci. U.S.* **50**, 148.

Mazia, D., and Roslansky, J. D. (1956). The quantitative relationship between total cell proteins and the proteins of the mitotic apparatus. *Protoplasma* **46**, 528.

Mazia, D., and Zimmerman, A. M. (1958). SH compounds in mitosis. II. The effect of mercaptoethanol on the structure of the mitotic apparatus in sea urchin eggs. *Exp. Cell Res.* **15**, 138.

Mazia, D., Blumenthal, G., and Benson, E. (1948). The activity and distribution of DNase and phosphatases in the early development of *Arbacia punctulata. Biol. Bull.* **95**, 250.

Mazia, D., Mitchinson, J. M., Medina, H., and Harris, P. (1961). The direct isolation of the mitotic apparatus. *J. Biophys. Biochem. Cytol.* **10**, 467.

Meeker, G. L., and Iverson, R. M. (1971). Tubulin synthesis in fertilized eggs. *Exp. Cell Res.* **64**, 129.

Mehl, J. W., and Swann, M. M. (1961). Acid and base production at fertilization in the sea urchin. *Exp. Cell Res.* **22**, 233.

Mende, T. J., and Chambers, E. L. (1953). The occurrence of arginine phosphate in echino-derm eggs. *Arch. Biochem. Biophys.* **45**, 105.

Menkin, V. (1959). Nature of factors regulating the rate of cell division. *J. Exp. Zool.* **140**, 441.

Mercer, E. H., and Wolpert, L. (1958). Electron microscopy of cleaving sea urchin eggs. *Exp. Cell Res.* **14**, 629.

Mercer, E. H., and Wolpert, L. (1962). An electron microscope study of the cortex of the sea urchin (*Psammechinus miliaris*) egg. *Exp. Cell Res.* **27**, 1.

Merriam, R. W. (1959). The origin and the fate of annulate lamellae in maturing sand dollar egg. *J. Biophys. Biochem. Cytol.* **5**, 117.

Mertes, D. H., and Berg, W. E. (1962). Prolongation of the life span of unfertilized sea urchin eggs with antibiotics and sulfonamides. *Acta Embryol. Morphol. Exp.* **5**, 280.

Messina, L. (1954). The metachromatic properties of the jelly coat of the sea urchinegg as a means for the study of the jelly coat sperm interaction. *Pubbl. Sta. Zool. Napoli* **25**, 454.

Metafora, S., Felicetti, L., and Gambino, R. (1971). The mechanism of protein synthesis activation after fertilization of sea urchin eggs. *Proc. Nat. Acad. Sci. U.S.* **68**, 600.

Metz, C. B. (1942). The inactivation of fertilizin and its conversion to "univalent" form by X-rays and ultraviolet light. *Biol. Bull.* **82**, 446.

Metz, C. B. (1957). Specific egg and sperm substances and activation of the egg. *In* "Beginnings of Embryonic Development," Publ. No. 48, pp. 23–69. Amer. Ass. Advance. Sci., Washington, D.C.

Metz, C. B. (1960). Investigation of the fertilization inhibiting action of *Arbacia* dermal secretion. *Biol. Bull.* **118,** 439.

Metz, C. B. (1961a). Use of inhibiting agents in studies on fertilization mechanisms. *Int. Rev. Cytol.* **11,** 219.

Metz, C. B. (1961b). Fertilization studies using inhibitors. *Symp. Int. Inst. Embryol., 1960* pp. 175–196.

Metz, C. B. (1967). Gamete surface components and their role in fertilization. *In* "Fertilization: Comparative Morphology, Biochemistry and Immunology" (C. B. Metz and A. Monroy, eds.), Vol. 1, pp. 163–236. Academic Press, New York.

Metz, C. B., and Köhler, K. (1960). Antigens of *Arbacia* sperm extracts. *Biol. Bull.* **119,** 202.

Metz, C. B., and Monroy, A., eds. (1967). "Fertilization: Comparative Morphology, Biochemistry and Immunology." Academic Press, New York.

Metz, Ch. B., and Thompson, P. H. (1967). Effect of papain-digested univalent antibody on the morphology, cleavage, and fertilizing capacity of sea urchins eggs. *Exp. Cell Res.* **45,** 433.

Metz, Ch. B., Schuel, H., and Bischoff, E. R. (1964). Inhibition of the fertilizing capacity of sea urchin sperm by papain-digested non-agglutinating antibody. *J. Exp. Zool.* **155,** 261.

Metz, Ch. B., Cone, M. V., and Bryant, J. (1968). Effect of proteolytic enzymes on the ultrastructure of antibody-treated sea urchin eggs. *J. Cell Biol.* **39,** 481.

Metz, C. W. (1938). Chromosome behaviour, inheritance and sex determination in *Sciara*. *Amer. Natur.* **72,** 485.

Michejda, J. W., and Hryniewiecka, L. (1969). Studies on dehydrogenases in early development of sea urchins. *Abstr. FEBS 6th Meet.* p. 317.

Miki, T. (1963). The ATPase activity of the mitotic apparatus of the sea urchin eggs. *Exp. Cell Res.* **29,** 92.

Miki, T. (1964). ATPase activity of the egg cortex during the first cleavage of sea urchin eggs. *Exp. Cell Res.* **33,** 575.

Miki-Nomura, T. (1965). Isolation of fine filaments from the mitotic apparatus of sea urchin eggs. *Embryologia* **9,** 98.

Miki-Nomura, T. (1968). Purification of the mitotic apparatus protein of sea urchin eggs. *Exp. Cell Res.* **50,** 54.

Miki-Nomura, T., and Oosawa, F. (1969). An actin-like protein of the sea urchin eggs. I. Its interaction with myosin from rabbit striated muscle. *Exp. Cell Res.* **56,** 224.

Millonig, G. (1966). The morphological changes of the nucleolus during oogenesis and embryogenesis of echinoderms. *Electron Microsc., Proc. Int. Congr., 6th, 1966* p. 345.

Millonig, G. (1969). Fine structural analysis of the cortical reaction in the sea urchin egg: After normal fertilization and after electric induction. *J. Subm. Cytol.* **1,** 69.

Millonig, G. (1970). A study on the formation and structure of the sea urchin spicule. *J. Subm. Cytol.* **2,** 157.

Millonig, G., and Giudice, G. (1967). Electron microscopic study of the reaggregation of cells dissociated from sea urchin embryos. *Develop. Biol.* **15,** 91.

Millonig, G., Bosco, M., and Giambertone, L. (1968). Fine structure analysis of oogenesis in sea urchins. *J. Exp. Zool.* **169,** 293.

Minganti, A. (1953). The action of proteolytic enzymes on the vitelline membrane of *Psammechinus miliaris* eggs. *Exp. Cell Res.* **5,** 492.

Minganti, A. (1958). Sulla costituzione chimica degli involucri ovulari negli animali. *Boll. Zool.* **25,** 55.

Minganti, A., and Vasseur, E. (1959). An analysis of the jelly substance of *Paracentrotus* eggs. *Acta Embryol. Morphol. Exp.* **2,** 195.

Mirsky, A. E., Burdick, C. J., Davidson, E. H., and Littau, V. C. (1968). The role of lysine-rich histone in the maintenance of chromatin structure in metaphase chromosomes. *Proc. Nat. Acad. Sci. U.S.* **61,** 592.

Mitchison, J. M. (1952). Cell membranes and cell division. *Symp. Soc. Exp. Biol.* **6,** 105.

Mitchison, J. M. (1953a). A polarized light analysis of the human red cell ghost. *J. Exp. Biol.* **30,** 397.

Mitchison, J. M. (1953b). Microdissection experiments on sea urchin eggs at cleavage. *J. Exp. Biol.* **30,** 515.

Mitchison, J. M. (1953c). The thickness of the sea urchin fertilization membrane. *Exp. Cell Res.* **5,** 536.

Mitchison, J. M. (1956). The thickness of the cortex of the sea-urchin egg and the problem of the vitelline membrane. *Quart. J. Microsc. Sci.* **97,** 109.

Mitchison, J. M., and Cummins, J. E. (1966). The uptake of valine and cytidine by sea-urchin embryos and its relation to cell surface. *J. Cell Sci.* **1,** 35.

Mitchison, J. M., and Swann, M. M. (1952). Optical changes in the membranes of the sea-urchin egg at fertilization mitosis and cleavage. *J. Exp. Biol.* **29,** 357.

Mitchison, J. M., and Swann, M. M. (1954a). The mechanical properties of the cell surface. I. The cell elastimeter. *J. Exp. Biol.* **31,** 443.

Mitchison, J. M., and Swann, M. M. (1954b). The mechanical properties of the cell surface. II. The unfertilized sea-urchin egg. *J. Exp. Biol.* **31,** 461.

Mitchison, J. M., and Swann, M. M. (1955). The mechanical properties of the cell surface. II. The sea-urchin egg from fertilization to cleavage. *J. Exp. Biol.* **32,** 734.

Miwa, M., Yamashita, H., and Mori, K. (1939). The action of ionizing rays on sea urchins. I. The effects of Roentgen, gamma, and beta rays upon the unfertilized eggs and sperms. *Gann* **33,** 1.

Miwa, M., Yamashita, H., and Mori, K. (1941). The sperm of sea urchins as a biological test object in Roentgen dosimetry. *Gann* **35,** 127.

Mizejewski, G. (1969). Effect of antimetabolites on developing sea urchin eggs. *Amer. Zool.* **9,** 599 (a).

Moav, B., and Nemer, M. (1971). Histone synthesis. Assignment to a special class of poly-ribosomes in sea urchin embryos. *Biochemistry* **10,** 881.

Mohri, H. (1959). Enzymic hydrolysis of phospholipides in sea urchin spermatozoa. *Sci. Pap. Coll. Gen. Educ., Univ. Tokyo* **9,** 269.

Mohri, H. (1964). Utilization of C^{14}-labelled acetate and glycerol for lipid synthesis during the early development of sea urchin embryos. *Biol. Bull.* **126,** 440.

Mohri, H. (1968). Amino acid composition of "Tubulin" constituting microtubules of sperm flagella. *Nature (London)* **217,** 1053.

Mohri, H., and Monroy, A. (1963). Lipid metabolism of sea urchin embryos. *Zool. Mag.* **72,** 265.

Molinaro, M., and Hultin, T. (1965). The anomalous potassium requirement of an amino acid-incorporating system from sea urchin eggs. *Exp. Cell Res.* **38,** 398.

Molinaro, M., and Mozzi, R. (1969). Heterogeneity of t-RNA during embryonic development of the sea urchin *Paracentrotus lividus*. *Exp. Cell Res.* **56,** 163.

Monné, L. (1944). Cytoplasmic structure and cleavage pattern of the sea urchin egg. *Ark. Zool., A* **35,** No. 13, p. 1.

Monné, L., and Härde, S. (1950). On the formation of the blastocoel and similar embryonic cavities. *Ark. Zool.* [2] **1,** 463.

Monné, L., and Härde, S. (1951). On the cortical granules of the sea urchin egg. *Ark. Zool.* [2] **1,** No. 31, 487.

Monné, L., and Slautterback, D. B. (1950a). The disappearance of protoplasmic acidophilia upon deamination. *Ark. Zool.* [2] **1**, 455.

Monné, L., and Slautterback, D. B. (1950b). Differential staining of various polysaccharides in sea urchin eggs. *Exp. Cell Res.* **1**, 477.

Monroy, A. (1947). Further observations on the fine structure of the cortical layer of unfertilized and fertilized sea urchin eggs. *J. Cell. Comp. Physiol.* **30**, 105.

Monroy, A. (1949). On the formation of the fertilization membrane in the sea urchin *Psammechinus microtuberculatus*. *Exp. Cell Res., Suppl.* **1**, 525.

Monroy, A. (1957a). Swelling properties of the mitochondria of unfertilized and newly fertilized sea urchin eggs. *Experientia* **18**, 398.

Monroy, A. (1957b). Adenosinetriphosphatase in the mitochondria of unfertilized and newly fertilized sea-urchin eggs. *J. Cell. Comp. Physiol.* **50**, 73.

Monroy, A. (1960). Incorporation of S^{35}-methionine in the microsomes and soluble proteins during the early development of the sea urchin egg. *Experientia* **16**, 114.

Monroy, A. (1965). "Chemistry and Physiology of Fertilization." Holt, New York.

Monroy, A. (1967). Fertilization. *Compr. Biochem.* **28**, 369–412.

Monroy, A., and Maggio, R. (1963). Biochemical studies on the early development of the sea urchin. *Advan. Morphog.* **3**, 95.

Monroy, A., and Nakano, E. (1959). Evaluation of the methods for the incorporation of radioactive compounds in the echinoderm eggs. *Pubbl. Sta. Zool. Napoli* **31**, Suppl., 95.

Monroy, A., and Ruffo, A. (1947). Hyaluronidase in sea urchin sperm. *Nature (London)* **159**, 603.

Monroy, A., and Runnström, J. (1948). Some experiments pertaining to the chemical changes occurring at the formation of the fertilization membrane of sea urchin egg. *Ark. Zool. A* **40**, No. 18, p. 1.

Monroy, A., and Tyler, A. (1963). Formation of active ribosomal aggregates (polysomes) upon fertilization and development of sea urchin eggs. *Arch. Biochem. Biophys.* **103**, 431.

Monroy, A., and Vittorelli, M. L. (1960). On a glycoprotein of the sea urchin eggs and its changes following fertilization. *Experientia* **16**, 56.

Monroy, A., Vittorelli, M. L., and Guarneri, R. (1961). Investigations on the proteins of the cell fluid during the early development of the sea urchin *Paracentrotus lividus*. *Acta Embryol. Morphol. Exp.* **4**, 77.

Monroy, A., Maggio, R., and Rinaldi, A. M. (1965). Experimentally induced activation of the ribosomes of the unfertilized sea urchin egg. *Proc. Nat. Acad. Sci. U.S.* **54**, 107.

Monroy-Oddo, A., and Esposito, M. (1951). Changes in the potassium content of sea urchin eggs on fertilization. *J. Gen. Physiol.* **34**, 285.

Moore, A. R. (1928). On the hyaline membrane and hyaline droplets of the fertilized egg of the sea urchin *Strongylocentrotus purpuratus*. *Protoplasma* **3**, 524.

Moore, A. R. (1930). Fertilization and development without fertilization membrane formation in the egg of the sea urchin *Strongylocentrotus purpuratus*. *Protoplasma* **9**, 18.

Moore, A. R. (1940). Osmotic and structural properties of the blastular wall in *Dendraster excentricus*. *J. Exp. Zool.* **84**, 73.

Moore, A. R. (1941). On the mechanism of gastrulation in *Dendraster excentricus*. *J. Exp. Zool.* **87**, 101.

Moore, A. R. (1943). Maternal and paternal inheritance in the plutei of hybrids of the sea urchins *Strongylocentrotus purpuratus* and *Strongylocentrotus franciscanus*. *J. Exp. Zool.* **94**, 211.

Moore, A. R. (1949). On the precursors of the fertilization and hyaline membranes in the egg of the sea urchin, *Strongylocentrotus purpuratus*. *Biodynamica* **6**, 197.

Moore, A. R. (1951). Action of trypsin on the eggs of *Dendraster excentricus*. *Exp. Cell Res.* **2**, 284.

Moore, A. R. (1957). Biparental inheritance in an interordinal cross of sea urchin and sand dollar. *J. Exp. Zool.* **135**, 75.

Moore, A. R., and Burt, A. S. (1939). On the locus and nature of the forces causing gastrulation in the embryos of *Dendraster excentricus*. *J. Exp. Zool.* **82**, 159.

Moore, R. O., and Villee, C. A. (1961). Malic dehydrogenase isozymes of *Asterias forbesi* and *Arbacia punctulata*. *Biol. Bull.* **121**, 398.

Moore, R. O., and Villee, C. A. (1962). Malic dehydrogenases in sea urchin eggs. *Science* **138**, 508.

Moore, R. O., and Villee, C. A. (1963). Malate dehydrogenase; multiple forms in separated blastomeres of sea urchin embryos. *Science* **142**, 389.

Morgan, T. H. (1893). Experimental studies on echinoderm eggs. *Anat. Anz.* **9**, 141.

Morgan, T. H. (1899). The action of salt solutions on the unfertilized and fertilized eggs of *Arbacia,* and of other animals. *Wilhelm Arch. Entwicklungsmech. Organismen* **8**, 448.

Morgan, T. H. (1909). The effects produced by centrifuging eggs before and during development. *Anat. Rec.* **3**, 155.

Mortensen, T. (1898). Die Echinodermen Larven der Plankton Expedition. *Ergeb. Plankton. Exp. Humbolt-Stift.* **2J**, 1.

Mortensen, T. (1920). Notes on the development and the larval forms of some Scandinavian echinoderms. *Vidensk. Medd. Dan. Naturh. Foren Copenhagen* **71**, 133.

Mortensen, T. (1921). "Studies of the Development of Echinoderms." G. E. C. Gad. Copenhagen.

Moser, F. (1939a). Studies on a cortical layer response to stimulating agents in the *Arbacia* egg. I. Response to insemination. *J. Exp. Zool.* **80**, 423.

Moser, F. (1939b). Studies on a cortical layer response to stimulating agents in the *Arbacia* egg. II. Response to chemical and physical agents. *J. Exp. Zool.* **80**, 447.

Moser, F. (1940). Studies on a cortical layer response to stimulating agents in the *Arbacia* egg. III. Response to non-electrolytes. *Biol. Bull.* **78**, 68.

Motomura, I. (1934). On the mechanism of fertilization and development without membrane formation in the sea urchin egg, with notes on a new method of artificial parthenogenesis. *Sci. Rep. Tohoku Univ., Ser. 4* **9**, 33.

Motomura, I. (1935). Determination of the embryonic axis in the eggs of Amphibia and echinoderms. *Sci. Rep. Tohoku Univ., Ser. 4* **10**, 211.

Motomura, I. (1941a). Materials of the fertilization membrane in the eggs of echinoderms. *Sci. Rep. Tohoku Univ., Ser. 4* **16**, 345.

Motomura, I. (1941b). Studies of cleavage. II. Cleavage of eggs of a sea-urchin, *Strongylocentrotus pulcherrimus,* in calcium-free sea water. *Sci. Rep. Tohoku Univ., Ser. 4* **16**, 283.

Motomura, I. (1949). Artificial alteration of the embryonic axis in the centrifuged eggs of sea urchins. *Sci. Rep. Tohoku Univ., Ser. 4* **43**, 117.

Motomura, I. (1950a). On the secretion of fertilizin in the eggs of a sea urchin, *Strongylocentrotus pulcherrimus*. *Sci. Rep. Tohoku Univ., Ser. 4* **18**, 554.

Motomura, I. (1950b). On a new factor for the toughening of the fertilization membrane of sea urchins. *Sci. Rep. Tohoku Univ., Ser. 4* **18**, 561.

Motomura, I. (1953a). Secretion of sperm agglutinin in the fertilized eggs of sea urchins. *Exp. Cell Res.* **5**, 187.

Motomura, I. (1953b). Secretion of the sperm agglutinin in the fertilized and denuded eggs of the sea urchin, *Strongylocentrotus nudus*. *Sci. Rep. Tohoku Univ., Ser. 4* **20**, 93.

Motomura, I. (1954). On a method of isolation of the egg cortex in the sea urchin egg. *Sci. Rep. Tohoku Univ., Ser. 4* **20**, 318.

Motomura, I. (1957). On the nature and localization of the third factor for the toughening of the fertilization membrane of the sea urchin egg. *Sci. Rep. Tohoku Univ., Ser. 4* **23**, 167.

Motomura, I. (1960a). Secretion of mucosubstance in the gastrula of the sea urchin embryo. *Bull. Mar. Biol. Sta. Asamushi, Tohoku Univ.* **10**, 165.

Motomura, I. (1960b). On the structure of the cortical granule in the sea urchin egg. *Sci. Rep. Tohoku Univ., Ser. 4* **26**, 367.

Müller, J. (1846–1855). Nine articles on echinoderms, mostly metamorphosis. *Abh. Köenig. Akad. Wiss. Berlin.*

Müller, W. E. G., Forster, W., Zahn, G., and Zahn, R. K. (1971). Morphologische und biochemische Charakterisierung der Entwicklung befruchteter Eier des Seeigels *Sphaerechinus granularis* Lam. I. Aufzucht, Morphologie und elektronische Stadien-bestimmung. *Wilhelm Roux' Arch. Entwicklungsmech. Organismen* **167**, 99.

Mullins, J. L. (1949). Apyrase distribution in sea-urchin eggs. *Experientia* **5**, 478.

Mulnard, J., Auclair, W., and Marsland, D. (1960). Metachromasia observed in the living eggs of *Arbacia punctulata* and its cytochemical analysis. *J. Embryol. Exp. Morphol.* **7**, 223.

Murthy, M. R. V., and Rappaport, D. A. (1965). Biochemistry of the developing rat brain. VI. Preparation and properties of ribosomes. *Biochim. Biophys. Acta* **95**, 132.

Mutolo, V., and Giudice, G. (1967). Experiments of hybridization of ribosomal RNA from different stages of sea urchin embryos. *Biochim. Biophys. Acta* **149**, 291.

Mutolo, V., Giudice, G., Hopps, V., and Donatuti, G. (1967). Species specificity of embryonic ribosomal proteins. *Biochim. Biophys. Acta* **138**, 214.

Nachtwey, D. S. (1965). Effects of mixed reactor radiation on cell division of synchronized *Tetrahymena pyriformis*. U.S. Naval Radiological Defense Lab. Rep. TR-865, May 27.

Nagano, H., and Mano, Y. (1968). Thymine kinase, thymidilate kinase and [^{32}Pi] and [^{14}C] thymidine incorporation into DNA during early embryogenesis of the sea urchin. *Biochim. Biophys. Acta* **157**, 546.

Nakano, E. (1954). Further studies on the fertilization of activated sea urchin eggs. *Jap. J. Zool.* **11**, 245.

Nakano, E., and Monroy, A. (1957). A method for incorporation of radioactive isotopes in the sea urchin egg. *Experientia* **13**, 416.

Nakano, E., and Monroy, A. (1958a). Incorporation of S^{35}-methionine in the cell fractions of sea urchin eggs and embryos. *Exp. Cell Res.* **14**, 236.

Nakano, E., and Monroy, A. (1958b). Some observations on the metabolism of S^{35}-methionine during development of the sea urchin eggs. *Experientia* **14**, 367.

Nakano, E., and Ohashi, S. (1954). On the carbohydrate component of the jelly coat and related substances of eggs from Japanese sea urchins. *Embryologia* **2**, 81.

Nakano, E., Giudice, G., and Monroy, A. (1958). On the incorporation of S^{35}-methionine in artificially activated sea urchin eggs. *Experientia* **14**, 11.

Nakano, E., Okazaki, K., and Iwamatsu, T. (1963). Accumulation of radioactive calcium in larvae of the sea urchin *Pseudocentrotus depressus*. *Biol. Bull.* **125**, 125.

Nakazawa, T., Asami, K., Shoger, R., Fujiwara, F., and Yasumasu, I. (1970). Ca^{2+} uptake, H$^+$ ejection and respiration in sea urchin eggs on fertilization. *Exp. Cell Res.* **63**, 143.

Neifakh, A. A. (1960). A study of nuclear function in the development of sea urchin *Strongylocentrotus droßachiensis* by radiational innativation. *Dokl. Biol. Sci.* **132**, 376.

Neifakh, A. A. (1963). The nuclear control of the development of respiration apparatus in in the cell. *Proc. Int. Biochem. Congr., 5th, 1961* No. 15.

Neifakh, A. A. (1964). Radiation investigation of nucleo-cytoplasmic interrelations in morphogenesis and biochemical differentiation. *Nature (London)* **201,** 880.

Neifakh, A. A., and Dontsova, G. V. (1962). Radiational study of the role of the nucleus in the increase in cytochrome oxidase activity in fish embryos. *Biokhimiya* **27,** 339.

Neifakh, A. A., and Krigsgaber, M. R. (1968). Protein synthesis in embryonic development of the sea urchin after inactivation of nuclei. *Dokl. Biol. Sci.* **183,** 639.

Nemer, M. (1962a). Characteristics of the utilization of nucleosides by embryos of *Paracentrotus lividus. J. Biol. Chem.* **237,** 143.

Nemer, M. (1962b). Interrelation of messenger polyribonucleotides and ribosomes in sea urchin egg during embryonic development. *Biochem. Biophys. Res. Commun.* **8,** 511.

Nemer, M. (1963). Old and new RNA in the embryogenesis of the purple sea urchin. *Proc. Nat. Acad. Sci. U.S.* **50,** 230.

Nemer, M., and Bard, S. G. (1963). Polypeptide synthesis in sea urchin embryogenesis: An examination with synthetic polyribonucleotides. *Science* **140,** 664.

Nemer, M., and Infante, A. A. (1965). Messenger RNA in early sea urchin embryos: size classes. *Science* **150,** 217.

Nemer, M., and Infante, A. A. (1967). Ribosomal RNA of the sea urchin egg and its fate during embryogenesis. *J. Mol. Biol.* **27,** 73.

Nemer, M., and Infante, A. A. (1968). Heterogenous ribonucleoprotein particles in the cytoplasm of the sea urchin embryos. *J. Mol. Biol.* **32,** 543.

Nemer, M., and Lindsay, D. T. (1969). Evidence that the s-polysomes of early sea urchin embryos may be responsible for the synthesis of chromosomal histones. *Biochem. Biophys. Res. Commun.* **35,** 156.

Nicotra, C., Tesoriere, G., Musotto, M. A., and Livrea, M. A. (1967). Sintesi di glucosamina 6-fosfato nelle uova e negli embrioni di *Paracentrotus lividus. Boll. Soc. Ital. Biol. Sper.* **44,** 273.

Nicotra, C., Tesoriere, G., Musotto, M. A., and Livrea, M. A. (1968). Sintesi di glucosamina 6-P per attività chinasica nelle uova e negli embrioni di *Paracentrotus lividus. Boll. Soc. Ital. Biol. Sper.* **45,** 170.

Nilsson, R. (1959). Acid-soluble nucleotides in the unfertilized eggs of the sea urchin *Paracentrotus lividus. Acta Chem. Scand.* **13,** 395.

Nilsson, R. (1961). Acid-soluble nucleotides during early embryonic development of the sea urchin *Paracentrotus lividus. Acta Chem. Scand.* **15,** 583.

Numanoi, H. (1959a). Studies on the fertilization substance. VII. Effect of acetylcholine esterase on development of sea urchin eggs. *Sci. Pap. Coll. Gen. Educ., Univ. Tokyo* **9,** 279.

Numanoi, H. (1959b). Studies on fertilization substance. VIII. Enzymic degradation of lecithin during development of sea urchin eggs. *Sci. Pap. Coll. Gen. Educ., Univ. Tokyo* **9,** 285.

Numanoi, H. (1959c). Studies on the fertilization substance. IX. Effect of intermediates split during fertilization. *Sci. Pap. Coll. Gen. Educ., Univ. Tokyo* **9,** 297.

Öhman, L. O. (1940). Über die Veränderung des Respiratorischen Quotienten Während der Frühentwicklung des Seeigeleis. *Ark. Zool., A* **32,** No. 15, 1.

Öhman, L. O. (1944). On the lipids of the sea urchin egg. *Ark. Zool., A* **36,** 1.

Öhman, L. O. (1947). On changes in the properties of the protoplasm in the one-cell stage of the fertilized sea urchin egg. *Ark. Zool., A* **39,** No. 11, 1.

Ohnishi, T., and Sugiyama, M. (1963). Polarographic studies of oxygen uptake of sea urchin eggs. *Embryologia* **8,** 79.

Okazaki, K. (1956a). Skeleton formation of sea urchin larvae. I. Effect of Ca concentration of the medium. *Biol. Bull.* **110,** 320.

Okazaki, K. (1956b). Exogastrulation induced by calcium deficiency in the sea urchin, *Pseudocentrotus depressus*. *Embryologia* **3**, 23.

Okazaki, K. (1960). Skeleton formation of sea urchin larvae. II. Organic matrix of the spicule. *Embryologia* **5**, 283.

Okazaki, K. (1961). Skeleton formation of sea urchin larvae. III. Similarity of effect of low calcium and high magnesium on spicule formation. *Biol. Bull.* **120**, 177.

Okazaki, K. (1962). Skeleton formation of sea urchin larvae. IV. Correlation in shape of spiculae and matrix. *Embryologia* **7**, 21.

Okazaki, K. (1965). Skeleton formation of sea urchin larvae. V. Continuous observation of the process of matrix formation. *Exp. Cell Res.* **40**, 585.

Okazaki, K., and Niijma, L. (1964). "Basement membrane" in sea urchin larvae. *Embryologia* **8**, 89.

Okazaki, K., Fukushi, T., and Dan, K. (1962). Cyto-embryological studies of sea urchins. IV. Correlation between the shape of the ectodermal cells and the arrangement of the primary mesenchyme cells in sea urchin larvae. *Acta Embryol. Morphol. Exp.* **5**, 17.

Okazaki, R. (1956). On the possible role of high energy phosphate in the cortical change of sea urchin eggs. 1. Effect of dinitrophenol and sodium azide. 2. Effect of uranyl nitrate. *Exp. Cell Res.* **10**, 476.

Olsson, T. (1965). Changes in metabolism of RNA during the early embryonic development of the sea urchin. *Nature (London)* **206**, 843.

O'Melia, A. F. (1971). Animalizing effects of Evans blue in embryos of *Arbacia punctulata*. *Exp. Cell Res.* **67**, 402.

Orengo, A., and Hnilica, L. S. (1970). *In vivo* incorporation of labeled amino acids into nuclear proteins of sea urchin embryos. *Exp. Cell Res.* **62**, 331.

Örström, A. (1935). Über Ammoniakbildung bei der Entwicklungserregung des Seeigeleies. *Ark. Zool., B* **28**, No. 6, 1.

Örström, A., and Lindberg, O. (1940). Über den Kohlen-hydratstoffwechsel bei der Befruchtung des Seeigeleies. *Enzymologia* **8**, 367.

Osanai, K. (1960). Development of the sea urchin egg with the inhibited breakdown of the cortical granules. *Sci. Rep. Tohoku Univ., Ser. 4* **26**, 77.

Oshima, H. (1921). Inhibitory effect of dermal secretion of the sea urchin upon the fertilizability of the egg. *Science* **54**, 578.

Ozaki, H. (1971). Developmental studies of sea urchin chromatin. Chromatin isolated from spermatozoa of the sea urchin *Strongylocentrotus purpuratus*. *Develop. Biol.* **26**, 209.

Ozaki, H., and Whiteley, A. H. (1970). *l*-Malate dehydrogenase in the development of the sea urchin *Strongylocentrotus purpuratus*. *Develop. Biol.* **21**, 196.

Ozernyuk, N. D. (1970). Role of ATP in regulation of respiration during maturation of sea urchin and loach eggs. *Dokl. Biol. Sci.* **190**, 23.

Palincsar, E. E. (1960). The effects of chloramphenicol on cleavage of *Arbacia* eggs. *Biol. Bull.* **119**, 329.

Paspaleff, G. (1927). Über Protoplasmareifung bei Seeigeleiren. *Pubbl. Sta. Zool. Napoli* **8**, 1.

Pasteels, J. J. (1955). Evolution de la métachromasie au bleu de toluidine suivie sur le vivant, au cours des premières phases du développement de l'Oursin et de la Pholade. *Bull. Cl. Sci., Acad. Roy. Belg. Sci.* [5] **41**, 761.

Pasteels, J. J. (1958). New studies on metachromasia *in vivo* and on the histochemistry of the normal and centrifuged egg of *Paracentrotus lividus*. *Arch. Biol.* **69**, 591.

Pasteels, J. J. (1965). Etude au microscope électronique de la réaction corticale. I. La réaction cortical de fécondation chez *Paracentrotus* et sa chronologie. II. La réaction corticale de l'oeuf vierge de *Sabellaria alveolata*. *J. Embryol. Exp. Morphol.* **13**, 327.

Pasteels, J. J., and Mulnard, J. (1957). La métachromasie *in vivo* au bleu de toluidine et son analyse cytochimique dans les oeufs de *Barnea candida, Gryphaea angulata* (Lamellibranches) et de *Psammechinus miliaris. Arch. Biol.* **68,** 115.

Pasteels, J. J., Cartiaux, P., and Vandermeerssche, G. (1958). Cytoplasmic ultrastructure and distribution of RNA in the normal and centrifuged fertilized eggs of *Paracentrotus lividus. Arch. Biol.* **69,** 627.

Patterson, J. B., and Stafford, D. W. (1970). Sea urchin satellite deoxyribonucleic acid. Its large-scale isolation and hybridization with homologous ribosomal ribonucleic acid. *Biochemistry* **9,** 1278.

Patterson, J. B., and Stafford, D. W. (1971). Characterization of sea urchin ribosomal satellite DNA. *Biochemistry* **10,** 2775.

Patton, G. W., Jr., Mets, L., and Villee, C. A. (1967). Malic dehydrogenase isozymes distribution in developing nucleate and anucleate halves of sea urchin eggs. *Science* **156,** 400.

Paul, J., and Gilmour, R. S. (1968). Organ-specific restriction of transcription in mammalian chromatin. *J. Mol. Biol.* **34,** 305.

Paul, J. S., Zuzolo, R. C, Fong, B. A., and Kopac, M. J. (1970). Laser induced changes in DNA synthesis and embryonic development in sea urchins. *Exp. Cell Res.* **60,** 166.

Paul, M., and Epel, D. (1971). Fertilization-associated light-scattering changes in eggs of the sea urchin *Strongylocentrotus purpuratus. Exp. Cell Res.* **65,** 281.

Pearse, J. S., and Giese, A. C. (1966). Food, reproduction and organic constitution of the common antarctic echinoid *Sterechinus neumayeri* (Meissner). *Biol. Bull.* **130,** 387.

Pease, D. (1939). An analysis of the factors of bilateral determination in centrifuged echinoderm embryos. *J. Exp. Zool.* **80,** 117.

Peltz, R., and Giudice, G. (1967). The control of skeleton differentiation in sea urchin embryos. A molecular approach. *Biol. Bull.* **133,** 479.

Penman, S. (1966). RNA metabolism in the HeLa cell nucleus. *J. Mol. Biol.* **17,** 117.

Penman, S., Vesco, C., and Penman, M. (1968). Localization and kinetics of formation of nuclear heterodisperse RNA, cytoplasmic heterodisperse RNA and polyribosome-associated messenger RNA in HeLa cells. *J. Mol. Biol.* **34,** 49.

Pequegnat, W. (1948). Inhibition of fertilization in *Arbacia* by blood extract. *Biol. Bull.* **95,** 69.

Perlmann, P. (1953). Soluble antigens in sea urchin gametes and developmental stages. *Exp. Cell Res.* **5,** 394.

Perlmann, P. (1954). Study on the effect of antisera on unfertilized sea urchin eggs. *Exp. Cell Res.* **6,** 485.

Perlmann, P. (1956). Response of unfertilized sea urchin eggs to antiserum. *Exp. Cell Res.* **10,** 324.

Perlmann, P. (1957). Analysis of the surface structures of the sea urchin egg by means of antibodies. *Exp. Cell Res.* **13,** 365.

Perlmann, P. (1959). Immunochemical analysis of the surface of the sea urchin egg — an approach to the study of fertilization. *Experientia* **15,** 41.

Perlmann, P., and Couffer-Kaltenbach, J. (1964). Antigens in eggs and developmental stages of the sea urchin. II. Localization. *J. Cell Biol.* **22,** 307.

Perlmann, P., and Gustafson, T. (1948). Antigens in the egg and early developmental stages of the sea urchin. *Experientia* **4,** 481.

Perlmann, P., and Perlmann, H. (1957a). Analysis of the surface structures of the sea urchins egg by means of antibodies. II. The J and A antigens. *Exp. Cell Res.* **13,** 454.

Perlmann, P., and Perlmann, H. (1957b). Analysis of the surface structures of the sea urchin egg by means of antibodies. III. The C and F antigens. *Exp. Cell Res.* **13,** 475.

Perlmann, P., Boström, H., and Vestermark, A. (1959). Sialic acid in the gametes of sea urchin. *Exp. Cell Res.* **17,** 439.

Perry, R. P., and Kelley, D. E. (1966). Buoyant densities of cytoplasmic RNP particles of mammalian cells: Distinctive character of ribosome subunits and the rapidly labeled components. *J. Mol. Biol.* **16,** 255.

Perry, R. P., and Kelley, D. E. (1968). Messenger RNA–protein complexes and newly synthesized ribosomal subunits: Analysis of free particles and components of poly-ribosomes. *J. Mol. Biol.* **35,** 37.

Perry, R. P., Cheng, T. Y., Freed, J. J., Greenberg, J. R., Kelley, D. E., and Tartof, K. D. (1970). Evolution of the transcription unit of ribosomal RNA. *Proc. Nat. Acad. Sci. U.S.* **65,** 609.

Pfohl, R. J. (1965). Changes in alkaline phosphatase during the early development of the sea urchin, *Arbacia punctulata. Exp. Cell Res.* **39,** 496.

Pfohl, R. J. (1972). In press.

Pfohl, R. J., and Giudice, G. (1967). The role of cell interactions in the control of enzyme activity during embryogenesis. *Biochim. Biophys. Acta* **142,** 263.

Pfohl, R. J., and Monroy, A. (1963). Alkaline phosphatase activity in the embryo of *Arbacia punctulata. Biol. Bull.* **125,** 367.

Piatigorsky, J. (1968). RNAase and trypsin treatment of ribosomes and polyribosomes from sea urchin eggs. *Biochim. Biophys. Acta* **166,** 142.

Piatigorsky, J., and Tyler, A. (1967). Radioactive labeling of RNAs of sea urchin eggs dur-ing oogenesis. *Biol. Bull.* **133,** 229.

Piatigorsky, J., and Tyler, A. (1968). Displacement of valine from intact sea-urchin eggs by exogenous amino acids. *J. Cell Sci.* **3,** 515.

Piatigorsky, J., and Tyler, A. (1970). Changes upon fertilization in the distribution of RNA-containing particles in sea urchin eggs. *Develop. Biol.* **21,** 13.

Piatigorsky, J., and Whiteley, A. H. (1965). A change in permeability and uptake of C^{14}-uridine in response to fertilization in *Strongylocentrotus purpuratus* eggs. *Biochim. Biophys. Acta* **108,** 404.

Piatigorsky, J., Ozaki, H., and Tyler, A. (1967). RNA and protein-synthesing capacity of isolated oocytes of the sea urchin *Lytechinus pictus. Develop. Biol.* **15,** 1.

Pictet, C. (1891). Recherches sur la spermotogenèse chez quelques invertébrés de la Méditerranée. *Mitt. Zool. Sta. Neapel* **10,** 75.

Pikò, L., and Tyler, A. (1965). Deoxyribonucleic acid content of unfertilized sea urchin eggs. *Amer. Zool.* **5,** 636.

Pikò, L., Tyler, A., and Vinograd, J. (1967). Amount location, priming capacity and other properties of cytoplasmic DNA in sea urchin eggs. *Biol. Bull.* **132,** 68.

Pikò, L., Blair, O. G., Tyler, A., and Vinograd, J. (1968). Cytoplasmic DNA in the un-fertilized sea urchin egg: Physical properties of circular mitochondrial DNA and the occurrence of catenated forms. *Proc. Nat. Acad. Sci. U.S.* **59,** 838.

Pinard, J., Bellemare, G., Aubin, A., Daigneault, R., and Cousineau, G. H. (1969). Uptake and incorporation of leucine and thymidine in developing sea urchin eggs. The effect of $D_2O. Exp. Cell Res.$ **56,** 254.

Pirrone, A. M., Sconzo, G., Mutolo, V., and Giudice, G. (1970). Effect of chemical ani-malization and vegetalization on the synthesis of ribosomal RNA in sea urchin embryos. *Wilhelm Roux'Arch. Entwicklungsmech. Organismen* **164,** 222.

Pirrone, A. M., Munisteri, A., Roccheri, M., Mutolo, V., and Giudice, G. (1971). Synthesis of RNA in isolated nuclei of sea urchin embryos. *Wilhelm Roux'Arch. Entwicklungs-mech. Organismen* **167,** 83.

Pitotti, M. (1939). Catalizzatori e determinazione negli embrioni di Echinodermi. *Pubbl. Sta. Zool. Napoli* **17,** 193.

Plough, H. (1929). Determination of skeleton forming material at the time of the first cleavage in the eggs of *Echinus* and *Paracentrotus*. *Wilhelm Roux'Arch. Entwicklungsmech. Organismen* **115**, 380.

Popa, G. T. (1927). The distribution of substances in spermatozoon (*Arbacia* and *Nereis*). *Biol. Bull.* **52**, 238.

Porath, J., and Flodin, P. (1959). Gel filtration: A method for desalting and group separation. *Nature (London)* **183**, 1657.

Prenant, M. (1926). L'étude cytologique du calcaire. III. Observation sur le déterminisme de la forme spiculaire chez larves pluteus d'oursins. *Bull. Biol. Fr. Belg.* **60**, 522.

Press, E. M., Porter, R. R., and Cebra, J. (1960). The isolation and properties of a proteolytic enzyme, cathepsin D, from bovine spleen. *Biochem. J.* **74**, 501.

Pucci-Minafra, I., Bosco, M., and Giambertone, L. (1968). Preliminary observations on the isolated micromeres from sea urchin embryos. *Exp. Cell Res.* **53**, 177.

Pucci-Minafra, I., Casano, C., and La Rosa, C. (1972). Synthesis of collagen and spicules formation in sea urchin embryos. *Cell Differ.* **1**, 157.

Raff, R. A., Penman, S., and Gross, P. R. (1970). The effect of 5-azacytidine on labelling of nucleic acids in embryos of the sea urchin *Arbacia punctulata. J. Cell Biol.* **47**, 166a.

Raff, R. A., Greenhouse, G., Gross, K. W., and Gross, P. R. (1971). Synthesis and storage of microtubule proteins by sea urchin embryos. *J. Cell Biol.* **50**, 516.

Raff, R. A., Colot, H. V., Selvig, S. E., and Gross, P. R. (1972). Oogenetic origin of mRNA for embryonic synthesis of microtubule proteins. *Nature (London)* **235**, 211.

Ranzi, S. (1957). Les changements protéiques au cours du développement embryonnaire et larvaire. *Annee Biol.* **30**, 523.

Rao, B. (1963). Analysis of X-ray-induced mitotic delay in sea urchin eggs. Ph.D. Thesis, Radiat. Lab. Publ. UCRL, University of California, Lawrence.

Rao, B., and Hinegardner, R. T. (1965). Analysis of DNA synthesis and X-ray-induced mitotic delay in sea urchin eggs. *Radiat. Res.* **26**, 534.

Rapkine, L. (1931). Sur les processes chimiques au cours de la division cellulaire. *Ann. Physiol. Physicochim. Biol.* **7**, 382.

Rappaport, R. (1961). Experiments concerning the cleavage stimulus in sand dollar eggs. *Exp. Zool.* **148**, 81.

Rappaport, R. (1964). Geometrical relations of the cleavage stimulus in constricted sand dollar eggs. *Exp. Zool.* **155**, 225.

Rappaport, R. (1965). Geometrical relations of the cleavage stimulus in invertebrate eggs. *J. Theor. Biol.* **9**, 51.

Rappaport, R. (1967). Geometrical analysis of establishment of the cleavage furrow in sea urchin egg. *J. Cell Res.* **35**, 109a.

Rappaport, R. (1968). Geometrical relations of the cleavage stimulus in flattened, perforated sea urchin egg. *Embryologia* **10**, 115.

Rappaport, R. (1969a). Division of isolated furrows and furrow fragments in invertebrate eggs. *Exp. Cell Res.* **56**, 87.

Rappaport, R. (1969b). Reversal of chemical cleavage inhibition in echinoderm eggs. *J. Cell Biol.* **43**, 111a.

Rappaport, R., and Ebstein, R. P. (1965). Duration of stimulus and latent periods preceding furrow formation in sand dollar eggs. *Exp. Zool.* **158**, 373.

Rappaport, R., and Ratner, J. H. (1967). Cleavage of sand dollar eggs with altered pattern of new surface formation. *Exp. Zool.* **165**, 89.

Rebhun, L. I., and Sawada, N. (1969). Argumentation and dispersion of the *in vivo* mitotic apparatus of living marine eggs. *Protoplasma* **68**, 1.

Reed, E. A. (1948). Ultraviolet light and permeability of sea urchin eggs. *J. Cell. Comp. Physiol.* **31**, 261.

Repsis, L. C. (1967). Acid soluble nuclear proteins in developmental stages of *Lytechinus variegatus*. *Exp. Cell Res.* **48**, 146.

Retzius, G. (1910). Zur Kenntnis der Spermien der Echinodermen. *Biol. Unters.* **15**, 55.

Rinaldi, A. M., and Monroy, A. (1969). Polyribosome formation and RNA synthesis in the early post-fertilization stages of the sea urchin egg. *Develop. Biol.* **19**, 73.

Rinaldi, R. A. (1967). Amino acid incorporation by cleaving ovum fragments of *Arbacia punctulata*. *J. Cell Biol.* **35**, 113a.

Ritossa, F. M., and Spiegelman, S. (1965). Localization of DNA complementary to ribosomal RNA in the nucleolus organizer region of *Drosophila melanogaster*. *Proc. Nat. Acad. Sci. U.S.* **53**, 737.

Robbie, W. A. (1946). The effect of cyanide on the oxygen consumption and cleavage of the sea urchin egg. *J. Cell. Comp. Physiol.* **28**, 305.

Rockstein, M. (1971). The distribution of phosphoarginine and phosphocreatine in marine invertebrates. *Biol. Bull.* **141**, 167.

Roeder, R. G., and Rutter, W. J. (1969). Multiple forms of DNA-dependent RNA polymerase in eukaryotic organisms. *Nature (London)* **224**, 234.

Roeder, R. G., and Rutter, W. J. (1970a). Specific nucleolar and nucleoplasmic RNA polymerases. *Proc. Nat. Acad. Sci. U.S.* **65**, 675.

Roeder, R. G., and Rutter, W. J. (1970b). Multiple RNA polymerases and ribonucleic acid synthesis during sea urchin development. *Biochemistry* **9**, 2543.

Roguski, H. (1960). The influence of nitrogen mustard on development of sea urchin eggs. *Folia Biol. (Prague)* **8**, 173.

Rosenkranz, H. S., Erlanger, B. F., Tanenbaum, S. W., and Beiser, S. M. (1964). Purine- and pyrimidine-specific antibodies: Effects on the fertilized sea urchin egg. *Science* **145**, 282.

Rossi, M., Geraci, G., and Scarano, E. (1967). Deoxycytidylate aminohydrolase. III. Modifications of the substrate sites caused by allosteric effectors. *Biochemistry* **6**, 3640.

Rothschild, Lord. (1949). The metabolism of fertilized and unfertilized sea-urchin eggs. *J. Exp. Biol.* **26**, 100.

Rothschild, Lord. (1951). Sea urchin spermatozoa. *Biol. Rev.* **26**, 1.

Rothschild, Lord. (1956). "Fertilization." Methuen, London.

Rothschild, Lord. (1958). Acid production after fertilization of sea urchin eggs. A reexamination of the lactic acid hypothesis. *J. Exp. Biol.* **35**, 843.

Rothschild, Lord, and Swann, M. M. (1949). The fertilization reaction in sea urchin egg. A propagated response to sperm attachment. *J. Exp. Biol.* **26**, 164.

Rothschild, Lord, and Swann, M. M. (1950). The fertilization reaction in the sea urchin egg. The effect of nicotine. *J. Exp. Biol.* **27**, 400.

Rothschild, Lord, and Swann, M. M. (1951a). The conduction time of the block to polyspermy in the sea urchin egg. *Exp. Cell Res.* **2**, 137.

Rothschild, Lord, and Swann, M. M. (1951b). The fertilization reaction in the sea urchin. The probability of a successful sperm-egg collision. *J. Exp. Biol.* **28**, 403.

Rothschild, Lord, and Swann, M. M. (1952). The fertilization reaction in the sea urchin. The block to polyspermy. *J. Exp. Biol.* **29**, 469.

Roy, H., and Giudice, G. (1967). Studies on the synthesis of ribosomes in sea urchin embryos. *Biol. Bull.* **133**, 481.

Rubenstein, B. B., and Gerard, R. W. (1934). Fertilization and the temperature coefficients of oxygen consumption in eggs of *Arbacia punctulata*. *J. Gen. Physiol.* **17**, 677.

Runnström, J. (1914). Analytische Studien über die Seeigelentwicklung. I. *Arch. Entwicklungsmech. Organismen* **40**, 526.

Runnström, J. (1917–1918). Zur Bioloogia und Physiologie der Seeigellarvae. Bergens Museum aarbok. *Naturvidensk. Raekke* 1, 1.

Runnström, J. (1926). Experimentelle Bestimmung der Dorso-Ventralachse bei dem Seeigelkeim. *Ark. Zool., A* 18, No. 4, 1.

Runnström, J. (1928a). Plasmbau und Determination bei dem Ei von *Paracentrotus lividus* L K. *Wilhelm Roux'Arch. Entwicklungsmech. Organismen* 113, 556.

Runnström, J. (1928b). Zur Experimentellen Analyse der Wirkung des Lithium auf den Seeigelkeim. *Acta Zool. (Stockholm)* 9, 365.

Runnström, J. (1928c). Ueber die Veränderung der Plasmakolloide bei der Entwicklungserregung des Seeigeleies. I. *Protoplasma* 4, 388.

Runnström, J. (1928d). Struktur und Atmung bei der Entwicklungserregung des Seeigeleies. *Acta Zool. (Stockholm)* 9, 445.

Runnström, J. (1930a). Spaltung und Atmung bei der Entwicklungserregung des Seeigels. *Ark. Zool., B* 21, No. 8, 1.

Runnström, J. (1930b). Atmungsmechamismus und Entwicklungserregung bei dem Seeigelei. *Protoplasma* 10, 106.

Runnström, J. (1933). Zur Kenntnis der Stoffwechselvorgänge bei der Entwicklungserregung des Seeigeleies. *Biochem. Z.* 258, 257.

Runnström, J. (1948a). Membrane formation in different stages of cytoplasmic maturation of the sea urchin egg. *Ark. Zool., A* 40, No. 19, 1.

Runnström, J. (1948b). On the action of trypsin and chymotrypsin on the unfertilized sea urchin egg. A study concerning the mechanism of the fertilization membrane. *Ark. Zool., A* 40, No. 17, 1.

Runnström, J. (1949). The mechanism of fertilization in metazoa. *Advan. Enzymol.* 9, 241.

Runnström, J. (1957). On the effect of porphyrexid and porphyrindin on the fertilization of the sea urchin egg. *Exp. Cell Res.* 12, 374.

Runnström, J. (1966a). Considerations on the control of differentiation in the early sea urchin development. *Arch. Zool. Ital.* 51, 239.

Runnström, J. (1966b). The vitelline membrane and cortical particles in sea urchin eggs and their function in maturation and fertilization. *Advanc. Morphog.* 5, 221–325.

Runnström, J. (1967a). Structural changes of the chromatin in early development of sea urchins. *Exp. Cell Res.* 48, 691.

Runnström, J. (1967b). The animalizing action of pretreatment of sea urchin eggs with thiocyanate in calcium-free sea water and its stabilization after fertilization. *Ark. Zool.* [2] 19, 251.

Runnström, J. (1969). The appearance of a type of cortical vesicles subsequent to fertilization of the sea urchin egg, their character and possible function. *Wilhelm Roux'Arch. Entwicklungsmech. Organismen* 162, 254.

Runnström, J., and Hagström, B. (1955). Studies on the action of the "*Fucus* fertilization inhibitor" on sea urchin eggs and sperm. *Exp. Cell Res.* 8, 1.

Runnström, J., and Immers, J. (1956). The role of mucopolysaccharides in the fertilization of the sea urchin egg. *Exp. Cell Res.* 10, 354.

Runnström, J., and Immers, J. (1966). On the animalizing action of trypsin on the embryos of the sea urchins (*Psammechinus miliaris* and *Paracentrotus lividus*). *Arch. Biol. (Liege)* 77, 365.

Runnström, J., and Immers, J. (1970). Heteromorphic budding in lithium-treated sea urchin embryos. A study of gene expression. *Exp. Cell Res.* 62, 228.

Runnström, J., and Immers, J. (1971). Treatment with lithium as a tool for the study of animal–vegetal interactions in sea urchin embryos. *Wilhelm Roux'Arch. Entwicklungsmech. Organismen* 167, 222.

Runnström, J., and Kriszat, G. (1950). On the effect of adenosine triphosphoric acid and of Ca on the cytoplasm of the egg of the sea urchin *Psammechinus miliaris*. *Exp. Cell Res.* **1**, 284.

Runnström, J., and Kriszat, G. (1953). The action of SH-reagents on the activation process in the sea urchin egg. *Ark. Zool.* [2] **4**, No. 10, 165.

Runnström, J., and Manelli, H. (1964). Induction of polyspermy by treatment of sea urchin egg with mercurials. *Exp. Cell Res.* **35**, 157.

Runnström, J., and Monné, L. (1945). On some properties of the surface layers of immature and mature sea urchin eggs, especially the changes accompanying nuclear and cyto-plasmic maturation. *Ark. Zool., A* **36**, No. 18, 1.

Runnström, J., Tiselius, A., and Vasseur, E. (1942). Zur Kenntnis der Gamonwirkungen bei *Psammechinus miliaris* und *Echinocardium chordatum*. *Ark. Kemi, Mineral. Geol.* **15**, No. 16, 1.

Runnström, J., Monné, L., and Wicklund, E. (1946). Studies on the surface layers and the formation of the fertilization membrane in sea urchin eggs. *J. Colloid Sci.* **1**, 421.

Runnström, J., Hagström, B. E., and Perlmann, P. (1959). Fertilization. *In* "The Cell" (J. Brachet and A. E. Mirsky, eds.), Vol. 1, pp. 327–397. Academic Press, New York.

Runnström, J., Hörstadius, S., Immers, J., and Fudge-Mastrangelo, M. (1964). An analysis of the role of sulfate in the embryonic differentiation of the sea urchin (*Paracentrotus lividus*). *Rev. Suisse Zool.* **71**, 21.

Rustad, R. C. (1959a). Consequences of unilateral ultraviolet irradiation of sea urchin eggs. *Biol. Bull.* **116**, 294.

Rustad, R. C. (1959b). Centriole damage: A possible explanation of radiation-induced mitotic delay. *Radiat. Res.* **11**, 465.

Rustad, R. C. (1959c). Induction of multipolar spindles by single X-irradiated sperms. *Experientia* **15**, 323.

Rustad, R. C. (1960a). Changes in the sensitivity to ultraviolet-induced mitotic delay during the cell division cycle of the sea urchin egg. *Exp. Cell Res.* **21**, 596.

Rustad, R. C. (1960b). X-ray-induced mitotic delay in the *Arbacia* egg. *Biol. Bull.* **119**, 337A.

Rustad, R. C. (1960c). Dissociation of the mitotic time schedule from the micromere "clock" with X-rays. *Acta Embryol. Morphol. Exp.* **3**, 155.

Rustad, R. C. (1961). Cytoplasmic radiation damage in *Arbacia punctulata*. *Biol. Bull.* **121**, 405.

Rustad, R. C. (1964). UV-induced mitotic delay in the sea urchin egg. *Photochem. Photo-biol.* **3**, 529.

Rustad, R. C. (1969). The independence of the mitotic rate of sea urchin eggs from ploidy and cytoplasmic volume. *Biophys. J.* **9**, 186A.

Rustad, R. C. (1970). Variations in the sensitivity to X-ray-induced mitotic delay during the cell division cycle of the sea urchin egg. *Radiat. Res.* **42**, 498.

Rustad, R. C. (1971). Radiation responses during the mitotic cycle of the sea urchin egg. *In* "Developmental Aspects of the Cell Cycle" (I. L. Cameron, G. M. Padilla, and A. M. Zimmerman, eds.), pp. 127–151. Academic Press, New York.

Rustad, R. C., and Burchill, B. R. (1966). Radiation-induced mitotic delay in sea urchin eggs treated with puromycin and actinomycin D. *Radiat. Res.* **29**, 203.

Rustad, R. C., and Failla, P. M. (1969). Protein synthesis and the recovery from γ-ray-induced delay in sea urchin eggs. *Radiat. Res.* **39**, 514.

Rustad, R. C., Yuyama, S., and Rustad, L. C. (1964). Nuclear-cytoplasmic relations in radiation sensitivity. *Biol. Bull.* **127**, 388.

Rustad, R. C., McGurn, E., Yuyama, S., and Rustad, L. C. (1966). Recovery from γ-ray and UV-radiation damage in unfertilized sea urchin eggs. *Radiat. Res.* **27**, 543.

Rustad, R. C., Yuyama, S., and Rustad, L. C. (1971). Nuclear–cytoplasmic relations in the mitosis of sea urchin eggs. III. γ-ray-induced damage to whole eggs and nucleate and anucleate half eggs. *J. Cell Biol.* **49**, 906.

Sachs, M. I., and Anderson, E. (1969). A cytological study of events associated with artificial parthenogenesis in the sea urchin *Arbacia punctulata. J. Cell Biol.* **43**, 121A.

Sachs, M. I., and Anderson, E. (1970). A cytological study of artificial parthenogenesis in the sea urchin *Arbacia punctulata. J. Cell Biol.* **47**, 140.

Sakai, H. (1960a). Studies on SH groups during cell division of sea urchin egg. II. Mass isolation of the egg cortex and its SH groups during cell division. *J. Biophys. Biochem. Cytol.* **8**, 603.

Sakai, H. (1960b). Studies on sulfhydryl groups during cell division of sea urchin egg. III. SH groups of KCl-soluble proteins and their change during cleavage. *J. Biophys. Biochem. Cytol.* **8**, 609.

Sakai, H. (1962a). Studies on SH groups during cell division of sea urchin egg. IV. Contractile properties. *J. Gen. Physiol.* **45**, 411.

Sakai, H. (1962b). Studies on SH groups during cell division of sea urchin egg. V. Change in contractility of the thread model in relation to cell division. *J. Gen. Physiol.* **45**, 427.

Sakai, H. (1963). Studies on sulfhydryal groups during cell division of sea urchin egg. VI. Behavior of—SH groups of cortices of eggs treated with ether–sea water. *Exp. Cell Res.* **32**, 391.

Sakai, H. (1965). Studies on sulfhydryl groups during cell division of sea urchin eggs. VII. Electron transport between two proteins. *Biochim. Biophys. Acta* **102**, 235.

Sakai, H. (1966). Studies on sulfhydryl groups during cell division of sea urchin eggs. VIII. Some properties of mitotic apparatus proteins. *Biochim. Biophys. Acta* **112**, 132.

Sakai, H. (1967). A ribonucleoprotein which catalyzes thioldisulfide exchange in the sea urchin egg. *J. Biol. Chem.* **242**, 1458.

Sakai, H. (1968). Contractile properties of protein threads from sea urchin eggs in relation to cell division. *Int. Rev. Cytol.* **23**, 89.

Sakai, H., and Dan, K. (1959). Sulfhydryl groups during cell division of sea urchin egg. I. Glutathione. *Exp. Cell Res.* **16**, 24.

Samarina, O. P., Krichevskaya, A. A., and Georgiev, G. P. (1966). Nuclear ribonucleoprotein particles containing messenger RNA. *Nature (London)* **210**, 1319.

Samarina, O. P., Molnar, J., Lukanidin, E. M., Bruskov, V. I., Krichevskaya, A. A., and Georgiev, G. P. (1967). Reversible dissociation of nuclear RNP particles containing mRNA into RNA and proteins. *J. Mol. Biol.* **27**, 187.

Samarina, O. P., Lukanidin, E. M., Molnar, J., and Georgiev, G. P. (1968). Structural organization of nuclear complexes containing DNA-like RNA. *J. Mol. Biol.* **33**, 251.

Sanchez, S. (1968). Effect de l'actinomycin D sur les constituants cellulaires et le metabolisme de l'ARN de l'ovocyte d'oursin (*Paracentrotus lividus*). *Exp. Cell Res.* **50**, 19.

Sanzo, L. (1904). Trasformazione sperimentale delle uova lecitiche diffuse in uova telolecitiche. *Ric. Lab. Anat. Norm. Univ. Roma* **10**, 263.

Sawada, N., and Rebhun, L. I. (1969). The effect of dinitrophenol and other phosphorylation uncouplers on the birefringence of the mitotic apparatus of marine eggs. *Exp. Cell Res.,* **55**, 33.

Scarano, E. (1958a). 5′-Deoxycytidylic acid deaminase. Enzymic production of 5′deoxyuridylic acid. *Biochim. Biophys. Acta* **29**, 459.

Scarano, E. (1958b). Deaminazione enzimatica dell'acido 5′-deossicitidilico. *Boll. Soc. Ital. Biol. Sper.* **34**, 499.

Scarano, E. (1958c). Preparazione enzimatica dell'acido 5′-deossiuridilico. *Boll. Soc. Ital. Biol. Sper.* **34**, 722.

Scarano, E. (1958d). Idrolisi enzimatica ed idrolisi acida dell'acido 5'-deossiuridilico. *Boll. Soc. Ital. Biol. Sper.* **34**, 724.

Scarano, E. (1958e). Caratteristiche spettrali dell'acido 5'-deossiuridilico nell'ultravioletto. *Boll. Soc. Ital. Biol. Sper.* **34**, 727.

Scarano, E. (1958f). Formazione enzimatica di acido timidilico dall'acido 5'-metil-5'-deossicitidilico. *Boll. Soc. Ital. Biol. Sper.* **34**, 945.

Scarano, E. (1969). Enzymatic modifications of DNA and embryonic differentiation. *Ann. Embryol. Morphol. Suppl.* **1**, 7.

Scarano, E. (1971). *Int. Symp. Cell Biol. Cytopharmacol., 1st, 1969* p. 13.

Scarano, E., and Augusti-Tocco, A. (1967). Biochemical pathways in embryos. *Compr. Biochem.* **28**, 55–111.

Scarano, E., and Kalckar, H. M. (1953). Nucleic acid synthesis in developing sea urchin embryos. *Pubbl. Sta. Zool. Napoli* **24**, 189.

Scarano, E., and Maggio, R. (1957). An exchange between ^{32}P-labeled pyrophosphate and ATP catalyzed by amino acids in unfertilized sea urchin eggs. *Exp. Cell Res.* **12**, 403.

Scarano, E., and Maggio, R. (1959a). Enzymatic deamination of 5-methyldeoxycytidylic acid to thymidylic acid. *Arch. Biochem. Biophys.* **79**, 392.

Scarano, E., and Maggio, R. (1959b). Enzymic deamination of 5'-deoxycytidylic acid and 5'-methyl-5'-deoxycytidylic acid in developing sea urchin embryo. *Exp. Cell Res.* **18**, 333.

Scarano, E., and Maggio, R. (1959c). Attivazione enzimatica dell'acetato nelle uova di riccio di mare. *G. Biochim.* **8**, 98.

Scarano, E., Bonaduce, L., and De Petrocellis, B. (1960). The enzymatic deamination of 6-aminopyrimidine deoxyribonucleotides. II. Purification and properties of a 6-aminopyrimidine deoxyribonucleoside 5'-phosphate deaminase from unfertilized eggs of sea urchins. *J. Biol. Chem.* **235**, 3556.

Scarano, E., Geraci, G., Polzella, A., and Campanile, E. (1963). The enzymatic amino-hydrolysis of 4-aminopyrimidine deoxyribonucleotides. IV. On the possibility of the occurrence of an allosteric site on 2'-deoxyribosyl 4-aminopyrimidine-2,5'-phosphate aminohydrolase. *J. Biol. Chem.* **238**, 1556.

Scarano, E., Geraci, G., and Rossi, M. (1964a). On the regulatory properties of deoxycytidylate aminohydrolase. *Biochem. Biophys. Res. Commun.* **16**, 239.

Scarano, E., De Petrocellis, B., and Augusti-Tocco, G. (1964b). Studies on the control of enzyme synthesis during the early embryonic development of the sea urchins. *Biochim. Biophys. Acta* **87**, 174.

Scarano, E., De Petrocellis, B., and Augusti-Tocco, G. (1964c). Deoxycytidylate amino-hydrolase content in disaggregated cells from sea urchin embryos. *Exp. Cell Res.* **36**, 211.

Scarano, E., Iaccarino, M., Grippo, P., and Winckelmans, D. (1965). On methylation of DNA during development of sea urchin embryos. *J. Mol. Biol.* **14**, 603.

Scarano, E., Geraci, G., and Rossi, M. (1967a). Deoxycytidylate aminohydrolase. II. Kinetic properties. The activatory effect of deoxycytidine triphosphate and the inhibitory effect of deoxythymidine triphosphate. *Biochemistry* **6**, 192.

Scarano, E., Geraci, G., and Rossi, M. (1967b). Deoxycytidylate aminohydrolase. IV. Stoichiometry of binding of isosteric and allosteric effectors. *Biochemistry* **6**, 3645.

Scarano, E., Iaccarino, M., Grippo, P., and Parisi, E. (1967c). The heterogeneity of thymine methyl group origin in DNA pyrimidine isostichs of developing sea urchin embryos. *Proc. Nat. Acad. Sci. U.S.* **57**, 1394.

Schäfer, A. (1966). Strukturwandlungen im Seeigelei nach der Befruchtung und während der ersten Teilungsschritte. *Protoplasma* **62**, 339.

Schechtman, A. M. (1937). Localized cortical growth as the immediate cause of cell division. *Science* **85,** 222.

Schmidt, G., Hecht, L., and Thannhauser, S. J. (1948). The behavior of the nucleic acid during the early development of the sea urchin egg (*Arbacia*). *J. Gen. Physiol.* **31,** 203.

Scholander, P. F., Claff, C. L., Sveinsson, S. L., and Scholander, S. I. (1952). Respiratory studies of single cells. III. Oxygen consumption during cell division. *Biol. Bull.* **102,** 185.

Scholander, P. F., Leivestad, H., and Sundnes, G. (1958). Cycling in the oxygen consumption of cleaving eggs. *Exp. Cell Res.* **15,** 505.

Sconzo, G. (1967). Thesis, Univ. of Palermo, Italy.

Sconzo, G., and Giudice, G. (1971). Synthesis of ribosomal RNA in sea urchin embryos. V. Further evidence for an activation following the hatching blastula stage. *Biochim. Biophys. Acta* **254,** 447.

Sconzo, G., Pirrone, A. M., Mutolo, V., and Giudice, G. (1970a). Synthesis of ribosomal RNA during sea urchin development. III. Evidence for an activation of transcription. *Biochim. Biophys. Acta* **199,** 435.

Sconzo, G., Pirrone, A. M., Mutolo, V., and Giudice, G. (1970b). Synthesis of ribosomal RNA in disaggregated cells of sea urchin embryos. *Biochim. Biophys. Acta* **199,** 441.

Sconzo, G., Vitrano, E., Bono, A., Di Giovanni, L., Mutolo, V., and Giudice, G. (1971). Synthesis of rRNA in sea urchin embryos. IV. Maturation of rRNA precursor. *Biochim. Biophys. Acta* **232,** 132.

Sconzo, G., Bono, A., Albanese, I., and Giudice, G. (1972). Studies on sea urchin oocytes. II. Synthesis of RNA during oogenesis. *Exp. Cell Res.* **72,** 95.

Scott, A. C. (1960a). Furrowing in flattened sea urchin eggs. *Biol. Bull.* **119,** 246.

Scott, A. C. (1960b). Surface changes during cell division. *Biol. Bull.* **119,** 260.

Selenka, E. (1883). "Die Kleimblätter der Echinodermen. Studien über die Entwicklungsgeschichte der Thiere," Vol. 1. Kreidel's Verlag, Wiesbaden.

Selvig, S. E., Gross, P. R., and Hunter, A. L. (1970). Cytoplasmic synthesis of RNA in the sea urchin embryo. *Develop. Biol.* **22,** 343.

Sevaljević, L., and Ruzdijic, S. (1971). The study of protein during early stages of embryogenesis of sea urchins. II. Combined electrophoretic and immunodiffusion investigations of S-100 fraction. *Wilhelm Roux'Arch. Entwicklungsmech. Organismen* **168,** 187.

Sevaljević, L., Ruzdijic, S., and Glisin, V. (1971). The study of proteins during early stages of embryogenesis of sea urchins. I. Investigations on the distribution of preexisting and *de novo* synthesized protein. *Wilhelm Roux'Arch. Entwicklungsmech. Organismen* **168,** 181.

Shapiro, H. (1935). The respiration of fragments obtained by centrifuging the egg of the sea urchin *Arbacia punctulata. J. Cell. Comp. Physiol.* **6,** 101.

Shapiro, H. (1939). Some functional correlatives of cellular metabolism. *Cold Spring Harbor Symp. Quant. Biol.* **7,** 406.

Shapiro, H., and Dawson, H. (1941). Permeability of the *Arbacia* egg to potassium. *Biol. Bull.* **8,** 295.

Sharma, O. K., Loeb, L. A., and Borek, E. (1971). Transfer RNA methylases during sea urchin embryogenesis. *Biochim. Biophys. Acta* **240,** 558.

Shaver, J. R. (1955). The distribution of mitochondria in sea urchin embryos. *Experientia* **11,** 351.

Shaver, J. R. (1957). Some observations on cytoplasmic particles in early echinoderm development. *In* "The Beginnings of Embryonic Development," Publ. No. 48, pp. 263–290. Amer. Ass. Advance. Sci., Washington, D.C.

Shearer, C. (1922a). On the oxydation processes of the echinoderm egg during fertilization. *Proc. Roy. Soc., Ser. B* **93,** 213.

Shearer, C. (1922b). On the heat production and oxidation processes of the echinoderm egg during fertilization and early development. *Proc. Roy. Soc., Ser. B* **93**, 410.

Shearer, C., and Lloyd, D. J. (1913). On methods of producing artificial parthenogenesis in *Echinus esculentus* and the rearing of parthenogenetic plutei through metamorphosis. *Quart. J. Microsc. Sci.* **58**, 523.

Shearer, C., De Morgan, W., and Fuchs, H. M. (1913). On the experimental hybridization of echinoids. *Phil. Trans. Roy. Soc. London, Ser. B* **204**, 255.

Shimamura, T. (1939). Cytological studies of polyploid induced by colchicine. *Cytologia* **9**, 486.

Shiokawa, K., and Yamana, K. (1967a). Pattern of RNA synthesis in isolated cells of *Xenopus laevis* embryos. *Develop. Biol.* **16**, 368.

Shiokawa, K., and Yamana, K. (1967b). Inhibitor of ribosomal RNA synthesis in *Xenopus laevis* embryos. *Develop. Biol.* **16**, 389.

Shiokawa, K., and Yamana, K. (1969). Inhibitor of rRNA synthesis in *Xenopus laevis* embryos. II. Effects on rRNA synthesis in isolated cells from *Rana japonica* embryos. *Exp. Cell Res.* **55**, 155.

Siekevitz, P., Maggio, R., and Catalano, C. (1966). Some properties of a rapidly labelled RNA species in *Sphaerechinus granularis*. *Biochim. Biophys. Acta* **129**, 145.

Silver, D. J., and Comb, D. G. (1966). Free amino acid pools in the developing sea urchin *Lytechinus variegatus*. *Exp. Cell Res.* **43**, 699.

Silver, D. J., and Comb, D. G. (1967). Acetic acid-soluble proteins in the developing sea urchin. *Develop. Biol.* **16**, 107.

Simmel, E. B., and Karnofsky, D. A. (1961). Observations on the uptake of tritiated thymidine in the pronuclei of fertilized sand dollar embryos. *J. Biophys. Biochem. Cytol.* **10**, 59.

Singh, U. N. (1968). Rate of flow of rapidly labelled RNA from nucleus to cytoplasm during embryonic development of sea urchin. *Exp. Cell Res.* **53**, 537.

Siskens, J. E., Wilkes, E., Donnelly, G. M., and Kakefuda, T. (1967). The isolation of the mitotic apparatus from mammalian cells in culture. *J. Cell Biol.* **32**, 212.

Skalka, A., Fowler, A. V., and Hurwitz, J. (1966). The effect of histones on the enzymatic synthesis of RNA. *J. Biol. Chem.* **241**, 588.

Slater, D. W., and Spiegelman, S. (1966a). An estimation of genetic messages in the unfertilized echinoid egg. *Proc. Nat. Acad. Sci. U.S.* **56**, 164.

Slater, D. W., and Spiegelman, S. (1966b). A chemical and physical characterization of echinoid RNA during early embryogenesis. *Biophys. J.* **6**, 385.

Slater, D. W., and Spiegelman, S. (1968). Template capabilities and size distribution of echinoid RNA during early development. *Biochim. Biophys. Acta* **166**, 82.

Slater, D. W., and Spiegelman, S. (1970). Transcriptive expression during sea urchin embryogenesis. *Biochim. Biophys. Acta* **213**, 194.

Slater, J. P., and Loeb, L. A. (1970). Initiation of DNA synthesis in eukaryotes: A model *in vitro* system. *Biochem. Biophys. Res. Commun.* **41**, 589.

Slater, J. P., Mildvan, A. S., and Loeb, L. A. (1971). Zinc in DNA polymerases. *Biochem. Biophys. Res. Commun.* **44**, 37.

Sofer, W. H., George, J. F., and Iverson, R. M. (1966). Rate of protein synthesis: Regulation during first division cycle of sea urchin eggs. *Science* **153**, 1644.

Solari, A. J. (1967). Electron microscopy of native DNA in sea urchin cells. *J. Ultrastruct. Res.* **17**, 421.

Soupart, P., Rinaldi, R. A., and Pickel, V. M. (1969). Amantadine hydrochloride inhibitor of cleavage and DNA synthesis in sea urchin ova. *J. Reprod. Fert.* **20**, 349.

Speidel, C. C., and Cheney, R. H. (1960). Comparative effect of X-ray and ultraviolet radiation of gametes on the developing sea urchin *Arbacia*. *Biol. Bull.* **119**, 338.

Spiegel, M., and Tyler, A. (1966). Protein synthesis in micromeres of the sea urchin egg. *Science* **151,** 1233.

Spiegel, M., Ozaki, H., and Tyler, A. (1965). Electrophoretic examination of soluble proteins synthesized in early sea urchin development. *Biochem. Biophys. Res. Commun.* **21,** 135.

Spiegel, M., Spiegel, E. S., and Meltzer, P. S. (1970). Qualitative changes in the basic protein fraction of developing embryos. *Develop. Biol.* **21,** 73.

Spirin, A. S. (1966). On "masked" forms of messenger RNA in early embryogenesis and in other differentiating systems. *Curr. Top. Develop. Biol.* **1,** 2.

Spirin, A. S., and Nemer, M. (1965). Messenger RNA in early sea urchin embryos: Cytoplasmic particles. *Science* **150,** 214.

Spirin, A. S., Belitsina, N. V., and Ajtkhozhin, M. A. (1964). Synthesis of messenger RNA (mRNA) and relation of mRNA to protein synthesizing structures of the cytoplasm were studied at different stages of early embryonic development of loach (*Misgurnus fossilis* L.). *Zh. Obshch. Biol.* **25,** 321.

Stafford, D. W., and Guild, W. R. (1969). Satellite DNA from sea urchin sperm. *Exp. Cell Res.* **55,** 347.

Stafford, D. W., and Iverson, R. M. (1964). Radioautographic evidence for the incorporation of leucine–carbon-14 into the mitotic apparatus. *Science* **143,** 580.

Stafford, D. W., Sofer, W. H., and Iverson, R. M. (1964). Demonstration of polyribosomes after fertilization of the sea urchin egg. *Proc. Nat. Acad. Sci. U.S.* **52,** 313.

Stavy, L., and Gross, P. R. (1967). The protein synthetic lesion in unfertilized eggs. *Proc. Nat. Acad. Sci. U.S.* **57,** 735.

Stavy, L., and Gross, P. R. (1969a). Protein synthesis *in vitro* with fractions of sea urchin eggs and embryos. *Biochim. Biophys. Acta* **182,** 193.

Stavy, L., and Gross, P. R. (1969b). Availability of mRNA for translation during normal and transcription-blocked development. *Biochim. Biophys. Acta* **182,** 203.

Stearns, L. W., Martin, W. E., Jolley, W. B., and Bamberger, I. W. (1962). Effects of certain pyrimidines on cleavage and nucleic acid metabolism in sea urchin, *Strongylocentrotus purpuratus,* embryos. *Exp. Cell Res.* **27,** 250.

Steinbruck, H. (1902). Über Bastardbildung zwischen *Strongylocentrotus* und *Sphaerechinus. Arch. Entwicklungsmech. Organismen* **14,** 1.

Steinhardt, R. A., Lundin, L., and Mazia, D. (1971). Bioelectric responses of the echinoderm egg to fertilization. *Proc. Nat. Acad. Sci. U.S.* **68,** 2426.

Stephens, R. E. (1965). Characterization of the mitotic apparatus protein and its subunits. *Biol. Bull.* **129,** 396A.

Stephens, R. E. (1967). The mitotic apparatus. Physical chemical characterization of the 22 S protein component and its subunits. *J. Cell Biol.* **32,** 255.

Stephens, R. E. (1968a). On the structural protein of flagellar outer fibers. *J. Mol. Biol.* **32,** 277.

Stephens, R. E. (1968b). Reassociation of microtubule protein. *J. Mol. Biol.* **33,** 517.

Stephens, R. E. (1970). Thermal fractionation of outer fiber doublet microtubules into A- and B-subfiber components: A- and B-tubulin. *J. Mol. Biol.* **47,** 353.

Stephens, R. E., Renaud, F. L., and Gibbons, I. R. (1967). Guanine nucleotide associated with the protein of outer fibers of flagella and cilia. *Science* **156,** 1606.

Stewart, D. R., and Jacobs, M. H. (1932). The effect of fertilization on the permeability of the eggs of *Arbacia* and *Asterias* to ethylene glycol. *J. Cell. Comp. Physiol.* **1,** 83.

Strathmann, R. (1968). Feeding of echinoderm larvae. *Amer. Zool.* **8,** 804.

Subirana, J. A. (1970). Nuclear proteins from a somatic and a germinal tissue of the echinoderm *Holothuria tubulosa. Exp. Cell Res.* **63,** 253.

Subirana, J. A., Palau, J., Cozcolluela, C., and Ruiz-Carrillo, A. (1970). Very lysine-rich histones of echinoderms and molluscs. *Nature (London)* **228**, 992.

Sugawara, H. (1943). Hatching enzyme of the sea urchin, *Strongylocentrotus pulcherrimus. J. Fac. Sci., Imp. Univ. Tokyo, Sect. 4* **6**, 109.

Sugino, Y. (1960). Studies on deoxynucleosidic compounds. II. Deoxycytidine diphosphate choline in sea urchin eggs. *Biochim. Biophys. Acta* **40**, 425.

Sugino, Y., Sugino, N., Okazaki, R., and Okazaki, T. (1960). Studies on deoxynucleosidic compounds. I. A modified microbioassay method and its application to sea urchin egg and several other materials. *Biochim. Biophys. Acta* **40**, 417.

Sugiyama, M. (1951). Re-fertilization of the fertilized eggs of the sea urchin. *Biol. Bull.* **101**, 335.

Sugiyama, M. (1953). Physiological analysis of the cortical response of the sea urchin egg to stimulating reagents. II. The propagating or non-propagating nature of the cortical changes induced by various reagents. *Biol. Bull.* **104**, 216.

Sugiyama, M. (1956). Physiological analysis of the cortical response of the sea urchin egg. *Exp. Cell Res.* **10**, 364.

Summers, K. E., and Gibbons, I. R. (1971). ATP-induced sliding of tubules in trypsin-treated flagella of sea urchin sperm. *Proc. Nat. Acad. Sci. U.S.* **68**, 3092.

Swan, E. (1953). The Strongylocentrotidae. *Evolution* 7, 269.

Swann, M. M. (1953). The mechanism of cell division. A study with carbon monoxide on sea urchin egg. *Quart. J. Microsc. Sci.* **94**, 369.

Swann, M. M. (1954). Secondary sex differences in five European species of sea urchin. *Pubbl. Sta. Zool. Napoli* **25**, 198.

Swann, M. M. (1955). The mechanism of cell division: the action of 2,4-dinitrophenol and certain glycolytic inhibitors on the sea urchin egg. *Proc. Phys. Soc. Edinburgh* **24**, 5.

Swann, M. M. (1957). The control of cell division: A review. I. General mechanisms. *Cancer Res.* **17**, 727.

Swann, M. M., and Mitchison, J. M. (1953). Cleavage of sea-urchin eggs in colchicine. *J. Exp. Biol.* **30**, 506.

Swann, M. M., and Mitchison, J. M. (1958). The mechanism of cleavage in animal cells. *Biol. Rev.* **33**, 103.

Swartz, M. N., Trautner, J. A., and Kornberg, A. (1962). Enzymatic snythesis of deoxyribonucleic acid. XI. Further studies on nearest neighbour base sequences in deoxyribonucleic acids. *J. Biol. Chem.* **237**, 1961.

Sy, J., and McCarty, K. S. (1968). Ribosomal RNA of *Arbacia punctulata. Biochim. Biophys. Acta* **166**, 571.

Sy, J., and McCarty, K. S. (1970). Characterization of 5.8 S RNA from a complex with 26 S ribosomal RNA from *Arbacia punctulata. Biochim. Biophys. Acta* **199**, 86.

Sy, J., and McCarty, K. S. (1971). Formation *in vitro* of a 5.8 S–26 S sea urchin rRNA complex. *Biochim. Biophys. Acta* **228**, 517.

Taguchi, S. (1962). Changes in the content of adenosine nucleotides during early development of the sea urchins, *Pseudocentrotus depressus* and *Hemicentrotus pulcherrimus. Annot. Zool. Jap.* **35**, 183.

Taguchi, S., Yasumasu, I., and Mohri, H. (1963). Changes in the content of adenine nucleotides upon aerobic incubation of sea urchin spermatozoa. *Exp. Cell Res.* **30**, 218.

Takashima, R. (1963). The egg-jelly and the fertilization in sea urchin. *Bull. Exp. Biol.* **13**, 11.

Takashima, R., and Takashima, Y. (1960). Electron microscopical observations on the fertilization phenomenon of sea urchins with special reference to the acrosome filament. *Tokushima J. Exp. Med.* **6**, 334.

Takashima, R., and Takashima, Y. (1965). Studies on submicroscopical structures of the nurse cells in sea urchin ovary, with special reference to the glycogen particles. *Okajimas Folia Anat. Jap.* **40,** 819.

Takashima, Y. (1960). Studies on the ultrastructure of the cortical granules in sea urchin eggs. *Tokushima J. Exp. Med.* **6,** 341.

Takashima, Y., and Takashima, R. (1966). Electron microscope investigation of the modes of yolk and pigment formation in sea urchin oocytes. *Okajimas Folia Anat. Jap.* **42,** 249.

Tamini, E. (1943). Ricerche sulla vegetativizzazione nello sviluppo dei ricci di mare. *Rendiconti* **76,** 363.

Tang, P. S. (1931). The oxygen tension–oxygen consumption curve of unfertilized *Arbacia* eggs. *Biol. Bull.* **60,** 242.

Tang, P. S. (1948). Rhythmic respiration in sea urchin. *Nature (London)* **162,** 189.

Tang, P. S., and Gerard, R. W. (1949). The oxygen tension–oxygen consumption curve of fertilized *Arbacia* eggs. *J. Cell. Comp. Physiol.* **1,** 164.

Taylor, E. W. (1965). The mitotic apparatus. Physical chemical factors controlling stability. *J. Cell Biol.* **25,** No. 1, 145.

Tennent, D. H. (1910). Echinoderm hybridization. *Carnegie Inst. Wash. Publ.* **132,** 117.

Tennent, D. H. (1911). A heterochromosome of male origin in echinoids. *Biol. Bull.* **21,** 152.

Tennent, D. H. (1912a). Studies in cytology. I. A further study of the chromosomes of *Toxopneustes variegatus.* II. The behaviour of the chromosomes in *Arbacia Toxopneustes* crosses. *J. Exp. Zool.* **12,** 391.

Tennent, D. H. (1912b). The behavior of the chromosomes in cross-fertilized echinoid eggs. *J. Morphol.* **23,** 17.

Tennent, D. H. (1912c). The correlation between chromosomes and particular characters in hybrid echinoid larvae. *Amer. Natur.* **46,** 68.

Tennent, D. H. (1913). Echinoderm hybridization. *Science* **37,** 535.

Tennent, D. H. (1922). Studies of the hybridization of echinoids, *Cidaris tribuloides.* *Carnegie Inst. Wash. Publ.* **312,** 1.

Tennent, D. H. (1923). Investigations on the hybridization of echinoids conducted at the Misaki Biological Station of Tokyo Imperial University, from April 24 to August 16, 1923. *Carnegie Inst. Wash., Yearb.* **22,** 169.

Tennent, D. H. (1929). Activation of the eggs of *Echinometra mathaei* by sperms of the crinoids *Comatula pectinata* and *Comatula purpurea. Carnegie Inst. Wash. Publ.* **391,** 105.

Tennent, D. H., and Ito, T. (1941). A study of oogenesis of *Mespila globulus* (Linné). *J. Morphol.* **69,** 347.

Tennent, D. H., Gardiner, M. S., and Smith, D. E. (1931). A cytological and biochemical study of the ovaries of the sea urchin *Echinometra lucunter. Pap. Tortugas Lab.* **27;** *Carnegie Inst. Wash. Publ.* **413,** 1.

Terman, S. A. (1970). Relative effect of transcription-level and translation-level control of protein synthesis during early development of the sea urchin. *Proc. Nat. Acad. Sci. U.S.* **65,** 985.

Terman, S. A., and Gross, P. R. (1965). Translation-level control of protein synthesis during early development. *Biochem. Biophys. Res. Commun.* **21,** 595.

Terni, T. (1914). Studio sulle larve atipiche (blastulae permanenti) degli Echinoidi. Analisi della limitata equipotenzialità dell'uovo di Echinoide. *Mitt. Zool. Sta. Neapel* **22,** 59.

Thaler, M. M., Cox, M. C. L., and Villee, C. A. (1969a). Actinomycin D: uptake by sea urchin eggs and embryos. *Science* **164,** 832.

Thaler, M. M., Cox, M. C. L., and Villee, C. A. (1969b). Isolation of nuclei from sea urchin eggs and embryos. *J. Cell Biol.* **42,** 846.

Thaler, M. M., Cox, M. C. L., and Villee, C. A. (1970). Histones in early embryogenesis. Developmental aspects of composition and synthesis. *J. Biol. Chem.* **245**, 1479.

Tilney, L. G., and Gibbins, J. R. (1968). Differential effects of antimitotic agents on the stability and behavior of cytoplasmic and ciliary microtubules. *Protoplasma* **65**, 167.

Tilney, L. G., and Gibbins, J. R. (1969a). Microtubules and filaments in the filopodia of the secondary mesenchyme cells of *Arbacia punctulata* and *Echinarachnius parma. J. Cell Sci.* **5**, 195.

Tilney, L. G., and Gibbins, J. R. (1969b). Microtubules in the formation and development of the primary mesenchyme in *Arbacia punctulata*. II. An experimental analysis of their role in development and maintenance of cell shape. *J. Cell Biol.* **41**, 227.

Tilney, L. G., and Goddard, J. (1970). Nucleating sites for the assembly of cytoplasmic microtubules in the ectodermal cells of blastulae of *Arbacia punctulata. J. Cell Biol.* **46**, 564.

Tilney, L. G., and Marsland, D. (1969). A fine structural analysis of cleavage induction and furrowing in the egg of *Arbacia punctulata. J. Cell Biol.* **42**, 170.

Timofeeva, M. Y., Ivanchik, J. A., and Neifakh, A. A. (1969). Change in the activity of high-polymer RNA synthesis in early embryonic development of the sea urchin *Strongylocentrotus nudus. Dokl. Biol. Sci.* **184**, 22.

Timourian, H. (1966). Protein synthesis during first cleavage of sea urchin embryos. *Science* **154**, 1055.

Timourian, H., and Watchmaker, G. (1970). Protein synthesis in sea urchin eggs. II. Changes in amino acid uptake and incorporation at fertilization. *Develop. Biol.* **23**, 478.

Timourian, H., and Watchmaker, G. (1971). Bipolar and tetrapolar cleavage time in sea urchin eggs. *Exp. Cell Res.* **68**, 428.

Tocco, G., Orengo, A., and Scarano, E. (1963). RNAs in the early embryonic development of the sea urchin. I. Quantitative variations and ^{32}P-orthophosphate incorporation studies of the RNA of subcellular fractions. *Exp. Cell Res.* **31**, 52.

Trinkaus, J. P. (1965). Mechanisms of morphogenetic movements. *In* "Organogenesis" (R. L. de Haan and H. Ursprung, eds.), pp. 55–104. Holt, New York.

Troll, W., Grossman, A., and Chasis, S. (1968). Fertilization-induced increase of trypsin-like activity in sea urchin "membrane" during embryogenesis. *Biol. Bull.* **135**, 440.

Tsukahara, J., and Sugiyama, M. (1969). Ultrastructural changes in the surface of the oocyte during oogenesis of the sea urchin *Hemicentrotus pulcherrimus. Embryologia* **10**, 343.

Tsuzuki, H., and Aketa, K. (1969). A study on the possible significance of carbohydrate moiety in the sperm-binding protein from sea urchin egg. *Exp. Cell Res.* **55**, 43.

Tyler, A. (1939). Crystalline echinochrome and spinochrome: Their failure to stimulate the respiration of eggs and sperm of *Strongylocentrotus. Proc. Nat. Acad. Sci. U.S.* **25**, 523.

Tyler, A. (1941). The role of fertilizin in the fertilization of eggs of the sea urchin and other animals. *Biol. Bull.* **81**, 190.

Tyler, A. (1946). Loss of fertilizing power of sea urchin and *Urechis* sperm treated with "univalent" antibodies vs. antifertilizin. *Proc. Soc. Exp. Biol. Med.* **62**, 197.

Tyler, A. (1948). Fertilization and immunity. *Physiol. Rev.* **28**, 180.

Tyler, A. (1949). Properties of fertilizin and related substances of eggs and sperm of marine animals. *Amer. Natur.* **83**, 195.

Tyler, A. (1956). Physicochemical properties of the fertilizins of the sea urchin *Arbacia punctulata* and the sand dollar *Echinarachnius parma. Exp. Cell Res.* **10**, 377.

Tyler, A. (1957). Immunological studies of early development. *In* "The Beginning of Embryonic Development," Publ. No. 48, pp. 341–382. Amer. Ass. Advance Sci., Washington, D.C.

Tyler, A. (1958). Changes in efflux and influx of potassium upon fertilization in eggs of *Arbacia punctulata* measured by use of K^{42}. *Biol. Bull.* **115**, 339.

Tyler, A. (1959). Some immunobiological experiments on fertilization and early development in sea urchins. *Exp. Cell Res., Suppl.* **7**, 183.

Tyler, A. (1963). The manipulation of macromolecular substances during fertilization and development of animal eggs. *Amer. Zool.* **3**, 109.

Tyler, A. (1965). Incorporation of amino acids into proteins by nonnucleate, nucleate and poly U-treated sea-urchin eggs. *Amer. Zool.* **5**, 34.

Tyler, A. (1966). Incorporation of aminoacids into protein by artificially activated non-nucleate fragments of sea urchin eggs. *Biol. Bull.* **130**, 450.

Tyler, A. (1967). Masked messenger RNA and cytoplasmic DNA in relation to protein synthesis and processes of fertilization and determination in embryonic development. *Develop. Biol., Suppl.* **1**, 170.

Tyler, A., and Brookbank, J. W. (1956a). Antisera that block cell division in developing eggs of sea urchins. *Proc. Nat. Acad. Sci. U.S.* **42**, 304.

Tyler, A., and Brookbank, J. W. (1956b). Inhibition of division and development of sea urchin eggs by antisera against fertilizin. *Proc. Nat. Acad. Sci. U.S.* **42**, 308.

Tyler, A., and Fox, S. W. (1940). Evidence for the protein nature of the sperm agglutinins of the keyhole limpet and sea urchin. *Biol. Bull.* **79**, 153.

Tyler, A., and Hathaway, R. R. (1958). Production of ^{35}S-labelled fertilizin in eggs of *Arbacia punctulata*. *Biol. Bull.* **115**, 369.

Tyler, A., and Humason, W. D. (1939). On the energetics of differentiation. VI. Comparison of the temperature coefficients of the respiratory rates of unfertilized and fertilized eggs. *Biol. Bull.* **73**, 261.

Tyler, A., and Metz, C. B. (1955). Effects of fertilizin treatment of sperm and trypsin treatment of eggs on homologous and cross-fertilization in sea urchin. *Pubbl. Sta. Zool. Napoli* **27**, 128.

Tyler, A., and Monroy, A. (1955). Apparent and real microinjection of echinoderm eggs. *Biol. Bull.* **109**, 370.

Tyler, A., and Monroy, A. (1956). Change in the rate of release of K^{42} upon fertilization in eggs of *Arbacia punctulata*. *Biol. Bull.* **111**, 296.

Tyler, A., and Monroy, A. (1959). Change in rate of transfer of potassium across the membrane upon fertilization of eggs of *Arbacia punctulata*. *J. Exp. Zool.* **142**, 675.

Tyler, A., and O'Melveny, K. (1941). The role of antifertilizin in the fertilization of sea urchin eggs. *Biol. Bull.* **81**, 364.

Tyler, A., and Pikò, L. (1968). Cytoplasmic DNA of sea urchins. XIIth International Congress of Cell Biology. *Excerpta Med. Int. Congr. Ser.* **166**, 85.

Tyler, A., and Spiegel, M. (1956). Elevation and retraction of the fertilization membrane of echinoderm eggs fertilized in papain solutions. *Biol. Bull.* **110**, 196.

Tyler, A., and Tyler, B. S. (1966). The gametes; some procedures and properties. *In* "Physiology of Echinodermata" (R. A. Boolotian, ed.), pp. 639–682. Wiley (Interscience), New York.

Tyler, A., Burbank, A., and Tyler, J. S. (1954). The electrophoretic mobilities of the fertilizin of *Arbacia* and *Echinarachinus*. *Biol. Bull.* **107**, 304.

Tyler, A., Monroy, A., and Metz, C. B. (1956a). Fertilization of fertilized sea urchin eggs. *Biol. Bull.* **110**, 184.

Tyler, A., Monroy, A., Kao, C. Y., and Grundfest, H. (1956b). Membrane potential and resistance of the starfish egg before and after fertilization. *Biol. Bull.* **111**, 153.

Tyler, A., Piatigorsky, J., and Ozaki, H. (1966). Influence of individual amino acids on uptake and incorporation of valine, glutamic acid and arginine by unfertilized and fertilized sea urchin eggs. *Biol. Bull.* **131**, 204.

Tyler, A., Tyler, B. S., and Piatigorsky, J. (1968). Protein synthesis by unfertilized eggs of sea urchins. *Biol. Bull.* **134,** 209.

Vacquier, V. D. (1968). The connection of blastomeres of sea urchin embryos by filopodia. *Exp. Cell Res.* **52,** 577.

Vacquier, V. D. (1969). The isolation and preliminary analysis of the hyaline layer of sea urchin eggs. *Exp. Cell Res.* **54,** 140.

Vacquier, V. D. (1971a). The appearance of β-1,3-glucanohydrolase activity during the differentiation of the gut of sand dollar plutei. *Develop. Biol.* **26,** 1.

Vacquier, V. D. (1971b). The effects of glucose and lithium chloride on the appearance of β-1,3-glucanohydrolase activity in sand dollar plutei. *Develop. Biol.* **26,** 11.

Vacquier, V. D., and Claybrook, J. R. (1969). Biochemical consequences of ethidium bromide treatment of sea urchin embryos. *Nature (London)* **224,** 706.

Vacquier, V. D., and Mazia, D. (1968a). Twinning of sand dollar embryos by means of dithiothreitol. The structural basis of blastomere interactions. *Exp. Cell Res.* **52,** 209.

Vacquier, V. D., and Mazia, D. (1968b). Twinning of sea urchin embryos by treatment with dithiothreitol. Roles of cell surface interactions and of the hyaline layer. *Exp. Cell Res.* **52,** 459.

Vacquier, V. D., Korn, L. J., and Epel, D. (1971). The appearance of α-amylase activity during gut differentiation in sand dollar plutei. *Develop. Biol.* **26,** 393.

Vanable, J. W., Jr. (1961). Hydroxyproline in the larval and adult forms of the sea urchin *Strongylocentrotus dröbachiensis. Exp. Cell Res.* **22,** 163.

Vasseur, E. (1947a). The sulfuric acid content of the egg coat of the sea urchin *Strongylocentrotus droebachiensis. Ark. Kemi, Mineral. Geol., B* **25,** No. **6,** 1.

Vasseur, E. (1947b). The spermatozoon of the sea urchin *Echinocardium cordatum* (Pennant). *Ark. Zool., B* **40,** No. 3, 1.

Vasseur, E. (1949). Chemical studies on the jelly coat of the sea urchin egg. *Acta Chem. Scand.* **2,** 900.

Vasseur, E. (1950). L-Galactose in the jelly coat of *Echinus esculentus. Acta Chem. Scand.* **4,** 1144.

Vasseur, E. (1952a). The chemistry and physiology of the jelly coat of the sea urchin eggs. Dissertation, pp. 1–32. Stockholm.

Vasseur, E. (1952b). Periodate oxidation of the jelly coat substance of *Echinocardium cordatum. Acta Chem. Scand.* **6,** 376.

Vasseur, E. (1952c). Geographic variation in the Norwegian sea urchins, *Strongylocentrotus droebachiensis* and *Strongylocentrotus pallidus. Evolution* **6,** 87.

Vasseur, E., and Immers, J. (1949). Hexosamine in the sea urchin jelly coat; a misinterpretation of the method of Elson and Morgan. *Ark. Kemi* **1,** 253.

Vercauteren, R. (1958). The mechanism of staining of the metachromatic granules of the sea urchin. *Arch. Biol.* **69,** 621.

Verhey, C. A., and Moyer, F. H. (1967). Fine structural changes during sea urchin oogenesis. *J. Exp. Zool.* **164,** 195.

Vernon, H. M. (1900). Cross-fertilization among echinoids. *Arch. Entiwickungsmech. Organismen* **9,** 464.

Vesco, C., and Penman, S. (1968). The fractionation of nuclei and the integrity of purified nucleoli in HeLa cells. *Biochim. Biophys. Acta* **169,** 188.

Villee, C. A., and Gross, P. R. (1969). Uptake of actinomycin by sea urchin eggs and embryos. *Science* **166,** 402.

Villee, C. A., and Villee, D. T. (1952). Studies on phosphorus metabolism in sea urchin embryos. *J. Cell. Comp. Physiol.* **40,** 57.

Villee, C. A., Lowens, M., Gordon, M., Leonard, E., and Rich, A. (1949). The incorporation of P³² into the nucleoproteins and phosphoproteins of the developing sea urchin embryo. *J. Cell. Comp. Physiol.* **33,** 93.

Villiger, M., Czihak, G., Tardent, P., and Baltzer, F. (1970). Feulgen microspectrophotometry of spermatozoa and blastula nuclei of different sea urchin species. *Exp. Cell Res.* **60,** 119.

Vincent, W. S., Halvorson, H. O., Chen, H. R., and Shin, D. (1968). Ribosomal RNA cistrons in single and multinucleolate oocytes. *Biol. Bull.* **135,** 441.

Vincent, W. S., Halvorson, H. O., Chen, H. R., and Shin, D. (1969). A comparison of ribosomal gene amplification in uni- and multinucleolate oocytes. *Exp. Cell Res.* **57,** 240.

Vittorelli, M. L. (1964). Phosphoproteinphosphatase activity in sea urchin embryos. *Experentia* **20,** 385.

Vittorelli, M. L., Caffarelli-Mormino, I., and Monroy, A. (1969). Poly U stimulation of single ribosomes and of ribosomes engaged in polysomes of sea urchin eggs and embryos. *Biochim. Biophys. Acta* **186,** 408.

von Ubisch, L. (1913a). Die Anlage und Ausbildung des Skeletsystems einiger Echiniden und die Symmetrieverhältnisse von Larvae und Imago. *Z. Wiss. Zool.* **104,** 119.

von Ubisch, L. (1913b). Die Entwicklung von *Strongylocentrotus lividus (Echinus microtuberculatus, Arbacia pustolosa). Z. Wiss. Zool.* **106,** 409.

von Ubisch, L. (1913c). Über das larvale Muskelsystem von *Arbacia pustolosa. Verh. Phys.-Med. Ges. Wurzburg* [N.S.] **42,** 127.

von Ubisch, L. (1925a). Entwicklungsphysiologische Studien an Seeigelkeimen. I. *Z. Wiss. Zool.* **124,** 361.

von Ubisch, L. (1925b). Entwicklungsphysiologische Studien an Seeigelkeimen. III. *Z. Wiss. Zool.* **124,** 469.

von Ubisch, L. (1925c). Über die Entodermisierung ektodermaler Bezirke des Echinoidenkeimes und die Reversion dieses Vorganger. *Verh. Phys.-Med. Ges. Wurzburg* [N.S.] **50,** 13.

von Ubisch, L. (1927). Über die Symmetrieverhältnisse von Larven und Imago bei regularen und irregularen Seeigeln. *Z. Wiss. Zool.* **129,** 541.

von Ubisch, L. (1929). Über die Determination der larvalen Organe und der Invaginanlage bei Seeigeln. *Wilhelm Roux' Arch. Entwicklungsmech. Organismen* **117,** 80.

von Ubisch, L. (1932a). Untersuchungen über Formbildung. II. *Wilhelm Roux' Arch. Entwicklungsmech. Organismen* **126,** 19.

von Ubisch, L. (1932b). Untersuchungen uber Formbildung. III. Ein vorwiegend spekulativer Beitrag zur Frage der Entstelung und systematischen Bedeutung der Seeigelplutei. *Wilhelm Roux' Arch. Entwicklungsmech. Organismen* **127,** 216.

von Ubisch, L. (1936). Über die Organization des Seeigelkeines. *Wilhelm Roux' Arch. Entwicklungsmech. Organismen* **134,** 599.

von Ubisch, L. (1937). Die normale Skelettbildung bei *Echinocyamus pusillus* and *Psammechinus miliaris* und die Bedeutung dieser Vorgänge für die Analyse der Skelette von Keimblatt-Chimaeren. *Z. Wiss. Zool.* **149,** 402.

von Ubisch, L. (1950). Die Entwicklung der Echiniden. *Verh. Kon. Ned. Akad. Wetenschap., Afd. Natuurk., Sect. 2* **47,** 1.

von Ubisch, L. (1954). Ueber Seeigelmerogone. *Pubbl. Sta. Zool. Napoli* **25,** 246.

von Ubisch, L. (1961). Über die Chromosomenzahl einiger Echinoidea. *Sarsia* **1,** 21.

Voroboyev, V. I. (1969). The effects of histones on RNA and protein synthesis in sea urchin embryos at early stages of development. *Exp. Cell Res.* **55,** 168.

Voroboyev, V. I., Gineitis, A. A., and Vinogradova, I. A. (1969a). Histones in early embryogenesis. *Exp. Cell Res.* **57,** 1.

Voroboyev, V. I., Gineitis, A. A., Kostyleva, E. I., and Smirnova, T. A. (1969b). The effect of histones on the early embryogenesis of sea urchins. *Exp. Cell Res.* **55,** 171.

Wada, K., Shiokawa, K., and Yamana, K. (1968). Inhibitor of rRNA synthesis in *Xenopus laevis* embryos. I. Changes in activity of the inhibitor during development and its distribution in early gastrulae. *Exp. Cell Res.* **52**, 252.

Warburg, O. (1908). Beobachtungen über die Oxydationprozesse im Seeigelei. *Hoppe-Seyler's Z. Physiol. Chem.* **57**, 1.

Warburg, O. (1910). Über die Oxydationen in lebenden Zellen nach Versuchen am Seeigelei. *Hoppe-Seyler's Z. Physiol. Chem.* **66**, 305.

Warburg, O. (1915). Notizen zur Entwicklungs-physiologie des Seeigeleies. *Pfluger's Arch. Gesamte Physiol. Menschen Tiere* **160**, 324.

Wartiowara, J., and Branton, D. (1970). Visualization of ribosomes by freeze-etching. *Exp. Cell Res.* **61**, 403.

Weinstein, R. S., and Herbst, R. R. (1964). Electron microscopy of cleavage furrows in sea urchin blastomeres. *J. Cell Biol.* **23**, 101A.

Weisenberg, R. C., and Taylor, E. W. (1968). Studies on ATPase activity of sea urchin eggs and the isolated mitotic apparatus. *Exp. Cell Res.* **53**, 372.

Weisenberg, R. C., Borisy, G. C., and Taylor, E. W. (1968). The colchicine-binding protein of mammalian brain and its relation to microtubules. *Biochemistry* **7**, 4466.

Weissman, G., Weck, S., Cagan, L. P., Troll, W., Levy, M., and Grossman, A. (1971). Redistribution of β-glucuronidase after fertilization of *Arbacia punctulata* eggs. *Biol. Bull.* **141**, 407 (a).

Wells, P. H., and Giese, A..C. (1950). Photoreactivation of ultraviolet light injury in gametes of the sea urchin *Strongylocentrotus purpuratus*. *Biol. Bull.* **99**, 163.

Went, H. A. (1959). Studies on the mitotic apparatus of the sea urchin by means of antigen–antibody reaction in agar. *J. Biophys. Biochem. Cytol.* **6**, 447.

Westin, M. (1969). Effect of actinomycin D on antigen synthesis during sea urchin development. *J. Exp. Zool.* **171**, 297.

Westin, M. (1970). Esterase active antigens in sea urchin eggs and embryos. *Exp. Cell Res.* **63**, 96.

Westin, M., Perlmann, H., and Perlmann, P. (1967). Immunological studies of protein synthesis during sea urchin development. *J. Exp. Zool.* **166**, 331.

Wheeler, M. B., Harding, C. V., Hughes, W. L., and Wilson, W. L. (1964). Developmental changes in the incorporation of 5-iododeoxyuridine by the embryo of *Arbacia punctulata*. *Exp. Cell Res.* **33**, 39.

Whitaker, D. M. (1933a). On the rate of oxygen consumption by fertilized and unfertilized eggs. IV. *Chaetopterus* and *Arbacia punctulata*. *J. Gen. Physiol.* **16**, 475.

Whitaker, D. M. (1933b). On the rate of oxygen consumption by fertilized and unfertilized eggs. V. Comparison and interpretation. *J. Gen. Physiol.* **16**, 497.

Whiteley, A. H. (1949). The phosphorus compounds of sea-urchin eggs and the uptake of radiophosphate upon fertilization. *Amer. Natur.* **83**, 249.

Whiteley, A. H., and Baltzer, F. (1958). Development, respiratory rate and content of deoxyribonucleic acid in the hybrid *Paracentrotus* ♀ *Arbacia* ♂. *Pubbl. Sta. Zool. Napoli* **30**, 402.

Whiteley, A. H., and Chambers, E. L. (1961). The differentiation of a phosphate transport mechanism in the fertilized egg of the sea urchin. *Symp. Int. Inst. Embryol., 1960* pp. 387–401.

Whiteley, A. H., and Chambers, E. L. (1966). Phosphate transport in fertilized sea urchin eggs. II. Effects of metabolic inhibitors and studies on differentiation. *J. Cell. Physiol.* **68**, 309.

Whiteley, A. H., McCarthy, B. J., and Whiteley, H. R. (1966). Changing populations of messenger RNA during sea urchin development. *Proc. Nat. Acad. Sci. U.S.* **55**, 519.

Whiteley, H. R., McCarthy, B. J., and Whiteley, A. H. (1970). Conservativism of base sequences in RNA for early development of echinoderms. *Develop. Biol.* **21**, 216.

Wicklund, E. (1948). Distribution of alkaline phosphatase in the eggs of a sea urchin. *Nature (London)* **161**, 556.

Wilson, E. B. (1901). Experimental studies in cytology. I. A cytological study of artificial parthenogenesis in sea urchin eggs. *Arch. Entwicklungsmech. Organismen* **12**, 529.

Wilson, E. B. (1902). Experimental studies in cytology. II. Some phenomena of fertilization and cell division in etherized eggs. *Arch. Entwicklungsmech. Organismen* **13**, 353.

Wilson, E. B. (1928). "The Cell Development and Heredity." Macmillan, New York.

Wilson, L., Bryan, J., Ruby, A., and Mazia, D. (1970). Precipitation of protein by vinblastine and calcium ions. *Proc. Nat. Acad. Sci. U.S.* **66**, 807.

Wilt, F. H. (1963). The synthesis of RNA in sea urchin embryos *(Strongylocentrotus purpuratus). Biochem. Biophys. Res. Commun.* **11**, 447.

Wilt, F. H. (1964). RNA synthesis during sea urchin embryogenesis. *Develop. Biol.* **9**, 299.

Wilt, F. H. (1970). The acceleration of RNA synthesis in cleaving sea urchin embryos. *Develop. Biol.* **23**, 444.

Wilt, F. H., and Ekenberg, E. E. (1971). Isolation of chromatin-bearing nascent RNA from nuclei of sea urchin embryos. *Biochem. Biophys. Res. Commun.* **44**, 831.

Wilt, F. H., and Hultin, T. (1962). Stimulation of phenylalanine incorporation by polyuridylic acid in homogenates of sea urchin eggs. *Biochem. Biophys. Res. Commun.* **9**, 313.

Wilt, F. H., Sakai, H., and Mazia, D. (1967). Old and new protein in the formation of the mitotic apparatus. *J. Mol. Biol.* **27**, 1.

Wolfson, N., and Wilbur, K. M. (1960). Sulfhydryl groups and the retardation of cleavage by extracts of sea urchin eggs. *Exp. Cell Res.* **21**, 219.

Wolpert, L. (1960). The mechanics and mechanism of cleavage. *Int. Rev. Cytol.* **10**, 164.

Wolpert, L. (1966). The mechanical properties of the membrane of the sea urchin egg during cleavage. *Exp. Cell Res.* **41**, 385.

Wolpert, L., and Gustafson, T. (1961a). Studies on the cellular basis of morphogenesis of the sea urchin embryo. *Exp. Cell Res.* **25**, 311.

Wolpert, L., and Gustafson, T. (1961b). Studies on the cellular basis of morphogenesis of the sea urchin embryo. *Exp. Cell Res.* **25**, 374.

Wolpert, L., and Mercer, E. H. (1961). An electron microscope study of fertilization of the sea urchin egg *Psammechinus miliaris. Exp. Cell Res.* **22**, 45.

Wolpert, L., and Mercer, E. H. (1963). An electron microscope study of the development of the blastula of the sea urchin embryo and its radial polarity. *Exp. Cell Res.* **30**, 280.

Wolpert, L., Marsland, D., and Hirshfield, M. (1971). The effect of high hydrostatic pressure on the mechanical properties of the surface of the sea urchin egg. *J. Cell Sci.* **8**, 87.

Wolsky, A., and de Issekutz Wolsky, M. (1961). The effect of actinomycin D on the development of *Arbacia* eggs. *Biol. Bull.* **121**, 414.

Woodward, A. E. (1918). Studies on the physiological significance of certain precipitates from the egg secretion of *Arbacia* and *Asterias. J. Exp. Zool.* **26**, 459.

Woodward, A. E. (1921). The parthenogenetic effect of echinoderm egg secretions on the eggs of *Nereis limbata. Biol. Bull.* **41**, 276.

Wyatt, G. R. (1951). The purine and pyrimidine composition of deoxypentose nucleic acids. *Biochem. J.* **48**, 584.

Yamashita, H., Mori, K., and Miwa, M. (1939). The action of ionizing rays on sea urchins. II. The effects of Roentgen, gamma and beta rays upon the fertilized eggs. *Gann* **33**, 117.

Yamashita, H., Mori, K., and Miwa, M. (1940). The action of ionizing rays on sea urchin. V. The mitotic observations on the effects of Roentgen rays upon the unfertilized eggs and sperm. *Gann* **34**, 239.

Yanagisawa, T. (1959). Studies on echinoderm phosphagens. I. Occurrence and nature of phosphagens in sea urchin eggs and spermatozoa. *J. Fac. Sci., Univ. Tokyo, Sect. 4* **8**, 473.

Yanagisawa, T. (1968). Studies on echinoderm phosphagens. IV. Changes in the content of arginine phosphate in sea urchin egg after fertilization and the effect of some metabolic inhibitors. *Exp. Cell Res.* **53**, 525.

Yanagisawa, T., and Isono, N. (1966). Acid-soluble nucleotides in the sea urchin egg. I. Ion exchange chromatographic separation and characterization. *Embryologia* **9**, 170.

Yanagisawa, T., Hasegawa, S., and Mori, H. (1968). The bound nucleotides of the isolated microtubules of sea urchin sperm flagella and their possible role in flagellar movement. *Exp. Cell Res.* **52**, 86.

Yang, S. S., and Comb, D. G. (1968). Distribution of multiple forms of lysyl t-RNA during early embryogenesis of the sea urchin *Lytechinus variegatus*. *J. Mol. Biol.* **31**, 139.

Yasumasu, I. (1958). Hatching enzyme of the sea urchin *Hemicentrotus pulcherrimus* and *Heliocidaris crassispina*. *Bull. Mar. Biol. Sta. Asamushi, Tohoku Univ.* **9**, 83.

Yasumasu, I. (1959). Spicules of the sea urchin larvae. *Zool. Mag.* **68**, 42.

Yasumasu, I. (1960). Quantitative determination of hatching enzyme activity of sea urchin blastulae. *J. Fac. Sci., Univ. Tokyo, Sect. 4* **9**, 39.

Yasumasu, I. (1963). Inhibition of the hatching enzyme formation during embryonic development of the sea urchin by chloramphenicol, 8-azaguanine and 5-bromo-uracil. *Sci. Pap. Coll. Gen. Educ., Univ. Tokyo* **13**, 241.

Yasumasu, I., and Koshihara, H. (1963). Aminoacyl RNA and transfer enzyme in sea urchin eggs. *Zool. Mag.* **72**, 259.

Yasumasu, I., and Nakano, E. (1963). Respiratory level of sea urchin eggs before and after fertilization. *Biol. Bull.* **125**, 182.

Yazaki, I. (1968). Immunological analysis of the calcium-precipitable protein of sea urchin eggs. 1) Hyaline layer substance. *Embryologia* **10**, 131.

Ycas, M. (1950). Studies on the respiratory enzymes of sea urchin eggs. Ph.D. Dissertation, California Institute of Technology, Pasadena.

Ycas, M. (1954). The respiratory and glycolytic enzymes of sea urchin eggs. *J. Exp. Biol.* **31**, 208.

Yoneda, M. (1960). Force exerted by a single cilium of *Mytilus edulis*. I. *J. Exp. Biol.* **37**, 461.

Yong Lee, S., and Brawerman, G. (1971). Pulse-labeled RNA complexes released by dissociation of rat liver polysomes. *Biochemistry* **10**, 510.

Young, C. W., Hendler, F. J., and Karnofsky, D. A. (1969). Synthesis of protein for DNA replication and cleavage events in the sand dollar embryo. *Exp. Cell Res.* **58**, 15.

Young, C. W., Hendler, F. J., Simmel, E., and Karnofsky, D. A. (1970). Studies on 2-piperidino-8-mercaptoadenine, a potent inhibitor of cleavage in echinoderm embryos. *Exp. Cell Res.* **60**, 45.

Yuyama, S. (1971). Delay and quadripartition in sea urchin eggs induced by short exposure to 2-mercaptoethanol. *Biol. Bull.* **140**, 339.

Zeikus, J. G., Taylor, M. W., and Buck, C. A. (1969). Transfer RNA changes associated with early development and differentiation of the sea urchin *Strongylocentrotus purpuratus*. *Exp. Cell Res.* **57**, 74.

Zeitz, L., Ferguson, R., and Garfinkel, E. (1968). Radiation-induced effects on DNA synthesis in developing sea urchin eggs. *Radiat. Res.* **34**, 200.

Zeitz, L., Ferguson, R., and Garfinkel, E. (1969). Incorporation of ^{3}H-TdR and ^{3}H-BUdR into sperm DNA of *Arbacia punctulata* after coelomic injection. *Exp. Cell Res.* **56**, 158.

Zeitz, L., Garfinkel, E., and Ferguson, R. (1970). Determination of the first S-period in sea urchin eggs by the uptake of labeled precursors. Differences found with different precursors. *Biophys. Soc. Abstr. Annu. Meet.* p. 141a.

Zeuthen, E. (1949). Oxygen consumption during mitosis; experiments on fertilized eggs of marine animals. *Amer. Natur.* **83**, 303.

Zeuthen, E. (1950). Respiration during cell division in the egg of the sea urchin *Psammechinus miliaris. Biol. Bull.* **98**, 144.

Zeuthen, E. (1951). Segmentation, nuclear growth and cytoplasmic storage in eggs of echinoderms and Amphibia. *Pubbl. Sta. Zool. Napoli, Suppl.* **23**, 47.

Zeuthen, E. (1953). Biochemistry and metabolism of cleavage in the sea urchin egg, as resolved into its mitotic steps. *Arch. Neerl. Zool., Suppl. 1* **10**, 31.

Zeuthen, E. (1955). Mitotic respiratory rhythms in single eggs of *Psammechinus miliaris* and of *Ciona intestinalis. Biol. Bull.* **108**, 366.

Zeuthen, E. (1960). Cycling in oxygen consumption in cleaving eggs. *Exp. Cell Res.* **19**, 1.

Zimmerman, A. M. (1960). Physicochemical analysis of the isolated mitotic apparatus. *Exp. Cell Res.* **20**, 529.

Zimmerman, A. M. (1963a). Chemical aspects of the isolated mitotic apparatus. *In* "The Cell in Mitosis" (L. Levine, ed.), p. 159. Academic Press, New York.

Zimmerman, A. M. (1963b). Incorporation of ³H-thymidine in the eggs of *Arbacia punctulata. Exp. Cell Res.* **31**, 39.

Zimmerman, A. M. (1964). Effects of mercaptoethanol on the furrowing capacity of *Arbacia* eggs. *Biol. Bull.* **127**, 345.

Zimmerman, A. M. (1971). High-pressure studies in cell biology. *Int. Rev. Cytol.* **30**, 1.

Zimmerman, A. M., and Marsland, D. A. (1956). Induction of premature cleavage furrows in the eggs of *Arbacia punctulata. Biol. Bull.* **111**, 317.

Zimmerman, A. M., and Marsland, D. A. (1960). Isolation of mitotic apparatus from pressurized *Arbacia* eggs. *Biol. Bull.* **119**, 352.

Zimmerman, A. M., and Marsland, D. A. (1964). Cell division: Effects of pressure on the mitotic mechanism of marine eggs *(Arbacia punctulata). Exp. Cell Res.* **35**, 293.

Zimmerman, A. M., and Silberman, L. (1964). Further studies on incorporation of H³-thymidine in *Arbacia* eggs under hydrostatic pressure. *Biol. Bull.* **127**, 355.

Zimmerman, A. M., and Zimmerman, S. B. (1960). Uptake of adenosine nucleotides in *Arbacia* eggs. *Biol. Bull.* **119**, 352.

Zimmerman, A. M., and Zimmerman, S. B. (1967). Action of colcemid in sea urchin eggs. *J. Cell Biol.* **34**, 483.

Zimmerman, A. M., Landau, J. V., and Marsland, D. A. (1957). Cell division: a pressure–temperature analysis of the effects of sulfhydryl reagents on the cortical plasmagel structure and furrowing strength of dividing egg *(Arbacia* and *Chaetopterns). J. Cell. Comp. Physiol.* **49**, 395.

Zimmerman, S. B., Murakami, T. H., and Zimmerman, A. M. (1968). The effect of selected chemical agents on furrow induction in the eggs of *Arbacia punctulata. Biol. Bull.* **134**, 356.

Zoja, R. (1895). Sullo sviluppo dei blastomeri isolati dalle uova di alcune meduse (e di altri organismi). II. *Arch. Entwicklungsmech. Organismen* **2**, 1.

Zotin, A. I. (1969). Cleavage-inhibiting thermolabile substances from sea urchin eggs. *Dokl. Biol. Sci.* **186**, 370.

Zotin, A. I., Milman, L. S., and Faustov, V. S. (1965). ATP level and cleavage of sea urchin eggs *Strongylocentrotus dröbachiensis* (O. F. Müller). *Exp. Cell Res.* **39**, 567.

Zotin, A. I., Faustov, V. S., Radzinskaya, L. I., and Ozernyuk, N. D. (1967). ATP level and respiration of embryos. *J. Embryol. Exp. Morphol.* **18**, 1.

Addendum

The following papers came to my attention too late to be included in the book. The reader is advised to look at them after reading the indicated chapters.

CHAPTER 1

Eckberg, W. R., and Ozaki, H. (1972). Temporal pattern of RNA synthesis in animalized sea urchin embryos. *Exp. Cell Res.* **73**, 177.

Gustafson, T., Lundgren, B., and Treufeldt, R. (1972). Serotonin and contractile activity in the echinopluteus. *Exp. Cell Res.* **72**, 115.

O'Melia, A. F., and Villee, C. A. (1972). Animalizing ability of Evans blue in embryos of *Arbacia punctulata*. Effect on ribosomal RNA synthesis. *Exp. Cell Res.* **72**, 276.

Stephens, R. E. (1972). Studies on the development of the sea urchin *Strongylocentrotus droebachiensis*. I. Ecology and normal development. *Biol. Bull.* **142**, 132.

CHAPTER 3

Ackerman, N. R., and Metz, C. B. (1971). Effects of multiple antibody layers on the morphology and fertilizability of sea urchin eggs. *Biol. Bull.* **141**, 376(a).

Ackerman, N. R., and Metz, C. B. (1972). Effects of multiple antibody layers on *Arbacia* eggs. *Exp. Cell Res.* **72**, 204.

Aketa, K., Onitake, K., and Tsuzuki, H. (1972). Tryptic disruption of sperm-binding site of sea urchin egg surface. *Exp. Cell Res.* **71**, 27.

Bryan, J. (1970). On the reconstitution of the crystalline components of the sea urchin fertilization membrane. *J. Cell Biol.* **45**, 606.

Citkowitz, E. (1972). Analysis of the isolated hyaline layer of sea urchin embryos. *Devel. Biol.* **27**, 494.

Inoue, S., Cousineau, G. H., and Krupa, P. L. (1971). Jelly coat material of *Arbacia* eggs: an electron diffraction study. *Biol. Bull.* **141**, 391.

Von Ledebur-Villiger, M. (1972). Cytology and nucleic acid synthesis of parthenogenetically activated sea urchin eggs. *Exp. Cell Res.* **72**, 285.

CHAPTER 4

Epel, D. (1972). Activation of an Na^+-dependent amino acid transport system upon fertilization of sea urchin eggs. *Exp. Cell Res.* **72**, 74.

Ito, S., and Yoshioka, K. (1972). Real activation potential observed in sea urchin egg during fertilization. *Exp. Cell Res.* **72**, 547.

Steinhardt, R. A., Shen, S., and Mazia, D. (1972). Membrane potential, membrane resistance and an energy requirement for the development of potassium conductance in the fertilization reaction of echinoderm eggs. *Exp. Cell Res.* **72,** 195.

Vacquier, V. D., Epel, D., and Douglas, L. A. (1972). Sea urchin eggs release protease activity at fertilization. *Nature (London)* **236,** 34.

Chapter 5

Forer, A., and Goldman, R. D. (1972). The concentration of dry matter in mitotic apparatuses *in vivo* and after isolation from sea-urchin zygotes. *J. Cell Sci.* **10,** 387.

Kane, R. E. (1970). Direct isolation of the hyaline layer protein released from the cortical granules of the sea urchin egg at fertilization. *J. Cell Biol.* **45,** 615.

Mazia, D., Petzelt, C., Williams, R. O., and Meza, I. (1972). A Ca-activated ATPase in the mitotic apparatus of the sea urchin egg (isolated by a new method). *Exp. Cell Res.* **70,** 325.

Petzelt, C. (1972). Ca^{2+}-activated ATPase during the cell cycle of the sea urchin *Strongylocentrotus purpuratus*. *Exp. Cell Res.* **70,** 333.

Schroeder, T. E. (1972). The contractile ring. II. Determining its brief existence, volumetric changes, and vital role in cleaving *Arbacia* eggs. *J. Cell Biol.* **53,** 419.

Stephens, R. E. (1972). Studies on the development of the sea urchin *Strongylocentrotus droebachiensis*. II. Regulation of mitotic spindle equilibrium by environmental temperature. *Biol. Bull.* **142,** 145.

Zeuthen, E. (1972). Inhibition of chromosome separation in cleaving *Psammechinus* eggs by elevated temperature. *Exp. Cell Res.* **72,** 337.

Chapter 6

Hynes, R. O., Raff, R. A., and Gross, P. R. (1972). Properties of three cell types in sixteen-cell sea urchin embryos: Aggregation and microtubule protein synthesis. *Devel. Biol.* **27,** 150.

Lallier, R. (1972). Effects of concanavalin A on the development of sea urchin egg. *Exp. Cell Res.* **72,** 157.

Kondo, K., and Sakai, H. (1971). Demonstration and preliminary characterization of re-aggregation-promoting substances from embryonic sea urchin cells. *Devel. Growth Diff.* **13,** 1.

Spiegel, M., and Rubinstein, N. A. (1972). Synthesis of RNA by dissociated cells of the sea urchin embryo. *Exp. Cell Res.* **70,** 423.

Tupper, J. T., and Saunders, Jr., J. W. (1972). Intercellular permeability in the early *Asterias* embryo. *Devel. Biol.* **27,** 546.

Chapter 7

Afzelius, B. A. (1972). Reactions of the sea urchin oocyte to foreign spermatozoa. *Exp. Cell Res.* **72,** 25.

Chapter 8

Goudsmith, E. M. (1972). Glycogen content of eggs and embryos of *Arbacia punctulata*. *Devel. Biol.* **27,** 329.

Chapter 9

Fitzmaurice, L. C., and Baker, R. F. (1972). Transcription ability of nuclear DNAs from different developmental stages of the sea urchin. *Biochim. Biophys. Acta* **272**, 510.

Slater, I., and Slater, D. W. (1972). DNA polymerase potentials of sea urchin embryos. *Nature (London) New Biol.* **237**, 81.

Tosi, L., Granieri, A., and Scarano, E. (1972). Enzymatic DNA modifications in isolated nuclei from developing sea urchin embryos. *Exp. Cell Res.* **72**, 257.

Chapter 10

Aoki, Y., and Koshihara, H. (1972a). Inhibitory effects of acid polysaccharides from sea urchin embryos in RNA synthesis *in vitro*. *Exp. Cell Res.* **70**, 431.

Aoki, Y., and Koshihara, H. (1972b). Inhibitory effects of acid polysaccharides from sea urchin embryos on RNA polymerase activity. *Biochim. Biophys. Acta* **272**, 33.

Aronson, A. I., Wilt, F. H., and Wartiovaara, J. (1972). Characterization of pulse-labeled nuclear RNA in sea urchin embryos. *Exp. Cell Res.* **72**, 309.

Bellemare, G., Cedergren, R. J., and Cousineau, G. H. (1972). Comparison of the physical and optical properties of *Escherichia coli* and sea urchin 5S ribosomal RNAs. *J. Mol. Biol.* **68**, 445.

Brandhorst, B. P., and Humphreys, T. (1972). Stabilities of nuclear and messenger RNA molecules in sea urchin embryos. *J. Cell Biol.* **53**, 474.

Hogan, B., and Gross, P. R. (1972). Nuclear RNA synthesis in sea urchin embryos. *Exp. Cell Res.* **72**, 101.

Hynes, R. O., Greenhouse, G. A., Minkoff, R., and Gross, P. R. (1972). Properties of the three cell types in sixteen-cell sea urchin embryos: RNA synthesis. *Devel. Biol.* **27**, 457.

Kronenberg, L. H., and Humphreys, T. (1972). Double-stranded RNA in sea urchin embryos. *Biochemistry* **11**, 2020.

Ruždijić, S., and Glišin, V. (1972). Towards a total analysis of polyribosome associated ribonucleoprotein particles of sea urchin embryos. *Biochim. Biophys. Acta* **269**, 441.

Selvig, S. E., Greenhouse, G. A., and Gross, P. R. (1972). Cytoplasmic synthesis of RNA in the sea urchin embryo. II. Mitochondrial transcription. *Cell Diff.* **1**, 5.

Chapter 11

Bryan, J. (1972). Vinblastine and microtubules. II. Characterization of two protein subunits from the isolated crystals. *J. Mol. Biol.* **66**, 157.

Easton, D., and Chalkey, R. (1972). High resolution electrophoretic analysis of the histones from embryos and sperm of *Arbacia punctulata*. *Exp. Cell Res.* **72**, 502.

Ecklund, P. S., and Pikò, L. (1972). *In vivo* radioactive labeling of *Arbacia* sperm histones. *Exp. Cell Res.* **71**, 477.

Terman, S. A. (1972). Extent of post-transcriptional level control of protein synthesis in the absence of cell division. *Exp. Cell Res.* **72**, 576.

Chapter 12

Noronha, J. M., Sheys, G. H., and Buchanan, J. M. (1972). Induction of a reductive pathway for deoxyribonucleotide synthesis during early embryogenesis of the sea urchin. *Proc. Nat. Acad. Sci. U. S.* **69**, 2006.

Subject Index

465